Principles of External Auditing

Second edition

Brenda Porter
Jon Simon
David Hatherly

JOHN WILEY & SONS, LTD

This publication is designed to provide accurate and authoritative information in regard to the subject
matter covered. It is sold on the understanding that the Publisher is not engaged in rendering professional
services. If professional advice or other expert assistance is required, the services of a competent
professional should be sought.

Other Wiley Editorial Offices

John Wiley & Sons Inc., 111 River Street, Hoboken, NJ 07030, USA

Jossey-Bass, 989 Market Street, San Francisco, CA 94103-1741, USA

Wiley-VCH Verlag GmbH, Boschstr. 12, D-69469 Weinheim, Germany

John Wiley & Sons Australia Ltd, 33 Park Road, Milton, Queensland 4064, Australia

John Wiley & Sons (Asia) Pte Ltd, 2 Clementi Loop #02-01, Jin Xing Distripark, Singapore 129809

John Wiley & Sons Canada Ltd, 22 Worcester Road, Etobicoke, Ontario, Canada M9W 1L1

Wiley also publishes its books in a variety of electronic formats. Some content that appears in print may not
be available in electronic books.

British Library Cataloguing in Publication Data

A catalogue record for this book is available from the British Library

ISBN 0-470-84297-0

Typeset in 11/13 Times Ten by Footnote Graphics Limited, Warminster, Wiltshire
Printed and bound in Great Britain by T. J. International Ltd, Padstow, Cornwall
This book is printed on acid-free paper responsibly manufactured from sustainable forestry
in which at least two trees are planted for each one used for paper production.

Contents

Contents _____ vii

Preface

This second edition of *Principles of External Auditing* follows the first edition which was published in 1996. Like its predecessor it describes and explains, in readily comprehensible, non-technical language, the nature of the audit function and the principles of the audit process. The book is designed for *anyone* who is interested in understanding the principles that underlie external auditing. It also provides an ideal foundation for all those studying auditing, and is particularly suitable as a text for introductory courses in universities and for professional examinations such as the ACCA's *Audit and Internal Review* (Part 2) and *Audit and Assurance Services* (Part 3). For more advanced courses the book may be supplemented by specialist articles and other reading material drawn from professional and academic journals. Some suitable references are indicated in the Additional Reading sections provided at the end of each chapter.

The fundamental principles of auditing as set out in the *The Auditor's Code*, published by the Auditing Practices Board (APB) in 1996, have remained and, as in the first edition, they are reproduced in the inside cover of this book. These fundamental principles are all pervasive but we have identified the chapter where each principle seems to have greatest application and have highlighted this principle at the beginning of the relevant chapter.

While the basic principles of auditing are unchanged since the first edition of this book, there have been a number of important developments. These are reflected in this second edition and they include:

- increased emphasis by auditors on the control environment, business risk, and understanding the client's business, as elements of the audit process;
- the auditing profession's response to society's increasing concern about corporate fraud;
- the debate over the auditor's independence from the client's management – a debate that has been given additional impetus by the Enron, WorldCom and similar experiences;[1]

---

[1] As the impact of the Enron, WorldCom and similar cases on the principles and practice of external auditing is, at the time of writing, still unfolding, we have not dealt with these cases in this edition of the book. In keeping with this, throughout the book we have referred to the Big Five auditing firms (that is, Andersen, Deloitte & Touche, Ernst & Young, KPMG and PricewaterhouseCoopers). As a result of the Enron case it is unlikely that Andersen will survive as a major international auditing firm.

- new responsibilities for external auditors in relation to corporate governance;
- changes in the regulatory regime for auditors (in particular, the establishment of The Accountancy Foundation);
- further development of the mechanisms for monitoring auditors;
- developments in the constitution and management of audit firms to limit their exposure to legal liability;
- developments in case law concerning auditors' liability.

The second edition of this book recognises the growing relevance of international auditing standards, the significance of which has increased as a consequence of the growth in global business and global capital. Reference to the relevant International Standards on Auditing issued by the International Federation of Accountants (IFAC), as well as Auditing Standards issued by the APB in the UK[2] is made at the beginning of each chapter. Additionally, footnotes explain the comparable requirements of the International Standards wherever the APB's Standards are cited in the text.

This book commences with five chapters that form the 'back-drop' for an understanding of the audit process. Greater emphasis is given to the conceptual framework of auditing, which now constitutes a separate chapter (Chapter 3), and a chapter is devoted to the important and topical issue of auditors' independence (Chapter 4). Chapter 6 gives an overview of the audit process, its staffing, documentation and administration.

In the next seven chapters (Chapters 7 to 13), the reader is taken step by step through the audit process – from gaining an initial understanding of the audit client to issuing reports to users of financial statements and to those charged with the entity's governance. It should be noted that, legally, a company's board of directors (comprising both executive and non-executive directors) is responsible for the company's governance. However, the board relies on senior executives (who may or may not be directors) to implement its policies and to ensure the smooth running of the company on a day-to-day basis. In this book we use the term 'management' to embrace executive and non-executive directors and non-director senior executives.

Chapter 14 examines the important issue of auditors' liability – in particular, how auditors' duty of care to third parties has evolved up to and since the

---

[2] Throughout this book we have referred to Statements of Auditing Standards (SASs) issued by the APB. The APB issues standards on behalf of the five Recognised Supervisory Bodies (RSBs) that have a statutory responsibility to govern external auditing in the UK and Ireland [that is, the Institutes of Chartered Accountants in England and Wales (ICAEW), of Scotland (ICAS), and in Ireland (ICAI), and the Chartered Association of Certified Accountants (ACCA) and the Association of Authorised Public Accountants (AAPA)].

landmark *Caparo* case. Chapter 15, following on from the examination of auditors' liability in Chapter 14, describes measures that auditing firms and the RSBs'[3] monitoring units have taken to monitor and improve audit quality and hence to help auditors avoid exposure to liability. The chapter provides an analysis of the findings of the RSB's monitoring units since their inception in 1992. It also provides an update on other measures that have been proposed or recently adopted as a means of limiting auditors' liability, namely, the use of limited liability companies, limited liability partnerships, the imposition of a statutory cap on damages, and the introduction of proportionate liability.

Prior to commencing the second edition of this book, we conducted extensive consultations with representatives of major auditing firms and academic colleagues. Those we consulted provided helpful and constructive feedback on the first edition of the book and how it should be revised. In this respect, our thanks go to Tony Bingham and Richard Pollard of PricewaterhouseCoopers, Tony Cabourn-Smith of Ernst & Young, Martyn Jones of Deloitte & Touche, Stuart Poyner of KPMG and Tony Upson of Pannell Kerr Forster.

Our consultations revealed a widely held view that the use of computers was now so pervasive in both the preparation and audit of financial statements that a separate chapter on 'Auditing and the Computer' is inappropriate. Accordingly, in Chapter 9 (Internal controls and the auditor), we have focused on internal controls in a computerised environment. Similarly, computer assisted audit techniques (CAATS) have been included with audit sampling in Chapter 10 and this chapter now deals with sophisticated techniques designed to access and examine accounting populations. Colleagues in the profession advised us that, in order to gain a thorough understanding of their audit clients' businesses, their 'new' audit methodologies placed greater emphasis than previously on their clients' business risks and their clients' management of those risks. Nevertheless, they stressed that the basic structure and emphasis of the audit process as reflected in this book remains intact.

Academic colleagues whom we consulted, who teach auditing courses in various universities in the UK and elsewhere, indicated that they did not require separate sections dealing with the audit of public sector entities. However, they stressed the importance, in today's environment, of providing material on internal and environmental audits. Accordingly we have included substantial new chapters (Chapters 16 and 17) devoted to these topics in this second edition. Chapter 16 was contributed by David Lewington, a very experienced internal auditor, and we are very grateful to him for his contribution.

---

[3] See footnote 2.

In addition to the academic and professional colleagues who provided us with invaluable feedback and guidance for this second edition, we would like to thank the numerous students whose insightful feedback on the first edition has been extremely helpful. We would also like to express special thanks to Steve Leonard, Stephen Thomas and John Young who have given us important and detailed comments on earlier drafts of various chapters of this edition of the book. Thanks are also due to our families and friends for their patience, understanding and support. Last, but certainly not least, special thanks go to Sheila Hart whose talent as an expert typist has been crucial to the preparation of this second edition.

Brenda Porter
Jon Simon
David Hatherly

1   What is Auditing?

LEARNING OBJECTIVES

After studying the material in this chapter you should be able to:

- explain the general nature of the audit function;
- distinguish between financial statement audits, compliance audits and operational audits;
- distinguish between external and internal audits;
- describe how auditing differs from accounting;
- explain why financial statement audits are necessary;
- discuss the benefits which arise from the external audit function for:
  - users of financial statements
  - the auditee (i.e. the entity whose financial statements are audited)
  - society as a whole.

The following fundamental principle included in *The Auditor's Code* (APB, 1996) is particularly relevant to this chapter:

Fundamental principle of external auditing: *Providing value*

1.1 INTRODUCTION

Under United Kingdom (UK) legislation, all companies with a turnover of £1 million or more,[1] and virtually all public sector entities, are required to produce annually, audited financial statements. The audits of these financial statements are big business. As shown in Figure 1.1, in 2000 the audit fees of just 10 of the largest companies listed on the London Stock Exchange amounted to nearly £63 million. It is therefore evident that the statutory audits of UK corporate entities as a whole involve a substantial amount of resources. But, what is an audit? Why are audits needed? Do they provide benefits commensurate with their cost?

We address these questions in this chapter. More specifically, we examine the nature of the audit function and distinguish between financial statement audits, compliance audits and operational audits, and also between external and internal audits. We consider the factors that make financial statement audits necessary and discuss their value for users of financial statements, for auditees (that is, the companies whose financial statements are audited), and for society as a whole.

Figure 1.1: Audit fees and non-audit fees paid to the auditors of 10 of the largest companies listed on the London Stock Exchange in 2000.[2]

Company	Audit fees £million	Non-audit fees paid to auditors £million	Auditor
BP plc	20.0	36.4	Ernst & Young
Vodafone Group plc	1.0	16.0	Deloitte & Touche
HSBC Holdings plc	18.4	10.7	KPMG
Astra Zeneca plc	2.3	9.9	KPMG
Royal Bank of Scotland plc	4.9	8.3	PricewaterhouseCoopers
Lloyds TSB plc	4.0	32.0	PricewaterhouseCoopers
Barclays Bank plc	4.6	27.0	PricewaterhouseCoopers
British Telecommunications plc	2.7	19.1	PricewaterhouseCoopers
Diageo plc	2.5	7.0	KPMG
Cable & Wireless plc	2.5	14.5	KPMG
Total	**£62.9**	**£180.9**	

Source: Relevant companies' annual reports

---

[1] See footnote 7.

[2] World-wide audit and non-audit fees paid by the relevant company.

1.2   WHAT IS AN AUDIT?

Anderson (1977) captured the essence of auditing when he stated:

> The practice of auditing commenced on the day that one individual assumed stewardship over another's property. In reporting on his stewardship, the accuracy and reliability of that information would have been subjected to some sort of critical review [i.e. an audit]. (p. 6)

The term 'audit' is derived from the Latin word meaning 'a hearing'. Auditing originated over 2,000 years ago when, firstly in Egypt, and subsequently in Greece, Rome and elsewhere, citizens (or, sometimes, slaves) entrusted with the collection and disbursement of public funds were required to present themselves publicly, before a responsible official (an auditor), to give an oral account of their handling of those funds.

In order to understand what an audit is and how it is conducted in the modern context, a definition is needed. A comprehensive definition of auditing with general application is as follows:

> Auditing is a systematic process of objectively gathering and evaluating evidence relating to assertions about economic actions and events in which the individual or organisation making the assertions has been engaged, to ascertain the degree of correspondence between those assertions and established criteria, and communicating the results to users of the reports in which the assertions are made.[3]

This definition conveys that:

- auditing proceeds by means of an ordered and structured series of steps;
- auditing primarily involves gathering and evaluating evidence. In pursuing this activity the auditor maintains an objective unbiased attitude of mind;
- the auditor critically examines assertions made by an individual or organisation about economic activities in which they have been engaged;
- the auditor assesses how closely these assertions conform to the 'set of rules' which govern how the individual or organisation is to act and/or report to others about the economic events which have occurred. This 'set of rules' comprises the established criteria which enable the auditor to evaluate whether the assertions represent the underlying events;
- the auditor communicates the results of this evaluation in a written report. The report is available to all users of the document(s) in which the assertions are made.

The major features of an audit are presented diagrammatically in Figure 1.2 below.

---

[3] Adapted from the definition provided by the American Accounting Association's (AAA) Committee on Basic Auditing Concepts (1973, p. 8).

Figure 1.2: Major features of an audit

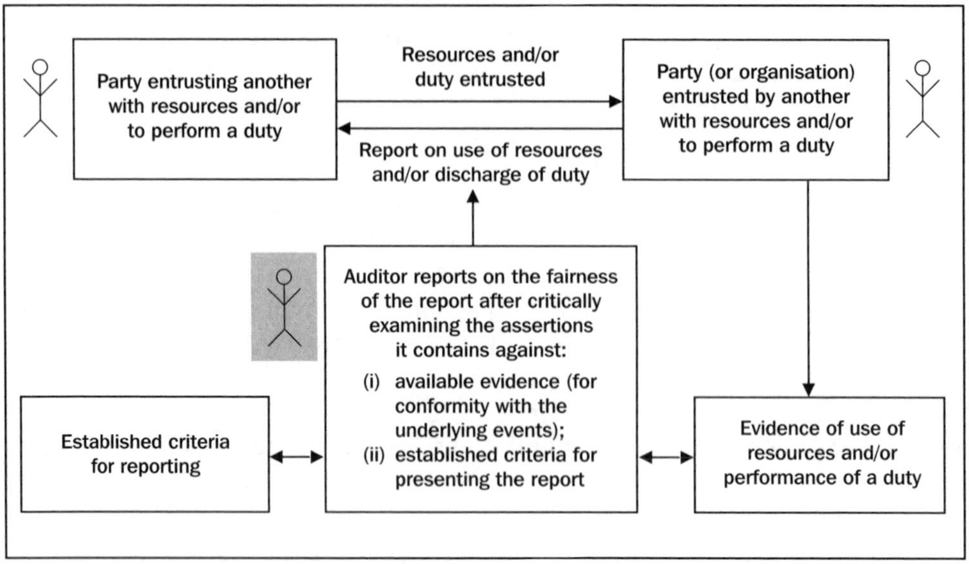

1.3 TYPES OF AUDIT

Audits may be classified in various ways. They may, for instance, be categorised according to:

- the primary objective of the audit; or
- the primary beneficiaries of the audit.

1.3.1 Classification by primary audit objective

Based on primary audit objective, three main categories of audits may be recognised, namely:

(i)   Financial statement audits,
(ii) Compliance audits,
(iii) Operational audits.

(i)   Financial statement audits

A financial statement audit is an examination of an entity's financial statements, which have been prepared by the entity's management/directors[4] for shareholders and other interested parties outside the entity, and of the

---

[4] In the Preface to this book it is noted that the term 'managers' is defined to mean a company's executive directors, non-executive directors, and non-director executives. Under the Companies Act 1985 (s.226) it is the responsibility of a company's directors to prepare the company's annual financial statements.

Figure 1.3: Major features of a financial statement audit

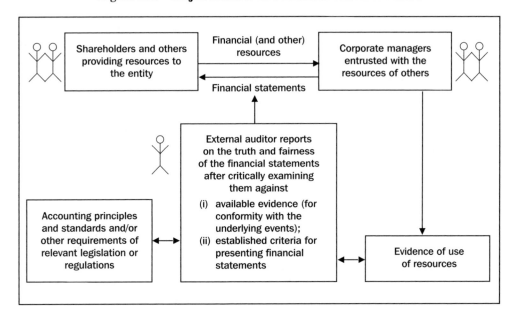

evidence supporting the information contained in those financial statements. It is conducted by a qualified, experienced professional,[5] who is independent of the entity, for the purpose of expressing an opinion on whether or not the financial statements provide a true and fair view of the entity's financial position and performance, and comply with relevant statutory and/or other regulatory requirements. The major features of a financial statement audit are presented in Figure 1.3.

Under section 226 of the Companies Act 1985, the directors of all companies are required to prepare annually, financial statements which include:
- a balance sheet, showing the entity's financial position (or 'state of affairs') as at the last day of the financial year;
- a profit and loss account, showing the results of the company's activities for the financial year.

Additionally, under section 235, auditors are required to report on these financial statements.[6] Thus, *prima facie*, all companies must, by law, subject their financial statements to an external audit. However, companies with a

---

[5] The term 'an auditor' usually refers to an audit firm. Although one person is responsible for the audit and signs the audit report, the audit is usually conducted by an audit team.

[6] The statutory and regulatory requirements applying to the audited financial statements of companies are discussed in greater detail in Chapter 5.

turnover of not more than £1 million and a balance sheet total of not more than £1.4 million are exempt from a statutory audit.[7]

Companies taking advantage of the audit exemption, and also partnerships and sole traders (which do not need to appoint an auditor), may still require financial statement audits for specific purposes. For example, if one of these entities approaches a bank for a loan, the bank may require audited financial statements as a basis for deciding whether or not to grant the loan. Further, it is usual for clubs and societies to include in their constitution a requirement for their annual financial statements to be audited.

(ii)   Compliance audits

The purpose of a compliance audit is to determine whether an individual or entity (the auditee) has acted (or is acting) in accordance with procedures or regulations established by an authority, such as the entity's management or a regulatory body. The audits are conducted by competent, experienced professionals (internal or external to the auditee) who are appointed by, and report to, the authority which set the procedures or regulations in place.

Examples of compliance audits include audits conducted by the Inland Revenue and by the Customs and Excise Department which are designed to ascertain whether individuals or organisations have complied with tax legislation or legislation governing imports and exports, as applicable. They also include audits conducted within companies, or other entities, to ascertain whether the entity's employees are complying with the system of internal control[8] established by management.

(iii)   Operational audits

An operational audit involves a systematic examination and evaluation of an entity's operations which is conducted with a view to improving the efficiency and/or effectiveness of the entity. Such audits are usually initiated by the entity's management and are conducted by competent, experienced professionals (internal or external to the organisation) who report their findings to

---

[7] In July 2001 the Company Law Review Steering Committee recommended that exemption from audit should be extended to companies that meet two of the following criteria: turnover of no more than £4.8 million, balance sheet total of no more than £2.4 million, no more than 50 employees.

The audit exemption is not available to a company if, at any time during the financial year, it was a public company, a banking or insurance company, an authorised person or appointed representative under the Financial Services Act 1986, a parent or subsidiary company (unless the group qualifies as a small group), or if members holding an aggregate of 10% or more of the nominal value of the company's issued shares request an audit (Companies Act 1985, s.249B).

[8] Internal control is discussed in Chapter 9.

management. An operational audit may apply to the organisation as a whole or to an identified segment thereof, such as a subsidiary, division or department. The objectives of the audit may be broad, for example, to improve the overall efficiency of the entity, or narrow and designed, for example, to solve a specific problem such as excessive staff turnover.[9]

1.3.2 Classification by primary audit beneficiaries

Based on primary audit beneficiaries (that is, those for whom the audit is conducted), audits may be classified as:

(i) external audits, or
(ii) internal audits.

(i) External audits

An external audit is an audit performed for parties external to the auditee. Experts, independent of the auditee and its personnel, conduct these audits in accordance with requirements which are defined by or on behalf of the parties for whose benefit the audit is conducted. Probably the best known, and most frequently performed, external audits are the statutory audits of companies' and public sector entities' financial statements (that is, financial statement audits). However, compliance audits conducted, for instance, by the Customs and Excise Department and the Inland Revenue, are also examples of external audits.

(ii) Internal audits

In contrast to external audits, internal audits are performed for parties (usually management) internal to the entity. They may be performed by employees of the entity itself or by personnel from an outside source (such as an accounting firm). However, in either case, the audit is conducted in accordance with management's requirements. These may be wide-ranging or narrowly-focused, and continuous (on-going) or one-off in nature. They may, for example, be as broad as investigating the appropriateness of, and level of compliance with, the organisation's system of internal control, or as narrow as examining the entity's policies and procedures for ensuring compliance with health and safety regulations.[10]

---

[9] In public sector entities, broadly-based operational audits (or value for money audits) are generally required as part of the statutory audit function. However, additional more specific operational audits may also be initiated by the entity's management and conducted along the lines of those undertaken in private sector entities.

[10] Internal audits are discussed in Chapter 16.

1.3.3   Common characteristics of audits

It should be noted that, although different categories and types of audit may be recognised, all audits possess the same general characteristics. Whether they are financial statement, compliance or operational audits, and whether they are conducted for parties external or internal to the entity, they all involve:

- the systematic examination and evaluation of evidence which is undertaken to ascertain whether statements or actions by individuals or organisations comply with established criteria; and
- communication of the results of the examination, usually in a written report, to the party by whom, or on whose behalf, the auditor was appointed.

1.4   AUDITING VS ACCOUNTING

This book is primarily concerned with the external financial statement audits of companies and, unless indicated otherwise, when we refer to 'audit' or 'auditor', these terms should be understood in that context. However, before focusing attention on these audits we need to distinguish between auditing and accounting.

Accounting data, and the accounting systems which capture and process this data, provide the raw materials with which auditors work. In order to understand these systems, and the data they process, an auditor must first be a qualified accountant. However, the processes involved in auditing and accounting are different. Accounting is essentially a *creative* process which involves identifying, organising, summarising and communicating information about economic events. Auditing, on the other hand, is essentially a *critical* (or *evaluative*) process. It involves gathering and evaluating audit evidence and communicating conclusions based on this evidence about the fairness with which the communication resulting from the accounting process (that is, the financial statements) reflects the underlying economic events.

1.5   WHY ARE EXTERNAL FINANCIAL STATEMENT AUDITS NEEDED?

1.5.1   The need to communicate financial information

Over the last 160 or so years, business organisations have grown from owner-operated entities, which employed a handful of family members, to vast multi-national companies staffed by thousands of employees. Such growth has been made possible by channelling financial resources from many thousands of small investors, through the financial markets and credit-granting institutions, to the growing companies.

As companies have grown in size, their management has passed from shareholder-owners to small groups of professional managers. Thus, company growth has been accompanied by the increasing separation of ownership interests and management functions. As a consequence, a need has arisen for company managers to report to the organisation's owners and other providers of funds such as banks and other lenders, on the financial aspects of their activities. Those receiving these reports (external financial statements) need assurance that they are reliable. They therefore wish to have the information in the reports 'checked out' or audited.

1.5.2 The need to have the communication examined

Three questions arise in relation to the 'checking out' of management's reports:
1. Why might the information in their reports not be reliable?
2. Why is it so important to the receivers of the reports that the information is reliable?
3. Why do the receivers of the reports not audit the information for themselves?

The answers to these questions may be found in four main factors, namely, a conflict of interests, consequences of error, remoteness, and complexity.

(i) Conflict of interests

A company's financial statements are prepared by its directors and these directors are essentially reporting on their own performance. Users of the financial statements want the statements to portray the company's financial performance, position and cash flows as accurately as possible. However, they perceive that the directors may bias their report so that it reflects favourably on their management of the company's affairs.

Thus, it can be seen that there is a potential conflict of interest between the preparers and users of the financial statements. The audit plays a vital role in helping to ensure that directors provide, and users are confident in receiving, information which is a fair representation of the company's financial affairs.

(ii) Consequences of error

If users of a company's external financial statements base their decisions on unreliable information, they may suffer serious financial loss as a result.

Therefore, before basing decisions on financial statement information, they wish to be assured that the information is reliable and 'safe' to act upon.

(iii) Remoteness

In general, as a consequence of legal, physical and economic factors, users of a company's external financial statements are not able to verify for themselves the reliability of the information contained in the financial statements. Even if, for example, they are major shareholders in a company, they have no legal right of access to the company's books and records. Further, they may be many miles distant from the company which prevents easy access to it, and/or they may not be able to afford the time and expense which would be involved in checking the information personally, should they have the legal right to do so.[11]

As a result of legal, physical and economic factors preventing users of external financial statements from examining personally the information provided by a company's directors, an independent party is needed to assess the reliability of the information on their behalf.

(iv) Complexity

As companies have grown in size, the volume of their transactions has increased. Further, especially in recent years, economic transactions, and the accounting systems which capture and process them, have become very complex. As a result of these changes, errors are more likely to creep into the accounting data and the resulting financial statements. Additionally, with the increasing complexity of transactions, accounting systems and financial statements, users of external financial statements are less able to evaluate the quality of the information for themselves. Therefore, there is a growing need for the financial statements to be examined by an independent qualified auditor, who has the necessary competence and expertise to understand the entity's business, its transactions and its accounting system.

1.6 BENEFITS DERIVED FROM EXTERNAL FINANCIAL STATEMENT AUDITS

In section 1.5 above, we noted that external financial statement audits are necessary because the ownership and management functions of companies

---

[11] However, it should be noted that many financial institutions, including pension funds, insurance companies and unit and investment trusts, which are significant shareholders of large UK companies, visit companies in which they have, or are considering, investment and question their managements. These institutions have considerable influence over the investee companies, especially if they are not performing adequately.

have become increasingly separated, and because of factors such as a potential conflict of interest between preparers and users of financial statements, and the inability of financial statement users to verify the information for themselves. In this section we consider the benefits derived from external financial statement audits by financial statement users, auditees, and society as a whole. These benefits are reflected in the fundamental principle of external auditing – *Providing value*:

> Auditors add to the reliability and quality of financial reporting [provided for external parties]; they [also] provide to directors and officers [of the auditee] constructive observations arising from the audit process; and thereby contribute to the effective operation of business, capital markets and the public sector. (APB, 1996)

1.6.1 Financial statement users

The value of an external audit for financial statement users is the credibility it gives to the financial information provided by the management of corporate entities. This credibility arises from three forms of control which an audit provides:

(i) *Preventive control:* Employees involved in the capture and processing of accounting data and/or the preparation of the entity's financial statements, who know their work will be subject to the scrutiny of an auditor, are likely to work more carefully than they would in the absence of an audit. It is probable that the extra care taken by employees prevents at least some errors from occurring.

(ii) *Detective control:* Even if employees in the auditee entity process the accounting data and prepare the financial statements carefully, errors may still occur. The auditor may detect these errors during the audit and draw them to management's attention. They may then be corrected prior to publication of the financial statements.

(iii) *Reporting control:* If the auditor detects material errors in the financial statements and refers them to management, but management refuses to correct them, the auditor draws attention to the errors by qualifying the audit report (that is, the auditor states that all is not well, giving reasons for this conclusion). In this way, users of the financial statements are made aware that, in the auditor's opinion, the information provided is not reliable.

It is interesting to note that, while UK legislation is silent on the qualifications of those who may prepare company financial statements, the Companies Act 1989 specifies that the auditor of these statements must hold an 'appropriate qualification' and be 'registered'.[12] This implies that, although the preparer of

---

[12] The required qualifications and registration of auditors is discussed in Chapter 5.

the financial statements need not be a qualified accountant, the auditor must be a well-qualified, competent and experienced professional. It therefore seems that Parliament looks to auditors to protect the interests of financial statement users by giving assurance that the financial statements are reliable, or providing a warning that they are not.

1.6.2 Auditees

During the course of an external financial statement audit, the auditor becomes very familiar with the organisation, its business, its accounting system and all aspects of its financial affairs. Added to this, the auditor is a qualified and experienced individual, who comes to the auditee as an independent objective outsider, divorced from the day-to-day running of the entity.

These factors place the auditor in an ideal position to observe where improvements can be made. (S)he is able to advise the auditee on matters such as strengthening internal control; the development of accounting or other management information systems; and tax, investment and financial planning. In addition (in cases where the issue arises for the auditee), the auditor is able to provide advice on matters such as how to proceed with a share float, businesses acquisition or divestment, or liquidation. The provision of these 'additional services' by the auditor is very valuable for the auditee. Indeed, as Anderson (1977) pointed out:

> In many cases, it is the presence of these collateral services which makes the audit an economical package from management's point of view. The professional auditor must always be alert for opportunities to be of service to his or her client while at the same time discharging conscientiously his or her responsibilities to the users of the audited financial statements. (p. 6)

Notwithstanding the value of these services for the auditee, there is a potential danger which auditors need to bear in mind. In recent years, the fees paid by audit clients to their auditors for non-audit services have grown to such an extent that in many instances, as indicated in Figure 1.1, they exceed the audit fee. This has led to concerns that auditors may not be sufficiently critical in their auditing duties for fear of upsetting the entity's management and consequently losing lucrative non-audit contracts.[13]

1.6.3 Society as a whole

The benefits flowing from audits for society as a whole fall into two broad groups:
(i)   those relating to the smooth functioning of financial markets; and
(ii) those relating to securing the accountability of corporate managements.

---

[13] The dangers to auditors' independence of providing non-audit services to audit clients is discussed in Chapter 4.

(i)   Smooth functioning of financial markets

The benefits – and importance – of audits helping to ensure the smooth functioning of financial markets was aptly conveyed by Turner (2001), Chief Accountant of the Securities and Exchange Commission in the United States of America (USA), when he stated:

> The enduring confidence of the investing public in the integrity of our capital markets is vital. In America today, approximately one out of every two adults has invested their savings in the securities markets, either [directly] through the purchase of individual stocks or [indirectly through investment] in a mutual fund or . . . pension plan. . . . These investments have provided trillions of dollars in capital for companies in the United States and around the globe. That capital is providing the fuel for our economic engine, funding for the growth of new businesses, and providing . . . job opportunities for tens of millions of workers. But . . . the willingness of investors to continue to invest their money in the markets cannot be taken for granted. . . . Public trust begins, and ends, with the integrity of the numbers the public uses to form the basis for making their investment decisions. . . . Accordingly, investors in the U.S. capital markets have depended for over a hundred years on an independent third party, an external auditor to examine the book and financial reports prepared by management. (pp. 1–2)

Thus, in the USA – and similarly in the UK and other countries throughout the Western world – continued investment in the capital markets is essential to the well-being of the economy – and to the financial well-being of those who invest directly or indirectly in the financial markets. Continued investment in the financial markets rests on investors having confidence in the financial infor-mation on which they base their investment decisions. This confidence, in turn, is derived from the audit function. Although not referred to by Turner, indirect investment includes investment by local authorities, and other public sector bodies, of funds (derived in the form of taxes but not yet needed to meet expenditures) provided by the vast majority of the public. Therefore, most members of society – directly or indirectly – benefit from external financial statement audits.

(ii)   Securing the accountability of corporate managements

Over the last 160 or so years, as financial, human and other non-financial resources have been channelled by individuals and groups in society to companies, so these entities have grown in size. As they have become larger, they have gained significant social, economic and political power. Today, large national and multinational companies dominate the lives, and control the well-being, of whole communities and have a major impact on society in general. However, in a democratic society, power is not absolute. Mindful of Lord Acton's dictum that 'power corrupts and absolute power corrupts absolutely', society has set in place checks and balances designed to prevent possible abuse of power. As one of the checks designed to ensure that company managements do not abuse the power bestowed upon them through the provision of resources, they are held accountable for the responsible use of the resources entrusted to them. This accountability is secured primarily by requiring company directors:

- to provide publicly available annual financial statements which report on their use of resources;
- to submit these financial statements to a critical examination by an independent expert (that is, an audit).

Thus, auditors may be seen as an integral part of the process of securing the accountability of company managements who control and use the resources of various groups in society such as shareholders, debt-holders, creditors, employees, suppliers, customers and the general public. Legally, a company auditor is appointed by, and reports to, shareholders. In reality, however, all stakeholders who provide resources to company managements (or who are otherwise affected by company managements' decisions) have an interest in the accountability process of which auditing is a part.

Therefore, in addition to protecting the interests of financial statement users by giving credibility to the financial statements, and providing ancillary services to auditee entities, the external audit, by helping to ensure the smooth functioning of financial markets, and by functioning as an element of social control within the corporate accountability process, is also of value to society as a whole.

1.7   SUMMARY

In this chapter we have considered the nature of the audit function and distinguished between financial statement audits, compliance audits and operational audits, and between external and internal audits. We have also noted the difference between accounting and auditing and discussed why external financial statement audits are needed. In the final section of the chapter we examined some of the benefits derived from these audits by financial statement users, auditees, and society as a whole.

In the next chapter we trace the development of auditing, noting in particular how auditing has responded over time to changes in its socio-economic environment.

SELF-REVIEW QUESTIONS

1.1   Give a comprehensive definition of auditing.

1.2   Explain briefly the following words and phrases included in the definition of auditing given in this chapter:

(i)   systematic process
(ii) objectively gathering and evaluating evidence
(iii) assertions
(iv) degree of correspondence between assertions and established criteria
(v)   communicating the results.
1.3 List the major elements which are present in all audits.
1.4 Explain briefly the major differences between the following types of audits:
(i)   Financial statement audits
(ii) Compliance audits
(iii) Operational audits.
1.5 Under the provisions of the Companies Act 1985 an auditor's report must be attached to a company's financial statements. Is this true for all companies? Explain.
1.6 Distinguish between:
(i)   auditing and accounting; and
(ii) internal and external audits.
1.7 Explain briefly why external financial statement audits are needed.
1.8 It is said that the value of an audit for financial statement users lies in the credibility it gives to the financial statements which are prepared by management. Explain briefly the three types of control which help an audit to give credibility to audited financial statements.
1.9 Explain briefly the benefits which an external financial statement audit provides for an auditee. Also explain any dangers which may result from auditors providing 'additional services' to auditees.
1.10 Explain briefly the value of external financial statement audits for society as a whole.

REFERENCES

Anderson, R.J. (1977) *The External Audit*. Toronto: Cropp Clark Pitman.
Auditing Practices Board (APB) (1996) *The Auditor's Code*. London: APB.
The Company Law Review Steering Group (2001) *Modern Company Law for a Competitive Economy: Final Report*. London: Department of Trade and Industry.
Turner, L.E. (2001) *Independence: A Covenant for the Ages*. Speech at the International Organisation of Securities Commissions, Stockholm, Sweden, 28 June.

ADDITIONAL READING

Bagshaw, K. (2001) One year on: changes in the audit exemption limit have raised a number of tricky issues. *Accountancy* **128**(1295), 154.
Benston, G. (1985) The market for public accounting services: Demand, supply and regulation. *Journal of Accounting and Public Policy* **4**, 33–79.

Commission on Auditors' Responsibilities (1978) *Report, Conclusions and Recommendations* (The Cohen Commission), pp. 3–12, New York: AICPA.

Hatherly, D. (1992a) Company auditing: a vision of the future. *Accountancy* **110**(1187), 75.

Hatherly, D. (1992b) Can auditing work without a break with tradition? *Accountancy* **110**(1189), 85.

Humphrey, C. & Moizer, P. (1990) From techniques to ideologies: An alternative perspective on the audit function. *Critical Perspectives on Accounting* **1**, 217–238.

Lee, T.A. (1998) A Stakeholder Approach to Auditing, *Critical Perspectives on Accounting* **9**, 217–226.

Pasewark. W.R., Shockley, R.A. & Wilkerson, J.E. (1995) Legitimacy claims of the auditing profession vis-à-vis the behaviour of its members: an empirical examination. *Critical Perspectives on Accounting* **6**, 77–94.

2 The Development of Auditing and Audit Objectives

LEARNING OBJECTIVES

After studying the material in this chapter you should be able to:

- describe and explain the changes which have taken place in audit objectives in the English-speaking world over the last 160 years;
- explain the relationship between changes in the external audit function and changes in the socio-economic environment of the English-speaking world over the last 160 years;
- discuss the differences between the audit risk and business risk approach to auditing.

The following fundamental principle included in *The Auditor's Code* (APB, 1996) is particularly relevant to this chapter:

Fundamental principle of external auditing: *Accountability*

2.1   INTRODUCTION

In this chapter we discuss the evolution of audit objectives in the English-speaking world, and examine the ways in which the external audit function has responded to changes in its socio-economic environment.

2.2   THE DEVELOPMENT OF AUDITING

2.2.1   An overview

Auditing, like all professions, exists to satisfy a need of society. It is therefore to be expected that auditing changes as the needs and demands of society change. Figure 2.1 shows the close link between auditing and the socio-economic environment it serves in the English-speaking world. In particular, it shows:

- how audit objectives have changed in response to changes in the socio-economic environment (in particular, to changes in the characteristics, and the accountability expected, of business enterprises);
- how the main centre of auditing development shifted from the United Kingdom (UK) to the United States of America (USA) as the centre of economic development moved across the Atlantic, and that it has become increasingly global in focus in recent years;
- how the procedures adopted by auditors accord with the objectives auditing is trying to meet.

Figure 2.1 also shows that the development of auditing can be considered conveniently in five phases:

- period up to 1844
- 1844–1920s
- 1920s–1960s
- 1960s–1990s
- 1990s–present.

2.2.2   Period up to 1844

During this earliest and longest phase in its development, auditing was primarily concerned with public accounts. Evidence, mainly in the form of markings on tablets and buildings, shows that over 2,000 years ago the Egyptians, Greeks and Romans all used systems to check the accounting of officials entrusted with public funds. In the Greek and Roman Empires, those responsible for public funds were required to appear periodically before a government official to give an oral presentation of their accounts. As noted in Chapter 1, the word 'audit' (derived from the Latin for 'a hearing') dates from these times.

Figure 2.1: The interrelationships of external auditing

Period	Main centre of audit development	Main characteristics of business enterprises and audit environment	Accountability of business enterprises		Audit objectives	Major characteristics of auditing techniques
			To whom	For what?		
Pre-1844	United Kingdom	• Cottage Industries • Individual trading ventures • Emergence of industrial organisations (with the Industrial Revolution).	• Owners • (Shareholders)	• Honest authorised use of funds	• Detection of fraud (Only Balance Sheet audited)	• Detailed checking of transactions and account entries • Concern for arithmetical accuracy and agreement between accounts and Balance Sheet
1844–1920s	United Kingdom	• Growth in number and size of companies • Separation of ownership and management (Emergence and increase in the number of professional accountants and auditors)	• Shareholders • Creditors	• Honest authorised use of funds	• Detection of fraud • Detection of errors • Determination of solvency/insolvency (Only Balance Sheet audited)	• Detailed checking of transactions and account entries • Little physical observation of assets or use of external evidence • Concern for arithmetical accuracy and agreement between accounts and Balance Sheet
1920s–1960s	Shift from United Kingdom to United States of America in the early 1920s	• Wall Street Crash (1929) and the depression • Increasing concentration of capital in, and the growth of, large corporations • Increasing separation of ownership and salaried managers • Emergence of Institutional Investors	• Shareholders • Creditors • Investors in general	• Honest authorised use of funds • Profitable use of resources	• Lending credibility to financial statements prepared by management • Fraud and error detection lost their significance as audit objectives and became of minor importance (Emphasis gradually shifted to Profit and Loss Statement but Balance Sheet remained important)	• Gradual change to reliance on internal controls combined with test checking of selected samples • Physical observation of external and other evidence outside the 'books of account' • Concern for the truth and fairness of financial information provided by management
1960s–1990s	United States of America	• Continued growth of large corporations (with many takeovers and mergers) • Companies increasingly multinational in nature • Dominance of professional management divorced from ownership interests • Increasing importance of taxation • Dominance of institutional investors • Increasing competition between business (and audit) firms • Stock Market Crash (1987)	• Shareholders • Creditors • Investors • Customers • Suppliers • Society in general	• Honest, authorised use of funds • Profitable use of resources • Wider social responsibilities (e.g. pollution)	• Lending credibility to financial statements prepared by management • Provision of management advisory services	• Audit based on – a thorough understanding of the client, its business and its industry – identification of audit risk through analytical review – assessment of reliance which can be placed on internal controls • Emergence and increasing significance of auditing by, and of, computers • Examination of evidence from a wide variety of sources – both internal and external to the entity
1990s–present	Primarily United States of America but increasingly global in focus	• Dominance of Western economies by multinational corporates (business and audit firms) • Technological advances affecting all aspects of the corporate/business environment • Increasing regulatory concern re corporate governance • Removal in the UK of audit requirement for small companies	• Shareholders • Creditors • Investors • Customers • Suppliers • Society in general	• Honest, authorised use of funds • Profitable use of resources • Responsible corporate governance • Wider social responsibilities	• Lending credibility to financial and non-financial information provided by management in annual reports • Provision of management advisory services • Increased responsibility for detecting fraud and reporting doubts about 'going concern' • Helping to secure responsible corporate governance • Reporting to regulatory authorities – fraud detected during an audit – doubts about auditees' solvency	• Emergence of audit methodologies focusing on clients' business risk (risk of auditees not meeting their objectives) • Audit based on – a thorough understanding of the client, its business, its industry and (especially) its risks – identification of audit risk through analytical review • Adaptation of auditing to the e-commerce/e-business environment

Similarly, in medieval times in England, government officials visited the various manors and estates to check the accounts (now in written form) to ensure that the funds collected and disbursed on behalf of the Crown were properly accounted for. Interestingly, as the following quotation reveals, the information collected for the Domesday Book in 1085 (which formed the initial basis for assessing the amounts due to the Crown from the manors and estates) was subject to audit.

> The Saxon Chronicle records that in 1085 at Gloucester,
>
>> at midwinter ... the King [William the Conqueror] had deep speech with his counsellors ... and sent men all over England to each shire ... to find out ... what or how much each landowner held ... in land and livestock, and what it was worth. The returns were brought to him.
>
> William was thorough. . . . [H]e also sent a second set of Commissioners to shires they did not know, where they themselves were unknown, to check their predecessors' survey, and report culprits to the King. (Reported and cited by Morris, 1977, p. 1, from Domesday Book, 20 Bedfordshire).

Prior to the industrial revolution (which began in the late eighteenth century), auditing had little commercial application. Industry was primarily based in cottages and small mills, located where water power was available. Individuals both owned and managed these small businesses and therefore there was no need for the business managers to report to the owners on their management of resources – and no need for such reports to be audited.

However, especially during the eighteenth century, overseas trading ventures became important. The captains of the ships engaged in these commercial ventures were required to account for the funds and cargos entrusted to their care, to those who had financed the undertaking. These accounts were subject to audit. Indeed, private commercial venture audits originate in the audits of the accounts of trading ships returning to Britain from the East and the New World.

During this pre-1844 period, concern centred on the honest authorised use of funds by those to whom the funds had been entrusted. Correspondingly, the main audit objective was the detection of fraud. In order to meet this objective, the accounts under audit were subjected to a detailed and thorough examination, with special emphasis on arithmetical accuracy and compliance with the authority given to the custodian of the funds.

2.2.3 1844–1920s

(i) Socio-economic developments

As in the latter stages of the pre-1844 period, economic and auditing development during the period from 1844 to the 1920s was centred in the UK.

This period, which followed the industrial revolution, saw far-reaching changes in the socio-economic environment. In particular, it witnessed the emergence of large-scale industrial and commercial enterprises and the displacement of individual (one-off) joint ventures by continuing corporations. Accompanying these changes, the period also witnessed a significant advancement in auditing.

In the late eighteenth century, the industrial revolution, with its associated large factories and machine-based production, led to a demand for vast amounts of capital. At the same time, a new 'middle class' emerged, with small amounts of surplus funds available for investment. As a result, small amounts of capital were contributed by many people, and these were channelled by financial entrepreneurs into large industrial and commercial undertakings. However, in the eighteenth and early nineteenth centuries, the share market was unregulated and highly speculative, and the rate of financial failure was high. At this time, liability was not limited and the treatment of debtors, including innocent investors who became debtors when 'their' business venture failed, was very harsh. Given this environment, it was clear that the growing number of small investors needed some protection.

(ii) Statutory developments

As a result of these socio-economic developments in the UK, the Joint Stock Companies Act was passed in 1844. This Act enabled companies to be formed and officially recognised merely by registration. Previously, companies could only become recognised as such by means of a Royal Charter or a Special Act of Parliament. The first option was very expensive; the latter very slow.

In return for gaining recognition through registration, companies had to comply with certain regulations. These included the following:
- each company's directors had to provide an annual balance sheet to their shareholders setting out the state of affairs of the company;
- an auditor had to be appointed by the company's shareholders. The auditor was empowered to examine the company's records at reasonable intervals throughout the year and was required to report to the company's shareholders whether, in his opinion, the balance sheet gave a 'full and fair' view of the company's state of affairs. Unlike today, the auditor was not required to be independent of the company's management, or a qualified accountant. In practice, a shareholder was usually appointed as auditor by his fellow members.

In 1856, the statutory provisions requiring compulsory audits were repealed. Subsequent events proved this move to be ill-advised: of 88,000 companies registered between 1862 and 1904, over 50,000 had come to an end by 1904

(Brown, 1905, p. 325). Not surprisingly, compulsory audits were re-introduced in the Companies Act of 1900. Under the auditing provisions of this Act, an auditor was still not required to be a qualified accountant but the need for auditors to be independent of management was recognised. The Act provided that neither a director nor an officer of the company could be appointed as auditor. The Act also provided that:

- auditors were to be given access to all of the company's books and records which they required to perform their duties as auditors. This included access to documents such as contracts and minutes of directors' meetings;
- auditors were to append a certificate to the foot of the audited balance sheet stating that all of their requirements as auditors had been met;
- in addition to the above certificate, auditors were to report to shareholders on the balance sheet stating whether, in their opinion, it conveyed a 'true and correct' view of the state of affairs of the company.

The Institute of Chartered Accountants in England and Wales (ICAEW) sought legal advice on the form the required certificate and report should take. This resulted in the adoption of a standard form of certificate and audit report. These were as follows:[1]

Auditor's Certificate

In accordance with the provisions of the Companies Act 1900, I certify that all my requirements as auditor have been complied with.

Auditor's Report

I have audited the above balance sheet and, in my opinion, such a balance sheet is properly drawn up, so as to exhibit a true and correct view of the state of affairs of the company, as shown by the books of the company.

The Companies Act 1900 was a prominent milestone in the history of company auditing. It established compulsory audits, the independence of auditors from company managements, and a standard form of audit report.

---

[1] Reported in an Editorial, *The Accountant's Magazine*, January 1901, p. 47.

(iii)   Corporate accountability and audit objectives

During the period from 1844 to the 1920s, companies generally remained relatively small and company managers were generally regarded as accountable only for the safe custody and honest, authorised use of funds entrusted to them. In accordance with society's needs and expectations of the time, audit objectives were designed to protect principally shareholders, but secondarily lenders/bankers, from unscrupulous acts by company managers who had custody of their funds. Hence the main audit objectives were:

- the detection of fraud and error; and
- the proper portrayal of the company's solvency (or insolvency) in the balance sheet.

In general, during this period company managers were considered to be accountable only to the company's shareholders. This is reflected in the fact that the balance sheet was regarded as a private communication between the company's management and its shareholders. Indeed, there was much debate in accounting circles about the auditor's report on the balance sheet. The Act only required that the report be read at the shareholders' annual general meeting and many professional accountants apparently thought it was wrong to also attach it to the published balance sheet. They feared that the auditor might have something to say in the report which, should it become public knowledge, might be injurious to the company; for example, comments which might cause creditors to panic and to demand that their claims be met immediately, causing the company to collapse. Others considered that, logically, the report should be combined and published with the auditor's certificate. In the event, the Companies Act 1908 settled the debate by supporting the latter view and requiring the auditor to provide just one (combined) report (Lee, 1970, p. 366).

(iv)   Development of auditors' duties

The decisions of the courts during the period from 1844 to 1920 served to clarify auditors' duties. The two most notable cases were those of *London and General Bank* (1895) and *Kingston Cotton Mill* (1896).

- In the renowned case of *Re London and General Bank (No. 2)* [1895] 2 Ch. 673, the auditor had discovered errors in the balance sheet. He had reported the facts to the directors but failed to report the matter to the shareholders. In his summing up, Lindley L J stated that it was not the duty of the auditor to see that the company and its directors acted prudently or imprudently, profitably or unprofitably, in performing their business activities, but it was the auditor's duty to report to shareholders any dishonest acts which had occurred and which affected the propriety of the information contained in the balance sheet. However, he also said that the auditor could not be expected to find every fraud and error committed within the company. That would be asking too much; the auditor was not an insurer or guarantor. What was expected of him was reasonable skill and care in the circumstances.

- In *Re Kingston Cotton Mill Co Ltd (No. 2)* [1896] 2 Ch. 279, Lopes L J elaborated on the remarks of Lindley L J (above). He stated:

  It is the duty of an auditor to bring to bear on the work he has to perform that skill, care and caution which a reasonably competent, careful and cautious auditor would use. What is reasonable skill, care and caution must depend on the particular circumstances of each case. An auditor is not bound to be a detective or ... to approach his work with suspicion or with a foregone conclusion that there is something wrong. He is a watchdog not a bloodhound. If there is anything to excite suspicion he should probe it to the bottom; but in the absence of anything of that kind he is only bound to be reasonably cautious and careful.

These two cases reinforced the audit objectives of detecting fraud and error and established the general standard of work expected of auditors. They established that auditors are not expected to ferret out every fraud but they are required to use reasonable skill and care in examining the relevant books and records.

Corresponding with the primary audit objective of detecting fraud and error, auditing procedures from 1844 to the 1920s involved close examination of the accounting entries and related internal documentary evidence, and detailed checking of the arithmetical accuracy of the accounting records. However, towards the end of the period, judgments by the courts made it clear that auditors were required to do more than merely check the company's books and records. In the case of *London Oil Storage Co Ltd v Seear, Hasluck & Co.* [1904] 31 Acct. LR 1, it was held that the auditor was liable for damage sustained by a company which resulted from his omission to verify the existence of assets stated in the balance sheet. It was established that the auditor, in ensuring that the information given in the audited balance sheet corresponded with the company's books and records, was not merely required to check the arithmetical accuracy of the entries; he was also required to ensure that the data in the books represented fact rather than fiction. This case made it clear, for the first time, that the auditor was required to go beyond the internal books and records of the company for evidence to support his audit opinion.

This position was confirmed and extended in *Arthur E. Green & Co. v The Central Advance and Discount Corporation Ltd* [1920] 63 Acct LR 1. In this case the court held that the auditor was negligent in accepting a schedule of bad debts provided by a responsible officer of the company when it was apparent that other debts not included in the schedule were also irrecoverable. The case established that, not only was the auditor required to go beyond the company's internal documentary evidence; he was also required to relate evidence obtained from different sources.

These cases indicate that, by the 1920s, auditing was rapidly developing into a technical process, requiring the skills of qualified accountants. However, many auditors were still laymen: frequently, they were merely shareholders chosen to be auditors by their fellow members. This reflects the key to this early period in the development of company audits. Company managers were regarded as accountable for the safe custody and honest, authorised use of the funds entrusted to them, primarily by shareholders. Audits were required to protect the interests of, and secure managers' accountability to, the company's share-holders.[2]

2.2.4   1920s–1960s

(i)   Socio-economic developments

During this period the centre of economic and auditing development shifted from the UK to the USA. The period was marked by the continued growth of companies and the development of sophisticated securities markets and credit-granting institutions, designed to serve the financial needs of the growing economic entities.

In the years of recovery following the 1929 Wall Street Crash and ensuing depression, investment in business entities grew rapidly and became wide-spread. Company ownership became highly diffused and a new class of small investors emerged. Unlike the shareholders of earlier years, who were few in number but closely bound to the companies they partially owned, the new breed of investors were little interested in the management or fortunes of

---

[2] Chandler *et al.* (1993) present a contrary view of audit objectives for the period from 1844 to the 1920s. They provide evidence to support the notion that verifying financial statements prepared by company managements, rather than fraud detection, was the chief audit objective during second and third quarters of the 19th century. However, they limit this suggestion to banking, railway and insurance companies which 'were generally much larger and possessed a much more widely dispersed shareholder group than the majority of industrial and manufacturing companies. [These] shareholders . . . tended to view themselves not so much as owners but as investors looking for the best return. . . . For the generality of companies, which remained relatively small, it was the auditor's fraud detection role which remained predominant' (Chandler *et al.*, 1993, pp. 444–445).

Thus, it seems that between 1844 and the 1870s the shareholders of banking, railway and insurance companies were similar to the typical investors of the 1920s to 1960s period – investors who required reliable (verified) information for their investment decisions. However, Chandler *et al.* note that during the latter part of the 19th century the primary audit objective, even for 'sectors of the economy where large (usually quoted) companies predominated' (p. 445) became fraud detection. They suggest the change can be traced to leading professional accountant-auditors (who were beginning to replace the amateur shareholder-auditors) becoming obsessed with fraud detection as a consequence of the frequency of corporate bankruptcy in the 1860s and 1870s, with fraud featuring as a major factor in the demise of the companies (p. 447). Professional accountants at this time were heavily involved in bankruptcy and insolvency work and thus many gained insight into the causes and adverse effects of fraud. The dominance of fraud detection as the chief audit objective at the turn of the century is reflected in Spicer and Pegler's 1911 textbook: 'In the minds of the public at large, and of the majority of clients, the discovery of fraud is so far the principal function of the Auditor as to overshadow his other duties entirely, and there can be no question that it is of primary importance' (p. 5).

'their' companies *per se*. They were primarily concerned with the return they could earn on their investment and, if they perceived that better returns could be earned elsewhere, they readily switched their allegiance to another company. With these developments, ownership interests and management functions of companies became increasingly separated. The management and control of companies gradually passed to small groups of qualified, professional, salaried managers who frequently owned no shares in the companies they managed.

In this new economic environment, the accountability of company managers was extended from the honest, authorised use of shareholders' funds, to include the profitable use of those funds; business managers became accountable for generating a reasonable return on the financial resources entrusted to them.

At the same time as shareholders became increasingly divorced from their companies, and companies grew in size and extended their influence in society, it came to be recognised that the survival and growth of companies rested, not only on the financial resources provided by shareholders, but on the joint contribution of all stakeholders, that is, all those with a particular 'stake' or interest in the company – shareholders, debtholders, employees, suppliers, customers and the government. As a consequence, many in society came to regard company managers as accountable to all of their company's stakeholders, and as having an obligation to ensure that each stakeholder group is sufficiently rewarded for its contribution so as to ensure it maintained its 'stake' in the company.

The trend towards society expecting increased accountability from company managers was re-inforced by events such as the 1929 Wall Street Crash and the questionable or downright dishonest acts of company directors which resulted in cases such as the *Royal Mail* case (1932) in the UK (see below) and the *McKesson & Robbins* case (1938) in the USA (see Chapter 5, section 5.3).

(ii)   Developments in auditing

During the period from the 1920s to the 1960s, in response to changes in the socio-economic environment, auditing changed in four main ways. These are as follows:

(a)   *Development of sampling techniques:* As companies grew in size, the volume of transactions in which they engaged made it progressively less feasible for auditors to check in detail all of the entries in the accounting records.

At the same time as companies grew in size, their managers found it necessary to delegate accounting and other duties to employees. With the growth in the volume of transactions and the delegation of responsibilities, errors in the company's records and also fraud became more likely. In order to prevent and/or detect errors and fraud, managements introduced systems of internal control.

As a result of these changes, auditing procedures changed from meticulous checking of accounting records to testing samples of transactions and accounting entries, combined with a review and evaluation of the company's system of internal control.

(b) *Increased emphasis on external audit evidence:* Particularly as a result of decisions in cases such as *London Oil Storage Co. Ltd* v *Seear Hasluck and Co.* (see above) and the *McKesson & Robbins* case (1938, USA), new emphasis was given to the physical observation of assets such as cash and stock, and to the use of external evidence (for example, confirmation of debtors). These duties came to be recognised as of equal importance to the auditor's traditional task of examining the company's internal books, records and documents.

(c) *Auditing the profit and loss statement:* As return on investment became the factor of prime importance for investors, and as companies' stakeholders focused their attention on receiving adequate compensation for their contribution to joint performance, so the emphasis of financial statement users shifted away from the balance sheet and ideas of solvency, towards the profit and loss statement and ideas of earning power.

This shift in emphasis was led from the USA but was dramatically reinforced in the UK by the *Royal Mail* case (*Rex* v *Kyslant* [1932] I KB 442; [1931] All ER 179) which, in the words of De Paula 'fell like an atom bomb and changed the face of the world of accounting' (as reported, Johnston *et al.*, 1982 p. 9). Similarly, Chandler *et al.* (1993) refer to it as 'perhaps the single most significant 20th century case in terms of its impact on the development of accounting thought and practice' (p. 454). They also attribute 'the transition from fraud detection to [financial] statement verification' as the primary audit objective in the 1930s 'mainly to the effects of the Royal Mail case' (p. 457).

The case principally revolved around the Royal Mail Steam Packet Company publishing profit and loss accounts between 1921 and 1928 which failed to show whether profits had or had not been earned, and paying dividends during these years, amounting to £5 million, funded largely from undisclosed transfers from secret reserves. Additionally, in 1928, the company published 'a prospectus inviting the public to subscribe to the issue of debenture stock . . . which . . . concealed the true position of the company, with intent to induce persons to entrust or advance property to the company' (Mr Justice Wright, presiding Judge). The profit and loss accounts and prospectus disclosed 'surpluses' for the years 1921 to 1928, ranging from £628,535 to £779,114 – implying that the company was profitable and a sound investment opportunity. In fact, the company made significant trading losses in each year from 1921 to 1928 ranging from £95,614 to £779,153.

The *Royal Mail* case, more than any other, highlighted the need for the profit and loss statement to be audited. Not surprisingly, the legislators introduced mandatory auditing of the profit and loss statement – in the USA in 1934, under the Securities and Exchange Commission Act, and in the UK in the Companies Act 1948.

(d) *Change in audit objectives:* Although the other changes which occurred in auditing between the 1920s and 1960s were significant, the greatest single change which took place was the change in audit objectives. The focus of auditing shifted away from preventing and detecting fraud and error towards assessing the truth and fairness of the information presented in companies' financial statements.

As noted above, as companies grew in size, their ownership and management functions became increasingly separated. In order to ensure that funds continued to flow from investors to companies, and that financial markets functioned smoothly, it was essential that participants in the financial markets were confident that company financial statements provided a true and fair portrayal of the relevant company's financial position and performance. Responding to these needs, auditors accepted as their primary audit objective, providing credibility to the financial statements prepared by company managers for their shareholders, which essentially reported on their own (that is, the managers') performance.

At the same time as providing credibility to externally reported financial information emerged as the chief audit objective, that of detecting fraud and error declined in importance. As Spicer and Pegler (1936) noted:

> The main object of an audit is the verification of accounts and statements prepared by a client or client's staff. Although of great importance the detection of fraud and error must be regarded as incidental to such main object. (p. 5)

The decline in the importance of fraud and error detection as the primary audit objective corresponded with the fact that, as companies grew in size:

- their managements established systems of internal control designed to prevent and detect fraud and error; and
- auditing procedures changed from detailed checking of the company's books and records to testing samples of transactions and accounting entries, combined with a review and evaluation of the company's system of internal control. This change reduced the likelihood of discovering fraud during an audit at the transaction and account level.

The changes indicated above also provided new opportunities for auditors. Through their review of their audit client's accounting system and related internal controls, and through the thorough knowledge of the client entity and its business which auditors gained during the course of their audit, they were ideally placed to offer ancillary services to the entity's managers. They were, for example, in an ideal position to suggest ways in which the efficiency and effectiveness of the accounting system and/or internal controls might be improved, and to offer assistance in areas such as financial and tax planning.

By the mid-1960s, companies had become an increasingly influential element in society and their managers were regarded as accountable to a wide range of interested parties, not only for the honest, authorised use of resources entrusted to their care, but also for the profitable use of the resources. Auditing had become well established as a profession and auditors' rights and duties, which still pertain today, were embodied in statute and case law. Nevertheless, since the 1960s further notable changes have occurred in the audit environment, audit objectives and auditing techniques.

2.2.5   1960s–1990s

(i)   Socio-economic developments

Since the 1960s, aided – and accelerated – by technological advances, companies have continued to grow in size and, particularly in the case of national and multinational companies, have become extremely powerful and influential forces in society. The extent of the power held by companies is reflected in the enormous share of the nation's resources which is invested in the corporate sector.

The social and economic influence of companies is also reflected in the effect they have in their local communities. This is not restricted to providing employment and generating a flow of funds in their neighbourhoods; they also have an impact through the presence and appearance of their grounds and buildings. Many provide sporting and cultural facilities. They use the local transport network and affect traffic volumes and flows. They produce goods and services desired by consumers. They purchase goods and services produced by suppliers. They may help to beautify, or to exploit and pollute, the local environment. When these and other factors are taken into consideration, it is clear that even a moderately-sized company can have a significant influence on the economic and social life of the community of which it is a part. Taken as a whole, the corporate sector has an enormous impact on the well-being of society in general. Given this level of power and influence in society, it is often argued that company managers should be held accountable for behaving in a socially responsible manner. Many believe that corporate managers have an obligation to consider the impact of their decisions on those who will be affected thereby, at the same time as they seek to accomplish their traditional economic goals, such as profit-making and long-term survival (see, for example, Davis, 1976; Demers and Wayland, 1982).

To an extent, this wider obligation to society is well established. Company managers are, for example, considered to have an obligation to prevent environmental pollution, to enhance employee and product safety, to adopt equal employment opportunities, and to protect consumers. The State has introduced a considerable volume of statutory regulation covering these and similar issues with which company managers must comply. The necessary compliance auditing, however, is not the responsibility of the company's financial statement auditors but may be undertaken by inspectors from a State agency.

Notwithstanding the extension of the accountability expected of company managers since the mid-twentieth century, legislation relating to external reporting by companies in the UK (as elsewhere) continues to focus on company managers' accountability to shareholders for financial performance. Nevertheless, the legislators have recognised that corporate managers are also accountable to their company's debenture-holders as, under the Companies Act 1985, s.238, companies are required to provide not only their shareholders, but also their debenture-holders, with a copy of their annual financial statements, directors' report and auditor's report.[3] However, they are not (as yet) required to report to a wider range of stakeholders and/or on their social activities, but these are possible developments for the future and many companies undertake such reporting voluntarily. The essence of the present position is reflected in the fundamental principle of external auditing – *Accountability*:

> Auditors act in the interests of primary stakeholders, whilst having regard to the wider public interest.

> The identity of primary stakeholders is determined by reference to the statute or agreement requiring an audit: in the case of companies, the primary stakeholder is the general body of shareholders. (APB, 1996)

Developments in auditing

As shown in Figure 2.1, three major developments in auditing techniques occurred during the 1960s–1990s period. These are:

- increased emphasis on examining audit evidence derived from a wide variety of sources, both internal and external to the auditee. (This is a continuation of the trend noted in the earlier phases of auditing's development);

---

[3] The statutory duties of companies with respect to external financial reporting are discussed in Chapter 5, section 5.2.

- the emergence and increasing significance of computers, both as an audit tool and as an element in auditee entities to be embraced by audit examinations;
- the development of risk-based auditing; in essence, assessing the likelihood of material misstatements occurring in the financial statements and focusing audit effort on those areas identified as most likely to contain error(s). This 'audit risk' approach seeks to reduce to an acceptable level the risk that the auditee's financial statements (to which a 'clean' audit report is attached) contain material misstatements.[4]

Adoption of risk-based auditing resulted in auditors needing to gain a thorough understanding of their audit clients (the organisation, key personnel, policies, procedures, etc.), their businesses and their industries. It also involved auditors understanding their clients' systems of internal financial controls and the extent to which these could be relied upon to prevent misstatements from occurring in the financial statements. Additionally, during the 1960s–1990s period, virtually all companies introduced computer systems to process their financial and other data, and to perform, monitor and/or control many (if not most) of their operational and administrative processes. These changes provided auditors with new opportunities to identify areas within their client companies where improvements could be made – for example, in their internal control and management information systems, in their tax and financial planning, and in aspects of their operations.

At the same time as changes in auditing presented opportunities for auditors to provide advisory services for management, fierce competition developed between businesses and between audit firms. This was largely prompted by advances in information technology and the phenomenal increase in the speed of information transfer which meant that businesses' products and services, prices, processes, etc. were quickly known by their competitors and others. In the case of audit firms, increased competition also resulted from mergers and acquisitions reducing the number of auditees. As a consequence of the competition, audit fees came under severe pressure. Auditors seeking to maintain (or increase) their fees emphasised to their clients' managements that, rather than being viewed as a 'statutorily required evil' to be secured at minimum cost, an audit should be viewed as a value-adding activity: valuable management advisory services could be provided as an outcome of the audit. As a consequence, the provision of advisory services for management emerged as a secondary audit objective.

---

[4] Risk-based auditing is discussed in detail in Chapter 8.

2.2.6 1990s–the present

(i) Socio-economic developments

Since the 1990s, the socio-economic developments of the 1960s–1990s period have continued at an accelerating pace. Today, developed economies are characterised by huge multinational companies, many other businesses are increasingly global in nature, and technology (and technical advances) pervades all aspects of the commercial environment.

As large companies have grown even larger in size, so they have further increased their power and influence in society. As seen in the aftermath of the 1987 Stock Market Crash and more recent well-publicised company failures, the demise of any large company has a major and widespread adverse impact on many individuals, groups and organisations in society. Responding to the unheralded failure of a number of large companies during the late 1980s and early 1990s, and evidence of misconduct, negligence, and/or recklessness, by senior company officials which came to light during investigations of the failed companies by the Department of Trade and Industry or similar agencies, regulators have sought to ensure that companies are governed properly. Hence, for example, all companies listed on the London Stock Exchange are required to comply with *The Combined Code*[5] (Committee on Corporate Governance, 1998b). This code of best corporate practice has been developed from a series of corporate governance reports, in particular, the reports of the Committee on the Financial Aspects of Corporate Governance (Cadbury Committee) (1992), the Study Group examining Directors' Remuneration (Greenbury Committee) (1995), and the Committee on Corporate Governance (Hampel Committee) (1998a). At the same time as regulators have become concerned with securing responsible corporate governance, large companies have come under increased societal and media pressure to conduct their business in a socially responsible manner.

(ii) Developments in auditing

As in the earlier periods of auditing development discussed above, since the early 1990s auditing has adapted and responded to changes in its environment. More specifically, the period has witnessed the emergence of a business risk approach to auditing. This is essentially a development of the audit risk approach which characterised the 1970s and 1980s (Lemon *et al.*, 2000). The business risk approach rests on the notion that a broad range of the client's business risks are relevant to the audit. Proponents point out that many business risks, if not controlled, will eventually affect the financial statements. They maintain that, by understanding the full range (and potential impact and likelihood of occurrence) of risks facing an auditee, the auditor is better able

---

[5] Or explain the provisions with which they have not complied and the reasons why.

(than under a narrow approach focusing directly on the financial statements) to identify matters of significance and relevance to the audit on a timely basis. While both approaches have as their ultimate objective expressing an opinion on the truth and fairness of the financial statements, the audit risk approach seeks to achieve this by focusing on the financial statements and assessing the likelihood of them being materially misstated, the business risk approach adopts a holistic business-wide perspective.

What prompted the development – and adoption – of the business risk approach? According to Lemon *et al.* (2000), it has resulted primarily from two sets of factors:

(a) those related to the effectiveness and efficiency of the audit;
(b) those related to the 'added value' dimension of the audit.

(a) Factors related to audit effectiveness and efficiency

Audit firms (especially the large firms) which have reviewed the causes of audit failure (that is, expressing a 'clean' audit opinion on financial statements that are materially misstated) have concluded that such failure does not generally stem from auditors' failure to detect accounting data recording or processing errors. Rather, it tends to result from matters associated with how the business is managed. As noted by Lemon *et al.* (2000, p. 10): 'factors such as the business environment, governance issues and the nature of managerial control will ultimately have significance for the financial statements – their accuracy, issues of fraud and going concern'. Thus, firms adopting the business risk approach have concluded: 'effective auditing [that is, expressing the appropriate audit opinion on the financial statements] requires greater attention to be paid to understanding the risks of the business' (Lemon *et al.*, 2000, p. 12).

Similarly, advances in computer technology have resulted in auditees' accounting records, and the processing of their routine data, being inherently less prone to error than formerly. Therefore detailed checking of this information is of less importance. Changes in the technology used by both auditees and auditors have provided greater scope for audit effort to be devoted to higher-level (less detailed and client-wide) analysis and assessment. This higher-level assessment generates more broadly-based evidence about the auditee and this, in turn, provides the auditor with a more broadly – and soundly – based context for making judgments about the truth and fairness of the auditee's financial statements.

(b) The added-value dimension of the audit

By considering a broad range of issues associated with the risks of an auditee's business, auditors increase their opportunities to assist the client avoid problems which would threaten achievement of its (the client's) objectives – or even its survival. As Lemon *et al.* (2000) explained:

Rather than an ex-post exercise to detect misstatement in financial statements, the audit is viewed as a means of influencing the conduct and control of business such that problems with financial statement information are less likely to arise. There is therefore an added-value or client service dimension to . . . the business risk audit approaches . . . [that is] consistent with a desire to ensure that the audit provides insights and information which is valued by the entity's management and contributes to the enterprise in some positive way. (pp. 10, 12)

Gaining greater knowledge of the client's business and attendant risks also accords with the emphasis placed by regulators and others on the need for responsible corporate governance – and the auditor's role in securing this.[6]

As indicated above and reflected in Figure 2.2, adoption of the business risk approach does not signal a change in the primary audit objective; that remains providing credibility to the financial statements prepared by management. However, it has facilitated auditors developing additional audit objectives. As

Figure 2.2: Comparison of the audit risk and business risk approach to auditing

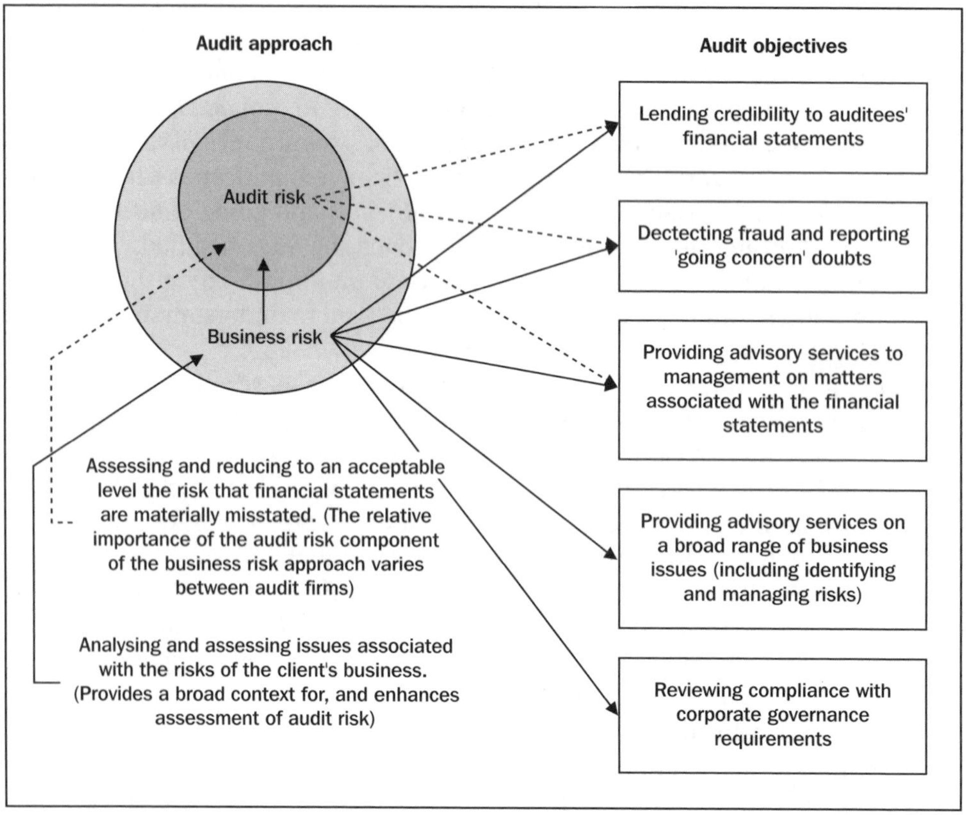

---

[6] This topic is discussed in greater detail in Chapter 5.

noted above, the approach has extended the objective of providing advisory services to management. Additionally, since the early 1990s, in conformity with society's and regulators' increasing concern about corporate governance matters, the auditing profession has acknowledged increased responsibility for detecting and reporting fraud[7] and for assessing, and reporting more explicitly, doubts about an auditee's ability to continue as a going concern.[8] Adoption of the business risk approach enhances auditors' ability to fulfil these responsibilities. Similarly, the approach assists auditors fulfil the audit requirements of the listing rules of the United Kingdom Listing Authority (UKLA) to review, for listed company clients, certain corporate governance disclosures in the auditees' annual reports.[9]

Despite the benefits claimed for the business risk approach, it is not without its critics. Perhaps most prominent among these are Levitt and Turner, former Chairman and Chief Accountant, respectively, of the Securities and Exchange Commission (SEC) in the USA. Turner (1999), for example, observed:

> Recent events[10] have caused the Commission and other securities regulators around the world to raise questions about the effectiveness of audits and the audit process, in particular, the perceived strengths and weaknesses of a [business] risk-based audit approach. . . . This approach requires an assessment of business risk within the business itself . . . [S]ome have argued that this approach, when coupled with firms' re-engineered audit approaches, has resulted in less verification of account balances by examining documentation from independent sources . . . Instead, the firms are relying on analytical analysis, inquiries of company personnel, and when appropriate control testing. . . . While some auditors have asserted that changes to their audit processes are responsive to the increased use of technology in financial reporting and accounting, other market participants have indicated a belief that the accounting profession is discarding the techniques that, in the past, made the financial statement audit a tool that enhances the reliability of information provided to investors. (pp. 3–6)

Along similar lines, Levitt observed:

> As firms increasingly have branched out to generate other sources of revenue, the basic audit model, not surprisingly, has undergone changes. In an era that calls for greater risk management the industry has migrated to what they call the '[business] risk-based' model. It sounds right on target . . . (Levitt, 1999, p. 2)

---

[7] The development of auditors' responsibilities for detecting and reporting fraud is discussed in detail in Chapter 5, section 5.9.

[8] The development of auditors' responsibilities in relation to auditees' going concern status is discussed in detail in Chapter 12, section 12.4.

[9] This topic is discussed in greater detail in Chapter 5.

[10] 'Recent events' refer, in particular, to some well-publicised audit failures such as Andersen's audit of Waste Management's 1992–1996 financial statements. In June 2001 the SEC settled enforcement actions against Arthur Andersen LLP amounting to $7 million. The SEC found that 'Arthur Andersen's reports on the financial statements for Waste Management Inc were materially false and misleading and that Andersen engaged in improper professional conduct' (SEC Press Release, 19 June 2001).

[R]ecent headlines of accounting failures [materially misstated financial statements with a 'clean' audit report] have led some people to question the thoroughness of audits. . . . We rely on auditors to put something like the good housekeeping seal of approval on the information investors receive. The integrity of that information must take priority over a desire for cost efficiencies or competitive advantage in the audit process. . . . As I look at some of the [audit] failures today, I can't help but wonder if the staff in the trenches of the profession have the training and supervision they need to ensure that audits are being done right. We cannot permit thorough audits to be sacrificed for re-engineered approaches that are efficient [that is, less costly] but less effective [that is, result in expressing an inappropriate opinion on financial statements]. (Levitt, 1998, p. 6)

In the light of implied criticism of the business risk approach by influential regulators such as the SEC, and some doubts expressed within the profession about its effectiveness as an audit approach, some of the larger firms in both the USA and UK appear to have reservations about its wholesale adoption. More particularly, they seem to see a need to strengthen, and make more explicit, the linkages between assessment of business risk and that of audit risk (that is, assessing the likelihood of the financial statements being materially misstated).

Notwithstanding the concerns expressed about the business-risk approach to auditing, the extension to audit objectives since the early 1990s has strengthened auditors' role in securing greater corporate accountability. Given the level of accountability expected of corporate managers (commensurate with the power and influence they command in society), it seems likely that the current trends in extending auditors' role in this regard will continue. Specific developments in auditors' responsibilities that might be expected in the future include the following:

- Expressing an audit opinion on auditees' financial statements that are published on the internet.[11] (In this regard it is pertinent to note that, in 2001, the Auditing Practices Board (APB) issued a bulletin: *The Electronic Publication of Auditors' Reports*).
- Reporting on the effectiveness of the auditee's procedures for identifying and managing risks and its system of internal control. [The responsibilities of company managements for reporting on these issues, and for auditors to express an opinion thereon, have been discussed in various corporate governance reports, such as Cadbury (1992), Hampel (1998) and Turnbull (1999), and have been hotly debated in corporate management and auditing circles].

---

[11] It is pertinent that the Company Law Review Steering Group (2001) has recommended 'for quoted companies (i.e. those listed or otherwise publicly traded) . . . [that their] full statements should be published as soon as practicable after they have been approved by the board and the auditors have made their report; this publication should be on a website . . . By full financial statements we mean the financial statements (accounts), and OFR [Operating and Financial Review] and any supplementary statement together with the auditors' report' (p. 196).

- Examining, and expressing an opinion about, the truth and fairness of all the information (financial and non-financial) provided by company managements in their annual reports. (The first tentative step in this direction seems to have been taken by the auditing profession in the explicit acknowledgement in the audit report that auditors 'read other information contained in the Annual Report and consider whether it is consistent with the audited financial statements'.[12]) It is also likely that the amount and range of information which company managements are required to provide in their annual reports will increase.[13]
- Performing management efficiency and effectiveness (or value for money) audits. Such audits are already required as part of the statutory audits of most public sector entities and it may be argued that, in order for audits to reach their potential as elements in the corporate accountability process, efficiency and effectiveness audits should also be required as part of the statutory audits of companies.

2.3 SUMMARY

In this chapter we have reviewed the development of auditing – more particularly, its development since the first introduction of compulsory audits in 1844 – and we have highlighted the close link between changes in the socio-economic environment of the English-speaking world and changes in audit objectives and techniques. We have noted that auditing continually evolves as it responds to, and utilises opportunities provided by, changes in its environment. We have also highlighted the relationship between auditing and the accountability expected of corporate managers.

We have noted that current legislation, which governs the preparation and audit of companies' financial statements, may not be attuned to the current level of accountability expected of company managers. It seems likely that in the future large national and multinational companies, at least, will be required

---

[12] This topic is discussed in detail in Chapter 13.

[13] It is relevant that the Company Law Review Steering Group (2001) has recommended that companies be required to include in their annual reports an Operating and Financial Review (OFR) 'to provide a discussion and analysis of the performance of the business and the main trends and factors underlying the results and financial position and likely to affect performance in the future . . .' (p. 181). The Group has also recommended that 'the OFR should be subject to review by the company's auditors for:

- the propriety of the directors' process for preparing it, i.e. how they have satisfied themselves that adequate, supportable information was considered in making their decisions as to inclusion of information; and how they have satisfied themselves that there is an adequate, supportable basis for statements made, whether factual or judgmental;
- consistency with the auditors' knowledge from the audit of the accounts . . . and from their review of the OFR itself; and
- compliance with any applicable standard' (pp. 190–191).

to produce, and external auditors will be required to audit, more comprehensive accountability (i.e. annual) reports. However, if legislators and, more particularly, regulators, seek to extend the role and responsibilities of auditors, they will need to be mindful of the costs associated with securing greater corporate accountability in this way, and ensure that the costs do not outstrip the benefits derived therefrom. It is arguable that the business risk approach described in this chapter prepares the auditing profession for a cost-effective approach to a wider set of responsibilities, but care must be taken to ensure that the financial statement audit, the essence of auditors' role in society, is not compromised.

SELF-REVIEW QUESTIONS

2.1 Briefly describe the audit environment in each of the following periods:
   (i)   pre-1844
   (ii) 1844–1920s
   (iii) 1920s–1960s
   (iv) 1960s–1990s
   (v)   1990s–present

2.2 Outline the major audit objectives in each of the following periods:
   (i)   pre-1844
   (ii) 1844–1920s
   (iii) 1920s–1960s
   (iv) 1960s–1990s
   (v)   1990s–present

2.3 State the major changes which have occurred in auditing techniques during the last 160 years. Explain briefly how changes in technology have impacted on the changes in auditing techniques.

2.4 Outline briefly the development of corporate accountability over the past 160 years.

2.5 Explain briefly the significance of the Joint Stock Companies Act 1844 to the development of auditing.

2.6 The Companies Act 1900 has been referred to as 'a prominent milestone in the history of company auditing'. List reasons which help to explain why this Act has been given this title.

2.7 Explain briefly the importance of the following cases to the development of auditors' responsibilities:
   (i)   Re London and General Bank (no.2) [1895];
   (ii) Re Kingston Cotton Mill Co. Ltd (no.2) [1896].

2.8 List reasons which help to explain why the detection of fraud and error lost its prominence as the primary audit objective during the 1920–1960s period.

2.9 'Changes in auditing reflect, and represent a response to, changes in the socio-economic environment'. Using an example to illustrate your answer, explain briefly the link between changes in auditing and changes in the socio-economic environment.

2.10 List three ways in which auditors' responsibilities are likely to change in the not too distant future.

REFERENCES

Auditing Practices Board (APB) (1996) *The Auditor's Code*. London: APB.

Auditing Practices Board (APB) (2001) *The Electronic Publication of Auditors' Reports*. Bulletin 2001/1. London: APB.

Brown, R. (1905) *History of Accounting and Accountants*. London: Jack.

Chandler, R.A., Edwards, J.R. & Anderson, M. (1993) Changing perceptions of the role of the company auditor, 1840–1940. *Accounting and Business Research* **23**(92), 443–459.

Committee on the Financial Aspects of Corporate Governance (Cadbury Committee) (1992) *Report of the Committee on the Financial Aspects of Corporate Governance*. London: Gee.

Committee on Corporate Governance (Hampel Committee) (1998a) *Final Report of the Committee on Corporate Governance*. London: The London Stock Exchange.

Committee on Corporate Governance (1998b) *The Combined Code*. London: The London Stock Exchange.

Company Law Review Steering Group (2001) Modern Company Law for a Competitive Economy: Final Report. London: Department of Trade and Industry.

Davis, K. (1976) Social responsibility is inevitable. *California Management Review,* – **X1X**(Fall), 14–20.

Demers, L. & Wayland, D. (1982) Corporate social responsibility: Is no news good news? *CA Magazine* **115** (January), 42–46; **115** (February), 56–60.

Greenbury, Sir Richard (1995) Directors' Remuneration: Report of a Study Group Chaired by Sir Richard Greenbury. London: Gee.

Johnston, T.R., Edgar, G.C. & Hays, P.L. (1982) *The Law and Practice of Company Accounting,* 6th ed. Wellington: Butterworths.

Lee, T.A. (1970). A brief history of company audits: 1840–1940. *The Accountant's Magazine* **74**(782), 363–368.

Lemon, W.M., Tatum, K.W. & Turley, W.S. (2000) *Developments in the Audit Methodologies of Large Accounting Firms*. London: APB.

Levitt, A. (1998) *The Numbers Game,* Remarks at the NYU Center for Law and Business, New York, 28 September.

Levitt, A. (1999) Remarks to the Panel on Audit Effectiveness of the Public Oversight Board, Public Oversight Hearings, New York, 7 October.

Morris, J. (1977) *Domesday Book 20 Bedfordshire*. Chichester: Philimore & Co. Ltd.

Spicer, E.E. & Pegler, E.C. (1911) *Practical Auditing*. London, UFL.

Spicer, E.E. & Pegler, E.C. (1936) *Practical Auditing*, 7th ed. Edited by W.W. Bigg, London, UFL.

Turner, L.E. (1999) Speech to the Panel on Audit Effectiveness, New York, 7 October.

Working Party on Internal Control (Turnbull Committee) (1999) *Internal Control: Guidance for Directors on the Combined Code*. London: ICAEW.

ADDITIONAL READING

Auditing Practices Board (APB) (1992) *The Future Development of Auditing.* London: APB.

Auditing Practices Board (APB) (1994) *The Audit Agenda.* London: APB.

Auditing Practices Board (APB) (1996) *The Audit Agenda – Next Steps.* London: APB.

Cadbury, A. (1992) Keeping the State from the corporate door. *Accountancy* **110**(1187), 71.

Chandler, R.A. (1997). Judicial views on auditing from the nineteenth century. *Accounting History* **2**(1), 61–80.

Chandler, R.A. (1997) Taking Responsibility: The early demand for institutional action to define an auditor's duties. *International Journal of Auditing* **1**(3), 165–174.

Chandler, R. & Edwards, J.R. (1996) Recurring issues in auditing: back to the future. *Accounting, Auditing and Accountability Journal* **9**(2), 4–29.

Edwards, R.J., Anderson, M. & Matthews, D. (1997) Accountability in a free-market economy: The British company audit, 1886. *Abacus* **33**(1), 1–25.

Elliott, R.K. (1994) Confronting the future: choices for the attest function. *Accounting Horizons* **8**(3), 106–124.

Elliott, R.K. (1995) The future of assurance services: implications for academia. *Accounting Horizons* **9**(4), 118–127.

Flint, D. (1971) The role of the auditor in modern society: An exploratory essay. *Accounting and Business Research* **1**(4), 287–293.

Hoskins, M. (1993) The future of auditing: a Big Six view. *Accountancy* **111**(1198), 88.

Institute of Chartered Accountants of Scotland (ICAS) (1993) *Auditing into the Twenty-first Century*. Edinburgh: ICAS.

Power, M. (1994) *The Audit Explosion*. London: Demos.

3 A Framework of Auditing Concepts

LEARNING OBJECTIVES

After studying the material in this chapter you should be able to:
- explain the meaning of, and relationship between, the social purpose of auditing, postulates of auditing, and key concepts of auditing;
- state seven postulates of auditing;
- explain and discuss the importance of the concepts relating to:
  - the credibility of auditors' work (Independence, Competence, Ethical Conduct);
  - the audit process (Evidence, Materiality, Audit Risk, Judgment, Scepticism);
  - auditors' communication (Reporting);
  - the standard of auditors' work (Due Care, Quality Control).

The following publications and fundamental principles of external auditing are relevant to this chapter:

Publications:
- Statement of Auditing Standards (SAS) 100: *Objective and general principles governing an audit of financial statements* (APB, 1995)
- Statement of Auditing Standards (SAS) 220: *Materiality and the audit* (APB, 1995)
- Statement of Auditing Standards (SAS) 240: *Quality control for audit work* (APB, 2000)
- Statement of Auditing Standards (SAS) 300: *Accounting and internal control systems and audit risk assessments* (APB, 1995)
- Statement of Auditing Standards (SAS) 400: *Audit evidence* (APB, 1995)
- International Standard on Auditing (ISA) 200: *Objective and general principles governing an audit of financial statements* (IAPC, 1994)
- International Standard on Auditing (ISA) 220: *Quality control for audit work* (IAPC, 1994)
- International Standard on Auditing (ISA) 320: *Audit materiality* (IAPC, 1994)
- International Standard on Auditing (ISA) 400: *Risk assessments and internal control* (IAPC, 1994)
- International Standard on Auditing (ISA) 500: *Audit evidence* (IAPC, 1994).

Fundamental principles of external auditing included in *The Auditor's Code* (APB, 1996)
- Objectivity and independence
- Competence
- Integrity
- Rigour
- Judgment
- Communication.

3.1 INTRODUCTION

During its long history, dating back some 3,000 years (see Chapter 1) and, more particularly, during the last 160 or so years which witnessed its very rapid development (see Chapter 2), auditing has developed in a very practical way. Perhaps surprisingly, given its importance to the smooth functioning of financial markets and the economy in general and the effort devoted to developing a coherent theory (or conceptual framework) of *accounting*, little attention has been given to developing a theory of *auditing*. Three notable exceptions to this are the classical works of Mautz and Sharaf (1961), the American Accounting Association's Committee on Basic Auditing Concepts (1973), and Flint (1988).

Why is a theory of auditing important? According to Mautz and Sharaf (1961):

> One reason ... for a serious and substantial investigation into the possibility and nature of auditing theory is the hope that it will provide us with solutions, or at least clues to solutions, of problems which we now find difficult. (p. 5)

They suggested adopting a philosophical approach and explained (p. 8):

1. Philosophy gets back to first principles, to the rationale behind the actions and thoughts which tend to be taken for granted.
2. Philosophy is concerned with the systematic organisation of knowledge in such a way that it becomes at once more useful and less likely to be self-contradictory.
3. Philosophy provides a basis whereby social relationships may be molded and understood.

Thus, auditing theory helps us to identify (and be cognisant of) basic assumptions which underpin auditing practice, to organise auditing knowledge so that it is useful and internally consistent, and to understand the social role and context of the audit function.

Flint (1988) shed more light on the issue when he stated:

> The purpose of theory in relation to auditing is to provide a coherent set of propositions about the activity which explains its social purpose and objectives, which furnishes a rational foundation and justification for its practices and procedures, relating them to the purposes and objectives, and which explains the place of the activity in the context of the institutions of society and the social, economic and political environment. (p. 9)

From this, a three-tier hierarchy of notions may be distilled. At the top is a statement of the social purpose and objectives of auditing. This is followed by the postulates or basic assumptions which underpin the social purpose of the audit function on the one hand and auditing practices and procedures on the other. At the bottom we have a coherent set of concepts which underpin (and

Figure 3.1: Hierarchy of notions underpinning a theory of auditing

Social purpose of auditing						
Auditors are agents of social control in the process of corporate accountability						

Postulates or auditing (Fundamental assumptions or truths)						
Accountability relationship	Subject matter remote, complex significant	Independence, investigatory and reporting freedom	Verifiable subject matter	Standards of accountability can be set, measured and compared with known criteria	Credibility given to financial and other information can be communicated	Provides an economic or social benefit

Key concepts of auditing

Credibility of work performed			Audit process					Communication	Standard of performance	
Independence	Competence	Ethical conduct, integrity	Evidence	Materiality	Audit risk	Judgment	Scepticism	Reporting	Due care	Quality control

help to explain and guide) auditing practice. This 'hierarchy of notions' is presented in outline form in Figure 3.1 and discussed below.

In this chapter we do not intend to provide a comprehensive theory of auditing. For this, reference may be made to the three 'classics' noted above. Rather, our purpose is to provide a basic framework for, and to discuss, key concepts which underpin auditing practice. We first outline the social purpose and postulates of auditing and provide a basic framework for the key auditing concepts. We then discuss 11 key concepts – their meaning and relevance for auditing – in greater detail. Most of the concepts have particular significance for material presented in subsequent chapters and these are cross-referenced to, and further developed, in the relevant later chapter.

3.2 SOCIAL PURPOSE, POSTULATES AND KEY CONCEPTS OF AUDITING

3.2.1 Social purpose of the audit function

As noted in Chapter 2, the primary objective of company statutory audits is to provide credibility to the financial statements prepared by the company's directors for use by parties external to the entity. In performing this function, auditors are one of the checks and balances imposed by society (through legislation) on company directors as a counter to the power and influence they wield in society. Thus, auditors' social purpose is to act as agents of social control in the process of corporate accountability.

3.2.2 Postulates of auditing

A postulate is defined by the Concise Oxford Dictionary as 'a thing assumed as a necessary condition especially as a basis for reasoning; a fundamental prerequisite or condition'. Mautz and Sharaf (1961) explain that postulates have five general characteristics. They state (p. 37):

Postulates are:
1. Essential to the development of any intellectual discipline.
2. Assumptions that do not lend themselves to direct verification.
3. A basis for inference.
4. A foundation for erection of any theoretical structure.
5. Susceptible to challenge in the light of later advancement of knowledge.

In the context of auditing, postulates may be defined as fundamental principles, assumed to be truths, which help to explain the social purpose of auditing and/or auditing practices. Flint (1988, pp. 21–22) identifies seven basic postulates. They are as follows:

1. The primary condition for an audit is that there is either
   (a) a relationship of accountability between two or more parties in the sense that there is a duty of acceptable conduct or performance owed by one party to the other party or parties;
   (b) a need by some party to establish the reliability or credibility of information for which they are responsible which is expected to be used and relied on by a specified group or groups of which the members may not be constant or individually identifiable, producing constructively a relationship of accountability; . . .
2. The subject matter of accountability is too remote, too complex and/or of too great a significance for the discharge of the duty to be demonstrated without the process of audit.
3. Essential distinguishing characteristics of audit are the independence of its status and its freedom from investigatory and reporting constraints.
4. The subject matter of audit, for example conduct, performance or achievement, or record of events or state of affairs, or a statement of facts relating to any of these, is susceptible to verification by evidence.
5. Standards of accountability, for example of conduct, performance, achievement and quality of information, can be set for those who are accountable; actual conduct, performance, achievement, quality and so on can be measured and compared with those standards by reference to known criteria; and the process of measurement and comparison requires special skill and the exercise of judgement.
6. The meaning, significance and intention of financial and other statements and data which are audited are sufficiently clear that the credibility which is given thereto as a result of audit can be clearly expressed and communicated.
7. An audit produces an economic or social benefit.

Reviewing these postulates, it may be seen that postulates 1, 2, 5 and 7 correspond with material presented in Chapter 1. The fundamental truth of the other postulates underpins, and should become evident as we discuss, the audit process in later chapters.

3.2.3 Concepts of auditing

Concepts of auditing are general notions that underlie audit practices and procedures. As indicated in Figure 3.1, the key concepts can usefully be categorised into four main groups, namely, those relating to:

- the credibility of auditors' work [auditors' independence, competence and ethical conduct (including integrity)];
- the audit process (evidence, materiality, audit risk, judgment and scepticism);
- the communication of audit conclusions (reporting);
- the standard of auditors' work [due care and quality control (including adherence to standards)].

Each of these concepts will be discussed below.

3.3 CONCEPTS RELATING TO THE CREDIBILITY OF AUDITORS' WORK

3.3.1 Concept of auditors' independence

3.3.1a Independence: the cornerstone of auditing

As may be seen from Figure 3.1, independence has a unique status within auditing. It figures amongst the postulates: it is assumed, as a fundamental truth, that the audit function is independent; it is also a key concept – a characteristic that is essential for ensuring the credibility of auditors' work. Indeed, independence has been referred to as 'the cornerstone [the very heart] of auditing' (Stewart, 1977; Levitt, 2000): without independence an audit is virtually worthless.

Let us examine this more closely. Auditors are intermediaries between the directors/senior managers of an entity and external parties interested in the entity. They have a duty to form and express an opinion as to whether the entity's financial statements (prepared by management for use by shareholders and others outside the entity) provide a true and fair view of the entity's financial position and performance. If users of the financial statements are to believe and rely on the auditor's opinion, it is essential that the auditor is, and is perceived to be, independent of the entity and its management. This is reflected in the fundamental principle of auditing – *Objectivity and independence* – which states:

> Auditors are objective. They express opinions independently of the entity and its directors. (APB, 1996)

If auditors are considered not to be independent of the client entity and its management, their opinion will carry little credibility and users of the financial statements will gain little, if any, assurance from the auditor's report about the truth and fairness (or otherwise) of the financial statements. As a consequence, the audit will have little purpose or value.

The importance of auditors' independence – to both investors and the wider economy – was succinctly conveyed by Turner (2001), former Chief Accountant of the Securities and Exchange Commission (SEC) in the USA, when he stated:

> The enduring confidence of the investing public in the integrity of our capital markets is vital. . . . [The capital they invest] is providing the fuel for our economic engine, funding for the growth of new businesses, . . . and job opportunities for tens of millions of workers. . . . [But] the willingness of investors to continue to invest ... cannot be taken for granted. . . . Public trust begins, and ends, with the integrity of the numbers the public uses to form the basis for making their investment decisions. . . . It is the report of the independent auditor that provides investors with the critical assurance that the numbers in the financial statements have been subjected to an impartial, unbiased and rigorous examination by a skilled professional. But in order for that report to have credibility with investors, to add value to the process and investors, it must be issued by a person or firm that the investor perceives is free of all conflicts – conflicts that may or will in part weight on or impair the auditor's judgments about the accuracy of the numbers. (pp. 1–2)

3.3.1b   Meaning of independence in the auditing context

Given the importance of independence to the audit function, it is clearly important to examine what the concept means.

It is well accepted that independence, in the sense of being self-reliant and not subordinating one's professional judgment to the opinions of others, is a fundamental hallmark of all professions. However, in auditing the term has come to have a special meaning. In essence it means maintaining an independent attitude of mind and avoiding situations which would tend to impair objectivity or create personal bias. As the Guide to Professional Ethics Statement (GPES) 1: *Integrity, Objectivity and Independence* (ICAEW, 1997) explains:

> Objectivity is essential for any professional person exercising professional judgment... Objectivity is the state of mind which has regard to all considerations relevant to the task at hand but no other. It is sometimes described as 'independence of mind'. (para 2)

With respect to auditing, if interested parties are to rely on the auditor's opinion, it is essential that the auditor is both:

- *independent in fact*, that is, the auditor maintains an objective unbiased attitude of mind which enables him or her to evaluate a set of financial statements (and supporting evidence) in an impartial manner, and to form and express an opinion in the audit report uninfluenced by personal bias; and
- *independent in appearance*, that is, avoiding situations which might cause others to conclude that the auditor might not be maintaining an objective unbiased attitude of mind; for example, by having mutual or conflicting interests with the audit client or its management.

Stipulating that auditors must be independent in both fact and appearance may seem to be a straightforward and, in view of the critical importance of independence to auditing, an obvious requirement. However, in practice, such independence may be difficult to achieve and easy to compromise. This issue is explored in detail in Chapter 4.

3.3.2 Concept of competence

If auditors' opinions are to have credibility, and be relied upon by users of financial statements, auditors must be regarded as possessing competence. According to Flint (1988): 'Audit competence requires both knowledge and skill, which are the products of education, training and experience' (p. 48). The fundamental principle of auditing – *Competence* – conveys similar ideas but goes a little further in explaining the requirements of auditors' competence:

> Auditors act with professional skill, derived from their qualification, training and practical experience. This demands an understanding of financial reporting and business issues, together with expertise in accumulating and assessing the evidence necessary to form an opinion. (APB, 1996)

The knowledge and skills required by auditors are acquired through a combination of general and technical education on the one hand, and work experience and work-related on-the-job training on the other. Flint (1988), observing that 'auditing is intellectually demanding, requiring a trained mind and the capacity for exercise of judgement' (p. 48), gives particular emphasis to the contribution of general education to auditors' competence. He notes:

> A broad general education cultivating the habit of systematic thinking and mental discipline, combined with a basic understanding of the principal fields of knowledge and ability for expression and communication orally and in writing, are an essential foundation . . . [A]uditing requires much more than a knowledge of its own theory ... and the principles of its own peculiar investigative process: it requires an understanding of the nature, structure, institutions and law of the society in which it is applied. And, in relation to particular audits it requires a knowledge of the activity in respect of which the conduct, performance or information has to be addressed. (pp. 48–49)

From a more practical standpoint, SAS 240: *Quality control for audit work* sheds rather more light on what the concept of competence embraces in the auditing context. It uses the term 'competencies' rather than competence but defines them in a similar manner to that conveyed for 'competence' in the fundamental principle of auditing (see above). Competencies are defined as 'the knowledge, skills and abilities of audit engagement partners and staff' (SAS 240, para 7).

SAS 240 specifies that 'audit staff with the appropriate competencies necessary to perform the audit work expected of them' are to be assigned to individual audit engagements (SAS 240, para 31).[1] Para 33 explains that when assessing whether or not staff members have the requisite competencies, consideration is to be given to their:

- understanding and practical experience of auditing;
- understanding applicable accounting, auditing, ethical and other technical standards;
- knowledge of specific industries;
- professional judgment;
- understanding the firm's quality control policy and processes.

SAS 240 also provides guidance on how auditors can acquire the required competencies. It explains (para 26):

> Competencies are developed through:
> a) *professional education and development* (including technical and management training, in-house courses and external training); all relevant members of a firm from the most junior to the most senior participate in training designed to enable the firm to perform audits in accordance with Auditing Standards;
> b) *work experience and coaching by other members of the audit team*; practical experience, especially in an environment in which team-working is encouraged helps the less experienced concerning the assessment of risk and adequacy of audit evidence.[2]

Thus, auditors acquire much of their required competence and, in particular, their technical education, and work experience and training, through in-house and external courses of study, and supervised practical experience. However, this 'competence acquisition' is not haphazard. As Flint (1988, p. 51) points out, if auditors are to gain the public's confidence in the credibility of their work,

---

[1] ISA 220: *Quality control for audit work* conveys similar ideas but does not define 'competence' or explain how it is acquired. It states: 'The firm is to be staffed by personnel who have attained and maintain the Technical Standards and Professional Competence required to enable them to fulfil their responsibilities with Due Care' [para 6(b)]; and 'Audit work is to be assigned to personnel who have the degree of technical training and proficiency required in the circumstances' [para 6(c)]. By implication, ISA 220 seems to equate 'competence' with 'technical training and proficiency'.

[2] The concepts of scepticism, judgment, audit risk and evidence are all shown in Figure 3.1 and discussed later in this chapter.

they must be able to demonstrate they have obtained a recognised reputable qualification – one that requires them to successfully complete a formalised programme of education, training and experience. Flint further notes:

> Audit is a matter of such social importance that the state has a responsibility to be satisfied in the public interest that appropriate standards of knowledge, training and experience are prescribed and that an adequate standard of proficiency is achieved. (p. 51)

As will be seen in Chapter 5 (section 5.2.3), in the UK this is achieved by legislation which requires auditors of companies to be 'registered auditors', and specifies, among other things, that in order to be 'registered', auditors must be suitably qualified and supervised.

The concept of competence is particularly relevant to the topics of 'staffing an audit' and 'controlling the quality of audit work' which are discussed in Chapters 6 and 15, respectively.

3.3.3   Concept of ethical conduct

As shown in Figure 3.1, the credibility of auditors' work rests on auditors being perceived as independent, competent, and adhering to ethical conduct. But what is ethical conduct? And how does it impact on the credibility of auditors' work?

Flint (1988) provides an answer when he states:

> Public trust and confidence in auditors are dependent on a continuing belief in their unqualified integrity, objectivity, and, in appropriate circumstances, acceptance of duty to the public interest, with a consequential subordination of self-interest. Creating and retaining trust and confidence, therefore, requires auditors to show certain characteristics which are those commonly associated with employments which are recognised and sanctioned by society as professions. (p. 87)

Thus, in order to retain the public's confidence in the credibility of their work, auditors must adhere to standards of ethical conduct: standards of conduct that embody and demonstrate integrity, objectivity, and concern for the public (rather than self-) interest.

In the UK, the fundamental principle of auditing – *Integrity* – captures many of the notions that comprise the concept of ethical conduct. It states:

> Auditors act with integrity, fulfilling their responsibilities with honesty, fairness and truthfulness. Confidential information obtained in the course of the audit is disclosed only when required in the public interest or by operation of law. (APB, 1996)

As for all other professions, the conduct expected of members of the auditing profession is set out in a Code of Ethics.[3] In 1996 the International Federation of Accountants (IFAC) published the *IFAC Code of Ethics for Professional Accountants.* (This was revised in 1998.) IFAC explains:

> [R]ecognizing the responsibilities of the accountancy profession . . . and considering its own role to be that of providing guidance, encouraging continuity of efforts, and promoting harmonization, [IFAC] has deemed it essential to establish an international Code of Ethics for Professional Accountants . . . This international Code is intended to serve as a model on which to base national ethical guidance. It sets standards of conduct for professional accountants and states the fundamental principles that should be observed by professional accountants in order to achieve common objectives. (IFAC, 1998, paras 3–4)

IFAC's Code provides guidance for its 153 member professional bodies in 113 countries, including the UK. For example, the *Guide to Professional Ethics* (1997) published (separately but in identical form) by the ICAEW, ICAS, ICAI is akin to IFAC's Code. It sets out guidance in the form of Fundamental Principles and Statements on the conduct expected of members of these bodies, as regards:

- their personal qualities (integrity, objectivity, professional competence and due care, confidentiality, professional behaviour, and adherence to technical standards); and
- their relations with other members of the profession, clients, and the public.

As noted in section 3.3.1 above, the *Guide to Professional Ethics* includes Statement 1 which provides guidance on auditors' independence. In Chapter 7 we will be referring to Statement 6 *Changes in a Professional Appointment* which explains the conduct expected of the preceding and succeeding auditor when the audit client is intending to appoint the latter in place of the former. A further key aspect of ethical conduct for auditors (as for other professional accountants) is that of client confidentiality. This was briefly referred to above, in the context of the fundamental principle of auditing – *Integrity*, and is discussed further in Chapter 6.

3.4 CONCEPTS RELATING TO THE AUDIT PROCESS

3.4.1 Concept of evidence

3.4.1a   Necessity of sufficient appropriate evidence for an audit

It was shown in Chapter 2 that the primary objective of an audit is to provide credibility to an auditee's financial statements (which are prepared by the

---

[3] A Code of Ethics may have various titles, for example, a Guide to Ethical Conduct, Code of Professional Conduct, Guide to Professional Ethics etc. but, in essence, the content is the same. It sets out the conduct expected of members of the profession (or of the professional body) in question.

auditee's management) by expressing an opinion on the truth and fairness (or otherwise) of the financial statements. Auditors can only express such an opinion if they are able to examine sufficient appropriate evidence to form an opinion. If no evidence exists in relation to the subject matter on which an auditor is to express an opinion, then there can be no audit. The fundamental necessity of the existence of evidence for an audit to take place is reflected in postulate 4 cited in section 3.2.2 above, i.e.:

> The subject matter of audit, for example conduct, performance or achievement, or record of events or state of affairs, or a statement of facts relating to any of these, is susceptible to verification by evidence.

SAS 400: *Audit evidence* requires auditors to:

> Obtain sufficient appropriate audit evidence to be able to draw reasonable conclusions on which to base the audit opinion. (para 2)

The Standard goes on to explain:

> Sufficiency and appropriateness are interrelated and apply to audit evidence obtained from both tests of control and substantive procedures.[4] Sufficiency is the measure of the quantity of audit evidence; appropriateness is the measure of the quality or reliability of audit evidence and its relevance to a particular assertion. (para 4)[5]

The Standard makes it clear that there is a direct relationship between audit tests or procedures, audit evidence and the auditor's opinion; the auditor performs compliance and substantive procedures to gather evidence on which to base an opinion about the financial statements. This relationship is presented diagrammatically in Figure 3.2.

Having established the necessity of sufficient appropriate evidence for an audit to take place, we need to consider the meaning and nature of audit evidence.

Figure 3.2:   Relationship between audit procedures, evidence and the auditor's opinion

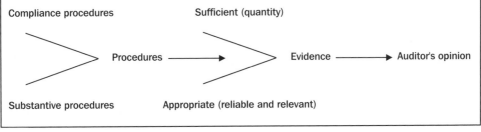

---

[4] These terms will be discussed in detail in Chapter 6. In essence.

- 'tests of control' refers to testing compliance with internal controls; and

- 'substantive procedures' refers to testing the financial statement amounts and other disclosures.

[5] The wording of SAS 400, paras 2 and 4 is almost identical to that in paras 2 and 7 of the International Standard, ISA 500: *Audit evidence*.

3.4.1b   Definition of audit evidence

A particularly useful definition of audit evidence has been provided by Anderson (1977). He defined it as:

> any perceived object, action or condition relevant to the formation of a knowledgeable opinion on the financial statements. Perceived objects may include certain tangible assets (such as cash funds, inventories and fixed assets), various documents, accounting records and reports, and written representations. Perceived actions generally consist of certain procedures performed by the client's employees. Perceived conditions may include the observed quality of assets, the apparent competence of employees met, the care with which procedures were seen to be performed, or an identified logical relationship with other facts known to the auditor. (p. 251)

Thus, in auditing, 'evidence' means all of the facts and impressions auditors acquire which help them to form an opinion about the truth and fairness of the financial statements under review and their compliance (or otherwise) with relevant legislation.

3.4.1c   The nature of audit evidence

Unlike scientific evidence, audit evidence does not consist of 'hard facts' which 'prove' or 'disprove' the accuracy of financial statements. Instead, it comprises pieces of information and impressions which are gradually accumulated during the course of an audit and which, taken together, persuade the auditor about the truth and fairness (or otherwise) of the financial statements under consideration. Thus, audit evidence is generally persuasive rather than conclusive in nature.

Furthermore, not all of the available evidence is examined by an auditor. The purpose of an audit is not to 'prove' or 'disprove' the accuracy of the financial statements. If it were, auditors would have to collect and evaluate as much evidence as possible. Instead, the objective is to form an *opinion* as to whether or not the financial statements under review give a true and fair view of the financial position and performance of the reporting entity. To accomplish this, auditors need only gather sufficient appropriate evidence to support their opinion. Thus, for example, rather than examining all of the evidence which is available, auditors usually test only samples of data.

Although only part, rather than all, of the available evidence is examined, when evidence derived from different sources is consistent, it has a reinforcing effect. Conversely, when evidence is inconsistent it has an undermining effect. An auditor may wish to reach a conclusion about a particular financial statement assertion (for example, about the ownership or value of an asset) using evidence from different sources and/or of different types. Where such evidence is consistent, (s)he gains cumulative assurance about the assertion in question.

(That is, the assurance the auditor gains regarding the truth and fairness of the assertion is greater than that obtained from the individual pieces of evidence by themselves.) However, when evidence from different sources or of different types is inconsistent, further evidence may need to be obtained in order to resolve the inconsistency.

The procedures used to gather audit evidence, and the various types and sources of evidence available to auditors, are discussed in detail in Chapter 6.

3.4.2   Concept of materiality

3.4.2a   Meaning of materiality in the auditing context

SAS 100: *Objective and general principles governing an audit of financial statements* states:

> In undertaking an audit of financial statements auditors should . . . carry out procedures designed to obtain sufficient appropriate audit evidence [so as] to determine with reasonable confidence whether the financial statements are free of *material* misstatement. (para 2, emphasis added)

The Standard does not explain what is meant by material but guidance on the meaning of the concept is provided in SAS 220: *Materiality and the audit*:

> 'Materiality' is an expression of the relative significance or importance of a particular matter in the context of financial statements as a whole. A matter is material if its omission. . . or misstatement . . . would reasonably influence the decisions of an addressee of the auditors' report . . . Materiality may also be considered in the context of any individual primary statement within the financial statements or of individual items included in them. Materiality is not capable of general mathematical definition as it has both qualitative and quantitative aspects. (para 3)

From this it may be seen that the term 'materiality' needs to be understood in the context of a user of the financial statements. Thus, as Flint (1988) observes:

> Materiality in accounting is a matter of materiality in auditing because it identifies the data or information which affect the information content of the financial statement, and which have the potential to affect the understanding and decisions of the persons for whom the data, information or financial statement are prepared. (p. 129)

The International Accounting Standards Committee (IASC) defines materiality in its *Framework for the preparation and presentation of financial statements* in similar terms:

> Information is material if its omission or misstatement could influence the economic decisions of users taken on the basis of the financial statements. Materiality depends on the size of the item or error judged in the particular circumstances of its omission or misstatement. Thus, materiality provides a threshold or cut off point rather than being a primary qualitative characteristic which information must have if it is to be useful. (as cited in ISA 320, para 3)

Notwithstanding the IASC's emphasis on the size of an item or error as a characteristic of materiality, SAS 220 states: 'The assessment of what is material is a matter of professional judgment and includes consideration of both the amount (quantity) and nature (quality) of misstatements' (para 4).[6]

It goes on to explain:

> Materiality is considered at both the overall financial statement level and in relation to individual account balances, classes of transactions and disclosures. Materiality may be influenced by considerations such as legal and regulatory requirements and considerations relating to individual financial statement account balances and relationships. This process may result in different materiality considerations being applied depending on the aspect of the financial statements being considered. For example, the expected degree of accuracy of certain statutory disclosures, such as directors' emoluments, may make normal materiality considerations irrelevant. (para 7)[7]

3.4.2b Characteristics of materiality

Having considered the meaning of materiality we can turn our attention to the characteristics of the concept in the context of auditing. From an analysis of the extracts from SAS 220 set out above, it is evident that materiality in the auditing context has a number of characterising features. These include the following:

(i)   deciding what is, and what is not, material (i.e. likely to affect the decision or action of a reasonable, legitimate financial statement user) in any given circumstance is a matter of professional judgment;

(ii)   an item may be material by virtue of its quantity or its quality;

(iii) the materiality of an item may be affected by legal and regulatory require-ments;

(iv) materiality needs to be considered at two levels:
   – the overall level: that is, in relation to the financial statements as a whole; and
   – the individual account or disclosure level.

Each of these characteristics is discussed below.

(i)   A matter of professional judgment

SAS 220 (and, similarly, ISA 320) does not provide numerical guidelines to assist auditors in deciding whether an item is or is not materially misstated.

---

[6] In similar vein, but still focusing on quantitative misstatement, ISA 320: *Audit materiality* (para 5) states: 'In designing the audit plan the auditor establishes an acceptable materiality level so as to detect quantitatively material misstatements. However, both the amount (quantity) and nature (quality) of misstatements need to be considered.'

[7] The wording of ISA 320, para 7, is almost identical to that in SAS 220, para 7, except that the final sentence of SAS 220 para 7 is omitted.

Indeed, it points out that 'materiality is not capable of general mathematical definition' (para 3). However, it is generally accepted that a useful starting point is to compare financial statement items with an appropriate base amount. For example:

- profit and loss statement items may be compared with profit before tax and exceptional items for the current year, or the average pre-tax profit for the last, say, three years (including the current year), whichever is the more relevant measure of profit having regard to the trend of business over the period;
- balance sheet items may be compared with the lower of:
  - total shareholders' funds; and
  - the appropriate balance sheet class total, for example, current assets, fixed assets, current liabilities, long-term liabilities.

Although SAS 220 does not provide numerical guidelines or endorse their use, in practice the following percentage limit guidelines are widely used:

- A variation of 10% or more of the relevant base amount may be presumed to be material, unless there is evidence to the contrary.
- A variation of 5% or less of the relevant base amount may be presumed to be immaterial, unless there is evidence to the contrary.
- For variations which lie between 5% and 10% of the relevant base amount, determination of materiality (or otherwise) depends on the particular circumstances.

It should be noted that these percentage guidelines are not 'magic numbers', and all of the circumstances surrounding the item in question, the reporting entity, and the financial statement users, need to be taken into account.

(ii) Quantity vs quality of an item

As noted in SAS 220, para 4 (quoted above), when assessing the materiality of a misstatement, it is not only its amount which is relevant. The nature or quality of the item is also significant. For example, a misstatement of directors' emoluments may be very small relative to the entity's profit and *prima facie* would be considered immaterial. However, the nature of the item may be of such sensitivity that even a small inaccuracy would be material. SAS 220, para 6 and ISA 320, para 5 also note that material misstatements include 'the inadequate or inaccurate description of an accounting policy when it is likely that a user of the financial statements could be misled by the description.'

(iii) Legal and regulatory requirements

Many financial statement disclosures are required by statute, regulation, and/or professional standards (primarily Financial Reporting Standards or Statements of Standard Accounting Practice). For example, disclosure of audit fees is required by the Companies Act 1985, s.390A, and disclosure by lessees of finance lease liabilities, classified into 'amounts payable in the next year, amounts payable in the second to fifth years inclusive from the balance sheet date, and the aggregate amount payable thereafter' is required by SSAP 21, para 52. In most cases, failure to disclose such item(s) will be regarded by the auditor as a material omission.

(iv) Overall and account level materiality

Overall materiality refers to the amount of error the auditor is prepared to accept in the financial statements as a whole while still concluding that they provide a true and fair view of the auditee's state of affairs (or financial position) and profit or loss. It is the amount of error the auditor considers may be present in the financial statements without affecting the decisions or actions of reasonable users of the statements.

Account level materiality refers to the amount of error an auditor will accept in an individual account balance, class of transactions or financial statement disclosure before concluding that the relevant financial statement account or disclosure may mislead reasonable financial statement users.

The issue of overall and account level materiality is discussed in detail in Chapter 8.

3.4.3 Concept of audit risk

3.4.3a Definition of audit risk

SAS 300: *Accounting and internal control systems and audit risk assessments* defines audit risk as 'the risk that auditors may give an inappropriate audit opinion on financial statements' (para 3). From this definition it is evident that audit risk has two forms:

- α risk: the risk that the auditor may express a *qualified* opinion (say something is amiss) on financial statements that are *not* materially misstated; and
- β risk: the risk that the auditor may express an *unqualified* ('clean') opinion on financial statements that *are* materially misstated.

The risk of an auditor expressing a qualified opinion on financial statements that are not materially misstated is very unlikely. Before qualifying the audit report, the auditor will need good reasons for doing so, and such reasons will need to be justified to the relevant company's directors. If the auditor has drawn invalid conclusions about the financial statements, these are likely to come to light during this 'justification process'. Thus, the term 'audit risk' is commonly used to mean β risk.[8] Ultimately, to the auditor, audit risk amounts to exposure to legal liability if, as a result of issuing a 'clean' audit report on financial statements which are materially misstated, a user of the financial statements is misled and suffers a loss as a consequence. However, as noted in section 3.4.1 above, auditors are required to *express an opinion* on the financial statements, not to *certify* their truth and fairness. As a result, some degree of audit risk is always present. Consequently, legal action against an auditor is likely to succeed only if the auditor deliberately or negligently accepts an unreasonably high level of audit risk (that is, the auditor fails to conduct an adequate audit before issuing a 'clean' audit report on materially misstated financial statements).

3.4.3b Components of audit risk

Audit risk comprises two main components, namely:
(i) the risk that material error is present in the (unaudited) financial statements. This risk of error occurring results from inherent risk and internal control risk;
(ii) the risk that the auditor will fail to detect material error which is present in the (unaudited) financial statements. This component is referred to as detection risk and comprises sampling risk and quality control risk.[9]

These components of audit risk are shown in Figure 3.3 and discussed below.

(i) The risk that material error is present (risk of error occurring)
The likelihood of material error occurring in the unaudited (or draft) financial statements is, for the most part, beyond the auditor's control. This component of audit risk results from two factors, inherent risk and internal control risk.

Inherent risk: This is the risk or likelihood of material error being present in the financial statements in the absence of internal controls (that is, controls designed to prevent errors from occurring). As may be seen from Figure 3.3, inherent risk derives from three main sources. These are as follows:

1. *Management integrity*: The likelihood of material error being present in the financial statements is strongly influenced by the integrity of the auditee's management. This integrity has two aspects:

---

[8] ISA 400: *Risk assessments and internal control* (para 3) defines audit risk as: 'The risk that the auditor gives an inappropriate opinion when financial statements are materially misstated.' Thus, it equates 'audit risk' with β risk.

[9] SAS 300 (and ISA 400) recognises as separate audit risk components inherent risk, control risk and detection risk. Control risk, as defined in SAS 300 (and ISA 400), equates with what we term internal control risk, and detection risk equates essentially to sampling risk.

Figure 3.3:   The components of audit risk

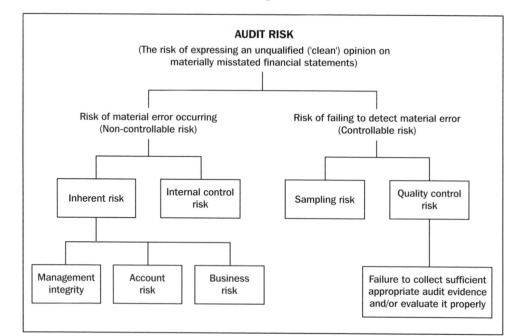

(a) *inherent integrity*: that is, management's moral and ethical stance; its 'natural' tendency towards being honest or dishonest; and

(b) *situational integrity*: that is, management's ability to withstand temptation to misrepresent the company's financial position and/or its profit or loss in situations of pressure. For example, when the entity has failed to meet profit forecasts, or when there are plans to float new shares and the year's profit has been small, management may be tempted to 'artificially improve' the entity's reported profit.

Where a company's management lacks integrity, the information reported in the (unaudited) financial statements may well be manipulated to the extent necessary to portray the company's state of affairs and profit or loss as desired by management.

2. **Account risk**: Material error may also occur in the financial statements as a result of account balances (or classes of transactions) being susceptible to misstatement. In the main, these are account balances which involve significant judgment (such as the provision for doubtful debts) or those where values are uncertain (for example, stands of unsold timber for which market demand is uncertain).[10]

3. **Business risk**: The likelihood of material error occurring in financial statements is also affected by the nature of the auditee's business. While some

---

[10] SAS 300 (and ISA 400) defines inherent risk in terms of account risk (see para 4).

businesses are not particularly vulnerable to changes in the state of the economy, competition and/or technological advances, the reverse is true for others. For example, jewellery outlets are affected by changes in consumer wealth; fashion-wear businesses are susceptible to changes in customer 'fads'; businesses in the electronics industry are prone to changes in technology and those in the oil industry are exposed to rapid and large changes in oil prices in world markets. In each case, a high risk attaches to the entity's stock valuation and possibly also to its ability to sustain operating cash flow at a level necessary to meet its debt obligations. In the latter instance, business risk may generate a situation in which management's integrity is put under pressure.

Internal control risk:[11] This is the risk that material misstatement will occur in the auditee's accounting data (and hence in its financial statements) because it is not prevented or detected and corrected by the company's internal controls. Some internal control risk will always be present because any internal control system has inherent limitations.[12] However, if a company has effective internal controls, the likelihood of error occurring in its unaudited financial statements can be reduced to a minimum.

In relation to the likelihood of error being present in an auditee's unaudited financial statements, it is pertinent to note that, although auditors have little or no direct control over inherent risk and internal control risk, they can and should be aware of the circumstances in which these risks are likely to be high. They can perform procedures to ascertain whether these circumstances are present in any given audit and adjust their audit effort and techniques accordingly. (Evaluating the integrity of the client's management and evaluating internal control risk are discussed in Chapters 7 and 9, respectively.)

(ii)   The risk that material error will not be detected (detection risk)
Unlike the risk of material error occurring in unaudited financial statements, the risk of auditors failing to detect such error is subject to their direct control. As Figure 3.3 shows, this component of audit risk derives from sampling risk and quality control risk.[13]

• **Sampling risk**: This is the risk that the auditor may fail to detect material error present in the financial statements because not all of the available

---

[11] As noted in footnote 9, SAS 300 (and ISA 400) terms this type of risk 'control risk'.

[12] The inherent limitations of internal control systems are discussed in Chapter 8.

[13] The definition of detection risk provided in SAS 300, para 6 (and ISA 400, para 6) is broad enough to embrace both of these components of detection risk. However, in SAS 300, para 50 (and ISA 400, para 41) emphasis is given to the sampling risk component.

evidence is examined and a particular transaction or account balance which is materially misstated is not included in the samples of transactions or balances examined during the audit. When statistical sampling techniques are used, sampling risk is quantifiable and controllable. As explained in Chapter 11, statistical sampling techniques enable sample sizes to be adjusted so that the level of audit (sampling) risk the auditor is prepared to accept may be achieved.

- **Quality control risk:**[14] This is the risk that the auditor will fail to detect material error which is present in the financial statements because sufficient appropriate audit evidence is not collected and/or is not evaluated properly. As with internal control risk, some quality control risk will always be present, simply because audits are conducted by humans (who are fallible) and they involve a considerable amount of judgment. Audit staff cannot be expected to make optimal judgments, and to perform with perfection, on every occasion throughout an audit. Some human error is inevitable!

As noted above, the risk of auditors failing to detect material misstatement present in financial statements is under their direct control. They should therefore seek to reduce sampling risk and quality control risk (that is, detection risk) to the level it is economically feasible to do so. As explained in Chapter 8, this level varies inversely with the auditor's assessment of inherent risk and internal control risk.

3.4.4 Concept of judgment

Judgment is a fundamental characteristic of all professions – including auditing. The concept encapsulates the notion of evaluating the circumstances and/or available evidence relevant to a known objective, and forming an opinion based on that evaluation. It contrasts with achieving an objective by means of following an established set of rules or procedures.

In order for a professional judgment to be sound it is essential that the person exercising it (for example, an auditor) has integrity, is competent, and maintains an objective unbiased attitude of mind – concepts, as we have already seen, that are central to the credibility of auditors' work.

Judgment pervades every stage of the audit process. As SAS 100: *Objective and general principles governing an audit of financial statements* observes:

> The work undertaken by auditors to form an opinion is permeated by the exercise of judgment, in particular regarding:
> a) the gathering of evidence; for example, in deciding the nature, timing and extent of audit procedures; and

---

[14] The concept of quality control is discussed in Section 3.6.2 below.

b) the drawing of conclusions based on the evidence gathered; for example, assessing the reasonableness of the estimates made by the directors in preparing the financial statements. (para 9)

More specifically, judgment must be exercised in relation to, for example, questions such as:

- how much effort (time and expertise) should be devoted to the audit in question?
- where should audit effort be focused?
- how much, what, and from where, should evidence be gathered?
- who should constitute the audit team (in terms of numbers of staff and their level of competence)?
- what conclusions about the truth and fairness of the financial statements (and each segment thereof) are supported by the evidence gathered?
- what opinion should be expressed in the audit report?

These, and numerous other questions that arise in any audit, do not have clear-cut answers that apply routinely in a given situation. Each audit is unique, and the circumstances of the particular audit must be considered when auditors exercise their judgment. However, one general factor that impacts and, to some extent, limits the exercise of auditors' judgment in all audits is the materiality of the matter in question. As the fundamental principle of auditing – *Judgment* – explains:

> Auditors apply professional judgment taking account of materiality in the context of the matters on which they are reporting. (APB, 1996)

Whether or not something is material is itself a matter for the auditor's judgment and, as noted in section 3.4.2 above, varies according to the circumstances of the auditee (particularly its size) and its financial statements.

The exercise of auditors' judgment is not only unique to the circumstances of each audit: it is also unique to each auditor. The ability of auditors to arrive at professional decisions and opinions, and the cognitive process by which they do so, varies according to a variety of environmental and personal factors. These include such things as the social, cultural and political environment in which the auditor (and auditee) operates, as well as the auditor's general and professional education, professional training and experience, problem-solving ability, the extent and detail of guidance provided in Auditing Standards and other professional promulgations, and the policies and culture of the auditor's firm.

3.4.5 Concept of scepticism

The first part of the fundamental principle of auditing – *Rigour* – states:

> Auditors approach their work with thoroughness and with an attitude of professional scepticism. (APB, 1996)

However, this leaves open the question of what is meant by 'professional scepticism'.

ISA 200: *Objective and general principles governing an audit of financial statements*, para 6 (revised, 2001)[15] explains the concept in the auditing context as follows:

> An attitude of professional scepticism means the auditor makes a critical assessment, with a questioning mind, of the validity of audit evidence obtained and is alert to audit evidence that contradicts or brings into question the reliability of documents or management representations. For example, an attitude of professional scepticism is necessary throughout the audit process for the auditor to reduce the risk of overlooking suspicious circumstances, of overgeneralizing when drawing conclusions from audit observations, and of using faulty assumptions in determining the nature, timing and extent of the audit procedures and evaluating the results thereof.

The APB, in its Consultation Paper: *Fraud and audit: choices for society* (1998) notes that 'scepticism is a personal quality that relates to the attitude of individual auditors: it is characterised by a questioning, probing – almost suspicious – approach being applied throughout the audit' (para 3.7). However, as indicated by Lopes L J in the *Kingston Cotton Mill* case [1896] 2 Ch. 279,[16] auditors are *not* required to 'approach [their] work with suspicion or with a foregone conclusion that there is something wrong'. This is beyond the concept of professional scepticism. Rather, auditors should be neutral in their approach: they should neither assume that the auditee's directors, executives and other employees are dishonest, nor should they assume unquestioned honesty. They should carefully evaluate (rather than merely accept) the evidence they gather, and the information and explanations provided by auditee personnel, with an objective, unbiased attitude of mind. They need to ask themselves: 'Given my knowledge of this auditee, its business, its circumstances, its operations, does the evidence (or information or explanations) obtained make sense?' If not, they should seek further evidence and ask probing questions to satisfy themselves as to its truth or otherwise.

Auditors' ability and propensity to evaluate evidence gathered and information provided, and to ask probing questions, is affected by a variety of environmental and personal factors. These factors tend to coincide with those (noted in section 3.4.4 above) that impact auditors' ability to, and the manner in which they, exercise judgment.

---

[15] ISA 200, para 6, was revised as an addendum to revised ISA 240: *The auditor's responsibility to consider fraud and error.*

[16] The key principles to emerge from this case are discussed in Chapter 5, section 5.3.

3.5   CONCEPTS RELATING TO AUDITORS' COMMUNICATION

3.5.1   Concept of reporting

Given that the key objective of an audit is to form and express an opinion (in an audit report) on the truth and fairness of the auditee's financial statements, reporting is clearly a concept that goes to the very heart of the audit function. However, it is not just a case of auditors completing their audit and issuing a report without regard to the readers of that report. Rather, it involves *communicating* essential information to users of the audited financial statements. As the fundamental principle of auditing – *Communication* – explains:

> Auditors' reports contain clear expressions of opinion and set out the information necessary for a proper understanding of that opinion. (APB, 1996)

When preparing their reports, auditors need to bear in mind that the users of the financial statements on which they are expressing an opinion, unlike themselves, do not have access to the auditee's accounting and other data, records and information, and frequently they have little (if any) technical accounting or auditing knowledge. Thus, they rely on auditors to report their opinion about the financial statements in which they are interested – and to do so in a manner which enables them to comprehend the opinion expressed, and the level of assurance it provides.

Flint (1988, p. 117) explains the importance of auditors' reports:

> Audit reports have potentially serious consequences for all parties involved. The inadequacy of a report and the failure to communicate successfully could result in consequences which were not justified by the facts, with injustice and damage to the interests of the parties.

This conveys the idea that, if users of financial statements rely on the auditor's report and make investment decisions based on their understanding of the message it contains, if their understanding is erroneous, their investment decisions could be unwise and have serious adverse financial consequences.

Flint's statement also indicates that to be effective, auditors' reports need to meet two key criteria: they need to be adequate in content and communicate successfully with users of the audited financial statements.

(a) Adequacy: To be of value to financial statement users, audit reports must contain sufficient information them to be left in no doubt as to the opinion (and any reservations) the auditor is expressing. They must be explicit and complete. As Flint (1988, p. 117–118) observes:

> Auditors are rarely in a position to engage in a dialogue with the parties who will use their report and, once released, the report is frequently public information. . . . An audit report must be complete and explicit so that any

reader at any time in the future knows fully and exactly what the auditors had to communicate as the outcome of the audit. It must be complete within itself, not requiring the reader to refer to any other document to understand its terms.

(b) *Communication:* In order to communicate a message to financial statement users, audit reports need to be explicit, precise, and comprehensible. However, meeting these requirements is no easy task.

The matters which are the subject of audit are frequently complex and highly specialised, and auditing itself is an advanced professional specialism. Auditors face the dilemma that they must communicate effectively with persons with limited or no technical understanding and at the same time must express themselves with sufficient technical precision to define precisely the terms and limits of the responsibility they undertake. ...

The audit report must be in terms which enable [financial statement users] to be informed ... whether or not accounts, reports or other statements provide the information they should, and in what respects, if any, there have been failures or defaults or any description in relation to matters with which recipients of the audit report are concerned. (Flint, 1988, pp. 118–119)

Since 1988 (when the 'long form' audit report was first adopted – in the USA; it was adopted in the UK in 1993), the auditing profession has made efforts to ensure that audit reports are adequate in content, complete, explicit, precise and comprehensible. Auditing Standards in the UK, as in most other countries of the developed world, have been revised with this objective in view. (The latest revision to the wording of auditors' reports in the UK was in 2001.)

As we will discuss in Chapter 13, auditors' reports, amongst other things:
- identify the financial statements which have been audited and about which the auditor is expressing an opinion;
- explain the respective responsibilities of the auditee's directors and the auditors with respect to the financial statements;[17]
- outline the audit process which forms the basis for the opinion expressed;
- express an opinion about the truth and fairness (or otherwise) of the financial statements.

3.6 CONCEPTS RELATING TO THE STANDARD OF AUDITORS' PERFORMANCE

3.6.1 Concept of due care

In order for an auditor's opinion to be respected and valued, those relying on that opinion must be able to assume it has been formed by an auditor who has

---

[17] An example of this statement of responsibilities is provided in Chapter 5, section 5.7.

conducted the underlying audit diligently, competently and with due care. But what does the term 'due care' mean in the auditing context?

Court decisions from the nineteenth and twentieth centuries shed some light on the meaning. For example, in *Re Kingston Cotton Mill (No. 2)* [1896] 2 Ch. 279, Lopes L J explained:

> It is the duty of an auditor to bring to bear on the work he has to perform, that skill, care and caution which a reasonably competent, careful and cautious auditor would use. What is reasonable skill, care and caution must depend on the particular circumstances of each case.

Pennycuick J in the case of *Re Thomas Gerrard & Son Ltd.* [1967] 2 All ER 525, further clarified the issue. He stated:

> I am not clear that the quality of the auditor's duty has changed in any relevant respect since 1896. Basically that duty has always been to audit the company's accounts with reasonable care and skill. The real ground on which *Re Kingston Cotton Mill Co. (No. 2)* is I think capable of being distinguished, is that the standards of reasonable care and skill are . . . more exacting today than those which prevailed in 1896.

Similar ideas were expressed by Moffit J *in Pacific Acceptance Corporation Ltd.* v *Forsyth and Others* (1970) 92 WN (NSW)29:[18]

> It is beyond question that when an auditor ... enters into a contract to perform certain tasks as auditor, he promises to perform such tasks using that degree of skill and care as is reasonable in the circumstances as they then exist. ... The legal duty, namely, to audit the accounts with reasonable skill and care remains the same, but ... reasonable skill and care calls for changed standards to meet changed conditions or changed understanding of dangers and in this sense standards are more exacting today than in 1896.

Moffit J goes on to observe that the auditing profession, by changing the guidance it has given to auditors, has recognised that changed conditions require changed audit procedures. However, he also gives a warning:

> [The] standards and practices adopted by the profession to meet current circumstances provide a sound guide to the court in determining what is reasonable. . . . [However] when the conduct of an auditor is in question in legal proceedings it is not the province of the audit profession itself to determine . . . what reasonable skill and care require to be done in a particular case. [This is the province of the court.]

So, what can we distil from the Judges' statements in the cases cited above about the concept of due care? It may be seen that it has four significant characteristics, namely:

1. it embodies the notion of auditors exercising reasonable skill, care and caution;
2. what is 'reasonable skill, care and caution' in any audit depends on the particular circumstances of the case;

---

[18] This case is also cited in Chapter 5.

3. the standard of 'reasonable skill, care and caution' has become more exacting over the past 100 or so years, as society, and more particularly the commercial and corporate worlds, have become more complex and dynamic;
4. although Auditing Standards and other professional promulgations provide guidance to the court on what may reasonably be expected of auditors, it is up to the court, not the profession, to determine whether an auditor has taken due care in any particular audit.

This concept is discussed further in Chapter 5, section 5.3, and in Chapter 15.

3.6.2   Concept of quality control

If the public is to have confidence in auditors' work it is essential that measures (or controls) are put in place to ensure that their work is consistently of high quality. Flint (1988) conveys succinctly the importance of quality control for auditing:

> Auditors have both a legal duty and a professional obligation to work to the highest standards which can reasonably be expected to discharge the responsibility that is placed on them. . . . In a profession whose authority is dependent among other things on public confidence . . . a demonstrable concern, individually and collectively on the part of the members of the profession, to control and maintain the highest quality in its work, is a matter of basic principle. The basis of continuing public confidence and trust in professional competence is a belief that the standards of the members of the profession will be maintained and can be relied on. (pp. 159, 161)

The auditing profession has tackled the issue of ensuring high quality audit work in two main ways, namely:

(i)   embodying requirements in SAS 240: *Quality control for audit work*;
(ii) implementing external monitoring of registered auditors' compliance with regulatory requirements, Auditing Standards, and other professional promulgations such as the Guide to Professional Ethics.

(i) SAS 240: Quality control for audit work requires audit firms to 'establish, and communicate to audit engagement partners and audit staff, and others who need to be aware of them, quality control policy and processes' (SAS 240, para 8). It defines quality control policy and processes as those 'designed to provide reasonable assurance as to the appropriateness of the auditors' report and of adherence to Auditing Standards, ethical and other regulatory requirements' (para 2).[19]

---

[19] ISA 220: *Quality control for audit work* requires audit firms to 'implement quality control policies and procedures designed to ensure that all audits are conducted in accordance with International Standards on Auditing or relevant national standards or practices' and to communicate the general quality control policies and procedures 'to its personnel in a manner that provides reasonable assurance that the policies and procedures are understood and implemented'. However, it does not define quality control procedures.

The need for audit firms to implement and maintain quality control measures derives from the fact that, apart from the smallest audit clients, audits are conducted by audit teams ranging from 2 or 3 members for fairly small auditees, to some 20 or more members for large clients. It is only by implementing quality control processes and procedures that audit firms can ensure that all members of all audit teams perform the same high quality standard of work. SAS 240 implicitly recognises that responsibility for securing high quality audit work lies at all levels of audit firms.

- Individual audit staff members should accept responsibility for performing their work in accordance with professional standards.
- The audit engagement partner (the partner responsible for the particular audit) has overall responsibility for ensuring the audit team adheres to procedures designed to ensure high quality audit work and for engendering a quality culture within the team.
- The audit team has collective responsibility for ensuring the audit is performed to a high standard: this includes confirming and consulting between themselves about issues arising during the audit – especially where they are difficult or contentious to resolve.
- At firm level, an important element in securing high quality audit work is building quality into the firm's policies and procedures and monitoring the results of audit work.

We discuss the requirements of SAS 240 in Chapter 15, but the following provisions are cited as illustrative examples:

- Before accepting a new audit engagement, firms should ensure that they are competent to undertake the work. [SAS 240, para 15(a)]
- Firms should assign audit staff with the competencies necessary to perform the audit work expected of them in individual audit assignments. (SAS 240, para 31)
- Audit engagement partners should ensure that audit work is directed, supervised and reviewed in a manner that provides reasonable assurance that the work has been performed competently. (SAS 240, para 49)
- Firms should appoint a senior audit partner to take responsibility for monitoring the quality of audits carried out by the firm. (SAS 240, para 67).

(ii) External monitoring: Not only has the profession sought to ensure that audits are performed to a high quality standard, but Parliament too, recognising the importance of the audit function to society,[20] has taken steps in this direction. As explained in Chapter 5, under the provisions of the Companies Act 1989, only 'registered auditors' may be appointed as auditors of companies. To become 'registered', an individual or firm must register with a Recognised Supervisory Body (RSB). One of the conditions of becoming an RSB is that

---

[20] See Chapter 1, section 1.6.3.

procedures must be in place for monitoring the performance of registrants. Thus the five RSBs[21] have established monitoring units which are responsible for monitoring registered auditors' compliance with all of the RSB's requirements. These include performing all audit work in accordance with Auditing Standards and other relevant professional promulgations. If registered auditors are found not to be complying with all of the RSB's requirements, they are subject to sanction – including the ultimate sanction of de-registration.

Monitoring of auditors' work is discussed in greater detail in Chapter 15.

3.7 SUMMARY

In this chapter we have laid the theoretical foundation for our study of the practice of auditing. We have noted the interrelationship between the social purpose, the postulates and the concepts of auditing. We have also described seven postulates and examined the meaning and importance to auditing of 11 concepts. We have seen that these concepts fall into four groups – credibility of auditors' work (independence, competence, ethical conduct), the audit process (evidence, materiality, audit risk, judgment, scepticism), communication (reporting), and standard of performance (due care, quality control) – and that each is of fundamental importance to the auditing function. We will study most of these concepts in greater detail in their relevant contexts in subsequent chapters. However, we devote all of the next chapter to the critically important issue of auditors' independence.

SELF-REVIEW QUESTIONS

3.1 State the social purpose of auditing and how this relates to the postulates and concepts of auditing.

3.2 (a) Explain briefly what is meant by a 'postulate'.
    (b) List four postulates of auditing.

3.3 Define and explain the importance of the concept of 'independence' as it relates to auditing. (Your definition should refer to both independence in fact and independence in appearance.)

3.4 Explain briefly the meaning and importance to auditing of the concept of competence.

3.5 Explain briefly the meaning and importance to auditing of the concept of ethical conduct.

---

[21] See Chapter 5, section 5.2.3, especially footnote 9.

3.6 Explain briefly the meaning and importance to auditing of the concept of evidence.

3.7 Explain briefly the meaning and importance to auditing of the concept of materiality.

3.8 Explain briefly the meaning and importance to auditing of the concept of audit risk.

3.9 (a) Distinguish between 'non-controllable' and 'controllable' risk.
     (b) Explain briefly the components of non-controllable and controllable risk.

3.10 Explain briefly the meaning and importance to auditing of the concepts of due care, and quality control.

REFERENCES

Anderson, R.J. (1977) *The External Audit*. Toronto: Cropp Clark Pitman.

Auditing Practices Board (APB) (1998) *Fraud and audit: choices for society.* Consultation Paper, London: APB.

Committee on Basic Auditing Concepts (1973) *A Statement of Basic Auditing Concepts.* New York: AAA.

Flint, D. (1988) *Philosophy and Principles of Auditing: An Introduction*. Basingstoke: Macmillan.

Levitt, A. (2000, 18 September) A Profession at the Crossroads. Speech by SEC Chairman to National Association of State Boards of Accountancy, Boston, MA.

Mautz, R.K. & Sharaf, H.A. (1961) *The Philosophy of Auditing.* New York: AAA.

Stewart, R.E. (1977) Independence: The auditor's cornerstone. *Accountants' Journal* **56**(9), 333–337.

Turner, L.E. (2001, 28 June) Independence: A Covenant for the Ages. Speech by SEC Chief Accountant to International Organization of Securities Commissions, Stockholm, Sweden.

ADDITIONAL READING

Church, B.K. & Schneider, A. (1993) Auditor objectivity: The effect of prior involvement in auditing programmes. *Accounting and Finance,* November, 61–78.

Iselin, E.R. & Iskandar, T.M. (2000) Auditors' recognition and disclosure materiality thresholds: their magnitude and the effects of industry. *British Accounting Review* **32**, 289–309.

4 Threats to, and Preservation of, Auditors' Independence

LEARNING OBJECTIVES

After studying the material in this chapter you should be able to:

- explain the critical importance to the audit function of auditors being independent in fact and in appearance;
- describe the circumstances in which auditors' independence may, or may appear to be, compromised;
- discuss measures taken by Parliament and the auditing profession which are designed to ensure auditors are (and remain) independent of their audit clients;
- outline arguments for and against (i) mandatory auditor rotation, (ii) auditors' appointment by the State (or a State agency), and (iii) auditors' appointment by a shareholder panel, as means of strengthening auditors' independence;
- explain the development, importance and principal responsibilities of audit committees – with particular reference to auditors' independence.

The following publications and fundamental principle of external auditing are relevant to this chapter:

Publications:
- Guide to Professional Ethics Statement (GPES) 1: *Integrity, Objectivity and Independence* (ICAEW, ICAS, ICAI;[1] 1997).
- *Code of Ethics for Professional Accountants* (IFAC, 1998)

Fundamental principle of external auditing included in *The Auditor's Code* (APB, 1996)
- Objectivity and independence

---

[1] GPES 1 is published separately, but in identical form, by each of the three Chartered Institutes: ICAEW, ICAS and ICAI and in similar form by the ACCA and AIA. In each case, the Guide to Professional Ethics is based on IFAC's Code of Ethics (as published, 1996)

4.1 INTRODUCTION

As noted in Chapter 3, auditors being independent of their audit clients, their clients' managements, and any other influences which might impair their objectivity and impartiality, is of critical importance to the audit function. If auditors are not perceived as independent by those who use and rely on audited financial statements, their opinion on those financial statements will lack credibility and thus the audit will be of little or no value.

Given the importance of auditors' independence to the audit function, stipulating that auditors must be independent both in fact and in appearance may seem to be an obvious requirement. However, in practice, such independence may be difficult to achieve and easy to compromise. In this chapter we discuss threats to auditors' independence – and steps taken, or proposed, which are designed to preserve and/or strengthen auditors' independence.

4.2 FACTORS THAT MAY COMPROMISE AUDITORS' INDEPENDENCE

For many years, politicians (such as Congressman Dingell in the USA and Austin Mitchell MP in the UK), regulators (such as the Department of Trade and Industry in the UK and the SEC in the USA) and various commentators (such as Briloff, 1986 and Mitchell and Sikka, 1993) have raised questions about auditors' ability to remain independent of their audit clients. They note that auditors are hired, fired and paid by their clients' managements, they work closely with them as they conduct their audits and, as a result, after a number of years of acting as auditor for the client they become very familiar with them. Further, auditors are frequently engaged by audit client managements to provide non-audit, in addition to, audit, services.

During the 1990s, the SEC in particular, became very concerned about the possible impairment of auditors' independence as a consequence of providing non-audit services to audit clients. For example, Levitt (2000), former Chairman of the SEC, observed:

> I cannot help but notice the many advertisements for the big accountancy firms. They seem to always extol their IT talents, corporate finance capabilities, and financial planning tools. But rarely do I see an advertisement that conveys to the public and their clients their passion for living up to their public mandate of keeping the sanctity of the numbers inviolate – never a mention of the public interest.
> [A]uditors who also provide consulting services for their audit clients must now serve two masters: a public obligation to shareholders, and a professional duty to management. And when the two come into conflict, the independent audit – dwarfed by the more lucrative consulting businesses – too often may be compromised. (pp. 2, 7)

While the SEC has focused principally on the increased provision of non-audit services to audit clients, the profession's Guide to Professional Ethics Statement (GPES) 1 has identified five broad 'threats' to auditors' independence, namely:

- *the self-interest threat* – the threat to auditors' independence resulting from a financial or other self-interest conflict (para 2.2);
- *the self-review threat* – the difficulty of maintaining objectivity in situations where a product or judgment of a previous audit, or non-audit, assignment needs to be challenged or re-evaluated in reaching audit conclusions (para 2.3);
- *the advocacy threat* – the threat to auditors' objectivity resulting from auditors becoming advocates for (or against) their client's position in any adversarial proceedings or situations (para 2.4);
- *the familiarity or trust threat* – the threat arising from auditors becoming over-influenced by the personality and qualities of their clients' directors and/or senior managers and consequently too sympathetic to their interest. Alternatively, auditors may become too trusting of management representations and, thus, insufficiently rigorous in their audit testing (para 2.5);
- *the intimidation threat* – the possibility that auditors may be intimidated by threat, by a dominating personality, or by other pressures, by a director or manager of their client or by some other party (para 2.6).

In addition to recognising these general situations which may endanger an auditor's independence, GPES 1 identifies more specific circumstances in which an auditor may find it difficult (or may be perceived as likely to find it difficult) to maintain an unbiased, objective attitude of mind. These include situations where the auditor:

- has some financial involvement with the audit client as a shareholder, debt holder or creditor;
- participates (or plans to participate) in the affairs of a client in a capacity other than that of auditor (for example, as a director of, or consultant to, the client);
- has a mutual business interest with the audit client, or with an officer or senior employee of the client;
- receives favourable treatment from the client in the form of goods, services or hospitality;
- is actually or potentially involved in litigation against the client.

Also where:

- the auditor (or the auditor's firm) depends on the audit client for a substantial portion of total fee income and/or provides non-audit services to the audit client.

4.3   STEPS TAKEN BY PARLIAMENT AND THE PROFESSION TO SECURE AUDITORS' INDEPENDENCE FROM THEIR AUDIT CLIENTS

From the above, it is clear that a wide range of circumstances may cause auditors' independence to be impaired. However, conscious of the importance of independence to the credibility of the audit function, both Parliament and the accounting profession have established measures designed to ensure that auditors are, and remain, independent of their audit clients. For example, the Companies Act 1989, s.27, stipulates that neither an officer or employee of the company, nor a partner or employee of an officer or employee of the company, may be appointed as auditor of a company. This provision is designed to ensure that the auditor is not exposed to a conflict of interest as a result of working for the company (directly or indirectly) in a capacity other than that of auditor. Additionally, the Companies Act 1985, s.390A, provides that a company must disclose in its annual report, the amount paid or payable to the auditor (or audit firm) in respect of audit fees and expenses for the year. Further, under regulations issued by the Secretary of State (in accordance with s.390B of the Companies Act 1985), companies are required to disclose in their annual report, fees and expenses paid to their auditors (or an associate thereof) for non-audit services. This requirement ensures that financial statement users are provided with information which enables them to assess the likelihood of auditor's independence being compromised as a consequence of too great an involvement with the audit client through the provision of non-audit services.

In addition to the statutory and regulatory requirements, the professional accountancy bodies have promulgated a series of 'rules' designed to prevent auditors' independence from being compromised. These are of two types:

(a) general environmental safeguards; and
(b) specific safeguards appropriate for identified situations where independence may be at risk.

(a)   General environmental safeguards

GPES 1 notes that certain safeguards for auditors' independence are embodied in the general environment of the auditing profession and audit firms. It notes, for example, that:

- qualified accountants are taught from the outset of their training to behave with integrity in all their professional and business relationships and to strive for objectivity in all professional and business judgments [para 3.3(i)];
- the profession has a long standing ethical code which imposes specific prohibitions in circumstances where the threat to auditors' objectivity is so

significant, or is generally perceived to be so, that no other appropriate safeguards would be effective [para 3.4(i)];
- firms establish internal procedures which help to provide reassurance that the required audit objectivity has been preserved. These include:
  - arrangements to ensure that staff are adequately trained and empowered to communicate any issue of objectivity that concerns them to a separate principal (or partner) of the firm;
  - the rotation of audit engagement partners and staff;
  - formal consideration of the propriety of accepting all potential and continuing audit engagements;
  - the overall control environment, starting with a professional approach towards matters of quality and ethics, and embracing staff training, development and performance appraisal (para 3.5).

(b)   Specific safeguards for identified situations of risk

These may be considered conveniently under the following headings:
(i)   financial involvement with an audit client;
(ii)   personal or business relationships with an audit client;
(iii)   favourable treatment from an audit client;
(iv)   litigation and other external pressures on the auditor;
(v)   undue dependence on an audit client for fee income;
(vi)   provision of non-audit services to an audit client.

(i)   Financial involvement with an audit client

Financial involvement with an audit client may arise through a shareholding in, or loan to or from, the client, or through any other direct or indirect beneficial interest in the client: this includes a beneficial interest arising through a trust (as trustee or beneficiary) or a Personal Equity Plan which has an audit client among its investments.

To safeguard auditors' independence from being comprised as a result of financial involvement with an audit client, GPES 1 provides that:
- except in cases where a client is in the business of borrowing and lending money (for example, a bank), no audit firm or principal of a firm should directly or indirectly make any loan to, or receive any loan from, an audit client, or give or accept any guarantee in relation to a debt of the client, firm or principal (paras 4.10 to 4.12);
- in cases where significant fees are overdue from an audit client, or group of connected clients, a principal not involved in the audit should undertake a review to ascertain whether the overdue fees, together with the fees for the current audit assignment, could be regarded as a significant loan (paras 4.13 and 4.14);

- no principal in an audit firm, nor anyone closely connected with a principal (such as a spouse and dependent children), should have any beneficial interest in shares or other direct investment in an audit client. Similarly, no principal in an audit firm should have a Personal Equity Plan which has any audit client among its investments (paras 4.31 and 4.36);
- if an employee in an audit firm, or a person closely connected with an employee, has a beneficial interest in shares or other investments of an audit client, that employee should not take part in the audit of that client (para 4.32);
- if a principal in an audit firm, or person closely connected with a principal, holds a beneficial interest in a trust which has a shareholding in an audit client, and the principal is a trustee of the trust, the audit firm should cease to be the auditor of the client. If the principal is not a trustee of the trust, the firm may retain the client but the principal should not be involved in the audit (paras 4.39 to 4.41);
- in cases where shares or other relevant investment(s) in an audit client are acquired involuntarily by a principal in an audit firm, for example, through inheritance, marriage or a takeover, the investment(s) should be disposed of at the earliest practicable date when the disposition would not be considered to amount to insider trading (para 4.37);
- in cases where the audit client's Articles of Association require the auditor to be a shareholder, the auditor should hold no more than the minimum number of shares necessary to comply with the provision in the Articles (para 4.38). Additionally, the auditor is precluded from voting at any general meeting of the company in relation to the appointment, removal or remuneration of the company's auditor(s) (para 4.49).

(ii)   Personal or business relationships with an audit client

As for financial involvement, the professional bodies have recognised that personal, family and business relationships with an audit client (or officer or senior employee of an audit client) may impair auditors' independence. GPES 1 stipulates, for example, that no member of the profession should personally take part in the audit of a company in which (s)he has been an officer or employee during the current accounting period or the preceding two years (para 4.24). Along similar lines, GPES 1 states that where a principal or senior employee of an audit firm joins an audit client, appropriate steps should be taken to sever any significant connections between that former principal or employee and the audit firm. Where such a person plans to join an audit client, (s)he should be removed from the audit team immediately this is known, and any significant audit judgments made by that person with respect to the client should be reviewed (paras 4.26 to 4.29).

(iii)   Favourable treatment from an audit client

The professional bodies have recognised that auditors' independence may be compromised as a result of receiving a benefit by way of goods, services or hospitality from an audit client. As a consequence, audit firms and persons closely connected with the firm (principals and employees) are prohibited from accepting such goods, services and hospitality from a client, except where 'the value of any benefit is modest' (GPES 1, para 4.15). What amounts to a 'modest benefit' is left to the auditor's (or audit firm's) judgment.

(iv)   Litigation and other external pressures

Where litigation between an auditor and audit client is in progress, or is likely to take place, it seems most unlikely that the auditor will be able to maintain an independent attitude of mind when evaluating the client's financial statements and supporting evidence. Even if the auditor is, in fact, able to maintain his or her objectivity, independence in appearance will be impaired. This applies whether the client has sued the auditor, for example, for negligence, or the auditor has brought a case against the client for occurrences such as fraud or deceit (GPES 1, paras 4.16 to 4.19).

The professional bodies have also recognised that an auditor's independence may be endangered as a result of pressures being exerted by an associated audit firm or by an outside source introducing business, such as bankers or solicitors. In this regard GPES 1 notes:

> The threat to objectivity [in such circumstances] will depend upon the closeness of the relationship and association, the strength of an associate's interest in the [audit] firm's retaining a client, and the extent to which the introduction of business by an outside source is able to affect the firm's fee income. (para 4.51)

In order to mitigate the likelihood of auditors' independence being compromised as a consequence of pressures being brought to bear by outside sources, the audit firm is precluded from employing on the relevant audit any person who is subject to such pressures. GPES 1 also notes that potential dangers to auditors' independence resulting from external pressures 'should be borne in mind and provided for in the [audit] firm's review machinery' (para 4.53) (that is, the measures incorporated in the audit firm's control environment, such as considering, prior to their acceptance, the propriety of accepting certain new or continuing audit engagements).

(v)   Undue dependence on an audit client for fee income

GPES 1 (para 4.1) recognises that auditors' objectivity may be threatened, or appear to be threatened, by undue dependence for fees on any one audit client or group of connected clients. While noting that new firms may not be able to meet the criteria, GPES 1 recommends that auditors should avoid situations where recurring fees (from audit and non-audit services) from one client, or group of connected clients, exceed 15% of the gross income of the practice. If the client is a listed company (or of particular interest to the public), the fees should not exceed 10% of the practice's gross income (para 4.2). GPES I emphasises that the 15% and 10% noted above 'indicate only the extremes beyond which the public perception of a member's objectivity is likely to be at risk'. It goes on to state that an audit firm:

> ... should, before accepting an audit appointment and as part of its annual review, carefully consider ... the propriety of accepting or retaining each audit client or group of connected clients the fees from which for audit and other recurring work ... represent 10 per cent or more of the gross practice income ... In the case of a listed company or other public interest company ... a figure of not more than 5 per cent is the appropriate point to initiate review. (para 4.9)

Although serious, dependence on a particular audit client (or group of connected clients) for a significant proportion of fee income is not the only threat to auditors' independence arising from audit fees. It is a widely held view that auditors are unlikely to be truly independent of their clients all the time audit fees are settled through direct negotiation with the client's management. Auditors are perceived as unlikely to bite the hand that feeds them!

A significant proposal designed to divorce company officials from negotiating the audit fee with their auditors is that of having audit fees determined according to a fixed scale. The main difficulty with this proposal is identifying a suitable base for developing a scale of fees. The most common suggestion has been the size of the audit client but there is no consensus as to the appropriate indicator of size. Should it be, for example, total assets? total revenue? total profits? and, if so, before or after exceptional items? before or after tax? etc.

Even if agreement could be reached about the 'best' indicator of size, this may not be an appropriate basis for determining audit fees. The time, effort and skills required for an audit frequently depend on factors other than size; for example, whether the audit is an initial or subsequent engagement (an initial audit requires additional time to become familiar with the client, its business, its accounting system, etc.); the complexity (or simplicity) of the client's organisational structure and business operations; the quality of the client's internal controls; the expertise of the client's accountancy staff; the presence (or absence) of circumstances which might motivate client-personnel to manipulate the financial statements (for example, plans to float shares or issue debentures during the ensuing accounting period, or managers' bonuses being tied to reported profits).

Further, even if a satisfactory scale of fees could be developed which accommodated factors recognised as affecting the time and skills needed for audits, there is the danger that auditors would be tempted to tailor individual audits to the set fees rather than to the particular circumstances of the audit. In some cases this could result in over-auditing: that is, auditors conducting audit tests beyond those which are strictly necessary because additional time is 'available' under the set fee. In other cases, under-auditing may result: auditors failing to perform tests which are required because the fee is insufficient to cover the time needed.

Direct negotiation of audit fees between auditors and audit-client managements is a serious obstacle to securing and maintaining auditors' independence and it is an obstacle that is difficult to overcome. A mechanism which can mitigate the difficulties, by ensuring that executives who are responsible for the day-to-day management of the entity are not involved in negotiating audit fees with the auditors, is that of an audit committee. This is discussed in section 4.4a below.

(vi)   Provision of non-audit services to an audit client

Like placing undue dependence on audit clients for fee income, the provision of non-audit services to audit clients is generally regarded as a serious threat to auditors' independence – both in fact and in appearance and, as noted above, the SEC in the USA is particularly concerned about this issue. However, there are two sides to the argument. These are as follows:

- As noted in Chapter 2, during the course of an audit, the auditor becomes familiar with all aspects of the audit client – its business, organisation, accounting system, internal controls, policies, key personnel, etc. This familiarity places the auditor in an ideal position to provide financial and management advice to the audit client. The auditor, unlike other outside consultants, does not have to spend time getting to know the client. This clearly reduces the costs involved. Furthermore, because the auditor is familiar with every aspect of the client's organisation, (s)he is able to anticipate the likely impact on all parts of the organisation, of any advice given to management. An outside consultant is likely to become familiar only with the aspect of the entity related to the particular task in hand. This consultant may not, therefore, appreciate wider ramifications within the organisation of advice given to the entity's management.
- While it is generally agreed that auditors are well placed to provide financial and management advice to their audit clients more efficiently and effectively than other outside consultants, providing these services is likely to be at the cost of at least some of the auditor's independence. The threat to auditors' independence comes from three main sources: self-interest, self-review of non-audit work, and familiarity.

- *Self-interest*: As GPES 1 (para 4.58) notes:

  All work that creates a financial relationship between the auditor and the audit client may appear to create a self-interest threat . . . [T]he auditor's objectivity might be impaired by a need to remain on good terms with the directors of the audited company in order to preserve a working relationship. The perceived threat grows with the size of the fees and is thus increased by work or services additional to the audit.

- *Self-review of non-audit work*: If an auditor (or audit firm) advises an audit client on – say – a new accounting system and the client, acting on that advice, installs the new system, in any subsequent audit the auditor (or members of the audit firm) will be reviewing the outcome of their own advice. In this circumstance, it is difficult to believe that the auditor will evaluate the system with the same level of objectivity as (s)he would apply had the advice on the system come from an outside consultant. Even if the auditor is, in fact, able to maintain an objective and unbiased attitude of mind, it may be difficult for an outside observer to accept that this is the case and so, as a minimum, independence in appearance is impaired.

  A similar situation exists when an auditor both prepares and audits a set of financial statements. Even if the auditor manages to maintain an impartial attitude of mind whilst performing the audit, it may be difficult for an outside observer to conclude that this is the case. The situation might be helped if some other person or group within the auditor's firm provides the advisory service or compiles the financial statements, as the case might be. However, independence in appearance, if not in fact, is still at a lower level than would apply if the audit firm were not involved in providing any advisory service or accounts preparation to the audit client (GPES 1, paras 4.60 to 4.63).

- *Familiarity threat:* If an auditor provides non-audit services to an audit client (s)he may be perceived as too closely involved with the audit client's management to be able to conduct the audit in an objective, unbiased manner.

Despite the potential threat to auditors' independence resulting from the provision of non-audit services to audit clients, the profession's ethical guidance is permissive in this regard. GPES 1 (para 4.56) for example, observes:

It is economic in terms of skill and effort for professional accountants in public practice to be able to provide other services to their clients since they already have a good knowledge of their business. Many companies (particularly smaller ones) would be adversely affected if they were denied the right to obtain other services from their auditors.

However, auditors are also warned: 'Care must be taken to ensure not to perform management functions or make management decisions' (para 4.56). They are also counselled to be mindful of the limits placed on the fee income which may be derived from an audit client (discussed above) and to ensure that safeguards are put in place to prevent the provision of non-audit services from adversely affecting their objectivity (see, for example, GPES 1 paras 4.58, 4.60 and 4.64).

The question of whether auditors' independence is or is not impaired by the provision of non-audit services to audit clients has been hotly debated for many years. Commentators such as Cowen (1980) have emphasised that there is little or no empirical evidence to suggest that the provision of non-audit services to audit clients impairs auditors' independence. Similarly, the Commission on Auditors' Responsibilities (1978) concluded that 'there is no evidence that provision of services other than auditing has actually impaired the independence of auditors' (p. 94). However, other commentators, both from inside the auditing profession, such as Briloff (1986), and from outside the profession, such as Congressman Dingell (a vocal critic of auditors in the USA) and Austin Mitchell MP (a vocal critic of auditors in the UK), are adamant that the provision of non-audit services to audit clients must, and does, impair auditors' independence.

Analysis of the arguments advanced by proponents of each viewpoint suggests that the answer to the question of whether auditors' independence is compromised by the provision of non-audit services to audit clients depends less on whether such services are provided than on the nature and amount of such services. As noted above, under the Companies Act 1989 (s.27) and regulations issued by the Secretary of State, companies are required to disclose in their annual reports, the amounts paid or payable to the auditor (or audit firm) for the year for audit fees and (separately) for non-audit services. By requiring companies to disclose this information, interested external parties are able to assess for themselves the extent of non-audit services provided by the auditor, and thus to form a judgment as to whether the auditor's independence is likely to have been impaired as a result.

However, in the USA, the SEC concluded that such disclosures are not enough. During the 1990s the Commission became so concerned about the growth in the provision of non-audit services to audit clients, and the resultant impairment of auditors' independence, that it introduced strict new independence rules (effective from 5 February 2001). Turner (2001) explains that, in formulating the rules, the SEC was guided by four principles that indicate a breach of auditors' independence:

> The four principles specify an auditor would not be considered independent when the auditor:
> 1. Has a mutual or conflicting interest with the audit client;
> 2. Is placed in the position of auditing his or her own work;
> 3. Acts as management or an employee of the audit client; or
> 4. Is in the position of being an advocate for the client. (p. 5)

Among other things, the SEC's auditor independence rules prohibit auditors from providing to SEC registrant audit clients (essentially all US public companies) legal and bookkeeping services, and from issuing appraisal or valuation reports and fairness opinions.[2] In relation to the provision of legal services, Turner (2000) explains:

> Fundamentally, a conflict exists between the role of an independent auditor and that of an attorney. The auditor's charge is to examine objectivity and report, regardless of the impact on the client, while the attorney's fundamental duty is to advance the client's interest . . . [The prohibition includes giving] clients legal advice and preparing legal opinions. (p. 2)

The SEC's independence rules also prohibit affiliate and business relationships with audit clients including joint ventures, limited partnerships, investments in supplier or customer companies, leasing interests, and sales by the auditor (or audit firm) of items other than professional services. Similarly, auditors are prohibited from undertaking any work for audit clients which involves a contingency fee.[3] In this regard, Turner (2000) explains that the SEC:

> Will look closely to determine whether a fee, such as those labelled 'value added' or 'performance based' is in fact or substance a contingent fee. (p. 4)

The rules further require audit committees to disclose in their annual proxy statements, among other things:

- fees billed for services rendered by the principal auditor. These are to be broken down into fees for:
  - the audit and review of the company's annual and quarterly financial statements;
  - information technology consulting; and
  - all other services;
- whether the audit committee considered the compatibility of non-audit services the company received from its auditor and the independence of the auditor.

4.4 OTHER PROPOSALS FOR STRENGTHENING THE INDEPENDENCE OF AUDITORS

Many members of the auditing profession, as well as a number of politicians, financial journalists and others, have recognised the importance of auditors'

---

[2] Appraisal and valuation services include any service valuing assets, both tangible and intangible, or liabilities. Fairness opinions or reports relate to opinions expressed on the adequacy of consideration in a transaction. The SEC considers that 'if an audit firm provided such services to an audit client, when it is time to audit the financial statements, the accountant could well end up reviewing his or her own work . . .' (SEC, 2000, p. 50).

[3] A contingency fee is defined as: 'any fee established for the provision of any service or product pursuant to an arrangement in which no fee will be charged unless a specified finding or result is attained, or in which the amount of the fee is otherwise dependent upon the finding or result of such service or product, including commissions and similar payments' (Turner, 2000, p. 4).

independence to the future of the audit function. They have also seen the dangers posed to that independence, particularly as a result of auditors becoming too familiar with their audit clients' managements, and being dependent on those managements for their fees and continued appointment. Commentators in the UK (as in many other countries in the English-speaking world) have expressed concern about the ineffectiveness of current legislative provisions and professional bodies' pronouncements (such as GPES 1) in dealing with the problem. As noted above, in the USA, the SEC – adopting the view that auditors are tending towards impairing their independence by putting their own (or their firm's) business interests ahead of the public's interests – have introduced strict new auditor independence rules. Elsewhere, predicated on the notion that the problem lies in auditors becoming too familiar with their audit clients, or auditees' managements being able to exert too much power over auditors, other proposals for maintaining and strengthening auditors' independence have been proposed. These include:

(a) mandatory auditor rotation;
(b) the appointment of auditors by the State or a State agency;
(c) appointment of auditors by a shareholder panel;
(d) audit committees.

(a)   Mandatory auditor rotation

Two forms of auditor rotation have been proposed:

(i)   rotating the partners responsible for a particular audit but retaining the audit within the audit firm;
(ii) rotating the firms responsible for a particular audit.

Support for both proposals has been expressed from time to time in most English-speaking countries – particularly by politicians such as Senator Metcalfe and Congressmen Moss and Dingell in the USA, and Austin Mitchell MP in the UK.

Four main arguments are usually advanced in favour of auditor rotation. These are as follows:

1. The quality and competence of auditors' work tends to decline over time as auditors become 'over-familiar' with particular audit clients and, as a consequence, begin to make unjustified assumptions. An auditor may, for example, make assumptions about such things as the effectiveness of certain internal controls and the reliability of management's representations based on the findings of previous audits, instead of objectively evaluating current evidence.

2. A long-term relationship with an audit client is likely to result in the development of a close personal relationship between the auditor and the

client's management. This is likely to cause some diminution in the auditor's objectivity and impartial attitude of mind when conducting the client's audits.

3. Many auditors provide (non-audit) management advisory services (MAS) to their audit clients and the extent of these services is likely to increase directly in proportion to the time the audit is retained. Proponents of mandatory auditor rotation contend that auditors are unlikely to evaluate the results of management advice they have given to their clients as objectively as they would the results of advice proffered by other, unrelated advisors.

4. The longer the auditor retains the audit of a particular client, the more significant MAS work is likely to become. As MAS work increases, so does the dependence of the auditor on the client for fee income. It seems likely that such dependence will cause some impairment of the auditor's independence – in appearance, if not in fact.

Reviewing these arguments it should be noted that, while rotation of audits amongst audit firms could be expected to reduce all four of the problems indicated, rotation of audits within firms affects only the first two – and it is the latter two which the SEC identified as the chief dangers to auditors' independence!

Those who oppose mandatory auditor rotation support their position with contrary arguments. These include the following:

1. The complexity of most modern business organisations renders short-term audit engagements inappropriate. It takes an auditor time to gain a thorough knowledge of a business, its policies, operations, accounting system, internal controls, key personnel, and so on – an essential requirement for an effective audit in today's environment. As Olson, then President of the American Institute of Certified Public Accountants (AICPA), stated to the US Senate Committee on Commerce in 1976:

> The most effective audits are generally performed by auditors who have acquired a thorough knowledge of the business entity under review. It is generally recognized that such knowledge is best gained through actual audit experience over a considerable period of years. (cited by Hoyle, 1978, p. 74)

If mandatory auditor rotation were introduced, a company might have to appoint new auditors just as the quality of audit work was improving.

2. Auditor rotation would result in significantly increased audit fees. The initial years of any audit are very costly. During these years the auditor must devote considerable time and effort to becoming familiar with the client and its business. This is not necessary in later years. With mandatory auditor rotation, the costly initial period of any audit would occur more frequently than at present, and the benefits to be gained from subsequent, lower cost years, would not be fully realised.

3. The overall quality of audits would fall. Opponents of mandatory auditor rotation contend that, because auditors would know that a particular audit engagement is to be terminated after a limited number of years, they would not be motivated to perform audits of the highest quality. *motivation problem.*

When evaluating the desirability (or otherwise) of mandatory auditor rotation, the benefits of such a measure need to be weighed against the costs. According to Hoyle (1978):

> Too many of the arguments for rotation have never been substantiated . . . [Further] to say that, [for example], the overall quality of audit work would improve under a rotation system ignores the problems of initial audit engagements and the complexity of the modern business organisation. The idea of mandatory rotation is somewhat like trying to swat a fly with a baseball bat. Although it is possible that the problem [of compromised auditor independence] may be solved, the accompanying damage may be irreparable. Mandatory auditor rotation is simply too drastic a step to take without proof that the benefits are worth the . . . costs. (p. 75)

Irrespective of how strong the arguments against auditor rotation may appear to be, it seems that the profession has been swayed by those advanced in favour of rotation of audit partners. In the UK, the profession was encouraged to move in this direction by the Committee on the Financial Aspects of Corporate Governance (CFACG, Cadbury Committee, 1992). This Committee looked specifically at ways of improving corporate governance in listed UK companies and considered, amongst many other things, mandatory auditor rotation. It decided against the compulsory rotation of audit firms but was favourably disposed towards the suggestion of rotating audit partners. It went so far as to ask the accountancy profession to produce guidelines with a view to implementing an appropriate scheme. Following on from this, in 1994, the Institutes of Chartered Accountants in England and Wales (ICAEW), of Scotland (ICAS), and in Ireland (ICAI) introduced a requirement (through GPES 1, para 4.80) for the engagement partner, responsible for the audit of a public listed company, to be rotated every seven years. This requirement was reduced to five years from 1 January 2003. A similar requirement was introduced in the USA for all firms joining the AICPA's Securities and Exchange Commission (SEC) Practice Section. All such firms are required, as a condition of membership of the Section, to rotate the audit engagement partner of an SEC-registered audit client every seven years (Wood and Sommer, 1985, p. 122).

(b) Appointment of company auditors by the State or a State agency

As noted earlier, it is a widely held view that auditors will not be truly independent of their audit clients' managements all the time those managements are influential in their (the auditors') appointment and payment. This has given rise to the suggestion that auditors' independence could be strengthened if company auditors were appointed by the State or by a State agency.

However, this suggestion is not without significant difficulties. For example, if the State were to control auditors' appointment and fees, then the State would, in effect, also control the audit function. This would introduce the possibility of auditors becoming susceptible to the political agenda of the day and of the audit profession losing its professional independence. Further, if auditors were appointed by a State agency, they would be accountable to the State through that agency. If, at the same time, the directors of companies remained accountable to their shareholders, a conflict of the directors' and auditors' accountabilities could arise, with consequential difficulties for the achievement of an effective audit.

(c) Shareholder/stakeholder panel

The potential conflict of directors' and auditors' accountabilities (resulting from auditors being appointed by a State agency) could be avoided if auditors were accountable to a panel of shareholders. The company's shareholders would appoint the panel (which would exclude directors) from amongst their membership to represent their interests in relation to appointing, remunerating, monitoring and appraising the company's auditor. In this way, both the directors and the auditor would be separately accountable to the company's shareholders.

The idea of shareholder panels was mooted by the APB (1992, 1994) and it was also suggested that it might, in time, develop into a stakeholder panel. Such a panel would represent a wider group of interests – those of the company's stakeholders (including the shareholders) – rather than those of the shareholders alone (Hatherly, 1995). However, one possible criticism of the stakeholder panel idea is that, by involving a wider set of stakeholders in the supervisory process, some conflict of accountability between the auditor and the directors is re-introduced. While the auditor would be accountable to the company's stakeholders (through the stakeholder panel) the directors would legally be accountable only to the shareholders.

From the perspective of strengthening auditors' independence, the shareholder/stakeholder panel is conceptually superior to the audit committee which is discussed in the next section. This is because, unlike stakeholders (or shareholders) who are outside – and independent of – the auditee's governance structure, the audit committee is a committee of the board of directors and it cannot therefore appraise, or support, the auditor independently of the board.

Although the audit committee should comprise mainly (or wholly) non-executive directors (who are independent of the day-to-day management of the company), it is the board as a whole – executive and non-executive directors – who are legally responsible for the overall performance, direction and conduct of the company. Nevertheless, despite its conceptual superiority for securing auditors' independence, to date the shareholder/stakeholder panel idea has not attracted much support and it is the audit committee that has been widely adopted.

(d)   Audit committees

Audit committees are probably the most widely adopted means of strengthening auditors' independence. An audit committee is a committee of the board of directors (or its equivalent) which has delegated responsibility from the board for, *inter alia*, overseeing the external financial reporting process – including the external audit.

Over the past three decades, the value of audit committees as a means of enhancing external financial reporting and ensuring the independence of external auditors has been recognised and these committees have become widely established in many parts of the world. Their development has varied from country to country but, interestingly, in each case it has been stimulated by unexpected corporate failure and/or reports of misconduct by senior executives or directors. It seems that politicians and the public believe that, if auditors had been properly independent of their audit client's managements, and had performed their duties with due skill and care, then warning bells would have been sounded in at least some of the cases. Following on from this, it is generally reasoned that if audit committees are established, with a majority of non-executive directors,[4] to oversee the appointment of external auditors and the external audit function, then unexpected corporate failure and undetected misconduct by senior officials will be significantly reduced.

Development of audit committees

Audit committees made their first significant appearance in Canada (the first country to introduce a legal requirement for audit committees) and the USA. During the 1970s, audit committees were established in these countries, largely as a result of 'several well-publicised instances of corporate wrongdoing and questionable conduct that severely tarnished the image of big business in North America' (CICA, 1981, p. 1). Following the collapse of Atlantic Acceptance

---

[4] Directors not involved in the day-to-day management of the entity.

Corporation Ltd in Canada in 1965, in 1971 audit committees became a legal requirement for public companies incorporated in Ontario. In 1973, a similar requirement became effective for public companies incorporated in British Columbia, and in 1975 for federally incorporated companies. Since then audit committees have become a universally accepted feature of corporate life in Canada.

In the USA, audit committees received their first major endorsement, from both the New York Stock Exchange (NYSE) and the SEC in the late 1930s as a result of the infamous *McKesson and Robbins* case. However, few audit committees were established until the 1970s, when interest in them was revived as a result of several factors, including a number of legal decisions (including the *BarChris Construction Corporation* case) which emphasised that executive and non-executive directors are equally responsible for the company's affairs, and equally liable for misleading financial statements. Other factors included the unexpected collapse of Penn Central Company, the notorious Equity Funding fraud, and the widespread incidents of corporate misconduct which came to light during the enquiries which led to the passing of the Foreign Corrupt Practices Act 1977 – in particular, the admittance by hundreds of companies that they had made significant unrecorded payments overseas (CICA, 1981, pp. 98–99).

In June 1978, largely as a result of pressure from politicians and the SEC for public companies to be required to establish audit committees, they became a listing requirement of the NYSE. Adoption of audit committees was further encouraged in 1987 when the National Commission on Fraudulent Financial Reporting (Treadway Commission, 1987) recommended that they be established by all public companies. Today, as in Canada, virtually all publicly traded companies in the USA have audit committees.

In the UK, adoption of audit committees did not begin in earnest until the late 1980s. Indeed, until 1987, neither the professional accountancy bodies nor the regulatory agencies (such as the Bank of England and the Department of Trade and Industry) seemed to give these committees serious consideration. However, in 1987, stimulated by the serious and growing size and incidence of corporate fraud, the ICAEW recommended that public companies be required to establish audit committees, and the Bank of England and PRO-NED[5] also urged these companies to adopt such committees. These moves were followed in 1988 by the introduction of a Private Member's Bill to Parliament which, if

---

[5] An organisation established in 1982 by the Stock Exchange, the Confederation of British Industry, the Bank of England and other financial institutions to promote the appointment of non-executive directors to Boards of Directors.

enacted, would have required large listed public companies in the UK to establish audit committees. The adoption of audit committees by all UK public companies received a further boost in 1992, when the Cadbury Committee included in its *Code of Best Practice*, the establishment of an audit committee of non-executive directors, with at least three members (CFACG, 1992, Code of Best Practice, clause 4.3).[6] Today, the United Kingdom Listing Authority (UKLA)[7] requires all companies listed on the London Stock Exchange to comply with the *Combined Code* (Committee on Corporate Governance, 1998) (which incorporates many of the provisions of the Cadbury Committee's Code of Best Practice). Under the Combined Code, listed companies must establish audit committees of at least three non-executive directors or disclose that they have not done so, and the reasons therefor.

Audit committees are not only a normal feature of corporate life in North America and the UK. They are similarly well established in Australia, New Zealand, and South Africa; they are a legal requirement for public companies in Singapore and a listing requirement for companies listed on the Kuala Lumpur Stock Exchange.

Duties of audit committees
Particularly during the early 1970s, the principal duties of audit committees were generally confined to matters related to external financial reporting and the external audit. They were, for example, typically expected to:
- select (and recommend to shareholders for approval) the company's external auditors;
- oversee the external financial reporting process – including the external audit; and
- review the external financial statements prior to their submission to the full board of directors for approval.

Since the mid-1970s, the value of audit committees for a much broader function has been recognised – that of securing responsible corporate governance. This broader function is reflected in the duties audit committees are now typically expected to perform. They include, for example:
- helping to establish an environment in which internal controls can operate effectively;

---

[6] In April 1993, the London Stock Exchange made it a listing requirement for companies to include in their annual reports a statement as to whether or not they had complied with the Code of Best Practice during the reporting period. If they had not done so, they needed to explain the respects in which they did not comply and the reasons why.

[7] In 2001 responsibility for the UKLA (and hence for the listing rules) passed from the London Stock Exchange to the Financial Services Authority.

- ensuring that an effective accounting system and related internal controls are maintained;
- reviewing the company's accounting policies and reporting requirements;
- assessing the adequacy of management reporting;
- selecting and recommending for appointment the external auditor(s), and recommending their remuneration;
- appointing the chief internal auditor;
- discussing with the chief internal auditor and external auditor, respectively, the intended scope of the internal and external audit and satisfying itself that no unjustified restrictions have been imposed by executive management;
- reviewing the findings of the internal and external auditors;
- reviewing the entity's financial statements and annual report prior to their submission to the full board of directors;
- reviewing public announcements relating to financial matters prior to their release;
- reviewing, and monitoring compliance with, the company's code of conduct;
- reviewing the company's compliance with legal and regulatory requirements.

In the USA, the NYSE, the National Association of Securities Dealers (NASD), the AICPA, and the SEC have sought to strengthen and clarify the role and responsibilities of audit committees. In 1999, the Blue Ribbon Committee on Improving the Effectiveness of Corporate Audit Committees (a committee established by the NYSE and NASD) published its Report and Recommendations (1999). This document contains five Guiding Principles for audit committee best practices (pp. 37–44). These may be summarised as follows:

- *Principle 1* discusses the audit committee's pivotal role in monitoring the other components of the audit. In particular, it notes that the audit committee oversees management which has primary responsibility for the financial statements, the external auditors on whom investors rely to provide an impartial, robust examination of the financial statements to ensure their credibility, and where they exist, internal auditors who provide a source of advice on information on the processes and safeguards that exist.
- *Principle 2* highlights the importance of independent communication and information flow between the audit committee and the company's internal auditors.
- *Principle 3* notes the need for independent communication and information flow between the audit committee and the external auditors.[8]
- *Principle 4* emphasises the need for candid discussions between the audit committee and, respectively, management, the internal auditors, and

---

[8] This topic is discussed in Chapter 13.

external auditors, regarding issues concerned with judgments used in, and the quality of, the company's financial statements.

- *Principle 5* underscores the need for effective audit committees, of diligent and knowledgeable audit committee members.

In August 2000, building on the work and recommendations of the Blue Ribbon Committee, the Panel on Audit Effectiveness (established in 1998 by the Public Oversight Board (POB)[9] in response to a request by the SEC) published its Final Report (2000). In its report, the Panel recommended, *inter alia*, that audit committees:

- obtain from management annually a written report on how effectively the company's internal controls are operating;
- review annually the performance of the external and internal auditors;
- be advised of plans to hire personnel of the external audit firm into high level positions within the company;
- be proactive in ensuring factors such as time pressures on auditors are addressed so as not to negatively impact the credibility of audits;
- pre-approve non-audit services to be provided by the external auditor above a specified threshold. In considering the appropriateness of a service, the audit committee should consider factors such as:
  - whether the service is being performed principally for the audit committee;
  - the effects of the service, if any, on audit effectiveness or on the quality and timeliness of the entity's financial reporting process;
  - whether the service would be performed by specialists (for example, technology specialists) who ordinarily also provide recurring audit support;
  - whether the service would be performed by audit personnel, and if so, whether it will enhance their knowledge of the entity's business and operations;
  - whether the role of those performing the service would be inconsistent with the auditors' role (i.e. a role where neutrality, impartiality and auditor scepticism are likely to be subverted);
  - whether the audit firm personnel would be assuming a management role or creating a mutual or conflicting interest with management;
  - whether the auditors, in effect, would be auditing their own work;
  - whether the audit firm has unique expertise in the service;
  - the size of the fee(s) for non-audit services.

---

[9] Following the Sarbanes-Oxley Act of 2002 the POB has been replaced by a new body, the Public Company Oversight Board.

4.5 SUMMARY

The issue of auditors' independence seems to be aptly summarised by Turner (2000):

> The independence of auditors of public companies has been and continues to be an issue of paramount importance ... It is a subject that cannot be a question, but rather must be a given. But all too often today, the question is being asked, 'Did the auditors provide an unbiased and truly independent report on the numbers?' To maintain their value to the capital markets and regain the confidence of investors, auditors around the globe must renew their covenant with investors; a covenant that says each auditor will remain ... free from a web of entanglements or arrangements that threaten the appearance of his or her objectivity; that with the auditor's stamp, the numbers speak the truth. (p. 7)

Maintaining auditors' independence, both in fact and in appearance, is clearly crucial to the credibility of the opinion expressed by auditors in their audit reports and, thus, to the future of the audit function and the well-being of financial markets. But, it is equally evident that a number of factors serve to undermine this independence – in particular, financial and personal involvement with the client, undue fee dependence, the influence of executive directors over the auditor's appointment and fees, and the provision of non-audit services to audit clients.

The professional bodies have attempted to prevent impairment of auditors' independence by publishing ethical guidelines. These guidelines identify threats, or perceived threats, to auditors' independence, and require auditors to review their exposure to such threats and to introduce appropriate safeguards. However, safeguards additional to those required by ethical guidelines may also be needed. Proposals advanced as means for securing the required level of auditors' independence include mandatory auditor rotation, the appointment of auditors by the State (or a State agency) or by a shareholder panel, and the establishment of audit committees. The suggestions of mandatory rotation of audit firms and the appointment of company auditors by a State agency or a shareholder panel have not received widespread support, but the rotation of audit partners within a firm responsible for the audits of public listed companies has been endorsed by the profession in both the UK and USA. Additionally, audit committees have been established in corporate entities in many parts of the world. These committees are regarded as valuable, not only for overseeing the external financial reporting process, but also as a means of securing responsible corporate governance. In the USA, steps taken by the SEC, the NYSE and NASD, and the AICPA to secure the independence of external auditors go further than those taken in the UK and elsewhere. However, given the propensity for characteristics of the corporate, regulatory and auditing environment to cross the Atlantic, the steps taken in the USA may well appear in a similar form in the UK in the future.

SELF-REVIEW QUESTIONS

4.1 Explain briefly the importance of auditors being independent in both fact and appearance.

4.2 List six factors that may result in an auditor's independence being compromised in fact or in appearance.

4.3 Distinguish between 'general environmental safeguards' and 'specific safeguards' in the context of auditors' independence.

4.4 List the restrictions placed on auditors by the professional accountancy bodies which are designed to prevent auditors' independence from being impaired through:
(i)   financial involvement with an audit client;
(ii) personal involvement with an audit client.

4.5 List the four principles that underpin the SEC's auditor independence rules.

4.6 List two advantages and two disadvantages attaching to audit fees being paid according to a scale of fees.

4.7 (a) Explain briefly two forms of 'mandatory rotation of auditors' and outline two arguments that have been advanced in favour of each.
    (b) Outline the requirements for auditor rotation that have been imposed by the profession in both the UK and the USA.

4.8 Discuss briefly how auditors being appointed by (i) the State or by a State agency or (ii) a shareholder panel, may help strengthen auditors' independence.

4.9 Explain briefly what is meant by an audit committee. (What is it and how many members does it usually have?)

4.10 Outline the principal responsibilities of audit committees and explain briefly how audit committees may help strengthen auditors' independence.

REFERENCES

Auditing Practices Board (APB) (1992) *Future Development of Auditing*. London: APB.

Auditing Practices Board (APB) (1994) *The Audit Agenda*. London: APB.

Blue Ribbon Committee on Improving the Effectiveness of Corporate Audit Committees (1999) *Report and Final Recommendations of the Blue Ribbon Committee*. New York: NYSE and NASD.

Briloff, A.J. (1986) *Corporate Governance and Accountability: Whose Responsibility?* Unpublished address delivered at the University of Connecticut, Storrs, Connecticut, April 1986.

Canadian Institute of Chartered Accountants (CICA) (1981) *Audit Committees: A Research Study*. Canada: CICA.

Commission on Auditors' Responsibilities (CAR) (1978) *Report, Conclusions and Recommendations* (The Cohen Commission). New York: AICPA.

Committee on Corporate Governance (1998) *The Combined Code.* London: The London Stock Exchange Limited.

Committee on the Financial Aspects of Corporate Governance (CFACG) (1992) *Report of the Committee on the Financial Aspects of Corporate Governance* (Cadbury Report). London: Gee.

Cowen, S.S. (1980) Non-audit services: How much is too much? *Journal of Accountancy* **150**(6), 51–56.

Hatherly, D.J. (1995) The case for the shareholder panel in the UK. *The European Accounting Review* **4**(3), 535–553.

Hoyle, J. (1978) Mandatory auditor rotation: The arguments and an alternative. *Journal of Accountancy* **146**(5), 69–78.

Levitt, A. (2000) *A Profession at the Crossroads.* Speech by SEC Chairman to National Association of State Boards of Accountancy, Boston, Massachusetts, 18 September.

Mitchell, A. & Sikka, P. (1993) Accounting for change: The institutions of accountancy. *Critical Perspectives on Accounting* **4**(1), 29–52.

National Commission on Fraudulent Financial Reporting (1987) *Report of the National Commission on Fraudulent Financial Reporting* (Treadway Commission). New York: AICPA.

Panel on Audit Effectiveness (2000) *Report and Recommendations.* New York: Public Oversight Board.

Securities and Exchange Commission (SEC) (2000) *Final Rule: Revision of the Commission's Auditor Independence Requirements.* New York: SEC.

Turner, L.E. (2000) *Current SEC developments: Independence 'Matters'.* Speech by SEC Chief Accountant to 28th National Conference on Current SEC Developments, 6 December.

Turner, L.E. (2001) *Independence: A Covenant for the Ages.* Speech by SEC Chief Accountant to International Organization of Securities Commissions, Stockholm, Sweden, 28 June.

Wood, A.M. & Sommer, Jr, A.A. (1985) Statement in quotes. *Journal of Accountancy* **156**(5), 122–131.

ADDITIONAL READING

Barkness, L. & Simnett, R. (1994) The provision of other services by auditors: independence and pricing issues. *Accounting and Business Research* **24**(94), 99–108.

Bartlett, R.W. (1991) A heretical challenge to the incantations of audit independence. *Accounting Horizons,* March, 11–16.

Bartlett, R.W. (1993) A scale of perceived independence: new evidence on an old concept. *Accounting, Auditing & Accountability Journal* **6**(2), 52–67.

Beattie, V., Brandt, R. & Fearnley, S. (1999) Perceptions of auditor independence: UK evidence. *Journal of International Acountancy, Auditing and Taxation* **8**(1), 67–107.

Calegari, M.J., Schatzberg, J.W. & Sevcik, G.R. (1998) Experimental Evidence of Differential Auditor Pricing and Reporting Strategies. *The Accounting Review* **73**(2), 255–275.

Carcello, J.V. & Neal, T.L. (2000) Audit committee composition and auditor reporting. *The Accounting Review* **75**(4), 453–467.

Chartered Accountants' Joint Ethics Committee (CAJEC) (1994) *The Framework – A New Approach to Professional Independence.* London: ICAEW.

Collier, P. (1993) Factors affecting the voluntary formation of audit committees in major UK listed companies. *Accounting and Business Research* **23**(91A), 421–430.

Collier, P. & Gregory. A. (1996) Audit committee effectiveness and the audit fee. *The European Accounting Review* **5**(2), 177–198.

Currie, B. (1994) The nature of independence. *Accountancy* **113**(1209), 93.

Davis. L.R., Ricchiute, D.N. & Trompeter, G. (1993) Audit effort, audit fees, and the provision of nonaudit services to audit clients. *The Accounting Review* **68**(1), 135–150.

Falk, H., Lynn, B., Mestelnan, S. & Skehata M. (1999) Auditor independence, self interested behaviour and ethics: Some experimental evidence. *Journal of Accountancy and Public Policy* **18**, 395–428.

Hatherly, D.J. (1992) Can auditing work without a break with tradition? *Accountancy* **110**(1189), 85.

Jeppesen, K.K. (1998) Reinventing auditing, redefining consulting and independence. *The European Accounting Review* **7**(3), 517–539.

Kalbers, L.P. & Fogarty, T.J. (1993) Audit committee effectiveness: an empirical investigation of the contribution of power. *Auditing: A Journal of Practice & Theory* **12**(1), 24–49.

Lee, C.J. & Gu, Z. (1998) Low balling, legal liability and auditor independence. *The Accounting Review* **73**(4), 533–555.

Magee, R.P. & Tseng, M. (1990) Audit pricing and independence. *The Accounting Review* **65**(2), 315–336.

McMullen, D.A. (1996) Audit committee performance: an investigation of the consequences associated with audit committees. *Auditing: A Journal of Practice & Theory* **15**(1), 87–103.

Miller, T. (1992) Do we need to consider the individual auditor when discussing auditor independence? *Accounting, Auditing & Accountability Journal* **5**(2), 74–84.

Parkash, M. & Venable, C.F. (1993) Auditee incentives for auditor independence: the case of nonaudit services. *The Accounting Review* **68**(1), 113–133.

Patel, C. & Psaros, J. (2000) Perceptions of external auditors' independence: some cross-cultural evidence. *British Accounting Review* **32**, 311–338.

Ponemon, L.A. & Gabhart, D.R.L. (1990) Auditor independence judgements: A cognitive-developmental model and experimental evidence. *Contemporary Accounting Review* **7**(1), 227–251.

Raghunandan, K., Read, W.J. & Rama, D.V. (2001) Audit committee composition, 'grey directors,' and interaction with internal auditors. *Accounting Horizons* **15**(2), 105–118.

Reynolds, J.K. & Francis, J.R. (2001) Does size matter? The influence of large clients on office-level auditor reporting decisions. *Journal of Accounting and Economics* **30**, 375–400.

Sikka, P. & Willmott, H. (1995) The power of 'independence': defending and extending the jurisdiction of accounting in the United Kingdom. *Accounting, Organizations and Society* **20**(6), 547–581.

Sweeny, J.T. & Roberts, R.W. (1997) Cognitive moral development and auditor independence. *Accounting, Organizations and Society* **22**(3/4), 337–352.

Sutton, M.H. (1997) Auditor independence: the challenge of fact and appearance. *Accounting Horizons* **11**(1), 86–91.

Wallman, S.M.H. (1996) The future of accounting, Part (iii): reliability and auditor independence. *Accounting Horizons* **10**(4), 76–97.

Wolnizer, P.W. (1995) Are audit committees red herrings? *Abacus* **31**(1), 45–66.

5 Legal and Professional Duties of Auditors

LEARNING OBJECTIVES

After studying the material in this chapter you should be able to:
- state which companies are required to have an audit;
- list the rights, responsibilities and duties of external auditors under:
  - (a) legislation;
  - (b) decisions of the courts;
  - (c) professional standards;
  - (d) regulatory requirements.
- describe the relationship between the auditor and the client;
- explain the auditor's, as compared with directors'/management's responsibility, for the financial statements;
- discuss the meaning, importance and structure of the audit expectation–performance gap;
- discuss the auditor's responsibility for detecting and reporting fraud.

The following statutes and professional publications are particularly relevant to this chapter:

- Companies Acts 1985 and 1989
- The scope and authority of Auditing Practices Board pronouncements (APB, 1993)
- Statement of Auditing Standards (SAS) 110: *Fraud and error* (APB, 1995)
- Statement of Auditing Standards (SAS) 120: *Consideration of law and regulations* (APB, 1995)
- Statement of Auditing Standards (SAS) 620: *The auditors' right and duty to report to regulators in the financial sector* (APB, 1994)
- *The Combined Code: Requirements of Auditors under the Listing Rules of the London Stock Exchange*, Bulletin 1999/5 (APB, 1999)
- *Revisions to the Wording of Auditors' reports on Financial Statements and the Interim Review Report*, Bulletin 2001/2 (APB, 2001)
- Preface to International Standards on Auditing and Related Services (IFAC, 1994)
- International Standard on Auditing (ISA) 120: *Framework of International Standards on Auditing* (IAPC, 1994)
- International Standard on Auditing (ISA) 240: *Fraud and error* (IAPC, 2001)
- International Standard on Auditing (ISA) 250: *Consideration of laws and regulations in an audit of financial statements* (IAPC, 1994).

5.1 INTRODUCTION

The rights, responsibilities and duties of auditors are defined by four separate institutions:

- Parliament – in statute law;
- The courts – in case (or common) law;
- The profession – represented in the United Kingdom and Ireland by the Auditing Practices Board (APB)[1] – in Auditing Standards and Guidelines;
- Regulators (whose authority is derived from statute) – in specific requirements which apply in the audits of regulated clients.

The impact of these institutions on auditors' duties is cumulative in the sense that:

- statute law requires the financial statements of companies to be audited and sets out the administrative details of the auditor's appointment, removal and remuneration. It also specifies who may be an auditor and outlines their rights and duties;
- case law expands on statute law by establishing the standard of work expected of auditors in the performance of their statutory duties;
- professional Standards and Guidelines provide more specific guidance to auditors on what is required of them when conducting an audit;
- regulations impose specific duties on auditors when auditing regulated entities.

The relationship between these institutions and auditors' legal and professional duties is presented diagrammatically in Figure 5.1.

In this chapter, we discuss the statutory requirement for the audit of companies' financial statements, and the rights and duties of auditors. We also consider the auditor's relationship with the client, examine the auditor's (*vis-à-vis* management's) responsibility for the audited financial statements, and discuss the audit expectation–performance gap – the gap between the duties society expects auditors to perform and what society perceives auditors actually deliver. This gap has serious consequences for the auditing profession as it helps fuel criticism of auditors and the undermining of confidence in their work. Before concluding the chapter we discuss in some detail the thorny issue of auditors' responsibility for detecting and reporting corporate fraud.

---

[1] The APB (which replaced the Auditing Practices Committee) was established in 1991 by the Consultative Committee of Accountancy Bodies. In 2002 the APB became a component of the newly established Accountancy Foundation. Since 1991 the Board has had authority to issue Auditing Standards on behalf of the accountancy profession [or, more strictly speaking, on behalf of the Recognised Supervisory Bodies (RSBs) with whom all company auditors are required to register]. RSBs are discussed in section 5.2.3. The composition and functions of the APB are discussed in section 5.4.

Figure 5.1:   Defining the legal and professional duties of auditors

```
                                    ┌──────────────┐
                                    │   AUDITOR    │
                                    └──────────────┘
              ┌───────────────────────────┼───────────────────────────┐
              ▼                           ▼                           ▼
      ┌──────────────┐           ┌──────────────┐           ┌──────────────┐
      │  Statute Law │           │  Common Law  │           │ Professional │
      │              │           │  (Case Law)  │           │  Standards   │
      └──────────────┘           └──────────────┘           └──────────────┘
```

COMPANIES ACT 1985 AND 1989

Administrative matters
• Who may be auditor (CA 1989, s.25–27)
• Appointment and remuneration (CA 1985, s.384–388, 390A)
• Resignation and removal (CA 1985, s.391–392A, 394)
• Duties and rights (CA 1985, s.235–237, 389A, 390)

Duties: What auditors must do
1) Form an opinion and report to shareholders as to whether the financial statements

- give a true and fair view of the company's state of affairs and profit or loss

- are properly prepared in accordance with the Companies Act 1985

2) Form an opinion as to whether
- required information and explanations have been received
- proper accounting records have been kept
- the financial statements agree with the accounting records
- proper returns adequate for the audit have been received from branches not visited
- the directors' report is consistent with the financial statements
- emoluments and other benefits of the directors and others have been disclosed in accordance with Sch. 6, Companies Act 1985

And report to shareholders in cases where the criteria in (2) above are not met

REGULATORS (whose authority is derived from statute)

Examples:
The Financial Services Authority (FSA) and United Kingdom Listing Authority (UKLA) impose specific duties on the auditors of auditees within their jurisdiction

Standard of work required Guidance on how duties are to be performed

OVERRIDING STANDARD
Reasonable skill, care and caution in the circumstances
(In re Kingston Cotton Mill [1896])

This standard changes as the socio-economic environment changes over time

INDIVIDUAL CASES define the standards required in specific areas of the audit, in specific circumstances, and at a specific time.

Examples:
• *London Oil Storage Co. Ltd* v *Seear Hasluck & Co.* (1904)
• *Arthur E Green & Co* v *The Central Advance and Discount Co* (1920)
• *McKesson & Robbins* case (1938) U.S.

LANDMARK CASES draw together and restate the principles enunciated in individual cases over preceding years.

Example:
Pacific Acceptance Corp. Ltd v *Forsyth and others* (1970) (Australia)

AUDITING STANDARDS
Principles and procedures indicating what is required of auditors to meet the standards of 'reasonable skill and care and caution'

GUIDE TO PROFESIONAL ETHICS
Guidance on ethical conduct expected:

Examples:
• Independence, Integrity and Objectivity
• Competence
• Communication between predecessor and successor auditor

ACCOUNTING STANDARDS (FRSs/SSAPs)
Compliance with accounting standards is, in general, required for financial statements to give a true and fair view

5.2   AUDITS AND AUDITORS' DUTIES UNDER STATUTE LAW[2]

5.2.1   Overview

The main statutory provisions governing the audits of companies are contained in the Companies Acts 1985 and 1989. These Acts require companies to provide audited financial statements annually to their shareholders and debenture holders. They also set out:

- who may be an auditor;
- who is responsible for appointing and remunerating auditors;
- how auditors may resign or be removed;
- the basic duties and rights of auditors.

Each of these matters is considered below.

5.2.2   Requirement for audited financial statements

Under the provisions of the Companies Act 1985 (CA 1985), two types of company are recognised, namely:

(i)   Public companies – companies with a memorandum stating that it is a public company and a name which must end with 'public limited company' (plc).

(ii)   Private companies – companies which are not public. In most cases, the name of these companies must end with the word 'limited'.

Only a public company may issue shares or loan stock to the general public.

The directors of all companies (whether public or private) must prepare and provide to all of the company's shareholders and debenture holders, and also to the Registrar of Companies, a balance sheet and profit and loss account for each financial year[3] (CA 1985, s.226, 238, 241, 242). These financial statements must present a true and fair view of the company's state of affairs as at the end of its financial year and its profit or loss for the financial year, and must also comply with the form and content requirements of Schedule 4 of the Companies Act 1985 (CA 1985, s.226).

---

[2] We restrict our discussion to all companies subject to audit. Other private sector organisations, such as building societies, trade unions and employer associations, housing associations, certain charities and unincorporated investment businesses, and also public sector entities, are subject to specific financial reporting and auditing requirements. These are usually enshrined in separate legislation.

[3] Companies with subsidiaries are also required to prepare and submit group financial statements (that is, financial statements which treat the parent company and its subsidiaries as a single entity) (CA 1985, s.227).

The meaning of 'true and fair view' has not been defined in legislation or by the courts but it is generally accepted that in order for financial statements to give a true and fair view they must comply with applicable Financial Reporting Standards (FRSs) and Statements of Standard Accounting Practice (SSAPs) issued by the Accounting Standards Board (ASB) and its predecessor body, the Accounting Standards Committee (ASC). Support for this stance seems to be provided by clause 36A of Schedule 4 of CA 1985 which requires financial statements to state whether they have been prepared in accordance with applicable accounting standards[4] and to provide details of any material departure from these standards together with the reasons for the departure. Nevertheless, CA 1985 also provides that, if compliance with its provisions is insufficient for a true and fair view of the company's state of affairs and profit or loss to be presented, additional information is to be provided so that a true and fair view is given [CA 1985, s.226(4)]. Further, if, in special circumstances, compliance with any of the Act's provisions would result in a true and fair view not being given, then that provision is to be departed from to the extent necessary for a true and fair view to be presented. Reasons for, and particulars of, any such departure are to be provided [CA 1985, s.226(5)].

In addition to requiring companies to prepare annual financial statements, CA 1985 requires these statements to be audited.[5] However, in 1994, CA 1985 was amended to relax the audit requirement for small companies.[6] Initially the exemption was limited to companies with a turnover of not more than £350,000 and a balance sheet total of not more than £1.4 million. However, between August 1994 and June 1997, companies with a turnover of between £90,000 and £350,00 were required to have an 'exemption report' prepared by a reporting accountant. In June 1997 the 'exemption report' requirement was dropped. In May 2000 the audit exemption was extended to companies with a turnover of not more than £1 million and a balance sheet total of not more than £1.4 million.[7]

---

[4] 'Applicable accounting standards' refers to the Standards issued by the ASB or, where they remain current, by the ASC.

[5] With the exception of the financial statements of a dormant company, that is, a company which has not undertaken any significant accounting transactions during the financial year.

[6] The audit exemption is not available to a company if, at any time during the financial year, it was a public company, a banking or insurance company, an authorised person or appointed representative under the Financial Services Act 1986, a parent or subsidiary company (unless the group qualifies as a small group), or if members holding an aggregate of 10% or more of the nominal value of the company's issued shares request an audit (CA 1985, s.249B).

[7] In July 2001 the Company Law Review Steering Committee recommended that exemption from audit should be extended to companies that meet two of the following criteria: turnover of no more than £4.8 million, balance sheet total of no more than £2.4 million, no more than 50 employees.

5.2.3 Who may be an auditor of a company?

The Companies Act 1989 (CA 1989) introduced a regime for regulating auditors which is in line with the Eighth European Union (EU) Company Law Directive. This regime is designed 'to ensure that only people who are properly supervised and appropriately qualified are appointed as company auditors, and that audits are carried out properly, with integrity and with the proper degree of independence' (Beattie, 1989, p. 5). Since 1991 (1993 in Northern Ireland), only 'registered auditors' have been eligible for appointment as company auditors (CA 1989 s.25). In order to become registered, an individual must first qualify with one of the six Recognised Qualifying Bodies (RQBs)[8] and then register with one of the five Recognised Supervisory Bodies (RSBs).[9] In order to become an RSB, a professional body must have, *inter alia*:

- rules relating to auditors being fit and proper persons, auditors maintaining their independence and integrity, and technical standards to be applied in audit work;
- procedures for admitting, disciplining and excluding members, and for maintaining auditors' competence;
- arrangements for monitoring and enforcing the RSB's rules, investigating complaints, and meeting claims arising out of audit work (professional indemnity insurance).

(Details of the requirements for recognition as an RSB are set out in CA 1989, Schedule 11, Part 11).

CA 1989 [s.25(2)] provides that either a firm or an individual may be appointed as a company's auditor. Under the Act, firms may be registered auditors if a majority of their principals are qualified individuals (that is, qualified with an RQB). In addition to being a registered auditor, in order to be appointed as a company's auditor, the individual or firm must *not* be:

(a) an officer or employee of the company;
(b) a partner or employee of an officer or employee of the company;
(c) a partnership in which a person included in (a) or (b) above is a partner (CA 1989, s.27(1)).

---

[8] The six RQBs are The Institute of Chartered Accountants in England and Wales (ICAEW), The Institute of Chartered Accountants of Scotland (ICAS), the Institute of Chartered Accountants in Ireland (ICAI), the Chartered Association of Certified Accountants (ACCA), the Association of Authorised Public Accountants (AAPA), and the Association of International Accountants (AIA).

[9] The five RSBs are ICAEW, ICAS, ICAI, ACCA and AAPA. Although most individuals qualify and register with the same professional body, this is not a requirement. They may, if they wish, qualify with one body and register as an auditor with another.

The purpose of the Companies Act specifying who may, and who may not, be appointed as a company's auditor is to ensure that auditors are:

(a) competent and experienced, and also bound by the rules and standards of the accountancy profession;
(b) independent of the entity to be audited.

5.2.4 Who is responsible for appointing and remunerating an auditor?

CA 1985 [s.385(2)] provides for a company's shareholders to appoint an auditor for the following financial year at the general meeting at which the financial statements for the year just ended are presented, and also to determine how the auditor's fees and expenses are to be fixed (s.390A). However, in practice, the company's directors usually decide who they wish to be appointed as auditor and their decision is merely ratified by the shareholders at the general meeting. Normally, the shareholders also delegate to the directors, responsibility for fixing the auditor's fees and expenses. However, as noted in Chapter 3, in order to secure 'transparency' with respect to the fees paid to the auditor, CA 1985 (s.390A) requires the company to disclose the audit fee (including sums paid in respect of expenses) in the notes to its financial statements. Additionally, under regulations issued by the Secretary of State (in accordance with CA 1985, s.390B), companies are required to disclose (separately from the audit fee) fees paid to the auditor (or audit firm) for non-audit work.

As noted above, auditors are appointed at each general meeting of the company where the annual financial statements are presented. They hold office from the conclusion of that meeting until the conclusion of the next such meeting and, in general, there is no automatic reappointment. However, under CA 1985 (s.386) a private company may dispense with the obligation to appoint an auditor annually and, in this case, the auditor is automatically reappointed.

Although shareholders are given responsibility for appointing the company's auditor annually, if an auditor ceases to act as such during the year (for whatever reason), the directors are permitted to appoint a replacement auditor. This auditor holds office until the conclusion of the following general meeting (at which an auditor is appointed in the usual way, i.e. by the shareholders). The directors are also permitted to appoint the first auditor of the company – to hold office until the end of the first general meeting of the company. If an initial auditor is not appointed by the directors, the shareholders are required to appoint the first auditor at a general meeting of the company. In any case where no auditor has been appointed, the Secretary of State may appoint an auditor (CA 1985, s.385, 387, 388).

5.2.5 How may an auditor resign or be replaced?

Auditors may resign by simply giving a written notice to this effect to the company (CA 1985, s.392). Alternatively, they may decline to seek re-election at the general meeting at which auditors are to be appointed, or the company may remove the auditor at any time by passing an ordinary resolution to this effect at a general meeting. Similarly, if a company wishes to appoint another auditor in place of the retiring auditor, it must pass a resolution to appoint another auditor at a general meeting. Resolutions to remove or replace an auditor may not be passed at a general meeting unless at least 28 days' notice of the resolution has been given to both the shareholders and the existing auditor and the latter has been given the opportunity to make representations to the shareholders on the intended resolution to remove or replace him or her (CA 1985, s.391A).

The provisions enabling auditors to inform shareholders of the reasons they perceive for their removal or replacement are particularly important where company directors wish to remove auditors for the wrong reasons – for example, because they have uncovered questionable acts by the directors or senior managers of which the shareholders are not aware and of which they would not approve. Directors lacking integrity may wish the company to engage less diligent auditors!

Whenever auditors cease to hold office (whether it be through resignation, failure to seek reappointment, removal or replacement), they are required to deposit at the relevant company's registered office a statement of any circumstances connected with their ceasing to hold office which they consider should be brought to the attention of the company's shareholders or creditors, or a statement that there are no such circumstances. If there are such circumstances, unless the company applies to the court for a judgment on whether the auditor is seeking needless publicity for defamatory matter, the company must send a copy of the auditor's statement to all those entitled to receive copies of the company's financial statements. If the company makes application to the court, the auditor must be notified accordingly. In the absence of such notice, auditors must send a copy of their statement to the Registrar of Companies (CA 1985, s.394). Additionally, in the case of a resigning auditor, if the notice of resignation is accompanied by a statement of circumstances which the auditor considers should be drawn to the attention of members or creditors of the company, the auditor may require the company's directors to convene an extraordinary general meeting to consider any such explanation of the circumstances as the auditor wishes to place before the meeting. The resigning auditor may also require the company to send to all shareholders a copy of the written statement of the circumstances connected with his or her resignation. Such statement must be sent prior to the extraordinary meeting or the general meeting at which a 'replacement auditor' (prompted by the resignation) would be appointed (CA 1985, s.392A).

5.2.6 Auditors' statutory duties

Auditors' primary duties are set out in CA 1985, sections 235 and 237. Under these provisions, auditors are required to report to the company's shareholders stating whether, in their opinion, the company's financial statements:

- give a true and fair view of the company's state of affairs as at the end of the financial year and its profit or loss for the financial year; and
- have been properly prepared in accordance with the Companies Act 1985.[10]

Auditors are also required to carry out investigations and form an opinion as to whether:

- proper accounting records have been kept by the company and proper returns, adequate for their audit, have been received from branches not visited by them;
- the financial statements are in agreement with the underlying accounting records;
- they have received all the information and explanations they required for the purpose of their audit;
- the information given in the directors' report is consistent with the financial statements.

In any case where auditors consider that one or more of the above requirements has not been met, they are required to state that fact in their audit report. Additionally, auditors are required to ensure that the disclosure requirements relating to directors' emoluments and other benefits specified in CA 1985, Schedule 6, have been made and, insofar as they have not, to provide the required particulars in their audit report.

Auditors (who, as noted earlier may be individuals or audit firms) must sign their audit report and state their names. A signed copy of the auditor's report must be sent with the audited financial statements to the Registrar of Companies (see below) but copies of the auditor's report which are circulated to shareholders and debenture holders, or published or issued, need only state the name(s) of the auditor(s) (for example, in typewritten form) (CA 1985, s.236).

---

[10] In applicable cases, auditors are also required to report whether group financial statements give a true and fair view of the state of affairs and profit or loss of the group of companies included in the consolidated financial statements, and whether they have been properly prepared in accordance with the Act.

It was noted in section 5.2.2 above that CA 1985 requires the directors of companies to prepare financial statements which give a true and fair view of the company's state of affairs and its profit or loss and that, in general, providing such a view requires the financial statements to be prepared in accordance with applicable accounting standards. It was also noted that if it is necessary, in order for financial statements to present a true and fair view, information additional to that required by the Companies Act should be provided and/or a provision of the Act should be departed from. It follows from this that auditors, in forming their opinion on the company's financial statements, need to assess:

(i)   whether the financial statements comply with applicable accounting standards and relevant provisions of CA 1985;

(ii) if they *do not so comply*, whether the departure is necessary in order for the financial statements to give a true and fair view;

(iii) if they *do comply*, whether compliance results in:

  – financial statements which do not contain sufficient information to provide a true and fair view. In this case, additional information and explanations should have been provided so that the financial statements give the required true and fair view;

  – financial statements which fail to give a true and fair view. In this case, which would arise only in extremely rare circumstances, the Act's provisions should have been departed from to the extent necessary for the financial statements to give a true and fair view.

Under CA 1985, s.233, a company's financial statements must be approved by the board of directors and the balance sheet must be signed on behalf of the board by one of the directors. This approval and signing signifies acceptance by the board for its responsibility of the financial statements. The board of directors must also send a signed copy of the financial statements, together with the auditor's report (complete with the auditor's name and signature) and a copy of the directors' report, to the Registrar of Companies, and also to all of the company's shareholders and debenture holders. In the latter cases, the circulated financial statements need show only the names of the auditors and the director(s) who signed the balance sheet: their signatures are not required. The audited financial statements and directors' reports must be sent to all those entitled to receive copies of these documents not less than 21 days before the general meeting at which copies of the documents are to be laid (s.236, 238, 242).

5.2.7   Auditors' statutory rights

CA 1985 provides auditors with rights which facilitate the performance of their duties. They are, for example, given a right of access, at all times, to all of a company's accounting records and other documents, and the right to require directors and employees of the company to provide any information and explanations they consider necessary for the performance of their duties as auditors (s.389A). They are also entitled to attend any general meeting of the company, to receive notices and other communications relating to any general meeting which a shareholder is entitled to receive, and to speak at any general meeting on matters that concern them as auditors (s.390).

5.3 AUDITORS' DUTIES UNDER COMMON LAW

Although statute law requires the financial statements of companies to be audited and specifies the duties auditors are to perform, it has been left to the courts to explain what is expected of auditors in the performance of their statutory duties.

The general standard of performance required of auditors was laid down by Lopes LJ in *Re Kingston Cotton Mill Co.(No.2)* [1896] 2 Ch. 279, when he said:

> It is the duty of an auditor to bring to bear on the work he has to perform that skill, care and caution which a reasonably competent, careful and cautious auditor would use. What is reasonable skill, care and caution must depend on the particular circumstances of each case.

Clearly, what is regarded as 'reasonable skill, care and caution in the circumstances' will change over time as changes occur in society, in society's attitudes and values, and in the 'technology' of auditing.

As noted in Chapter 2, until the 1920s, auditors were primarily concerned with detecting fraud and error and ensuring that the solvency position of the reporting entity was fairly portrayed in the balance sheet. In accordance with this, during the nineteenth century, auditors carefully checked the detailed entries in, and arithmetical accuracy of, the company's books and made sure that the amounts shown in the balance sheet corresponded with the ledger account balances. If this was all that auditors did today they would be regarded as grossly negligent. They are now expected to examine sufficient appropriate evidence, drawn from a variety of sources (from both inside and outside the entity), on which to base an opinion about the truth and fairness of the auditee's financial statements – including the profit and loss account and cash flow statement in addition to the balance sheet.

Over the years, various parties who have suffered loss after relying on audited financial statements have taken auditors to court on claims of negligence; that is, on grounds that the auditors did not perform their duties properly and, as a result, failed to detect material error in the financial statements. Many of these cases have helped to clarify specific duties of auditors. The following cases serve as examples.

- In *Leeds Estate Building and Investment Co. v Shepherd* (1887) 36 Ch. D 787, the auditor (a bank clerk) was found to be negligent for failing to ensure that the audited balance sheet was drawn up in accordance with the company's Articles of Association (which the auditor had, in fact, never seen). The auditor claimed that his duty was to see that the balance sheet represented, and was a true result of what appeared in the books of the company, and that his certificate went no further than that. However the judge (Sterling J) thought otherwise. He stated:

  > [It was] the duty of the auditor not to confine himself merely to the task of verifying the arithmetical accuracy of the balance sheet, but to enquire into its substantial accuracy, and to ascertain that it contained the particulars specified in the articles of association . . . and was properly drawn up so as to contain a true and correct representation of the state of the company's affairs. (at 802)

- As in the *Leeds Estate* case, in *Re London and General Bank* (No. 2) (1895) 2 Ch. 677, (which concerned a bank whose loans to other companies were of doubtful recoverability) the auditor, in phrasing his audit report, tried unsuccessfully to limit his duty to a comparison of the balance sheet with the books of account. Lindley LJ made it clear that more was expected of auditors. He stated (at 682–3):

  > [An auditor's] business is to ascertain and state the true financial position of the company at the time of the audit and his duty is confined to that. But then comes the question: How is he to ascertain such position? The answer is: By examining the books of the company. But he does not discharge his duty by doing this without enquiry, and without taking any trouble to see that the books of the company show the company's true position. He must take reasonable care to ascertain that they do. Unless he does this, his duty will be worse than a farce.

  The *London and General Bank* case, which confirmed the *Leeds Estate* case, is a landmark in that it established that auditors had to examine the auditee's books and records and to form an opinion as to whether they 'truly' reflected the substance of the company's financial position.

- In *The London Oil Storage Co. Ltd v Seear, Hasluck & Co.* (1904) Acc LR 30, it was established that auditors are required to verify the existence of assets stated in the balance sheet. In this case the cash book balance did not agree with the physical cash balance, a fact that the auditors failed to check or discover. This case is particularly significant as it was the first time that the court made it clear that auditors are expected to go beyond the books and records of the client company for evidence to support their opinion about the truth and fairness of the financial statements.

- In *Arthur E Green & Co. v The Central Advance and Discount Corporation Ltd* (1920) 63 Acc LR 1, an auditor was held to be negligent for accepting a schedule of bad debts provided by a responsible officer of the company when it was apparent that other debts not included in the schedule were also irrecoverable. The case settled that auditors may not blindly accept evidence given to them by officers of the auditee. They must properly relate it to other evidence gathered during the course of the audit.

- In the infamous *McKesson and Robbins* case (US, 1938), the auditor failed to uncover a massive fraud involving fictitious accounts receivable (debtors) and inventory (stock). The court held that auditors have a duty to verify the existence of these assets. This extended the *London Oil Storage Company* case, making it clear that auditors must verify assets stated in the balance sheet, even when those assets are at a distant location.

Occasionally when a case comes before the court, the judge takes the opportunity to bring together the specific duties of auditors settled in a number of previous cases, and to enunciate general principles. One of the most renowned cases of this type is the Australian case, *Pacific Acceptance Corporation Limited v Forsyth and Others* (1970) 92 WN (NSW) 29.

In his long judgment, Moffit J provided comprehensive guidance on auditors' duties and responsibilities. Among the important legal principles he confirmed or established are the following:

1. When auditors accept an engagement to conduct a statutory financial statement audit they can be taken to have promised, not only to make the report required by legislation (for example, by s.235 of CA 1985), but also to conduct such examination as is necessary to form their opinion, and to exercise due skill and care in so doing.
2. Auditors' duties are not confined to an examination of the company's books and records at balance sheet date, but extend to an audit of the company's financial affairs in general, and for the whole of the relevant financial period.
3. The duty to audit involves a duty to pay due regard to the possibility that fraud may have occurred. The audit programme and audit tests should be structured so that the auditor has a reasonable expectation of detecting material fraud if it exists.
4. Auditors have a duty to make prompt and frank disclosure, to the appropriate level of management, of material matters discovered during the course of an audit. This includes a duty to report promptly to the company's directors if suspicious circumstances are encountered.
5. The auditor's duty to report includes a duty to report to shareholders at their general meeting any material matters discovered during the audit. This responsibility cannot be shirked on the grounds that it involves an adverse reflection on the board, a director, or a senior executive, or on the pretext that public disclosure may damage the company.
6. The auditor has a paramount duty to check material matters for him or herself. However, reliance may be placed on enquiries from others where it

is reasonable to do so. Nevertheless, reliance on others is to be regarded as an aid to, and not a substitute for, the auditor's own procedures.

7. The use of inexperienced staff or the failure to use an adequate audit programme do not, of themselves, establish negligence. However, if audit failure occurs (that is, a material misstatement in the financial statements is not uncovered by the audit), then the use of such staff and/or the absence of a satisfactory audit programme may be taken as evidence that the failure occurred as a result of negligence.

In his judgment, Moffit J noted that professional standards and practice must change over time, to reflect changes in the economic and business environment. He further observed that the courts, in trying to ascertain what qualifies as 'reasonable skill, care and caution', are guided by professional standards and best auditing practices of the time. However, he emphasised that the courts are not bound by these standards and, if they see fit, they will go beyond them. It is the courts, not the profession, which determine, in the light of society's prevailing norms, what is reasonable skill, care and caution in the particular circumstances of the case.

The relevance of these points is evident when it is realised that the duties which Moffit J attributed to auditors were not generally practised at the time (1970). Indeed, Kenley (1971, pp. 153–161) noted that the case brought to light key matters which required the immediate attention of auditors. These included:

1. The need to have an adequate written audit programme, and the need to correlate this with a review of the audit client's system of internal controls, and to modify it as necessary during the course of the audit to ensure that it adequately covers all material aspects of the entity.
2. The need to ensure that audit samples are drawn from records and events that cover the entire financial period, not just the period around the balance sheet date.
3. The need to ensure that audit staff are properly supervised by both partners and managers, and that proper instructions are given to assistants who have limited qualifications and/or experience.
4. The need to carefully assess the level of management from which the auditor seeks information, and the need to record appropriate details of responses to enquiry in the audit working papers.
5. The need to report promptly and forthrightly to the appropriate level of the audit client's management, deficiencies in transactions or accounting records examined by the auditor.

Today all of these matters have become what is regarded as 'usual practice'. Indeed, the *Pacific Acceptance* case has had a profound impact on auditing, as the principles enunciated by Moffit J underlie the Auditing Standards which have been promulgated by professional accountancy bodies throughout the English-speaking world.

5.4 AUDITORS' DUTIES UNDER PROFESSIONAL AUDITING STANDARDS AND GUIDELINES

Unlike statute and case law, which impose duties on auditors from outside the profession, Auditing Standards and Guidelines have been set, monitored and amended (as appropriate) by the auditing profession itself.[11] Rather than each of the professional bodies in the UK and Ireland setting its own Auditing Standards and Guidelines, these bodies established in 1991 the Auditing Practices Board (APB) to perform this function. In 2001, the APB became a component of the Accountancy Foundation. It has 15 members of whom no more than 6 (40%) may be eligible for appointment as a company auditor. The membership also includes 'persons from the business and academic worlds, the public sector and the legal profession' (APB, 1993a, para 2, 3).

In its *Scope and Authority of APB Pronouncements* (1993b, paras 1 and 18), the APB explains that its pronouncements fall into three principal categories:

- Statements of Auditing Standards (SASs);
- Practice Notes, which 'assist auditors in applying Auditing Standards of general application to particular circumstances and industries'; and
- Bulletins, which 'provide auditors with timely guidance on new or emerging issues'.

The APB also explains that:

SASs contain basic principles and essential procedures ('Auditing Standards') . . . with which auditors are required to comply, except where otherwise stated in the SAS concerned, in the conduct of any audit of financial statements. (para 4)
SASs also include explanatory and other material which, rather than being prescriptive [that is, mandatory], is designed to assist auditors in interpreting and applying Auditing Standards. (para 6)

The APB has issued its SASs in a structured series. This is shown in Figure 5.2.

It should be noted that compliance with the 'basic principles and essential procedures' within the SASs is mandatory. (These are printed in bold type and constitute the actual Auditing Standards.[12]) If auditors fail to comply with these

[11] Or, more correctly, the RSBs which, as seen in section 5.2.3, coincide with the professional bodies whose members may register as auditors, i.e. ICAEW, ICAS, ICAI, ACCA, AAPA (see footnote 9).

[12] In common parlance, entire SASs (Auditing Standards and explanatory material) are referred to as 'Auditing Standards'. In this book we use the terms 'Auditing Standard' and 'the Standard' in a similar manner; i.e. to refer to the relevant SAS in its entirety.

Figure 5.2: Structure of the APB's Statements of Auditing Standards (SASs) and corresponding International Standards on Auditing (ISAs)

APB's SASs			ISAs	
Series	Title	Date Issued	ISA no	Title
001/099	**Introductory matters**			
010	The scope and authority of APB pronouncements	May 1993		Preface to International Standardsof Auditing and Related Services
011	The Auditor's Code	February 1996	–	–
–	–	–	100	Assurance engagements
–	–	–	120	Framework of International Standards of Auditing
100/199	**Responsibility**			
100	Objective and general principles governing an audit of financial statements	March 1995	200	Objective and general principles governing an audit of financial statements
110	Fraud and error	January 1995	240	Fraud and error
120	Consideration of law and regulations	January 1995	250	Consideration of laws and regulations in an audit of financial statements
130	The going concern basis in financial statements	November 1994	570	Going concern
140	Engagement letters	March 1995	210	Terms of audit engagements
150	Subsequent events	March 1995	560	Subsequent events
160	Other information in documents containing audited financial statements (revised)	October 1999	720	Other information in documents containing audited financial statements
200/299	**Planning, controlling and recording**			
200	Planning	March 1995	300	Planning
210	Knowledge of the business	March 1995	310	Knowledge of the business
220	Materiality and the audit	March 1995	320	Audit materiality
230	Working papers	March 1995	230	Documentation
240	Quality control for audit work (revised)	September 2000	220	Quality control for audit work
300/399	**Accounting systems and internal control**			
300	Accounting and internal control systems and audit risk assessments	March 1995	400	Risk assessments and internal control
–	–	–	401	Auditing in a computer information systems environment
400/499	**Evidence**			
400	Audit evidence	March 1995	500	Audit evidence
–	–		501	Audit evidence – Additional considerations for specific items
–			505	External confirmations
410	Analytical procedures	March 1995	520	Analytical procedures
420	Audit of accounting estimates	March 1995	540	Audit of accounting estimates
430	Audit sampling	March 1995	530	Audit sampling and other selective testing procedures
440	Management representations	March 1995	580	Management representations
450	Opening balances and comparatives	March 1995	510	Initial engagements – Opening balances
			710	Comparatives
460	Related parties	November 1995	550	Related parties
470	Overall review of financial statements	March 1995	–	–
480	Service organisations	January 1999	402	Audit considerations relating to entities using service organisations
500/599	**Using the work of others**			
500	Considering the work of internal audit	March 1995	610	Considering the work of internal auditing
510	The relationship between principal auditors and other auditors	March 1995	600	Using the work of another auditor
520	Using the work of an expert	March 1995	620	Using the work of an expert
600/699	**Reporting**			
600	Auditors' reports on financial statements	May 1993	700	The auditor's report on financial statements
601	Imposed limitation of audit scope	January 1999	700	Para 41
610	Communication of audit matters to those charged with governance (revised)	June 2001	260	Communications of audit matters with those charged with governance and
			400	Section entitled 'Communication of weaknesses'
620	The auditor's right and duty to report to regulators in the financial sector	March 1994	–	–

Standards, disciplinary action may be taken against them by the RSB with which they are registered. Such disciplinary action may result in withdrawal of registration and hence of the auditor's eligibility to perform company audits (APB, 1993b, paras 9 and 11).

It may thus be seen that Auditing Standards serve two main purposes: (i) they inform individual auditors about the standard of work required of them in the performance of their duties, and (ii) they help to protect the reputation of the profession as a whole. As the standard of work required of auditors is set out clearly, and as this is binding on all members of the profession in the conduct of all audits, any auditor falling short of the required standards when performing an audit is exposed to disciplinary action. This helps to ensure that all members of the profession perform their duties in accordance with the profession's standards.

It is pertinent to observe that, although the explanatory material included in SASs and the APB's Practice Notes and Bulletins is persuasive rather than mandatory, the APB notes that *all* of its pronouncements 'are likely to be taken into account when the adequacy of the work of auditors is being considered in a court of law or in other contested situations' (APB, 1993b, para 13).

In addition to the APB's SASs, Practice Notes and Bulletins, just one Auditing Guideline (issued by the APB's predecessor body, the Auditing Practices Committee) remains current – this provides guidance to auditors on *Attendance at stocktaking.*

International Standards on Auditing (ISAs) and International Auditing Practice Statements are issued by the International Auditing Practices Committee (IAPC), a committee of the Council of the International Federation of Accountants (IFAC). All 153 member bodies of IFAC (in 113 countries – including the professional bodies in the UK and Ireland) are expected to comply with ISAs to the extent they are able to do so.

In its Preface to ISAs, IFAC (1994) explains:

The IAPC believes that the issue of international [auditing] standards and state-ments will improve the degree of uniformity of auditing practices ... throughout the world. (para 3).

ISAs contain basic principles and essential procedures ... together with related guidance in the form of explanatory and other material. The basic principles and essential procedures are to be interpreted in the context of the explanatory and other material that provide guidance for their application. (para 10)

ISAs do not override the local regulations ... governing the audit of financial or other information in a particular country. To the extent that ISAs conform with local regulations on a particular subject, the audit of financial or other information in that country in accordance with local regulations will automatically comply with the ISA regarding that subject. In the event that the local regulations differ from, or conflict with, ISAs on a particular subject, member bodies should comply with the obligations of membership . . . [i.e. to] support the work of IFAC . . . by using their best endeavors . . . to incorporate in their national auditing standards the principles on which are based International Standards on Auditing developed by IFAC. (para 16)

Thus, as a consequence of the UK professional bodies' membership of IFAC, except where UK laws and regulations are inconsistent with ISAs, UK SASs should be very similar to the related ISAs. Each UK SAS includes a paragraph headed 'Compliance with International Standards on Auditing'. This paragraph explains the respects in which the particular UK SAS differs from the corresponding ISA. In most cases the paragraph reads: 'Compliance with this SAS ensures compliance in all material respects with International Standard on Auditing [relevant number and title]'.

5.5 AUDITORS' DUTIES UNDER REGULATORY REQUIREMENTS

Certain regulatory bodies, such as the Financial Services Authority (FSA),[13] have been given authority under relevant statutes to impose requirements on entities under their jurisdiction and also on the auditors of these entities. Most of the regulatory requirements are limited in their application to entities within certain industrial sectors (for example, the financial services sector) and it is outside the scope of this book to discuss auditing requirements that are specific to any particular sector. However, the requirements of the UKLA are wide-ranging in their application, as they apply to all companies listed on the London Stock Exchange.

Under the UKLA's Listing Rules, listed companies are required to comply with the Combined Code (Committee on Corporate Governance, 1998b) which essentially consolidates the recommendations of the Cadbury (Committee on the Financial Aspects of Corporate Governance, 1992), Greenbury (Study Group on Directors' Remuneration, 1995) and Hampel (Committee on Corporate Governance, 1998a) reports. The Combined Code requires listed companies to include in their annual reports a statement of their compliance (or otherwise) with the Code's provisions. If a company chooses not to comply with one or more of the provisions, it is required to state that it has not so complied and the reason(s) for the departure. The Code also requires the auditors of listed com-

---

[13] Regulatory responsibility for companies listed on the London Stock Exchange passed from the London Stock Exchange to the Financial Services Authority (FSA) in 2000. The FSA has delegated its responsibilities for listed companies to the United Kingdom Listing Authority (UKLA). To all intents and purposes the UKLA constitutes a division of the FSA.

panies to review these clients' compliance (or disclosure of non-compliance) with just seven of the Code's provisions. These are as follows:

A.1.2 The board [of directors] should have a formal schedule of matters specific- ally reserved to it for decision.

A.1.3 There should be a procedure agreed by the board for directors in the furtherance of their duties to take independent professional advice if necessary, at the company's expense.

A.6.1 Non-executive directors should be appointed for specified terms subject to re-election and to Companies Act provisions relating to the removal of a director, and re-appointment should not be automatic.

A.6.2 All directors should be subject to election by shareholders at the first oppor- tunity after their appointment, and to re-election thereafter at intervals of no more than three years. The names of directors submitted for election or re-election should be accompanied by sufficient biographical details to enable shareholders to take an informed decision on their election.

D.1.1 The directors should explain their responsibility for preparing the accounts and there should be a statement by the auditors about their reporting responsibilities.

D.2.1 The directors should, at least annually, conduct a review of the effectiveness of the group's system of internal controls and should report to shareholders that they have done so. The review should cover all controls, including financial, operational and compliance controls and risk management.

D.3.1 The board should establish an audit committee of at least three directors, all non-executive, with written terms of reference which deal clearly with its authority and duties. The members of the committee, a majority of whom should be independent non-executive directors, should be named in the report and accounts.

The APB, in Bulletin 1999/5: *The Combined Code: Requirements Under the Listing Rules of the London Stock Exchange,* has provided guidance for auditors in relation to their review of their listed company clients' compliance (or disclosure of non-compliance) with these seven provisions. It states:

> In relation to all elements of the corporate governance disclosures relating to the Code provisions that are within the scope of their review, the auditors obtain appropriate evidence to support the compliance statement made by the company. [It then sets out procedures that should usually be performed to obtain the 'appropriate evidence']. (para 17)
> Where the auditors become aware of any Code provision with which the company has not complied, and that is within the scope of their review, they satisfy them- selves that the departure is described in the directors' statement of compliance. ... Where there is a departure from a Code provision specified for the auditors' review but there is proper disclosure of this fact and of the reasons for the departure . . . the auditors do not report this in their report on the financial statements. However, where the auditors consider that there is not proper disclosure of a departure from a Code provision specified for their review the auditors' report this in the opinion section of their report on the financial statements.[14] (paras 19–21)

---

[14] Auditors' reports on financial statements are discussed in Chapter 13.

5.6 AUDITOR–CLIENT RELATIONSHIP

The legal relationship between the auditor and the client company, and the auditor and the company's shareholders, is somewhat unusual. It was noted in section 5.2 that, under the provisions of the Companies Act 1985, shareholders are responsible for appointing the auditor and it is implicit in the statutory provisions that the auditor is appointed primarily to protect shareholders' interests. However, after being appointed at the company's general meeting, the auditor has no contact with the shareholders until the brief audit report is sent to them (after the end of the financial period), together with the audited financial statements.

Notwithstanding that auditors are appointed by the company's shareholders (at least, technically), the contractual arrangement for the audit is between the auditor and the client company. As a result, the auditor owes a contractual responsibility to the company *per se*, not to its shareholders. Further, in conducting the audit, a close working relationship necessarily develops between the auditor and the company's management, and it is the company's management (not its shareholders) who receive the auditor's management letter – a detailed report of the auditor's findings.[15] The auditor's relationship with the client company and its shareholders is represented diagrammatically in Figure 5.3.

Given auditors' dual relationship with the company and its shareholders, it is essential that they adhere strictly to the profession's fundamental principle of objectivity and independence: that they remain objective and independent of the entity and directors.

5.7 AUDITORS' *VIS-À-VIS* DIRECTORS'/ MANAGEMENT'S RESPONSIBILITY FOR THE FINANCIAL STATEMENTS

Responsibility for the preparation of a company's financial statements lies squarely with the company's directors. As noted in section 5.2 above, the Companies Act 1985 requires the directors of all companies to provide financial statements annually to their shareholders and debenture holders. It also requires all companies to keep proper accounting records. These are records which, among other things, facilitate both the preparation and audit of the company's annual financial statements (CA 1985, S.221).

---

[15] Management letters are discussed in Chapter 13.

Figure 5.3:   The auditor's relationship with the client company and its shareholders

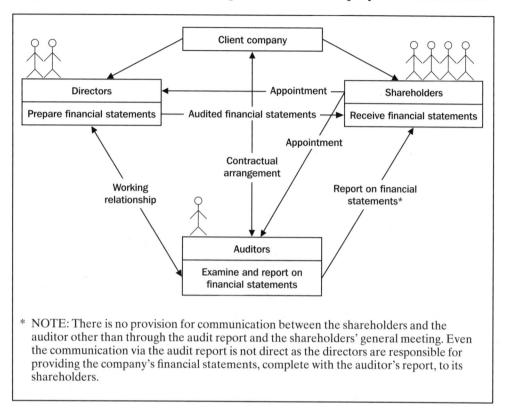

* NOTE: There is no provision for communication between the shareholders and the auditor other than through the audit report and the shareholders' general meeting. Even the communication via the audit report is not direct as the directors are responsible for providing the company's financial statements, complete with the auditor's report, to its shareholders.

The APB, in SAS 600: *Auditors' reports on financial statements* (discussed in Chapter 13), requires auditors to distinguish, in their audit reports, between their responsibilities and those of the auditee's directors for the audited financial statements. It states:

> (a) Auditors should distinguish between their responsibilities and those of the directors by including in their report
>   (i)   a statement that the financial statements are the responsibility of the reporting entity's directors;
>   (ii) a reference to a description of those responsibilities when set out elsewhere in the financial statements or accompanying information; and
>   (iii) a statement that the auditors' responsibility is to express an opinion on the financial statements.
> (b) Where the financial statements or accompanying information (for example the directors' report) do not include an adequate description of directors' relevant responsibilities, the auditors' report should include a description of those responsibilities. (SAS 600, para 20)

A typical statement of directors' responsibilities is that provided in the Annual Report of Diageo plc for 2001:

Directors' responsibilities in relation to financial statements

The following statement, which should be read in conjunction with the report of the auditors set out below, is made with a view to distinguishing for shareholders the respective responsibilities of the directors and of the auditors in relation to the financial statements.

The directors are required by the Companies Act 1985 to prepare financial statements for each financial year which give a true and fair view of the state of affairs of the company and the group at the end of the financial year and of the profit or loss for the financial year. The directors, in preparing these financial statements, consider that the company has used appropriate accounting policies, consistently applied and supported by reasonable and prudent judgements and estimates, and that all applicable accounting standards have been followed.

The directors have responsibility for ensuring that the company keeps accounting records which disclose with reasonable accuracy the financial position of the company and which enable them to ensure that the financial statements comply with the Companies Act 1985. The directors have general responsibility for taking such steps as are reasonably open to them to safeguard the assets of the group and to prevent and detect fraud and other irregularities.

The audit report (which is presented immediately following the statement set out above) includes the following statement:

Respective responsibilities of the directors and auditors

The directors are responsible for preparing the Annual Report and Accounts. As described above this includes responsibility for preparing the financial statements in accordance with applicable United Kingdom law and accounting standards. Our responsibilities, as independent auditors, are established in the United Kingdom by statute, the Auditing Practices Board, the Listing Rules of the Financial Services Authority, and by our profession's ethical guidance.

We report to you our opinion as to whether the financial statements give a true and fair view and are properly prepared in accordance with the Companies Act. We also report to you if, in our opinion, the directors' report is not consistent with the financial statements, if the company has not kept proper accounting records, if we have not received all the information and explanations we require for our audit, or if information specified by law or the Listing Rules regarding directors' remuneration and transactions with the group is not disclosed.

We review whether the statement on page 11 reflects the company's compliance with the seven provisions of the Combined Code specified for our review by the Financial Services Authority, and we report if it does not. We are not required to consider whether the board's statements on internal control cover all risks and controls, or form an opinion on the effectiveness of the group's corporate governance procedures or its risk and control procedures.

We read the other information contained in the Annual Report, including the corporate governance statement, and consider whether it is consistent with the audited financial statements. We consider the implications for our report if we become aware of any apparent misstatements or material inconsistencies with the financial statements.

The above statement of the respective responsibilities of directors and auditors included in KPMG's audit report on Diageo plc's 2001 financial statements substantially follows the wording in the example audit report in Appendix 1, APB Bulletin 2001/2: *Revisions to the Wording of Auditors' Reports on Financial Statements and the Interim Review Report.*

Statements explaining the respective responsibilities of directors and auditors for the financial statements are helpful in informing users about these matters. Research conducted prior to publication of SAS 600 indicated that many financial statement users were not aware that it is the directors, and not the auditors, who are responsible for preparing the financial statements. A survey conducted by Lee and Tweedie (1975), for example, found that one quarter of institutional investors and more than half of private investors had little or no understanding of who is legally responsible for the preparation of company financial statements. Research conducted by Porter and Gowthorpe (2001) indicates that, notwithstanding statements to the contrary in company annual reports, the situation remains essentially unchanged: in 2000 just over a quarter of both financial community and non-financial audit beneficiaries were of the opinion that auditors are responsible for preparing company financial statements.

5.8   THE AUDIT EXPECTATION–PERFORMANCE GAP

5.8.1   Importance of the audit expectation–performance gap

Although auditors spell out their responsibilities in some detail in their audit reports, there is a mismatch (or gap) between the duties society expects of auditors and what it perceives it receives from them. This phenomenon, known as the audit expectation–performance gap, is not new nor is it confined to the UK. It has existed for more than 100 years (Chandler and Edwards, 1996) and it has been recognised and studied in many countries of the world – for example, in the USA, Canada, South Africa, New Zealand, Australia, Singapore, Denmark, the Netherlands, Spain and Finland.

Why has this gap prompted so much attention? And why is it of concern to the auditing profession? It is because auditors' failure to meet society's expectations of them has resulted in severe criticism of, and litigation against, auditors and this, in turn, has served to undermine confidence in the audit function. According to Russell (1986, p. 58) auditors face 'a liability crisis and a credibility crisis'. Some 70 years ago, Limperg (1932) explained:

> The [audit] function is rooted in the confidence that society places in the effectiveness of the audit and in the opinion of the accountant . . . if the confidence is betrayed, the function, too, is destroyed, since it becomes useless. (as reproduced in Limperg Instituut 1985, p. 16)

He went on to explain that auditors have a dual responsibility: not to arouse 'in the sensible layman' greater expectations than can be fulfilled by the work done, and to carry out the work in a manner that does not betray the expectations evoked. In other words, it is the responsibility of auditors to ensure that society does not have unreasonable expectations of them and to satisfy its reasonably held expectations.

It follows from the above that, if the auditing profession is to narrow the audit expectation–performance gap (and thereby reduce criticism and loss of confidence in its work), it needs to ascertain:
(i)   the duties society expects auditors to perform,
(ii) which of these duties it is reasonable to expect of auditors,
(iii) the extent to which society's reasonable expectations are satisfied (or, more pertinently, not satisfied) by auditors.

This brings us to examining the structure and composition of the audit expectation–performance gap.

5.8.2 Structure and composition of the audit expectation–performance gap

Analysis of the audit expectation–performance gap reveals that it has two major components (Porter, 1991, 1993):
1. The *'reasonableness gap'* – the gap between the duties society expects auditors to perform and those it is reasonable to expect of auditors. Thus, this component comprises the duties that society *un*reasonably expects auditors to perform.
2. The *'performance gap'* – the gap between the duties society reasonably expects of auditors and what it perceives auditors actually accomplish. This component may be subdivided into:
    (a) the *'deficient standards gap'* – the gap between the duties reasonably expected of auditors and auditors' existing duties as defined by auditing standards, other professional promulgations, the law, and regulations;
    (b) the *'deficient performance gap'* – the gap between the standard of performance of auditors' existing duties expected by society and auditors' performance of those duties as perceived by society.

The structure of the audit expectation–performance gap is depicted in Figure 5.4.

Having established the structure of the audit expectation–performance gap, we can examine the duties comprising, and the relative extent of, each component. The starting point is to ascertain the duties society expects auditors to perform (i.e. the right end of the gap depicted in Figure 5.4). Research conducted in the

Figure 5.4:   The structure of the audit expectation–performance gap

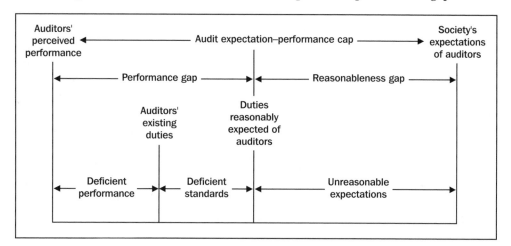

UK, as well as elsewhere in the world, has established that society expects auditors to perform a very wide range of duties. These include auditors' actual existing duties, duties which are reasonably expected of auditors (even though they are not required to perform them under auditing standards, other professional promulgations, the law, or regulations), and those that are unreasonably expected of auditors.

Reasonableness gap

The next step is to determine the duties that are reasonable to expect of auditors. It seems logical that, in order for duties to be reasonably expected of auditors, they should be cost-beneficial for auditors to perform:[16] the benefits derived by financial statement users, auditees and society as a whole from auditors performing the duty should be equal to, or greater than, the costs incurred of auditors so doing. Research conducted by Porter and Gowthorpe (2001) suggests that, at least in the UK in 2000, society expects auditors to perform some 47 duties and that just over half of these (24 of the 47 duties[17]) are not cost-beneficial for auditors to perform; that is, just over half of the duties are unreasonably expected of auditors. These duties, which constitute the reasonableness gap, fall into two broad groups:

(a) those that are not economically feasible for auditors to perform – for example, verifying *every* transaction of the auditee; *guaranteeing* the accuracy of the auditee's financial statements and/or its solvency; detecting and reporting minor theft of auditee assets, and detecting other illegal acts

---

[16] The surrogate for cost-benefit analysis is explained in Porter and Gowthorpe (2001).

[17] The number of duties at each division, and comprising each component, of the audit expectation–performance gap are shown in Figure 5.5.

by the company's directors/senior managers that only indirectly impact on the financial statements;

(b) those relating to issues that have only recently emerged as significant in the corporate arena – for example, examining and reporting on the auditee's IT systems, the adequacy of its risk management procedures, the effectiveness of its internal non-financial controls, and the efficiency and effectiveness of its management; examining and reporting on the reliability of the auditee's financial information on the internet and all of the information in its annual report, in particular, about its equal employment opportunities, product safety, and occupational health and safety. In time, as these recently emerging issues become more commonplace, it may be that benefits to be derived from auditors performing related duties will be more widely recognised and, thus, the duties will cross the cost-benefit threshold to be reasonably (rather than unreasonably) expected of auditors.

Deficient standards gap

Of the duties that are reasonably expected of auditors, Porter and Gowthorpe's research indicates that a little over half are existing duties. (Porter and Gowthorpe found that 13 of the 23 reasonably expected duties are existing duties of auditors.) The remainder (i.e. 10 duties) are reasonably expected but not required of auditors: these constitute the 'deficient standards gap'. Like the duties comprising the 'reasonableness gap', the 'deficient standards gap' duties, in the main, fall into two broad groups:

(a) those that involve disclosing in the audit report, or to an appropriate authority, matters of concern that are uncovered during an audit. These include theft of a material amount of the auditee's assets; other illegal acts by the company's directors/senior managers which directly impact on the financial statements; deliberate distortion of the financial statements; and doubts about the entity's continued existence. (In the latter two cases, auditors have an existing duty to report their findings in the audit report but they are not required also to report them to an 'appropriate authority');

(b) those that relate to corporate governance issues; for example, examining and reporting on the effectiveness of the company's internal financial controls, and its compliance with the Stock Exchange's governance requirements; and also examining and reporting (to the company's directors) on the adequacy of a company's risk management procedures.

Deficient performance gap

Turning to consider how well society considers that auditors perform their existing duties, Porter and Gowthorpe's (2001) research indicates that society is satisfied with the performance of about half of their duties. Six of auditors' 13 existing duties were considered by society to be performed satisfactorily; seven were judged to be performed deficiently. These (deficiently performed) duties constitute the deficient performance gap. They include detecting the theft of a material amount of the company's assets by the entity's employees or by its directors or senior managers; reporting to an appropriate authority illegal acts by the entity's directors or senior managers; and disclosing in the audit report doubts about the company's continued existence.

Relative extent of the gap's components

If auditors fail to perform a duty expected of them by society, or they fail to perform an existing duty to society's satisfaction, society has unfulfilled expectations with respect to these duties. Based on a measure (proposed by Porter and Gowthorpe, 2001) of 'unfulfilled expectations' attaching to each duty constituting the components of the audit expectation–performance gap,[18] it appears that about 50% of the audit expectation–performance gap derives

Figure 5.5:   The relative extent of the components of the audit expectation–performance gap in the UK in 2000

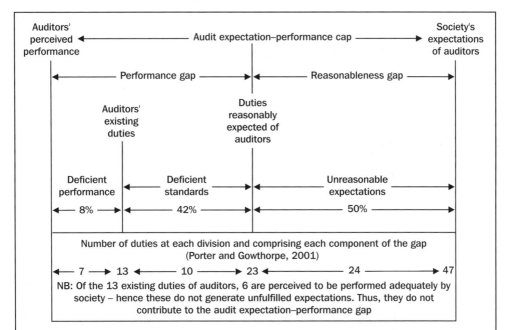

[18] The measure of unfulfilled expectations attaching to each duty constituting the audit expectation–performance gap is derived from the proportion of the society group (auditees, financial community audit beneficiaries and non-financial community audit beneficiaries) who signified that the duty in question should be performed by auditors (in the case of the reasonableness gap and deficient standards gap duties) or that auditors perform the duty poorly (in the case of the deficient performance gap duties).

from society having unreasonable expectations of auditors, 42% from auditors not being required to perform duties that are reasonably expected of them, and 8% from auditors' deficient performance. These proportions are shown in Figure 5.5.

5.8.3 Comparison of the gap in the UK in 2000 and New Zealand in 1989

Porter and Gowthorpe's study of the audit expectation–performance gap in the UK in 2000 replicated research conducted in New Zealand (NZ) a decade earlier (reported in Porter, 1993). Although the audit environments in the UK and NZ are not identical, the two countries are very similar culturally, socially, politically and economically. As a result, by comparing the findings of the NZ study conducted in 1989 with those of the 2000 UK study, we can glean some useful insights into changes that have occurred in the audit expectation–performance gap. The most striking change is in the relative contribution of the three components to the overall expectation–performance gap: while the performance gap decreased from 69% in 1989 in NZ to 50% in 2000 in the UK (with the deficient performance and deficient standards components falling from 11% to 8% and 58% to 42% respectively), the reasonableness gap increased from 31% to 50%. Thus, while auditors' performance (in terms of the duties required and standard of auditors' work) appears to have improved over the decade from 1989 to 2000, the resultant narrowing of the audit expectation–performance gap has been more than offset by a broadening of society's (unreasonable) expectations of auditors. Indeed, Porter and Gowthorpe found that, despite the marked reduction in the performance gap, the overall expectation–performance gap in the UK in 2000 was 34% wider than that pertaining in NZ in 1989. Society's increased expectations of auditors are primarily associated with corporate governance matters that were not significant in the auditing arena in 1989.

5.8.4 Narrowing the audit expectation–performance gap

Knowledge of the structure and composition of the audit expectation–performance gap provides insight into how the gap may be narrowed. The more auditors' performance is aligned to society's expectations, the greater the reduction in society's unfulfilled expectations – and the less criticism auditors will face. As a corollary, the more society's confidence in the audit function can be expected to increase.

Reviewing the three components that constitute the audit expectation–performance gap, the required corrective action is evident. In order to narrow the deficient performance gap, auditors need to be better informed about their existing duties under statute and case law, regulations and professional promulgations,[19] and also about the standard of work that is expected of them. Additionally, improved quality control procedures need to be established and maintained in order to ensure that all auditors perform their work to the required standard. In this they should be assisted by the APB's revised SAS 240: *Quality control for audit work,* issued in 2000.[20]

In order to narrow the deficient standards gap, auditing standards need to be extended to embrace the duties that are not required of auditors but are cost-effective for auditors to perform. Most of the duties constituting the deficient standards gap have featured prominently in recent corporate governance or other similar debates and it might be anticipated that, in the future, these duties will change their status from being reasonably expected but not required, to existing duties of auditors.

The effect on the audit expectation–performance gap of improving quality controls over auditors' work and of developing new auditing standards is reflected in the marked narrowing of the deficient performance and deficient standards components of the gap between 1989 and 2000. Since 1989, monitoring of auditors' work has been introduced in both the UK[21] and NZ, and it seems likely that this is responsible, at least in part, for the apparent improvement in auditors' performance. This conclusion accords with the opinions of the monitoring units in the UK – as reflected in their annual reports to the Department of Trade and Industry. Similarly, since 1989, new auditing standards have been responsible for changing the status of two duties that were reasonably expected but not required of auditors in 1989 into existing duties. These are reporting theft, and other illegal acts, by company officials discovered during an audit to an appropriate authority when it is in the public interest to do so. Additionally, SAS 130: *The going concern basis in financial statements* was issued in the UK in 1994 (i.e. post 1989) and this provides much clearer guidance to auditors than its predecessor did as to what is required of them in this regard. It is notable that society's dissatisfaction with auditors' performance of their duty 'to disclose in the audit report doubts about the continued existence of the auditee' has declined significantly over the period 1989 to 2000.

Although further improvement in auditors' performance would help to narrow the audit expectation–performance gap, the greatest challenge facing the

---

[19] Porter and Gowthorpe (2001) found that, in 2000, some 15% of auditors were uncertain or incorrect about their existing duties.

[20] SAS 240 and the concept and application of quality control are discussed in Chapters 3, 6 and 15.

[21] In the UK the RSBs are required to monitor the work of auditors registered with them (see section 5.2.3 above). The Joint Monitoring Unit (JMU) performs this function for the ICAEW, ICAS and ICAI; the ACCA monitoring unit performs the same function for the ACCA and AAPA.

auditing profession is reducing the reasonableness gap: reducing society's unreasonable expectations of auditors by engaging with members of society about the audit function and what it can – and cannot – be reasonably expected to achieve. As indicated above, the set of duties comprising the reasonableness gap has expanded as new issues, particularly those related to corporate governance, have moved into the domain where society expects auditors to play a part.

As noted in section 5.7, the profession has taken steps to educate financial statement users about the respective responsibilities of auditors, and the auditee's directors, for the auditee's financial statements, and also about the audit process. However, it seems that more is needed – particularly in educating those who are indirect (non-financial community) audit beneficiaries who seem unlikely to read auditors' reports. It is perhaps pertinent to note that, should auditors be taken to court for apparent failure to perform their duties to the expected standard, the jury will almost certainly comprise a cross-section of society. Those both with, and without, knowledge of the audit function and what is reasonable to expect of auditors are likely to be represented. Similarly, when a company fails unexpectedly – particularly if the failure is accompanied by allegations of fraud or other forms of misconduct by the company's senior officials, 'where were the auditors?' the cry will (almost certainly) be heard. This will reflect unfulfilled expectations of auditors which will, in turn, fuel criticism of auditors and undermine confidence in their work.

5.9 AUDITORS' RESPONSIBILITY TO DETECT AND REPORT FRAUD

5.9.1 Fraud defined

Before considering auditors' duties with respect to fraud, we need to establish what is meant by 'fraud' in the auditing context. There are basically three types of corporate fraud. These are as follows:

(i) *Misappropriation of corporate assets*. Evidence suggests that this type of fraud is most likely to be committed by non-managerial employees. However, if it is carried out by senior company officials (directors or senior managers) it can be on a massive scale. Misappropriation (theft) of company assets is usually undertaken for personal gain and is an action against the company. It should be noted that some company assets, such as cash, stock and certain computer hardware (such as laptop computers) and software are particularly prone to theft.

(ii) *Manipulation of accounting information*. This type of fraud (which is usually referred to as fraudulent financial reporting) is intended to result in financial statements which give a misleading impression of the company's financial affairs. It is almost always perpetrated by management but, rather than being committed for direct personal financial gain, it is usually motivated by what the individual concerned considers to be in his or her own best interests in terms of reporting the company's financial position or (more commonly) its performance in a particularly favourable (or in some instances, unfavourable) light. Management may, for instance, feel pressured to report earnings (or net profit after tax) in line with the financial market's expectations – especially if the company plans to raise new share or debt capital during the next financial year – when the 'actual' earnings figure is significantly below that which management feels motivated to report.[22]

(iii) *Deception of a third party.* This generally involves misappropriation of a third party's assets and/or deception through the provision of false information to a third party. The person committing the fraud may believe (s)he is acting in the company's best interests. An example is making false representations to the Inland Revenue in order to minimise the company's tax liability.

5.9.2 A controversial and evolving issue

Auditors' responsibility for detecting fraud is one of the most controversial issues in auditing. The Commission on Auditors' Responsibilities (CAR, 1978: the Cohen Commission), for example, reported:

> Court decisions, criticism by the financial press, actions by regulatory bodies, and surveys of users indicate dissatisfaction with the responsibility for fraud detection acknowledged by auditors. Opinion surveys . . . indicate that concerned segments of the public expect independent auditors to assume greater responsibility in this area. Significant percentages of those who use and rely on the auditor's work rank the detection of fraud among the most important objectives of an audit. (p. 31)

The stance of the auditing profession in relation to detecting and reporting fraud has changed markedly over the last 160 or so years. As noted in Chapter 2, from the time compulsory audits were first introduced in 1844 until the 1920s, the prevention and detection of fraud and error were regarded as primary audit objectives. Nevertheless, as also noted in Chapter 2, it was decided in the *Kingston Cotton Mill* case (1896) that auditors are not required to nose out every fraud (auditors are 'watchdogs not bloodhounds'), but they are expected to exercise reasonable skill, care and caution appropriate to the particular circumstances. Further, if anything comes to their attention which arouses their

---

[22] As explained in section 5.9.4, fraudulent financial reporting often develops from aggressive earnings management.

suspicions, they are expected to 'probe the matter to the bottom' and to report it promptly to the appropriate level of management.

Between the 1920s and 1960s the importance of fraud detection as an audit objective was steadily eroded. During this period companies grew in size and complexity and, as a consequence, company managements set in place accounting systems to capture and process accounting data. These systems incorporated internal controls designed to prevent or detect error and fraud and thus to protect the integrity of the accounting information. At the same time, growth in the volume of company transactions made it impractical, within the limits of reasonable time and cost constraints, for auditors to check every entry in the accounting records. Auditing procedures changed accordingly, from meticulous checking of every transaction to techniques based on testing samples of transactions, combined with a review and evaluation of the effectiveness of the accounting system and its internal controls (see Chapter 2, section 2.2.4).

Given this environment, auditors argued that preventing and detecting fraud were the responsibility of management and that they were best achieved through the maintenance of a good system of internal control. They also argued that auditing procedures were not designed, and could not be relied upon, to detect fraud. The general attitude of the profession from the 1940s to 1960s is reflected in the AICPA's *Codification of Statements on Auditing Procedure*, published in 1951. It states:

> The ordinary examination incident to the issuance of an opinion respecting financial statements is not designed and cannot be relied upon to disclose defalcations and other similar irregularities, although their discovery frequently results. In a well-organized concern reliance for the detection of such irregularities is placed principally upon the maintenance of an adequate system of accounting records with appropriate internal control. If an auditor were to discover defalcations and similar irregularities he would have to extend his work to a point where its cost would be prohibitive. (paras 12–13)

By the 1960s the profession's position on fraud was subject to criticism from both inside and outside the profession. Since that time, as corporate fraud has grown in both incidence and size, so dissatisfaction with the extent of responsibility for detecting fraud acknowledged by auditors has increased. The level of discontent is evident from the following illustrations:

• Woolf (1978) drew attention to the pertinent question raised by the investment analyst whose solo efforts were responsible for exposing the notorious *Equity Funding* fraud in the USA in the early 1970s:

> If routine auditing procedures cannot detect 64,000 phony insurance policies [two thirds of the total number], $25 million in counterfeit bonds, and $100 million in missing assets, what is the purpose of audits? (p. 62)

- In similar vein, Carty (1985), a member of the Auditing Practices Committee (the predecessor of the APB), observed:

   [T]he public do not readily accept the limitations on the scope of an audit that the auditors inevitably build into their approach. Whenever there is a revelation in the press of a fraud, there is public outcry and the usual question, 'Why didn't the auditors pick this up years ago?' (p. 30)

During the past couple of decades, pressure has mounted, especially in the UK and USA, for auditors to assume greater responsibility for detecting fraud. In the mid-1980s, faced by the rising wave of corporate fraud in the UK, Fletcher and Howard, successive Ministers of Corporate and Consumer Affairs, made it clear that they viewed auditors as being in the front line of the public's defences in the fight against corporate fraud, and they called upon auditors to extend their duties in this regard. Their stance was supported by fraud investigators who stated that they considered it both practical and desirable, within the limits of cost and auditing procedures, for auditors to accept a general responsibility to detect fraud (Smith, 1985, p. 10).

Similar opinions have been expressed more recently in the USA by senior staff of the SEC. For example, Walker (1999a), former Director of the SEC's Division of Enforcement, stated:

   The Commission looks to auditors to combat fraud. . . . The Commission, with its small staff and limited resources . . . necessarily must rely heavily on the accounting profession to perform its tasks diligently and responsibly. In short, auditors are the first line of defence. (p. 2)

He also noted (1999b) that:

   [There] are indicators that financial fraud is still occurring at too great a pace. . . . National Economic Research Associates (NERA) [have] issued a report on recent trends in securities litigation. NERA found that a whopping 55 percent of all securities claims actions in the first half of 1999 were based on claims of fraudulent accounting. (p. 2)

Although he did not say so directly, Walker implied that the instances of fraudulent financial reporting should have been detected by the relevant company's auditors.

Turner (1999), former Chief Accountant of the SEC, was more direct in his criticism of auditors for failing to detect fraud – in particular, fraudulent financial reporting:

   You only have to look as far as the March 1999 report sponsored by the Committee of Sponsoring Organizations of the Treadway Committee (COSO) on fraudulent financial reporting to understand the problems with today's audits. One startling fact in that report, which summarizes fraud cases from 1987–1998, is that over 80% of the fraud cases involved the highest levels of management . . . the very group responsible for ensuring the adequacy of the control environment. The irony of today's audit processes is that significant audit assurance is derived from internal controls; however, the very group . . . charged with ensuring the effectiveness of internal controls is responsible for committing fraud. (p. 4)

In Turner's (2000) view, auditors should be required to perform additional forensic-type procedures during their audits, specifically designed to detect fraudulent activities by management.

In the UK, as in the USA, corporate fraud is a very serious issue. KPMG (1997, 2001) reported that between 1987 and 2000, 855 fraud cases were taken to court in the UK, with the associated fraud charges amounting to some £4,177 million. Among these frauds are the well-publicised cases of the Bank of Credit and Commerce International (BCCI), Ferranti, Guinness Peat, and Maxwell Communications. However, what is particularly startling (apart from the number and value of the fraud cases) is that, according to Ernst & Young (2000), 82% of all identified corporate frauds are committed by employees and almost one third of these are committed by management. This proportion of management fraud is lower than that noted by Turner in the USA (see quotation above) but is still very high – and is very worrying, given auditors' reliance on management's responses to enquiries in relation to many aspects of the audit.

5.9.3 Recent developments in auditors' responsibilities to detect and report corporate fraud

Faced by the evidence of increasing incidence and size of frauds, and the significant involvement of management, auditors have come under mounting pressure from politicians, the media, and influential commentators in society (such as Turner and Walker quoted above) to play a more active role in combating corporate fraud. In response, the auditing profession, in many parts of the English-speaking world, has acknowledged greater responsibility for detecting fraud and, additionally, for reporting fraud to both shareholders (via the audit report) and to regulatory authorities. For example, in the USA, the AICPA, in SAS 53, *The auditor's responsibility to detect and report errors and irregularities* (issued in 1988) adopted a new positive approach in defining auditors' duties with respect to fraud. In place of its former defensive tone and insistence that audits cannot be relied on to disclose irregularities, it stated:

> Because of the characteristics of irregularities, particularly those involving forgery and collusion, a properly designed and executed audit may not detect a material irregularity. [However], the auditor should exercise (a) due care in planning, performing and evaluating the results of audit procedures, and (b) the proper degree of professional skepticism to achieve reasonable assurance that material errors or irregularities will be detected. (paras 7–8)

The AICPA strengthened its recognition of auditors' role in detecting fraud in

SAS 82: *Consideration of fraud in a financial statement audit* (published in 1997). Unlike its predecessor (SAS 53), which embraced both errors and irregularities, SAS 82 deals only with fraud in financial statement audits. Further, SAS 82 (unlike SAS 53) seems to go beyond requiring auditors to plan and perform their audits to obtain reasonable assurance that the financial statements are free of material misstatement: it seems also to require them to actively search for fraud. The Standard requires auditors to assess, specifically, the risk of material misstatement in the financial statements due to fraud and to consider that assessment when planning and performing the audit. In making their assessment, auditors are required to:

(i) consider whether risk factors that might indicate the existence of fraud are present, and
(ii) make enquiries of management to obtain management's understanding and assessment of the likelihood of fraud occurring within the entity.

To assist auditors in their fraud risk assessment, SAS 82 provides an extensive list of fraud risk factors they are to consider in making this assessment. SAS 82 also explicitly requires auditors to respond appropriately to the risk factors they have identified, and to document:

(i) the performance of their fraud risk assessment,
(ii) the specific risk factors they identified, and
(iii) their response to those factors.

At the conclusion of their audits, auditors are required to reassess, in the light of all the evidence gathered during the audit, the risk of material misstatement in the financial statements as a consequence of fraud.

ISA 240: *Fraud and error* (as revised, 2001) is similar to SAS 82 in many respects. However, unlike SAS 82, rather than being confined to fraud, ISA 240 covers both fraud and error in financial statement audits. Reminiscent of auditing standards in previous decades, ISA 240 notes that primary responsibility for the prevention and detection of fraud and error rests with management and those charged with the governance of the entity (para 10). It also observes that, although audits conducted in accordance with ISAs are designed to provide reasonable assurance that the financial statements are free from material misstatement, whether caused by fraud or error, because of the inherent limitations of an audit, there is an unavoidable risk that some material misstatements may not be detected (paras 13–14).

Having given a caveat that properly planned and conducted audits may not detect material misstatement in financial statements, ISA 240 provides some exacting requirements for auditors which are designed to ensure that, if a significant fraud has been committed within the auditee, they will have a reasonable chance of detecting it. For example, the Standard requires auditors, when planning their audits, to make enquiries of management (para 22). Such enquiries are designed to enable the auditor, among other things:

(i) to obtain an understanding of management's assessment of the risk that the financial statements may be materially misstated as a result of fraud, and the accounting and internal control systems management has put in place to address such risk;

(ii) to determine whether management is aware of any known fraud that has affected the entity, or suspected fraud that the entity is investigating.

ISA 240 also requires auditors to obtain written representations from management (para 51):

(i) acknowledging its (management's) responsibility for the implementation and operation of accounting and internal control systems that are designed to prevent and detect fraud and error;

(ii) stating it has disclosed to the auditor:

(a) all significant facts relating to any frauds or suspected frauds known to management that may have affected the entity; and

(b) the results of its assessment of the risk that the financial statements may be materially misstated as a result of fraud.

The Standard explains that it is important for auditors to obtain written representations from management on the above matters 'because of the nature of fraud and the difficulties encountered by auditors in detecting material misstatements . . . resulting from fraud' (para 55). Nevertheless, it also acknowledges that, although enquiries of management (and their written representations) may provide useful information about the risk of material misstatement resulting from employee fraud, they are unlikely to provide useful information on management fraud. Hence, following up fraud risk factors that relate to management fraud is of particular importance (para 27).

While observing: 'The fact that fraud is usually concealed can make it very difficult to detect' (para 34), ISA 240 notes that by using his or her knowledge of the business:

> The auditor may identify events or conditions that provide an opportunity, a motive or a means to commit fraud, or indicate that fraud may have already occurred. Such events or conditions are referred to as 'fraud risk factors'. For example, a document may be missing, a general ledger may be out of balance, or an analytical procedure may not make sense. . . . Fraud risk factors do not necessarily indicate the existence of fraud, however, they often have been present in circumstances where frauds have occurred. (para 34)

Like SAS 82, in order to assist auditors identify fraud risk factors – and thus increase the likelihood of their detecting fraud if it is present – ISA 240 provides an extensive list of examples of fraud risk factors.

If fraud risk factors are identified within an auditee, auditors are required, when designing their audit procedures,[23] to make an appropriate response. In some cases auditors may consider that the procedures already planned provide sufficient response to the identified fraud risk factors. In other cases, they may conclude that the nature, timing and/or extent of their procedures need modifying in order to address adequately the fraud risk factors that are present (paras 40–41).

To demonstrate that they have addressed properly the possibility of the financial statements being materially misstated as a result of fraud, auditors are required to document the fraud risk factors they identified as being present during their fraud risk assessment process and also their response to those factors. Further, if during the course of the audit fraud risk factors are identified that cause the auditor to perform additional procedures, the presence of those fraud risk factors, and the auditor's response thereto, are to be documented (para 49).

Like SAS 82, ISA 240 states that if auditors:

- identify a fraud, whether or not it results in a material misstatement in the financial statements, or
- obtain evidence that indicates a fraud may exist (even if the potential effect on the financial statements would not be material),

they should communicate these matters to the appropriate level of management on a timely basis, and consider the need to report such matters to those charged with the entity's governance (i.e. the board of directors or, possibly, the audit committee if the company has one) (para 62). According to the Standard, the 'appropriate level of management' is ordinarily at least one level above the person(s) who appears to be involved in the misstatement or fraud. Regarding communication with those charged with governance, ISA 240 observes (para 58) that what is communicated is a matter for the auditor's professional judgment but it is affected by any understanding between the auditor and board of directors (and/or audit committee) about the matters to be communicated. Nevertheless, ordinarily such matters would include:

(i) questions regarding management competence and integrity;
(ii) fraud involving management;

---

[23] Audit procedures (tests of control and substantive procedures) are discussed in Chapter 6.

(iii) other fraud that results in the financial statements being materially misstated; and

(iv) misstatements that indicate material weaknesses in the internal controls, including the design and operation of the entity's financial reporting process.

In the event that auditors encounter circumstances that indicate the financial statements may be materially misstated as a result of fraud or error, they are required to perform procedures to determine whether or not the financial statements are materially misstated (para 42). If the procedures confirm that the financial statements are materially misstated, or fail to enable the auditor to form a conclusion on the matter, the auditor is required to 'consider the implications for the audit report' (para 48). However, either outcome would result in a modified audit report (a qualified, adverse, or disclaimer of, opinion depending on the seriousness of the misstatement or inability to form a conclusion thereon).[24]

As indicated above, the general requirements of ISA 240 and SAS 82 are broadly similar. Each has introduced explicit, and fairly rigorous, requirements of auditors in relation to detecting fraud. Each requires auditors to undertake a formal fraud risk assessment process and to respond appropriately to the fraud risk factors that are found to be present. Further, both Standards preclude auditors from hiding behind the excuse of lack of materiality[25] when encountering evidence that fraud may exist. If auditors find evidence that indicates that fraudulent financial reporting or misappropriation of assets may have caused the financial statements to be misstated, they are required to pursue it even if it seems minor in isolation.

ISA 240 and, more particularly, SAS 82 (which deals only with fraud, rather than both fraud and error) seem to take a (tentative) step towards recognising a general duty for auditors to detect fraud. Although each Standard carefully couples fraud (and, in the case of ISA 240, error) with material misstatement in the financial statements, they provide far more guidance than hitherto on detecting fraud and their tenor is indicative of a more general duty to detect fraud.

In the UK, SAS 110: *Fraud and error* (published in 1995 – thus pre-dating SAS 82 and ISA 240) is less explicit and less demanding in its requirements of auditors as regards detecting fraud. It requires auditors to 'plan, perform and

---

[24] Modified audit reports are discussed in Chapter 13.

[25] The meaning and importance of this concept is discussed in Chapter 3.

evaluate their audit work in order to have a reasonable expectation of detecting material misstatements arising from error and fraud' (para 18). But, it does not require auditors to make a formal fraud risk assessment or to respond, specifically, when planning or performing their audits, to fraud risk factors that are identified.

However, with respect to auditors reporting detected or suspected fraud encountered during an audit, SAS 110 seems to go beyond the requirements of ISA 240 and SAS 82. SAS 110 requires auditors:

- if they suspect or discover fraud, to communicate their findings as soon as practicable to the appropriate level of management, the board of directors or the audit committee. Even if the potential effect of a fraud or suspected fraud is immaterial to the financial statements, the auditor should still report it to the appropriate level of management (para 41);
- to qualify their audit report when they form the opinion that, as a result of fraud, the financial statements do not give a true and fair view. Similarly, they should qualify the audit report if they disagree with the accounting treatment, or with the extent or lack of disclosure, of the fraud or its consequences (para 45).

Thus far the reporting requirements of SAS 110 are very similar to those of ISA 240 and SAS 82. However, SAS 110 goes further: it also recognises that there may be circumstances in which auditors should go beyond their duty as outlined above and report suspected or actual instances of fraud to an appropriate external authority. The Standard requires auditors who encounter suspected or actual fraud during an audit to consider whether the matter ought to be reported 'to a proper authority in the public interest' (para 50). In normal circumstances, the auditor's duty of confidentiality to the client is paramount and, in accordance with this, SAS 110 notes that 'confidentiality is an implied term of the auditor's contract'. However, it goes on to state: 'In certain exceptional circumstances auditors are not bound by their duty of confidentiality and have the right or duty to report matters to a proper authority in the public interest' (para 53). In particular:

> When a suspected or actual instance of fraud casts doubt on the integrity of the directors, auditors should make a report direct to a proper authority in the public interest without delay and without informing the directors in advance. (para 52)

Provided that auditors report an actual or suspected fraud encountered during an audit to a proper authority in the public interest, and the disclosure is not motivated by malice, they are protected from the risk of liability for breach of confidence or defamation (para 55).

When deciding whether disclosure of a detected or suspected fraud to a proper authority in the public interest is justified, the auditor is required to consider factors such as (para 56):

- the extent to which the fraud is likely to affect members of the public;
- whether the directors are taking corrective action or are likely to do so;
- the extent to which non-disclosure of the fraud is likely to enable it to recur with impunity;
- the gravity of the matter;
- the weight of evidence and degree of suspicion that fraud has occurred.

Acceptance of a duty to report to a proper authority when it is in the public interest to do so, represents a significant extension to the responsibility to report fraud previously acknowledged by auditors.[26] Prior to issuance of SAS 110, auditing standards in the UK interpreted public interest reporting as a right rather than a duty, and the reporting of fraud to anyone outside the entity was generally considered by auditors as likely to be perceived as a breach of their duty of confidentiality.

Since publication of SAS 110, the issue of auditors' responsibility for detecting and reporting fraud has remained high on the APB's list of priorities. In 1998 it published a Consultation Paper: *Fraud and audit: choices for society,* in which it reported that research it had undertaken had shown, *inter alia,* that most material frauds involve management; more than half of frauds involve misstated financial reporting (i.e. fraudulent financial reporting) but do not involve diversion of funds from the company (i.e. theft of company assets); and management fraud is unlikely to be found in a financial statement audit. (These findings coincide with those reported in the USA, and by Ernst & Young in the UK, noted above.) The APB also reported that 'a review of the effectiveness of new Auditing Standards on fraud [i.e. SAS 110] indicates that auditors have increased the emphasis they place on fraud in the course of their work' (p. 5). However, the APB further notes that, despite the steps taken by both the APB and audit firms to improve performance in this regard, there is a continuing gap between society's expectations of auditors and auditors' performance. It reports that although society expects auditors to find fraud, 'particularly when a fraud involves factors that threaten the entity's ability to continue in business . . . auditors cannot ensure that they will discover management fraud' (p. 15). It cites factors that hamper auditors in detecting fraud, for example:

---

[26] SAS 120: *Consideration of law and regulations* also imposes a duty on auditors to report to an appropriate authority when they encounter suspected or actual non-compliance with law and regulations relating to the preparation of, or disclosure of items in, the financial statements and it is in the public interest to so report.

- the nature of evidence[27] available to auditors which results in them rarely having sufficient evidence to resolve suspicions that fraud may have occurred;
- directors and senior management can over-ride the auditee's internal controls;
- external financial statements – and the audit thereof – focuses on the provision of a 'true and fair view' rather than on the incidence of fraud. Company law does not require directors or auditors to report on fraud discovered within an auditee;
- time constraints for publishing audited financial statements (which may result in severe consequences if delayed) can be exploited by auditees to discourage auditors from seeking evidence to resolve suspicions of fraud.

These are the 'inherent limitations' of an audit referred to in ISA 240, para 14 (noted above) that result in the possibility that a properly planned and performed audit will not detect material misstatements caused by fraud.

Notwithstanding these and other difficulties, the APB suggests ways in which auditors' performance in detecting corporate fraud might be brought more into line with public expectations. More specifically it suggests:

i) Auditing Standards might be changed, for example
- to increase the emphasis placed on professional scepticism[28]
- to introduce more specific requirements for particular types of evidence to be gathered or procedures to be performed;

ii) the auditor's role in detecting fraud within an entity might be extended by, for example:
- requiring auditors to report to boards of directors and audit committees on the adequacy of controls within the entity to prevent and detect fraud;
- encouraging the use of forensic fraud reviews based on an assessment of the risks of fraud that are inherent in an auditee;
- considering whether it would be beneficial to extend auditors' responsibility for reporting fraud – including suspected fraud. In this regard the APB explains:

  Auditors of regulated entities are normally required to report frauds. Current Auditing Standards require auditors of other entities who suspect fraud to report to an appropriate authority if they consider it necessary in the public interest. There may be benefit in reviewing these arrangements to determine whether auditors should report suspicions in a wider range of circumstances . . . (p. 27)

Although the APB has not (yet) revised SAS 110, the suggestions included in its Consultation Paper may well provide some insight into changes that might

---

[27] The concept of audit evidence is discussed in Chapter 3.

[28] The concept of professional scepticism is discussed in Chapter 3.

be forthcoming in the not-too-distant future – changes that seem all the more likely given the revision of ISA 240 (in 2001) and the issue of SAS 82 in the USA in 1997.

5.9.4 Aggressive earnings management

In 2001, the APB issued a further Consultation Paper: *Aggressive earnings management*. This seems to be linked to the research finding noted above, namely, 'more than half of frauds involved misstated[29] financial reporting . . .' (APB, 1998, p. 5) and the findings of research conducted in the USA, such as that by NERA (see section 5.9.2 above).

Aggressive earnings management is defined as:

> [A]ccounting practices including the selection of inappropriate accounting policies and/or unduly stretching judgments as to what is acceptable when forming accounting estimates. These practices, while presenting the financial performance of the compan[y] in a favourable light, [do] not necessarily reflect the underlying reality. (APB, 2001, paras 4–5)

The APB explains that as a result of, and in response to, commercial pressures (for example, to report earnings in line with the market's expectations, or to conform with legal and/or regulatory requirements to meet specific financial thresholds or ratios), a company may begin in a small legitimate way to ensure that it reports the 'desired results'. However, over time, manipulation of the financial statements may increase until it 'crosses the border of acceptability' (APB, 2001, p. 7). Thus 'aggressive earnings management' may be seen as a rung on the ladder leading to fraudulent financial reporting. An example of how aggressive earnings management can develop into 'unacceptable financial reporting' (as provided in the APB's Consultation Paper) is presented in Figure 5.6.

In its Consultation Paper, the APB asserts that it wishes auditors to be alert to, and respond to, the risk of aggressive earnings management, and reports that it will consider whether auditing standards need to be enhanced in order to ensure that auditors:

- better understand the pressures on directors and management to report a specific level of earnings;
- act with greater scepticism when circumstances are encountered that may be indicative of aggressive earnings management;

---

[29] The APB explains: 'Misstatements include (1) errors, (2) other inaccuracies (whether intentional or not), and (3) with regard to estimates and amounts dependent upon an exercise of judgment, unreasonable differences between (a) the amount intended to be included in the financial statements [by the directors] and (b) the auditors' assessment of what that amount should be based on the available audit evidence' (APB, 2001, p. 9).

Figure 5.6:   Example to demonstrate how legitimate business practices can develop into unacceptable financial reporting

Year ended 31 December XXXI

A listed manufacturing company has thrived in an economic expansion and announced a series of record-breaking results. Analysts believe earnings will continue their strong upward trend and have forecast the results for the year and the earnings per share to the penny. Shareholders see increased earnings producing an ever-higher share price.

Management perceives a slow-down in its business and is very concerned about the impact on the share price if the analysts' forecasts are not met. Departmental heads are told to pull out all the stops; targets are set; management will see missing the target as a failure. The pressure is on.

Being a manufacturing company, earnings are based on completed items shipped and invoiced. In this instance, for the earnings target to be met, overtime is authorised and worked to accelerate completions so that the necessary shipments are made, and invoices raised before the year-end.

Year ended 31 December XXX2

The analysts, seeing their forecast met by the company at December XXX1, project a further increase in the company's earnings in line with its record-breaking past. Management, believing, or hoping, that any slow-down will be temporary, issues departments with new targets to enable it to meet the analysts' forecast for the next year-end.

Unfortunately, the business slow-down turns out not to be temporary. Not only have completions and shipments failed to increase to meet the new forecast but some method has to be found to make up in this year for the sales and profit which were accelerated into the previous year. The pressure is now greater than at the previous year-end.

Overtime is again authorised to increase shipments but will not be enough to meet the target. To further stimulate sales the company announces a price discount that will apply to sales and shipments made in December. In addition to the continued efforts to accelerate shipments for completed goods, the provisions for bad debts, returns and warranty costs are also reduced. While individually each provision can be justified, each has been calculated on the basis of the most optimistic view of the ranges of possible outcomes. No disclosures are given in the financial statements, nor in the other information published with the financial statements, of the actions taken to stimulate sales or the fact that each provision is determined on the most optimistic basis.

Year ended 31 December XXX3

A year later the position has escalated out of control and many employees are now involved. In addition to all the actions taken in XXX2, goods are now being shipped on sale or return (without a provision for returns) and fictitious shipments are made close to the year-end on the basis of false documentation, both being designed to deceive the auditors.

At some point the 'balloon goes up', the police are called in and, inevitably, the cry goes up 'what were the directors doing and where were the auditors?'

Source: APB Consultation Paper: *Aggressive earnings management*

- take a more robust attitude with directors when seeking adjustments for misstatements identified by the audit; and
- communicate openly and frankly with those charged with the entity's governance – and, more particularly, with its audit committee (if it has one).[30]

By tackling 'aggressive earnings management' as soon as they suspect that an auditee may be engaging in it, auditors may well prevent their client from sliding down the slippery slope to cross the boundary between 'undesirable practices' and fraudulent financial reporting.

5.10 SUMMARY

In this chapter auditors' legal and professional duties have been reviewed. It has been shown that auditors' duties are derived from statute law, case law, professional promulgations and regulations. Statute law (primarily embodied in the Companies Act 1985, as amended by the Companies Act 1989) provides that (subject to certain exemptions) companies' financial statements are to be audited, and it sets out the administrative framework for the auditor's appointment, remuneration, rights, duties, resignation or removal. Statute law is silent on the standard expected of auditors in the performance of their statutory duties but case law provides guidance on what is required. Auditing standards issued by the APB in the UK, and the IAPC in the international arena, provide further and more detailed guidance to auditors on what is required of them when conducting an audit. When required by regulations, auditors' duties are usually defined very specifically but they only apply to the audits of entities within the jurisdiction of the relevant regulatory body.

In this chapter we have also discussed the three-way relationship between auditors, the client company and the company's shareholders, and emphasised that responsibility for a company's financial statements, lies with its directors and not with the auditors. The auditor's responsibility is limited to forming and expressing an opinion on the truth and fairness of the company's financial statements and their compliance (or otherwise) with relevant legislation. We have shown that the directors' and auditors' responsibilities are required to be spelt out clearly in the company's annual report and/or audit report.

Notwithstanding the explanation of auditors' responsibilities which is provided in each audit report, there is a gap between what society expects from auditors and what it perceives it receives from them (i.e. an audit expectation–

---

[30] SAS 610: *Communication of audit matters to those charged with governance* is discussed in Chapter 13.

performance gap). We have described the structure and composition of the gap as it existed in the UK in 2000 and we compared this with the composition of the gap that pertained in NZ in 1989. We reported that, although society appears to perceive that auditors' performance has improved quite markedly over the decade 1989–2000, its (unreasonable) expectations of auditors have grown to a greater extent. Thus, although the 'performance gap' has narrowed, this has been more than offset by a widening of the 'reasonableness gap'.

In the final section of the chapter we have examined the controversial issue of auditors' duties in relation to corporate fraud. We noted that auditors today acknowledge greater responsibility than they did 30 or so years ago to detect fraud and also to report detected or suspected fraud to an appropriate level of management within the entity. Further, in cases where fraud (or suspected fraud) is material to the financial statements, and is not appropriately dealt with in those financial statements, auditors are required to report this to share-holders by qualifying their audit report. Additionally, in the UK, when it is in the public interest to do so, auditors are required to report detected or suspected fraud to an appropriate authority.

We have also observed that, given the requirements of (revised) ISA 240 and SAS 82, together with statements made by the APB in Consultation Papers in 1998 and 2001, extension to auditors' responsibilities to detect and report fraud in the UK might be expected in the not-too-distant future.

SELF-REVIEW QUESTIONS

5.1 State the institutions which define the rights and responsibilities of auditors and the particular part played by each.
5.2 (a) State who may, and who may not, be appointed as an auditor of a company.
    (b) List those parties who may:
        (i) appoint the auditor,
        (ii) remove the auditor from office,
        and the circumstances in which these parties can exercise their rights.
5.3 List the items which the Companies Act 1985 requires auditors to include in their reports to shareholders.
5.4 State the fundamental standard required of auditors in the performance of their duties as laid down in the *Kingston Cotton Mill* case (1896).
5.5 Explain briefly:
    (i) the purpose of the profession's Auditing Standards;
    (ii) how Auditing Standards differ from Auditing Guidelines.

5.6 Explain the responsibilities of a company's:
   (i) directors; and
   (ii) its auditors,
   with respect to the company's financial statements.

5.7 Explain briefly what is meant by 'the audit expectation–performance gap' and describe its basic structure.

5.8 Distinguish briefly between the three types of corporate fraud.

5.9 The importance of detecting fraud as an audit objective has changed markedly over the period from 1844 to the present time. State the significance of fraud detection as an audit objective in each of the following periods:
   (i) 1844–1920s
   (ii) 1920s–1960s
   (iii) 1960s–1990s
   (iv) 1990s–present.
   List reasons to explain the change in the importance of fraud detection as an audit objective during each of these periods.

5.10 Describe briefly the changes to auditors' responsibilities in respect of detecting fraud:
   (i) introduced in (revised) ISA 240: *Fraud and error*;
   (ii) indicated in the APB's Consultative Papers: *Fraud and audit: choices for society* and *Aggressive earnings management*.

REFERENCES

Auditing Practices Board (APB) (1993a) The Auditing Practices Board. *Auditing and Reporting 2001/2002*, London: ICAEW, 5–6.

Auditing Practices Board (APB) (1993b) The scope and authority of APB pronouncements. *Auditing and Reporting 2001/2002*, London: ICAEW, 6–8.

Auditing Practices Board (APB) (1998) *Fraud and audit: choices for society.* Consultation Paper. London: APB.

Auditing Practices Board (APB) (2001) *Aggressive earnings management.* Consultation Paper. London: APB.

Beattie, A. (1989) Regulation of auditors; how will it affect you? *The Accountant's Magazine* **93**(999), 45.

Carty, J. (1985) Fraud and other irregularities. *Certified Accountant*, 30 September.

Chandler, R. & Edwards, J.R. (1996). Recurring issues in auditing: back to the future? *Accounting, Auditing & Accountability Journal* **9**(2), 4–29.

Commission on Auditors' Responsibilities (CAR) (1978) *Report, Conclusions and Recommendations* (The Cohen Commission). New York: AICPA.

Committee on the Financial Aspects of Corporate Governance (1992) *Report of the Committee on the Financial Aspects of Corporate Governance* (Cadbury Committee). London: Gee.

Committee on Corporate Governance (1998a) *Final Report of the Committee on Corporate Governance* (Hampel Committee). London: The London Stock Exchange Ltd.

Committee on Corporate Governance (1998b) *The Combined Code.* London: The London Stock Exchange Ltd.

Ernst & Young (2000) *Fraud, The Unmanaged Risk: An International Survey of the Effect of Fraud on Business.* London: Ernst & Young.

Kenley, W. J. (1971) Legal decisions affecting auditors. *The Australian Accountant* **41**(4), 153–161.

KPMG. (1997) *Fraud still costs the UK dear, despite lowest figures for seven years.* News release, 28 April.

KPMG. (2001) *Fraud case values decreased by two thirds during 2000, says KPMG's Fraud Barometer.* News release, 12 February.

Lee, T.A. & Tweedie, D.P. (1975) Accounting information: An investigation of private shareholder usage. *Accounting and Business Research* **5**(20), 289–291.

Limperg, T. (1932) *The Social Responsibility of the Auditor.* Reproduced in Limperg Instituut (1985). The Netherlands: Limperg Institute.

Porter, B.A. (1991) Narrowing the expectation–performance gap: A contemporary approach. *Pacific Accounting Review* **3**(1), 1–36.

Porter, B.A. (1993) An empirical study of the audit expectation–performance gap. *Accounting and Business Research* **24**(93), 49–68.

Porter, B.A. & Gowthorpe, C. (2001) *The audit expectation–performance gap: Some new evidence from the United Kingdom.* Paper presented at the National Auditing Conference, Leicester, March 2001.

Russell, G. (1986) All eyes on accountants. *Time* **58**, 21 April.

Smith, T. (1985) Expectation gap trips up fraud fight's 'front line'. *Accountancy Age*, 22 August, p. 10.

Study Group on Directors' Remuneration (1995) *Report of the Study Group on Directors' Remuneration* (Greenbury Committee). London: Gee.

Turner, L.E. (1999) *Remarks to the panel on audit effectiveness.* USA: New York, 7 October.

Turner, L.E. (2000) *Remarks to the panel on audit effectiveness.* USA: New York, 10 July.

Walker, R.H. (1999a) *Behind the numbers of the SEC's recent financial fraud cases.* Speech, 27th National AICPA Conference on Current SEC Developments, 7 December.

Walker, R.H. (1999b). *Remarks to the panel on audit effectiveness.* USA: New York, 9 October.

Woolf, E. (1978) Profession in peril – Time running out for auditors. *Accountancy* **89**(1014), 58–65.

ADDITIONAL READING

Beasley, M.S. (1996) An empirical analysis of the relation between the board of director composition and financial statement fraud. *The Accounting Review* **71**(4), 443–465.

Beattie, V. & Fearnley, S. (1993) Audit regulator dominance in the UK listed market. *Accountancy* **111**(1194), 71–73.

Bingham, A., Huntington, I. & Jones, M. (1996) *Taking Fraud Seriously.* London: Audit Faculty of the Institute of Chartered Accountants in England and Wales.

Bloomfield, R.J. (1997) Strategic dependence and the assessment of fraud risk: a laboratory study. *The Accounting Review* **72**(4), 517–538.

Bonner, S.E., Palmrose, Z. & Yound, S.M. (1998) Fraud type and auditor litigation: an analysis of SEC accounting and auditing enforcement releases. *The Accounting Review* **73**(4), 503–532.

Canadian Institute of Chartered Accountants (1978) *Report of the Special Committee to Examine the Role of the Auditor* (Adams Committee). Toronto: CICA.

Canadian Institute of Chartered Accountants (1988) *Report of the Commission to Study the Public's Expectations of Audits* (Macdonald Commission). Toronto: CICA.

DeFond, M. I. & Jiambalvo, J. (1993) Factors related to auditor–client disagreements over income-increasing accounting methods, *Contemporary Accounting Research* **9**(2), 415–431.

Deshumukh, A., Karim, K.E. & Siegel, P.H. (1998) An analysis of efficiency and effectiveness of auditing to detect management fraud: A signal detection theory approach. *International Journal of Auditing* **2**, 127–138.

Eining, M.M, Jones, D.R. & Loebbecke, J.K. (1997) Reliance on decision aids: an examination of auditors' assessment of management fraud. *Auditing: A Journal of Practice & Theory* **16**(2), 1–19.

Garcia Benau, M.A., Humphrey, C.G., Moizer, P. & Turley, W.S. (1993) Auditing expectations and performance in Spain and Britain: A comparative analysis. *International Journal of Accounting* **28**, 281–307.

Gloek, J.D. & Jager, H. (1993) *The Audit Expectation Gap in the Republic of South Africa*, Working Paper, School of Accountancy, University of Pretoria, South Africa.

Hirst, D.E. (1994) Auditor sensitivity to earnings management. *Contemporary Accounting Research* **11**(I-II), 405–422.

Hooks, K.L., Kaplan, S.E. & Schultz, Jr, J.J. (1994) Enhancing communication to assist in fraud prevention and detection. *Auditing: A Journal of Practice & Theory* **13**(2), 86–117.

Humphrey, C. (1997) Debating audit expectations. In M. Sherer and S. Turley (eds) *Current Issues in Auditing*, 3rd ed., Chapter 1. London: Paul Chapman Publishing.

Humphrey, C.G., Moizer, P. & Turley, W.S. (1992) The audit expectations gap – plus ça change, plus c'est la même chose. *Critical Perspectives on Accounting* **3**, May, 137–161.

Humphrey, C., Turley, S. & Moizer, P. (1993) Protecting against detection: The case of auditors and fraud? *Accounting, Auditing & Accountability Journal* **6**(1), 39–62.

Johnson, P.E., Grazioli, S. & Jamal, K. (1993) Fraud detection: Intentionality and deception in cognition. *Accounting Organization and Society* **18**(5), 467–488.

Jupe, R.E. & Rutherford, B.A. (1997) Watchdogs or straw dogs? A critical appraisal of the UK regulatory framework with respect to (non-)compliance with Financial Reporting Standard No. 1. *International Journal of Auditing* **1**(3), 205–223.

Knox, J. (1996) Prosecution for deception of auditors. *Accountancy* **117**(1232), 79.

Krull, Jr, G., Reckets, P.M.J. & Wong-On-Wing, B. (1993) The effect of experience, fraudulent signals and information presentation order on auditors' beliefs. *Auditing: A Journal of Practice & Theory* **12**(2), 143–153.

Land, N. (1995) The future of audit regulation, *Accountancy*. **116**(1223), 92.

Low, A.M., Foo, S.L. & Koh, H.C. (1988) The expectation gap between financial analysts and auditors – some empirical evidence. *Singapore Accountant* **4**, May, 10–13.

Martinis, M.D. & Kim, E. (2000) An examination of the audit expectation gap in Singapore. *Asian Review of Accounting* **8**(1), 59–82.

McAlpine, S. (1995) When fraudster and auditor meet. *Accountancy* **115**(1219), 100.

Mitchell, A. (1995) The Auditing Practices Board: an assessment. *Accountancy* **115**(1218), 76–77.

Porter, B.A. (1997) Auditors' responsibilities with respect to corporate fraud: A controversial issue. In M. Sherer and S. Turley (eds) *Current Issues in Auditing*, 3rd ed., Chapter 2. London: Paul Chapman Publishing.

Shelton, S.W., Whittington, O.R. & Landsitter, D. (2001) Auditing firms' fraud risk assessment practises. *Accounting Horizons* **15**(1), 19–33.

Sikka, P., Puxty, A, Willmott, H. & Cooper, C. (1998) The impossibility of eliminating the expectations gap: some theory and evidence. *Critical Perspectives on Accounting* **9**, 299–330.

Society of Certified Practising Accountants and The Institute of Chartered Accountants in Australia (1994) *A Research Study on Financial Reporting and Auditing – Bridging the Expectation Gap.* Melbourne: ASCPA, Sydney: ICAA.

Troberg, P. & Viitanen, J. (1999) *The Audit Expectation Gap in Finland in an International Perspective.* Research Report, Swedish School of Economics and Business Administration, Helsinki.

Woolf, E. (1996) A practical approach to standards. *Accountancy* **118**(1238), 80–81.

Woolf, E. & Hindson, M. (2000) Lessons in fraud. *Accountancy* **126**(1283), 128–129.

6 Overview of the Audit Process, Audit Evidence: Staffing and Documenting an Audit

LEARNING OBJECTIVES

After studying the material in this chapter you should be able to:
- outline the steps in the audit process from 'Appointment' to 'Reporting';
- list and describe audit procedures which are used to gather evidence;
- discuss the different sources of audit evidence;
- explain the factors which should be considered when deciding which audit evidence to seek;
- discuss the requirements with respect to auditors' competence;
- explain auditors' responsibilities when part of an audit is performed by other auditors and/or experts;
- explain the importance of auditors directing, supervising and reviewing the work of audit staff;
- discuss the purpose and importance of audit working papers;
- explain the importance of working paper review;
- discuss auditors' duty of confidentiality to their clients.

The following publications and fundamental principle of auditing are particularly relevant to this chapter:

Publications:
- Statement of Auditing Standards (SAS) 120: *Consideration of law and regulations* (APB, 1995).
- Statement of Auditing Standards (SAS) 230: *Working papers* (APB, 1995)
- Statement of Auditing Standards (SAS) 240: *Quality control for audit work* (APB, 2000)
- Statement of Auditing Standards (SAS) 400: *Audit evidence* (APB, 1995).
- Statement of Auditing Standards (SAS) 510: *The relationship between principal auditors and other auditors* (APB, 1995)
- Statement of Auditing Standards (SAS) 520: *Using the work of an expert* (APB, 1995)
- Guide to Professional Ethics Statement 5: *Confidentiality* (ICAEW, ICAS, ICAI; 1997)
- International Standard on Auditing (ISA): 220: *Quality control for audit work* (IFAC, 1994)
- International Standard on Auditing (ISA): 230: *Documentation* (IFAC, 1994)
- International Standard on Auditing (ISA): 250: *Consideration of laws and regulations in an audit of financial statement* (IFAC, 1994)
- International Standard on Auditing (ISA): 500: *Audit evidence* (IFAC, 1994)
- International Standard on Auditing (ISA): 600: *Using the work of another auditor* (IFAC, 1994)
- International Standard on Auditing (ISA): 620: *Using the work of an expert* (IFAC, 1994)

Fundamental principle of external auditing included in *The Auditor's Code* (APB, 1996)
Integrity

6.1   INTRODUCTION

It was shown in Chapter 5 that auditors are required, among other things, to form and express an opinion on whether or not their audit clients' financial statements provide a true and fair view of their financial position and performance. In order to form this opinion, auditors must gather and evaluate sufficient appropriate evidence. This evidence is collected through the audit process. Although the audit process is very similar in all audits, audit clients differ markedly in size, nature and complexity. In order to ensure that audits are conducted effectively and efficiently they must be carefully planned and controlled. This involves, *inter alia*, ensuring they are properly staffed and documented.[1]

In the next seven chapters of this book we describe and discuss the various stages of the audit process. However, in this chapter, we set the scene by providing a general overview. We also discuss important administrative aspects of an audit. More particularly, we examine the requirements with respect to the skills and competence an auditor must possess, the principal auditor's responsibilities when part of an audit is performed by other auditors or experts, and the importance of auditors directing, supervising and reviewing work delegated to audit staff.

We also consider the importance, purpose, content and preparation of audit working papers and discuss the process of working paper review. Before concluding the chapter we address the important, but sometimes rather controversial, issue of the auditor's duty of confidentiality to their clients.

6.2   OVERVIEW OF THE AUDIT PROCESS

As may be seen from Figure 6.1, the audit process comprises a series of logical well-defined steps and each step has a specific objective or purpose and is performed using appropriate audit procedures. In order to illustrate the relationship between the audit steps, their objectives, and the procedures used to achieve those objectives, we will refer to Step 3 of the audit process – 'Gain an understanding of the client, its activities and its circumstances' (see Figure 6.1).

What is the objective of this step? Why is it performed? It is performed so as to ensure the auditor understands events, transactions and practices of (or affecting) the auditee which may have a significant impact on its financial statements. The auditor needs this understanding, amongst other reasons:

---

[1]   As noted in Chapter 3, an important aspect of ensuring that audits are conducted effectively and efficiently is the implementation and operation of proper quality control policies and procedures. This issue is discussed in Chapter 15.

Figure 6.1: Summary of the audit process

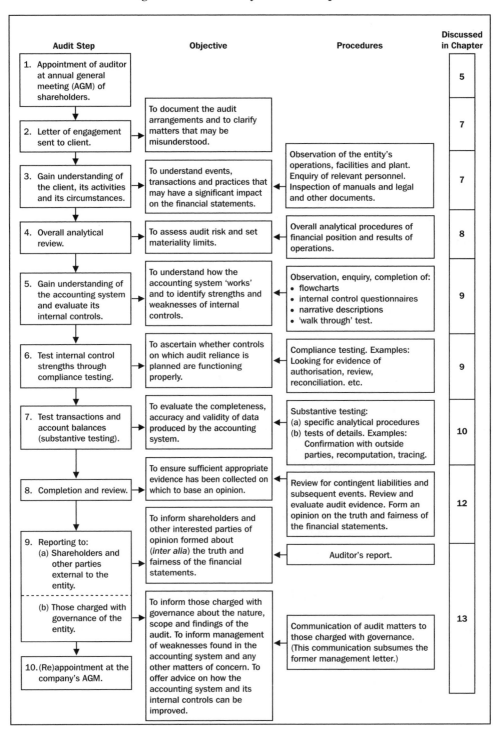

Audit Step	Objective	Procedures	Discussed in Chapter
1. Appointment of auditor at annual general meeting (AGM) of shareholders.			5
2. Letter of engagement sent to client.	To document the audit arrangements and to clarify matters that may be misunderstood.		7
3. Gain understanding of the client, its activities and its circumstances.	To understand events, transactions and practices that may have a significant impact on the financial statements.	Observation of the entity's operations, facilities and plant. Enquiry of relevant personnel. Inspection of manuals and legal and other documents.	7
4. Overall analytical review.	To assess audit risk and set materiality limits.	Overall analytical procedures of financial position and results of operations.	8
5. Gain understanding of the accounting system and evaluate its internal controls.	To understand how the accounting system 'works' and to identify strengths and weaknesses of internal controls.	Observation, enquiry, completion of: • flowcharts • internal control questionnaires • narrative descriptions • 'walk through' test.	9
6. Test internal control strengths through compliance testing.	To ascertain whether controls on which audit reliance is planned are functioning properly.	Compliance testing. Examples: Looking for evidence of authorisation, review, reconciliation. etc.	9
7. Test transactions and account balances (substantive testing).	To evaluate the completeness, accuracy and validity of data produced by the accounting system.	Substantive testing: (a) specific analytical procedures (b) tests of details. Examples: Confirmation with outside parties, recomputation, tracing.	10
8. Completion and review.	To ensure sufficient appropriate evidence has been collected on which to base an opinion.	Review for contingent liabilities and subsequent events. Review and evaluate audit evidence. Form an opinion on the truth and fairness of the financial statements.	12
9. Reporting to: (a) Shareholders and other parties external to the entity.	To inform shareholders and other interested parties of opinion formed about (*inter alia*) the truth and fairness of the financial statements.	Auditor's report.	
(b) Those charged with governance of the entity.	To inform those charged with governance about the nature, scope and findings of the audit. To inform management of weaknesses found in the accounting system and any other matters of concern. To offer advice on how the accounting system and its internal controls can be improved.	Communication of audit matters to those charged with governance. (This communication subsumes the former management letter.)	13
10. (Re)appointment at the company's AGM.			

- to ascertain whether there are circumstances which increase (or reduce) the likelihood of misstatements being present in the financial statements;
- to provide a background against which evidence gathered during the audit can be evaluated to see if it 'makes sense' and 'looks right'.

How is this objective achieved? Audit procedures used to gain this under-standing of the client include the following:

- Gathering information (from a very wide range of sources – including, for example, the internet, relevant trade magazines, making enquiries from relevant knowledgeable people) about the client's industry and its operating, economic, legislative and regulatory environment;
- Observing the client's operations, facilities and plant; i.e. visiting the client, touring the premises and meeting key personnel (for example, the managing director, financial director, marketing manager, sales manager, production manager, and personnel manager).
- Making enquiries of relevant personnel; i.e. discussing with key personnel matters such as the trading and financial position of the entity during the past year, and any significant changes in business, accounting or personnel policies and procedures which occurred during the year.
- Inspecting the entity's manuals and legal and other documents; i.e. reviewing the organisation's legal documents, policy and procedures manuals, minutes of directors' meetings or those of significant committees, and any important commercial agreements (for example, franchise agreements).

It should be noted that the summary of the audit process presented in Figure 6.1 is designed to give a general overview of the process. It is intended to pro-vide a contextual setting for the detailed discussion of the individual steps in the process which are the subject of Chapters 7 to 13 of this book. The chapter in which each step is considered is indicated in the rightmost column of Figure 6.1.

Before moving on to discuss the collection of evidence through the audit process, we will clarify the meaning of some troublesome jargon.

6.3 CLARIFICATION OF SOME JARGON

Considerable confusion seems to exist in relation to the terms 'audit objectives' and 'audit procedures'. This seems to stem from three main causes, namely:

(i)   failure to distinguish between audit objectives and audit procedures;
(ii) use of different terms to mean the same thing;
(iii) use of the single term 'audit objective' when separate levels of objectives exist.

(i)   Failure to distinguish between audit objectives and audit procedures: The term 'compliance tests' or 'compliance procedures' provides an example of this cause of misunderstanding. The term refers to audit procedures which are used to meet the objective of ascertaining whether entity personnel have complied with identified internal controls. The audit procedures adopted (such as enquiry) are not restricted to compliance testing: they are also used to meet other audit objectives. Thus the term 'compliance testing' does not denote a particular set of audit procedures; rather, it indicates the objective or purpose for which the procedures are employed.

(ii)   Use of different terms to mean the same thing: This cause of confusion may be illustrated by reference to the use, by different authors, of the terms 'audit procedures' 'audit tests', and 'audit techniques', to convey essentially the same meaning, that is, methods used to gather audit evidence. Indeed, the terms are frequently used interchangeably.

Similarly, as illustrated in Figure 6.3, different authors use different terms to refer to the same audit procedure. For example, Anderson (1977) uses the term 'vouching' to refer to the inspection of source documents, but Arens and Loebbecke (1991) and the APB's SAS 400: *Audit evidence* use the terms 'Documentation' and 'Inspection', respectively, for this audit procedure. (The various audit procedures are outlined in section 6.4.2 below.)

(iii)   Use of the single term 'audit objective' when separate levels of objectives exist: Notwithstanding use of the term 'audit objective', as shown in Figure 6.2 three distinct levels of audit objectives may be distinguished: the overall audit objective, general audit objectives and specific audit objectives.

An audit objective is the object of the auditor's investigation: it is what the auditor is trying to find out and the purpose for which audit procedures are performed. It is often helpful to express an audit objective in the form of a question.

From Figure 6.2 it can be seen that at the highest level is the overall audit objective. This is reflected in the question: Do the financial statements give a true and fair view of the entity's state of affairs and its profit or loss?

In order to answer this question, and thus accomplish the overall audit objective, further, more detailed, questions need to be asked. For example, do the financial statements comply with accounting standards? Have the entity's internal controls operated effectively throughout the reporting period? Is the amount shown in the financial statements for, say, sales or trade debtors fairly stated? Questions of this general nature reflect general audit objectives.

Figure 6.2: Hierarchy of audit objectives

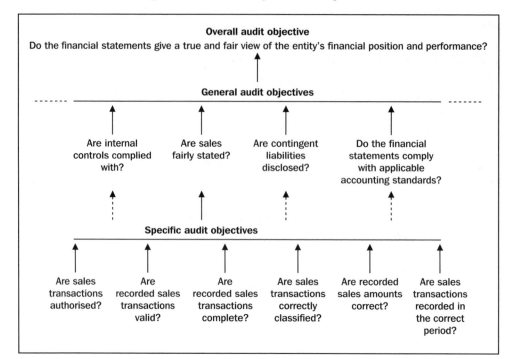

To accomplish these general objectives, even more specific questions need to be asked. These are expressions of the specific audit objectives. For example, to accomplish the general objective of ascertaining whether sales are fairly stated in the financial statements, the auditor needs to determine whether:

- sales transactions have been properly authorised;
- recorded sales transactions are valid;
- all valid sales transactions have been recorded;
- sales transactions have been properly classified;
- sales transactions have been recorded at their proper amount;
- sales transactions have been recorded in their proper accounting period.

Each of these factors constitutes a specific audit objective.

6.4   AUDIT EVIDENCE

6.4.1   General requirement

As auditors proceed through the audit process, they accumulate audit evidence to meet specific audit objectives and thereby form conclusions about the related general audit objectives. Eventually, they will have sufficient appropriate audit evidence to support their opinion as to whether or not the financial statements provide a true and fair view of the entity's financial position and performance. As discussed in Chapter 3 (section 3.4.1), SAS 400: *Audit evidence* requires the auditor to:

> [O]btain sufficient appropriate audit evidence to be able to draw reasonable conclusions on which to base the audit opinion (para 2).

6.4.2 Audit procedures

Audit procedures are the methods used to gather audit evidence. As noted above, the terms 'audit tests' and 'audit techniques' are frequently used in place of, or interchangeably with, 'audit procedures' and different terms are used by different authors for the same procedure. Figure 6.3 shows the relationship between the terms used for audit procedures by Anderson (1977), Arens and Loebbecke (1991), SAS 400: *Audit evidence* (APB, 1995) and ISA 500: *Audit evidence* (IAPC, 1994).

The APB defines the terms used in SAS 400 as follows (paras 20 to 25).[2]

Inspection

20. Inspection consists of examining records, documents or tangible assets. Inspection of records and documents provides audit evidence of varying degrees of reliability depending on their nature and source and the effectiveness of internal controls over their processing.

    Three major categories of documentary audit evidence, listed in descending degree of reliability as audit evidence, are evidence:

    a) created and provided to auditors by third parties;

    b) created by third parties and held by the entity; and

    c) created and held by the entity.

    Inspection of tangible assets provides reliable audit evidence about their existence but not necessarily as to their ownership or value.

Observation

21. Observation consists of looking at a process or procedure being performed by others, for example the observation by auditors of the counting of stock [inventories] by the entity's staff or the performance of internal control procedures, in particular those that leave no audit trail.

Enquiry and confirmation

22. Enquiry consists of seeking information of knowledgeable persons inside or outside the entity. Enquiries may range from formal written enquiries addressed to third parties to informal oral enquiries addressed to persons

---

[2] With the exception of 'analytical procedures', the definitions in ISA 500: *Audit evidence* (IAPC, 1994) (paras 20–25) are virtually the same as those in SAS 400: *Audit evidence* (paras 20–25). ISA 500 defines analytical procedures as follows:

> Analytical procedures consist of the analysis of significant ratios and trends including the resulting investigation of fluctuations and relationships that are inconsistent with other relevant information or deviate from predicted amounts.

Figure 6.3: Different terms for the same audit procedure

Anderson (1977)	Arens and Loebbecke (1991)	SAS 400 (APB 1995) and ISA 500 (IAPC 1994)
Enquiry	Enquiry	Enquiry
Confirmation	Confirmation	Confirmation
Reperformance (of accounting routines)	Mechanical accuracy	Computation
Vouching (of source documents)	Documentation	Inspection
Physical examination (of assets)	Physical examination	Inspection
Inspection (of other documents)	Observation	Observation
Observation (of activities)	Observation	Observation
Scrutiny of accounting records	Analytical procedures	Analytical procedures
Analysis (into components)	Analytical procedures	Analytical procedures

inside the entity. Responses to enquiries may provide auditors with information not previously possessed or with corroborative audit evidence.

23. Confirmation consists of the response to an enquiry to corroborate information contained in the accounting records. For example, auditors may seek direct confirmation of debts by communication with debtors.

Computation

24. Computation consists of checking the arithmetical accuracy of source documents and accounting records or performing independent calculations.

Analytical procedures

25. Analytical procedures consist of the analysis of relationships between items of financial data, or between items of financial and non-financial data, deriving from the same period, or between comparable financial information deriving from different periods or different entities, to identify consistencies and predicted patterns or significant fluctuations and unexpected relationships, and the results of investigations thereof.

6.4.3 Further clarification of the jargon

Those first encountering auditing jargon frequently find the distinction and relationship between (a) compliance and substantive procedures, and (b) between tests of details, tests of transactions and tests of balances far from clear. The relationship between these terms and some specific audit procedures, is depicted in Figure 6.4.

Figure 6.4: Relationship between compliance and substantive procedures, tests of detail, tests of transactions and tests of balances

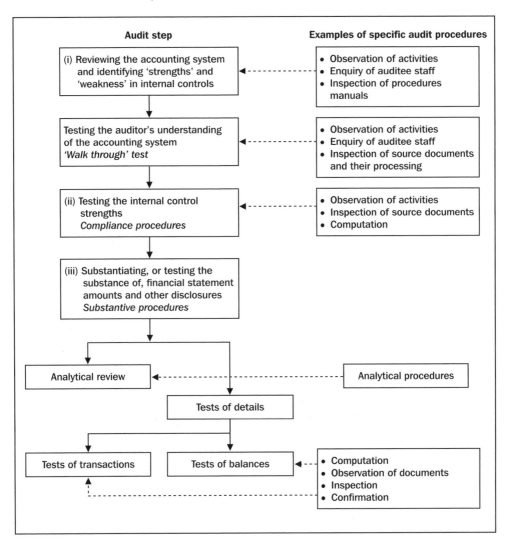

(a) *Compliance vs substantive procedures*

In order to form an opinion as to whether or not the financial statements under audit give a true and fair view of the auditee's financial position and performance, the auditor needs to establish, amongst other things, whether each financial statement amount and disclosure is fairly stated (i.e. not materially misstated).

Auditors can reduce their work in determining whether each financial state-ment amount and disclosure is fairly stated if they can assure themselves that the auditee's business processes and, particularly, its accounting system incorporates effective internal controls which can be relied on to prevent and/or detect errors and irregularities in the accounting data. If such internal controls are in place and working effectively, the auditor can feel reasonably assured that the accounting data passing through the system and presented in the financial statements is reliable and accurate.

Thus, an audit includes the following three distinct steps:

(i) *A review of the accounting system* [see Figure 6.4(i)]: This review is undertaken for two main purposes, namely:

(a) to enable the auditor to understand how the accounting system captures and processes the accounting data, and how it converts the data into the information which is presented in the entity's financial statements;

(b) to identify the system's 'strengths' and 'weaknesses', that is, internal controls which, if operating properly, can be relied upon to prevent and/or detect errors and irregularities in the accounting data (strengths), and internal controls which are needed, but which are absent or ineffective (weaknesses).

In order to ensure the auditor has a proper understanding of the accounting system and its internal controls, a 'walk through' test is conducted. This test consists of following one or two transactions through the entire accounting system - from their initial recording on source documents to their final inclusion in the financial statements.

(ii) *Testing internal control 'strengths'* [see Figure 6.4(ii)]: As noted above, during the initial review of the accounting system, the auditor identifies internal control 'strengths'. These controls, if operating properly, will help to ensure that the data which passes through the accounting system is complete, valid, and accurate as to amount, account classification and reporting period. However, before the auditor can rely on these internal controls to protect the integrity of the accounting data, they must be tested to establish that they are, in fact, operating effectively and that they have been so operating throughout the reporting period. Such tests are referred to as compliance procedures (or tests of control): they are tests or procedures which are performed in order to ascertain whether the internal controls on which the auditor plans to rely have been complied with by personnel within the reporting entity.[3]

(iii) *Testing the financial statement amounts and other disclosures* [see Figure 6.4(iii)]: The auditor is required to form and express an opinion on the truth and fairness of the financial statements rather than on the internal controls. Therefore, irrespective of how effective an entity's internal

---

[3] Compliance procedures are discussed in Chapter 9.

controls may appear to be, tests must always be performed to substantiate, or to test the substance of, the information presented in the financial statements. Such tests are referred to as substantive procedures.[4]

The relationship between the results of compliance procedures (or testing) and substantive procedures is reflected in SAS 400: *Audit evidence,* para 14:

Where tests of control provide satisfactory evidence as to the effectiveness of accounting and internal control systems, the extent of relevant substantive procedures may be reduced, but not entirely eliminated.

(b) *Tests of detail, tests of transactions and tests of balances*

Substantive procedures fall into two broad categories:

(i)   analytical procedures;
(ii) tests of details.

(i)   *Analytical procedures* analyse meaningful relationships between accounting data (and also between financial and non-financial data) in order to establish the 'reasonableness' of financial statement amounts. For example, the relationship between average debt and average interest rates can be used to provide an estimate of an entity's interest expense. If, based on this estimate, the interest expense looks 'reasonable', this may be the extent of the audit tests conducted to substantiate this balance. If, however, there is a marked discrepancy between the estimated amount and the financial statement amount, this discrepancy will need to be investigated.

(ii) *Tests of details:* Two subsets of tests of details may be distinguished, namely, tests of transactions and tests of balances.

(a) *Tests of transactions* are audit tests or procedures which are applied to transactions, or rather, to the source documents which provide evidence of the transactions. Transaction testing is normally used to substantiate revenue and expense account balances in the profit and loss account (income statement), however, it may also be used to substantiate (indirectly) balance sheet account balances. This is because, if the opening balance of a particular balance sheet account is accurate (substantiated by the previous year's audit) and all of the transactions affecting that account during the reporting period are complete, accurate and valid, then the balance shown in the closing balance sheet must also be correct.

(b) *Tests of balances* are audit tests or procedures which, rather than testing the transactions which constitute particular financial statement

[4] Substantive procedures are discussed in detail in Chapter 10.

balances, directly test the completeness, accuracy and validity of the balances themselves. An example is debtors' confirmation, where the auditor writes to an entity's debtors requesting them to confirm their outstanding account balance with the audit client.

In relation to tests of transactions, it is important to note that source documents used to substantiate the completeness, accuracy and validity of transactions may also be used for compliance tests. For example, a customer order and a despatch note may be used to substantiate the validity of a sale (a substantive test). The same source documents might also be examined for evidence indicating that an internal control, designed to ensure that despatches are only made against customer orders, has been complied with (that is, for compliance testing).

6.4.4 Different sources and types of audit evidence

It was noted in Chapter 3 that auditors generally examine only part of the evidence available to them. They may select evidence from different sources and of different types. Which evidence they decide to collect depends on a number of factors, in particular, its relevance, reliability, availability, timeliness and cost.

- *Relevance of evidence* refers to how closely the evidence relates to the particular objective the auditor is trying to accomplish. For example, observation is a useful procedure for verifying the existence, but not the ownership, of stock. To establish ownership, relevant purchase (or similar) documents need to be scrutinised.
- *Reliability of evidence* refers to how confident the auditor is that the evidence reflects the facts of the matter being investigated. For example, the auditor can have greater confidence in bank reconciliations (s)he has performed personally, than in assurances from client personnel that the entity's bank statements and bank balances have been reconciled. Similarly, as SAS 400: *Audit evidence* points out:
  > Evidence in the form of documents and written representations is more reliable than oral representations, and original documents are more reliable than photocopies, telexes and facsimiles. (para 16)
- *Availability* of evidence refers to how readily the auditor can acquire the evidence. For example, the auditor has ready access to the client's accounting records – including the balances of individual trade debtors. Evidence of these balances, obtained by confirming them with the individuals concerned, is less readily available.
- *Timeliness* of evidence refers to how quickly the evidence can be obtained. For example, the auditor may be aware that the amount of a contingent

liability arising from disputed tax will be clarified when the case is heard by the relevant taxation authority. However, if the case is to be deferred for some months, the auditor may decide to forgo that evidence. If audited financial statements are to be useful to external parties interested in the reporting entity, they must be made available – and hence the audit must be completed – on a timely basis.

- *Cost* of evidence. The auditor generally has a choice of evidence which may be used to establish, for example, whether internal controls have been complied with or financial statement amounts are fairly stated. Therefore, the cost of obtaining particular evidence should be weighed against its benefits; that is, the contribution the evidence may make towards the auditor forming an opinion about the degree of compliance with the internal controls, or the truth and fairness of the financial statement amounts, under investigation.

Reviewing the above factors it may be seen that, with the exception of relevance, they are all affected by the source from which the evidence is derived. As is shown in Figure 6.5, audit evidence may be obtained from three sources:

(i)   direct personal knowledge;
(ii) sources external to the client;
(iii) sources internal to the client.

Evidence obtained by direct personal knowledge is the most reliable evidence. It is generally readily available on a timely basis, but it is very costly to acquire. At the other extreme, evidence obtained from sources internal to the client is the least reliable, but it is generally readily available on a timely basis and is the least costly evidence to obtain. Evidence derived from sources external to the client has an intermediate placing in terms of reliability and cost, but is frequently less readily available and is less timely to acquire than evidence obtained from the other two sources (see Figure 6.5).

SAS 400: *Audit evidence* (and ISA 500, para 2) requires auditors to 'obtain sufficient appropriate evidence to be able to draw reasonable conclusions on which to base the audit opinion' (SAS 400, para 2). SAS 400 (para 6) and ISA 500 (para 9) go on to explain that what amounts to sufficient appropriate evidence in any particular case is influenced by a number of factors. These include the following:

- the assessment of the nature and degree of risk of misstatement at both the financial statement level and the account balance or class of transactions level;

Figure 6.5: **Sources of evidence and accompanying characteristics**

	Sources of evidence		
	Direct personal knowledge	**External to the client**	**Internal to the client**
Examples	• *Observation* • *Computation*	• *Confirmation from third parties* • *Documents (e.g. invoices) from third parties*	• *Accounting records* • *Responses to enquiries by auditee personnel*
Characteristics of evidence			
Reliability	High level of reliability	High to medium level of reliability	Low level of reliability
Availability	Readily available	Less readily available	Readily available
Timeliness	Available on a timely basis	May not be available on a timely basis	Available on a timely basis
Cost	High cost	High to medium cost	Low cost

- the nature of the accounting and internal control systems, including the control environment;
- the materiality of the item being examined;
- the experience gained during previous audits and the auditors' knowledge of the business and industry;
- the findings from audit procedures, and from any audit work carried out in the course of preparing the financial statements, including indications of fraud or error; and
- the source and reliability of information available.

Notwithstanding that the factors indicated above (and other similar factors) affect what amounts to 'sufficient appropriate evidence' in particular cases, for any given set of circumstances there is a trade-off between the quantity of evidence that is required (its sufficiency) and its relevance and reliability (its appropriateness). The greater the relevance and reliability of evidence, the less that is needed to enable the auditor to form an opinion about the truth and fairness of the financial statements. This trade-off is depicted in Figure 6.6. All points on the curve represent combinations of quantity and quality of evidence which meet the 'sufficient appropriate' requirement of SAS 400. The particular combination the auditor selects will be affected by consideration of factors such as availability, timeliness, and cost of the evidence. The auditor will seek the combination which will provide a sufficient amount of reliable evidence,

Figure 6.6:   Sufficient appropriate evidence trade-off

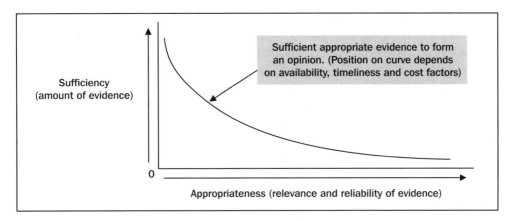

relevant to the objective under investigation, within a reasonable time – at the lowest possible total cost.

6.5   STAFFING AN AUDIT

Having discussed the meaning and some important aspects of audit evidence, we need to consider who actually collects this evidence. Although 'the auditor' is the person responsible for the audit, an audit team (varying from two or three to about 20 people – depending on the size, complexity and specific circumstances of the audit) is usually involved in collecting the audit evidence.

When considering audit teams we need to distinguish between three categories of audit personnel, namely:

- *the auditor (or audit engagement partner)*: This is the person who is responsible for the audit and who signs the audit report;
- *audit staff*: These are the professional staff members employed by the audit firm who assist on the audit. They range from new entrants to the firm (trainees) to highly experienced audit managers;
- *other auditors and experts*: These are auditors and experts from outside the audit firm who, for a variety of reasons, may be employed by the audit engagement partner to perform some part(s) of the audit.

In order for an audit to be performed effectively and efficiently, it is essential that:

(i)   it is adequately staffed by personnel who possess the skills and competence required for the tasks to be performed, and

(ii)   any work assigned to audit staff is properly directed, supervised and reviewed.

(i)   Requirements with respect to skills and competence

In order to perform an audit to the expected standard, an audit team – and members comprising the team – must possess the necessary skills and competence. SAS 240: *Quality control for audit work* requires audit firms to ensure they have sufficient audit engagement partners and audit staff with the competencies necessary to meet their needs (SAS 240, para 24). Further, before accepting an audit engagement, audit firms are required to ensure they are competent to undertake the work involved [SAS 240, para 15(a)]. This does not mean that audit partners and staff must possess all of the skills and competencies required for all audits, particularly if these are of a highly specialised or technical nature. However, where a firm lacks the particular skills and/or competencies required to complete an audit satisfactorily, it should ensure it can – and does – acquire the required advice or assistance from outside the firm. For example, if the audit firm lacks the competence needed to perform part of an audit, technical advice may be sought from experts such as lawyers, actuaries, engineers and valuers. This would probably apply, for example, in an audit of a company specialising in jewellery. If the audit firm lacks the competence to evaluate the company's valuation of, say, its stocks of diamonds, the auditor may (indeed, should!) seek assistance from a jewellery valuation expert. If the firm does not possess, and cannot acquire, the necessary skills and/or competence to perform or complete a particular audit to the required standard, the audit engagement should be declined or discontinued (as applicable).

It should be noted that, under SAS 520: *Using the work of an expert* (para 1), when an auditor seeks advice or assistance from an expert, the auditor remains responsible for all aspects of the audit. It is incumbent upon the auditor to be satisfied that the expert possesses the required degree of skill and competence to perform the task in question, and to obtain reasonable assurance that the work is performed to the appropriate standard. More specifically, SAS 520 requires the auditor:

- to be satisfied that the expert is properly qualified. Evidence of this may be obtained, for example, through professional certification, licensing by, or membership of, an appropriate professional body, and/or through the expert's experience and reputation in the field (para 11);
- to be satisfied that no relationship exists between the expert and the client such that the objectivity of the expert is likely to be impaired (para 12);
- to be reasonably assured that the expert's work constitutes appropriate audit evidence for the financial statement assertion being considered. Such assurance should be gained by considering:
  - the source data used by the expert;
  - the assumptions and methods used by the expert;
  - when the expert carried out the work;

- the reasons for any changes in the expert's assumptions and methods compared with those used in the prior period;
- the results of the expert's work in the light of the auditor's overall knowledge of the business and the results of other audit procedures (para 17).

Similar conditions apply when an auditor relies upon the work of another auditor. This may arise, for example, when a branch, division or subsidiary of the audit client is located at a distant geographical location and the auditor relies on another auditor to gather evidence in relation to that branch, division or subsidiary. (SAS 510: *The relationship between principal auditors and other auditors* deals with this issue.)

In addition to audit firms possessing, or acquiring (from outside the firm), sufficient competent personnel to complete their audit engagements, it is essential that they assign their audit staff appropriately to audits according to the work they will be required to do. As noted in Chapter 3 (section 3.3.2), SAS 240 specifies that audit staff with the competencies necessary to perform the audit work expected of them are to be assigned to individual audit engagements (SAS 240, para 31).[5]

(ii)   Directing, supervising and reviewing the work of audit staff

Audit work must not only be appropriately assigned to audit staff members, it must also be 'directed, supervised and reviewed in a manner that provides reasonable assurance that the work has been performed competently' (SAS 240, para 49).

SAS 240 explains that 'direction' means more than merely informing audit staff of their responsibilities and tasks to be performed. It also involves providing them with background information about both the client and the audit so that they can understand the importance and context of the audit procedures they are asked to perform. Audit staff should, for example, be provided with information about the nature of the entity's business, accounting or auditing problems that may arise, and the overall audit plan (SAS 240, para 50). The Standard makes particular reference to the importance of junior audit staff understanding the objectives of the work they are to perform – because such staff 'possess limited audit experience and may draw inappropriate conclusions as a result of misunderstandings' (para 51).

---

[5] ISA 220: *Quality control for audit work* has similar requirements to SAS 240 as regards the staffing of audits. It states:

The firm is to be staffed by personnel who have attained and maintain the Technical Standards and Professional Competence required to enable them to fulfil their responsibilities with Due Care. [para 6(b)]

Audit work is to be assigned to personnel who have the degree of technical training and proficiency required in the circumstances. [para 6(c)]

With respect to supervision of audit work, SAS 240 (para 53) notes that this includes:

(a) considering [monitoring] the progress of the audit;
(b) considering whether audit staff have the competencies necessary to perform the audit work expected of them and sufficient time to carry out their work, whether they understand their instructions and whether the work is being carried out in accordance with the overall audit plan and audit programme;
(c) addressing significant accounting and auditing questions raised during the audit, assessing their significance and modifying the overall audit plan and audit programme as appropriate; and
(d) identifying matters for further consideration during the audit.

As regards the review of audit work, SAS 240 specifies that work performed by audit staff is to be reviewed by other more senior audit staff or the engagement partner (para 54).[6] The reviewers are to consider, amongst other things, whether:

(i)   the work has been performed in accordance with the audit firm's (quality control) procedures and the audit programme;
(ii) the objectives of audit procedures have been met, the work performed is adequate in the light of the results obtained from the audit procedures, and conclusions reached are consistent with the results;
(iii) significant audit matters have been raised for further consideration; and
(iv) the audit work performed, results obtained and conclusions reached are adequately documented.

The review of audit work by more senior audit staff is not a remote and post-event process. Rather, those who have performed the work discuss it, upon completion, directly with the more senior audit team member. This enables the reviewer to question the more junior staff member about the work performed and results obtained – and this, in turn, enables any audit issues to be identified and followed up on a timely basis. It also facilitates developing the skills of, and providing training for, the more junior staff member.

The provisions of SAS 240 relating to audit staff are clearly very important. If an audit is to be conducted effectively, efficiently and with due professional care but much (most) of the work is to be performed by audit staff, it is essential that care is taken to ensure that work delegated to audit staff:

• is within their skills and competence to perform; and
• is carefully directed, supervised and reviewed.

---

[6] In addition to ensuring the work performed by audit staff is properly reviewed, the audit engagement partner is responsible for conducting an overall review of the audit working papers (SAS 240, para 55). Further details of this aspect of the review of audit work are provided in footnote 12 and discussed in Chapter 15, section 15.2.2.

If these responsibilities are not discharged properly, the audit is in danger of being performed inadequately and the door may be opened to allegations of negligence.

6.6 DOCUMENTING AN AUDIT

6.6.1 Definition, purpose and importance of audit working papers

It was noted in section 6.5 above that one of the matters reviewers of audit work are to consider is whether audit work performed, results obtained and conclusions reached are all adequately documented. It is essential that audit work is fully and properly documented in audit working papers. As SAS 230: *Working papers* indicates, such documentation provides evidence that the audit has been conducted in accordance with Auditing Standards (para 3).

SAS 230 explains (paras 3–4) that audit working papers are records, in written or electronic form, which are prepared or obtained (and retained) by auditors in order to provide a record of:

- the planning, performance, supervision and review of audit work, and
- the evidence resulting from audit work performed which supports the opinion expressed in the audit report.

Working papers should contain all of the information auditors consider relevant to their audits – including their 'reasoning on all significant matters which require the exercise of judgment, and their conclusions thereon' (SAS 230, para 6). However, the Standard observes:

> The extent of working papers is a matter of professional judgment since it is neither necessary nor practical to document every matter auditors consider. Auditors base their judgment as to the extent of working papers upon what would be necessary to provide an experienced auditor, with no previous connection with the audit, with an understanding of the work performed and the basis of the decisions taken. (para 7)

The primary purpose of audit working papers is to provide evidence that work performed during the audit, the results obtained, and the conclusions reached, all accord with Auditing Standards. However, they also serve other more specific purposes. For example, they provide:

(i) *a basis for planning the audit*: Records of preliminary discussions with the client, notes relating to the assessment of audit risk and the setting of materiality limits, and other similar documentation, provide a basis for planning the nature, timing and extent of audit procedures to be performed;

(ii) *a basis for performing the audit*: The audit programme (an important working paper) provides directions on the audit procedures to be performed. Other documents provide evidence of procedures already completed and conclusions reached based on the results of those procedures. Additionally, the audit working papers include notes on any particular matters audit staff need to consider or accommodate when performing certain procedures listed in the audit programme;

(iii) *a basis for reviewing work done and evidence gathered*: The audit working papers provide a record of work done by audit staff in relation to particular audit objectives. They therefore provide a means of assessing the adequacy of work performed, the quality of results obtained, and the validity of conclusions reached;

(iv) *a means of supervising more junior members of the audit team:* This purpose of audit working papers is closely related to that outlined in (iii) above. Because audit working papers record audit procedures to be performed and audit work completed, they enable personnel responsible for supervising the work of more junior members of the audit team to monitor and assess the work performed by their subordinates;

(v) *an aid to planning subsequent audits*: The findings of previous audits, as recorded in the audit working papers, provide a good basis from which to begin the initial planning of a subsequent audit.

6.6.2   Form and content of audit working papers

The form and content of audit working papers vary from audit to audit, reflecting such things as the size, nature and complexity of the client's activities; the nature and quality of the client's record-keeping, accounting system and internal controls; and the needs of audit team members for direction, supervision and review of audit work (SAS 230, para 10). Nevertheless, certain documents are present in virtually every audit and these are arranged logically in either the permanent file or the current file.

(i)   The permanent audit file

As Figure 6.7 indicates, the permanent audit file contains documents of a 'permanent' nature which are required in every audit of the client. Typical permanent audit file documents include the following:

(a) *Legal documents* – extracts or copies of legal documents such as the entity's Memorandum and Articles of Association, contracts (including, for example, pension plans and leases), agreements (such as loan agreements), and debenture deeds. A copy of the audit engagement letter is also frequently kept in this section of the audit file.

(b) *General information about the client's industry, business and operations* – information relating to the auditee's industry; its business, economic, legislative and regulatory environment; its historical development; and its

Figure 6.7: Form and content of audit working papers

Permanent audit file   **Examples of content**

• Legal documents
• General information about the client's industry, business and operations
• Administrative details of the client
• Information about the client's business processes and its procedures for identifying, evaluating and managing its risks
• Information about the client's accounting systems and internal controls
• Information relating to audit risk and materiality limits in previous audits
• Accounts of continuing interest

Current audit file

• Current year's financial statements
• General information relating to the current year
• Planning memoranda
• Audit programme
• Difficult issues and issues still to be resolved
• Summary of adjustments and reclassifications
• Working trial balance
• Supporting schedules (grouped to reflect financial statement categories, i.e. revenues, direct costs, indirect expenses, current assets, fixed assets, etc.)

present organisational and operational structure. This information includes details of the company's board of directors and board committees, details of any subsidiaries, divisions or departments (their geographical location, size, principal products, etc.), and details of key suppliers, customers, competitors, bankers, solicitors, etc.

(c) *Administrative details of the client* – documents reflecting the client's administrative structure, for example, its organisation chart, chart of accounts, policies and procedures manuals, job descriptions.

(d) *Business processes and risks* – information gathered during previous audits about the auditee's business processes and its procedures for identifying, evaluating and managing its business, financial, operational and other risks.

(e) *Accounting systems and internal controls* – information relating to the client's accounting systems and internal controls, including flowcharts, internal control evaluations and narrative descriptions, completed during previous audits. Also, notes made in previous audits about strengths and weaknesses identified in the internal controls, and copies of management letters sent to the client's directors, audit committee and/or senior executives.[7]

(f) *Information on audit risk and materiality limits* – the results of analytical review and other information relating to the assessment of audit risk and setting of materiality limits in previous audits.

(g) *Accounts of continuing interest* – analyses from previous audits of accounts that are of continuing importance to the auditor. These include shareholders' equity accounts, long-term liabilities, tangible and intangible fixed assets.

(ii)   The current audit file

As may be seen from Figure 6.7, the current audit file (which is usually in electronic form, accessible to all members of the audit team) contains information pertaining to the current year's audit. It includes documents such as:

(a) *The financial statements under examination.*

(b) *General information* – information of a general nature relating to the current year's audit. This includes, for example, notes on discussions with the client about business, financial, operational and other matters which have occurred during the reporting period; abstracts or copies of directors' (and similar) meetings; abstracts or copies of contracts or agreements not included in the permanent file; and comments on the current year's evaluation of the auditee's internal controls and risk management procedures.

(c) *Planning memoranda relating to the current audit* – notes on audit team planning meetings where matters such as relevant features of the audit client (its industry, business, operations, and organisation), the audit strategy, matters of particular audit interest or concern, and the planned nature, timing and extent of audit tests are discussed.[8]

(d) *The audit programme* – a list of the audit procedures to be performed. As the audit progresses, each staff member performing a procedure initials and dates the audit programme to indicate that the procedure has been completed.

(e) *Difficult and unresolved issues* – comments arising from the review of working papers and conclusions reached in relation to various segments of the audit and, more particularly, notes on:

(i)   difficult issues which have arisen during the audit and how they have been resolved, and

(ii) issues remaining to be resolved prior to completion of the audit.

---

[7] Internal controls, and audit documents relating thereto, are discussed in Chapter 9. Management letters are discussed in Chapter 13.

[8] Planning the audit (and planning memoranda) are discussed in Chapter 8.

(f) *Summary of adjusting and reclassification entries* – as the audit proceeds, audit team members almost invariably encounter accounting entries which require correction as to amount or classification – for example, a direct payment into the client's bank account by a credit customer on balance sheet date may not have been recorded as a receipt in the current period, or office equipment purchased during the year may have been recorded as 'repairs and maintenance' instead of 'office equipment'. All errors discovered during the audit which require adjustment or reclassification are recorded on a summary schedule. Such a summary enables the engagement partner (or another senior member of the audit team) to assess at a glance the significance of individual errors, and the cumulative effect of errors, in relation to the financial statements as a whole and the affected components thereof, such as net or gross profit, current assets, long-term liabilities, etc.

Although the audit team will find and note errors as the audit progresses, no adjustments to the client's ledger accounts or financial statements can be made without the consent of the client's directors. As noted in Chapter 5, maintaining the accounting records and preparing the financial statements are the responsibility of the directors. The auditor will request the directors to effect adjusting entries to correct errors discovered during the audit. In many cases no difficulty is encountered and the directors approve the changes. If the directors refuse to correct what the auditor considers to be a material error, the auditor will have little choice but to issue a qualified audit report. (This type of report is discussed in Chapter 13.)

(g) *Working trial balance:* Usually, as soon as possible after balance sheet date, the auditor obtains or prepares a list of general ledger accounts and their year-end balances. This is known as a working trial balance.

Frequently, the working trial balance is in the form of a list of balances which appear in the financial statements. Each line of the trial balance is supported by a lead schedule. This lists the general ledger accounts (and their balances) which constitute the relevant financial statement balance. (For example, the 'Cash' balance in the financial statements may comprise petty cash and a number of current and deposit account balances held at a number of banks – possibly in different currencies in different countries.)

Each significant account shown in the lead schedule is, in turn, supported by detailed working papers. These show the audit work performed in relation to the account in question, the results obtained, and the conclusion reached as regards the validity (or otherwise) of the account balance.

The relationship between the financial statements, the working trial balance, the lead schedule and supporting schedules is shown in simplified form in Figure 6.8. This shows that the cash balance presented in the financial statements for 20x3 and recorded in the working trial balance is

£154,370. The composition of this balance is detailed in the 'Lead Schedule: Cash'. Audit work has revealed that a receipt from a customer of £120 has not been recorded in the correct period and, as a consequence, an adjusting entry is required.

(h) *Supporting schedules:* The supporting schedules which provide details of audit work performed in relation to individual financial statement balances constitute the major part of the current audit file. Frequently they are grouped in the file in sections which reflect financial statement categories. There may, for example, be sections for revenues, direct costs, indirect expenses, current assets, tangible fixed assets, investments, intangible fixed assets, current liabilities, long-term liabilities and shareholders' funds. Each of these sections may be subdivided into groups of related accounts. The amount of subdivision will largely depend on the size and complexity of the particular audit.

Each group of accounts has a lead schedule which is cross-referenced to both the working trial balance, relevant 'working accounts' and supporting schedules (see, respectively, C-1, B-1 and C-2 to C-4 in Figure 6.8 and Figure 6.9). Each supporting schedule presents, in relation to an individual account balance, details of:

- the objective(s) of audit procedures performed[9]
- the procedures performed
- the results of the procedures
- relevant comments
- the conclusion reached with respect to the account balance investigated.

These features are reflected in Figure 6.9.

6.6.3 Preparation of audit working papers

It was noted in section 6.6.1 above that the primary objective of audit working papers is to provide evidence that the audit has been conducted in accordance with Auditing Standards. In order for such evidence to be provided, it is essential that audit working papers are properly prepared.

Although the details of working papers vary according to the nature of the schedule concerned and the specific audit objectives being met, audit working papers should always contain certain features. These are discussed below and illustrated in Figure 6.9.

---

[9] The objectives of audit procedures, and the procedure to be performed, may be specified in the audit programme rather than in the relevant supporting schedule.

Figure 6.8: Simplified representation of the relationship between the financial statements and audit working papers

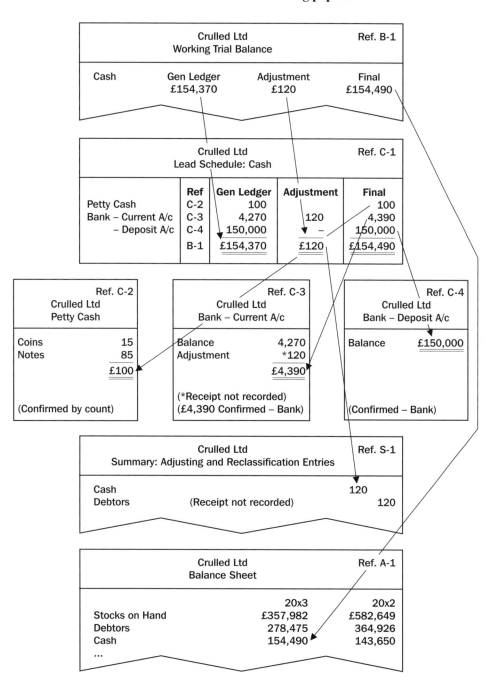

(i) Each working paper should be clearly headed to indicate:
- the name of the client;
- the audit area (or account) to which the working paper (schedule) relates;
- the relevant accounting period.

(ii) Each working paper should have a unique reference number and be cross-referenced to the relevant lead schedule, working trial balance and/or other related working papers.

(iii) Completed working papers must show:
- the initials (or name) of the preparer, and date of preparation;
- the initials (or name) of the reviewer and date of the review.

(iv) Audit working papers also need to show:
- the audit objectives of the procedures performed;[10]
- the audit procedures performed (these should be cross-referenced to the audit programme);
- the results of the audit procedures (these frequently involve the use of tick marks or symbols, and all such notation must be clearly explained);
- the conclusion(s) reached in terms of the objectives, based on the results of the audit procedures performed.

(v) Where sampling is used, the relevant working paper should indicate the population from which the sample was drawn, the size of the sample and the means by which the sample was selected.

(vi) Where any deviation from the expected result of an audit procedure is encountered, such deviation, and an explanation thereof, should be clearly recorded in the relevant working paper. In cases where some follow-up is required, the person undertaking the follow-up must initial and date the relevant working paper entry to indicate that the follow-up has been performed.

6.6.4 Working paper review

It was noted in section 6.5 that SAS 240: *Quality control for audit work* (and, similarly, ISA 220) requires the work of audit staff to be reviewed. Such review should ensure, *inter alia*, that audit objectives have been met, audit procedures performed and results obtained have been properly documented, and conclusions reached are consistent with the results obtained and support the opinion expressed in the audit report.

It was also noted in section 6.5 (and Chapter 3) that conducting an audit requires specialised skills and competence. Further, in Chapter 3 we discussed the importance of, and necessity for, the exercise of professional judgment in all

---

[10] See footnote 9.

Figure 6.9: Common features of audit working papers

		Working paper reference
Name of client	**CRULLED LIMITED**	
Audit area	**Stock Purchases and Cash Payments**	REF: K-2
Accounting period	**Year to 31 March 20x3**	Prepared by: RB ←
		Date: 10.4.x3 ←
		Reviewed by: MC ←
		Date: 16.4.x3 ←

Preparer and Preparation date

Reviewer and Review date

Audit objectives:
* To verify that merchandise is properly ordered and received and is for legitimate business purposes.
* To verify that expenses (purchases) and assets (stock) are properly valued and classified
* To verify that cash payments are for legitimate liabilities and properly valued.

Audit procedures:
\#   Traced payment to purchase invoice. Agreed invoice with amount of cheque and payment date. Each payment is 5% less than invoice amount as cash discount received. Recalculated all discounts. (A-6) ← *Audit programme reference*
<   Compared invoice prices with master price list. All agreed except those marked*. (A-7)
Ø   Examined purchase invoices for evidence that company employee verified prices, extensions and footings. Markings or initials present in all cases. (A-8)
>   Verified arithmetical accuracy of extensions and footings of invoices. (A-9)
v   Examined cancelled cheques for amounts, dates, signatures, and payee. (A-10)
t   Examined receiving report for agreement with purchase invoice as to description and quantity. All reports were properly signed by Backhouse (Receiving Officer). (A-11)
@   Examined purchase order with receiving report and invoice. Verified account code. All orders agreed with receiving report and were properly approved except those marked + and }. (A-12)

Sample selection:[11]
Population: All purchases were from Yumslip Products, Western Corporation and Capers Ltd.
Sample: Judgmental. Selected 12 payments for merchandise beginning with cheque 1690 from Cash Payments Journal.

Results of procedures:

		Cheque					Audit Procedure			
Date	Payee	No.	Amount	1	2	3	4	5	6	7
10-4-x2	Western Corporation	1690	£1,432.67	#	<	Ø	>	v	t	@
9-5-x2	Yumslip Products	1725	£2,568.91	#	<*	Ø	>	v	t	@+
15-6-x2	Western Corporation	1744	£1,021.05	#	<	Ø	>	v	t	@
6-7-x2	Yumslip Products	1769	£456.26	#	<	Ø	>	v	t	@}
10-8-x2	Capers Ltd	1780	£461.34	#	<	Ø	>	v	t	@}
8-9-x2	Yumslip Products	1795	£1,263.76	#	<*	Ø	>	v	t	@
14-10-x2	Western Corporation	1841	£1,246.34	#	<	Ø	>	v	t	@
17-11-x2	Yumslip Products	1860	£319.38	#	<	Ø	>	v	t	@}
9-12-x2	Capers Ltd	1887	£248.21	#	<	Ø	>	v	t	@}
15-1-x3	Yumslip Products	1898	£1,219.47	#	<	Ø	>	v	t	@
13-2-x3	Western Corporation	1924	£2,639.31	#	<	Ø	>	v	t	@
15-3-x3	Yumslip Products	1953	£1,632.19	#	<	Ø	>	v	t	@

NOTE: Symbols used are shown alongside relevant audit procedure.

Comments:
*   Prices on purchases of 9-5-x2 and 8-9-x2 do not agree with master price list by £56.00 and £124.34 respectively. According to Smithson (Purchasing Officer) the differences represent special prices available in May and September which differed from price list. (Confirmed with Yumslip.)
+   Purchase order does not agree with receiving report for one item. Smithson indicated that replacement (similar) item was supplied as a result of a stock-out. (Confirmed replacement item ordered.)
}   Four orders were approved by Thomas (Chief Accountant) instead of Mates (Finance Director). According to Smithson only orders in excess of £1,000 need be approved by Mates. (Confirmed with Mates.)
NOTE: Need to alter flowchart to reflect this. (MC 15-4-x3) ← *Follow-up by audit staff member*

Conclusions:
(1)   The purchases are properly ordered and received and are for legitimate purposes.
(2)   Purchases are properly valued and classified.
(3)   Payments are properly valued and are for legitimate liabilities.
(4)   Purchases and payments transactions are fairly stated in the accounts. (K-1) ← *Lead schedule reference*

---

[11]   Sample sizes and selection are discussed in Chapter 11.

stages of an audit – a fact that will become increasingly evident as we study the steps in the audit process in more detail. These characteristics of an audit, combined with the fact that members of audit teams are human (and therefore prone to make mistakes and faulty judgments), mean that reliance cannot be placed on audit staff correctly identifying audit objectives, performing appropriate audit procedures, and drawing correct conclusions, on *every* occasion. Clearly, if an effective audit is to be conducted, it is essential that the work of each audit staff member is reviewed by a more senior member of the audit team. This is usually effected in the following manner.

(i) As each section of the audit is completed, the working papers of the relevant audit staff member are discussed with, and reviewed by, a more senior member of the audit team. The audit procedures performed are compared with those set down in the audit programme, and the results obtained and conclusions reached (based on those results) are evaluated. The working papers are also reviewed for completeness, orderly presentation and cross-referencing to other relevant working papers.

(ii) *The reviewer* (the more senior audit team member) prepares summary notes on each segment of the audit for which (s)he is responsible, regarding:
   (a) the evidence gathered and conclusions reached;
   (b) any problems encountered and how they were dealt with;
   (c) matters requiring the attention of the audit manager (usually the most senior member of the audit team other than the engagement partner) or the engagement partner;
   (d) matters to be included in the management letter.

(iii) *The audit manager* (or another senior member of the audit team) reviews the summary notes prepared by the reviewer of the audit work performed. (S)he also reviews the detailed working papers prepared by the audit staff member(s) who undertook the work to ensure they contain evidence indicating they have been reviewed, and to evaluate the reviewer's findings. The manager discusses with the audit staff members who performed and/or reviewed the audit work any matters which require clarification, any difficult audit issues and how they were resolved, and any issues remaining to be resolved.

(iv) The audit manager prepares summary notes on each major segment of the audit and on the audit as a whole. (S)he comments on:
   (a) the sufficiency and appropriateness of the audit evidence gathered;
   (b) conclusions reached, based on that evidence;
   (c) problems encountered and how they were resolved;
   (d) any outstanding unresolved difficulties.
   The audit manager also prepares the management letter. (This frequently amounts to approving or amending a draft letter prepared by a senior audit staff member).

The audit manager will be particularly concerned to see that:
(a) all audit problems have been adequately dealt with;
(b) any unresolved difficulties are either resolved or passed on, by way of audit working paper note, to the audit engagement partner;
(c) sufficient appropriate evidence has been obtained in each audit segment and for the audit as a whole;
(d) the conclusions reached are supported by the evidence gathered.

(v) *The audit engagement partner* considers, in detail, the final draft of the financial statements, and the summary notes and management letter prepared by the audit manager. (S)he also
(a) reviews the audit working papers for completeness, orderliness, adequacy, cross-referencing and evidence of review, and
(b) discusses with the audit manager and/or relevant audit staff members any matters that require clarification, and/or difficult or unresolved audit issues.[12]

The audit partner's main concerns are to ensure that:
(a) (s)he can form an appropriate opinion on the financial statements under examination based on the evidence recorded in the audit working papers, assessed against a background of his or her knowledge of the client, its operations and its financial affairs;
(b) if the adequacy of the audit is challenged in a court of law, the working papers will:
• stand up to the scrutiny of the court;
• clearly show that the opinion expressed in the audit report is supported by audit evidence that is both sufficient and appropriate.

For all but small audits, in order to ensure that objectives (a) and (b) above are met, most audit firms require the audit working papers to be reviewed by a second audit partner who has not had any involvement in the audit in question. Indeed, SAS 240: *Quality control of audit work*[13] specifies that:

> Firms should ensure that an independent review is undertaken for all audit engagements where the audited entity is a listed company. In addition, firms

---

[12] As noted in footnote 6, the audit engagement partner is required to conduct an overall review of the audit working papers. SAS 240, para 55, states:

> The review is sufficient for [the audit engagement partner] to be satisfied that the working papers contain sufficient appropriate evidence to support the conclusions reached and for the auditors' report to be issued. Although the review may not cover all working papers, it covers:
> • all critical areas of judgement, especially any relating to difficult or contentious matters identified during the audit;
> • audit evidence relating to high risk areas;
> • any other areas which the audit engagement partner considers important.

The engagement partner's review of the audit working papers is discussed in greater detail in Chapter 15, section 15.2.2.

[13] It is pertinent to note that ISA 220: *Quality control for audit work* does not contain provisions similar to those in SAS 240 paras 58–62.

should establish procedures setting out the circumstances in which an independent review should be performed for other audit engagements, whether on grounds of public interest or audit risk. (para 58)

The Standard explains (paras 60–61) that the independent review is to be conducted by 'one or more independent partners having sufficient experience and authority to fulfil the role' and that the following matters are to be considered:

(a) the objectivity of the audit engagement partner and key audit staff and the independence of the firm . . .;

(b) the rigour of the planning process including the analysis of the key components of audit risk identified by the audit team and the adequacy of the planned responses to those risks;

(c) the results of audit work and the appropriateness of the key judgements made, particularly in high risk areas;

(d) the significance of any potential changes to the financial statements that the firm is aware of but which the management of the audited entity has declined to make;

(e) whether all matters which may reasonably be judged by the auditors to be important and relevant to the directors, identified during the course of the audit, have been considered for reporting to the board of directors and/or the audit committee . . .; and

(f) the appropriateness of the draft auditors' report.

The Standard further explains:

> The independent review does not involve a detailed review of all audit working papers, nor does it affect the responsibilities of the audit engagement partner. Its purpose is to provide an independent assessment of the quality of the audit including the key decisions and significant judgements made. The extent of the review depends of the complexity of the engagement, the risks associated with the audit and the experiences of the audit engagement partner and the audit staff. (para 62)

A second (independent) audit partner, and/or possibly a relevant committee of the audit firm, may also be consulted if the audit requires particularly difficult judgments to be made, especially where there is also disagreement with the auditee's management.

6.6.5 Ownership and retention of audit working papers

Working papers prepared in relation to an audit engagement, including those prepared by the client at the request of the auditor, are the property of the auditor. The only time anyone else has a legal right to examine the working papers is when they are subpoenaed by a court of law or (for clients in regulated industries) demanded by a relevant regulator. However, SAS 230: *Working papers* makes it clear that, auditors may, if they wish, make parts of, or extracts from, their audit working papers available to the audit client, 'provided such disclosure does not undermine the independence or the validity of the audit process' (para 19).

The Standard also requires auditors to 'adopt appropriate procedures for maintaining the confidentiality and safe custody of their working papers' (para 16). It further notes:

> There are no specific statutory requirements regarding the period of retention of audit working papers. Auditors exercise judgment to determine the appropriate period of retention bearing in mind possible needs of their client, for example that audited information may need to be included in a prospectus at some future date, and their own needs, including any regulatory requirements. (para 17)[14]

6.7 AUDITORS' DUTY OF CONFIDENTIALITY TO CLIENTS

During the course of an audit, members of the audit team become very knowledgeable about the client's business, its operations, and its financial affairs. It is imperative that audit staff respect the confidential nature of this knowledge.

Without discounting the importance of the principle of confidentiality, disclosure of information is generally permitted (according to the Guide to Professional Ethics Statement 5: *Confidentiality,* ICAEW, ICAS, ICAI, 1997) in the following situations:

- when the client consents to the auditor disclosing information;
- if the auditor has a legal duty to disclose information, for example, to enable documents to be located or to give evidence in legal proceedings;
- if an auditor has a professional duty to disclose otherwise confidential information, for example, in order to comply with ethical requirements.

However, apart from very limited circumstances, such as those referred to above, auditors are required to respect the confidentiality of information which comes to their notice as a result of their audits. Nevertheless, in recent years this duty of confidentiality to audit clients has been increasingly questioned. This has occurred, in particular, when cases of corporate fraud and other illegal acts by company directors or senior executives have come to light and politicians, the courts, financial journalists and the public have asked why the company's auditor did not discover such acts and report them to an appropriate authority. Auditors, in response, have traditionally emphasised that, in the absence of a legal requirement to do so, their duty of confidentiality to their clients is paramount and precludes them from reporting matters of concern discovered during an audit to third parties – including authorities such as the Serious Fraud Office, the police, or the Department of Trade and Industry.

---

[14] ISA 230: *Documentation* (paras 13–14) contains similar provisions to those in SAS 230 paras 16–19.

It was largely in response to public and political pressure that the APB included certain provisions in SAS 110: *Fraud and error* and SAS 120: *Consideration of law and regulations*.[15] As noted in Chapter 5, SAS 110 imposes a duty on auditors to report suspected or actual fraud discovered during an audit to a proper authority, whenever it is in the public interest to do so. SAS 120 similarly requires auditors to step outside their duty of confidentiality to their audit clients in certain circumstances. The Standard deals with two situations, namely:

(i) where auditors have a statutory duty to report to an appropriate authority (for example, under the Financial Services Act 1986); and

(ii) where auditors have no statutory duty to report to any party outside the client.

SAS 120 states that when auditors encounter actual or suspected instances of non-compliance with the law or regulations which give rise to a statutory duty to report to an appropriate authority, they should so report without undue delay (para 56). In this case, the need for auditors to override their duty of confidentiality to their client is clear-cut. However, the Standard also requires auditors who become aware of non-compliance with the law and/or regulations which does not give rise to a statutory duty to report, to consider whether the matter ought to be reported to a proper authority in the public interest (para 59). In general, the matter should first be discussed with the audit client's board of directors (including any audit committee). If, after considering any views expressed on behalf of the entity (and in the light of any legal advice obtained), the auditors conclude that the matter ought to be reported to an appropriate authority in the public interest, they should notify the directors of their view, in writing. If the entity does not itself report the matter to an appropriate authority, then the auditors should do so (paras 59 and 60). Further, if the suspected or actual instance of non-compliance with the law or regulations is such as to undermine the auditors' confidence in the integrity of the entity's directors, then, according to SAS 120, the matter should be reported directly to a proper authority without discussing it with the entity (para 61). An example of this kind of event could be money laundering.

From the above it is clear that, normally, auditors adhere to their duty of confidentiality to their client. However, when a statutory or regulatory duty exists, or it is in the public interest to do so, auditors should subordinate this duty of confidentiality and disclose matters of concern to an appropriate

---

[15] The relevant provisions were, in fact, first promulgated by the APB's predecessor, the Auditing Practices Committee (APC) in 1990 in Auditing Guideline: *The auditor's responsibility in relation to fraud, other irregularities and errors.* The APB carried forward the relevant provisions from the APC's Auditing Guideline into SAS 110: *Fraud and error* and SAS 120: *Consideration of law and regulations.*

authority. The position is reflected in the second portion of the fundamental principle of external auditing – *Integrity*:

> Confidential information obtained in the course of an audit is disclosed only when required in the public interest, or by operation of law.

6.8 SUMMARY

In this chapter we have reviewed the audit process, discussed the meaning and nature of audit evidence, and examined some important administrative aspects of auditing – in particular, staffing and documenting an audit, and auditors' duty of confidentiality to their clients.

We have seen that the audit process comprises a series of well-defined steps through which auditors proceed, gradually gathering evidence to enable them to form an opinion on (amongst other things) whether the financial statements under examination provide a true and fair view of the entity's financial position and performance and comply with relevant legislation.

We have also drawn a distinction between audit objectives (the purpose for which audit evidence is obtained) and audit procedures (the methods by which the evidence is gathered). Additionally, we have identified three levels of audit objectives (overall, general and specific objectives), outlined some common audit procedures, and explained terms such as compliance and substantive procedures, tests of transactions and tests of balances. We have also examined some characteristics of evidence obtained from different sources and explored factors affecting auditors' choice of evidence, namely, reliability, relevance, availability, timeliness and cost. We have observed that there is a trade-off between the quantity of evidence an auditor needs to gather (sufficiency) and the relevance and reliability (appropriateness) of the evidence.

In relation to staffing an audit we have considered the skills and competence required of auditors, auditors' responsibilities in cases where they rely on other auditors or experts to perform part of an audit, and the need for audit engagement partners to carefully assign, direct, supervise and review work delegated to audit staff. As regards documenting an audit, we have discussed the purpose and importance of audit working papers; their form, content and preparation; and also working paper review and ownership.

From our examination of these topics it is evident that, in order for an audit to be conducted effectively, efficiently and with due professional care, it must be adequately staffed by personnel who possess the personal qualities of integrity, objectivity and independence, and who also have the skills and competence required to perform the tasks assigned to them. Additionally, work assigned to audit staff must be carefully directed and supervised and all audit work must be fully and properly documented and carefully reviewed. Proper documentation is also required to provide evidence that sufficient appropriate audit evidence was gathered during the audit and that the conclusions reached accord with that evidence and support the opinion expressed in the audit report.

In the concluding section of the chapter, we highlighted the confidential nature of knowledge gained by audit team members and the importance of audit staff respecting their duty of confidentiality to the client. However, we also observed that auditors may have an overriding duty to report to third parties (such as regulatory authorities) when there is a statutory duty to so report or when it is in the public interest to do so.

SELF-REVIEW QUESTIONS

6.1   Identify the major steps in the audit process.
6.2   Briefly explain the objective of:
      (i)   compliance procedures; and
      (ii)   substantive procedures.
      For each of these objectives give one example of an audit procedure which is designed to meet that objective.
6.3   Indicate the audit procedure(s) you would use to verify each of the following items. Briefly explain each procedure, indicating how it would be applied in the particular situation.
      (i)   Value of office supplies on hand at year end.
      (ii)   Value of a trade debtor's balance outstanding at year end.
      (iii) Fire insurance expenses for the year under audit.
      (iv)   Value of raw materials purchased for the year under audit.
      (v)   The liability arising from long service leave available to employees at year end.
6.4   State whether you agree or disagree with the following statement. Briefly explain your answer.
           Gathering evidence in accordance with Auditing Standards requires the auditor to obtain the strongest possible evidence for each item in the financial statements regardless of cost or difficulties that may be encountered.
6.5   Explain how an auditor might acquire evidence about each of the following transactions:
      (i)   Equipment   £3,000
             Cash   £3,000

	(ii)	Equipment	£4,000	
		Creditors		£4,000
	(iii)	Depreciation expense	£2,000	
		Accumulated depreciation – equipment		£2,000
	(iv)	Insurance expense	£1,000	
		Prepaid insurance		£1,000

6.6 Outline the requirements of SAS 240: *Quality control for audit work* with respect to:
(i) directing,
(ii) supervising, and
(iii) reviewing
the work of audit staff.

6.7 Briefly explain the responsibilities of the audit engagement partner when (s)he relies on the work of experts to perform part of an audit.

6.8 (a) Define 'audit working papers', and
(b) List five specific purposes of audit working papers.

6.9 (a) Distinguish between information contained in:
(i) the permanent audit file;
(ii) the current audit file.
(b) Provide two examples of the information contained in each of the above files.

6.10 (a) Outline the requirements of SAS 230: *Working papers* with respect to ownership and custody of audit working papers.
(b) Describe briefly the circumstances in which auditors may have a duty to override their duty of confidentiality to their client and report matters of concern encountered during the audit to an appropriate authority. (In your answer you should refer, specifically, to relevant provisions in SAS 110 and SAS 120.)

REFERENCES

Anderson, R.J. (1977) *The External Audit.* Toronto: Cropp Clark Pitman.
Arens, A.A. & Loebbecke, J.K. (1991) *Auditing: An Integrated Approach*, 5th ed. New Jersey: Prentice-Hall.

ADDITIONAL READING

Asare, S.K. & McDaniel, L.S. (1996) The effects of familiarity with the preparer and task complexity on the effectiveness of the audit review process. *The Accounting Review* **71**(2), 139–159.
Cunningham, L. (1999) How much is enough? *Accountancy* **124**(1275), 116–117.

Frederick, D.M., Heiman-Hoffman, V.B. & Libby, R. (1994) The structure of auditors' knowledge of financial statement errors. *Auditing: A Journal of Practice & Theory* **13**(1), 1–21.

Harding, N. & Trotman, K.T. (1999) Hierarchical differences in audit working paper review performance. *Contemporary Accounting Research* **16**(4), 671–684.

Institute of Chartered Accountants in England and Wales (ICAEW) (2000) *Towards Better Auditing*. London: ICAEW, Audit Faculty.

Maroney, J.J. & Bedard, J.C. (1997) Auditors' use of inconsistent evidence. *International Journal of Auditing* **1**(3), 187–204.

McMillian, J.J. & White, R.A. (1993) Auditors' belief revisions and evidence search: the effect of hypothesis frame, confirmation bias, and professional skepticism. *The Accounting Review* **68**(3), 443–465.

Messier, Jr, W.F. (1992) The sequencing of audit evidence: its impact on the extent of audit testing and report formulation. *Accounting and Business Research* **22**(86), 143–150.

Pratt, J. & Stice, J. D. (1994) The effects of client characteristics on auditor litigation risk judgements, required audit evidence, and recommended audit fees. *The Accounting Review* **69**(4), 639–656.

Rudolph, H.R. & Welker, R.B. (1998) The effects of organizational structure on communication within audit teams. *Auditing: A Journal of Practice & Theory* **17**(2), 1–14.

Salterio, S. & Koonce, L. (1997) The persuasiveness of audit evidence: the case of accounting policy decisions. *Accounting, Organizations and Society* **22**(6), 573–587.

Scott, A. (1997) What to record and what to keep. *Accountancy*, **120** (1249), 140.

Shelton, S.W. (1999) The effect of experience on the use of irrelevant evidence in auditor judgement. *The Accounting Review* **74**(2), 217–224.

Tan H. & Jamal, K. (2001) Do auditors objectively evaluate their subordinates' work? *The Accounting Review* **76**(1), 99–110.

Tubbs, R.M. (1992) The effect of experience on the auditor's organisation and amount of knowledge. *The Accounting Review* **67**(4), 783–801.

Tuckey, D. (1996) Proof beyond reasonable doubt. *Accountancy* **117**(1232), 88–90.

Woolfe, E. (1994) Auditing standards: Can small firms comply? *Accountancy* **113**(1209), 84–86.

Woolfe, E. (1994) Where's the evidence? *Accountancy* **113**(1210), 93–94.

Woodrow, M. (1997) The Audit Process in Practice. In M. Sherer and S. Turley (eds) *Current Issues in Accounting*, 3rd ed., Chapter 12. London: Paul Chapman Publishing.

7 Commencing an Audit: Engagement Procedures and Gaining an Understanding of the Client

---

LEARNING OBJECTIVES

After studying the material in this chapter you should be able to:
- outline the reasons for, and the process of, pre-engagement investigations;
- discuss the purpose and content of audit engagement letters;
- explain the importance of gaining a thorough understanding of the client, its business (including its processes, operations and risks), and its industry;
- identify and discuss external and internal environmental factors which impact on an entity and its external audit;
- outline the audit procedures used to gain an understanding of the client and its business.

The following publications are particularly relevant to this chapter:
- Statement of Auditing Standards (SAS) 140: *Engagement letters* (APB, 1995)
- Statement of Auditing Standards (SAS) 210: *Knowledge of the business* (APB, 1995)
- Statement of Auditing Standards (SAS) 240: *Quality control for audit work* (APB, 2000)
- Statement of Auditing Standards (SAS) 450: *Opening balances and comparatives* (APB, 1995)
- Guide to Professional Ethics Statement (GPES) 6: *Changes in a Professional Appointment* (ICAEW, ICAS, ICAI, 1997).
- International Standards on Auditing (ISA) 210: *Terms of audit engagements.* (IFAC, 1994)
- International Standards on Auditing (ISA) 310: *Knowledge of the business.* (IFAC, 1994)
- International Standards on Auditing (ISA) 510: *Initial engagements.* (IFAC, 1994).

7.1 INTRODUCTION

In this chapter we begin our journey through the audit process. We assume that an auditor (an individual or an audit firm) has been approached by a company to accept appointment as its auditor. We discuss the steps the auditor should take before accepting the engagement, the audit engagement letter (s)he should prepare, and the all-important audit step of gaining a thorough understanding of the client, its business (including its processes, operations and risks), and its industry.

7.2 PRE-ENGAGEMENT INVESTIGATION

7.2.1 The need for a pre-engagement investigation

In a competitive environment it is not always easy to obtain and retain audit clients. Nevertheless, when auditors are offered a new or continuing audit engagement they should consider carefully whether it is prudent to accept the offer. It is, for example, generally unwise to accept (or continue with) an audit client whose management lacks integrity, or constantly argues about the proper conduct of the audit and/or the audit fees. Equally, it is important that an audit engagement is not accepted if the audit cannot be adequately staffed with personnel possessing the necessary levels of independence, skills and competence. As noted in SAS 240: *Quality control for audit work* (para 15):

> Before accepting a new engagement firms should ensure that they:
> (a) are competent to undertake the work;
> (b) consider carefully whether there are any threats to their independence and objectivity and, if so, whether adequate safeguards can be established;
> (c) assess the integrity of the owners, directors and management of the entity; and
> (d) comply with the ethical requirements of the professional accountancy bodies in relation to changes in appointment.
> Firms should also ensure that they reconsider these matters, before the end of their term of office, when deciding whether they are willing to continue in office as auditor.

Particularly in the light of the requirements of SAS 240 cited above, it is convenient to discuss the elements of a pre-engagement investigation under the following headings:

- assessing the auditor's independence and competence to perform the audit;
- evaluating the integrity of the client's owners, directors and management;
- changes in appointment: communicating with the predecessor auditor.

7.2.2 Assessing the auditor's independence and competence to perform the audit

In Chapters 3 and 4 we examined in some detail the importance of auditors (engagement partners and audit staff) being independent of their audit clients and the clients' managements. We noted several threats that may endanger auditors' independence – in appearance if not in fact, and various requirements the law and the accountancy profession have imposed on auditors in order to protect and/or strengthen their independence. Similarly, in Chapters 3 and 6 we noted the importance of auditors possessing (or, in the case of specialised skills and knowledge, having available) the skills and competence required to complete the audit.

Our earlier discussions of these matters highlight the need for an audit firm, before accepting a new or continuing audit engagement, to consider carefully whether it (or, more pertinently, the audit engagement partner):

- possesses the required degree of independence from the (potential) audit client, in both fact and appearance;
- possesses the required levels of training, experience and competence to perform the audit satisfactorily. This includes possessing both:
  - technical skills and experience in auditing; and
  - adequate knowledge of the (potential) client's industry;
- has available, at the appropriate time, adequate audit staff who possess the required degree of independence from the (potential) client, and the skills and competence necessary to perform the work to be assigned to them;
- is able to direct, supervise and review the work of audit staff as required by SAS 240: *Quality control for audit work;*
- has available, at the appropriate time, assistance from other auditors and/or experts, if they are to perform part of the audit.

Additionally, before accepting a new audit client, an audit firm needs to consider the impact of the engagement on its audit portfolio. In particular, the firm should consider whether acceptance of the client would give rise to any conflict of interest with existing clients and whether it would adversely affect its ability to service existing clients properly.

7.2.3 Evaluating the integrity of the client's owners, directors and management

It has been noted in earlier chapters that an auditor is required, *inter alia*, to examine financial statements prepared by an audit client's management for parties external to the entity, and to form and express an opinion on whether or not these financial statements present a true and fair view of the entity's financial position and performance and comply with relevant legislation.

Over the past 30 to 40 years, deliberate manipulation of financial statement information has become a problem in many parts of the English-speaking world. Indeed, the problem was so serious in the United States in the mid-1980s that, in 1986, the National Commission on Fraudulent Financial Reporting (the Treadway Commission, 1987) was established to investigate it. In some cases, entity managements have manipulated financial statement information in order to cover up a fraud (as, for example, in the infamous *Equity Funding* case); in other cases, management has been motivated by a desire to portray the entity's financial position and performance in a more favourable light than is warranted by the underlying facts. This has arisen from management's wish to avoid events such as a decline in the value of the company's shares, or public criticism of its performance; or its desire to secure outcomes such as a bonus which is linked to reported profits, or raising new debt or equity capital in financial markets on favourable terms.

In the UK (as elsewhere in the world), deliberate but legal manipulation of financial statements (somewhat flatteringly entitled 'creative accounting') has received considerable attention. The Accounting Standards Board has sought to eliminate so-called 'creative practices' by issuing more tightly prescribed accounting standards. However, in recent years 'aggressive earnings management', a variant of creative accounting, has emerged as a significant problem and, as noted in Chapter 5, the APB is keen for auditors to be alert to, and respond to, the risk of clients engaging in this activity – an activity which may, unless checked, progress into fraudulent financial reporting.

If an entity's management lacks integrity, there is a fairly high probability that some manipulation of financial statement information will occur whenever the management perceives it advantageous so to do. Additionally, such a management is likely to be at pains to deceive the auditor to the extent necessary to ensure that (s)he does not discover the underlying situation. In this regard it is pertinent to observe that in many of the court cases where auditors have faced charges of negligence as a result of failing to uncover management fraud, it has been revealed that the senior executives and/or directors who were responsible for the fraud had a past history of such deeds. Arens and Loebbecke (1980), amongst others, have drawn attention to this phenomenon. They state:

> An analysis of recent court cases involving management fraud shows that in most instances the individuals responsible for the fraud had also been previously involved in illegal or unethical business practices. (p. 176)

A specific example of such a case is afforded by de Angelis, instigator of the massive salad oil fraud in the 1960s at the Allied Crude Vegetable Oil Refining

Corporation of New Jersey. During the court hearing it was revealed that de Angelis had a string of previous convictions for fraud and other illegal acts committed whilst acting as a company director.

The importance of auditors evaluating the integrity of a potential client's management is emphasised by Pratt and Dilton-Hill (1982). They suggest that management integrity is probably the single most important factor in the potential for (intentional) material misstatements in financial statements. They also draw attention to the extent to which an auditor relies on information and responses provided by the auditee's management. The nature of an audit is such that auditors make many decisions based on discussions with management. If an auditee's management lacks integrity, information and responses given to the auditor may be untrustworthy and, as a result, erroneous audit decisions may be made. Examples of cases in the UK where auditors have found themselves in court for alleged negligence, in which the integrity of the directors is highly questionable, include Maxwell Communications, Polly Peck and the Bank of Credit and Commerce International (BCCI).

For a continuing audit engagement, the auditor should evaluate the integrity of the client's management by reviewing his or her past experience with that management. However, if significant changes have occurred amongst the client's senior executives and/or directors, further investigation may be necessary, similar to that undertaken for a new audit engagement.

In the case of a new engagement, if the potential client has been audited previously, information pertaining to the integrity of its management can usually be obtained from the predecessor auditor. As we explain in section 7.2.4 below, before a proposed auditor can accept an audit engagement, (s)he is required by the profession's Guide to Professional Ethics to communicate with the auditor who is to be replaced. One of the matters to be communicated by the incumbent (or predecessor) auditor to the proposed auditor is any doubts the former auditor may have regarding the integrity of the auditee's directors and/or senior managers.

Additionally, SAS 240: *Quality control for audit work* requires audit firms which are approached to accept a new audit engagement to enquire into the reasons for the proposed appointment and the reasons for the retirement or removal of the incumbent auditor (para 16). Further, as noted in section 7.2.1 above, SAS 240 also requires audit firms which are deciding whether or not to accept (or retain) an audit client to assess the integrity of the client's owners, directors and management. The Standard explains:

> [Audit] firms make enquiries to help them assess the integrity of the owners, directors and management of the entity . . . Such enquiries may involve discussions with third parties, the obtaining of written references and searches of relevant databases. (para 17)

The third parties to whom enquiries may be directed include the prospective client's bankers, legal advisors, and others in the financial or business community who may have relevant knowledge about the prospective client. The search of relevant databases includes searching for references in the media during the past three to five years to the potential client or any of its directors, senior executives or influential shareholders, to ascertain whether there is any information in the public domain which indicates that they may have been associated with anything untoward (in particular, with any unethical or illegal activities).

In the United States, some auditors and audit firms consider the integrity of a potential client's management to be so important that they hire professional investigators to obtain information about the reputation and background of key members of its management. In the UK, it is not usual to go to those lengths but, faced by the spate of unexpected company failures and allegations of corporate fraud which have occurred in recent years, audit firms in the UK have become more diligent than formerly about investigating the integrity of senior executives and directors of potential audit clients and more willing to refuse to accept nomination to act as auditors for companies where that integrity is in doubt.

7.2.4 Changes in appointment: communicating with a predecessor auditor

When an audit firm is invited to accept nomination for appointment as auditor for a potential client, in addition to evaluating the firm's independence and competence to complete the work, and assessing the integrity of the potential client's management and influential shareholders, if the entity has been audited previously the audit firm is required to comply with the relevant professional body's guidance relating to changes in a professional appointment[1] [SAS 240 para 15(d)]. The Institute of Chartered Accountants in England and Wales' (ICAEW's) Guide to Professional Ethics Statement (GPES) 6: *Changes in a Professional Appointment*,[2] for example, states that, before accepting nomination to replace an existing auditor, a prospective auditor should communicate with the existing auditor to ascertain whether there are any considerations which might affect his or her decision to accept (or not accept) appointment (para 1.0).

GPES 6 explains:

> The purpose of finding out the background to the proposed change is to enable the [prospective auditor] to determine whether, in all the circumstances, it would be proper for him or her to accept the assignment. In particular, [prospective] auditors will wish to ensure that they do not unwittingly become the means by which any unsatisfactory practices of the company or any impropriety in the conduct of its

---

[1] The relevant professional body is the Recognised Supervisory Body (RSB) with which the auditor (or audit firm) is registered (see Chapter 5, section 5.2.3).

[2] The Guide to Professional Ethics Statement 6: *Changes in a professional appointment* is published in identical form by the ICAEW, ICAS and ICAI.

affairs may be enabled to continue, or may be concealed from shareholders or other legitimately interested persons. Communication is meant to ensure that all relevant facts are known to the [prospective auditor] who, having considered them, is then entitled to accept the nomination if he wishes so to do. (para 1.3)

The Ethics Statement requires prospective auditors, when first approached by a client to accept nomination to act as auditor, to explain that they have a professional duty to communicate with the existing auditor. They are also required to request the prospective client to inform the existing auditor of the proposed change and to give the existing auditor written authority to discuss the client's affairs with the proposed auditor. If the client fails or refuses to grant the existing auditor permission to discuss its affairs with the proposed auditor, the latter should not accept nomination (para 1.7).

Once the existing auditor receives permission from the client to disclose information to the proposed auditor, GPES 6 requires the existing auditor to advise the proposed auditor 'without delay' of 'factors within his knowledge of which, in his opinion, the latter should be aware' (para 1.8). If there are no such factors, this should be conveyed to the proposed auditor.

Normally the communication between the existing and proposed auditor is a matter of routine and nothing of significance need be reported by the former to the latter. However, as GPES 6 indicates, occasionally circumstances arise which are likely to affect the proposed auditor's decision to accept or reject the nomination. These are the matters the incumbent auditor should communicate to the proposed auditor. They include the following (para 1.15):

i)   reasons for [the] change [of auditor] advanced by the client of which the existing auditor is aware are not in accordance with the facts (as understood by the latter);

ii) the proposal to displace the existing auditor arises in his opinion because he has carried out his duties in the face of opposition or evasion/s in which important differences of principle or practice had arisen with the client;

iii) the client, its directors, or employees may have been guilty of some unlawful act or default, or [some] aspect of their conduct which is relevant to the carrying out of an audit [and] ought, in the opinion of the existing auditor, to be investigated further by the appropriate authority;

iv) the existing auditor has unconfirmed suspicions that the client or its directors or employees have defrauded the Inland Revenue, Customs and Excise or others . . .;

v)   the existing auditor has serious doubts regarding the integrity of the directors and/or senior managers of the client;

vi) the client, its directors, or employees have deliberately withheld information required by the existing auditor for the performance of his duties or have limited or attempted to limit the scope of his work;

vii) the existing auditor proposes to bring to the attention of members or creditors circumstances surrounding the proposed change of auditor [i.e. file a 'statement of circumstances' in accordance with the Companies Act 1985, section 394: see Chapter 5, section 5.2.5].

From the above, it is evident that the communication between the proposed and existing auditor serves two main purposes, namely:

(i) it reduces the likelihood of the prospective auditor accepting an audit nomination in circumstances where all of the pertinent factors are not known; and

(ii) it protects the interests of the existing auditor when the proposed change arises from, or is an attempt to interfere with, the conscientious exercise of the existing auditor's duty to act as an independent professional.

It is frequently contended that a new auditor should not succeed another if the prospective client owes fees to the existing auditor. However, in relation to this issue, GPES 6 states:

> The existence of unpaid fees is not of itself a reason why a prospective auditor should not accept nomination/appointment. If he does accept, it may be appropriate for him to assist in any way open to him towards achieving a settlement of outstanding fees; whether or not he does so is entirely a matter for his own judgement in the light of all the circumstances. (para 1.17)

A further matter relating to a change of auditors concerns the incoming auditor substantiating the balances presented in the financial statements of the period preceding that in which (s)he is appointed. In this regard, SAS 450: *Opening balances and comparatives* (para 8) requires auditors to:

obtain sufficient appropriate evidence that:

(a) opening balances have been appropriately brought forward;

(b) opening balances do not contain errors or misstatements which materially affect the current period's financial statements; and

(c) appropriate accounting policies are consistently applied or changes in accounting policies have been properly accounted for and adequately disclosed.[3]

---

[3] ISA 510: *Initial engagements – opening balances* (para 2) similarly requires auditors to:

obtain sufficient appropriate audit evidence that:

(a) the opening balances do not contain misstatements that materially affect the current period's financial statements;

(b) the prior period's closing balances have been correctly brought forward to the current period, or when appropriate have been restated; and

(c) appropriate accounting policies are consistently applied or changes in accounting policies have been properly accounted for and adequately disclosed.

It also notes:

When the prior period's financial statements were audited by another auditor, the current auditor may be able to obtain sufficient appropriate audit evidence regarding opening balances by reviewing the predecessor auditor's working papers. In these circumstances, the current auditor would also consider the professional competence and independence of the predecessor auditor. (para 6)

Prior to communicating with the predecessor auditor, the current auditor will need to consider the Code of Ethics for Professional Accountants issued by the International Federation of Accountants (IFAC). (The Guide to Professional Ethics issued by each of the UK professional accountancy bodies is based on, and very similar to, IFAC's Code of Ethics.) (para 7)

SAS 450 provides details of procedures designed to achieve the above objectives and then goes on to note:

> [These] procedures normally enable incoming auditors to obtain sufficient appropriate audit evidence about the opening balances, and consultations with predecessor auditors are not normally necessary. Except in the case of certain public sector appointments, predecessor auditors have no legal or ethical obligation to provide information and do not normally allow access to their working papers. However, they are expected to co-operate with incoming auditors to provide clarification of, or information on, specific accounting matters where this is necessary to resolve any particular difficulties. (para 14)

Along similar lines, GPES 6 (para 3.0) observes:

> The incoming auditor often needs to ask his predecessor for information as to the client's affairs, lack of which might prejudice the client's interests. Such information should be promptly given and unless there is good reason to the contrary, such as a significant amount of work involved, no charge should be made.

7.3   AUDIT ENGAGEMENT LETTERS

Once the pre-engagement investigation is complete and the auditor has decided to accept the engagement, an engagement letter should be prepared. As SAS 140: *Engagement letters* explains, the purpose of this letter is to document and confirm the auditor's acceptance of the appointment and to ensure there is no misunderstanding between the auditor and the client as regards the auditor's and directors' responsibilities, the scope of the audit engagement, and the form of the reports the auditor is to provide at the conclusion of the audit (para 14).[4]

Although the details of engagement letters vary according to the circumstances of the particular audit, certain items are almost invariably included. These are as follows:

- A statement emphasising that entity's directors (or their equivalent) are responsible for maintaining proper accounting records and for preparing financial statements that give a true and fair view of the entity's state of affairs and profit or loss and comply with relevant legislation.
- A statement drawing attention to the directors' responsibility to ensure that all of the company's records and documents, and any other information requested in connection with the audit, are made available to the auditors.
- A statement outlining the auditor's statutory and professional responsibilities, including his or her responsibility to form and express an opinion on the financial statements and to report if the financial statements do not comply

---

[4] ISA 210: *Terms of audit engagements*, para 5, is the same in all essential respects as SAS 140, para 14.

in any material respects with applicable accounting standards, unless the auditor considers that non-compliance is justified in the circumstances.

- A statement outlining other matters the auditor must consider and may need to refer to in the audit report – for example, whether proper accounting records have been kept by the entity, whether information given in the directors' report is consistent with the financial statements, and whether the financial statements give details of the directors' remuneration required by the Companies Act 1985.
- A statement explaining the scope (extent) of the audit and that the audit will be conducted in accordance with Auditing Standards. Reference is also made to any work the auditor is to do in addition to that required for a statutory audit.
- An indication of how the auditor will approach the audit and the work to be done. Also, in appropriate cases, reference is usually made to the involvement of other auditors or experts in certain aspects of the audit.
- A warning that the audit is not designed to detect significant weaknesses in the company's systems. However, it is noted that any such weaknesses which come to light during the audit will be reported to the directors.
- A statement informing the directors (or their equivalent) that the auditor may request written confirmation of certain oral representations expressed by them to the auditor during the course of the audit. Attention is also drawn, in appropriate cases, to the legislative provision under which it is an offence for an officer of the entity to mislead the auditors (for example, Companies Act 1985, s.389A).
- A statement informing the directors that the auditor will request sight of all documents or statements (such as the directors' report and operating and financial review) to be issued in the entity's annual report along with the financial statements.
- A statement to the effect that responsibility for safeguarding the entity's assets and preventing and detecting fraud, error, and non-compliance with the law or regulations rests with management. However it is also pointed out that the audit will be planned so as to have a reasonable expectation of detecting material misstatements in the financial statements or accounting records – including those resulting from fraud, error, or non-compliance with legal requirements.
- A statement informing the directors that the auditor's responsibility for the financial statements for the year in question ceases once the audit report has been issued but requesting that the auditor be informed of any material event occurring between the issue of the audit report and the entity's annual general meeting.
- A statement outlining the form of any reports or other communications to be provided by the auditor in relation to the conduct and findings of the audit.

- A statement confirming any verbal agreements with the client, including the basis on which fees are to be charged.[5]

An example of an audit engagement letter is provided in Figure 7.1. The auditor prepares two copies of the letter: they are both sent to the client for signing; one is retained by the client, the other is returned to the auditor for inclusion in the permanent audit file.

In the case of a continuing audit engagement, the auditor may decide that an engagement letter is not needed. However, SAS 140 (para 8) notes that, as part of the annual planning process, the auditor should consider whether a new engagement letter is required and points out that certain factors make such a letter appropriate. The factors include the following:

- any indication that the client misunderstands the objective and scope of the audit;
- a recent change of management, board of directors or audit committee;
- a significant change in ownership, such as a new holding company;
- a significant change in the nature or size of the client's business; and
- any relevant change in legal or professional requirements.

The Standard also notes that:

It may be appropriate to remind the client of the original letter when the auditors decide a new engagement letter is unnecessary for any period. (para 8)[6]

Before leaving the subject of audit engagement letters, it should be noted that these letters do not absolve the auditor from any duties in relation to the audit. Their principal purpose is to clarify the objective and scope of the audit and to ensure that the client's directors/management are aware of the nature of the audit engagement and of their own responsibilities with respect to the financial statements and other matters noted in the engagement letter.

7.4 UNDERSTANDING THE CLIENT, ITS BUSINESS AND ITS INDUSTRY

7.4.1 Importance of gaining an understanding of the client and its business

In order to perform an effective and efficient audit it is essential that the auditor gains a thorough understanding of the client (its organisation, strategy, key personnel, etc.), its business, its business processes and risks, and its industry. SAS 210: *Knowledge of the business* states:

---

[5] The principal contents of audit engagement letters set out in ISA 210: *Terms of audit engagements*, paras 6, 7 and 8, are similar in all material respects to those outlined above and contained in the example audit engagement letter shown in Figure 7.1.

[6] ISA 210 paras 10 and 11 are almost identical in content to SAS 140 para 8.

Figure 7.1: Example of an audit engagement letter (for a limited company client)
(This specimen letter is modified to meet the needs of specific circumstances)

To the directors of Foolproof plc

The purpose of this letter is to set out the basis on which we are to act as auditors of the company and its subsidiary undertakings and the respective areas of responsibility of the directors and of ourselves.

Responsibilities of directors and auditors

1.1 As directors of Foolproof plc, you are responsible for ensuring that the company maintains proper accounting records and for preparing financial statements which give a true and fair view and have been prepared in accordance with the Companies Act 1985. You are also responsible for making available to us, as and when required, all the company's accounting records and all other relevant records and related information, including minutes of all management and shareholders' meetings.

1.2 We have a statutory responsibility to report to the members whether, in our opinion, the financial statements give a true and fair view and whether they have been properly prepared in accordance with the Companies Act 1985. In arriving at our opinion, we are required to consider the following matters, and to report on any in respect of which we are not satisfied:

   a) whether proper accounting records have been kept by the company and proper returns adequate for our audit have been received from branches not visited by us;

   b) whether the company's balance sheet and profit and loss account are in agreement with the accounting records and returns;

   c) whether we have obtained all the information and explanations which we consider necessary for the purposes of our audit; and

   d) whether the information given in the directors' report is consistent with the financial statements.

In addition, there are certain other matters which, according to the circumstances, may need to be dealt with in our report. For example, where the financial statements do not give details of directors' remuneration or of their transactions with the company, the Companies Act 1985 requires us to disclose such matters in our report.

1.3 We have a professional responsibility to report if the financial statements do not comply in any material respect with applicable accounting standards, unless in our opinion the non-compliance is justified in the circumstances. In determining whether or not the departure is justified we consider:

   a) whether the departure is required in order for the financial statements to give a true and fair view; and

   b) whether adequate disclosure has been made concerning the departure.

1.4 Our professional responsibilities also include:

• including in our report a description of the directors' responsibilities for the financial statements where the financial statements or accompanying information do not include such a description; and

• considering whether other information in documents containing audited financial statements is consistent with those financial statements.

Scope of audit

2.1 Our audit will be conducted in accordance with the Auditing Standards issued by the Auditing Practices Board, and will include such tests of transactions and of the existence, ownership and valuation of assets and liabilities as we consider necessary. We shall obtain an understanding of the accounting and internal control systems in order to assess their adequacy as a basis for the preparation of the financial statements and to establish whether proper accounting records have been maintained by the company. We shall expect to obtain such appropriate evidence as we consider sufficient to enable us to draw reasonable conclusions therefrom.

2.2 The nature and extent of our procedures will vary according to our assessment of the company's accounting system and, where we wish to place reliance on it, the internal control system, and may cover any aspect of the business's operations that we consider appropriate. Our audit is not designed to identify all significant weaknesses in the company's systems but, if such weaknesses come to our notice during the course of our audit which we think should be brought to your attention, we shall report them to you. Any such report may not be provided to third parties without our prior written consent. Such consent will be granted only on the basis that such reports are not prepared with the interests of anyone other than the company in mind and that we accept no duty or responsibility to any other party as concerns the reports.

2.3 As part of our normal audit procedures, we may request you to provide written confirmation of certain oral representations which we have received from you during the course of the audit on matters having a material effect on the financial statements. In connection with representations and the supply of information to us generally, we draw your attention to section 389A of the Companies Act 1985 under which it is an offence for an officer of the company to mislead the auditors.

2.4 In order to assist us with the examination of your financial statements, we shall request sight of all documents or statements, including the chairman's statement, operating and financial review and the directors' report, which are due to be issued with the financial statements. We are also entitled to attend all general meetings of the company and to receive notice of all such meetings.

2.5 The responsibility for safeguarding the assets of the company and for the prevention and detection of fraud, error and non-compliance with law or regulations rests with yourselves. However, we shall endeavour to plan our audit so that we have a reasonable expectation of detecting material misstatements in the financial statements or accounting records (including those resulting from fraud, error or non-compliance with law or regulations), but our examination should not be relied upon to disclose all such material misstatements or frauds, errors or instances of non-compliance as may exist.

2.6 Once we have issued our report we have no further direct responsibility in relation to the financial statements for that financial year. However, we expect that you will inform us of any material event occurring between the date of our report and that of the Annual General Meeting which may affect the financial statements.

Other services

3. You have requested that we provide other services in respect of taxation advice. The terms under which we provide these other services are dealt with in a separate letter.

Fees

4. Our fees are computed on the basis of the time spent on your affairs by the partners and our staff and on the levels of skill and responsibility involved. Unless otherwise agreed, our fees will be billed at appropriate intervals during the course of the year and will be due on presentation.

Applicable law

5. This engagement letter shall be governed by, and construed in accordance with, English law. The Courts of England shall have exclusive jurisdiction in relation to any claim, dispute or difference concerning the engagement letter and any matter arising from it. Each party irrevocably waives any right it may have to object to an action being brought in those Courts, to claim that the action has been brought in an inconvenient forum, or to claim that those Courts do not have jurisdiction.

Agreement of terms

6. Once it has been agreed, this letter will remain effective, from one audit appointment to another, until it is replaced. We shall be grateful if you could confirm in writing your agreement to these terms by signing and returning the enclosed copy of this letter, or let us know if they are not in accordance with your understanding of our terms of engagement.

Yours faithfully

We agree to the terms of this letter

....
Signed for and on behalf of (company)

Source: Adapted from SAS 140: *Engagement letters*, Appendix.

Auditors should have or obtain a knowledge of the business of the entity to be audited which is sufficient to enable them to identify and understand the events, transactions and practices that may have a significant effect on the financial statements or the audit thereof. (para 2)

Knowledge of the business is used by auditors in, for example, assessing risks of error, in determining the nature, timing and extent of audit procedures and in considering the consistency and reliability of the financial statements as a whole when completing the audit. (para 3)

The auditors' level of knowledge for an engagement normally includes a general knowledge of the economy and the industry within which the entity operates, and a more particular knowledge of how the entity operates. (para 4)[7]

Although the auditor needs to understand the client and its business in order to identify factors that may have a significant effect on the financial statements (that is, for the reason stated in SAS 210, para 2 above), this does not reflect the fundamental, all-pervasive importance of auditors possessing this understanding. The explanation provided in para 3 is closer to it but still does not seem to get to the heart of the matter. By becoming thoroughly familiar with all aspects of the client, and the internal and external factors which affect it, the auditor can understand 'how the client ticks' and (s)he is provided with a background (or context) against which the credibility of evidence gathered during the audit (and responses given by the client's management and employees to the auditor's enquiries) can be evaluated. (In the light of his or her knowledge of the business, its circumstances, and its internal and external environment, does the evidence gathered and responses given 'make sense' and 'ring true'?)

As indicated in SAS 210, para 3, the auditor's understanding of the client also provides a basis for:

- assessing whether circumstances exist which increase the likelihood of errors being present in the financial statements; and
- determining the nature, timing and extent of audit procedures for the audit as a whole and for each audit segment.

By gaining knowledge of the client the auditor may, for example, ascertain that the control environment and the internal financial controls are somewhat weak in a certain division of the business, or (s)he may identify circumstances (such as trading conditions being less good than expected during the previous six months but a planned share float is to go ahead) that may motivate management towards 'gently bending' (if not actually manipulating) the financial statements. In circumstances such as these, the likelihood of the financial statements containing material misstatement is higher than might otherwise be expected. Where the likelihood of material misstatements is high, the auditor will need to ensure that the audit procedures applied are particularly rigorous

---

[7] ISA 310: *Knowledge of the business* paras 2 and 3 are identical in content to SAS 210 paras 2–4.

and that they are focused on the segments of the audit where the risk is considered to be particularly high.[8]

Further, as explained in Chapter 2 (section 2.2.6), gaining an understanding of the client, its business, its business processes, its operational, financial and compliance risks, and its economic, commercial and competitive environment, helps the auditor identify matters of significance and relevance to the financial statements on a timely basis. Expressed in a slightly different way, such knowledge of the business can operate as an 'early warning system' for the auditor, enabling him or her to be alert, and respond appropriately, to factors that may threaten the integrity of the financial statement information. (It may be recalled that an in-depth and wide-ranging knowledge of the client underlies the business risk approach to auditing.)

7.4.2 Obtaining knowledge of the client and its business

In order to understand the client, its business, its business processes and risks, and its industry, the auditor must obtain knowledge of the environmental factors – both external and internal – which affect it.

(i)   External environmental factors include:

- the general economic and competitive conditions of the industry within which the client operates, and the industry's vulnerability to changing economic and political factors;
- the presence or absence of characteristics such as changes in product or process technology, cyclical or seasonal activity, business risk (for example, products prone to consumer fads or rapid obsolescence or deterioration), rapidly declining or expanding markets, that may typify the client's industry;
- environmental considerations that affect the industry in general and/or the client in particular;
- major policies and practices of the industry and industry-specific accounting policies (if any);
- governmental or other regulatory requirements which affect the client and its industry;
- the client's reporting obligations to external parties such as shareholders, debenture holders, regulators (in the case of clients in regulated industries); the Inland Revenue, Department of Trade and Industry, and the Companies Registrar.

---

[8] Assessing the risk of the financial statements being materially misstated and the relationship of such risk and the nature, timing and extent of audit procedures is discussed in detail in Chapter 8.

(ii)   Internal environmental factors include:

- the ownership interests of the client entity;
- the client's organisational structure and management characteristics;
- the relationship between the client's owners, directors and non-director executives;
- the influence of stakeholders other than shareholders;
- the client's financial characteristics – in particular its financial structure and solvency;
- the client's operating characteristics;
- the ethical tone, and strength of the control environment, within the client entity;
- the directors' objectives, philosophy, strategic plans and general approach (for example, entrepreneurial or conservative, planned or haphazard management).[9]

A variety of procedures are available to assist auditors obtain knowledge about their clients and the environmental factors which affect them. These include the following:

(i)   visiting the client and touring the premises;
(ii)   having discussions with key personnel inside and outside the entity;
(iii) reviewing the client's documentation;
(iv)   reviewing industry and business publications and data;
(v)   reviewing previous years' audit working papers.

(i)   Visiting the client and touring the premises: By visiting the client, touring the premises and meeting key personnel (such as the chief executive officer, finance director, marketing, production and personnel department managers, and the chief internal auditor), the auditor can become familiar with the client's layout, organisation and operations.

A tour of the premises enables the auditor to obtain knowledge about the client's production or service provision processes, its storage facilities and its dispatching procedures. It also enables him or her to gain insight into the security (or otherwise) of stocks-in-hand and supplies, and the quantity and quality of stocks-on-hand and fixed assets. Additionally, it enables the auditor to obtain information about the client's accounting records, information technology, and the expertise and work habits of its accounting and other personnel. Further, it provides the opportunity to gauge (by observation of activities) the general attitude of the client personnel to the control environment and the care with which they discharge their responsibilities.

---

[9] SAS 210 and ISA 310 each has an appendix (which are virtually identical in content) listing matters auditors should consider when seeking to gain knowledge of the client's business.

(ii)   Having discussions with key personnel inside and outside the entity: By having discussions with key personnel inside the client entity (for example, the chief executive officer, the finance director, the sales and production managers, and the chief internal auditor), the auditor is able to learn about the entity's policies and procedures, and any changes thereof which have occurred during the reporting period or are expected to occur in the current or future periods. Such discussions also enable the auditor to ascertain the views of key personnel about the entity's financial position and performance during the past year, and any changes in its operations, organisation, financial structure or personnel which are planned or expected in the near to medium term future. Discussions with these key personnel should embrace topics such as likely changes in premises or plant facilities, divisions or departments; expected developments in technology, products or services, or production and distribution methods; and any planned changes to the client's accounting system, information technology, management information systems and internal controls. It also affords the opportunity to gauge the objectives, philosophy, and strategic plans and general approach/attitudes of key executives within the entity.

Discussions with significant people outside the client, such as economists and industry regulators, as well as other auditors, legal, financial and other advisors who have provided services to the client or within the industry, enables the auditor to gain some understanding of the external factors affecting the client – and may also provide some insight into how other external parties view the client, its directors and its senior executives.

(iii)   Reviewing the client's documentation: The auditor may gain considerable knowledge about internal aspects of the client by reviewing its documentation. Such documentation includes its legal documents (for example, Memorandum and Articles of Association, and any debenture trust deeds or other loan agreements); significant commercial agreements; its organisation chart, policies and procedures manuals, and job descriptions; its code of corporate conduct and compliance procedures; minutes of directors' and other (especially board committee) meetings; reports to shareholders and to regulatory agencies (such as the Inland Revenue); promotional material (in hard and electronic form); internal financial management reports, budgets, and chart of accounts; marketing, sales and production plans; and internal audit reports.

(iv)   Reviewing industry and business publications and data: A review of industry and business data, reading trade journals and magazines, and similar publications relating to the client or its industry, and also visiting relevant internet sites, provides the auditor with information which is helpful in understanding the general economic, political, commercial and competitive

factors and processes which are likely to affect the client's operational and financial well-being – and, hence, its financial statements.

(v) Reviewing previous years' audit working papers: Reviewing previous years' audit working papers may highlight problems encountered during previous audits which need to be followed up, or watched for, during the current audit. It may also reveal planned or expected developments which are of significance to the present year's audit – for example, plans disclosed during the previous year to expand or change production and sales, to amend distribution policies, to develop new products, processes and/or markets, or to alter the accounting system, are likely to have an impact on this year's audit.

It should be noted that acquiring knowledge and understanding of a client, its business and its industry is not a one-off event which is completed at the commencement of an audit. Rather, it is a continuous and cumulative process which proceeds as the audit progresses. Although information is gathered and assessed as a basis for planning the audit, it is usually refined and added to as the auditor and audit staff learn more about the client and its business (SAS 210, para 9; ISA 310, para 6).

Clearly, for a new audit engagement, the auditor (more specifically, the audit engagement partner and senior members of the audit team) will need to expend considerable time and effort in establishing a sound understanding of the client, its business and its industry. For continuing engagements, less time and effort may be devoted to this audit step but it should not be skipped altogether. The auditor needs to update and re-evaluate information gathered in previous audits to determine whether it is still valid and relevant. Additionally, the auditor should perform audit procedures which are designed to identify any significant changes that have affected the client, its business or its industry since the last audit (SAS 210, para 10; ISA 310, para 7).

It is important to note that knowledge of the client, its business, its business processes and risks, and its industry are not the prerogative of the audit engagement partner and senior members of the audit team. SAS 210 (and ISA 310) highlight the importance of all members of the audit team having sufficient relevant knowledge to enable them to perform effectively audit work assigned to them. More specifically, SAS 210 states:

> The audit engagement partner should ensure that the audit team obtains such knowledge of the business of the entity being audited as may reasonably be expected to be sufficient to enable it to carry out the audit work effectively. (para 14)
> Such knowledge may be transmitted initially by means of the overall audit plan or an audit briefing meeting and subsequently during the course of the audit. (para 15)

The audit engagement partner also ensures that the audit team understands the need to be alert for and to share additional information. (para 16)[10]

7.5 SUMMARY

In this chapter we have discussed the first steps in the audit process. We have considered why an auditor should conduct an investigation before accepting an audit engagement and pointed out that this investigation involves assessing the auditor's independence (in both fact and appearance) and competence to perform the audit, evaluating the integrity of the (potential) client's management, and communicating with the predecessor auditor. We have also discussed the purpose and content of audit engagement letters, and examined the importance of the auditor gaining a thorough understanding of the client, its business and its industry and how this understanding may be obtained. It has been emphasised that gaining an understanding of the client, its business, its business processes and risks, and its industry is essential for the performance of an efficient and effective audit. More specifically, it has been noted that this understanding provides a sound basis for planning the audit and a background (or context) against which the credibility of audit evidence may be evaluated.

SELF-REVIEW QUESTIONS

7.1 List three elements of the auditor's pre-engagement investigation.

7.2 List five factors auditors should consider before concluding that they are sufficiently independent and competent to accept a particular audit engagement.

7.3 Explain briefly why it is advisable for an auditor to investigate the integrity of a (prospective) client's management before accepting an audit engagement.

7.4 Explain briefly the purpose of a proposed auditor communicating with the existing or predecessor auditor, and list three pieces of information the proposed auditor should seek.

7.5 Explain briefly the purpose of audit engagement letters.

7.6 List five topics which are usually referred to in audit engagement letters.

7.7 Explain briefly the importance of an auditor gaining a thorough understanding of his or her client, its business, business processes and risks, and its industry.

7.8 List five external environmental factors and five internal environmental factors which are likely to affect an entity and its external audit.

---

[10] ISA 310 para 11 contains virtually identical wording to that in SAS 210 paras 14 and 16.

7.9 List five audit procedures which may be used to gain an understanding of the client, its business, and its industry.

7.10 Explain briefly the importance of each of the following procedures for gaining an understanding of the client and its business:
(i) touring the client's premises;
(ii) reading trade journals and magazines;
(iii) visiting relevant internet sites.

REFERENCES

Arens, A.A. & Loebbecke, J.K. (1980) *Auditing: An Integrated Approach*, 2nd ed. New Jersey: Prentice-Hall.

National Commission on Fraudulent Financial Reporting. (1987) *Report of the National Commission on Fraudulent Financial Reporting* (Treadway Commission). New York: AICPA.

Pratt, M.J. & Dilton-Hill, K. (1982) The elements of audit risk. *The South African Chartered Accountant* **18**(4), 137–141.

ADDITIONAL READING

Eilifsen, A., Knechel, W.R. & Wallage, P. (2001) Application of the business risk audit model: a field study. *Accounting Horizons* **15**(3), 193–207.

Gambling, A.A., Schatzberg, J.W., Bailey, AD., Jr & Zhang, H. (1998) The impact of legal liability regimes and differential client risk on client acceptance, audit pricing, and audit effort decisions. *Journal of Accounting, Auditing & Finance* **13**(1), 437–460.

Gendon, Y. (2001). The difficult client-acceptance decision in Canadian audit firms: A field investigation. *Contemporary Accounting Research* **18**(2), 283–310.

Grant Thornton (1990) *Audit Manual*. Chapter 9: Knowledge of the Business and Environmental Assessment. London: Longman, pp. 115–132.

Huss, H.F. & Jacobs, F.A. (1991) Risk containment: exploring auditor decisions in the engagement process. *Auditing: A Journal of Practice & Theory* **10**(2), 16–32.

Miller, K. (1996) ISO 9000 and the external auditor. *Accountancy* **117**(1233), 136.

Stice, J.D. (1991) Using financial and market information to identify pre-engagement factors associated with lawsuits against auditors. *The Accounting Review* **66**(3), 516–533.

8 Planning the Audit and Assessing Audit Risk

LEARNING OBJECTIVES

After studying the material in this chapter you should be able to:
- differentiate between the two phases of planning an audit;
- explain what is meant by the auditor's desired level of assurance (or desired level of audit risk) and factors which affect this;
- distinguish between planning materiality and tolerable error;
- discuss the relationship between the auditor's desired level of audit risk, inherent risk, internal control risk and detection risk;
- discuss the importance of overall analytical review for assessing audit risk and identifying high-risk audit areas;
- describe procedures commonly used for overall analytical review.

The following publications are particularly relevant to this chapter:
- Statement of Auditing Standards (SAS) 100: *Objective and general principles governing an audit of financial statements* (APB, 1995)
- Statement of Auditing Standards (SAS) 200: *Planning* (APB, 1995)
- Statement of Auditing Standards (SAS) 220: *Materiality and the audit* (APB, 1995)
- Statement of Auditing Standards (SAS) 300: *Accounting and internal control systems and audit risk assessments* (APB, 1995)
- Statement of Auditing Standards (SAS) 410: *Analytical procedures* (APB, 1995)
- International Standards on Auditing (ISA) 200: *Objective and basic principles governing an audit of financial statements* (IFAC, 1994)
- International Standards on Auditing (ISA) 300: *Planning* (IFAC, 1994)
- International Standards on Auditing (ISA) 320: *Audit materiality* (IFAC, 1994)
- International Standards on Auditing (ISA) 400: *Risk assessments and internal control* (IFAC, 1994)
- International Standards on Auditing (ISA) 520: *Analytical procedures* (IFAC, 1994).

8.1 INTRODUCTION

If a task is to be accomplished effectively and efficiently it must be carefully planned. This is no less true for an audit than it is for a social event such as a party. The auditor needs to plan what evidence to collect in order to be able to express an opinion on whether or not the financial statements give a true and fair view of the state of affairs and profit or loss of the reporting entity, and how and when to collect this evidence.

Planning an audit has two phases – audit strategy development and audit programme design. Each of these phases is outlined in this chapter but, as audit programme design is discussed in Chapter 9, it is not considered in detail here. This chapter focuses on developing the audit strategy. More specifically, it explains the importance of the auditor's desired level of assurance (or desired level of audit risk), materiality limits, and the auditor's assessment of inherent and internal control risk to the audit strategy. The chapter discusses factors that affect the auditor's desired level of assurance (or desired level of audit risk), the distinction between planning materiality and tolerable error, and the relationship between inherent and internal control risk on the one hand and detection risk on the other. It also explores the interrelationship between materiality, audit risk and audit planning, examines the meaning and importance of analytical review, and considers the assessment of audit risk through overall analytical review.

8.2 PHASES OF PLANNING AN AUDIT

8.2.1 Benefits and characteristics of audit planning

Statement of Auditing Standards (SAS) 200: *Planning* states:

> Auditors should plan the audit work so as to perform the audit in an effective manner. The audit work planned should be reviewed and, if necessary, revised during the course of the audit. (paras 2 and 16)[1]

The Standard explains that planning is necessary to ensure that appropriate attention is devoted to the different areas of the audit, potential problems are identified, and the work is completed in an efficient and timely manner (para 5) (ISA 300 para 4). It also notes that obtaining knowledge of the entity's business is an important part of planning the audit and that the extent of audit planning will vary according to the size of the auditee and the complexity of the audit (paras 7 and 8) (ISA 300, paras 5 and 6).

---

[1] The wording of ISA 300: *Planning,* paras 2 and 12, is very similar to that of SAS 200, paras 2 and 16.

SAS 200, para 3 (and ISA 300, para 3) observes that planning an audit entails two distinct phases, namely:

- developing a general strategy (an overall audit plan); and
- developing a detailed approach for the expected nature, timing and extent of audit procedures (an audit programme).

SAS 200 explains:

> Auditors formulate the general audit strategy in an overall audit plan, which sets the direction for the audit and provides guidance for the development of the audit programme. The audit programme sets out the detailed procedures required to implement the strategy. (para 4)

The Standard also emphasises that planning is not a 'one-off' event at the start of the audit but should continue throughout an audit. It notes that if changed conditions are encountered and/or audit procedures generate unexpected results, the audit strategy and/or the audit programme may need to be revised (para 17) (ISA 300, para 12).

8.2.2 The audit strategy (overall audit plan)

Once the auditor has gained a thorough understanding of the client and its business (as outlined in Chapter 7), the audit strategy can be developed. That is, the scope and conduct of the audit can be determined or, more specifically, plans can be made regarding:

- how much and what evidence to gather;
- how and when this should be done.

In essence, developing the audit strategy depends on factors such as the following:[2]

- general economic factors and industry conditions affecting the entity's business and important characteristics of the entity, its business, its financial position and performance and its statutory, regulatory and reporting requirements. (These factors largely coincide with those identified in Chapter 7 in relation to Understanding the client, its business and its industry);
- the level of assurance (or level of confidence) the auditor wishes to gain regarding the appropriateness of the opinion expressed in the audit report (or, alternatively, the level of risk (s)he is prepared to accept that the opinion expressed in the audit report may be inappropriate). (This factor is discussed in section 8.3);

---

[2] SAS 200, para 12 (and ISA 300, para 9) provides a comprehensive list of items the auditor should consider when developing an audit strategy.

- the limits beyond which errors in the financial statements as a whole, and in individual financial statement amounts, are to be regarded as 'material'. (This factor is discussed in section 8.4);
- the likelihood of material errors being present in the (unaudited) financial statements as a whole, and in certain sections thereof (that is, the level of inherent risk and internal control risk). (This factor is discussed in section 8.5);
- the appropriate segments into which the audit should be divided to facilitate the conduct of audit work. (This factor is discussed in Chapter 9);
- the availability of audit evidence from different sources and of different types. (This factor is discussed in Chapter 6);
- the likely impact of the use of information technology by the entity or by the auditor;
- the availability of suitable audit staff and, where applicable, other (outside) auditors and experts. (This factor is discussed in Chapter 6.)

Once factors such as those outlined above have been determined, the overall audit plan can be developed. This sets out in broad terms:

(i)   the nature of audit procedures to be performed – in particular, the expected emphasis to be placed on, respectively, testing compliance with internal controls and substantive testing of transactions and account balances;
(ii) the timing of audit procedures – the procedures expected to be performed during the interim audit (the part of the audit generally performed some months before the client's year end) and the final audit (performed at and/or shortly after the client's year end);[3]
(iii) the extent of audit procedures – the amount of audit evidence expected to be collected in relation to each audit segment.

8.2.3   The audit programme

The audit programme, in effect, operationalises the audit strategy. It sets out in detail the audit procedures to be performed in each segment of the audit, indicating those to be performed during the interim audit and those to be performed during the final audit. It frequently also includes details of such things as the size of samples to be tested and how the samples are to be selected.

As noted in Chapter 6, the audit programme often lists audit procedures in the form of instructions audit staff can follow. As the procedures are performed, they are signed off by the staff member concerned and cross-referenced to relevant audit working papers. (Developing the audit programme is discussed in Chapter 9.)

---

[3] In general, the interim audit focuses on understanding the entity's accounting system and testing compliance with internal controls; the final audit focuses more particularly on substantive testing.

8.3 DESIRED LEVEL OF ASSURANCE (DESIRED LEVEL OF AUDIT RISK)

8.3.1 Meaning of desired level of assurance (desired level of audit risk)

The Companies Act 1985 requires auditors to state in their audit reports, amongst other things:

- whether, *in their opinion,* the financial statements give a true and fair view of the state of affairs of the company (and, in relevant cases, of the Group) and its (or the Group's) profit or loss;
- whether, *in their opinion,* the financial statements have been properly prepared in accordance with the Companies Act. (emphasis added)

It should be noted that auditors are required to express an opinion, not to certify that the financial statements give a true and fair view and comply with the Companies Act. Thus it seems that, in passing the legislation, Parliament did not expect auditors to reach a state of certainty with respect to the matters in question. This conclusion is reflected in SAS 100: *Objective and general principles governing an audit of financial statements,* which states:

> The auditors' opinion enhances the credibility of the financial statements by pro-viding *reasonable assurance* from an independent source that they present a true and fair view. . . An audit carried out in accordance with Auditing Standards is designed to provide *reasonable assurance* that the financial statements taken as a whole are free from material misstatement. The term 'reasonable assurance' is therefore central to an audit undertaken in accordance with Auditing Standards. (paras 5 and 8, emphasis added).

But, what is reasonable assurance? Let us first look at what Auditing Standards tell us. SAS 100 (para 8) explains:

> The view given in financial statements is itself based on a combination of fact and judgment and, consequently, cannot be characterised as either 'absolute' or 'correct'. When reporting on financial statements auditors provide a level of assurance which is reasonable in that context but, equally, cannot be absolute.

This does not seem to shed much light on the meaning of 'reasonable assur-ance'. ISA 300: *Objective and general principles governing an audit of financial statements* also seems to be unhelpful in this regard. It states (para 8):

> Reasonable assurance is a concept relating to the accumulation of the audit evi-dence necessary for the auditor to conclude that there are no material misstate-ments in the financial statements taken as a whole. Reasonable assurance relates to the whole audit process.

If Auditing Standards do not enlighten us, what can we deduce about the mean-ing of this important concept? We have seen that auditors are not expected to be *certain* that financial statements, which they report as giving a true and fair view of the entity's financial position and performance and as complying with the Companies Act 1985, are not materially misstated. However, they clearly want to be reasonably confident that this is indeed the case. The level of confidence they wish to attain (to be 'reasonably' confident or assured about the 'correctness' of the opinion they express on the financial statements) is known as their desired level of assurance. Arens and Loebbecke (1980) define the concept as follows:

> The *desired level of assurance* is the subjectively determined level of confidence that the auditor wants to have about the fair presentation of the financial statements after the audit is completed. The higher the level of assurance attained, the more confident the auditor is that the financial statements [on which a 'clean' opinion is expressed] contain no material misstatements or omissions. (p. 142).

They also note:

> Complete assurance of the accuracy of the financial statements is not possible. . . . the auditor cannot guarantee the complete absence of material errors and irregularities. (p. 142)

This theme is echoed by Anderson (1977) who states:

> Absolute certainty in the presentation of audited financial statements is neither possible nor its pursuit economically desirable. The auditor's report adds credibility to the statements to which it is appended, but it cannot add complete certainty. . . . [Audit procedures could be extended, but] the cost of such an extension [beyond some point] would be out of all proportion to the minuscule increment in credibility thereby achieved. (pp. 129–130)

It should be noted that the auditor's desired level of assurance (the auditor's desired level of confidence about the 'correctness' of the opinion expressed on the financial statements) is the complement of his or her desired level of audit risk. It was noted in Chapter 3 (section 3.4.3) that SAS 300: *Accounting and internal control systems and audit risk assessments* defines audit risk as 'the risk that auditors may give an inappropriate opinion on financial statements'. Thus, if, for example, the auditor wishes to be 95% assured (or confident) that the financial statements on which (s)he expresses a 'clean' audit opinion are free of material misstatements, this means that (s)he is prepared to accept a 5% risk that the financial statements, in fact, contain such errors and, therefore, a 'clean' opinion is inappropriate.

8.3.2 Factors affecting the auditor's desired level of assurance (or desired level of audit risk)

An auditor's desired level of assurance will always be high (or, alternatively stated, his or her desired level of audit risk will always be low). It is frequently expressed in quantitative terms (a 95% level of assurance or 5% level of audit risk is often quoted as a rule of thumb) but it is clearly difficult to pinpoint when a particular numeric level of assurance has been reached. As a result, in practice, auditors often adopt a qualitative approach and think in terms of a 'high' or 'medium' level of assurance (or 'medium' or 'low' level of risk) rather than in precise percentage terms.

In certain circumstances auditors wish to attain a particularly high level of assurance (a particularly low level of audit risk). This applies, for example, in cases where a large number of users are likely to rely on the financial statements, and/or where heavy reliance is placed upon the statements by one or more users (such as when a takeover is contemplated), and/or where there is doubt about the client's ability to continue as a going concern. In each of these cases, if the auditor signifies that the financial statements give a true and fair view of the entity's state of affairs and profit or loss when they contain a material error or omission, or a materially inadequate disclosure, serious consequences may ensue for both the financial statement user(s) and for the auditor.

Generally speaking, the larger the entity (in terms of total revenues or total assets), and the more widely disbursed its ownership and its debts, the greater the number of users of its audited financial statements. A large listed public company, such as BP, Diageo, HSBC or British Telecom, which has extensive economic resources and numerous shareholders, debtholders and creditors, is likely to have its audited financial statements used far more widely than are companies with few shareholders and/or few debtholders and other creditors. Private companies, wholly owned subsidiaries, and companies whose directors hold a large proportion of the company's equity and debt (as applies in some smaller companies) are likely to have relatively few financial statements users who are remote from the company. As Arens and Loebbecke (1991) point out:

> When the [financial] statements are heavily relied on, a great social harm could result if a significant error were to remain undetected. . . . The cost of additional evidence [that is, raising the auditor's level of assurance] can be more easily justified when the loss to users from material errors is [likely to be] substantial. (p. 258)

Additionally, where audited financial statements have a large number of users, each of whom may suffer loss if the auditor fails to detect a material error, omission or inadequate disclosure and inappropriately issues a 'clean' audit report thereon, the auditor may have a wide exposure to potential liability for negligence.[4] Thus, where a large number of users rely on financial statements, it may be in the auditor's own interest to seek a particularly high level of assurance (low level of audit risk). The same is true where one or more users place heavy reliance on the audited financial statements when making a major investment decision (such as in a takeover situation). If the potential investors decide to make the investment and the audited financial statements on which they rely subsequently prove to be materially misstated, they are likely to suffer serious financial loss. As a result, they are likely to seek redress from the auditors for the loss they sustain.

---

[4] In the UK the *Caparo* case has limited the parties to whom auditors owe a duty of care and thus their exposure to potential liability. This is discussed in detail in Chapter 14.

Another situation in which the auditor may desire a particularly high level of assurance about the truth and fairness of the financial statements before issuing a 'clean' audit report is where there is some doubt about the entity's status as a going concern. This is because, if a client is forced into liquidation shortly after receiving a 'clean' audit report and the financial statements are subsequently found to contain material errors, omissions, or inadequate disclosures, the auditor may be exposed to litigation, brought by the company's liquidator or by those who suffer loss as a result of the entity's collapse. If, in such circumstances, the auditor raises his or her desired level of assurance (reduces his or her desired level of audit risk), he will gather more evidence than would otherwise be the case and be particularly concerned to see that the nature of the going concern problem is adequately disclosed in the notes to the financial statements. As a result of these actions, the auditor will be more likely to detect material errors, omissions, and/or inadequate disclosures in the financial statements and, failing this, will be better placed to defend the quality of the audit should a challenge arise.[5]

8.4   IMPACT OF MATERIALITY ON PLANNING AN AUDIT

8.4.1   Planning materiality and tolerable error

It was noted in Chapter 3 (section 3.4.2) that auditors are required 'to determine with reasonable confidence whether the financial statements are free of *material* misstatement' (SAS 100, para 2, emphasis added) and that a 'matter is material if its omission . . . [or] misstatement . . . would reasonably influence the decisions of an addressee of the auditors' report' (SAS 220, para 3).

From these quotations it is evident that, when planning their audits, auditors need to form a judgment as to what is 'material' in the context of a particular audit. In Chapter 3 we explained that in forming this judgment auditors need to consider both the quantity and quality of financial statement items and both overall and account level materiality. The distinction between overall and account level materiality is of particular significance to planning an audit.

(i)   Overall materiality

This refers to the amount of error the auditor is prepared to accept in the financial statements as a whole while still concluding that they provide a true and fair view of the state of affairs and profit or loss of the reporting entity. The auditor needs to estimate this level of error, or materiality level, prior to commencing the audit, based on his understanding of the client, its business and

---

[5] Auditors' responsibilities as regards assessing audit clients' 'going concern' status are discussed in Chapter 12.

its industry, and on his or her assessment of the decision needs of users of the auditee's financial statements. It is often referred to as 'planning materiality' or, in terms of SAS 220: *Materiality and the audit* (para 9), as the 'preliminary materiality assessment'. It provides a basis for planning the nature, timing and extent of procedures to be performed during the audit. The lower the level of planning materiality (the smaller the amount of error in the financial statements as a whole which qualifies as 'material'), the greater the amount and/or the more appropriate the evidence[6] that needs to be collected to ensure that the combined errors in the financial statements do not exceed it.

However, planning materiality must not be viewed as a fixed monetary amount which, if exceeded even by a small margin, will necessarily cause the auditor to conclude that the financial statements do not give a true and fair view, but which, if not exceeded, will lead to the contrary conclusion. When forming an opinion on a set of financial statements, the auditor considers a myriad of factors – including the size and direction of the difference between the actual error estimated to exist in the financial statements (as estimated at the conclusion of the audit) and the auditor's preliminary estimate of error (planning materiality) which would be accepted while still concluding the financial statements are 'true and fair'. Planning materiality provides a starting point for the auditor's conclusion.

To emphasise the imprecise nature of planning materiality, auditors frequently express it as a range of monetary amounts, rather than as a single figure. Auditing Standards do not require auditors to quantify planning materiality, however, in practice, most auditors do so. Surveys in the USA, New Zealand (NZ), and elsewhere have shown that auditors use a variety of bases for this purpose. A survey conducted in the USA by Read *et al.* (1987), for example, found that the 97 auditors surveyed used 9 different bases to establish planning materiality. The most popular base was pre-tax operating income (used by 45% of respondents), followed by total revenue (used by 15%), and after-tax operating income (used by 10%). Other bases used include total assets, current assets, current liabilities and long-term liabilities. Interestingly, 12% of the auditors surveyed did not use a financial statement amount to arrive at a figure (or range of figures) for planning materiality but relied instead on judgment (or 'instinct'). The study also showed that even where different auditors adopted the same financial statement base to estimate their planning materiality (such as pre-tax operating income), they applied a variety of percentages to the base.

In NZ, a survey conducted by Pratt and Cuthbertson in 1988 (reported in Pratt, 1990) found that the 'Big 7' international accounting firms then represented in

---

[6] The relationship between the sufficiency and appropriateness of evidence is discussed in Chapter 6.

Figure 8.1: Planning Materiality Guidelines used by the 'Big 7' accounting firms in New Zealand in 1988 (figures are percentages)

Criteria	Accounting firms						
	1	**2**	**3**	**4**	**5**	**6**	**7**
Net profit – before tax	10*	9–10		5		5–10	5
– after tax			5–10		5–10		
Sales (or turnover)	1–1½		½–1	¼–½		$ #	½
Gross profit				1–2			
Total assets	1		1–2	½	1		½
Current assets				1			
Working capital						$ #	
Shareholders' funds			2–5	1–5		$ #	

Notes: * The materiality level can be increased to 12½% for subsidiaries within a group.
　　　　# Consideration is given to the dollar amounts involved when determining materiality.

New Zealand[7] used the guidelines shown in Figure 8.1 for determining their planning materiality.

From Figure 8.1 it may be seen that:

- the seven firms used a fairly wide range of bases for establishing their planning materiality and that, in general, these coincided with the bases used by the auditors in the US study;
- the percentages applied by different firms to the same financial statement base varied quite widely. For example, the percentages applied to net profit before tax ranged from 5%, used by Firms 4 and 7, to 10%, adopted by Firm 1. Similarly, the percentages applied to sales ranged from ¼–½%, applied by Firm 4, to 1–1½%, used by Firm 1;
- most of the firms arrived at a figure (or range of figures) for planning materiality by reviewing the estimates derived from the various bases and exercising judgment. Only Firm 2 relied on just one base, namely, net profit before tax.

From discussions with senior audit partners in the 'Big 5' international accounting firms in the UK in 2001, a similar variety of bases, and similar range of percentages applied to the bases, are used by these firms for setting their planning materiality limits.

---

[7] The seven firms included in the survey were Arthur Young, Coopers & Lybrand, Deloitte Haskins & Sells, Ernst & Whinney, KPMG Peat Marwick, Price Waterhouse and Touche Ross.

(ii)   Account level materiality

The monetary amount or range established for planning materiality not only defines the amount of error the auditor is prepared to accept in the financial statements as a whole before concluding they are not 'true and fair'; it also provides the basis for establishing the maximum amount of error the auditor will tolerate in an individual account balance, class of transactions, and/or other financial statement disclosure before concluding that the relevant balance or disclosure is materially misstated. Similarly, while the overall level of materiality helps to determine the amount of audit effort required for the audit as a whole, the account level materiality determines the nature, timing and extent of audit procedures to be performed in relation to each account balance, or class of transactions and related disclosures. Use of the term 'tolerable error' for the account level estimate of materiality is a useful means of distinguishing between this level of materiality and overall (or planning) materiality. We therefore adopt this term for use in this book.

At the outset, it must be emphasised that setting the tolerable error for individual accounts (or class of transactions) is never easy and always involves considerable judgment by the auditor. It should also be noted that different audit firms approach the task in different ways. However, in general, as a starting point, tolerable error for each account balance or class of transactions is set at a selected level (for example, it may be set at 60% or 75%) of planning materiality.[8] The monetary amount thus established may then be adjusted upwards or downwards for individual accounts for factors which are specific to that account. In this way, tolerable error is established for each financial statement account balance.

Factors auditors will take into consideration when setting the tolerable error for individual accounts include the following:

- the significance of the financial statement account balance to the decisions of users of the financial statements. The cash balance, for instance, with its implications for company liquidity and flexibility may be more material to financial statement users than – say – prepaid expenses. The more important a particular financial statement account balance is to users, the more important it is that it is stated accurately; hence, the smaller the tolerable error;
- the size of the account balance. For example, if the debtors balance is £700,000 and the stock balance is £1,500,000, the tolerable error in the

---

[8] If planning materiality is the maximum amount of error the auditor will allow in the financial statements as a whole while still concluding that they give a true and fair view of the financial position and performance of the reporting entity, it is clear that the tolerable error (the maximum amount of error the auditor will tolerate in an account balance or class of transactions while concluding that the relevant balance is true and fair) cannot exceed the monetary amount of planning materiality.

debtors account (in monetary terms) is likely to be set at a lower level than for the stock account;

- the auditability of the account. Certain accounts such as cash and loans are capable of more accurate verification than others, such as debtors and depreciation, where provisions need to be estimated. This variation should be reflected in the expectations of financial statement users with respect to the accuracy of account balances. The greater the expected accuracy of an account balance, the smaller the tolerable error;
- the relative significance of understatement and overstatement of an account balance. In general, overstatements of assets and understatements of liabilities are more likely to be material to financial statement users than their counterparts (understatements of assets and overstatements of liabilities), and this can be reflected in the materiality limits. Tolerable error may, therefore, be set at different levels for understatements and overstatements in certain account balances.

Some of the ideas presented above in relation to planning materiality and tolerable error may, perhaps, be best understood if illustrated by an example. Let us assume that, from calculations based on net profit after tax, sales, total assets and shareholders' funds, planning materiality for a particular set of financial statements is estimated at £70,000. Let us also assume that, given the particular circumstances of the audit, the auditor considers it appropriate to set tolerable error initially at 70% of planning materiality (£49,000). If the account being considered is, say, stock (or inventories), the auditor will be aware of, amongst other things, the difficulty of auditing this account as a consequence of, for example, assessing the condition of the stock, possible obsolescence, etc. Given such factors, the initial estimate of tolerable error may be adjusted downwards by a relatively small amount, say to £45,000. On the other hand, if the account being considered is cash, the significance of this account balance for users of the financial statements and their likely expectation that the balance will be stated fairly accurately, is likely to result in the initial estimate of tolerable error being adjusted downwards by a significant amount – to, say, £10,000. In this case, if the stock or cash balance is found to be misstated by an amount in the region of £45,000 or £10,000, respectively, the auditor is likely to require the auditee's directors to adjust the errant account balance before an unqualified (or 'clean') audit report will be issued.

It should be noticed that we have referred to the stock and cash account balances causing concern for the auditor when they are misstated by an amount *in the region of* £45,000 or £10,000, respectively. This underscores the point that (like planning materiality) the limit set for tolerable error in each account is an estimate, not a 'magic number', which, if exceeded by even a minuscule amount will cause the auditor to require the account balance to be adjusted but which, if not exceeded, prompts no action. Indeed, all errors that are found, even if less than tolerable error, need to be investigated to establish their cause and the likely implications for the estimated error in the account.

As for determining planning materiality, estimating tolerable error for individual financial statement account balances is an important step in planning the audit; the magnitude of the tolerable error has a direct impact on what qualifies as 'sufficient appropriate amount of audit evidence' (see Chapter 6) that must be gathered. The smaller the tolerable error, the more relevant and reliable and/or the greater the amount of evidence the auditor must collect in order to be assured that errors in the account in question do not exceed the materiality limit.

8.4.2 Amending materiality estimates

When considering materiality in the auditing context it is important to remember that neither planning materiality nor tolerable error are 'magic numbers'. They are limits set by the auditor during the planning phase of the audit which reflect his or her judgment as to the level of misstatement in the financial statements as a whole, and in individual financial statement account balances, at which the decisions or actions of reasonable users of the financial statements are likely to be affected.

The quantitative limits of planning materiality and tolerable error are determined as objectively as possible. Planning materiality, for example, as explained in section 8.4.1, is frequently established by applying pre-set percentages to pre-selected financial statement bases. However, notwithstanding auditors' efforts to arrive at materiality estimates, objectively this does not mean they should be regarded as fixed and unalterable. As explained in Chapter 3 (section 3.4.2), qualitative characteristics of financial statement items are also important and, when the materiality (or otherwise) of a misstatement is evaluated, as much attention should be given to the nature of the misstatement as to its amount.

Further, as the audit progresses, the auditor may find that the level of planning materiality and/or tolerable error in one or more account balance or class of transactions needs to be changed. This may occur, for instance, because one of the bases used to establish planning materiality is amended (for example, sales or pre-tax profits) and/or because new information comes to light which causes the auditor to conclude that planning materiality or tolerable error was established at a level which is too high or too low. SAS 220 explains, for example:

> The assessment of materiality during audit planning may differ from that at the time of evaluating the results of audit procedures. This may be because of a change in circumstances or a change in the auditors' knowledge as a result of the

216 _____ Principles of External Auditing

audit, for example if the actual results of operations and financial position are different from those they expected when the auditor was planned. (para 10)[9]

If, during the audit, factors come to the auditor's attention which suggest that planning materiality, and/or tolerable error in one or more account balance or class of transactions, is set at too high or too low a level, the bases on which the materiality estimates were established need to be re-evaluated. If, upon examining the bases in the light of the new knowledge, the auditor considers that a change in the materiality limits is appropriate, then the change should be made – and the implications of the change for the planned audit procedures (their nature, timing and extent) – should be considered and any necessary modifications made.

In general, auditors find it easier to adjust materiality estimates upwards. They tend to be less willing to adjust them downwards or to maintain those which are found to have been exceeded. This asymmetry arises because, the lower the materiality limit:

- the greater the amount and/or the more appropriate (relevant and/or reliable) the audit evidence that needs to be collected to make sure the limit has not been exceeded. (The lower the materiality limit, the smaller the margin of error within which the auditor must work – and, thus, the more 'careful' the auditor must be to establish, through the collection of evidence, that the limit has not been exceeded); and
- the more likely it is that misstatements which are discovered will exceed the limit and thus qualify as 'material'. Such (material) errors, if not adjusted by the reporting entity, should give rise to a qualified audit report.

The effect of lowering materiality limits is explained in SAS 220 (para 11) as follows:

> [I]f, after planning for specific audit procedures, [auditors] determine that the acceptable materiality level is lower than was previously assessed, the risk of failing to detect a material misstatement necessarily increases. They compensate for this by carrying out more audit work. (para 11)

Clearly, raising the materiality limits has the reverse impact.

---

[9] ISA 320 (para 11) provides a rather fuller explanation:

> The auditor's assessment of materiality . . . may be different at the time of initially planning the engagement from at the time of evaluating the results of audit procedures. This could be because of a change in circumstances or because of a change in the auditor's knowledge as a result of the audit. For example, if the audit is planned prior to period end, the auditor will anticipate the results of operations and the financial position. If actual results of operations and financial position are substantially different, the assessment of materiality . . . may also change. Additionally, the auditor may, in planning the audit work, intentionally set the acceptable materiality level at a lower level than is results of the audit. This may be done to reduce the likelihood of undiscovered misstatements and to provide the auditor with a margin of safety when evaluating the effect of misstatements discovered during the audit

The auditor will not relish having to increase the extent or amend the nature of planned audit procedures, largely because such extension or amendment will have an adverse impact on audit time and cost. Similarly, the auditor will not welcome having to put pressure on the reporting entity's management (if this becomes necessary) to correct misstatements in the financial statements which are judged by the auditor to be material and, in the event of the auditee's directors not making the required amendments, issuing a qualified audit report. Such eventualities almost invariably cause a strain in the relations between the auditor and the entity's management.

Thus, when factors are encountered during an audit which raise questions about the propriety of materiality estimates established in the planning phase of the audit, justification for amending those estimates must be considered carefully. Upward adjustments should only be made, and downward adjustments should not be resisted, when examination of the bases on which planning materiality and tolerable error in individual financial statements account balances were determined, reveals that the initial materiality estimates were inappropriate. In particular, when the auditor finds that misstatements in individual account balances, or in the financial statements as a whole, exceed the pre-set materiality limits, (s)he must avoid any temptation to adopt spurious arguments to justify adjusting the relevant estimate(s) upwards (and thus avoid additional audit work).

8.5 IMPACT OF AUDIT RISK ON PLANNING AN AUDIT

8.5.1 Risk-based approach to auditing

In section 8.3, we noted that audit risk (the risk of the auditor expressing an inappropriate opinion on a set of financial statements)[10] is the complement of the auditor's level of assurance (the auditor's level of confidence about the appropriateness of the opinion expressed). Ultimately, to the auditor, audit risk amounts to exposure to legal liability if, as a result of issuing a 'clean' audit report on financial statements which are materially misstated, a user of the financial statements is misled and suffers a loss as a consequence.[11] However, as noted in section 8.3, an auditor *expresses an opinion* on the financial statements;

---

[10] As explained in Chapter 3 (section 3.4.3), because the likelihood of the auditor expressing a qualified audit opinion when the financial statements are, in fact, not materially misstated is so small that the term 'audit risk' is usually taken to mean the risk of an auditor expressing an unqualified (i.e. 'clean') audit opinion on financial statements that are materially misstated. Similarly, the term 'the auditor's level of assurance' is usually taken to mean the auditor's level of confidence that the financial statements on which (s)he expresses a 'clean' opinion are not materially misstated.

[11] As noted in footnote 4, in the UK the *Caparo* case has limited the parties to whom auditors owe a duty of care, and thus their exposure to potential liability.

(s)he does not *certify* their truth and fairness. As a result, some degree of audit risk (forming the 'wrong' opinion) is unavoidable and legal action against an auditor should succeed only if the auditor wittingly or negligently accepts an unreasonably high level of audit risk (i.e. forms an opinion based on evidence (s)he knows to be inadequate or does not care whether or not it is adequate).

In today's highly competitive audit environment, audit firms have focused their attention on conducting efficient, cost-effective audits. This has led to them adopting a risk-based approach to auditing; that is, assessing the risk of the unaudited financial statements being materially misstated and tailoring their audit procedures accordingly.

Like establishing materiality thresholds, the risk of errors (or omissions) occurring in the unaudited financial statements (which may be referred to as pre-audit risk) is considered at two levels; the overall (financial statement) level and the individual financial statement account or class of transactions level.

- *Pre-audit risk at the overall level* refers to the risk of material misstatement being present in the financial statements as a whole (that is, the likelihood of planning materiality being exceeded) and, based on this, determining the total amount of effort (or work) required for the audit as a whole. (The higher the likelihood of material misstatement being present, the greater the amount of audit work required.)
- *Pre-audit risk at the individual financial statement account balance or audit segment level* refers to identifying high audit-risk areas; that is, identifying specific accounts or class of transactions where material misstatement is most likely to occur (or, in other words, where tolerable error is most likely to be exceeded). Once these areas have been identified, total audit effort may be allocated so as to ensure that audit work is concentrated primarily in the high-risk areas.

The objective of risk-based auditing is to achieve maximum effectiveness and efficiency (that is, to arrive at the appropriate audit opinion whilst incurring least cost). It is designed to ensure that neither the financial statements as a whole, nor any segment thereof, are under- or over-audited; that is, that neither too little, nor too much, audit evidence is gathered to achieve the auditor's desired level of audit risk (or desired level of assurance). Too little audit evidence leaves the auditor with greater exposure to audit risk than (s)he wishes to accept; too much evidence means the auditor's exposure to risk is reduced to beyond the level (s)he is prepared to accept and, as a result, represents unnecessary expenditure of audit time and cost.

The auditor assesses the overall risk of material error being present in the unaudited financial statements, and identifies high audit-risk areas through:

- gaining a thorough understanding of the client, its business, its industry and its key personnel (see Chapter 7);
- performing analytical procedures (discussed in section 8.6) and evaluating the client's system of internal control (see Chapter 9).

8.5.2 Relationship between inherent risk, internal control risk and detection risk

In Chapter 3 (section 3.4.3) we noted that audit risk comprises two main components:

- the risk that the unaudited financial statements are materially misstated in one or more respects. (This is a function of inherent risk and internal control risk); and
- the risk that the auditor will fail to detect a material misstatement which is present. (This is a function of sampling and quality control risk, collectively referred to as detection risk.[12])

The relationship between audit risk and its components may be presented (in simplified form) as follows:

Risk of the auditor expressing a 'clean' opinion on materially misstated financial statements	=	Risk of material error being present in the unaudited financial statements	+	Risk of failing to detect material error
Audit risk	=	Inherent risk + internal control risk	+	detection risk

At this point it may be helpful to recall (from Chapter 6) that audit procedures are basically of two kinds: compliance procedures and substantive procedures.

- *Compliance procedures* are designed to ascertain whether the entity's internal controls are operating effectively (that is, are being complied with) and have been so operating throughout the reporting period. In the context of the audit risk equation (above), compliance procedures are particularly relevant to the evaluation of internal control risk.
- *Substantive procedures* are designed to substantiate, or to evaluate the substance (validity, completeness and accuracy) of, financial statement balances. They fall into two broad categories, namely:
  - specific analytical procedures; and
  - tests of details. These tests are of two types: tests of transactions and direct tests of account balances.

---

[12] Inherent risk, internal control risk, sampling risk and quality control risk are discussed in Chapter 3, section 3.4.3.

Substantive procedures have a direct bearing on detection risk. In general, the lower the levels of inherent risk and internal control risk (that is, the lower the risk of material error being present in the unaudited financial statements), the less than substantive procedures which are required to confirm that the financial statements are, in fact, free of material error. In other words, where the auditor believes there is little likelihood of material misstatement occurring in the financial statements (inherent and internal control risk are low), the greater the risk (s)he is prepared to accept that a material error, if present, will not be detected (high detection risk). Therefore, the less the substantive procedures that will need to be performed.

When considering the relationship between the components of audit risk it should be borne in mind that:

- inherent risk is the risk of material error being present in the unaudited financial statements in the absence of internal controls. Thus, conceptually, the auditor assesses the likelihood of error occurring in the unaudited financial statements in two stages:
  (i)   first, inherent risk is assessed; then
  (ii) the extent to which the entity's internal controls reduce the likelihood of error occurring in the unaudited financial statements is evaluated;
- gaining an understanding of the client and performing analytical procedures are particularly important for assessing inherent risk; evaluating the client's internal control system and testing for compliance with its internal controls (performing compliance procedures) are the primary means of determining internal control risk;
- inherent risk and internal control risk are beyond the direct control of the auditor. As a consequence, the auditor must adjust detection risk (primarily by increasing or reducing the extent and/or appropriateness of substantive procedures) in order to achieve his or her desired level of audit risk (or alternately stated, his or her desired level of assurance);
- inherent risk and internal control risk may both be assessed as high, or may both be assessed as low, or one may be assessed as high and the other as low. But, whatever their combined level of risk, this directly impacts the extent of the substantive procedures the auditor must conduct in order to achieve his desired level of audit risk.

The conceptual aspects of the relationships indicated above may be illustrated (in simplified form) by reference to numerical examples.

Example 1:   Assume the following facts:
- The auditor's desired level of audit risk is 5% (desired level of assurance is 95%).

- After assessing inherent risk the auditor believes there is a 60% risk of material misstatement being present in the unaudited financial statements.
- After evaluating the entity's internal controls, the auditor reduces his or her assessment of the risk of material misstatement occurring in the unaudited financial statements to 20% (a reduction of 40 percentage points).

Given the facts outlined above, it is evident that in order to achieve a desired level of audit risk of 5%, the auditor must reduce his assessment of audit risk by a further 15 percentage points through the performance of substantive procedures.

Desired level of audit risk	=	Inherent risk	−	Risk reduction through internal control assessment	−	Risk reduction through substantive audit procedures
5%	=	60%	−	40%	−	15%

Example 2: Assume the following facts:

- The auditor's desired level of audit risk is 5% (desired level of assurance is 95%).
- After assessing inherent risk, the auditor believes there is an 85% risk of material misstatement being present in the unaudited financial statements.
- After assessing the effectiveness of the entity's internal controls, the auditor assesses the risk of material misstatement occurring in the unaudited financial statements as 75% (a reduction of 10 percentage points).

Given the above facts, it is evident that, in order to achieve a desired level of audit risk of 5%, the auditor must reduce audit risk by a further 70 percentage points through the performance of substantive procedures.

Desired level of audit risk	=	Inherent risk	−	Risk reduction through internal control assessment	−	Risk reduction through substantive audit procedures
5%	=	85%	−	10%	−	70%

In the first example the auditor plans to use substantive procedures to reduce overall audit risk by 15 percentage points, whereas in the second case such procedures need to reduce audit risk by 70 percentage points. It follows that in the second case the substantive procedures need to be significantly more extensive than in the first.

The above examples illustrate how, conceptually, inherent risk (the risk or likelihood of errors being present in the financial data in the absence of internal controls) is reduced to the auditor's desired level of audit risk in two stages:

(i) by assessing the likelihood of errors present in the financial data not being detected by the internal controls and thus occurring in the unaudited financial statements; and

(ii) by performing substantive procedures to reduce the likelihood of undetected errors remaining in the financial statements on which the auditor expresses a 'clean' audit opinion.

Although we have represented this risk reduction process conceptually as two sequential subtractions from inherent risk, a simple probability multiplication rule is more appropriate (and is adopted as guidance by some firms) to determine the level of detection risk which should be planned for in order to reduce audit risk to the desired level. In statistics, the probability of two events (A and B) both happening is the multiple of the probability of A [p(A)] and the probability of B [p(B)]. Thus the multiple of the risk (or probability) of a material error occurring in the unaudited financial statements, and the risk (or probability) of the substantive tests failing to detect it, gives the risk of the auditor failing to qualify materially misstated financial statements (that is, audit risk). This reasoning underlies what is commonly referred to as the 'audit risk model' which may be represented as follows:[13]

Desired level of audit risk	=	Risk of material error occurring in the unaudited financial statements	×	Risk of failing to detect material error
Audit risk	=	Inherent risk × Control risk	×	Detection risk
AR	=	IR × CR	×	DR

Applying this to the figures given in the examples set out above:

Example 1:

Desired level of audit risk	=	Risk of material error occurring in the unaudited financial statements	×	Risk of failing to detect material error
Audit risk	=	Inherent risk × Control risk	×	Detection risk
AR	=	IR × CR[14]	×	DR
5%	=	60% × 34%	×	DR

---

[13] The audit risk model is widely cited in auditing literature as a useful audit planning tool. However, it is not without its critics. As indicated above, the model is grounded in probability theory and, in order for it to be valid, the probability of events IR, CR and DR must be independent of each other. A number of commentators have raised doubts about the independence of IR, CR and DR and thus about the validity of the audit risk model. Nevertheless, the model provides useful insights into the relationship between inherent risk, internal control risk, detection risk and the auditor's desired level of audit risk.

[14] $[IR = 60\% \times CR = 34\%]$ = Risk of error occurring in unaudited financial statements = 20% (as in previous Example 1).

Rearranging the equation to find detection risk:

$$DR = \frac{5\%}{60\% \times 34\%} = 25\%$$

Example 2:

Desired level of audit risk	=	Risk of material error occurring in the unaudited financial statements	×	Risk of failing to detect material error
Audit risk	=	Inherent risk × Control risk	×	Detection risk
AR	=	IR × CR[15]	×	DR
5%	=	85% × 88%	×	DR

Rearranging the equation to find detection risk:

$$DR = \frac{5\%}{85\% \times 88\%} = 6.7\%$$

It may be seen that in Example 1 the auditor can accept a 25% risk of failing to detect material error, whereas in Example 2 such detection risk falls to 6.7%.

From Examples 1 and 2 it is evident that the greater the likelihood of material error occurring in the unaudited financial statements (the higher the combined level of inherent and internal control risk), the lower the risk the auditor can take of not detecting material error which is present. The lower the detection risk the auditor can accept, the more extensive the substantive audit procedures (s)he must conduct.

We can use a town's water supply (see Figure 8.2) to illustrate the inverse relationships between:
(a) inherent risk and internal control risk on the one hand and detection risk on the other; and
(b) detection risk and the amount of substantive testing.

For the purpose of illustration, assume that:
• the population of Jolleytown derives its water supply from Smillie Reservoir;
• three rivers flow into Smillie Reservoir; and
• the water from the rivers passes through a purification filter before it passes into the reservoir.

---

[15] [IR = 85% × CR = 88%] = Risk of error occurring in unaudited financial statements = 75% (as in previous Example 2).

Figure 8.2: Jolleytown's water supply

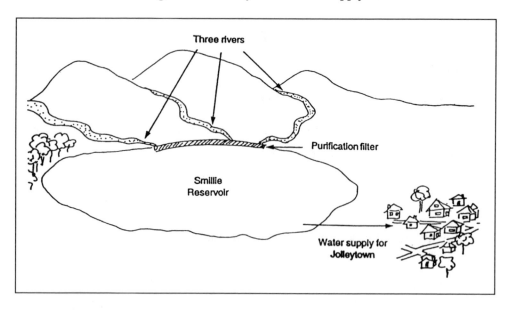

Jolleytown's water supply	*Parallel in audit risk terms*
Situation 1	
1. The rivers (mountain streams) flowing down towards the purification filter are crystal clear.	1. Management integrity appears to be high, there are no apparent pressures likely to motivate management to manipulate the financial statement information, and business risk is low. (Inherent risk is low.)
2. The purification filter is in excellent order and can be relied upon to filter out impurities in the river water.	2. Internal controls appear to be effective in preventing and detecting errors in the accounting data. (Internal control risk is low.)
3. In order for the authorities to be assured that the water in Smillie Reservoir is safe for the population of Jolleytown to drink, relatively little testing will be required.	3. The auditor, having assessed the inherent risk and internal control risk, will be fairly confident that the financial statements are not materially misstated. Thus (s)he will conduct relatively little substantive testing to confirm that material error is not present.
Because the authorities believe the reservoir water is 'pure', they will not test it extensively. They thus run the risk of failing to detect impurities which may have slipped through the system.	By conducting relatively little substantive testing, the auditor runs the risk of not detecting material misstatement which may have slipped through the system. Thus detection risk is high.

Jolleytown's water supply	*Parallel in audit risk terms*
Situation 2	
1. The three rivers flowing down from the hills towards the purification filter are muddy and carry lots of impediments such as rocks, stones and vegetation.	1. Management integrity appears to be fairly low and business risk is high. The risk of material error occurring in the unaudited financial statements in the absence of internal controls (i.e. inherent risk) is high.
2. The purification filter is not in a good state of repair. A number of holes have developed and the filter needs to be replaced.	2. Internal controls do not appear to be effective: they seem unlikely to prevent and detect errors which are present in the accounting data. (Internal control risk is high.)
3. Before the water in the reservoir can be accepted as safe for Jolleytown residents to drink, extensive testing will be required. (A large number of water samples will need to be taken from various parts of the reservoir.)	3. Before the financial statements can be adjudged 'true and fair', the financial statement account balances will need to be tested extensively.
As a result of the extensive testing, the failure to detect impurities in the water (if they are present) will be fairly low.	As a result of the extensive (substantive) testing, the chances of failing to detect material error is fairly low (i.e. low detection risk).

8.5.3   Audit risk at the overall and individual account (or audit segment) level

The discussion in section 8.5.2 focused on assessing inherent risk and internal control risk at the overall (financial statement) level and considers the extent of substantive procedures required to reduce detection risk, and thus audit risk, to the desired level for the audit as a whole.

However, as noted in section 8.5.1, audit risk is also considered at the individual account or class of transactions level. The principles explained in relation to overall audit risk apply equally to audit risk at the more detailed level. Indeed, in practice, the audit risk equation and determination of the substantive procedures required to reduce detection risk to the desired level probably has greater application at the individual account (or class of transactions) level than at the overall (financial statement) level.

8.5.4   Relationship between materiality, audit risk and audit planning

It follows from our discussion of audit risk that the relationship between the audit risk components has a significant impact on audit planning. Audits must be planned so as to ensure that:

- inherent risk is properly assessed;
- internal control risk is properly evaluated (which includes planning, performing and evaluating compliance procedures); and
- sufficient appropriate substantive procedures are performed so that detection risk – and thus audit risk – is reduced to the level desired by the auditor.

Hence, in order to reduce audit risk to the desired level, the auditor must carefully plan the nature, timing and extent of audit procedures.

The relationship between the components of audit risk and planning of audit procedures is reflected in the following extracts from SAS 300: *Accounting and internal control systems and audit risk assessments*:

> When planning their audit, auditors consider the likelihood of error [occurring in the financial statements] in the light of inherent risk and the system of internal control (control risk) in order to determine the extent of work (and hence the level of detection risk) required to satisfy themselves that the risk of error in the financial statements is sufficiently low. (para 12)
> If auditors ... expect to be able to rely on their assessment of control risk to reduce the extent of their substantive procedures, they should make a preliminary assessment of control risk . . . and should plan and perform tests of control to support that assessment. (para 27)[16]
> Auditors should consider the assessed levels of inherent and [internal] control risk in determining the nature, timing and extent of substantive procedures . . . to be performed to reduce detection risk, and therefore audit risk, to an acceptably low level. (paras 49 and 51)

Like audit risk, the level at which materiality limits (planning materiality and tolerable error) are set affects the planning of audit procedures – their nature, timing and extent. In section 8.4.1 we noted that an error, omission or inadequate disclosure in the financial statements is material if it is likely to affect the decisions or actions of a reasonable user of those financial statements. We also noted that the level at which the auditor sets the limits for planning materiality and tolerable error affects the amount and/or appropriateness of the evidence the auditor must collect: the lower the materiality limits the more (or more relevant and reliable) the evidence the auditor must collect to ensure those limits are not exceeded.

Expressed in terms of audit risk, we can say that the lower the materiality limits, the greater the likelihood that errors (or omissions) will occur in the financial statements that will exceed those limits and thus qualify as material misstatements. (Expressed in terms of risk, the lower the materiality limits, all other

---

[16] Assessing internal control risk and performing tests of control (compliance procedures) are discussed in detail in Chapter 9.

things remaining constant, the higher the auditor's assessment of inherent and control risk.) Additionally, the lower the materiality limits, the more 'careful' the auditor will need to be in determining whether or not those limits are exceeded. Thus, the auditor will wish to reduce detection risk to a level lower than would otherwise be the case – and, accordingly, plan to perform more extensive substantive procedures.

Following the reasoning set out above we can see there is an inverse relationship between materiality and audit risk and thus between materiality and the extent of substantive procedures. This relationship may be represented as in Figure 8.3.

The relationship between materiality, audit risk and audit planning is explained by ISA 320 *Audit materiality* as follows:

> When planning the audit, the auditor considers what would make the financial statements materially misstated. The auditor's assessment of materiality, related to specific account balances and classes of transactions, helps the auditor . . . to select audit procedures that, in combination, can be expected to reduce audit risk to an acceptably low level. (para 9)
> There is an inverse relationship between materiality and the level of audit risk, that is the higher the materiality level, the lower the audit risk and vice versa. The auditor takes the inverse relationship between materiality and audit risk into account when determining the nature, timing and extent of audit procedures. For example, if, after planning for specific audit procedures, the auditor determines that the acceptable materiality level is lower, audit risk is increased. The auditor would compensate for this by either:
> (a) reducing the assessed level of control risk, where this is possible, and supporting the reduced level by carrying out extended or additional tests of control; or
> (b) reducing detection risk by modifying the nature, timing and extent of planned substantive procedures. (para 10)

Figure 8.3: The effect on audit risk and planned audit procedures of setting materiality limits at different levels

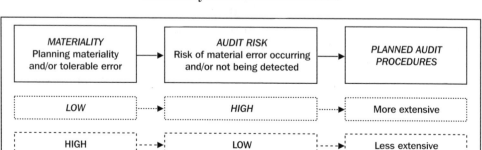

8.6   ANALYTICAL PROCEDURES

8.6.1   The meaning of analytical procedures

Analytical procedures are the means by which meaningful relationships and trends in both financial and non-financial data may be analysed, actual data may be compared with budgeted or forecast data, and the data of an entity may be compared with that of similar entities and industry averages.

The procedures consist primarily of ratio, percentage, trend and comparative analyses, although they also include more sophisticated statistical techniques such as regression analysis.

SAS 410: *Analytical procedures* (paras 5 and 6)[17] explains:

> Analytical procedures include the consideration of comparisons of the entity's financial information with, for example:
> - comparable information for prior periods;
> - anticipated results of the entity, from budgets or forecasts;
> - predictive estimates prepared by the auditors, such as an estimation of the depreciation charge for the year; and
> - similar industry information, such as a comparison of the entity's ratio of sales to trade debtors with industry averages, or with the ratios relating to other entities of comparable size in the same industry.
>
> Analytical procedures also include consideration of relationships:
> - between elements of financial information that are expected to conform to a predicted pattern based on the entity's experience, such as the relationship of gross profit to sales; and
> - between financial information and relevant non-financial information, such as the relationship of payroll costs to number of employees.

It should be noted that in financial accounting the term 'interpretation and analysis' is used to mean essentially the same thing as 'analytical procedures' in auditing. Since the ratios, percentages, trends and comparisons used by financial statement users in the interpretation of financial statements are essentially the same as those used in analytical procedures, it follows that analytical procedures prompt consideration of the size of errors which would be material to financial statement users. For example, the auditor would seek an explanation for a gross profit percentage which moved from, say, 18% to 20% if such a change would cause financial analysts to change their assessment of the entity's financial performance. In this case, it follows that any error in the sales or cost of sales which caused such a shift in the gross profit percentage would be material.

---

[17] Almost identical wording is contained in ISA 520: *Analytical procedures*, paras 4 and 5.

8.6.2 Importance of analytical procedures

Analytical procedures are generally regarded as highly efficient and effective audit tests, however, it must be borne in mind that their effectiveness is always dependent on the quality of the underlying data. As indicated above, these procedures provide a useful means of establishing whether financial statement amounts display unexpected characteristics; that is, whether they deviate from the auditor's expectations, given his or her understanding of the client, its business, its industry, and detailed knowledge of events which have affected the client's financial position and/or performance over the reporting period.

As shown in Figure 8.4, analytical procedures are used at three different stages during an audit to achieve three different objectives.

1. *During the planning stage* they are used to help gain an understanding of the client's business, to help assess the likelihood of errors being present in the unaudited financial statements, to help determine appropriate levels of materiality and to help determine the nature, timing and extent of audit procedures.
2. *During the substantive testing stage* they are used to obtain audit evidence in relation to individual account balances and classes of transactions.

Figure 8.4: The use of analytical review procedures in an audit

Stage of the audit	Objective	Nature of procedures used
Planning the audit	• To understand the client's business • To assess the likelihood of errors being present in the unaudited financial statements • To set materiality limits • To identify high risk audit areas • To plan the nature, timing and extent of audit procedures	• Trend analysis • Ratio analysis of entity data • Comparative analysis of entity data with that of other similar entities and industry averages (Focus is on the entity's overall financial position and performance)
Substantive procedures	To obtain evidence to confirm (or refute) individual account balances	Ratio analysis based on direct relationships amongst individual accounts (Focus is on the reasonableness of individual account balances)
Final review	To confirm conclusions reached with respect to the truth and fairness of: • profit and loss statement amounts • balance sheet amounts • cash flow statement amounts • financial statement note disclosures	• Trend and percentage analysis of individual accounts • Ratio analysis of financial statement data (Focus is on the truth and fairness of the financial statements as a whole in portraying the entity's financial position, performance and cash flows)

3. *During the final review stage* they are used to help confirm (or challenge) conclusions reached by the auditor regarding the truth and fairness of the financial statements.

The use of analytical procedures as substantive tests and in the final review of the financial statements is discussed in Chapters 10 and 12, respectively.

8.6.3   Analytical procedures in planning the audit

SAS 410 (paras 9 and 11) (and ISA 520, para 8) notes that:

> Auditors should apply analytical procedures at the planning stage [of an audit] to assist in understanding the entity's business [and] in identifying areas of potential audit risk, . . . Application of analytical procedures may indicate aspects of the entity's business of which the auditors were previously unaware and assist in determining the nature, timing and extent of other audit procedures.

On the basis of his or her general understanding of the client and its business, and knowledge of events and significant transactions which have affected the client's financial position and performance during the reporting period, the auditor will have certain expectations regarding the results of the analytical procedures performed during the planning stage of the audit. Where the results differ from the auditor's expectations, they raise questions about the accuracy of the financial and/or non-financial data used in the analysis (and, hence, about the accuracy of the financial statements) and/or about information previously obtained by the auditor on which his or her understanding of the entity and its financial affairs is based. Thus, analytical procedures performed in the planning phase of an audit are useful for confirming or challenging the auditor's understanding of the entity's business and its financial position and performance as well as for ascertaining whether it is likely that the unaudited financial statements are materially misstated in one or more respects, and for identifying the accounts or classes of transactions in which material error is most likely to occur. Once the likelihood of errors being present in the financial statements has been established, the auditor can determine the areas in which audit effort is to be concentrated and plan the nature, timing and extent of audit procedures to be performed during the rest of the audit.

The analytical procedures performed during the planning phase of the audit concentrate on the overall financial position and performance of the entity. The analysis focuses in particular on the entity's liquidity, solvency (or capital adequacy) and profitability.

(i)   Liquidity

When analysing the entity's liquidity, the auditor is primarily interested in the entity's ability to meet its short-term financial obligations when they fall due.

Two ratios in particular are used by auditors to assess an entity's liquidity, namely:

- current (or working capital) ratio [current assets/current liabilities]; and
- quick assets ratio (or acid test), [(current assets minus stocks and prepayments)/current liabilities].

In order to assess the results of these ratios, the auditor needs to consider:

- the quality of current assets – for example, whether debtors are stated at their net realisable value and how quickly they and stocks are likely to generate cash; and
- the nature of current liabilities – for example, how quickly they will have to be paid and whether unused bank overdraft (or other short-term funding) facilities are available.

To help evaluate these factors, the auditor usually calculates additional ratios, such as:

- the number of days debtors' balances are outstanding [(average debtors over the reporting period /sales) $\times$ 365];
- the number of days trade creditors' balances are outstanding [(average trade creditors over the reporting period/purchases) $\times$ 365];
- the rate of stock turn [cost of goods sold/average stocks held over the reporting period].

(ii) Solvency (or capital adequacy)

When analysing the entity's solvency, the auditor is primarily interested in the entity's ability to continue in operation even if it encounters adverse trading conditions and experiences exceptional losses. The auditor wishes to assess, in particular, the ease with which the entity can meet its financing commitments, and the ease with which it is likely to be able to raise new capital should the need arise.

To assess an entity's solvency, auditors usually calculate ratios such as the following:

- asset structure [current assets/total assets; fixed assets/total assets];
- financial structure [current liabilities/total funds; long-term liabilities/total funds; shareholders' funds (or equity)/total funds];
- times interest earned [earnings before interest and tax[18]/interest paid];
- debt to equity ratio [total debt/total equity].

---

[18] Earnings before interest and tax is alternatively referred to as 'operating profit'.

(iii)   Profitability

Probably the most widely used measure of an entity's profitability is the return it earns on its assets (ROA) [operating profit (or, alternatively net profit after tax)/average total assets held over the reporting period].[19] This ratio is, in fact, built up from two other ratios, each of which provides a useful measure of profitability, namely:

- operating profit (or, alternatively net profit) margin [operating profit (or net profit after tax)/sales]; and
- asset turnover [sales/average total assets held over the reporting period].

Other measures of profitability frequently used by auditors include:

- gross profit margin [gross profit/sales];
- sales to current assets [sales/average current assets held over the reporting period];
- sales to fixed assets (sales/average fixed assets held over the reporting period];
- return on shareholders' funds [net profit after tax/average shareholders' funds held over the reporting period].

8.7   SUMMARY

In this chapter we have identified the two phases involved in planning an audit – developing the audit strategy and designing the audit programme – and we have discussed various aspects of developing the audit strategy. More specifically, we have examined the auditor's desired level of assurance (desired level of audit risk), the distinction between planning materiality and tolerable error, and the setting of materiality thresholds. We have also discussed the relationship between inherent risk, internal control risk and detection risk and noted that, in order to achieve his or her desired level of audit risk, the auditor needs to assess inherent risk and internal control risk (over which (s)he has no direct control) and then to plan the nature, timing and extent of audit procedures so as to ensure that detection risk, and hence audit risk, is reduced to the desired level. We have additionally observed the inverse relationship between materiality and audit risk, and the relationship between these factors and the extent of substantive testing.

In the final section of this chapter we considered the meaning and importance of analytical procedures and discussed the use of these procedures in the planning phase of an audit.

---

[19] As a result of the equivalence of total assets and total funds invested, this ratio is also referred to as 'return on investment' (ROI) [operating profit (or, alternatively, net profit after tax)/average total funds invested in the entity over the reporting period].

Figure 8.5: **Relationship between steps in the audit process,[20] planning the audit, establishing materiality thresholds and assessing audit risk.**

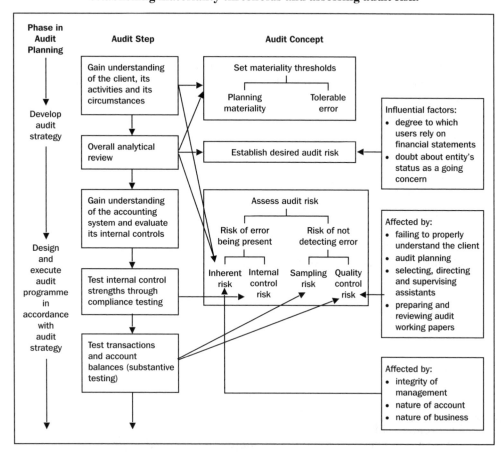

A summary of the main ideas discussed in this chapter (and some of the notions considered in Chapters 3 and 6) is presented in Figure 8.5.

SELF-REVIEW QUESTIONS

8.1 State the two main phases in planning an audit and outline the main objective of each.

8.2 Define the auditor's 'desired level of assurance'. Explain how this relates to the auditor's desired level of audit risk.

8.3 Explain briefly the circumstances in which the auditor's desired level of assurance is likely to be particularly high.

---

[20] As shown in Figure 6.1.

8.4 Define 'materiality' and explain briefly the distinction between:
(i) planning materiality, and
(ii) tolerable error.
8.5 Explain briefly how setting materiality limits at different levels affects planned audit procedures.
8.6 Explain briefly how the auditor's assessment of inherent risk and internal control risk affects his or her planning of substantive procedures.
8.7 Explain briefly the relationship between materiality limits, audit risk and audit planning.
8.8 When planning an audit, the auditor must consider:

- the extent of audit procedures
- the timing of audit procedures
- the nature of audit procedures
  (i) Briefly explain the meaning of each of these terms.
  (ii) Give one example for each term to illustrate its effect on planning an audit.

8.9 Define 'analytical procedures' and list three different ways in which these procedures are used in an audit.
8.10 List four ways in which analytical procedures can assist an auditor during the planning stage of an audit.

REFERENCES

Anderson, R.J. (1977) *The External Audit.* Toronto: Cropp Clark Pitman.
Arens, A.A. & Loebbecke, J.K. (1980) *Auditing: An Integrated Approach*, 2nd ed. New Jersey: Prentice-Hall.
Arens, A.A. & Loebbecke, J.K. (1991) *Auditing: An Integrated Approach*, 8th ed. New Jersey: Prentice-Hall.
Pratt, M.J. (1990) *External Auditing: Theory and Practice in New Zealand.* Auckland: Longman Paul.
Read, J.W., Mitchell, J.E. & Akresh, A.D. (1987) Planning materiality and SAS No. 47. *Journal of Accountancy* **164**(12), 72–79.

ADDITIONAL READING

Ameen, E.C. & Strawser, J.R. (1994) Investigating the use of analytical procedures: an update and extension. *Auditing: A Journal of Practice & Theory* **13**(2), 69–76.
Anderson, U. & Koonce, L. (1995) Explanation as a method for evaluating client-suggested causes in analytical review. *Auditing: A Journal of Practice & Theory* **14**(2), 124–132.
Anderson, U., Koonce, L. & Merchant, G. (1994) The effects of source-competence information and its timing on auditors' performance of analytical procedures. *Auditing: A Journal of Practice & Theory* **13**(1), 137–148.

Asare, S.K. & Wright, A. (1997) Hypothesis revision strategies in conducting analytical procedures. *Accounting, Organizations and Society* **22**(8), 737–755.

Bloomfield, R. (1995) Strategic dependence and inherent risk assessments. *The Accounting Review* **70**(1), 71–90.

Carpenter, B.W., Dirsmith, M.W. & Gupta, P.P. (1994) Materiality judgments and audit firm culture: social-behavioural and political perspectives. *Accounting, Organizations and Society* **19**(4/5), 355–380.

Christ, M.Y. (1993) Evidence on the nature of audit planning problem representation: an examination of auditor free recalls. *The Accounting Review* **68**(2), 304–322.

Colbert, J.L. (1987) Audit risk – tracing the evolution. *Accounting Horizons,* September, 49–57.

Dusenbury, R., Reimers, J.L. & Wheeler, S. (1996) An empirical study of belief-based and probability-based specifications of analytical review. *Auditing: A Journal of Practice & Theory* **15**(2), 12–28.

Glover, S.M., Jiambalvo, J. & Kennedy, J. (2000) Analytical procedures and audit-planning decisions. *Auditing: A Journal of Practice & Theory* **19**(2), 27–45.

Hirst, D.E. & Koonce, L. (1996) Audit analytical procedures: a field investigation. *Contemporary Accounting Research* **13**(2), 457–486.

Houston, R.W., Peters, M.F. & Pratt, J.H. (1999) The audit risk model, business risk and audit-planning decisions. *The Accounting Review* **74**(3), 281–298.

Koonce, L. (1993) A cognitive characterization of audit analytical review. *Auditing: A Journal of Practice & Theory* **12**(Supp.), 57–76.

Lea, R.B., Adams, S.J. & Boykin, R.F. (1992) Modelling of the audit risk assessment process at the assertion level within an account balance. *Auditing: A Journal of Practice & Theory* **11**(Supp.), 152–179.

Martinov, N. & Roebuck, P. (1998) The assessment and integration of materiality and inherent risk: an analysis of major firms' audit practices. *International Journal of Auditing* **2**, 103–126.

Monroe, G.S. & Ng, J. (2000) An examination of order effects in auditors' inherent risk assessments. *Accounting and Finance* **40**, 153–168.

Nelson, M.W. (1993) The effects of error frequency and accounting knowledge on error diagnosis in analytical review. *The Accounting Review* **68**(4), 804–824.

Nelson, M.W., Libby, R. & Bonner, S.E. (1995) Knowledge structure and the estimation of conditional probabilities in audit planning. *The Accounting Review* **70**(1), 27–47.

Schulz, A.K.D. & Booth, P. (1995) The effects of presentation format on the effectiveness and efficiency of auditors' analytical review judgements. *Accounting and Finance* May, 107–131.

Strawser, J.R. (1991) Examination of the effect of risk model components on perceived audit risk. *Auditing: A Journal of Practice & Theory* **10**(1), 126–135.

Taylor, M.H. (2000) The effects of industry specialization on auditors' inherent risk assessments and confidence judgements. *Contemporary Accounting Research* **17**(4), 693–712.

Waller, W.S. (1993) Auditors' assessments of inherent and control risk in field settings. *The Accounting Review* **68**(4), 783–803.

Wheeler, S. & Pany, K. (1990) Assessing the performance of analytical procedures: A best case scenario. *The Accounting Review* **65**(3), 557–577.

9 Internal Controls and the Auditor

LEARNING OBJECTIVES

After studying the material in this chapter you should be able to:
- explain what is meant by 'an accounting system';
- explain why the accounting system is divided into sub-systems for audit purposes and the basis on which this is done;
- describe the techniques for reviewing and documenting the accounting system and its internal controls;
- explain what is meant by 'a walk through test' and why it is conducted;
- explain how an audit programme is developed;
- explain what is meant by 'an internal control system', 'the control environment' and 'control procedures';
- describe the elements of a good system of internal control;
- describe the objectives of internal accounting controls;
- discuss the inherent limitations of all systems of internal control;
- discuss the importance of the auditor identifying the strengths and weaknesses of the client's system of internal control;
- explain the meaning of the term 'compliance testing';
- describe the audit procedures used for compliance testing.

The following publications are particularly relevant to this chapter:
- Statement of Auditing Standards (SAS) 200: *Planning* (APB, 1995)
- Statement of Auditing Standards (SAS) 300: *Accounting and internal control systems and audit risk assessments* (APB, 1995)
- International Standards on Auditing (ISA) 300: *Planning* (IFAC, 1994)
- International Standards on Auditing (ISA) 400: *Risk assessments and internal control* (IFAC, 1994)
- Institute of Chartered Accountants in England and Wales (ICAEW): *Internal Control: Guidance for Directors on the Combined Code* (Turnbull Report) (ICAEW, 1999)

9.1   INTRODUCTION

As the auditor has journeyed through the audit process to reach the present stage, (s)he has gained an understanding of the client and its activities, established a desired level of audit risk, defined materiality thresholds, assessed the likelihood of material error being present in the financial statements, and identified the accounts or classes of transactions where error seems most likely to occur (see Chapter 6, Figure 6.1, Audit Steps 1–4).

The auditor will now wish to obtain a detailed knowledge of the client's accounting system and evaluate the effectiveness of its internal controls. Once the auditor has assessed the level of reliance (s)he can place on the entity's internal controls to eliminate errors from the accounting data, the audit programme can be designed; that is, the nature, timing and extent of audit procedures to be performed during the rest of the audit can be planned in detail.

In this chapter we examine what is meant by an accounting system and how the system is segmented for audit purposes. We explore some conceptual aspects of internal control, and discuss how the auditor gains knowledge of the client's accounting system and evaluates its internal controls. We also investigate how the auditor develops an audit programme. Before concluding the chapter, we consider the tests auditors conduct in order to determine whether the internal controls on which they plan to rely (in order to reduce their substantive tests) are operating as effectively as their preliminary evaluation suggested.

9.2   THE ACCOUNTING SYSTEM

Like all systems, the accounting system has an input, a processing and an output stage. As Figure 9.1 indicates:

- *the input stage* involves capturing a mass of accounting data from either:
  - source documents, which are completed when transactions take place; or
  - memoranda generated by the entity's accountant. These generally record non-transaction data, for example, writing off bad debts and period end adjustments;
- *the processing stage* involves converting the mass of raw data into useful information. This may be achieved using manual, mechanical or, as in most cases today, electronic data processing methods but, in each case, it is accomplished through recording, classifying and summarising the data;
- *the output stage* involves preparing the accounting information in a form useful to those who wish to use it; that is, appropriately classifying, grouping and heading the information in a meaningful manner.

Figure 9.1: The accounting system

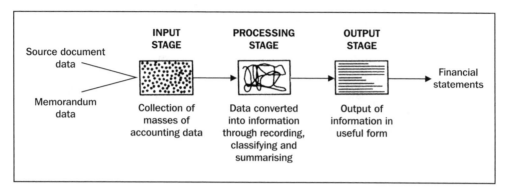

In order to ensure that all relevant data are captured as input to the accounting system, and to ensure that the data are properly and correctly processed during their conversion into output in the form of financial statements, special checking mechanisms or internal controls are built into the system. The characteristics and objectives of internal control systems are discussed in section 9.3 below.

The auditor has the task, *inter alia*, of forming an opinion on whether or not the entity's financial statements give a true and fair view of its financial position and performance. In order to reach this opinion, the auditor needs to understand the system which generates the financial statements. If the auditor tried to gain this understanding by approaching the entity's accounting system as a single unit, (s)he would find it extremely cumbersome and inefficient. In order to facilitate the audit (or to put it on a more practical footing), the auditor (conceptually) dissects the accounting system into sub-systems or audit segments.

The audit segments recognised for any audit vary according to the nature, size and complexity of the audit client and its activities; however, they are almost invariably based on either transaction categories (such as sales, purchases, administration expenses, long-term loans, etc.) or (more commonly) accounting cycles. When they are based on accounting cycles, groups of closely related accounts and associated transactions are audited as a single unit. As an example of audit segments based on accounting cycles, in an audit of a wholesale or retail business the following segments may be recognised:

- Sales-debtors-receipts cycle;
- Purchases-creditors-payments cycle;
- Stock-warehousing cycle;
- Payroll and personnel cycle;
- Financing and investing cycle.

These audit segments are depicted in Figure 9.2. To illustrate related accounts which constitute audit segments, the accounts comprising the sales-debtors-receipts cycle are shown in Figure 9.3.

It should be noted that, until audit segments are identified during the review of the entity's accounting system, the audit is approached holistically. As is shown in Figure 9.2, the auditor gains an understanding of the client and its activities, establishes a desired level of audit risk, defines materiality thresholds, and assesses the likelihood of material error being present in the financial statements, based on the client as a whole. Once audit segments have been recognised, obtaining detailed knowledge of the accounting system, evaluating and testing its internal controls, and assessing the accuracy, validity and completeness of financial statement balances, revolve around particular audit segments. When the detailed segment-based work is complete, the auditor reviews as a whole the evidence gathered in the segments, and conducts the remaining audit procedures on an entity-wide basis. These final steps of the audit constitute the review and completion stage which is discussed in Chapter 12.

Figure 9.2: Steps in audit process conducted on entity-wide and audit segment basis

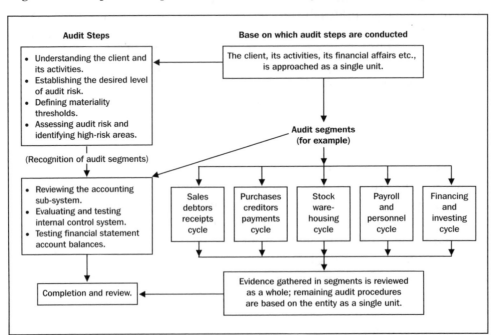

Figure 9.3:   Accounts comprising the sales-debtors-receipts cycle

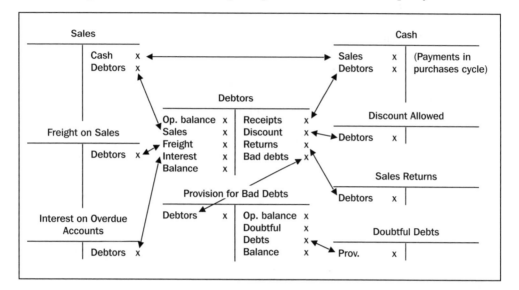

9.3   CONCEPTUAL ASPECTS OF INTERNAL CONTROL

9.3.1   The meaning and importance of an 'internal control system' and 'internal controls'

When an entity is small, its owner or manager can personally perform, or directly oversee, all of its functions. However, as the entity grows larger it becomes necessary to delegate functional responsibilities to employees. Once this occurs, mechanisms need to be introduced which enable the performance of the employees to be checked, to ensure they are fulfilling their responsibilities as intended. As Anderson (1977) explains:

> With the best of intentions, most people make mistakes. The mistakes may be errors in the end results of their work, needless inefficiencies in achieving those end results, or both. And sometimes, without the best of intentions, a few people deliberately falsify. Any organisation wishing to conduct its business in an orderly and efficient manner and to produce reliable financial accounting information, both for its own and for others' use, needs some controls to minimise the effects of these endemic human failings. When such controls are implemented within the organisation's systems they are described as internal controls ... (p. 143)

It is significant that Anderson refers to internal controls as controls which are implemented within the *organisation's* systems rather than within its *accounting* system. This recognises the fact that internal controls are mechanisms designed to control *all* of an entity's functions, not just its accounting function. The wide application of the term is reflected in the definition of internal control proposed by the Committee of Sponsoring Organisations of the Treadway Commission (COSO, 1992):

Internal control is broadly defined as a process, effected by an entity's board of directors, management and other personnel, designed to provide reasonable assurance regarding the achievement of objectives in the following categories:
- Effectiveness and efficiency of operations.
- Reliability of financial reporting.
- Compliance with applicable laws and regulations.

The first category addresses an entity's basic business objectives, including performance and profitability goals and safeguarding of resources. The second relates to the preparation of reliable published financial statements, including interim and condensed financial statements and selected financial data derived from such statements, such as earnings releases, reported publicly. The third deals with complying with those laws and regulations to which the entity is subject. (p. 1)

Since the COSO report was published in 1992, the issue of internal controls has gained prominence in the UK as a result of the requirements of the Combined Code (Committee on Corporate Governance, 1998) and their adoption by the UK listing authority (UKLA). In respect of internal control the Code states:

Principle D.2: The board [of directors] should maintain a sound system of internal control to safeguard shareholders' investment and the company's assets.

Provision D.2.1: The directors should, at least annually, conduct a review of the effectiveness of the group's system of internal control [i.e. that of the parent company and its subsidiaries] and should report to shareholders that they have done so. The review should cover all controls, including financial, operational and compliance controls and risk management.

Under the UKLA's rules, companies listed on the London Stock Exchange are required to include in their annual report a governance statement setting out how they have applied the Code's principles (including Principle D.2, cited above) and stating whether or not they have complied with the principles throughout the accounting period – and, if not, the respects in which they have not done so and the reasons therefor. Additionally, auditors are required to review the company's governance statement insofar as it relates to seven of the Combined Code's provisions – including Provision D.2.1 (cited above).

Companies have been provided with guidance on implementing the Combined Code's Principle D.2 and Provision D.2.1 by the ICAEW's *Internal Control: Guidance for Directors on the Combined Code* (Turnbull Report, 1999). Like COSO (1992), the Turnbull Report defines internal control in very broad terms (para 20):

An internal control system encompasses the policies, processes, tasks, behaviours and other aspects of a company that, taken together:
- facilitate its effective and efficient operation by enabling it to respond appropriately to significant business, operational, financial, compliance and other risks to achieving the company's objectives. . . .;
- help ensure the quality of internal and external reporting. . . .;
- help ensure compliance with applicable laws and regulations . . .

However, unlike COSO, the Turnbull Report explicitly links internal control with risk management. This is reflected, for example, in its explanation of the importance of a company's system of internal control and its financial controls:

> A company's system of internal control has a key role in the management of risks that are significant to the fulfilment of its business activities. A sound system of internal control contributes to safeguarding the shareholders' investment and the company's assets. (para 10)
> Effective financial controls, including the maintenance of proper accounting records, are an important element of internal control. They help ensure that the company is not unnecessarily exposed to avoidable financial risks and that financial information used within the business and for publication is reliable. They also contribute to the safeguarding of assets, including the prevention and detection of fraud. (para 12)

When referring to 'internal control' it is important to distinguish between the broadly defined internal control system, the control environment, and control procedures (or internal controls). Statement of Auditing Standards (SAS) 300: *Accounting and internal control systems and risk assessments* explains:

> [An] 'internal control system' comprises the control environment and control procedures. It includes all the policies and procedures (internal controls) adopted by the directors and management of an entity to assist in achieving their objective of ensuring . . . the orderly and efficient conduct of its business, including adherence to internal policies, the safeguarding of assets, the prevention and detection of fraud and error, the accuracy and completeness of the accounting records, and the timely preparation of reliable financial information. (para 8)

> 'Control environment' means the overall attitude, awareness and actions of directors and management regarding internal controls and their importance in the entity. The control environment . . . provides the background against which the various other controls are operated. . . . Factors reflected in the control environment include:
> - the philosophy and operating style of the directors and management;
> - the entity's organisational structure and methods of assigning authority and responsibility . . .; and
> - the directors' methods of imposing control, including the internal audit function, the functions of the board of directors and personnel policies and procedures. (para 9)

> 'Control procedures' are those policies and procedures in addition to the control environment which are established to achieve the entity's specific objectives. They include in particular procedures designed to prevent or to detect and correct errors. . . . Specific control procedures include:
> - approval and control of documents;
> - controls over computerised applications and the information technology environment;
> - checking the arithmetical accuracy of the records;
> - maintaining and reviewing control accounts and trial balances;
> - reconciliations;
> - comparing the results of cash, security and stock counts with accounting records;

- comparing internal data with external sources of information; and
- limiting direct physical access to assets and records. (para 10)[1]

The 'controls over computerised applications and the information technology environment' referred to in SAS 300, para 10, are usually referred to separately as:

(i) general controls, and

(ii) application controls.

General (computer environment) controls

General controls are designed to control both the IT environment and the development and maintenance of computer systems. They include:

- restricting access to the computer, data, programs and files to authorised personnel;
- ensuring that duties are clearly assigned and that incompatible duties are segregated; for example, assigning systems analyst, programming, program testing, computer operating and library (storage) duties to different employees;
- ensuring that there are adequate back-up facilities for both software and hardware, should they be needed;
- ensuring that the development or acquisition of new programs (or packages), and the testing and implementation of new programs and program changes, are properly authorised and adequately planned;
- ensuring that all computer applications, and modifications thereof, are properly and fully documented;
- ensuring that computer systems are used only for authorised purposes, and that only authorised programs and data are used.

(ii) Application controls

Application controls are controls over the input, processing and output of accounting applications. More particularly, they are controls which are designed to ensure that:

- all transactions input to the system are properly authorised;
- input data is complete;
- invalid and incorrect data is rejected;
- transactions are completely, properly and accurately processed (in particular, they are accurate as to their amount, account classification and reporting period);
- processing errors are identified and corrected on a timely basis;
- data files are properly maintained and protected;
- output is checked against input data;

---

[1] ISA 400: *Risk assessments and internal control*, para 8, contains similar wording to SAS 300, paras 8–10.

- output is provided to appropriate, authorised personnel on a timely basis;
- exception reports are acted on promptly and appropriately;
- only the latest versions of programs and data are used for processing.

The relationship between the components of an internal control system are shown in Figure 9.4.

It should be noted that, although we can distinguish the control environment from the control procedures, both components are essential for an effective internal control system. If the control environment is weak or defective, it is likely that the control procedures will not be applied properly and the internal control system as a whole will be not be effective in meeting its objectives (as

Figure 9.4:   Relationship between the components of an internal control system

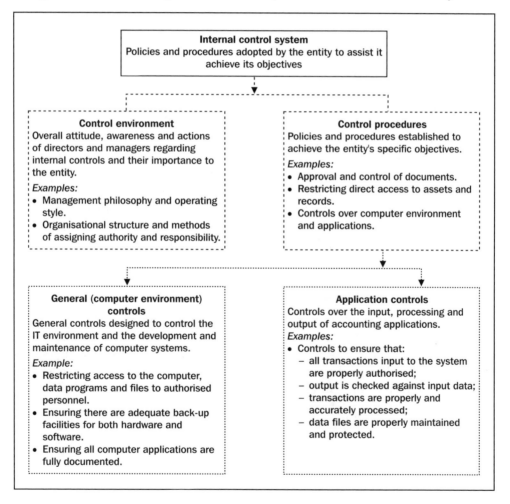

outlined by COSO and the Turnbull Report). Similarly with the general (computer environment) controls and the application controls. If the general (computer environment) controls are weak or defective, it is likely that the application controls will not be applied properly. Weaknesses in the control environment or general (computer environment) controls cannot be adequately compensated for by 'foolproof' control procedures or application controls, respectively. By the same token, the existence of a strong control environment and 'perfect' general (computer environment) controls do not, of themselves, mean that control procedures and application controls are unnecessary. They remain essential components of an effective internal control system. The control environment and general (computer environment) controls set the culture and context within which the more specifically targeted control procedures and application controls operate: each component of the internal control systems complements the other components.

Where entities have internal auditors, these auditors are generally responsible for implementing, monitoring and maintaining all aspects of the internal control system.[2] External auditors need to be familiar with the internal control system and they need to evaluate the quality of the control environment, but they are primarily concerned with the internal controls which relate to the accounting function – in particular, those relating to safeguarding the entity's assets and accounting records, and the provision of reliable financial information. External auditors are less concerned with the entity's operational and compliance controls. However, for listed company audit clients, they also need to be sufficiently acquainted with the design and operation of the company's internal control system to be able to review, in an informed manner, the directors' report on their review of the effectiveness of the company's internal control system (i.e. review the directors' compliance with the Combined Code's Provision D.2.1) as required by the UKLA's listing rules.

9.3.2 Characteristics of a good system of internal control

If an entity's control environment possesses certain characteristics and certain control procedures are present, then it is likely that the entity's assets will be adequately safeguarded and its accounting data (and thus its financial statements) will be reliable. (Expressed in terms of audit risk, control risk will be low.) These internal control characteristics are as follows:

(i)   competent, reliable personnel who possess integrity;
(ii) clearly defined areas of authority and responsibility;
(iii) proper authorisation procedures;

---

[2] The role of internal audit in these regards is discussed in Chapter 16.

(iv) adequate documentation and records;
(v)   segregation of incompatible duties;
(vi) independent checks on performance;
(vii) physical safeguarding of assets and records.

(i)   *Competent, reliable personnel who possess integrity:* The most important factor in safeguarding an entity's assets and records and in securing reliable financial data is the quality of the entity's personnel. If the entity's directors, managers and other employees are competent, they are able to fulfil their responsibilities efficiently and effectively; if they are also reliable and possess integrity, they will fulfil their responsibilities carefully and honestly. Indeed, if this control characteristic is satisfied, it is probable that the entity's assets will remain safe and its financial data will be free of material errors, even if the other elements are missing or weak.

(ii) *Clearly defined areas of authority and responsibility:* Irrespective of how competent and reliable an entity's personnel may be, in order to ensure that all necessary tasks are performed – and performed in an efficient, timely manner – it is important that the authority and responsibility of each employee is clearly defined. This not only ensures that employees know what is expected of them, it also facilitates pinpointing responsibility in cases where tasks are not performed properly. Such identification of responsibility motivates employees to work carefully and also enables management to ascertain where corrective action is required.

(iii) *Proper authorisation procedures:* In order to safeguard its physical assets and protect the integrity of its records, an entity must have proper authorisation procedures. For example, procedures must be established to ensure that all transactions are initiated or approved by a person who has the requisite authority. For example, an entity may establish procedures for approving credit sales whereby:

- all credit sales have to be authorised in writing by the credit manager before the goods are sold;
- the credit manager has discretion to extend credit to individual customers up to a maximum of, say, £5,000;
- if the £5,000 limit is to be exceeded, written authority for this to happen must be obtained from the managing director.

Similarly, a purchases manager may be granted authority to purchase stocks and/or supplies up to the value of a specified amount, or a departmental manager may be authorised to purchase capital equipment for his or her department up to a specified value. If the purchases or departmental manager wish to exceed their authorised limit, they must seek approval to do so from a higher authority, such as a divisional manager, managing director or the Board of Directors (depending on the procedures established in the entity).

Procedures must also be established to ensure that the acquisition or development of all new computer programs or packages, and their testing and implementation, are properly authorised. The same applies to all program changes. Even small errors in computer programs can cause considerable 'harm' in an organisation. For example, they can result in erroneous data (and hence, in faulty decisions based on that data) and cause much wasted organisational effort in locating and correcting the errors and in rectifying the damage they have done. This may extend to faulty documents being sent to third parties and, thereby, damage to the entity's reputation.

(iv) *Adequate documentation and records:* If an entity is to secure reliable financial data and safeguard its assets, it is essential that it maintains adequate documents and records. This includes ensuring that:

- the entity's documents (such as order forms, receiving reports, sales invoices, receipts, and payments vouchers, whether they be in paper or electronic form) are numbered consecutively and are designed so that they may be completed easily and fully at the time the transaction takes place;
- every transaction is supported by a source document in paper or electronic form;
- all accounting entries are supported by a source document (for transactions) or a memorandum generated by the entity's accountant (for non-transactions, such as period end adjustments and writing off bad debts);
- authorisations are supported by appropriate and adequate evidence;
- an adequate chart of accounts is maintained to facilitate recording transactions in the correct accounts;
- adequate procedures manuals and job descriptions are maintained to ensure that employees:
  - know (or can find out) the procedures to follow when undertaking organisational activities; and
  - are aware of the requirements of their own position in the entity and how this relates to the duties attaching to associated positions.
- in the IT area, the specifications and authorised application of computer programs (and any modifications thereof) are properly and fully documented.

(v) *Segregation of incompatible duties:* When defining areas of responsibility and assigning tasks to employees, it is essential that incompatible duties are vested in different people. In particular:

- no one person should have custody of assets and also maintain the records of those assets. For example, the cashier (who handles money) should not record cash received or paid. If the same person performs these duties (s)he is able to steal cash and cover his or her traces by making appropriate adjustments in the cash records;

- no one person should have custody of assets and also authorise transactions relating to those assets. For example, the stores manager should not be given the task of authorising purchases or sales of items under his control. If these tasks are vested in the same person it enables that person to obtain assets for his or her personal benefit by authorising fictitious transactions;
- no one person should be given responsibility for both software design and computer programming; or for both computer programming and computer operations; or for computer programming and software testing. In each of these cases, if the responsibilities are assigned to one person, it enables them to manipulate computer programs to their own advantage and/or to leave any undiscovered errors they may have made;
- no one person should have responsibility for all of the entries in the accounting records. Careful allocation of accounting duties enables the work of different employees to be organised so that the work of one automatically cross-checks the work of another. This facilitates the detection of unintentional errors.

(vi) *Independent checks on performance:* Even if personnel are competent, reliable and trustworthy, and their responsibilities are clearly defined and carefully assigned so as to avoid one person performing incompatible duties, there remains the possibility that errors will occur. All employees are humans, not robots, and humans are prone to making mistakes. Unintentional errors may occur, for example, as a result of tiredness, boredom, or failure to concentrate fully on the task in hand. On occasions, employees may become careless in following defined procedures or may deliberately fail to do so, either because they perceive an 'easier' way to accomplish the task or because they wish to defraud the entity. In any event, if financial data are to be reliable, and the entity's assets and records are to be safeguarded, it is important that independent checks on employees' performance take place.

One means of achieving these checks is to assign accounting duties so that the work of one employee automatically cross-checks the work of another – a process known as 'internal check'. For example, one accounts clerk may maintain the Debtors Subsidiary Ledger and another the Debtors Control account in the General Ledger. Similarly, before preparing a cheque, the payments clerk may be required to match the supplier's invoice with a copy of the relevant order form (from the purchases department) and receiving note (from the receiving department), to check for authorised signatures on the order form and receiving note, and to verify and reconcile the items, quantities and monetary amounts shown on the documents.[3] In

---

[3] In computerised systems, the computer can be programmed so that a cheque is prepared (electronically) once the purchase order, receiving report and supplier's invoice (all in electronic form) have been properly authorised and 'matched' by the computer.

other situations, two employees may be involved in a single task, so that each provides a check on the performance of the other; for example, two employees may be involved in opening the mail when it is expected to contain remittances from debtors. A further means of checking employees' performance is for supervisors to review the work of subordinates; for example, the financial controller may review journal and ledger entries and completed bank reconciliations.

(vii) *Physical safeguarding of assets and records:* As noted above, one of the objectives of an internal control system is to safeguard the entity's assets and records. The most effective way to achieve this objective is to provide physical protection for assets and records, combined with restricted access. For example, stocks and supplies may be stored in a locked store room with access restricted to a limited number of authorised personnel; cash, cheques, marketable securities and similar items may be kept in a fireproof safe, with few personnel having access to the safe keys or being privy to the combination lock number; the entity's land and buildings may be protected by such things as fences, locked entry doors, closed circuit television, burglar and fire alarms, smoke detectors, water sprinklers and similar devices. SAS 300 para 24 (and ISA 400, para 13) notes that, in order to ensure that physical assets are in agreement with the records thereof, the two should be compared at reasonable intervals and appropriate action should be taken in respect of any differences.

An entity's legal, accounting and other documents are important components of its assets and should be protected in the same way as its other assets; that is, facilities should be provided for their safekeeping and access should be strictly limited to authorised personnel. The same applies to computer hardware, programs, data and files. Additionally, back-up copies should be kept of entity information generated or stored in computers, and emergency use of computer facilities should be arranged in case the entity's system should fail.

It was noted in section 9.3.1 above that internal controls become necessary when an entity grows beyond the size at which the owner or manager can personally perform or oversee all of the entity's functions, and functional responsibilities have to be delegated to employees. It follows from this that the extent of internal controls and their degree of formalisation are likely to vary according to the size of the entity. However, once functional responsibilities are delegated to employees, it is necessary to institute control procedures and, irrespective of the entity's size, if the internal control system possesses the seven characteristics outlined above, then it is likely that the entity's assets and records will be adequately safeguarded and its financial data (and hence its financial statements) will be reliable.

9.3.3 Objectives of internal accounting and application controls

As explained in section 9.2 above, an entity's accounting system is designed to capture accounting data and to convert and output this data as useful financial information. In order for financial information to be useful, it must be reliable. Thus, the underlying accounting data must be valid, complete and accurate. To secure data which meets these criteria, internal controls are built into the accounting system. These controls, which we refer to as 'internal accounting controls', are designed, in particular, to ensure that transactions which give rise to the accounting data are:

(i) properly recorded; that is, all relevant details of transactions are recorded at the time the transactions take place;

(ii) properly authorised; that is, all transactions are authorised by a person with the requisite authority;

(iii) valid; that is, transactions recorded in the accounting system represent genuine exchanges with *bona fide* parties;

(iv) complete; that is, all genuine transactions are input to the accounting system; none are omitted;

(v) properly valued; that is, transactions are recorded at their correct exchange value;

(vi) properly classified; that is, transactions are recorded in the correct accounts;

(vii) recorded in the correct accounting period.

Since practically all entities' accounting systems are now largely or wholly computerised, these internal controls are, in essence, application controls. If the objectives of the internal accounting controls (outlined above) are met, it is probable that the information presented in the financial statements will be reliable. If the seven characteristics of a good internal control system are present (as outlined in section 9.3.2), then it is likely that the internal accounting control objectives will be met.

In addition to controls designed to ensure that all transactions are properly recorded (i.e. all data input to the accounting system are valid, complete and accurate), controls are needed to ensure that the transactions (or input data) are properly processed. Thus, application controls need to be established to ensure that, for example:

- invalid and incorrect data is rejected;
- processing errors are identified and corrected on a timely basis;
- data files are properly maintained and protected;
- exception reports are acted on promptly and appropriately;
- only the latest versions of programs and data are used for processing.

9.3.4 Inherent limitations of internal control systems

Irrespective of how well designed an internal control system may be, and how effectively it operates, it will always possess inherent limitations. These may be illustrated by the following examples:

(i)   The extent of an entity's internal control procedures depends on their cost-effectiveness. Beyond some point, the cost of instituting additional controls will exceed the benefits to be gained from more accurate financial data or increased safeguarding of assets. There is, for example, little point in installing a £50,000 surveillance system to prevent the theft of, say, one 20p Biro each week!

(ii) Internal controls are designed to prevent and detect errors and irregularities in the normal, frequently recurring transactions. However, errors are more likely to occur in relation to infrequent, unusual transactions – for the very reason that they are unusual.

(iii) The potential for error is always present because accounting personnel are human and therefore prone to make mistakes. Thus, internal controls may not always operate as intended.

(iv) There is the possibility that management will override the controls; alternatively, there may be collusion between two or more employees which results in the controls being circumvented.

(v)   Internal control procedures may become inadequate or inappropriate as a result of changes in the entity's internal and/or external environment and, as a consequence, compliance with the controls may deteriorate.[4]

Because of the inherent limitations of all internal control systems, irrespective of how 'perfect' a system may appear to be, an auditor can never rely on the system to prevent and/or detect *all* material errors and irregularities in the accounting data. (S)he will always have to evaluate, at least to some extent, the accuracy, validity and completeness of the information presented in the financial statements; that is, some substantive audit procedures will always be necessary.

9.3.5 The significance of internal controls to the external auditor

External auditors are not responsible for establishing or maintaining an entity's internal control system: that is the responsibility of the entity's management. Nevertheless, the quality of the internal control system can, and usually does, have a significant impact on the audit.

If the internal control system is well designed (if it contains the seven characteristics of a good system of internal control outlined in section 9.3.2),

---

[4] These inherent limitations of internal controls are noted in SAS 300, para 25, and ISA 400, para 14.

and if it operates effectively to meet the seven internal accounting control objectives set out in section 9.3.3, then the auditor will gain a high level of assurance that any material errors or irregularities which might be present in the accounting data will be eliminated as the data passes through the accounting system. Thus, the auditor will feel fairly confident that the financial statements are free of material misstatement. Expressed in terms of audit risk, where an entity has a well designed and effective internal control system, the risk of material errors in the accounting data not being eliminated (that is, internal control risk) will be fairly low. However, as noted earlier, as a consequence of the inherent limitations of all internal control systems, this risk can never be reduced to zero. As demonstrated in Chapter 8, when inherent risk and internal control risk are low, there is little likelihood of material error being present in the (pre-audited) financial statements and, as a result, substantive procedures need not be extensive.

However, if an entity's internal control system is poorly designed and/or is ineffective in meeting the internal accounting control objectives, the auditor will gain little assurance that the financial statements are free of material error (that is, internal control risk will be assessed as high). As a consequence, before a 'clean' audit report can be issued, the auditor will need to conduct extensive substantive tests in order to gain sufficient assurance that the financial statements are, in fact, free of material misstatement (see Chapter 8, section 8.5).

9.4   REVIEWING THE ACCOUNTING SYSTEM AND EVALUATING ITS INTERNAL CONTROLS

9.4.1   Understanding the accounting sub-systems and control environment

In section 9.2, we pointed out that in order to facilitate the audit, auditors (conceptually) divide their auditees' accounting system into sub-systems or audit segments. They then conduct their detailed audit examination based on these audit segments.

As the starting point of the detailed examination, auditors seek to understand and to document the entity's accounting sub-systems, and to conduct a preliminary evaluation of the related internal controls. In order to make this preliminary evaluation, auditors need, amongst other things, to understand the control environment. SAS 300: *Accounting and internal control systems and audit risk assessments* specifies:

> In planning the audit, auditors should obtain and document an understanding of the accounting system and control environment sufficient to determine their audit approach. (para 16)

It goes on to explain the understanding that is required:

> Auditors obtain an understanding of the accounting system sufficient to enable them to identify and understand:
> (a) major classes of transactions in the entity's operations;
> (b) how such transactions are initiated;
> (c) significant accounting records, supporting documents and accounts in the financial statements;
> (d) the accounting and financial reporting process from the initiation of significant transactions and other events to their inclusion in the financial statements. (para 17)
>
> An understanding of the control environment enables auditors to assess the likely effectiveness of control procedures. . . . As control procedures are often incorporated within accounting systems, gathering information to obtain the understanding of the accounting system is likely to result in some understanding of specific control procedures. In any event, as the accounting system, control environment and control procedures are closely related, auditors often seek to obtain information about all the relevant aspects of the accounting and internal control systems . . . as one exercise. However, in order to design and select appropriate audit tests it may be necessary for them to undertake additional work to obtain a more detailed understanding of specific control procedures. (paras 18 and 20)[5]

How, then, do auditors obtain their understanding of the accounting systems (or, more correctly, accounting sub-systems) and related internal controls?

An initial understanding is gained primarily through the following audit procedures:

(i) *Enquiries of client personnel:* Auditors ask questions of relevant personnel from management, supervisory and staff levels of the audit client about various aspects of the sub-system. For example, they enquire how accounting data are captured and input to the accounting sub-system and how the data are recorded, classified and summarised within the sub-system. Auditors also make enquiries as to which employees are responsible for what duties, how employees know what to do, how much guidance is provided by procedures manuals and similar documents, and what reviews of employees' work take place.

(ii) *Inspection of client documents:* Auditors gain significant insight into the structure and operation of accounting sub-systems by consulting their clients' documents. They examine, for example, the auditee's organisation

---

[5] The content of ISA 400: *Risk assessments and internal control* paras 18 and 20 is very similar to that of SAS 300 paras 17 and 20, respectively. However, ISA 400 does not contain a provision equivalent to SAS 300 para 16 but, unlike SAS 300, it sheds additional light on what is expected of auditors in respect of understanding the control environment. It states:

> The auditor should obtain an understanding of the control environment sufficient to assess directors' and management's attitudes, awareness and actions regarding internal controls and their importance in the entity.

chart, its chart of accounts and guidance given on account classification of transactions, and the client's policies and procedures manuals insofar as they relate to the accounting sub-system. Auditors also inspect more detailed documents such as source documents, journals, ledgers and trial balances, and discuss the various documents with client personnel to ascertain how well they are used and understood.

(iii) *Observation of client personnel:* In addition to asking client personnel about their various duties, and inspecting documents which specify the duties which should be performed, auditors observe personnel at various levels of the organisation carrying out their normal accounting and review functions.

9.4.2 Documenting the accounting sub-systems

Once auditors have gained a preliminary understanding of the accounting sub-system, they document that understanding (or, more usually, obtain relevant documents from the audit client and check their understanding against those documents). Two primary forms of documentation are used, namely:

(i) narrative descriptions,
(ii) flowcharts.

(i) Narrative descriptions

A narrative description is a detailed description of the accounting routines which take place within an accounting sub-system. An example of part of a narrative description from the purchases-creditors-payments cycle is provided in Figure 9.5.

A narrative description should include details of:

(a) all of the documents (whether in paper or electronic form) which are used in the accounting routine. For example, in a purchases routine the narrative description should refer to order forms, receiving reports, suppliers' invoices and credit notes, payments vouchers, etc. The description should detail how each document is initiated, the steps through which it passes between initiation and filing, where and how it is filed (for example, the name of the relevant file and whether it is arranged alphabetically or by document number or date), and who is responsible for preparing, reviewing, using and filing the document;

(b) all of the processes which take place within the routine. For example, what triggers goods to be ordered, how a supplier is selected, how quantities to be ordered are determined, how price is ascertained, how goods received are checked against goods ordered, how discrepancies between goods ordered and received are handled and so on;

Figure 9.5: Narrative description of part of a purchases-creditors-payments cycle

When the issue of a regular item of stock results in the re-order point for that stock item being reached, the staff member in the Stores Department responsible for that stock item prepares a requisition. The requisition is sent electronically to the manager or assistant manager of the Stores Department. He authorises the requisition and sends a copy to the Purchasing Department. A copy is also filed (by requisition number) in the Approved Requisitions (Pending) file. The filed copy is subsequently matched by the Stores Department with a copy of the purchases order and receiving report and moved to a Goods Received file. Discrepancies between goods requested, ordered and received are reported (by means of a computer-generated exception report) to the Stores Department, Purchasing Department, Receiving Department and Creditors Ledger clerk and filed with the relevant (matched) documents.

On receiving a copy of the approved requisition, the Purchasing Department prepares a purchase order. Copies are sent electronically to the supplier, the Stores Department (see above), the Receiving Department and the Creditors Ledger clerk. A copy is also filed in the Purchase Orders (Pending) file according to the purchase order number.

The Receiving Department files the purchase order (by number) pending the arrival of the goods. On arrival, the goods are inspected and counted and compared with the purchase order. A receiving report is prepared and copies are sent to the purchasing Department, Creditors Ledger clerk and Stores Department (see above). A copy is also filed, by receiving report number, together with purchase order, in a Goods Received file, . . .

(c) internal control procedures. The narrative should refer to internal control procedures such as the segregation of incompatible duties, authorisation procedures, procedures which provide independent checks on performance, and safeguards for assets and records (for example, the use of locked storerooms and fireproof safes, and access being restricted to authorised personnel, etc).

As a means of documenting the entity's accounting sub-systems, compared to flowcharts narrative descriptions are generally less time-consuming and less technically demanding to prepare. However, they do not convey the sequence of processes or document flows as clearly as flowcharts, they are time-consuming to read, they may be difficult to comprehend, and the key points may not be readily apparent.

Narrative descriptions are appropriate for describing simple accounting routines or sub-systems, but their use requires a careful balance between giving sufficient detail to provide an adequate description, and giving too much detail, which mitigates clarity and ease of comprehension. Narrative descriptions are frequently used, and are useful, as supplements to flowcharts, to expand on elements of a flowchart where additional detail or explanation is considered necessary.

(ii) Flowcharts

A flowchart is a diagrammatic representation of the flow of documents or information through an accounting sub-system and the processes which take place in the system. An example of a flowchart of part of a purchases-creditors-payments cycle is presented in Figure 9.6.[6,7]

The prime advantages of a flowchart are the clear overview it provides of the accounting system and the ease with which internal control strengths and weaknesses can be identified. Compared with a narrative description, a flowchart is easier to read and understand and, when changes are made to the accounting system, it is easier to update. However, on the downside, a flowchart is time-consuming and technically demanding to prepare and its preparation is, therefore, costly. It is largely for these reasons (together with the inefficiency of duplicating effort) that external auditors obtain and use (at least as a starting point) flowcharts of the accounting sub-systems which are prepared by their audit clients (usually their internal audit function) for their own internal use.

9.4.3 Walk through test

Once auditors have documented (or checked, using the auditees' documentation) their understanding of the accounting sub-system, they will test this understanding against the system itself. They achieve this by means of a 'walk through test' (also known as a 'cradle to the grave test'). One or two transactions of each major type (for example, credit sales, credit purchases, cash received, cash paid) are traced through the entire accounting system, from their initial recording at source to their final destination as a component of an account balance in the financial statements.

It should be noted that a walk through test is not an audit procedure designed to test financial statement balances: instead, it is a procedure designed to confirm

---

[6] The narrative description provided in Figure 9.5 describes part of the system depicted in Figure 9.6. This is for illustrative purposes only. In practical situations, one or other method would be adopted to represent the system. However, this is not to say that one form may not be used to supplement the other. For example, a narrative description may be provided to clarify an element of a flowchart. Similarly, a flowchart component may be used to clarify a point in a narrative description.

[7] Although Figure 9.6 depicts the flow of documents through part of the purchases-creditors-payments cycle, it could equally depict the flow of information in electronic form from one department to another. The basic principles remain unchanged.

Figure 9.6: Flowchart of part of a purchases-creditors-payments cycle

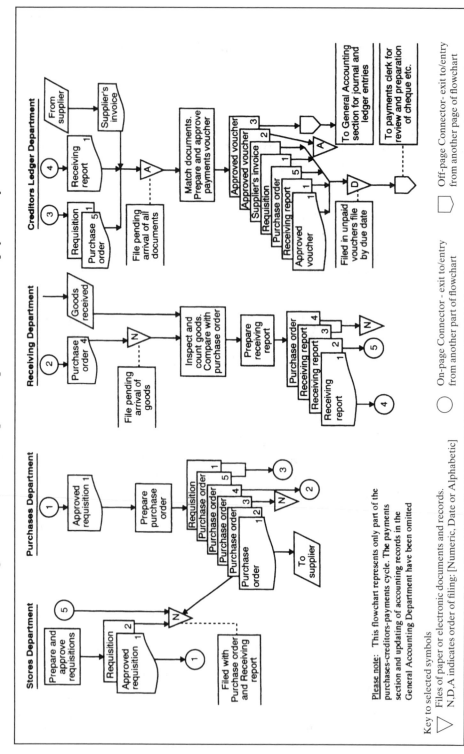

Please note: This flowchart represents only part of the purchases-creditors-payments cycle. The payments section and updating of accounting records in the General Accounting Department have been omitted

Key to selected symbols

▽ Files of paper or electronic documents and records.
N,D,A indicates order of filing: [Numeric, Date or Alphabetic]

○ On-page Connector - exit to/entry from another part of flowchart

⬠ Off-page Connector - exit to/entry from another page of flowchart

(or correct) the auditor's understanding of the flow of transactions data through the client's accounting system and the accuracy of their (or their clients') documents (narrative description and/or flowcharts) recording the system.

9.4.4 Evaluating internal controls

Having gained an understanding of the accounting sub-systems and related internal controls, and documented that understanding, auditors are required to evaluate and test, as appropriate, the operation of those internal control procedures upon which reliance is to be placed to reduce (potentially costly) substantive testing. In the words of SAS 300:

> If auditors, after obtaining an understanding of the accounting system and control environment, expect to be able to rely on their assessment of [internal] control risk to reduce the extent of their substantive procedures, they should make a preliminary assessment of [internal] control risk for material financial statement assertions,[8] and should plan and perform tests of control [compliance tests] to support that assessment. (para 27)[9]

This makes it clear that auditors are required to undertake two processes:

i)   a preliminary assessment of the effectiveness of internal controls in preventing material misstatements in the financial statements;[10]
ii) testing those controls on which they plan to place reliance to reduce substantive testing.

In this section we are concerned with the preliminary assessment.

The key purpose of the preliminary assessment of internal controls within the accounting system (or sub-system) is to identify internal control strengths and weaknesses.

- *Strengths* are internal control procedures which operate effectively to prevent or detect errors and irregularities in the accounting data which pass through the control point. These are the controls on which the auditor may plan to rely to prevent material misstatement from occurring in the financial statements and thus to reduce substantive tests.

---

[8] Financial statement assertions are explained in Chapter 10.

[9] ISA 400, para 22 contains similar wording to that in SAS 300, para 27. However, ISA 400 (para 24) further specifies:

> The preliminary assessment of control risk for a financial statement assertion should be high unless the auditor:
> (a) is able to identify internal controls relevant to the assertion which are likely to prevent or detect and correct a material misstatement [known as an internal control strength]; and
> (b) plans to perform tests of control to support that assessment.

[10] In this regard it should be recalled from Chapter 8 that, where auditors consider the accounting and internal control systems are effective in preventing and correcting material misstatements, control risk is assessed as low.

- *Weaknesses* are points in the accounting system which are prone to errors or irregularities but effective controls to prevent or detect such occurrences are absent.

In order to identify the internal control strengths the auditor needs to:

(i) gather information about the relevant internal control procedures;
(ii) evaluate their effectiveness in preventing and detecting errors.

(i)   Gathering information

The primary means of gathering information about an entity's internal control procedures is an internal control questionnaire (ICQ). This consists of a series of questions relating to control procedures which are normally considered necessary to prevent or detect and correct errors and irregularities occurring in each major type of transaction. The questions are usually phrased so that they require a 'yes' or 'no' response. As a result, ICQs are generally simple (and quick) to complete. A useful way to organise the questions, so as to ensure good coverage of each audit segment, is to link them to the internal accounting control objectives outlined in section 9.3.3 above. An example of part of an ICQ prepared on this basis, relating to purchase transactions, is presented in Figure 9.7.

It should be noted that, although gathering information about the internal controls has been presented here as an audit step subsequent to the auditor gaining an understanding of, and documenting, the client's accounting system (or, more correctly, sub-system), ICQs are commonly completed during the 'understanding and documenting' stage. (This was indicated in SAS 300, para 20, cited in section 9.4.1.)

(ii)   Assessing the adequacy of internal controls

Once information about the client's internal controls has been gathered, the auditor evaluates the adequacy of the control procedures. In conducting this evaluation the auditor considers, in particular:

- the errors and irregularities that could occur in each audit segment;
- whether effective control procedures are present to prevent or detect and correct such occurrences;
- where effective control procedures appear to be absent, whether there are compensating controls which overcome the internal control weakness.

Once the auditor has identified internal control procedures which appear to be effective in preventing material misstatement from occurring in the financial statements, (s)he must decide whether (s)he wishes to rely on any of these procedures to reduce substantive testing. This decision affects the nature, timing and extent of audit tests.

Figure 9.7:   Part of an ICQ relating to the purchases-creditors-payments cycle

Internal Control Questionnaire Purchases				Ref: C-4
Client: Jasper Limited Period: Year to 31 March 2003		Prepared by: RB Reviewed by: MC		Date: 12/12/02 Date: 15/12/02

Control Procedure	Yes	No	N/A	Remarks
1. Are sequentially numbered requisitions used to initiate purchase orders?	✓			
2. Are all numbered requisitions accounted for?	✓			Copies are filed numerically. Cancelled requisitions also filed (marked to indicate cancellation)
3. Are requisitions approved by a responsible official?	✓			Manager or Assistant Manager of Stores Department
4. Is initiation of requisitions limited to authorised personnel?		✓		All Stores Department employees have access
5. Can purchase orders be prepared without a requisition?		✓		
6. Are purchase orders sequentially numbered?	✓			
7. Are all numbers accounted for?	✓			Copies are filed numerically (including cancelled order forms)
8. Are purchase orders prepared by a responsible official?	✓			Manager or Assistant Manager of Purchasing Department
9. Is initiation of purchase orders restricted to authorised personnel?	✓			
10. Do all purchase orders show: (a) Quantities ordered? (b) Prices of goods ordered? (c) Special terms of the order? (d) Initials of preparer? (e) Date of preparation?	✓ ✓ ✓ ✓ ✓			
11. Is there a limit to the value of goods that may be ordered?	✓			Maximum order size £5,000
12. Is a copy of the purchase order sent to: (a) Stores Department? (b) Receiving Department? (c) Creditors Ledger Clerk?	✓ ✓ ✓			

9.4.5 Internal control evaluation and audit planning

Irrespective of how effective internal control procedures may appear to be in preventing material misstatements from occurring in the financial statements, before the auditor can rely on them to reduce related substantive tests, (s)he must test them to obtain evidence that they are working as effectively as his or her preliminary evaluation suggests, and that they have been so working throughout the reporting period. As SAS 300, para 35, explains:

> Tests of control are performed to obtain audit evidence about the effective operation of the accounting and internal control systems – that is, that properly designed controls identified in the preliminary assessment exist in fact and have operated effectively throughout the relevant period. They include tests of elements of the control environment where strengths in the control environment are used by auditors to reduce [internal] control risk assessments.[11]

ISA 400, para 31, adds to this by stating:

> The auditor should obtain audit evidence through tests of control to support any assessment of control risk which is less than high. The lower the assessment of control risk, the more support the auditor should obtain that accounting and internal control systems are suitably designed and operating effectively.

Thus, the greater the reliance the auditor plans to place on internal controls to eliminate material misstatements from the financial statements (and thus reduce substantive tests), the more extensive the tests of those controls (i.e. compliance tests) that need to be performed.

Further, when the auditor considers that internal controls can be relied upon, a significant proportion of the audit procedures may be conducted during an interim audit; that is, about three months prior to the end of the client's financial year. This enables the audit to be completed in a timely manner following the end of the financial year. It also facilitates efficient scheduling of audit work (and thus audit staff) over the calendar year and avoids 'bottlenecks' occurring when the balance sheet dates of a number of audit clients coincide.

It can be seen that when an auditor considers a client's internal controls can be relied upon, compliance procedures will be given greater emphasis, total audit testing will be less extensive,[12] and more audit procedures will be conducted during an interim (rather than year end) audit, than would otherwise be the case. Thus, the auditor's evaluation of the client's internal controls clearly has a direct impact on audit planning and, once the evaluation is complete, the auditor proceeds to develop the audit programme.

---

[11] ISA 400, para 27 is similar in content to SAS 300, para 35.

[12] As explained in Chapter 8, low internal control risk results in the auditor's desired level of audit risk being attained with less substantive testing than is needed when internal control risk is assessed as higher.

When considering the detailed audit procedures to be included in the audit programme, the following points need to be borne in mind:

(a) Irrespective of how effective a client's internal controls may appear to be, the auditor may not rely upon them to reduce substantive procedures until they have been tested and found to be operating effectively – and operating in this manner throughout the reporting period. This may appear to preclude the planning of substantive procedures until compliance testing is complete. However, such a delay would introduce inefficiencies into the audit process. As a consequence, the auditor develops the audit programme on the assumption that the internal control procedures on which (s)he plans to rely operate generally as indicated by his or her preliminary assessment and that they have functioned effectively throughout the reporting period. Nevertheless, the auditor must remain alert to the possibility that compliance tests may reveal that internal control procedures are not as effective as was first thought, and so adjustments to the audit programme may be necessary.

(b) Although particular internal control procedures may appear to be operating effectively, the auditor may decide not to rely on them to reduce substantive procedures because (s)he considers that the audit effort required to test compliance with the controls is likely to exceed the reduction in effort (in terms of reduced substantive testing) that would be achieved through reliance upon the controls. In this case, no testing of the relevant controls is undertaken and internal control risk is assumed to be high. In the words of SAS 300, para 28:

> If, as a result of their work on the accounting system and control environment, auditors decide it is likely to be inefficient or impossible to rely on any assessment of control risk to reduce their substantive procedures, no such assessment is necessary and control risk is assumed to be high.

9.5 DEVELOPING THE AUDIT PROGRAMME

The audit programme consists of a set of detailed audit procedures designed to meet the specific audit objectives of each audit segment. According to SAS 200: *Planning:*

> Auditors should develop and document the nature, timing and extent of planned audit procedures. ... The documentation may take the form of an audit programme which sets out the audit procedures the auditors intend to adopt and includes reference to other matters such as the audit objectives, timing, sample size and basis of selection for each area. It serves as a set of instructions to the audit team and as a means to control and record the proper execution of the work. The level of detail in the audit programme depends on the complexity of the audit, the extent of other documentation and the experience of the members of the audit team. (paras 13 and 15)

The audit programme is usually prepared (at least conceptually) in two stages as follows:

(i) planning format;
(ii) performance format.

(i)   Planning format

In this stage, the audit objectives for each class of transactions and each financial statement balance within an audit segment are identified. For example, audit objectives for purchase transactions might be ascertaining whether:

• purchase transactions are recorded;
• purchase transactions are authorised;
• recorded purchase transactions are valid;
• recorded purchase transactions are complete;
• purchase transactions are properly classified;
• purchase transactions are stated at their correct amount;
• purchase transactions are recorded in their correct accounting period.

Based on the auditor's understanding of the client, the results of overall analytical review procedures, and his or her preliminary evaluation of the client's internal controls, the auditor determines how each identified audit objective is best met through compliance and/or substantive procedures, and identifies the specific procedure(s) to be performed. Certain procedures may be identified as appropriate for meeting more than one objective.

This process is repeated systematically for each audit segment.

(ii)   Performance format

Once the lists of audit procedures to be performed have been compiled, the procedures are arranged in a logical sequence and any overlapping procedures are eliminated. This results in a list of audit procedures which are set out in a manner suitable for their performance. This is the audit programme.

Although we can identify (and describe) two stages in preparing the audit programme, where audit programmes are generated electronically (which is normally the case) the two stages may occur concurrently (that is, the 'planning format' procedures are concurrently arranged in their performance format).

The final document (whether in paper or electronic form) specifies for each audit segment:

- the audit objectives to be met;
- the procedures to be performed (both compliance and substantive procedures) to meet the stated objectives; and
- the timing of the procedures, that is, whether they are to be performed during the interim or final (year end) audit.

An example of part of an audit programme relating to purchase transactions is presented in Figure 9.8.

Review of audit programme

The audit programme is not a document which is prepared near the commencement of an audit and then followed slavishly. Rather, it is kept under continuous review. Its adequacy and appropriateness are re-evaluated as evidence is gathered, and it is revised as and when this is found to be necessary. ISA 300 *Planning* explains:

> The overall audit plan and the audit programme should be revised as necessary during the course of the audit. Planning is continuous throughout the engagement because of changes in conditions or unexpected results of audit procedures. The reasons for significant changes would be recorded. (para 12).

SAS 200 expands on this, stating:

> Changes in conditions, or unexpected results of audit procedures, may require changes to the overall audit plan or the planned audit procedures. Changes to the planned audit procedures are documented so that there is an accurate record of the nature, timing and extent of the audit procedures performed. (para 17)

9.6   COMPLIANCE TESTING

9.6.1   Purpose of compliance procedures

As noted in section 9.4.4, during the preliminary evaluation of the client's internal controls, the auditor identifies internal control strengths; that is, internal control procedures which appear to be operating effectively to meet certain audit objectives. Two examples are set out below:

Audit objective	Internal control procedures meeting audit objective
1. Sales transactions are properly authorised.	The credit manager approves all credit sales before goods leave the premises, and initials the sales document to indicate approval.
2. Sales transactions are properly valued.	All sales invoices are checked (prices are checked against price lists, and extensions and additions are checked) by an independent person, prior to the invoice being sent to the customer. The 'checker' initials the invoice to indicate that it has been checked.

Figure 9.8: Part of an audit programme for purchase transactions

	Procedure	Completed by	Date	Workpaper Ref.
1	**Test sequence of purchase orders.** Randomly select five purchase orders from total. Test number sequence – five forwards and five backwards.			
2	**Test purchase order approval.** (See 3(i) below)			
3	**Test adherence to authority limits and compatibility with nature of client's business.** Randomly select 25 purchase orders: (i) Vouch for initials of purchasing officer. (ii) Compare value of order with authorised limit. (iii) Evaluate compatibility of goods ordered with nature of client's business.			
4	**Test sequence of receiving reports.** Randomly select five receiving reports from total. Test number sequence – five forwards and five backwards.			
5	**Test for matching of purchase orders with receiving reports.** Randomly select 25 receiving reports: (i) Check for matching with purchase orders. (ii) Vouch for independent check of items and quantities ordered and received.			
6	**Test sequence of purchase returns records.** Randomly select three purchases returns records. Test number sequence – five forwards and five backwards.			
7	**Test for matching of purchases returns records and suppliers' credit notes.** Randomly select 15 purchases returns records: (i) Check for matching with credit notes. (ii) Vouch for independent check of items and quantities returned and credited.			

8	**Test suppliers' invoices and payments vouchers.**
	Randomly select 25 payments vouchers:
	(i) Check for matching with
	    – supplier's invoice
	    – purchase order
	    – receiving report
	    – purchase returns report
	    – supplier's credit note.			

9	(ii) Vouch supplier's invoice for evidence of independent check of:
	    – items, quantities and prices of goods ordered and received
	    – extensions and footings.
	(iii) Vouch payments vouchers for:
	    – account classification shown
	    – evidence of independent check of:
	       • amount of payment
	       • account codes.
	(iv) Test accuracy of amounts and account classifications:
	    – recalculate extensions and footings on supplier's invoices and credit notes
	    – recalculate VAT on invoices and credit notes
	    – check propriety of account codes.
	
	Review all outstanding purchase orders at year end.
	Check for goods in transit at year end.
	•
	•
	•			

However, we noted in section 9.4.5 that, irrespective of how effective internal controls may appear to be, before the auditor can rely on them to eliminate errors and irregularities from the accounting data, their effectiveness must be tested, that is, confirmed through compliance procedures.

9.6.2   Types of compliance procedures

Compliance procedures fall into two main categories:

(i)   those performed where the internal control procedures leave no audit trail; and

(ii) those performed where an audit trail is left.

(i)   Procedures where the internal controls leave no audit trail

The primary compliance procedures performed where the internal controls leave no audit trail are enquiry, observation and – for certain computer applications – reperformance. For example, in order to ascertain whether controls that are designed to secure the segregation of incompatible duties are being complied with, the auditor will enquire and observe which personnel perform what duties, and when and how these duties are performed. In order to determine whether controls designed to protect assets and records are being complied with, the auditor will observe if access to restricted areas is limited to authorised personnel. Additionally, tests may be performed on specific computer applications or over the general control environment; for example, the auditor can check on whether access is restricted to hardware, computer files and data, and to implementation of program changes by trying to gain access thereto.

(ii) Procedures where the internal controls leave an audit trail

Where an audit trail is available (that is, where there is tangible evidence that a control procedure has or has not been performed), the primary audit tests are enquiry and observation (as for cases where no audit trail is left), vouching of source documents, inspection of other documents and reperformance. For example, in addition to enquiring and observing who performs what duties, and how and when the duties are performed, source documents are vouched for evidence of compliance with authorisation procedures and independent verification of prices, quantities, extensions and additions (such as the initials of the person performing the control procedure). Similarly, other documents, such as reconciliations, journals and ledgers, are inspected for evidence indicating that independent review procedures have been performed. Reperformance of control procedures may take the form of, for example, reperforming bank reconciliations to ascertain whether they have been performed correctly, and trying to gain unauthorised access to computer hardware, files and data.

SAS 300 (para 39) and ISA 400 (para 32) note that, when obtaining evidence about the effective operation of internal controls (i.e. performing compliance procedures):

> . . . relevant factors for auditors to consider are how . . . [the internal controls] were applied, the consistency with which they were applied during the period and by whom they were applied. The concept of effective operation recognises that some deviations may have occurred. Deviations from prescribed controls may be caused by such factors as changes in key personnel, significant seasonal fluctuations in volume of transactions and human error.

The Standards point out that particular attention needs to be given to the possibility that deviations from the internal controls may occur as a result of staff changes in key control functions (for example, a change of credit manager). Such staff changes may be permanent or temporary; they may occur, for example, during holiday periods. Care must be taken to ensure that compliance procedures cover any periods of change.

9.6.3   Follow-up to compliance procedures

Having performed sufficient appropriate compliance procedures and evaluated their results, the auditor will either:

- accept that the internal controls (or certain controls) are effective and reliable; or
- reject them as not operating effectively. In this situation the auditor should ascertain whether there is another relevant control on which reliance might be placed. (Any such alternative control(s) need to be appropriately tested before a conclusion may be reached about its/their effectiveness and reliability.) Alternatively, the auditor should modify the nature, timing and/or extent of substantive audit procedures to ensure that the relevant financial statement assertion is not materially misstated. Such modification will require the audit programme to be adjusted.

9.7   REPORTING INTERNAL CONTROL WEAKNESSES TO MANAGEMENT

Weaknesses identified in the internal control system (that is, points in the accounting system where errors and irregularities could arise and/or be present but not detected) are not compliance-tested by the auditor. The controls are absent or ineffective and therefore they cannot be relied upon to meet audit objectives. However, the auditor does not ignore them. Identified internal control weaknesses are reported to management or to the audit committee (if the entity has one) at the earliest opportunity, preferably in writing, so that appropriate corrective action may be taken as soon as possible. Similarly, deficiencies in internal controls discovered during compliance testing, and errors in the financial statements (resulting from weaknesses in the internal controls) discovered during substantive testing, are likewise reported to management or the audit committee. Suitable action to correct internal control weaknesses is usually suggested by the auditor at the same time as the weaknesses are reported.

At the conclusion of the audit these internal control weaknesses, together with other matters of concern arising during the audit, are documented in a formal management letter. (This letter is discussed in Chapter 13.)

9.8 SUMMARY

In this chapter we have discussed what is meant by an accounting system and considered why and how a client's system is divided into sub-systems (or audit segments) for audit purposes. We have also examined the process by which an auditor gains a detailed understanding of each audit segment, and documents and tests this understanding.

Additionally, we have explored the issue of internal control. We have noted that the internal control system comprises the control environment and control procedures, that the control procedures include general (computer environment) controls and application controls, and that the internal control system embraces all of the controls which are instituted within an organisation's systems.

While the entity's internal audit function is responsible for establishing and maintaining the organisation's entire internal control system, the external auditor is particularly interested in those controls which are designed to safeguard the entity's assets and ensure that its accounting data are free of material errors. (We have referred to the latter set of controls as 'internal accounting controls'.) We have discussed the seven characteristics of a good internal control system, identified the seven objectives of internal accounting and application controls, and observed that, irrespective of how effective a system of internal control may appear to be, it will always possess certain inherent limitations. We have also examined why and how the auditor conducts a preliminary evaluation of the internal controls in each audit segment.

Once the auditor has identified internal control strengths (controls which are effective in preventing or detecting errors in the accounting data) and weaknesses (controls which are required to prevent or detect errors but which are either absent or ineffective), the auditor is in a position to develop the audit programme. This is accomplished (at least on a conceptual level) in two stages, a planning stage and a performance stage, and the final document comprises a list of audit procedures set out in a format which audit staff can follow.

We have emphasised throughout this chapter that, although certain internal controls may appear to be operating effectively, the auditor may not rely on them to prevent material misstatements from occurring in the financial statements until their effectiveness and reliability have been tested. We have discussed compliance procedures (that is, procedures designed to test whether the internal controls on which the auditor plans to rely are operating as effectively as his preliminary evaluation suggests) and whether they have been so operating throughout the reporting period. If the compliance procedures confirm that internal controls are operating effectively, this will result in reduced substantive testing – the topic of the next chapter.

SELF-REVIEW QUESTIONS

9.1 Explain briefly what is meant by 'an accounting system'.

9.2 Explain briefly why a client's accounting system is divided into sub-systems (or audit segments) for audit purposes. State two bases on which this sub-division may be based.

9.3 Describe briefly two procedures which are used to document clients' accounting sub-systems.

9.4 Explain briefly the purpose of a 'walk through test' and how it is conducted.

9.5 Explain briefly the meaning of each of the following terms:
   (i)   internal control system
   (ii)   control environment
   (iii) control procedures
   (iv)   general (computer environment) controls
   (v)   application controls
   (vi)   internal accounting controls.

9.6 Outline the seven characteristics of a good internal control system.

9.7 Define in relation to internal controls:
   (i)   a strength
   (ii)   a weakness.

9.8 List five examples of inherent weaknesses of internal control systems.

9.9 (a) Explain briefly the purpose of 'compliance procedures'.
   (b) Give two examples of compliance procedures and link each to the audit objective it is designed to test.

9.10 (a) Describe briefly what is meant by 'an audit programme'.
    (b) State the two stages in which an audit programme is developed.

REFERENCES

Anderson, R.J. (1977) *The External Audit.* Toronto: Cropp Clark Pitman.

Committee of Sponsoring Organisations of the Treadway Commission (COSO) (1992) *Integrated Control – Integrated Framework.* Executive Summary. New Jersey: COSO.

Committee on Corporate Governance (1998) *The Combined Code.* London: The London Stock Exchange.

Institute of Chartered Accountants in England and Wales (ICAEW) (1999) *Internal Control: Guidance for Directors on the Combined Code* (Turnbull Report). London: ICAEW.

ADDITIONAL READING

Frederick, D.M. (1991) Auditors' representation and retrieval of internal control knowledge. *The Accounting Review* **66**(2), 240–258.

Grant Thornton (1990) *Audit Manual.* Chapter 14, Internal control as a source of audit reliance. London: Longman.

Hermanson, H.M. (2000) An analysis of the demand for reporting on internal control. *Accounting Horizons* **14**(3), 325–341.

Leonard, S. (1995) The internal control debate: Will public reporting on internal control effectiveness inhibit auditors and distract audit committees? *Accountancy* **115**(1222), 74–75.

Leonard, S. (2001) Keep it long. *Accountancy* **128**(1298), 127.

McMullen, D.A., Raghunandan, K. & Rama, D.A. (1996) Internal control reports and financial reporting problems. *Accounting Horizons* **10**(4), 67–75.

Srinidhi, B. (1994) The influence of segregation of duties on internal control judgements. *Journal of Accounting, Auditing & Finance* **9**(3), 423–444.

Waggoner, J.B. (1990) Auditor detection rates in an internal control test. *Auditing: A Journal of Practice & Theory* **9**(2), 77–89.

Wright, A. & Wright, S. (1996) The relationship between assessment of internal control strength and error occurrence, impact and cause. *Accounting and Business Research* **27**(1), 58–71.

10 Testing the Financial Statement Assertions: Substantive Testing

LEARNING OBJECTIVES

After studying the material in this chapter you should be able to:

- explain the significance of substantive testing in the audit process;
- explain the term 'financial statement assertions';
- state the audit objectives of substantive procedures;
- discuss the purpose and importance of analytical procedures as substantive tests (specific analytical procedures);
- explain what is meant by 'testing the details' of financial statement balances;
- distinguish between the two approaches to 'testing the details' – testing transactions generating account balances and testing account balances directly;
- describe common audit procedures used to test the details of financial statement balances;
- discuss the importance of, and procedures used for, confirming the existence, ownership and value of stocks;
- discuss the importance and performance of confirmations as a substantive test of debtors;
- explain the factors the auditor should consider when assessing the adequacy of the client's allowance for bad debts.

The following publications are particularly relevant to this chapter:

- Statement of Auditing Standards (SAS) 300: *Accounting and internal control systems and audit risk assessments* (APB, 1995)
- Statement of Auditing Standards (SAS) 400: *Audit evidence* (APB, 1995)
- Statement of Auditing Standards (SAS) 410: *Analytical procedures* (APB, 1995)
- Auditing Guideline (AG) 405: *Attendance at stocktaking* (APC, 1983)
- International Standards on Auditing (ISA) 400: *Risk assessments and internal control* (IFAC, 1994)
- International Standards on Auditing (ISA) 500: *Audit evidence* (IFAC, 1994)
- International Standards on Auditing (ISA) 501: *Audit evidence – additional considerations for specific items* (IFAC, 1994)
- International Standards on Auditing (ISA) 505: *External confirmations* (IFAC, 2001)
- International Standards on Auditing (ISA) 510: *Analytical procedures* (IFAC, 1994)

10.1 INTRODUCTION

The financial statements of a corporate entity comprise a set of statements by the entity's directors which, taken together, provide a picture of the entity's financial position, the results of its operations, and (in applicable cases) its cash flows. These statements are presented as account balances (appropriately grouped and classified), a statement of accounting policies and notes to the financial statements. The accounting policies and notes explain, among other things, the bases on which the financial statements have been prepared. In presenting the financial statement balances (and accompanying notes), the entity's directors are making implicit assertions about the balances and the items they represent. More particularly, they are implicitly asserting that the balances are valid, complete and accurate.

The auditor is required, *inter alia,* to express an opinion as to whether or not the financial statements give a true and fair view of the entity's state of affairs and its profit or loss. To accomplish this, the auditor conducts substantive tests – tests which examine the substance of (or assertions embodied in) the financial statement balances.

In this chapter we examine the significance of substantive testing in the audit process and discuss the objectives of substantive procedures. We also explore the different approaches which may be taken to test the financial statement balances and explain the audit procedures commonly adopted for each approach. More particularly, we discuss specific analytical procedures and procedures used for testing the details of the financial statement balances – whether this be through testing the transactions which generate the balances or testing the balances directly. After studying the principles of substantive testing, we examine in more detail the application of substantive procedures in auditing the balances of the stock and debtors accounts.

10.2 SIGNIFICANCE OF SUBSTANTIVE TESTING IN THE AUDIT PROCESS

When considering the significance of substantive testing in the audit process, it is important to appreciate the integrative character of an audit. The nature, timing and extent of substantive procedures are essentially determined by the preceding audit steps, particularly:

- understanding the client, its industry, its business and its activities;
- establishing the desired level of audit risk (or desired level of assurance) and setting materiality thresholds;

- assessing inherent risk; that is, assessing the likelihood of material error being present in the financial statements in the absence of internal controls;
- evaluating the effectiveness of the client's internal control system;
- testing the control procedures on which the auditor plans to rely to prevent material misstatement from occurring in the financial statements and, thus, to reduce substantive testing.

From Figure 10.1 it may be seen that both the auditor's evaluation of the effectiveness of the internal control system and the results of testing the control procedures on which (s)he plans to rely have a particularly significant impact on the nature, timing and extent of substantive testing.

If, based on his evaluation of the client's internal control system, the auditor concludes the control procedures are not effective in preventing material error from occurring in the financial statements or, alternatively, having initially concluded that the control procedures are effective but the results of compliance tests prove this not to be the case, the auditor will need to perform extensive substantive procedures before attaining his desired level of assurance that the financial statements are not materially misstated. Further, this testing will need to be as close as possible to the end of the accounting period.

Figure 10.1:   Impact of internal control evaluation and testing on substantive testing

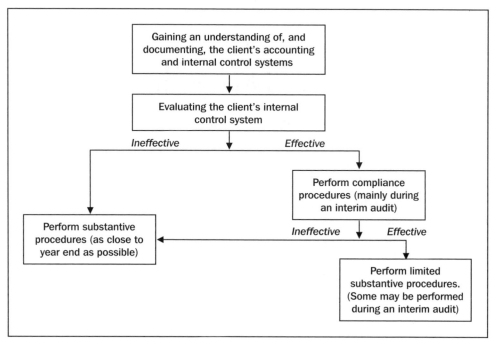

Conversely, if the auditor concludes that the client's internal control system is effective and this belief is supported by the results of compliance tests, (s)he will feel reasonably confident that the information contained in the financial statements is valid, complete and accurate. As a result, the auditor will perform more limited substantive testing than would otherwise be the case. However, substantive tests may not be omitted altogether. The auditor is required to form and express an opinion about the truth and fairness of the financial statements *per se* – not about inherent risk or the effectiveness of the client's internal control system. Further, as noted in Chapter 9, no internal control system is perfect; they all possess some inherent limitations. Therefore, irrespective of how confident the auditor may be that the financial statements are not materially misstated, in order to form and express the required opinion, some substantive testing of the financial statement balances and related notes is always necessary.

These ideas are conveyed in Statement of Auditing Standards (SAS) 300: *Accounting and internal control systems and audit risk assessments,* which states:[1]

> The auditors' control risk assessment, together with the inherent risk assessment, influences the nature, timing and extent of substantive procedures to be performed to reduce detection risk, and therefore audit risk, to an acceptably low level. (para 51)
> The assessed levels of inherent and control risks cannot be sufficiently low to eliminate the need for auditors to perform any substantive procedures . . . Regardless of the assessed levels of inherent and control risks, auditors should perform some substantive procedures for financial statement assertions of material account balances and transaction classes. (paras 54 and 53)

10.3 OBJECTIVES OF, AND APPROACHES TO, SUBSTANTIVE TESTING

10.3.1 Objectives of substantive procedures

The overall objective of substantive testing is to verify the validity, completeness and accuracy of the financial statement balances and note disclosures. More specifically, the objective is to confirm (or refute) the assertions embodied in the financial statement balances; namely, to verify that:

- the account balances are valid; that is, they represent *bona fide* transactions: no fictitious amounts are included;
- the account balances are complete; that is, they include all relevant amounts: none have been omitted;

---

[1] ISA 400: *Risk assessments and internal control*, paras 41 and 45, contain similar wording to that in SAS 300 paras 51, and 53 and 54, respectively.

- the account balances represent items that are owned by the entity (or, as in the case of leased assets, the entity has rights to control the items which are similar to rights normally associated with ownership);
- the account balances are arithmetically accurate;
- items included in the account balances are properly valued;
- items included in the account balances are correctly classified;
- items included in, or excluded from, the account balances are allocated to the correct accounting period;
- the account balances, and any requisite notes, are properly disclosed.

Verifying each of these assertions constitutes a specific audit objective. If the specific audit objectives are met, the overall objective of confirming the validity, completeness and accuracy of the financial statement balances will also be met.[2]

10.3.2 Alternative approaches to substantive testing

Although all substantive testing has, as its objective, determining the validity, completeness and accuracy of financial statement balances, two basic approaches may be adopted, namely:

(i) specific analytical procedures;
(ii) tests of details.

(i) Specific analytical procedures: Where this approach is adopted, meaningful relationships between account balances, or between financial and non-financial information, are examined to ascertain the reasonableness (or otherwise) of the relevant financial statement amounts.

---

[2] Statement of Auditing Standards (SAS) 400: *Audit evidence*, paras 10 and 11, and ISA 500: *Audit evidence*, paras 12 and 13, convey similar ideas but express them differently. (The wording in SAS 400 and ISA 500 also differs slightly). SAS 400 paras 10 and 11 state:

> In seeking to obtain audit evidence from substantive procedures, auditors should consider the extent to which that evidence together with any evidence from tests of controls supports the relevant financial statement assertions.

> Financial statement assertions are the representations of the directors that are embodied in the financial statements. . . . These representations or assertions may be described in general terms ... as follows:
>
> a) existence: an asset or a liability exists at a given date;
> b) rights and obligations: an asset or a liability pertains to the entity at a given date;
> c) occurrence: a transaction or event took place which pertains to the entity during the relevant period;
> d) completeness: there are no unrecorded assets, liabilities, transactions or events, or undisclosed items;
> e) valuation: an asset or liability is recorded at an appropriate carrying value;
> f) measurement: a transaction or event is recorded at the proper amount and revenue or expense is allocated to the proper period; and
> g) presentation and disclosure: an item is disclosed, classified and described in accordance with the applicable reporting framework (for example relevant legislation and applicable accounting standards).

(ii) Tests of details: This approach may take one of two forms:

(a) testing the transactions which give rise to the account balances;
(b) testing the closing account balances directly.

(a) Where the transactions approach is adopted, attention is focused on the opening balance of the account in question and the transactions which affect the account during the reporting period. If the opening balance and the transactions are recorded and added correctly, the closing balance must, of necessity, be correct.[3]

(b) Where closing account balances are tested directly, components of the balance are usually tested. For example, individual debtors' account balances are tested as a means of substantiating the debtors account balance in the balance sheet.

Regarding the selection of the appropriate approach to substantive testing, International Standards on Auditing (ISA) 510: *Analytical procedures*, explains:

> The auditor's reliance on substantive procedures to reduce detection risk relating to specific financial statement assertions may be derived from tests of details, from analytical procedures, or from a combination of both. The decision about which procedures to use to achieve a particular audit objective is based on the auditor's judgment about the expected effectiveness and efficiency of the available procedures in reducing detection risk for specific financial statement assertions. (para 10)[4]

Although different approaches to substantive testing may be adopted, it should be recognised that they are frequently complementary and interlock in a mutually supportive manner. This may be illustrated by reference to the sales-debtors-receipts cycle, as shown in Figure 10.2.

Specific analytical procedures may be used to ascertain the reasonableness of the debtors closing balance. If it appears to be reasonable, the extent of further detailed testing may be reduced. Conversely, if analytical procedures indicate that the balance may be materially misstated, more extensive testing will be required to identify the nature and extent of any error(s). Specific analytical procedures may also be used to substantiate less material account balances

---

[3] In the case of balance sheet accounts, the opening balance is established from the audited closing balances of the previous period; for profit and loss statement accounts, the opening balance is, of course, zero.

[4] SAS 410: *Analytical procedures,* para 12, conveys similar notions to ISA 510, para 10, but focuses more explicitly on analytical procedures. It states:
> The decision about whether to use analytical procedures as substantive procedures and the nature, timing and extent of their use is based on the auditor's judgment about the expected effectiveness and efficiency of the available procedures in reducing detection risk for specific financial statement assertions.

Figure 10.2: Substantive testing of debtors and related accounts

Verified by	Debtors		Verified by
Previous year's audit →	Opening bal x	Receipts x Discount x ←	Testing cash receipts transactions
Testing sales transactions →	Sales x		
Analytical procedures or testing transactions → (depending on materiality)	Freight x Interest x	Returns x Bad debts x ←	Analytical procedures or testing transactions (depending on materiality)
Analytical procedures → (for reasonableness) and direct tests of balance	= Closing bal x	=	

NB: Verification of complementary account balances (such as sales) simultaneously helps to confirm the debtors account balance.
Verification of the debtors account balance (through direct testing) simultaneously helps to confirm the balances of related accounts (such as sales).

such as 'interest on overdue accounts' and 'freight charged to credit customers'. (Specific analytical procedures are discussed in section 10.4.2 below.)

In order to determine the validity, completeness and accuracy of the sales account balance, the period's sales transactions are tested. Similarly cash receipts, discount received and sales returns transactions may be tested to substantiate their respective account balances. It should be noted that testing these transactions serves two purposes: it confirms the relevant account balance in the profit and loss statement and simultaneously provides support for an element of the debtors account. If the balance of the debtors account is also confirmed through direct testing this, by implication, provides support for the accuracy of the related (component) accounts. By obtaining mutually supportive evidence in this manner, the auditor can feel confident that all of the accounts constituting the sales-debtors-receipts cycle are fairly stated.

It should be noted that substantive testing is concerned with the validity, completeness and accuracy of information presented in the financial statements. Its objective is very different from that of compliance testing. In compliance testing, the auditor is concerned to confirm that internal controls on which (s)he plans to rely to prevent material error from occurring in the financial statements are operating effectively and have been so operating throughout the reporting period. Thus, compliance procedures conducted in relation to, for example, sales transactions, seek evidence which indicates, *inter alia*, that sales transactions have been authorised, and that extensions, additions, and account codings shown on sales invoices have been independently checked. By contrast, substantive procedures are concerned with examining the monetary amounts and correctness of recording of transactions.

Confusion between the two types of procedures frequently arises in relation to testing transactions. This is because the source documents recording transactions are used for both types of tests. For example, copies of sales invoices may be vouched to see if initials are present which indicate that extensions, additions and account classifications have been checked by an independent person. In this case, evidence of compliance with an internal control procedure is sought. The same document may be used for substantive testing; that is, for the auditor to check for him/herself that the extensions and additions are arithmetically correct, and that the transaction has been correctly classified. The same source document (and transaction) is used for two entirely different purposes.

10.4   SUBSTANTIVE AUDIT PROCEDURES

10.4.1   Overview of substantive audit procedures

We noted above that there are two broad categories of substantive tests – specific analytical procedures and tests of details. We also noted that tests of details may be either tests of transactions or direct tests of account balances. The relationship between these types of substantive tests, and the procedures used for each, are depicted in Figure 10.3.

10.4.2   Specific analytical procedures

During the planning stages of an audit, analytical procedures are used to assist the auditor understand the client's business, assess the likelihood of material error being present in the (pre-audited) financial statements, to identify high-risk audit areas and to plan the nature, timing and extent of other audit procedures. At this stage, broad entity measures are important such as the current ratio, debt to equity ratio, gross profit percentage, return on assets, and return on shareholders' funds. During the substantive testing stage, the focus of attention is on individual account balances. To distinguish between the two uses of analytical procedures, the term 'overall analytical procedures' is frequently applied to the broad risk assessment procedures and 'specific analytical procedures' to the narrow account-focused substantive tests.

Statement of Auditing Standards (SAS) 410: *Analytical procedures*, explains that when analytical procedures are used as substantive tests:

Figure 10.3: Overview of substantive audit procedures

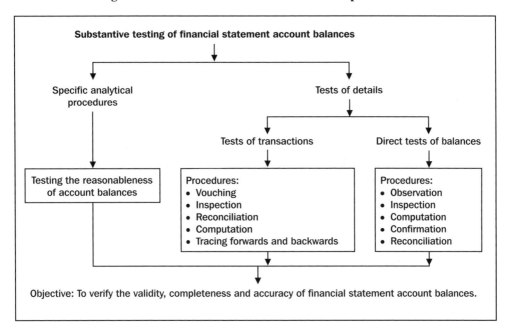

Auditors usually enquire of management as to the availability and reliability of information needed to apply analytical procedures and the results of any such procedures performed by the entity. It may be efficient to use the analytical data prepared by the entity, provided the auditors are satisfied that such data is properly prepared. (para 12)

It further notes:

When intending to apply analytical procedures as substantive procedures, auditors need to consider a number of factors such as:
- the plausibility and predictability of the relationships identified for comparison and evaluation . . .;
- the objectives of the analytical procedures and the extent to which their results are reliable;
- the degree to which information can be disaggregated, for example analytical procedures may be more effective when applied to financial information on individual sections of an operation. . .;
- the availability of information, both financial (such as budgets or forecasts) and non-financial (such as the number of units produced or sold);
- the relevance of the information available, for example whether budgets are established as results to be expected rather than as goals to be achieved; . . . (para 13)

The application of [specific] analytical procedures is based on the expectation that relationships between data exist and continue in the absence of known conditions to the contrary. ... However, reliance on the results of [specific] analytical procedures depends on the auditors' assessment of the risk that the analytical procedures may identify relationships as expected whereas, in fact, a material mis-statement exists. (para 16)[5]

Specific analytical procedures are usually used during the substantive testing phase of an audit in two different ways – as preliminary tests for account balances where more extensive substantive procedures are required and as complete tests where less extensive procedures are needed.

(i)   Specific analytical procedures as preliminary tests

For accounts where extensive substantive testing is required (such as debtors and stock), specific analytical procedures are generally used as preliminary tests – to test the reasonableness of the account balances as a basis for deciding the extent to which further substantive testing is required. When an account balance appears to be reasonable, material misstatement is generally unlikely. In these cases, less substantive testing is needed than in situations where material error seems likely. The use of specific analytical procedures as a preliminary test in auditing stock is illustrated in section 10.6 below.

(ii)   Specific analytical procedures as complete tests

For accounts where less extensive substantive testing is required (such as often applies in the case of prepaid expenses and interest paid), specific analytical procedures are frequently used to test the reasonableness of their balances. If they appear to be reasonable, no further testing is undertaken. However, if error appears likely, then the relevant account is subjected to more detailed testing.

The following two examples illustrate ways in which specific analytical procedures may constitute complete substantive tests.

1. Historically, sales returns may possess a fairly stable relationship with sales. Thus, assuming that nothing has come to the auditor's attention which suggests that the relationship may not hold in the current year, if the sales returns account balance is calculated as a percentage of sales, the result should be similar to that for previous years. If it is, the account balance is will probably be assumed to be reasonable and accepted as 'true and fair'.
2. The balance of the interest-paid account may be estimated by using a known relationship between two variables. More specifically, the average debt and the average interest rate for the reporting period may be ascertained, and the average interest rate then applied to the average debt. This provides an estimate of the interest-paid account balance. In the absence of exceptional

---

[5] ISA 510 paras 11, 12 and 14 are very similar to SAS 410 paras 12, 13 and 16. However, interestingly, unlike SAS 410 para 13, ISA 510, para 12, includes as a factor auditors need to consider when intending to use specific analytical procedures, '[the] reliability of information available, for example, whether budgets are prepared with sufficient care'.

circumstances known to the auditor, if the interest-paid account balance is close to the estimated amount, it will probably be judged to be reasonable and accepted as 'true and fair'.

10.4.3 Tests of details

As noted in section 10.3 above, substantive tests of details may involve testing the transactions which give rise to an account balance or directly testing the balance itself. The approach adopted is generally that which provides the most efficient means of determining the validity, completeness and accuracy of the account balance in question.

(i) Testing transactions

Profit and loss statement accounts (i.e. revenue and expense accounts) commence the accounting period with a zero balance and the transactions comprising the account are generally of a similar type. For example, entries in sales and purchases accounts are usually confined to cash and credit sales and purchases, respectively. Such similarity of transactions facilitates their testing and results in testing of the transactions generally being more efficient than directly testing the relevant account balances.

The same applies for some balance sheet accounts. Where the number of transactions affecting the account during the reporting period is small relative to the size of the account balance, testing the transactions affecting the account may be more efficient than directly testing the closing balance. An example is afforded by the motor vehicle account in entities which have large fleets of vehicles but relatively few additions and disposals (such as British Telecom). In the case of balance sheet accounts, the opening balance was verified during the previous year's audit and, as for the revenue and expense accounts, if the opening balance and the transactions affecting the account are recorded and added correctly, the closing balance must be correct.

As shown in Figure 10.3, the primary procedures for testing the accuracy, validity and completeness of transactions are vouching, inspection, reconciliation, computation and tracing. All of these procedures, other than tracing, are directed towards examining the accuracy of financial statement account balances – their accuracy as to amount, account and reporting period. These audit procedures may be illustrated as follows:

- *Vouching* of source documents may be used to determine whether transactions are *bona fide* and if they have been recorded in the correct account and period. The auditor checks the account code classifications of the transactions and, particularly for transactions near year end, examines the dates and terms of the transactions to ascertain the period to which they relate.

- *Inspection* of documents such as price lists may be used to check that correct prices have been applied to goods and services bought and sold.
- *Reconciliation* may be used, for example, to ensure that related purchase orders, receiving reports, suppliers' invoices and payments vouchers all match – that the quantities and prices of goods ordered and received, invoiced and paid for, are in agreement. Similarly, source document totals are reconciled with journal entries, and journal entries are reconciled with ledger records.
- *Computation* of items such as extensions and additions on source documents may be performed by the auditor in order to check that transactions have been recorded at their correct amount.

Tracing backwards and forwards are substantive procedures designed to test the validity and completeness, respectively, of recorded transactions, rather than their accuracy.

- *Tracing backwards* involves tracing selected entries back through the accounting records, from the financial statements, through the ledgers and journals, to the source documents. This procedure is designed to check that the amounts recorded in the financial statements represent *bona fide* transactions and that financial statement account balances are not overstated. Because of the (usual) desirability of having more rather than less assets and revenue, there may be an incentive to inflate asset and revenue accounts. Tracing backwards has particular application in ensuring that asset and revenue account balances are valid and not overstated.
- *Tracing forwards* involves tracing selected transactions forwards through the accounting records, from source documents, through the journals and ledgers, to the financial statements. This procedure is designed to check that financial statement account balances include all relevant transactions and that they are not understated. Because of the desirability of having less rather than more liabilities and expenses, there may be an incentive to understate liability and expense accounts. Tracing forwards has particular application for testing the completeness of liability and expense account balances, and ensuring that they are not understated.

(ii)   Direct tests of balances

For some accounts it is more efficient to audit the closing balance directly rather than examine the transactions that constitute the balance. This applies, for example, to many balance sheet accounts such as stock, debtors, investments and loans.

The primary audit procedures used to examine the validity, completeness and accuracy of account balances are observation, inspection, computation, confirmation and reconciliation. These may be illustrated as follows:

- *Observation* is used, for example, to establish the existence, quantity and quality of stock and of fixed assets such as plant, equipment and motor vehicles. (In some cases, observation extends to observing identification numbers of fixed assets, for example, the engine and chassis numbers of motor vehicles.)
- *Inspection* of documents, such as marketable securities and loan, lease and hire purchase contracts, is used to confirm the existence of the items concerned and to ascertain their terms and conditions.
- *Computation* of accounts such as depreciation and accumulated depreciation, doubtful debts and allowance for bad debts, is used to confirm the arithmetical accuracy of their balances.
- *Confirmation* is used to confirm certain information with parties outside the audit client, for example, the balance of debtors' and bank accounts, and items such as contingent liabilities and commitments. (Confirmation of debtors is discussed in detail in section 10.7 below and confirmation of contingent liabilities and commitments is considered in Chapter 12.)
- *Reconciliation* is used, for example, to reconcile the bank account balance in the general ledger with the confirmation letter received from the bank, and to reconcile subsidiary ledger totals with the relevant control account in the general ledger.

10.5 INTRODUCTION TO SUBSTANTIVE TESTING OF STOCK AND DEBTORS

To illustrate the application of substantive procedures to direct tests of balances, some aspects of auditing stock and debtors are discussed in detail in sections 10.6 and 10.7 below. These accounts frequently constitute the greatest proportion of a company's current assets and represent its chief source of short-term cash. They are also accounts which are prone to misstatement. In the case of stock this arises, in particular, from possible over-valuation of stock resulting from stock obsolescence. For debtors, it results primarily from the subjectiveness involved in estimating the allowance for bad debts. As a consequence of these factors, the stock and debtors account balances almost always attract considerable audit attention. Particular interest in these accounts arose as a result of the infamous *McKesson & Robbins* case in the US in the 1930s. Subsequent to this case, which involved many millions of dollars worth of fictitious stock and debtors, auditors have generally attended stocktakes and confirmed debtors in all audits where these items are material which, as noted above, is usually the case.

10.6   SIGNIFICANT ASPECTS OF AUDITING STOCK

10.6.1   Overview of auditing stock

When auditing stock, the auditor is particularly concerned to confirm its existence, ownership and value. As shown in Figure 10.4, each of these audit objectives requires a different set of audit procedures.

Before testing the details of the stock account balance, in order to ascertain whether misstatement seems likely, specific analytical procedures may be performed. For example, the ratio of stock to cost of goods sold (COGS) may be calculated for each significant type of stock, at each significant location. The trend for the current and past years may then be plotted and the resultant picture evaluated in the light of the auditor's understanding of the client's business and its operations. Some possible scenarios (where no change in the ratio was expected) are as follows:

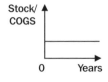

(1) A steady relationship between stock and COGS is indicated, suggesting that significant misstatement is unlikely.

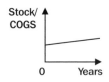

(2) A steady increase in stock levels is indicated suggesting the possibility of overstocking. This may indicate that stock obsolescence is a problem and that some write-down in value may be necessary.

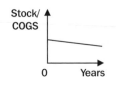

(3) A steady decrease in stock levels is indicated suggesting the possibility of stockouts. This may indicate that future sales and profits are threatened. The reduction in stocks may signal liquidity problems.

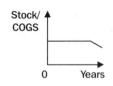

(4) A marked decline in stock in the current year is indicated. This raises the possibility of theft, a material error in the accounts, or a reduction in stock in anticipation of a decline in sales.

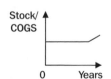

(5) A marked increase in stock in the current year is indicated. This raises the possibility of manipulation of the accounts by senior management, a material error in the accounts, or an increase in stock in anticipation of an increase in sales.

Figure 10.4: Procedures for auditing stock

Assertion/Audit Objective	Audit Procedures
Existence – Does stock exist?	Observation (attendance at stocktake)
Ownership – Is stock owned?	Vouching of source documents and inspection of other documents for dates and terms of 'purchase' of stock
Valuation – Is stock correctly valued?	• Observation of quality of stock and degree of completion of work-in-progress • Vouching of source documents and inspection of price lists for cost of stock • Computation of stock valuation

When assessing the results of specific analytical procedures (such as those set out above) it is essential that they are not viewed in isolation. The auditor must evaluate the results within the context of his or her understanding of the client, and must give due consideration to all of the relevant external and internal environmental factors. For example, the above graphs need to be assessed on the basis of the stock item(s) and/or location(s) to which they apply and how they compare with the graphs of other stock items and/or locations. Consideration must be given to pertinent policy decisions of management, such as planned changes in product mix, changes in target market(s), and/or changes in purchases and sales policies. Similarly, due allowance must be made for local and national economic, competitive and other factors which may have a bearing on stock levels.

It is important that specific analytical procedures be regarded, not as a source of answers, but as a means of identifying questions which need to be asked.

10.6.2 Ascertaining the existence of stock

The primary means by which an auditor ascertains that stock exists is attending the client's stocktake.[6] International Standards on Auditing (ISA) 501: *Audit evidence – additional consideration for specific items* recognises the importance of this audit procedure. It states:

> When inventory is material to the financial statements, the auditor should obtain sufficient appropriate audit evidence regarding its existence and condition by

---

[6] It should be noted that this applies whether the client uses a periodic or a perpetual system of recording stock. In relation to a perpetual system, ISA 501 explains:

> [W]hen the entity operates a perpetual system and the auditor attends a count one or more times during the year, the auditor would ordinarily observe count procedures and perform test counts. (para 9)

attendance at physical inventory counting unless impracticable. Such attendance will enable the auditor to inspect the inventory, to observe compliance with the operation of management's procedures for recording and controlling the results of the count and to provide evidence as to the reliability of management's procedures. (para 5)[7]

Audit procedures relating to a stocktake fall into three main groups:

(i)   those conducted prior to the commencement of the stocktake;
(ii) those conducted during the stocktake; and
(iii) those conducted when the stocktake is completed.

(i)   Procedures conducted prior to the stocktake

Prior to the commencement of the stocktake the auditor should review the client's stocktaking procedures to ensure they are adequate. The auditor needs to establish, for example:

- when the stocktake is to take place and whether sufficient time has been allowed to enable the task to be completed satisfactorily;
- which personnel are to be involved in the count, their seniority and experience, and whether they are to work in pairs;
- how the count is to be performed; whether, for example, stocksheets are to be used;
- whether the instructions given to the stocktaking teams are clear, easily understood and complete;
- whether management's control procedures are adequate; whether, for example, appropriate procedures have been established to facilitate accounting for used and unused stocksheets, for counting and recounting stock, and to prevent stock from being counted twice, or omitted from the count;
- whether management has established adequate procedures for identifying the stage of completion of work-in-progress, obsolete or damaged items, and/or stock owned by a third party (such as goods held on consignment);
- whether appropriate arrangements have been made regarding the movement of stock between locations (or areas within one location), just prior to, during and following the stock count, and the despatch and receipt of stock before and after the cut-off date.[8]

---

[7] Auditing Guideline (AG) 405: *Attendance at stocktaking* similarly recognises the importance of the auditor attending stocktakes but expresses the point slightly differently. It states:

> Where stocks are material in the enterprise's financial statements, and the auditor is placing reliance upon management's stocktake in order to provide evidence of existence, then the auditor should attend the stocktaking. This is because attendance at stocktaking is normally the best way of providing evidence of the proper functioning of management's stocktaking procedures, and hence of the existence of stocks and their condition. (para 5)

[8] 'Cut-off' date is the end of the accounting period. It defines (or 'cuts off') the stock (and other assets and liabilities) owned – and those not owned – by the entity at the balance sheet date. Only (but all) stock owned by the entity at the end of the accounting period should be included in the stock count.

If, having reviewed the client's stocktaking procedures, the auditor is of the opinion that they are not adequate, (s)he should discuss these concerns with management so the deficiencies can be rectified before the stocktake begins.

Where stock is held at several locations, the auditor needs to decide at which locations audit attendance is appropriate. In making this decision, (s)he should consider (among other things) the materiality of the stock held, and the assessment of inherent and internal control risk at each location. Audit staff should attend the stock count at each location where the stock held is material and/or inherent and internal control risk are assessed as high.

(ii) Procedures conducted during the stocktake

During the stocktake the auditor should observe whether the client's employees adhere to management's procedures, and he should also perform test counts. ISA 501 explains:

> To obtain assurance that management's procedures are adequately implemented, the auditor would observe employees' procedures and perform test counts. When performing counts the auditor would test both the completeness and the accuracy of the count records by tracing items selected from those records to the physical inventory and items selected from the physical inventory to the count records. The auditor would consider the extent to which copies of such count records need to be retained for subsequent testing and comparison. (para 13)[9]

AG 405 adds to this, noting:

> The auditor should determine whether the procedures for identifying damaged, obsolete and slow moving stock operate properly ... [and] should consider whether management has instituted adequate cut-off procedures, i.e. procedures intended to ensure that movements into, within and out of stocks are properly identified and reflected in the accounting records. ...[T]he auditor should [also] test the arrangements made to segregate stocks owned by third parties and he should identify goods movement documents for reconciliation with financial records of purchases and sales. (paras 16 and 17)

Many stocktakes are conducted with the aid of stocksheets. In an effective stocksheet system:

- all stocksheets are pre-numbered sequentially and a record is kept of the stocksheets which are issued to identified members of the stocktaking team;
- all items of stock at a location are identified and listed on the stocksheets;
- working in pairs, one team of stocktakers counts the stock and records the quantity on the stocksheets;
- a second team of stocktakers (also working in pairs) recounts the stock and records the quantity on duplicate stocksheets;

---

[9] Similar ideas are conveyed in AG 405, para 15.

- the completed (and unused) stocksheets are returned to the stocktaking clerk who checks off the returned stocksheet numbers and compares the stock counts recorded by the two teams of stocktakers;
- any significant discrepancies in the counts recorded by the two teams are investigated and the affected stock items are recounted to establish the correct quantity.

(iii)   Procedures following completion of the stocktake

When the stocktake is complete, a master stock listing is prepared. The auditor should test this listing to determine whether it accurately reflects the stock counts. (S)he should also compare the quantities listed on the master listing with the perpetual stock records. Discrepancies between the physical count and perpetual records should be noted and investigated. Additionally, the accounting records should be inspected to ascertain whether they have been adjusted appropriately.

Because the balance of the stock account presented in the financial statements reflects the stock held at the balance sheet date, stocktaking is usually undertaken at, or as close as possible to, the end of the accounting period. However, ISA 501 recognises that this is not always practical. It observes:

> For practical reasons, the physical inventory count may be conducted at a date other than period end. This will ordinarily be adequate for audit purposes only when [internal] control risk is assessed at less than high. The auditor would assess whether, through the performance of appropriate procedures, changes in inventory between the count date and period end are correctly recorded. (para 15)

ISA 501 also provides guidance for auditors in situations where the counting of stock is not feasible. It notes:

> If the entity uses procedures to estimate the physical quantity [of stock], such as estimating a coal pile, the auditor would need to be satisfied regarding the reasonableness of the procedures. (para 10)

10.6.3   Ascertaining ownership of stock

Stock recorded as a current asset in the financial statements should reflect the value of stock owned by the company at balance sheet date. It should not include stock which is not owned by the company: neither should it exclude stock which is owned. Therefore, as part of the audit of stock, the auditor vouches source documents and inspects other relevant documents in order to determine stock ownership. Two situations are of particular concern to the auditor:

(i)   *The ownership of goods bought and sold near year end.* The auditor needs to determine, for example, whether legal title to goods purchased, but in transit on balance sheet date, had passed to the client by that date. [This usually depends on whether the terms of the contract are f.o.b. (free on board) at shipping point or destination.] The auditor must also ascertain whether the goods in question have been properly included in or, excluded from, the client's stock listing at balance sheet date.

Similarly, the auditor needs to ensure that where goods have been sold (and legal title has passed to the customer) but the goods are still on the client's premises awaiting delivery at balance sheet date, these goods have not been recorded as part of the client's stock.

(ii) *Goods on consignment.* The auditor needs to ascertain whether any stock included in the client's stock listing is held on consignment, or under a franchise agreement, whereby title to the goods does not pass to the client until a specified condition is met; for example, the goods are sold to a third party. Such goods are not owned by the client and, therefore, do not form part of the client's stock.

By the same token, the auditor needs to ensure that stock owned by the client which is held on consignment, or under a franchise agreement, by a third party is included as part of the client's stock.

10.6.4 Ascertaining that stock is correctly valued

In addition to establishing the quantity and ownership of stock, the auditor must verify that it is correctly valued. To accomplish this audit objective, the auditor performs the following procedures. (S)he:

- determines the valuation method adopted by the client and confirms that this method:
  - is in accordance with Statement of Standard Accounting Practice (SSAP) 9: *Stocks and Long Term Contracts;*
  - has been applied consistently across all stock items;
  - is consistent with previous years;
- vouches suppliers' invoices and inspects price lists and other relevant documents to determine the cost of items held as stock;
- computes the value of stock based on its quantity (from the master listing), cost information, and the valuation method adopted;
- establishes that the degree of completion of work-in-progress has been determined appropriately, and that raw materials, work-in-progress and finished goods stock are properly classified;
- assesses the quality, condition and possible obsolescence of stock items, and determines whether the net realisable value of stock is lower than its cost;
- determines whether 'the lower of cost or market' rule has been applied correctly.

In relation to assessing the value of stock, it is important that the auditor evaluates his or her competence to estimate its value and, if necessary, seeks assistance from an appropriate expert. The most commonly cited example to illustrate this point is the auditor's inability, in general, to distinguish between diamonds and glass. The following case, reported in a BBC news broadcast in 1983, also provides a pertinent example. In this case the problem was an inability to distinguish between brass and gold.

> A North Wales jeweller committed suicide when it was discovered that his company's stock of gold was really brass. The Chester coroner was told that the jeweller had instructed his staff not to use the stock of what he said was gold wire, but when the bank sent investigators around, he admitted to a friend that the stock had been over-valued by £1 million. He then drove to a hotel where he drank a solution of cyanide poison. (BBC 'News about Britain', August 1983)

10.7 SIGNIFICANT ASPECTS OF AUDITING DEBTORS

10.7.1 Overview of auditing debtors

The debtors account balance is audited as an element of the sales-debtors-receipts cycle. Auditing this cycle involves, *inter alia*:

- performing specific analytical procedures to test the reasonableness of relevant profit and loss statement and balance sheet accounts (for example, sales, sales returns, doubtful debts, allowance for bad debts and debtors);
- verifying the validity, completeness and accuracy of sales and cash receipts transactions;
- directly testing the debtors account balance.

In this section, our focus of attention is the debtors account balance. When auditing this balance the auditor is concerned, in particular, to verify the existence, ownership and value of debtors. As for auditing stock, each of these audit objectives (or management assertions) requires a different set of audit procedures. These are shown in Figure 10.5.

10.7.2 Confirmation of debtors

As noted in section 10.5 above, confirmation of debtors became a standard audit procedure as a result of the *McKesson & Robbins* case in the US in the 1930s. ISA 505: *External confirmations,* explains the procedure as follows:[10]

> External confirmation is the process of obtaining and evaluating audit evidence through a direct communication from a third party in response to a request for information about a particular item affecting assertions made by management in the financial statements. (para 4)

_____

[10] It should be noted that, at the time of writing, there is no UK SAS equivalent to ISA 505.

Figure 10.5:   Procedures for auditing debtors

Assertion/Audit Objective	Audit Procedures
Existence – Do debtors exist?	Confirmation
Ownership – Are debtors owned?	Enquiry and inspection of documents for possible factoring of debtors
Valuation – Are debtors correctly valued?	• Confirmation • Computation of allowance for bad debts

It also notes:

> [A]udit evidence from external sources is more reliable than audit evidence generated internally, and written evidence is more reliable than oral evidence. Accordingly, audit evidence in the form of written responses to confirmation requests received directly by the auditor from third parties who are not related to the entity being audited . . . may assist in reducing audit risk for the related assertions to an acceptably low level. (para 3)

ISA 505 specifically affirms the value of confirmations in the audit of debtors, observing:

> External confirmation of an account receivable [i.e. a debtor's account] provides strong evidence regarding the existence of the account as at a certain date. Confirmation also provides evidence regarding the operation of cut-off procedures. (para 13)

However, the Standard also warns that confirmations do not usually provide evidence as to the collectibility, and hence the value, of debtors, pointing out: 'it is not practicable to ask the debtor to confirm detailed information relating to its ability to pay the account' (para 13). Further, ISA 505 indicates that auditors should not confirm debtors' balances as a matter of course but should consider whether this is the most efficient way to obtain evidence to meet their audit objective(s). It states:

> The auditor should determine whether the use of external confirmation is necessary to obtain sufficient appropriate audit evidence to support certain financial statement assertions. In making this determination, the auditor should consider materiality, the assessed level of inherent and control risk, and how the evidence from other planned audit procedures will reduce audit risk to an acceptably low level for the applicable financial statement assertions. (para 2)

Whilst acknowledging the caveats contained in ISA 505, it should be appreciated that confirmations provide the most widely used, and the most reliable, audit procedure available for verifying the existence and accuracy of debtors. However, auditors also heed the advice provided by ISA 505, para 4:

> In deciding to what extent to use external confirmations the auditor considers the characteristics of the environment in which the entity being audited operates and the practice of potential respondents in dealing with requests for direct confirmation.

Hence, the extent of reliance on confirmation as a procedure in auditing debtors varies from audit to audit.

Seven steps may be identified in the confirmation process. These are as follows:
(i)   designing the confirmation request;
(ii)   deciding on the timing of confirmations;
(iii)   selecting the sample of debtors;
(iv)   preparing and despatching the confirmations;
(v)   following up non-responses;
(vi)   analysing discrepancies;
(vii)   drawing conclusions with respect to the accuracy of the debtors' account balance.

(i)   Designing the confirmation request

The auditor should tailor external confirmation requests to the specific audit objective. When designing the request, the auditor considers the assertions being addressed and the factors that are likely to affect the reliability of the confirmations. Factors such as the form of the external confirmation request, prior experience on the audit or similar engagements, the nature of the information being confirmed, and the intended respondent, affect the design of the requests because these factors have a direct effect on the reliability of the evidence obtained through external confirmation procedures. (ISA 505, para 17)

The auditor may use positive or negative external confirmation requests or a combination of both. A positive external confirmation request asks the respondent to reply to the auditor in all cases either by indicating the respondent's agreement with the given information, or by asking the respondent to fill in information. . . . A negative external confirmation request asks the respondent to reply only in the event of disagreement with the information provided in the request. (ISA 505, paras 20–22)

From the above passage, it is evident that confirmations may be of two types, positive and negative. Positive confirmations are generally considered to provide more reliable evidence as the debtor is requested to respond as to whether the amount stated in the confirmation request is correct or incorrect. This enables the auditor to perform follow-up procedures in cases where responses are not received. However, the auditor also needs to bear in mind the possibility that a respondent may reply to a confirmation request without actually verifying that the information is correct. Where the auditor considers this is likely, instead of stating an amount in the confirmation request, the respondent may be asked to fill in the relevant amount. The problem with this type of 'blank' confirmation request is that it may result in a reduced response rate because more is required of the respondents.

Where negative confirmations are used, debtors are asked to respond only if the amount stated in the confirmation request is incorrect. Thus, all non-responses must be treated as if the amount stated in the confirmation request is correct – even though the debtor may have merely ignored the request. However, negative confirmations are less expensive than positive confirmations (because there are no follow-up procedures for non-responses) and, therefore, for a given total cost, more negative than positive confirmation requests may be sent. Nevertheless, because negative confirmations provide less reliable evidence than positive confirmations, the auditor needs to consider whether other substantive procedures are required to supplement the negative confirmations (ISA 505, para 22).

Determining which type of confirmation to use in any given audit is a matter of judgment. Nevertheless, it is generally accepted that positive confirmations are appropriate when the following circumstances apply:

- A small number of large accounts represent a significant proportion of the total debtors balance.
- The auditor has reason to believe that there may be disputed or inaccurate accounts. (For example, when internal controls are weak.)
- The auditor has good reason to expect that recipients of confirmation requests will not give them reasonable consideration. (For example, low response rates have been experienced in previous years. In this circumstance negative confirmations are not appropriate.)

By way of contrast, it is generally accepted that negative confirmations are appropriate in the following circumstances:

- The auditor considers that internal controls are reliable and that, as a result, material error in debtors' accounts is unlikely.
- The auditor has no reason to believe that recipients will disregard the confirmation request or fail to treat it seriously.
- A large number of small balances is involved.

It is pertinent to note that in some audits a combination of positive and negative confirmations is used. For example, where the total debtors' account balance comprises a small number of large balances and a large number of small balances, positive confirmations may be used for all or a sample of large balances and negative confirmations for a sample of small balances.

A further factor auditors should consider when designing confirmation requests is the type of information respondents will be able to confirm readily. For example, certain respondents' accounting systems may facilitate the confirmation of single transactions rather than account balances. Where this is the case, the confirmation request should contain details of one or more transactions rather than the relevant account balance. If information is sought in confirmations that is not readily available to the respondent, this is likely to result in a reduced response rate.

(ii)   Deciding on the timing of confirmations

There is little doubt that the most reliable evidence from confirmations is obtained when requests are sent close to balance sheet date. When this occurs, the debtors' balances are tested directly, without any inferences having to be made about transactions which take place between the confirmation date and balance sheet date. However, in order to complete the audit on a timely basis, and to facilitate scheduling of audit staff workloads, it is often convenient to confirm debtors at an interim date (generally, two to three months prior to year end). This timing of confirmations is acceptable provided that the client's internal controls are evaluated as effective and the auditor can be reasonably assured that sales, sales returns and cash receipts transactions are properly recorded between the confirmation and balance sheet dates.

(iii)   Selecting the sample of debtors

In order to select the sample of debtors to be confirmed, two separate decisions need to be made, namely:

(a)   how large the sample is to be;
(b)   how the sample is to be selected.[11]

The auditor also needs to consider characteristics of the intended respondents.

(a)   *The size of the sample* will depend on a number of factors, including the following:
   - the materiality of the total debtors' account balance. (The more material the balance, the larger the sample size);
   - the number of accounts that constitute the total debtors balance;
   - the size distribution of individual debtors' account balances;
   - the results of specific analytical procedures and internal control evaluation which indicate the likelihood (or otherwise) of the debtors' accounts being materially misstated;
   - the results of confirmations in previous years;
   - the type of confirmation being used.
(b)   *The sample selection* usually involves some stratification of the total population of debtors. In most audits where confirmation is adopted as an audit procedure, the population is stratified based on size and age of outstanding balances. Emphasis is given to testing large and old accounts as these accounts are the most likely to contain a material error. (Old accounts may

---

[11] Determining sample size and selecting samples are discussed in detail in Chapter 11.

indicate a dispute between the company and debtor about the amount or even the existence of the debt, or may raise other questions about its collectibility.) However, it is important that the auditor's sample includes some items from every material stratum of the population.

In most cases, the auditor confirms all balances which exceed some designated monetary amount and all accounts beyond a specified age limit (for example, 90 days), and selects a random sample from the remainder.

(c) *Characteristics of respondents*: In this regard ISA 505 points out:

> The reliability of evidence provided by a confirmation is affected by the respondent's competence, independence, authority to respond, knowledge of the matter being confirmed and objectivity. . . . The auditor also assesses whether certain parties may not provide an objective or unbiased response to a confirmation request. . . . The auditor also considers whether there is sufficient basis for concluding that the confirmation request is being sent to a respondent from whom the auditor can expect a response that will provide sufficient appropriate evidence. (paras 28 and 29)

(iv)   Preparing and despatching the confirmations

Once the auditor has decided on the type of confirmation to be used and selected the sample of debtors to be confirmed, the confirmation requests are prepared.

A confirmation request is a letter, sent to a selection of the client's customers, which sets out the amount owed by the customer to the client as shown in the client's accounts on a specified date (the confirmation date). As noted earlier, if a positive confirmation is used, the debtor is generally requested to confirm that the amount stated in the letter is correct or indicate that it is not correct. If the auditor considers that the debtor may not verify the amount stated in the confirmation request before confirming it, the debtor may be asked to fill in the amount owed on confirmation date. If a negative confirmation is used, the debtor is asked to respond only if the amount stated is not correct. In either case, if the amount is incorrect, the debtor is asked to state what (s)he believes the correct amount to be. The letter is frequently prepared on the client's letterhead but, in any event, it should include an authorisation from the client to the debtor to disclose the requested information to the auditor.

Notwithstanding the use of the client's letterhead, it is essential that all aspects of the confirmation process remain completely under the control of the auditor. This includes preparing the confirmation requests, placing them in envelopes, stamping and posting the envelopes. A stamped addressed envelope should be enclosed with the confirmation request, with the envelope addressed to the audit firm. Additionally, the audit firm's address should be shown as the return address on the outside of the envelope addressed to the debtor. This is to ensure that any undelivered requests are returned to the audit firm.

When a confirmation request is returned as undelivered mail, the reason for the non-delivery needs to be carefully evaluated. In most cases it represents a customer who has moved away without settling his or her account, but there is always the possibility that it represents a fictitious account. Further, even if the debtor is valid, a large number of undelivered confirmation requests could signal errors in the client's debtors' address records and a consequential collectibility problem. This will need to be reflected in the auditor's allowance for bad debts.

(v)   Following up non-responses

As noted above, when negative confirmations are used it is assumed that amounts stated in confirmations which are not returned are correct. Non-responses are not followed up. However, when positive confirmations are used, no assumption is made as to the correctness or otherwise of amounts stated in confirmations which receive no response. Instead, second, and in some cases even third, confirmation requests are sent.

If a debtor still fails to respond, the auditor has to rely on alternative audit procedures to confirm the amounts in question. (S)he will, for example, examine the cash receipts records to ascertain whether the debtor paid an amount subsequent to the date of the confirmation. However, receipt of cash from the debtor does not necessarily establish that the amount being investigated was owed at confirmation date: it could relate to a subsequent sale. Therefore, in addition to examining the cash receipts records, the auditor needs to examine copies of:

- sales invoices – to confirm that the customer was billed for the relevant goods or services;
- despatch records – to confirm that the goods were despatched to the customer;
- sales returns records – to confirm that the goods were not returned by the customer.

In each case, careful attention must be paid to the dates and details of the records to ensure that they all relate to the same transaction(s).

Inspection of correspondence in a disputed accounts file may also provide evidence that a debtor who failed to respond to a confirmation request owed the amount in question at the confirmation date.

During the 'following up' stage of the confirmation process:

> [t]he auditor considers whether there is any indication that external confirmations received may not be reliable. . . . The auditor may choose to verify the source and contents of a response in a telephone call to the purported sender. . . . With ever-increasing use of technology, the auditor considers validating the source of

replies received in electronic format (for example, fax or electronic mail). . . . If the information in the oral confirmations is significant, the auditor requests the parties involved to submit written confirmation of the specific information directly to the auditor. (ISA 505, para 33)

The extent and nature of follow-up procedures largely depend upon the materiality of the non-responses, the types of errors discovered in the confirmed responses, subsequent cash receipts from non-respondents, and the auditor's evaluation of the quality of the client's internal controls. However, in order for valid conclusions to be drawn about the population of debtors from the sample of accounts examined, all of the unconfirmed balances (following positive confirmation requests) should be investigated using alternative procedures, even if the amounts involved are small.

(vi)   Analysing discrepancies

When confirmations are returned by debtors to the auditor, any disagreements with amounts stated in the confirmation requests must be analysed carefully. In many cases these will result from timing differences between the customer's and the client's records (for example, a payment by a debtor may not have been recorded in the client's records by the confirmation date). However, in other cases, disagreements may signal errors in the client's accounts. These may arise, for example, from incorrect recording of amounts (that is, clerical errors), or from failure to record certain transactions, such as goods returned by the customer. Alternatively, they may reflect disputed amounts, where the customer claims, for instance, that the wrong price has been charged, incorrect quantities or items were received, or the goods arrived in a damaged condition.

All disagreements with amounts in confirmation requests should be investigated to determine whether the client's records are in error and, if this is the case, by how much. Generally, the auditor asks the client to perform the necessary reconciliation but, if necessary, will communicate with the customer to settle discrepancies that have come to light.

(vii)   Drawing conclusions with respect to the debtors' account balance

When all discrepancies found in the sample of debtors have been explained, including those discovered as a result of procedures performed as a follow-up to non-responses, the auditor needs to:

- re-evaluate the client's system of internal control and determine whether detected errors are consistent with the auditor's original assessment of the controls;
- generalise from the sample of debtors examined to the total population of debtors;

- draw conclusions as to whether sufficient appropriate evidence has been gathered regarding the assertions being tested (i.e. the existence and accuracy of debtors' balances recorded in the client's accounts). ISA 505 (para 34) notes:

  > In forming the conclusion, the auditor considers:
  > (a) reliability of the confirmations and alternative procedures;
  > (b) nature of any exceptions, including the implications, both quantitative and qualitative of those exceptions; and
  > (c) evidence provided by other procedures.

If the auditor concludes that the confirmation process and any alternative or additional procedures have not provided sufficient appropriate evidence regarding the assertions, additional procedures will need to be performed.

10.7.3 Adjusting debtors for doubtful debts

Based on evidence gathered by the confirmation process and any additional procedures the auditor considered necessary, the auditor may conclude that the debtors' balances shown in the client's records are fairly stated. However, before concluding that the value of debtors is presented fairly in the financial statements, the auditor must assess the adequacy of the client's allowance for bad debts. To make this assessment, the auditor needs to consider whether, compared with previous years, there has been any change in factors such as the following:

- the client's credit policy;
- the client's credit approval procedures;
- the level of compliance by employees with the credit approval procedures;
- the number of days debtors' account balances are overdue (the longer debtors' balances are overdue, the greater the probability that they will never be paid);
- the volume of credit sales;
- general economic conditions which are likely to affect debtors' ability to meet their financial obligations.

Giving due weight to these and similar factors, the auditor will assess the propriety of the percentage applied by the client to gross debtors to establish the current year's allowance for bad debts. The auditor will also reperform the relevant calculation.

10.7.4 Ownership of debtors

In most cases ownership of debtors does not give rise to problems: the amounts owed by debtors are owed to the client. However, particularly where there is evidence that the client has cash flow problems, the auditor must remain alert to the possibility that all or part of the client's debtors may have been factored (that is, sold to a financial institution at a discount). When this occurs, customers are frequently not aware of the change in the ownership of their debt because they continue to make payments to the client. As a consequence, factoring does not, in general, come to light through the confirmation process. The most common means of the auditor discovering that factoring has occurred is through discussions with management and inspection of documents such as minutes of directors' meetings, and correspondence.

10.8   SUMMARY

In this chapter we have discussed substantive testing; that is, testing the substance of (or assertions embodied in) the financial statement account balances. It is these balances about which the auditor is required to form and express an opinion and, irrespective of how 'perfect' a client's internal control system may appear to be, some substantive testing is always necessary.

We have noted that substantive testing may take one of two basic forms: specific analytical procedures or tests of details, and that tests of details may involve testing the transactions which give rise to a financial statement account balance or testing the balance directly. However, whichever form of substantive testing is used, the objective is always the same; namely, to test the validity, completeness and accuracy of the financial statement disclosures.

In addition to discussing the general principles of substantive testing, we have discussed the application of commonly used substantive audit procedures (for example, observation, inspection, computation, tracing, confirmation and reconciliation) and examined in some detail the significant aspects of auditing stock and debtors.

SELF-REVIEW QUESTIONS

10.1   Explain briefly the significance of substantive testing in the audit process.
10.2   State the overall audit objective of substantive testing.
10.3   Explain the meaning of the term 'financial statement assertions' and list seven such assertions.
10.4   Explain briefly what is meant by 'tests of details'.
10.5   Explain briefly the two ways in which specific analytical procedures are used as substantive tests.

10.6 (a) Describe briefly how the following audit procedures are performed:
   (i) tracing forwards
   (ii) tracing backwards.
   (b) Using a specific example to illustrate your answer, explain the purpose of each of the above audit procedures.

10.7 Describe briefly the 'stocksheet system' which may be used for a client's stocktaking.

10.8 Explain briefly two special considerations the auditor must take into account when testing the audit objective: is stock owned by the client?

10.9 In relation to auditing debtors, distinguish between a positive confirmation and a negative confirmation.

10.10 (a) List five aspects of the process of confirming debtors which must remain under the auditor's control.
   (b) Explain briefly why it is important that audit-client personnel are not permitted to assist the auditor in the process of confirming debtors.

ADDITIONAL READING

Bagshaw, K. (1994) Evidence: How much is enough? *Accountancy* **113**(1209), 80–82.

Grant Thornton. (1990) *Audit Manual.* Chapter 16, Tests of Details, and Chapter 29, Sales Cycle. London: Longman.

Hodgkinson, R. (1993) Taking stock. *Accountancy* **112**(1203), 90.

Krogstad, J.K. & Romney, H.B. (1980) Accounts receivable confirmation – An alternative auditing approach. *Journal of Accountancy* **149**(2), 68–74.

Lee, K. (1998) Taking stock, *Accountancy* **122**(1263), 90–1.

Littrell, E.K. (1982) Creative accounting – Getting a bang out of inventory. *Management Accounting* **63**(10), 56.

11 Introduction to Audit Sampling and Computer Assisted Auditing Techniques (CAATs)

LEARNING OBJECTIVES

After studying the material in this chapter you should be able to:
- explain what is meant by 'sampling' and why this technique is important in auditing;
- explain the meaning of the basic terminology used in sampling;
- distinguish between judgmental and statistical sampling and explain the advantages and disadvantages of each;
- describe the methods commonly used for selecting samples;
- distinguish between attributes sampling and variables sampling;
- explain the process of attributes sampling;
- explain the basic principles of sampling with probability proportional to size (monetary unit sampling);
- discuss the follow-up to the results obtained by sampling;
- explain what is meant by 'computer assisted auditing techniques' (CAATs);
- distinguish between 'test data' and 'audit software' and explain how each technique may be used in audit testing; and
- discuss the use and control of CAATs in auditing.

The following publications are particularly relevant to this chapter:
- Statement of Auditing Standards (SAS) 430: *Audit sampling* (APB, 1995);
- International Standards on Auditing (ISA) 530: *Audit sampling and other selective testing procedures* (IFAC, 1999).

11.1   INTRODUCTION

In this chapter we consider two audit techniques that traverse both compliance and substantive testing, namely, audit sampling and computer-assisted auditing techniques. We explain the meaning and importance of sampling in auditing, the meaning of basic terminology relating to sampling, and the differences between, and advantages and disadvantages of, judgmental and statistical sampling. We also discuss factors affecting the size of samples and describe some commonly used methods of selecting samples. Additionally, we examine in more detail some aspects of statistical sampling. More particularly, we discuss the difference between attributes and variables sampling, and describe the application of attributes sampling to compliance testing and sampling with probability proportioned to size (PPS; monetary unit sampling) to substantive tests. Before concluding this part of the chapter, we discuss the ways in which the auditor follows up the results obtained by sampling.

In the second part of the chapter, we explain what is meant by computer assisted auditing techniques (CAATs) and discuss the meaning and use of 'test data' and 'audit software' in relation to audit procedures. We also examine the use and control of CAATs during an audit.

11.2   MEANING AND IMPORTANCE OF SAMPLING IN AUDITING

ISA 530: *Audit sampling and other selective testing procedures* defines audit sampling as follows:

> 'Audit sampling' (sampling) involves the application of audit procedures to less than 100% of items within an account balance or class of transactions such that all sampling units have a chance of selection. This will enable the auditor to obtain and evaluate audit evidence about some characteristic of the items selected in order to form or assist in forming a conclusion concerning the population from which the sample is drawn. Audit sampling can use either a statistical or non-statistical approach. (para 3)[1]

Expressed in more general terms, sampling is the examination of a few items (or sampling units) drawn from a defined mass of data (or population), with a view to inferring characteristics about the mass of data as a whole. This may be illustrated by reference to a simple example.

Example: Assume that a client has 200,000 suppliers' invoices and that the auditor wishes to ascertain:

---

[1] SAS 430: *Audit sampling*, para 4, defines audit sampling in similar, but slightly briefer, terms.

(i) whether, before payment, the invoices were:
- matched with purchase orders and receiving reports;
- checked for correct extensions and additions;
- checked for correct account classifications; and

(ii) whether:
- the extensions and additions are arithmetically correct;
- the transactions have been coded to the correct accounts;
- the correct amounts have been recorded in the accounting records;
- the transactions have been recorded in the correct accounting period.

Reviewing these audit objectives, it should be noted that the first group relates to the client's internal control procedures. In order to test the level of compliance with these procedures, the auditor will perform compliance tests. The second group of objectives relates to the accuracy of the recorded amounts, account classifications, and accounting periods of the transactions. To test these, the auditor will perform substantive tests.

Clearly, it is not feasible for the auditor to apply the seven tests to all 200,000 invoices. Instead, (s)he will select a sample of, say, 40 invoices, and will perform the seven tests on these. Based on the results of the tests, the auditor will draw conclusions about the population of suppliers' invoices with respect to each of the characteristics tested. (That is, for each characteristic tested, the results obtained from testing 40 invoices will be inferred for the population as a whole.)

Sampling has been an accepted auditing technique since the early part of the twentieth century and today is recognised as an essential feature of most audits. Three main reasons account for its importance:

- in the modern business environment, it is not economically feasible to examine the details of every transaction and account balance.
- testing a sample of transactions is faster and less costly than testing the whole population.
- the auditor is required to form an opinion about the truth and fairness of the financial statements. (S)he is not required to reach a position of certainty or to be concerned about the statements' absolute accuracy. The task can be accomplished by testing samples of evidence and there is no need to test the whole. This point is reflected in SAS 400: *Audit evidence*, which states:

> Auditors seek to provide reasonable, not absolute, assurance that the financial statements are free from material misstatement. In forming their audit opinion, therefore, auditors do not normally examine all of the information available. Appropriate conclusions can be reached about a financial statement assertion using a variety of means of obtaining evidence, including sampling. (para 5)

Notwithstanding its undoubted advantages, reliance on sampling procedures introduces a matter of concern to the auditor. It exposes the auditor to sampling risk; that is, the risk of reaching a conclusion based on the sample which may differ from that which would have been reached had the entire population been subjected to the same audit procedure. Expressed in different terms, it is the risk that the auditor will draw inappropriate conclusions about the population because the sample examined is not representative of the population.

ISA 530 notes that there are two types of sampling risk and that each has an adverse impact on the audit. It explains the two types of risk as follows:[2]

    (a)   the risk the auditor will conclude, in the case of a test of control, that control risk is lower than it actually is, or in the case of a substantive test, that a material error does not exist when in fact it does. This type of risk affects audit effectiveness and is more likely to lead to an inappropriate audit opinion; and

    (b)   the risk the auditor will conclude, in the case of a test of control, that control risk is higher than it actually is, or in the case of a substantive test, that a material error exists when in fact it does not. This type of risk affects audit efficiency as it would usually lead to additional work to establish that initial conclusions were incorrect. (para 7)

Sampling risk cannot be avoided altogether if sampling procedures are used but it can be reduced by increasing the size of the sample and by selecting sample units at random (see section 11.5.3). Additionally, sampling risk may be quantified and controlled through the use of statistical sampling techniques.

It should be recognised that sampling techniques only apply when less than 100% of items comprising a population are examined. As SAS 430 explains:

> Tests performed on 100% of the items within a population do not involve sampling. Likewise applying audit procedures to all items within a population which have a particular characteristic (for example, all items over a certain amount) does not qualify as audit sampling with respect to the portion of the population examined, nor with regard to the population as a whole, since the items were not selected from the total population . . . (para 5)

11.3 BASIC TERMINOLOGY RELATING TO SAMPLING

In order to understand the fundamental principles of audit sampling, it is necessary to have a good grasp of a few of the terms which are commonly used. These include the following:

- *Population*: This refers to all of the items within an account balance or class of transactions which display a particular characteristic about which the auditor wishes to draw a conclusion.

---

[2] SAS 430, para 15, conveys broadly similar ideas but relates sampling risk more directly to tests of control and substantive tests rather than to audit effectiveness and efficiency.

- *Frame*: This is the physical representation of the population. For example, if the auditor is interested in the initials of the credit manager on sales invoices as evidence of compliance with authorisation procedures, the sales invoices are the frame. If the auditor is interested in the accuracy of debtors' account balances, subsidiary debtors' ledger records may be the frame.
- *Sample unit*: A sample unit is a unit selected from the population which is included in the sample to be examined.
- *Characteristic of interest*: This term refers to the characteristic the auditor wishes to test. There are two basic characteristics of interest, an *attribute* and a *variable*.
  - An *attribute* is a characteristic of the population which is either present or absent. Attributes sampling measures how frequently the characteristic is present (or absent); for example, how frequently the credit manager's initials, signalling approval of the credit sale, are present (or absent) on sales invoices.
  - A *variable* is a measurement which is possessed by every member of the population but which can take any one of a wide range of values. An example of a variable is the monetary amount of a transaction or account balance. In variables sampling, the auditor is concerned with estimating a monetary value; for example, the auditor may wish to estimate the balance of the stock account, or estimate the amount by which this balance may be in error.
- *Stratification:* This refers to dividing a single population into sub-populations of sampling units with a similar characteristic. It is undertaken to improve audit efficiency and effectiveness. As ISA 530 explains:

  > The objective of stratification is to reduce the variability of items within each stratum and therefore allow sample size to be reduced without a proportional increase in sampling risk . . . When performing substantive procedures, an account balance or class of transactions is often stratified by monetary value. This allows greater audit effort to be directed to the larger value items which may contain the greatest potential monetary error in terms of overstatement. Similarly, a population may be stratified according to a particular characteristic that indicates a higher risk of error, for example, when testing the valuation of accounts receivable, balances may be stratified according to age. (paras 36 and 37)[3]

  Debtors' account balances may, for example, be stratified according to size and/or age. Balances exceeding some monetary amount, and balances beyond some age limit (say, 90 days) may be subjected to 100% testing (that is, no sample will be selected and the entire population will be tested). The remaining balances will be treated as a homogeneous population from which a sample may be selected and tested.

---

[3] SAS 430, para 11, conveys similar ideas but in less detail.

An important advantage of stratification is that it permits allowance to be made for variations in the risk attaching to identifiable components of the population. In the debtors example cited above, the risk of material error being present is higher for large and old account balances than it is for balances which are smaller and those which have been outstanding for a shorter period.

- *Precision limits*: This term refers to how closely the results obtained from the sample of items examined match the results that would have been obtained had the total population been tested. For example, in attributes sampling, if the sample shows that a particular characteristic occurs in 2% of cases, how closely this reflects the rate of occurrence which would have been found had every item in the population been checked. Alternatively, in variables sampling, if, based on testing a sample of items, the auditor estimates the balance of the stock account as £750,000, how close this is to the amount that would have been arrived at had the value of every individual item of stock been ascertained and added.

- *Confidence level (or level of sampling risk)*: This term refers to how confident the auditor wishes to be that the sample units examined will have the desired precision. For example, if the auditor wishes to estimate the balance of the stock account and specifies a precision limit of £10,000 with a 95% level of confidence, this means that the auditor wishes his estimate of stock to be within £10,000 of the actual value of stock, at least 95 times out of every 100. By inference, it also means that the auditor is prepared to accept that, on five occasions out of 100, his estimate of stock (based on the sample units examined) may differ from the actual value of stock by more than £10,000. This 5% risk of the results derived from the sample falling outside the specified precision limits is known as *sampling risk*. Expressed in alternative terms, there is a 5% risk of the sample selected not being representative of the population from which it is drawn.

11.4 JUDGMENTAL SAMPLING VS STATISTICAL SAMPLING

When discussing audit sampling, it is important to distinguish between judgmental and statistical sampling.

(i) Judgmental sampling

Judgmental sampling refers to the use of sampling techniques in circumstances where the auditor relies on his judgment to decide:

- how large the sample should be;
- which items from the population should be selected;
- whether or not to accept the population as reliable, based on the results obtained from the sample units examined.

This sampling method has advantages over statistical sampling in that it is generally faster, and therefore less costly, to apply. Additionally, it enables the auditor to incorporate in the sampling procedures, allowance for factors of which (s)he is aware as a result of earlier audit steps such as gaining an understanding of the client and its business, and evaluating its internal control system. However, unlike statistical sampling, the method provides no measure of sampling risk and, should the auditor's judgment be challenged (particularly in a court of law), the conclusions reached with respect to the sample may be difficult to defend. Further, when using judgmental sampling it is difficult not to introduce bias – whether it be in relation to sample size, the items selected, or the conclusions reached with respect to the population.

Statistical sampling

Statistical sampling refers to the use of sampling techniques which rely on probability theory to help determine:

- how large the sample should be;
- whether or not to accept the population as reliable based on the results obtained from the sample units examined.

It should be noted that when statistical sampling is used, sample units must be selected at random. (Random sample selection is discussed in section 11.5.3.)

This sampling method has three important advantages over judgmental sampling:

- it is unbiased;
- should aspects of the sampling be challenged, it is readily defensible;
- it permits quantification of sampling risk. For example, if a sample is selected on the basis of a 95% confidence level, there is a 5% sampling risk; that is, there is a 5% risk that the sample is not representative of the population and, as a result, inappropriate conclusions may be drawn about the population.

However, statistical sampling has the disadvantages that it is more complex and costly to apply than judgmental sampling. Further, in general, only large entities have populations which are sufficiently large and homogeneous for the full application of statistical sampling methods. As a consequence, in many audits where statistical sampling is applied, it tends to be applied in a modified form.

In relation to statistical sampling it is pertinent to note that, notwithstanding the distinction made between statistical and judgmental sampling, significant elements of judgment are involved in applying statistical sampling techniques. This will be evident from our discussion of attributes and PPS sampling procedures presented in section 11.7 below.

11.5 DESIGNING AND SELECTING SAMPLES

11.5.1 Designing a sample

When designing a sample the auditor must consider:

- the audit objective(s) to be met by testing a sample of items, and
- the attributes of the population from which the sample is to be drawn.

The audit objective largely determines the audit procedure(s) to be applied. In applying the audit procedure(s), the auditor needs to define what constitutes an error and this, in turn, affects the population to be used for sampling. For example, if the objective of a compliance test relating to credit sales is to ascertain whether credit sales are properly authorised, and the client's control procedures include requiring the credit manager to initial sales invoices to signify approval of the sales, an appropriate audit procedure is to vouch a sample of copies of sales invoices for the credit manager's initials. In this case, the absence of the credit manager's initials would constitute an error, and the population comprises copies of all sales invoices issued during the accounting period. If, however, the objective of a substantive test is to ascertain whether sales invoices have been properly extended (price per item multiplied by quantity sold) and totalled, an appropriate audit test is to reperform the extensions and additions on a sample of copies of sales invoices. In this case, an error is an arithmetical error in an extension or in the total of a sales invoice and the population is, once again, copies of all the sales invoices issued during the accounting period.[4]

11.5.2 Sample size

Once the auditor has decided to apply a certain audit procedure to a sample of items in a population, (s)he must decide how many sampling units to include in the sample. As SAS 430 explains, this decision will be affected by three factors: 'sampling risk, the amount of error that would be acceptable [in the population], and the extent to which they [auditors] expect to find errors' (para 12).

(i) *Sampling risk:* The size of a sample is affected by the level of sampling risk the auditor is willing to accept. The smaller the risk the auditor wishes to accept that conclusions reached based on testing a sample of items will differ from those that would have been reached had all items in the population been examined, the larger the sample will need to be (and vice versa).

(ii) *Acceptable error rate:* The maximum error in the population the auditor is willing to accept, while still concluding the audit objective has been

---

[4] The design of samples is discussed further in SAS 430, paras 7 and 8, and ISA 530, paras 31–33.

reached, also affects sample size. This maximum amount of error may be referred to as tolerable error. SAS 430 observes:

> In tests of control, the tolerable error is the maximum rate of deviation from a prescribed control procedure that auditors are willing to accept in the population and still conclude that the preliminary assessment of control risk is valid. In substantive procedures, the tolerable error is the maximum monetary error in the account balance or class of transactions that auditors are willing to accept so that, when the results of all the audit procedures are considered, they are able to conclude, with reasonable assurance, that the financial statements are not materially misstated. (para 18) [5]

The smaller the tolerable error, the larger the sample the auditor needs to select.

(iii) *Expected error rate:* The size of samples is also affected by the rate of errors the auditor expects to find in the population. If errors are expected, a larger sample of items will need to be examined (than if no errors are expected) to enable the auditor to conclude that the actual error rate in the population does not exceed his or her tolerable error. When no errors are expected in the population, sample sizes may be smaller. SAS 430 explains:

> In determining the expected error in a population, auditors consider such matters as the size and frequency of errors identified in previous audits, changes in the entity's procedures and evidence available from other procedures. (para 19)

As is shown in section 11.7, when statistical sampling methods are used, sampling risk, tolerable error and expected population error rate are incorporated within the sampling method. When judgmental sampling methods are used, the auditor needs to take these three factors into consideration when determining sample size.

11.5.3   Sample selection

Once the auditor has determined the size of the sample to be selected, (s)he needs to decide how the items are to be selected. ISA 530, para 42, specifies:

> The auditor should select items for the sample with the expectation that all sampling units in the population have a chance of selection. Statistical sampling requires that sample items are selected at random so that each sampling unit has a known chance of being selected. The sampling units might be physical items (such as invoices) or monetary units. With non-statistical sampling, an auditor uses professional judgment to select the items for a sample. Because the purpose of sampling is to draw conclusions about the entire population, the auditor endeavors to select a representative sample by choosing sample items which have characteristics typical of the population, and the sample needs to be selected so that bias is avoided. [6]

---

[5] As noted in Chapter 8, section 8.4.1, in relation to substantive procedures, tolerable error is equivalent to the auditor's judgment as to what is material for the particular account balance or class of transactions.

[6] SAS 430, para 20, contains similar wording to the first sentence of ISA 530, para 42. However, SAS 430 does not contain the rest of the paragraph.

Figure 11.1: Methods of selecting audit samples

Broad groups of sample selection methods	Sub-groups of sample selection methods
Random selection	• Unrestricted random selection • Systematic sampling – Cluster sampling is a variation of systematic sampling • Selection with probability proportional to size
Non-random selection	• Haphazard selection • Judgmental selection

There are numerous methods for selecting audit samples but the most commonly used fall into two groups. These are shown in Figure 11.1 and discussed below.

(a) Random selection

The key feature of random sample selection is that each item in the population has an equal chance of selection. While maintaining this characteristic, three variations of random selection may be recognised, namely:

(i)   unrestricted random selection;
(ii) systematic selection;
(iii) selection with probability proportional to size (PPS selection).

(i) Unrestricted random selection

This method of selection treats the total population as a homogeneous mass of data, and random number tables or computer-generated random numbers are used to select the required number of sampling units.

(ii) Systematic selection

For systematic selection, a sampling interval is first determined by dividing the population to be tested by the required sample size. For example, if the population comprises 2,625 sales invoices and the sample size is 125, the selection interval is: $2{,}625/125 = 21$.

A number between 0 and 21 is selected at random by the auditor or (preferably, if the sample is to be truly random) by means of random number tables or a computer-generated random number, and this gives the starting point. Every twenty-first item in the population is then selected, beginning with that point.

Systematic selection is simple to use, and is generally quicker, and therefore less costly, than unrestricted random selection. However, it has the disadvantage that it can introduce bias into the sample if the characteristic of interest is not randomly distributed through the population. For example, the use of systematic selection to select a sample of sales invoices to check for authorisation of credit sales will not generally cause any problems. However, if every twenty-fifth person on the payroll is fictitious, systematic selection using a sampling interval of 25 could result in a sample consisting entirely of fictitious employees. Alternatively, by selecting a different starting point and using a sampling interval of 25, the sample may fail to include any of the fictitious employees (a situation which is potentially more serious for the auditor).

Cluster selection

As noted in Figure 11.1, cluster selection is a variation of systematic selection. This method of sample selection involves selecting clusters of items in the population (or groups of contiguous items or records) rather than individual items. For example, if a sample of 125 units is required, 25 clusters of five units may be selected. If the first unit in each cluster is selected using random number tables or a computer-generated random number, then the sample is regarded as a random sample.

This method of selection provides a straightforward and relatively quick means of selecting a sample. However, in some circumstances it may be less efficient than samples comprising individually selected items, as it may result in a larger sample size. For example, if a sample of sales invoices is to be checked for authorisation (for example, the credit manager's initials signalling authorisation), a sample of 125 units selected individually may provide good coverage of invoices issued during the accounting period. However, 25 clusters of five units may not give adequate coverage and the number of clusters may need to be increased. In other cases cluster selection may be particularly appropriate, for example, in testing for completeness of records. If the auditor wishes to check that all sales invoices, purchase orders, stocktaking sheets and similar documents are accounted for (that is, documents which are numbered sequentially), (s)he may check the number sequence of 125 documents in 25 clusters of five.

(iii)   Selection with probability proportional to size (PPS selection)
When PPS selection is used, each individual monetary unit (that is, each individual £1) in a population is regarded as a separate unit within the population and each has an equal chance of selection. This method may be explained by reference to the following simple example.

Figure 11.2:   PPS selection: population of debtors

Account	Recorded balance	Cumulative total (pounds units)	Location of sample units
	£	£	
1	276	276	✓
2	1,194	1,470	✓
3	683	2,153	✓
4	25	2,178	
5	1,221	3,399	✓
6	94	3,493	
7	76	3,569	
8	684	4,253	✓✓
9	135	4,388	
10	302	4,690	

Example: Assume that the debtors account balance in a client's balance sheet comprises 10 individual debtors' accounts and that the balances of these accounts at the balance sheet date are as set out in Figure 11.2. Also assume that a sample of six units is required for testing.

The accounts are recorded in the order in which they appear in the subsidiary ledger and the cumulative pounds (£s) in the accounts are calculated (see Figure 11.2, column 3). These cumulative pounds constitute the population of 4,690 individual pounds. Pounds 1 to 276 are contained in account 1, pounds 277 to 1,470 in account 2, and so on. Unrestricted random sampling or systematic sampling is used to select the required number of sample units; that is, individual identified pounds.

With reference to Figure 11.2, assume that unrestricted random sampling generated the following random numbers: 2997, 3595, 3762, 2003, 0023, 0444. These random numbers correspond to individual pounds in the cumulative total and result in accounts 5, 8, 8, 3, 1 and 2 being selected for examination. Account 8 is a 'double hit' but it is, of course, only examined once.

The advantage of PPS selection is that larger account balances have a greater chance of selection and it is these balances which, because of their size, are more likely to contain a misstatement which is material. However, the method also has the disadvantage that small balances have a low probability of being included in the sample, yet a small balance may be small because it is significantly understated; additionally, a series of errors in small balances may together constitute a material misstatement. These concerns may be overcome by stratifying the population and treating balances which are smaller than a specified limit as a separate population. A sample may then be selected from this (sub)population of small balances using, for example, unrestricted random sampling.

Another problem of PPS sampling is its inability to include negative balances, for example, debtors accounts with credit balances. A possible approach to this difficulty is to treat negative balances as if they were positive, and to include them in the cumulative total on that basis.

(b) *Non-random selection*

As shown in Figure 11.1, there are two main methods of non-random sample selection:

- haphazard selection;
- judgmental selection.

(i) *Haphazard selection*[7]

When using haphazard selection, the auditor attempts to replicate random sample selection but without using a random number table or computer-generated random numbers. The auditor selects items from the population haphazardly, without regard to the size, source, date or any other distinguishing feature of the items constituting the population.

This method of sample selection is simple and quick but has the disadvantage that unintended bias may be introduced into the sample. Certain items in the population tend to have a greater chance of being selected than others; for example, the auditor may have a propensity to select (or avoid) items at the top, bottom or middle of a page; known (or unknown) persons; names which attract attention for some reason, and so on.

(ii) *Judgmental sample selection*

When using judgmental selection, the auditor deliberately tries to select a sample which is representative of the population and/or includes those items which (s)he considers require close attention.

When attempting to select a representative sample, the auditor will be particularly concerned to include, for example:

- a selection of items representing transactions occurring in each month (or even in each week) of the accounting period, and for each employee who has been involved in handling the transactions during the period;

---

[7] It should be remembered that non-random selection is not appropriate when using statistical sampling methods.

- a selection of account balances or transactions which are representative of those in the population. Thus, the proportion of large and small account balances included in the sample will reflect the proportion of these balances in the population.

When the auditor wishes to select a sample that emphasises high-risk areas, care will be taken to include:

- a large proportion of large transactions or account balances, as an error in a large transaction or balance is more likely to be material;
- items representative of periods when internal control procedures may have been functioning less effectively than normal; for example, when the key control person (such as the credit manager, or supervisor responsible for reviewing bank reconciliations and journal entries) was on holiday or absent through illness.

The major advantage of judgmental sample selection is that it enables the auditor to tailor his sample to the unique circumstances of the client. However, it also has the significant disadvantage (which it shares with haphazard sampling) that, should the sample be challenged (for example, in a court of law), it may be more difficult to defend than random sample selection.

11.5.4 Documentation of sample selection

Before leaving the subject of sample selection, it should be noted that all aspects of selecting a sample should be clearly and fully documented in the audit working papers. The documentation should include details of the size of:

- the sample selected – and how this was determined,
- the method of sample selection.

When random sampling is used, the source of random numbers (for example, random number table or computer program) should be noted. When a population is stratified, the basis of, and rationale for, the stratification should be noted. Similarly, when judgmental sample selection is used, factors the auditor took into account when exercising his or her judgment should be recorded.

11.6 JUDGMENTAL SAMPLING AND AUDIT PROCEDURES

As noted in section 11.2, sampling is used to facilitate the performance of a compliance or a substantive audit procedure: instead of applying the audit procedure to all of the items constituting the population, the procedure is applied to a sample of the items. The results obtained by applying the procedure to the sample of items are then inferred into (or extrapolated to) the population as a whole.

When judgmental sampling is adopted, the sampling process rests on the exercise of the auditor's judgment. The steps in the process are as follows:

(i) the sample size is determined judgmentally.
(ii) the sample is selected using a random or a non-random sample selection method.
(iii) the sample is examined for the characteristic being tested; that is, compliance with a specific internal control procedure, or the validity, completeness and/or accuracy of the monetary amount of a class of transactions or account balance.
(iv) the sample results are extrapolated to the population and, based on these results, the population is accepted – or not accepted – as 'satisfactory'; that is, exercising judgment, the auditor concludes that the control being tested has (or has not) been adequately complied with, or the class of transactions or account balance is (or is not) free of material misstatement.

As will be seen in the next section, when statistical sampling techniques are used, steps (i) and (iv) above are determined by applying probability theory, and step (ii) must be performed using random selection methods.

11.7 INTRODUCTION TO STATISTICAL SAMPLING

11.7.1 Sampling plans

Statistical sampling is undertaken by means of sampling plans (or methods). The most common fall into two main categories, namely, attributes sampling plans and variables sampling plans. Banks (1979, p. 113) provides a clear explanation of the difference between the two. He says:

> From a practical audit point of view, generally the extrapolation of the sample results to arrive at a population conclusion is limited to the following two techniques:
> (a) sampling for Attributes (how many);
> (b) sampling for Variables (how much).
> In the case of attribute sampling the type of conclusion one would reach might read as follows:
>> 'I am 95% confident, based upon the results of the bias-free [i.e. random] sample selected, that the population error rate will not exceed five per cent in respect of those attributes being tested.'
> With the variable sampling techniques the type of conclusion one might reach would read as follows:
>> 'I am 95% confident, based upon the sample selected without bias, that the total monetary value of the entire population will be within the range of (say) $293,789 and $316,323.'

Figure 11.3: Relationship between sampling methods[8]

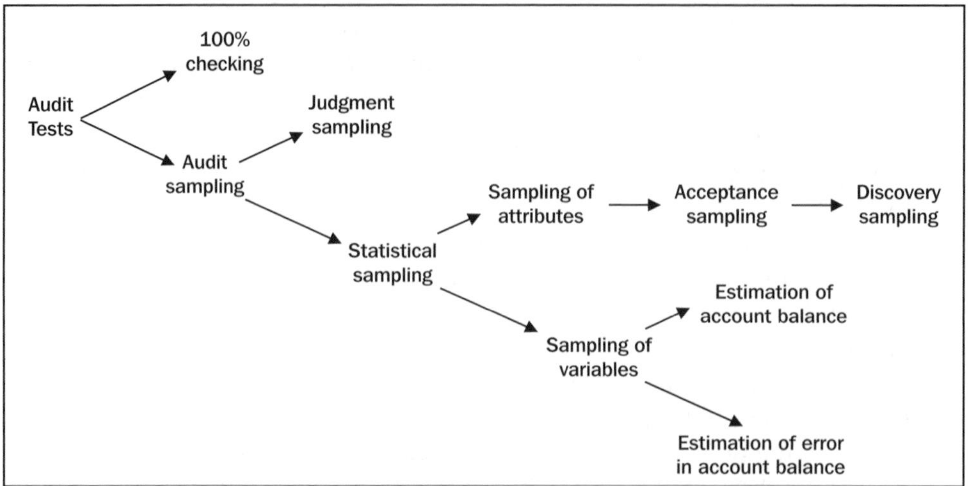

Note: PPS, or monetary unit, sampling is a hybrid of attributes and variables sampling. It is variables sampling in the sense that it measures monetary amounts, but attributes sampling techniques are employed to determine sample size and evaluate the sample results.

As may be seen from Figure 11.3, although the sampling plans used in auditing fall into two broad categories, different variations of attributes and variables sampling may be recognised.

11.7.2 Attributes sampling plans

As noted above, attributes sampling is concerned with ascertaining whether a characteristic of interest is present or absent. Because evidence of compliance with internal control procedures (such as the credit manager's initials on sales invoices signifying authorisation of credit sales) is generally either present or absent, attributes sampling has particular application in compliance testing.

Two variations of attributes sampling are often used in auditing, namely, acceptance sampling and discovery sampling. Each of these is discussed below.

- *Acceptance sampling*: as a prerequisite to using acceptance sampling, the auditor needs to specify:
  1. the tolerable error rate in the population (i.e. the rate of error in the population the auditor will accept while still concluding the control can be relied upon);
  2. the expected error rate in the population (i.e. the rate of error the auditor expects to exist in the population, given his or her assessment of inherent

[8] Adapted from McRae (1971, p. 376).

audit risk and preliminary evaluation of the client's internal control system); and

3. the desired level of confidence (i.e. the level of confidence the auditor wishes to have that the conclusion reached, based on the results of examining a sample of items, is valid. (Alternatively stated, the level of risk the auditor is prepared to accept that the conclusion reached based on the sample results is not valid.)

As shown in the detailed example of attributes sampling provided below, using this information, the auditor can use statistical sampling tables to determine the appropriate size of the sample of items to be tested.

The sample is then selected, using a random selection method, and examined for the characteristic being tested. Based on the presence (or more usually the absence) of the characteristic in the sample, statistical sampling tables are used to determine the maximum rate of error in the population. This sampling method gives rise to a statement such as: 'I am 95% confident that the rate of sales invoices not carrying the credit manager's initials does not exceed 2.0%.' (Alternatively stated, 'There is a 5% risk that the rate of sales invoices not carrying the credit manager's initials exceeds 2.0%.')

The estimated maximum population error rate is compared with the tolerable error and if the former does not exceed the latter, the auditor will probably accept the population as reliable (that is, the auditor will conclude that the internal control procedure can be relied upon).

- *Discovery sampling*: this is a subset of acceptance sampling where the expected error rate in the population is set at zero. This gives the smallest sample size possible under acceptance sampling but, if a single error is found in the sample, then the tolerable error rate will be exceeded and the population cannot be accepted (or the relevant internal control procedure cannot be relied upon) without further investigation.

As the discovery of a single error in a sample results in the population not being accepted by the auditor (at least, not without further investigation), discovery sampling reduces the number of populations which are accepted on the basis of the sample examined. However, discovery sampling is particularly useful to the auditor as it involves small samples, and errors which are discovered in the sample provide guidance as to the nature and cause of errors in the population. Discovery sampling is thus useful in directing the auditor's attention to areas that require more detailed investigation.

Detailed illustration of attributes sampling

In order to provide an overview of attributes sampling, the procedure for acceptance sampling is set out below. For purposes of illustration, it is assumed that the audit client has 20,000 sales invoices and that the auditor wishes to establish whether or not the internal control procedure for authorising credit sales is effective.

The steps involved in acceptance sampling are as follows:

Steps involved in acceptance sampling	Illustration
1. Define the objective of the audit procedure.	To ascertain whether credit sales are properly authorised.
2. Define the attribute of interest.	Initials of credit manager on sales invoices signalling approval of credit sales.
3. Define the population (or, more correctly the frame).	Sales invoices issued during the accounting period. These are numbered from 24,494 to 44,501.
4. Specify the tolerable error rate in the population.	4% tolerable error rate. The auditor will tolerate up to 4% of sales invoices not showing the credit manager's initials and still conclude the control can be relied upon.
5. Specify the desired level of confidence (or, alternatively, the desired level of sampling risk).	A 95% confidence level is required. The auditor wishes to be 95% confident that if, based on the results of the sample, (s)he concludes the error rate in the population does not exceed 4%, this conclusion is valid. [This is equivalent to the auditor accepting a 5% risk that the error rate in the population may, in fact, exceed 4% and thus, based on the sample, (s)he may incorrectly conclude that the control procedure can be relied upon.]
6. Estimate the population deviation rate. (This is an estimation of the error rate based on the auditor's preliminary evaluation of the client's compliance with internal control procedures.)	It is estimated that 1% of sales invoices in the population do not contain the credit manager's initials.
7. Use the relevant table to determine the required sample size.	See Figure 11.4 for the table entitled 'Sample size for attributes sampling'. [A different table exists for each desired level of confidence. The greater the desired level of confidence (or the lower the level of sampling risk), other things being held constant, the larger the sample size.]

Steps involved in acceptance sampling	Illustration
8. Using the table and the parameters established by judgment noted above, ascertain the sample size.	Tolerable error rate is 4% (see step 4 above). This identifies the relevant column in the table. The estimated population deviation rate is 1% (see step 6 above). This identifies the relevant row in the table. The required sample size is located at the intercept of the relevant column and row. It is seen to be 156.
9. Randomly select a sample of the required size.	Using computer-generated random numbers, identify and select a sample of 156 sales invoices.
10. Perform the relevant audit procedure and record deviations.	Vouch the 156 sales invoices and record all invoices which do not show the credit manager's initials. Assume one such invoice is found.
11. Generalise from the sample to the population using the relevant table for evaluating attributes sampling results.	See Figure 11.5. (A different table exists for each desired level of confidence/desired level of sampling risk.) The actual number of deviations found identifies the relevant column in the table. (In our example, one deviation is assumed: see step 10.) The sample size identifies the relevant row in the table. (In our example this is 150, being the closest to 156: see step 8.) From the table it is seen that (given our assumptions) the projected maximum error rate in the population (% of invoices without the sales manager's initials) is 3.1%. (This is not the most likely error rate but a 'worst case' possibility or upper limit of the error rate.)
12. Analyse detected deviations to ascertain whether they result from 'one-off' situations, or whether they are indicative of a more widespread problem; for example, the control procedure failing to function properly when the key control person is absent.	Investigate the cause of the deviation detected. Assume this is found to be an isolated incident of control failure. (For example, two sales invoices were presented to the credit manager at one time for approval. (S)he reviewed both, but only initialled one invoice.)

Steps involved in acceptance sampling	Illustration
13. Apply the decision rule for acceptance sampling. If the projected maximum population error rate shown in the sample results evaluation table exceeds the tolerable error rate, conclude that the control procedure may not be reliable. If the projected maximum population error rate is less than the tolerable error rate, subject to the analysis of detected deviations (see step 12), conclude the control procedure can be relied upon.	The projected maximum error rate in the population is 3.1%. This is less than the 4% tolerable error rate specified as acceptable by the auditor (see step 4). Additionally, the deviation detected has been found to be an isolated incident of control failure (see step 12). As a consequence of these findings, the auditor concludes that the control procedure may be relied upon.

Figure 11.4:   Sample size for attributes sampling

95% confidence level (5% sampling risk)											
Expected population deviation rate (in percentage)	Tolerable deviation rate (in percentage)										
	2	3	4	5	6	7	8	9	10	11	12
0.00	149	99	74	59	49	42	36	32	29	19	14
0.25	236	157	117	93	78	66	58	51	46	30	22
0.50	*	157	117	93	78	66	58	51	46	30	22
0.75	*	208	117	93	78	66	58	51	46	30	22
1.00	*	*	156	93	78	66	58	51	46	30	22
1.25	*	*	156	124	78	66	58	51	46	30	22
1.50	*	*	192	124	103	66	58	51	46	30	22
1.75	*	*	227	153	103	88	77	51	46	30	22
2.00	*	*	*	181	127	88	77	68	46	30	22
2.25	*	*	*	208	127	88	77	68	61	30	22
2.50	*	*	*	*	150	109	77	68	61	30	22
2.75	*	*	*	*	173	109	95	68	61	30	22
3.00	*	*	*	*	195	129	95	84	61	30	22
3.25	*	*	*	*	*	148	112	84	61	30	22
3.50	*	*	*	*	*	167	112	84	76	40	22
3.75	*	*	*	*	*	185	129	100	76	40	22
4.00	*	*	*	*	*	*	146	100	89	40	22
5.00	*	*	*	*	*	*	*	158	116	40	30
6.00	*	*	*	*	*	*	*	*	179	50	30
7.00	*	*	*	*	*	*	*	*	*	68	37

Figure 11.5: Evaluating attributes sampling results

	95% confidence level (5% sampling risk)										
	Actual number of deviations found										
Sample size	**0**	**1**	**2**	**3**	**4**	**5**	**6**	**7**	**8**	**9**	**10**
25	11.3	17.6	*	*	*	*	*	*	*	*	*
30	9.5	14.9	19.5	*	*	*	*	*	*	*	*
35	8.2	12.9	16.9	*	*	*	*	*	*	*	*
40	7.2	11.3	14.9	18.3	*	*	*	*	*	*	*
45	6.4	10.1	13.3	16.3	19.2	*	*	*	*	*	*
50	5.8	9.1	12.1	14.8	17.4	19.9	*	*	*	*	*
55	5.3	8.3	11.0	13.5	15.9	18.1	*	*	*	*	*
60	4.9	7.7	10.1	12.4	14.6	16.7	18.8	*	*	*	*
65	4.5	7.1	9.4	11.5	13.5	15.5	17.4	19.3	*	*	*
70	4.2	6.6	8.7	10.7	12.6	14.4	16.2	18.0	19.7	*	*
75	3.9	6.2	8.2	10.0	11.8	13.5	15.2	16.9	18.4	20.0	*
80	3.7	5.8	7.7	9.4	11.1	12.7	14.3	15.8	17.3	18.8	*
90	3.3	5.2	6.8	8.4	9.9	11.3	12.7	14.1	15.5	16.8	18.1
100	3.0	4.6	6.2	7.6	8.9	10.2	11.5	12.7	14.0	15.2	16.4
125	2.4	3.7	4.9	6.1	7.2	8.2	9.3	10.3	11.3	12.2	13.2
150	2.0	3.1	4.1	5.1	6.0	6.9	7.7	8.6	9.4	10.2	11.0
200	1.5	2.3	3.1	3.8	4.5	5.2	5.8	6.5	7.1	7.7	8.3

11.7.3 Variables sampling plans

As noted earlier, variables sampling is concerned with estimating the monetary value of a financial statement balance, or estimating the amount by which it might be in error. Because it focuses on monetary amounts, variables sampling has particular application for substantive testing.

As may be seen from Figure 11.3, variables sampling includes estimation sampling which may take the form of estimating an account balance or estimating the maximum amount of error in an account balance.

- *Estimating an account balance.* In this form of variables sampling, the auditor selects a sample of items (that is, a sample of transactions or components of an account balance, such as items of stock) and, based on this sample, estimates the range of values (between upper and lower limits) within which the financial statement account balance should fall. This form of estimation sampling might give rise to a statement such as: 'From the items of stock examined, I am 95% confident that the value of the stock account balance lies between an upper limit of £765,000 and a lower limit of £683,000.' (Alternatively stated: 'There is a 5% risk that the value of the stock account balance exceeds £765,000 or is less than £683,000.')

- *Estimating the maximum error in an account balance:* In this case, rather than estimating the value of an account balance, the auditor estimates the maximum amount of error which may exist in the balance. It might give rise to a statement such as: 'From the items of stock examined, I am 95% confident that the amount of error in the stock account balance does not exceed £50,000.' (Alternatively stated: 'There is a 5% risk that the amount of error in the stock account balance is greater than £50,000.')

Although variables sampling is a useful auditing technique, for many populations application of variables sampling procedures results in a sample size which is impractically large. As a result, PPS (or monetary unit) sampling is often preferred to variables sampling.

11.7.4 Probability proportional to size (PPS, or monetary unit) sampling

As noted in Figure 11.3, PPS (or monetary unit) sampling is a hybrid of attributes and variables sampling. It is a technique based on monetary values in a population, and therefore possesses elements of variables sampling; however, attributes sampling techniques are employed in determining the sample size and evaluating the sample results.

In order to provide an overview of monetary unit sampling, the procedure followed is set out below. For purposes of illustration, it is assumed that the client's pre-audited balance sheet shows total debtors at an amount of £3,198,426. The auditor wishes to confirm that this balance is not materially misstated.

The steps involved in PPS (monetary unit) sampling are as follows:

Steps involved in PPS sampling	Illustration
1. Define the objective of the audit procedure.	To reach a conclusion as to whether the debtors balance of £3,198,426 is materially misstated
2. Define the population (or, more correctly the frame).	3,198,426 individual £1 monetary units. (Each pound in the population is treated as equivalent to a physical unit in attributes sampling.)
3. Specify the tolerable error rate in the population.	Assume a tolerable error rate of 4%, i.e. an upper and lower materiality limit of £128,000 (4% of £3,198,426).

Steps involved in PPS sampling	Illustration
4. Specify the desired level of confidence (or alternatively, the desired level of sampling risk).	Assume a confidence level of 95% is required (or a sampling risk of 5%).
5. Estimate the expected error rate in the population. This is an estimate of the error rate in pounds (based on prior audit work). It is equivalent to the expected population deviation rate in attributes sampling.	Assume the expected error rate in the population is 1%; i.e. the auditor expects the population to contain a misstatement of £32,000 (1% of £3,198,426) above or below the stated balance £3,198,426.
6. Use the relevant table to determine the required sample size.	See Figure 11.4 for the table entitled 'Sample size for attributes sampling'.
7. Using the table and the parameters established by judgment noted above, ascertain the sample size.	Tolerable error rate is 4% (see step 3 above). This identifies the relevant column in the table. The estimated population deviation rate is 1% (see step 5 above). This identifies the relevant row in the table. The required sample size is located at the intercept of the relevant column and row. It is seen to be 156.
8. Randomly select a sample of the required size.	Using PPS selection, select a sample of 156 pounds and identify the individual debtors' account balances in which they are contained (see section 11.5.3).
9. Perform the relevant audit procedure and record errors (deviations.)	Confirm the debtors' balances containing the 156 sample pounds using confirmation techniques or alternative procedures in the normal way. Assume that one debtors' account balance recorded as £20,000 should be £10,000 and that no other errors are found.
10. Generalise from the sample to the population using the relevant table for evaluating attributes sampling results.	See Figure 11.5, entitled 'Evaluating attributes sampling results'. The actual number of errors (deviations) found identifies the relevant column in the table. (In our example, one deviation is assumed. Although the debtors' total balance of £20,000 is checked, only one of these 20,000 pounds was included in the sample. It is this one pound which is in error) (see step 9).

Steps involved in PPS sampling	Illustration
10. *Continued*	The sample size identifies the relevant row in the table. (In our example 150, being the closest to 156: see step 7.) From the table it is seen that (given our assumptions) the projected maximum error rate in the population (% of pounds misstated) is 3.1%.
11. Analyse detected errors to ascertain whether they result from 'one-off' situations, or whether they are indicative of a more widespread problem; for example, a control failing to function properly when the key control person is absent.	Investigate the cause of the error detected. Assume this is found to be an isolated incident of control failure. (For example, two sales invoices of £10,000 were paid but only one was recorded as paid in the debtors' ledger.)
12. Apply the decision rule for acceptance sampling. If the projected maximum population error rate shown in the sample results evaluation table exceeds the tolerable error rate, conclude that the account may be misstated. If the projected maximum population error rate is less than the tolerable error rate, subject to the analysis of the detected errors (see step 11), conclude the account is not materially misstated.	The projected maximum error rate in the population of 3.1% is less than the 4% tolerable error rate specified as acceptable by the auditor (see step 3). Additionally, the error detected has been found to be an isolated incident of control failure (see step 11). As a consequence of these findings, the auditor concludes that the debtors' balance of £3,198,426 is not materially misstated

Two points should be made in respect of this illustration. These are as follows:

1. It was noted in section 11.5.3 that PPS selection gives small balances a low probability of being included in the sample. It might be necessary, therefore, to supplement the sample of 156 account balances with a selection of small account balances to investigate the possibility of small balances being significantly understated.
2. The error found in the illustration was a debtors' balance recorded as £20,000 instead of £10,000. This was treated as one deviation, being one debtor's pound included in the sample which was in error (step 10). Thus, to ascertain

the projected maximum population error rate, the relevant column in Figure 11.5 is that for error (deviation) actually found. In reality the debtors' balance is not completely in error but 50% in error, since the £20,000 recorded should not be zero but £10,000. This is known as a 'partial' error. For such a 50% error (or 0.5 error) it is possible to 'interpolate' between the columns in Figure 11.5 for 0 errors and for 1 error, giving a maximum projected error rate in the population of 2.55% [that is, halfway between the projected error rate for 0 errors (2.0%) and for 1 error (3.1%)]. Such a refinement in respect of partial errors can reduce the projected maximum population error rate (from 3.1% to 2.55% in our example). This can affect the auditor's conclusion with respect to the acceptability of the population.

11.8 FOLLOWING UP SAMPLE RESULTS

Irrespective of whether judgmental or statistical sampling techniques are used, the auditor need not slavishly follow the sampling method's accept/not accept rule. For example, if the projected maximum population deviation rate in acceptance sampling is less than the specified tolerable deviation rate, this does not mean the auditor will automatically accept the internal control procedure as functioning effectively throughout the reporting period. Similarly, if the estimated value of an account balance falls within the auditor's specified tolerable error range, this does not automatically result in the conclusion that it is fairly stated. Instead, the auditor remains alert to the possibility that the control procedure under investigation may not have functioned effectively throughout the reporting period, or the account balance being examined may be materially misstated. Thus, for example, as noted in sections 11.7.2 and 11.7.3 above, *all* deviations detected during the examination of sample units in acceptance and monetary unit sampling are analysed to ascertain their cause, irrespective of whether the auditor's tolerable error rate is, or is not, exceeded.

However, assuming that nothing has come to the auditor's attention to cause him or her to conclude otherwise, if a sample produces results which accord with the sampling method's 'accept' rule, the auditor will generally conclude that the internal control procedure on which (s)he plans to rely to prevent material errors from occurring in the financial statements is functioning effectively, or that the account balance examined is not materially misstated. Nevertheless, the auditor remains aware of his or her exposure to sampling risk and continues to watch for evidence which suggests that his or her conclusion about the internal control procedure or account balance may be invalid.

Where a sample's results indicate that an internal control procedure cannot be relied upon, or an account balance may be materially misstated, this finding must be followed up by alternative auditing techniques. In the case of an internal control procedure which is found not to be operating effectively, other control procedures might be found and tested to see if reliance can be placed on them to detect or prevent the relevant (potential) error, or substantive tests may be extended. If the sample indicates that an account balance might be materially misstated, alternative techniques must be employed to ascertain whether this is, or is not, the case.

11.9 COMPUTER ASSISTED AUDIT TECHNIQUES

11.9.1 Meaning and types of computer assisted audit techniques (CAATs)

Like audit sampling, CAATs are audit techniques that apply to both compliance and substantive procedures. In brief, they are audit procedures which use computer facilities to investigate the reliability (or otherwise) of the client's accounting system and the information it generates. The two most well known CAATs are:

(i)   test data (or test decks or test packs); and
(ii) audit software.

(i)   Test data

The test data technique is primarily designed to test the effectiveness of internal control procedures which are incorporated in the client's computer programs. Thus, it is essentially a compliance procedure.

The technique involves entering data (such as a sample of transactions) into, and having the data processed by, the client's (computerised) accounting system, and comparing the output with predetermined results. The data may be used to test the effectiveness of control procedures, such as online passwords which are designed to restrict access to specified data and programs to authorised personnel. Alternatively, the data may comprise a set of transactions representing all types of transactions normally processed by the client's programs, and incorporating a variety of errors. These transactions (and errors) are designed to ascertain whether programmed control procedures are operating effectively; for example, whether exception reports are generated in appropriate cases, and whether transaction dates and amounts lying outside specified parameters are rejected.

Use of the test data technique is generally straightforward and does not require the auditor to possess a sophisticated knowledge of computer processes. Further, the tests are usually fairly quick to perform and generally cause little or no disruption to the client's normal processing schedules. However, a major disadvantage of the technique is that the test data are usually processed separately from the client's normal processing runs. Although the auditor can establish whether the control procedures are, or are not, operating effectively at the time the audit procedure is performed, (s)he does not know whether the procedures operate effectively at other times.

In order to overcome this disadvantage, the test data technique can be extended to an 'integrated test facility' (ITF). This involves establishing a 'dummy' department, employee or other unit appropriate for audit testing. Transactions affecting the dummy unit are interspersed among, and processed with, the client's ordinary transactions. The resultant output, relating to the dummy unit, is compared with predetermined results.

When the ITF technique is used, the auditor must be alert to the danger of contaminating the client's files and care must be taken to reverse out all of the audit test transactions.

(ii) Audit software

In contrast to the test data technique, which requires the auditor to input test data to be processed by the client's computer programs, the audit software technique involves the auditor using audit software to process the client's accounting data. Audit software is of three main types. These are as follows:

(a) *Utility programs and existing programs used by the entity:* In this case, general (non-audit specific) application programs, or enquiry facilities available within a software package, are used to perform common data-processing functions such as sorting, retrieving and printing of computer files. These programs may assist the auditor perform a variety of audit procedures but they are not specifically designed for audit purposes and, in general, their audit application is limited. They are used principally to extend or to speed up procedures which would otherwise be performed manually (for example, accessing and printing all or part of the debtors' account balances or items comprising the stock account balance).

(b) *General audit software:* This software consists of generally available computer packages which have been specially designed to perform a variety of functions for audit purposes. These include reading computer files, selecting and retrieving desired information and/or samples, performing various calculations, making comparisons and printing required reports.

(c) *Specialised audit software:* This software comprises specially developed programs which are designed to perform audit tests in specific circumstances – usually those pertaining to a particular entity. These programs may be prepared by the auditor (or auditor's firm), the entity's computer (IT) personnel, or by an outside programmer engaged by the auditor.

Although the development of specialised audit software may be appropriate for certain clients (for example, clients in specialised industries such as banking or mining), and may be a desired ideal in other cases, developing such software is extremely expensive and is often beyond the expertise of the auditor. Nevertheless, whenever specialised audit software is to be developed for use in certain audits, it is essential that the auditor is actively involved in designing and testing the programs. This is necessary to ensure that the auditor fully understands the operation (and limitations) of the software and also to ensure that it meets the requirements of the audit.

During recent years, the availability of general audit software has increased significantly and these packages are now used extensively to assist auditors perform a wide range of audit procedures. They are used, for example, for performing analytical procedures, for selecting and testing a sample of transactions or account balances, and for performing statistical sampling techniques such as monetary unit sampling.

Audit software is invaluable in most audits today as computers are used to process accounting data in virtually all audit clients. However, its use may be resisted by an entity's management or IT personnel because running additional programs for audit purposes may interrupt and cause delays to the entity's normal processing. Be that as it may, where an entity's accounting system involves extensive use of computer processing (as is normally the case), manual audit procedures may be rendered inappropriate, and application of audit software may be the only means by which a satisfactory audit can be conducted. In such circumstances, if the client's management restricts the use of audit software, this could amount to a limitation on the scope of the audit and give rise to a qualified audit report.[9]

11.9.2 Use and control of CAATs

CAATs may be used to assist the auditor with a variety of audit procedures. They may, for example, assist the auditor perform:
- compliance tests of general (computer environment) controls – for example, to analyse processing or access logs, or to review the effectiveness of library (or other storage facility) access procedures;
- compliance tests of application controls – for example, using test data to test the effectiveness of programmed controls such as the rejection of data outside specified parameters;
- analytical procedures – for example, using audit software to calculate specified financial statement ratios and to identify unusual fluctuations or items;

---

[9] Limitation on the scope of an audit, and its impact on the audit report, is discussed in Chapter 13.

- detailed tests of transactions and balances – for example, using audit software to test all (or a sample) of transactions in a computer file, or to perform statistical sampling routines to estimate account balances or the maximum error in account balances or classes of transactions.

CAATs are generally user-friendly so auditors do not require specialised computer knowledge in order to apply them. Although this is clearly an advantage to many auditors, it also carries the danger that auditors may be lulled into a false sense of security. This danger is particularly high when auditors require the co-operation of client computer (IT) personnel (who have an extensive and detailed knowledge of the client's system) in order to use CAATs, or where they use the client's own enquiry facilities. Such an enquiry facility could, for example, be programmed by client staff not to reveal certain records when accessed by means of the auditor's password.

Before using test data or audit software, the auditor must ensure that (s)he understands the process by which the computer performs the relevant audit procedures and the limitations of, or pitfalls related to, the process. If the auditor has limited computer knowledge, (s)he should obtain assistance from, or have ready access to, assistants within the audit firm who have computer expertise, or suitable experts from outside the firm. The auditor should guard against the temptation to rely upon the client's IT personnel for explanations in circumstances which render it inappropriate to do so. As for all audit procedures, the auditor must ensure that the performance of CAATs remains under his or her control and that client personnel are not able to improperly influence the results obtained therefrom.

When planning an audit in which CAATs are to be used, the auditor must be cognisant of the fact that certain computer files, such as transaction files, may be retained by the client for only a short period of time. In such cases, the auditor may need to make special arrangements for certain data to be retained, or to alter the timing of audit work, in order to facilitate the testing of data while it is still available.

An interesting sideline to the advent of CAATs is that they are once again making possible, for some audit tests, an examination of *all* accounting data, instead of just samples thereof.[10] This, as in the nineteenth and early twentieth centuries when detailed checking of all transactions was the norm, may increase the likelihood of detecting certain types of corporate fraud (although not

---

[10] This can happen whenever the audit procedure does not require reference to evidence held outside the computer system. For example, a CAAT can check calculations on the value of all stock items, but it cannot check on the condition or ownership of the stock.

necessarily computer fraud). Further, this is occurring at a time when the courts, politicians, the public, and a significant number of individual auditors are pressing the profession to assume greater responsibility for detecting fraud. However, it is also happening at a time when the increasing sophistication of computer networks is opening up new possibilities for computer fraud. This seems likely to present new challenges – and difficulties – for auditors.

It is suggested that it is likely that the development of CAATs and the increasing sophistication of IT systems, combined with the demand for auditors to accept greater responsibility to detect corporate fraud, will add impetus to the move towards re-establishing fraud detection as an important audit objective.[11] It was noted in Chapter 2 that history shows that changes in the audit environment, changes in audit techniques and changes in audit objectives go hand in hand. It appears that this is being demonstrated at the present time in relation to corporate fraud.

11.10 SUMMARY

This chapter has provided an introduction to audit sampling and computer-assisted auditing techniques – two somewhat specialised techniques that traverse both compliance and substantive procedures. The first part of the chapter focused on audit sampling. We explained the meaning and importance of sampling and the meaning of terms associated with this technique. We also considered the distinction between judgmental and statistical sampling, and the advantages and disadvantages of each. Additionally, we identified factors affecting the size of audit samples and described some of the commonly used methods of selecting samples (randomly and non-randomly). Further, we provided an overview of the application of attributes sampling to compliance testing and of PPS (monetary unit) sampling to substantive testing, and discussed the auditor's follow-up to sample results.

In the second part of the chapter we turned our attention to CAATs. We briefly explored the meaning and use of CAATs and saw that these techniques are of two main types – test data and audit software. We also noted that CAATs are equally applicable in compliance testing and substantive testing, and mentioned some of the ways in which CAATs can assist auditors. In the concluding section of the chapter, we discussed the importance of auditors understanding fully the application of CAATs and the dangers of relying on clients' IT personnel for assistance.

---

[11] This phenomenon is discussed in Chapter 5.

SELF-REVIEW QUESTIONS

11.1 Explain briefly what is meant by 'audit sampling'.

11.2 In relation to audit sampling, explain briefly what is meant by:
(i) precision limits;
(ii) confidence levels (and sampling risk);
(iii) tolerable error;
(iv) stratification.

11.3 Distinguish between judgmental sampling and statistical sampling, and list two advantages and two disadvantages of each approach.

11.4 State the characteristic feature of random sample selection and list three methods (or variations) of random sample selection.

11.5 Distinguish between:
(i) haphazard sample selection; and
(ii) judgmental sample selection.

11.6 Explain briefly the essential difference between attributes sampling and variables sampling.

11.7 (i) Define a sampling plan;
(ii) Explain briefly the key features of three sampling plans.

11.8 Explain briefly why PPS (monetary unit) sampling can be referred to as a hybrid of attributes and variables sampling.

11.9 With reference to CAATs, explain briefly:
(i) the test data technique;
(ii) three types of audit software.

11.10 List five ways in which CAATs may assist the auditor during an audit.

REFERENCES

Banks, A. (1979) Current status of statistical sampling. *Accountants' Journal* **58**(3), 113.
McRae, T.W. (1971) Applying statistical sampling in auditing: Some practical problems. *The Accountant's Magazine* **LXXV**(781), 369–377.

ADDITIONAL READING

Anderson, J.C. & Kraushaar, J.M. (1993) Auditing measurement error and statistical sampling: The dependently occurring case. *Journal of Accounting, Auditing & Finance* **8**(1), 53–75.
Cosserat, G. (1983) Judgmental sampling rules OK! *Accountancy* **94**(1076), 91–92.
Fischer, M.J. (1996) 'Real-izing' the benefits of new technologies as a source of audit evidence: an interpretive field study. *Accounting, Organisations and Society* **21**(2/3), 219–242.

Grant Thornton. (1990) *Audit Manual.* Chapter 18, Statistical Sampling. London: Longman.

Kashelmeier, S.J. & Messier, Jr, W.F. (1990) An investigation of the influence of a nonstatistical decision aid on auditor sample size decisions. *The Accounting Review* **65**(1), 209–226.

Nelson, M.K. (1995) Strategies of auditors: evaluation of sample results. *Auditing: A Journal of Practice & Theory* **14**(1), 34–49.

Ponemon, L.A. & Wendell, J.P. (1995) Judgement versus random sampling in auditing: An Experimental Investigation. *Auditing: A Journal of Practice & Theory* **14**(2), 17–34.

Prawitt, D.F. (1995) Staffing assignments for judgement-orientated audit tasks: The effect of structured audit technology and environment. *The Accounting Review* **70**(3), 443–465.

Robertson, J.C. & Rouse, R. (1994) Substantive audit sampling – The challenge of achieving efficiency along with effectiveness. *Accounting Horizons* **18**(1), 35–44.

Vagge, R. (1980) Towards understanding statistical sampling. *CPA Journal* **50**(5), 13–19.

Vasarhelyi, M.A. & Halper, F.B. (1991) The continuous audit of online systems. *Auditing: A Journal of Practice & Theory* **10**(1), 110–125.

Woolf, E. (1983) Audit sampling – without tears (or tables). *Accountancy* **94**(1076), 84–87.

Wurst, J., Neter, J. & Godfrey, J. (1991) Effectiveness of rectification in audit sampling. *Accounting Review* **66**(2), 333–346.

12 Completion and Review

LEARNING OBJECTIVES

After studying the material in this chapter you should be able to:
- explain the position and importance of completion and review procedures within the audit process;
- discuss the importance of, and procedures used for, the review for contingent liabilities and commitments;
- discuss the importance of, and procedures used for, the review for subsequent events;
- distinguish between subsequent events which necessitate adjustments to the financial statements and those which require only note disclosure;
- discuss the action auditors should take in relation to events which come to light after the audit report has been signed;
- explain the importance of re-assessing, during the completion stage of the audit, the validity of basing the financial statements on the going concern assumption;
- explain the nature and importance of management representation letters;
- discuss the nature and importance of the final review of audit working papers;
- explain the significance of dating the audit report.

The following publications and fundamental principle of external auditing are particularly relevant to this chapter:

Publications:
- Statement of Auditing Standards (SAS) 130: *The going concern basis in financial statements* (APB, 1994)
- Statement of Auditing Standards (SAS) 150: *Subsequent events* (APB, 1995)
- Statement of Auditing Standards (SAS) 160: *Other information in documents containing audited financial statements* (APB, 1999)
- Statement of Auditing Standards (SAS) 440: *Management representations* (APB, 1995)
- Statement of Auditing Standards (SAS) 470: *Overall review of financial statements* (APB, 1995)
- International Standards on Auditing (ISA) 501: *Audit evidence – additional considerations for specific items* (IFAC, 1994)
- International Standards on Auditing (ISA) 560: *Subsequent events* (IFAC, 1994)
- International Standards on Auditing (ISA) 570: *Going concern* (IFAC, 1994)
- International Standards on Auditing (ISA) 580: *Management representations* (IFAC, 1994)
- International Standards on Auditing (ISA) 720: *Other information in documents containing audited financial statements* (IFAC, 1994)

Fundamental Principle of External Auditing included in *The Auditor's Code* (APB, 1996): Association.

12.1   INTRODUCTION

As explained in Chapter 9, in order to conduct the detailed work of evaluating and testing the effectiveness of the client's internal control system and verifying the validity, completeness and accuracy of transactions and account balances, the auditor divides (conceptually) the client's accounting system into sub-systems, or audit segments. Once the detailed audit work is complete, the auditor approaches the audit holistically (as is the case for the early part of the audit), and the completion and review stage is conducted on an entity-wide basis.

As shown in Figure 12.1, the completion and review phase of an audit comprises four main steps, namely:
(i)   the review for contingent liabilities and commitments;
(ii)   the review for subsequent events and reassessment of the validity of basing the financial statements on the going concern assumption;
(iii)   the review of the financial statements and audit working papers;
(iv)   evaluation of the audit evidence and formation of the audit opinion.

In this chapter we discuss each of these important audit steps.

Figure 12.1:   Place of completion and review in the audit process

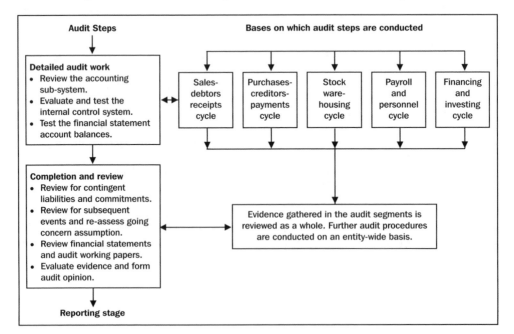

12.2   REVIEW FOR CONTINGENT LIABILITIES AND COMMITMENTS

Before considering the importance of the auditor's review for contingent liabilities and commitments, we need to clarify the meaning of these terms.

- *Contingent liabilities* are possible obligations that arise from past events but which, at the balance sheet date, are uncertain as to existence and/or amount. Their existence and/or amount are contingent upon the occurrence or non-occurrence of some uncertain future event not wholly within the entity's control. Examples include taxation in dispute, and pending litigation for infringement of, for example, environmental, product safety, or product description regulations.[1]
- *Commitments* are contractual undertakings. Examples include bonus and profit sharing schemes, and agreements to purchase raw materials or other stock at a fixed price at a particular date in the future, or to lease or buy fixed assets or to sell a certain quantity of goods, at an agreed price on a specified future date.

The auditor faces two major problems in relation to the review for contingent liabilities and commitments, namely:

(i)   management may not feel disposed to disclose them in the financial statements;

(ii) they do not involve transactions which are recorded in the accounting system. It is generally more difficult for the auditor to discover events and agreements which lie outside the accounting records.

Nevertheless, the existence of contingent liabilities and commitments may have a significant impact on the assessment of a reporting entity's financial position and performance by a user of its financial statements. Therefore, in order to provide a true and fair view of the entity's financial affairs, its financial statements must disclose any material contingent liabilities and commitments. As a consequence, when forming an opinion on the financial statements, the auditor has an obligation to determine the client's position with respect to these items.

The procedures most commonly adopted by auditors to ascertain the existence (or otherwise) of contingent liabilities and commitments include the following:

- enquiries of management;
- reviewing the minutes of directors' meetings;

---

[1]   A full definition of contingent liabilities may be found in FRS 12, para 2.

- reviewing correspondence files [and, in particular, correspondence between the client and its solicitor(s)];
- reviewing the current and previous years' tax returns;
- reviewing the current year's audit working papers for any information that may indicate a potential contingent liability;
- obtaining confirmation from the client's solicitor(s) regarding any known existing, pending or expected contingent liabilities (especially arising from litigation) and commitments.

With respect to the last procedure noted above, International Standards on Auditing (ISA) 501: *Audit evidence – additional considerations for specific items* states:

> When litigation or claims have been identified or when the auditor believes they may exist, the auditor should seek direct communication with the entity's lawyers. (para 33)

> The letter, which should be prepared by management and sent by the auditor, should request the lawyer to communicate directly with the auditor. When it is considered unlikely that the lawyer will respond to a general inquiry, the letter would ordinarily specify:

> - A list of litigation and claims.
> - Management's assessment of the outcome of the litigation or claim and its estimate of the financial implications, including costs involved.
> - A request that the lawyer confirm the reasonableness of management's assessments and provide the auditor with further information if the list is considered by the lawyer to be incomplete or incorrect. (para 34)

12.3   REVIEW FOR SUBSEQUENT EVENTS

12.3.1   Events between the balance sheet date and audit report date

The auditor has a responsibility to form and express an opinion as to whether or not the auditee's financial statements give a true and fair view of its financial position and performance as at the balance sheet date. As a result, the auditor has an obligation to consider events which take place between the balance sheet date and the date on which the audit report is signed, which might affect a financial statement user's assessment of the entity's financial position and/or performance as at the balance sheet date.

The auditor's responsibility to review events which occur subsequent to the balance sheet date is normally limited to the period between that date and the date of the audit report. The review normally takes place during the final two to three weeks before the audit report is signed. The timing of the subsequent events review is depicted in Figure 12.2.

Figure 12.2: Timing of the subsequent events review

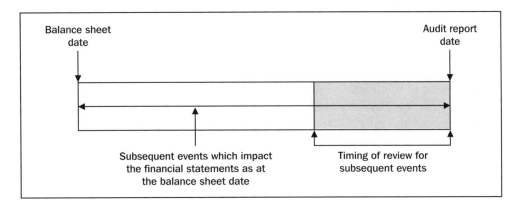

Subsequent events may be of two types, namely:
(i)   adjusting events
(ii) non-adjusting events.

(i)   Adjusting events

Adjusting events are events that clarify conditions which existed at the balance sheet date and/or which permit more accurate valuation of accounts in the financial statements at the balance sheet date. These events require the financial statements to be adjusted so that they reflect as accurately as possible the entity's financial position and performance as they existed at the end of the reporting period.

Examples of adjusting events include the resolution of tax disputes and litigation which existed at the balance sheet date but the amount of which was then uncertain, and the unexpected collapse of a material debtor which was regarded as 'good' at the balance sheet date. This latter event is classified as an adjusting event if the conditions which caused the customer's collapse existed at the balance sheet date.[2] If the conditions arose subsequent to the balance sheet date, the event is classified as a non-adjusting event.

(ii) Non-adjusting events

Non-adjusting events are events that relate to conditions which arose subsequent to the balance sheet date. These events represent changes in the situation as it existed at the end of the reporting period and, as a result, they

---

[2] It should be noted that, as the customer's collapse arose subsequent to the balance sheet date, the debt was not 'bad', and therefore the account should not be written off at year end. However, if the relevant conditions causing the collapse existed at the balance sheet date, the debt was under threat at that time and an adjustment should be made to the allowance for bad debts.

should not be incorporated in the financial statements as adjustments to account balances. However, if these events are considered to be material to financial statement users, in that they may affect users' evaluation of the financial position and/or future prospects of the entity, the events should be disclosed by way of a note to the financial statements.

Examples of non-adjusting events include a major fire or flood in the auditee subsequent to the balance sheet date where the resultant loss is not covered by insurance, and the entry of the entity into a significant transaction subsequent to the balance sheet date (such as the purchase or divestment of a subsidiary) which has a material impact on the entity's resources.

Statement of Auditing Standards (SAS) 150: *Subsequent events* outlines procedures auditors should perform in order to identify subsequent events. These include:

- enquiring into, and considering the effectiveness of, the procedures management has established to ensure that subsequent events are identified;
- reading minutes of the meetings of members, the board of directors and audit and executive committees held after period end and enquiring about matters discussed at meetings for which minutes are not yet available;
- reviewing relevant accounting records and reading the entity's latest available financial information, such as interim financial statements, budgets, cash flow forecasts and other related management reports; and
- making enquiries of management as to whether any subsequent events have occurred which might affect the financial statements. (para 7)

Examples of specific enquiries which may be made of management are:

- the current status of items involving subjective judgment or which were accounted for on the basis of preliminary data, for example litigation in progress;
- whether new commitments, borrowings or guarantees have been entered into;
- whether sales of assets have occurred or are planned;
- whether the issue of new shares or debentures, or an agreement to merge or to liquidate, has been made or is planned;
- whether any assets have been destroyed, for example by fire or flood;
- whether there have been any developments regarding risk areas and contingencies;
- whether any unusual accounting adjustments have been made or are contemplated; and
- whether any events have occurred or are likely to occur which might bring into question the appropriateness of accounting policies used in the financial statements as would be the case, for example, if such events might call into question the validity of the going concern basis. (para 8)[3]

---

[3] ISA 560: *Subsequent events*, para 5, contains similar wording to SAS 150, paras 7 and 8. However, unlike SAS 150, it also includes among the procedures auditors should perform in order to identify subsequent events: 'Inquiring, or extending previous oral or written enquiries, of the entity's lawyers concerning litigation and claims'.

As explained in section 12.5 below, when auditors need to rely on management's responses to enquiries (because alternative audit evidence is not available), they seek to have any significant responses (or representations) confirmed in writing in a management representation letter. However, whenever possible, they endeavour to substantiate significant responses by management by seeking information from alternative sources.

12.3.2   Events subsequent to the date of the audit report

(i) Prior to the issue of the financial statements to the entity's shareholders

The auditor has an obligation to seek out events which occur between the balance sheet date and the date of the audit report which might necessitate adjustment to, or disclosure in, the financial statements. However, (s)he does not have a responsibility to perform procedures to identify events after the audit report has been signed. Nevertheless, events may come to the auditor's attention after signing the audit report, but before the financial statements are issued to the shareholders, which (s)he considers should be reflected in the financial statements. In this circumstance, the auditor is required to discuss with the auditee's directors the possibility of amending the financial statements. If the financial statements are amended, the subsequent period is, in effect, extended to a later date. Appropriate subsequent events procedures should be performed relative to this extended period and the date of the audit report adjusted accordingly (SAS 150, paras 11 and 12; ISA 560, paras 9 and 10).

If management refuses to amend the financial statements, the auditor's future action depends on whether the audit report has been released to the client.

(i)   If the audit report has not been released to the client, and the auditor considers that the circumstances warrant a qualified or adverse audit opinion, such an opinion should be expressed.[4]

(ii) If the audit report has been released to the client but the financial statements have not been issued to the entity's shareholders, the auditor should: 'notify [he directors] . . . not to issue the financial statements and the auditor's report thereon' (ISA 560, para 12). If the directors have issued the financial statements to the shareholders prior to receiving (or after receiving but choosing to ignore) the auditor's notice, but the statements have not yet been laid before the members' annual general meeting, then:

the auditors consider steps to take on a timely basis to prevent reliance on their report. For example, they may consider making an appropriate

---

[4] These forms of audit opinion are discussed in Chapter 13.

statement at the annual general meeting. They may also consider taking legal advice on their position. (SAS 150, para 19)

(ii) Subsequent to the issue of the financial statements to the entity's shareholders

Occasionally, a matter may come to the auditor's attention after the financial statements have been issued to the entity's shareholders which materially affects the truth and fairness of those financial statements. If this occurs, the auditor should discuss the situation with the client's directors and consider the implications for the audit report. The directors may decide to make an appropriate statement at the annual general meeting. Alternatively, or additionally, they may decide to issue a revised set of financial statements. If the latter course of action is followed, SAS 150, para 17, notes that the auditor should take the following steps:

- carry out the audit procedures necessary in the circumstances;
- [for listed companies, consider] whether Stock Exchange regulations require the revision [of the financial statements] to be publicised;
- [for] businesses authorised under the Financial Services Act 1986 or other regulated businesses, [consider whether there is any requirement] to communicate with the appropriate regulator;
- review the steps taken by the directors to ensure that anyone in receipt of the previously issued financial statements, together with the auditor's report thereon, is informed of the situation;
- issue a new report on the revised financial statements.

SAS 150, para 18, further explains:

When auditors issue a new report, they:
(a) refer in their report to the note to the financial statements which more extensively discusses the reason for the revision of the previously issued financial statements, or set out such reason in their report;
(b) refer to the earlier report issued by them on the financial statements;
(c) date their new report not earlier than the date the revised financial statements are approved; and
(d) have regard to the guidance relating to reports on revised annual financial statements and directors' reports as set out in the APB's Practice Note 8: 'Reports by auditors under company legislation in the United Kingdom'.

If the auditee's directors do not take adequate steps to ensure that those in receipt of the (original) financial statements are notified that the information in those statements has been superseded (whether by issuing amended statements, or otherwise), the auditor should notify the directors that (s)he will take action to prevent future reliance on the audit report. ISA 560 observes:

The action taken will depend on the auditor's legal rights and obligations and the recommendations of the auditor's lawyers. (para 17)

The 2000 financial statements of Wiggins Group plc provide an example of revised financial statements accompanied by a revised audit report. These financial statements are the last in a series of revisions which commenced with the 1995 financial statements. As the Wiggins Group Chairman explains:

> The Financial Reporting Review Panel ('the Panel') opened an enquiry following the publication in August 2000 of our accounts for the year ended March 2000. The Panel had previously opened an enquiry into our accounts for the year ended March 1999 and had, by a letter of 27 June 2000, extended its enquiry in respect of the treatment of revenue from contracts for the sale of land to our accounts for the years ended March 1996 to 1998. . . . The Company announced on 22 December 2000 that it had decided to accept the Panel's position with respect to all the matters in dispute and that it was going to issue restated accounts for the years 1996 to 2000. On March 6 2001, the Company issued restated accounts for the years 1996 to 2000. The Company also issued restated accounts for the year ended March 1995 as it was appropriate to reclassify a particular transaction originally recorded in that year.

In respect of the revised accounts for the year to March 2000, the Wiggins Group directors, in an explanatory note,[5] provide details of a number of issues to which the Panel took exception. These include:

1. adoption of an inappropriate accounting policy for start-up costs;
2. premature recognition of revenue on contracts for the sale of land;
3. non-compliance with FRS 5 in respect of a fee paid to purchasers of land;
4. non-compliance with FRS 14 in respect of calculating diluted earnings per share;
5. inappropriate treatment of a pension scheme.

For each of the above issues, the directors explain the company's reasons for the treatment of the item in the original accounts, the grounds for the Panel's objection, and the remedial action taken by the company in the revised accounts. They also explain, in the following words, the manner in which they have revised the Group's 2000 financial statements and the effect of the revisions on profit:

> The directors are, by this [supplementary] note, revising the directors' report and accounts in accordance with Statutory Instrument 2570 Companies (Revision of Defective Accounts and Report) Regulations 1990, which permits revision by way of supplementary note. . . . As a result of the revisions, the profit on ordinary activities before taxation originally stated of £25,077,000 (1999: £12,113,000) is changed to a loss of £9,898,000 (1999: revised loss of £5,127,000). The original tax charge of £2,066,000 (1999: £3,295,000) has been revised to a credit of £24,000.

The directors have presented a set of revised financial statements and amended a paragraph in the Directors' Report headed 'Review of the business and future trading prospects'. The auditors (HLB Kidsons) have issued a revised audit

---

[5] The explanatory note precedes the formal 'Supplementary note' to the 2000 financial statements. The supplementary note supplements the original 2000 financial statements and comprises the revised 2000 financial statements (including the related notes) and an amended paragraph of the Directors' Report.

report that complies with the requirements of SAS 150. This is reproduced in Figure 12.3.

12.4   (RE)ASSESSMENT OF THE GOING CONCERN ASSUMPTION

An important audit step performed during the completion and review stage of the audit is assessing the propriety of the auditee preparing its financial statements on the basis that it is a going concern. Financial Reporting Standard (FRS) 18: *Accounting Policies,* explains that 'going concern' means 'the entity is to continue in operational existence for the foreseeable future' (para 22).

When financial statements are prepared on the basis of the going concern assumption, assets and liabilities are recorded at the amounts which can reasonably be expected to be realised or discharged (as applicable) in the ordinary course of business. These amounts may differ quite significantly from those that would apply in the event of the entity's liquidation. Thus, when forming an opinion about the truth and fairness (or otherwise) of the entity's financial statements, the auditor must consider whether adherence to the going concern assumption is justified.

Until SAS 130: *The going concern basis in financial statements,* came into effect in 1995, during the planning and evidence gathering stages of an audit, the auditor was merely required to remain alert to the possibility that the going concern assumption may not be valid. If something came to light which raised doubt in the auditor's mind regarding the ability of the entity to continue as a going concern, the auditor was required to perform specific audit procedures to assess the entity's going concern status. However, in the absence of such doubt, formal assessment of the propriety of adopting the going concern basis for the financial statements was left until the completion and review stage of the audit.

If, having evaluated the entity's going concern status, the auditor had doubts about the ability of the entity to continue in operation for the foreseeable future, (s)he was required to perform audit procedures to resolve those doubts. If, after conducting those procedures and evaluating management's plans for the future, the auditor still had doubts about the ability of the entity to continue as a going concern, (s)he was required to express those doubts in the audit report. This duty was unequivocal. However, during the 1980s and early 1990s (particularly following the Stock Market Crash in October 1987), auditors in the UK, USA and elsewhere, were severely criticised for not fulfilling this duty adequately; that is, for not expressing doubts about the going concern status of

Figure 12.3: Auditors' report on Wiggins Group plc's 2000 revised financial statements

Report of the auditors to the shareholders of Wiggins Group plc
We have audited the revised accounts of Wiggins Group plc for the year to 31 March 2000 which have been prepared under the historical cost convention and accounting policies set out on pages 38 to 40 in the original accounts and on page 10 of these revised accounts. The revised accounts replace the original accounts approved by the directors on 26 July 2000 and consist of the attached supplementary note together with the original accounts, which were dated 26 July 2000.

Respective responsibilities of directors and auditors
The directors are responsible for preparing the Annual Report, including, as described on page 27 of the original accounts, the accounts. Our responsibilities, as independent auditors, are established by statute, the Auditing Practices Board, the Listing Rules of the Financial Services Authority, and by our profession's ethical guidance.

We report to you our opinion as to whether the accounts give a true and fair view and are properly prepared in accordance with the Companies Act. We also report to you if, in our opinion, the directors' report is not consistent with the accounts, if the Company has not kept proper accounting records, if we have not received all the information and explanations we require for our audit, or if information specified by law or the Listing Rules regarding directors' remuneration and transactions with the Group and the Company is not disclosed. We are also required to report whether in our opinion the original accounts failed to comply with the requirements of the Companies Act in the respects identified by the directors.

We review whether the corporate governance statement on pages 24 to 26 of the original accounts reflects the Company's compliance with those provisions of the Combined Code specified for our review by the Financial Services Authority, and we report if it does not. We are not required to consider whether the Board's statements on internal control cover all the risks and controls, or form an opinion on the effectiveness of the Company's corporate governance procedures or its risk and control procedures.

We read the other information contained in the annual report, including the corporate governance statement, and consider whether it is consistent with the audited accounts. We consider the implications for our report if we become aware of any apparent misstatements or material inconsistencies with the accounts.

Basis of opinion
We conducted our audit in accordance with Auditing Standards issued by the Auditing Practices Board. An audit includes examination, on a test basis, of evidence relevant to the amounts and disclosures in the accounts. It also includes an assessment of the significant estimates and judgements made by the directors in the preparation of the accounts, and of whether the accounting policies are appropriate to the Group's and the Company's circumstances, consistently applied and adequately disclosed. The audit of the revised accounts includes the performance of additional procedures to assess whether the revisions made by the directors are appropriate and have been properly made.

We planned and performed our audit so as to obtain all the information and explanations which we considered necessary in order to provide us with sufficient evidence to give reasonable assurance that the revised accounts are free from material misstatement, whether caused by fraud or other irregularity or error. In forming our opinion we also evaluated the overall presentation of information in the revised accounts.

Opinion
In our opinion the revised accounts give a true and fair view, seen as at 26 July 2000, the date the original accounts were approved, of the state of the Group's and the Company's affairs as at 31 March 2000 and of the Group's loss and cash flows for the year then ended and have been properly prepared in accordance with the provisions of the Companies Act 1985 as they have effect under The Companies (Revision of Defective Accounts and Report) Regulations 1990.

In our opinion the original accounts for the year ended 31 March 2000 failed to comply with the requirements of the Companies Act 1985 for the reasons identified by the directors on pages 1 to 4 of the supplementary note.

Ocean House	HLB Kidsons
Waterloo Lane	Registered Auditors
Chelmsford	Chartered Accountants
Essex CM1 1BD	
Date: 6 March 2001	

entities that received 'a clean bill of health one day and collapse[d] just one day later' (Congressman Dingell, 1985, p. 22).[6]

Responding to the criticism, the auditing profession in the UK and USA (and elsewhere) developed new – more stringent and explicit – 'going concern' auditing standards. Instead of merely requiring auditors to remain alert to the possibility that the going concern assumption may be subject to question, SAS 130 requires auditors to be pro-active.[7] They are now required to assess the auditee's going concern status by performing certain procedures at various stages of the audit. These procedures are shown in Figure 12.4.

SAS 130 explains:

> [T]he auditors' procedures . . . are intended to provide them with assurance that:
> (a) the going concern basis used in the preparation of the financial statements as a whole is appropriate; and
> (b) there are adequate disclosures regarding that basis [i.e. going concern basis] in the financial statements in order that they give a true and fair view. (para 7)
> The auditors' procedures necessarily involve consideration of the entity's ability to continue in operational existence for the foreseeable future. In turn, this necessitates consideration both of the current and the possible future circumstances of the business and the environment in which it operates. (para 8)
> Any consideration involving the foreseeable future involves making a judgment at a particular point of time, about future events which are inherently uncertain. The following facts are relevant.
> (a) In general terms, the degree of uncertainty increases significantly the further into the future the consideration is taken. . . .
> (b) Any judgment about the future is based on information available at the time at which it was made. Subsequent events can overturn a judgment which was reasonable at the time it was made. (para 10)[8]

It is pertinent to recall that preparation of the auditee's financial statements (and adoption – or otherwise – of the going concern assumption) is the

---

[6] Research conducted into the audit expectation–performance gap in New Zealand in 1989 found that auditors were more severely criticised for not performing adequately their responsibility to report doubt they had (or should have had) about the going concern status of auditees than in respect of any other of their responsibilities. Even the auditor survey group was highly critical of auditors in this regard (see Porter, 1993).

[7] ISA 570: *Going concern*, contains similar provisions to SAS 130 and, thus, also requires auditors to be pro-active in assessing audtiees' going concern status.

[8] ISA 570, para 7, conveys similar ideas to those in SAS 130, para 10. However, it emphasises that the judgment regarding the validity of adopting the going concern assumption is that of management. It also refers to uncertainty being 'associated with the outcome of an event or condition' and adds a third relevant factor, namely: 'The size and complexity of the entity, the nature and condition of its business and the degree to which it is affected by external factors all affect the judgment regarding the outcome of events or conditions.'

Figure 12.4: Assessment of the auditee's going concern status

Audit steps		Audit phase
Undertake preliminary assessment of the risk that the client may be unable to continue as a going concern based on understanding the client's business, assessing risk factors, and discussions with the directors.		Planning phase
Perform specific procedures regarding the client's going concern status.	Perform other routine audit procedures	Evidence-gathering phase
Decide on the need for a bankers' confirmation or meeting.		
Consider and, if necessary, revise the preliminary going concern assessment. Determine and document the extent of concern (if any).		Completion and review phase
Decide on the need for formal representations from the client's directors		
Assess the need for, and adequacy of, disclosures relating to the client's going concern status.		
Express the appropriate opinion and, if necessary, make relevant disclosures regarding going concern uncertainties in the audit report.		Reporting Phase

responsibility of the directors (not the auditor). Before adopting the going concern assumption, the directors should explicitly assess the ability of the entity to continue in operation for the foreseeable future. Indeed, under the provisions of *The Combined Code* (Committee on Corporate Governance, 1998) the directors of all companies listed on the London Stock Exchange are required to report that the company is a going concern, noting supporting assumptions or qualifications as appropriate.[9]

---

[9] As a condition of listing, the directors of companies listed on the London Stock Exchange must either comply with the provisions of *The Combined Code* – and state in their company's annual report that they have done so, or disclose the respects in which they have not done so and the reasons therefor.

Auditors' responsibility for assessing the auditee's going concern status needs to be considered against this background. ISA 570 explains their responsibility particularly succinctly:

> The auditor's responsibility is to consider the appropriateness of management's use of the going concern assumption in the preparation of the financial statements, and consider whether there are material uncertainties about the entity's ability to continue as a going concern that need to be disclosed in the financial statements. (para 9)

As shown in Figure 12.4, auditors perform procedures to assess the appropriateness of the going concern assumption during (i) the planning phase, (ii) the evidence-gathering phase, (iii) the completion and review phase of the audit, and (iv) the reporting phase.

(i) Planning phase

During the planning phase the auditor undertakes a preliminary assessment of the auditee's going concern status – or, more correctly, the risk that the entity may be unable to continue as a going concern. This assessment is based on the auditor's understanding of the client, its business and its industry; identifying and evaluating events or conditions that may cast doubt on its ability to continue in operation; and discussions with the directors about the entity's current and future prospects and the basis for their intended adoption of the going concern assumption. ISA 570 (para 13) notes that considering the going concern issue during the planning process 'allows for more timely discussions with management,[10] review of management's plans and resolution of any identified going concern issues'. It also observes that during their early discussions with management, auditors can ascertain whether management has made a preliminary assessment of the entity's going concern status and, if so, they can review this assessment 'to determine whether management has identified events or conditions [that may cast significant doubt about the going concern assumption] and management's plans to address them' (para 14). If management has not undertaken the preliminary assessment, the auditor can establish when they plan to do so and whether they are aware of relevant events and conditions the auditor has identified.

(ii) Evidence-gathering phase

During the evidence-gathering phase of the audit, the auditor is primarily concerned to evaluate the directors' assessment of the entity's ability to continue as a going concern: more particularly, the process the directors followed

---

[10] It should be recalled that in the Preface to this book we noted that the term 'management' embraces non-director executives and both non-executive and executive directors.

in making their assessment, the assumptions on which their assessment is based and their plans for future action (ISA 570, paras 17 and 20). SAS 130, para 21, spells out auditors' responsibilities in this regard in some detail. It states:

> The auditors should assess the adequacy of the means by which the directors have satisfied themselves that:
> (a) it is appropriate for them to adopt the going concern basis in preparing the financial statements; and
> (b) the financial statements include such disclosures, if any, relating to going concern as are necessary for them to give a true and fair view.
> For this purpose:
> (i) the auditors should make enquiries of the directors and examine appropriate available financial information; and
> (ii) having regard to the future period to which the directors have paid particular attention in assessing going concern, the auditors should plan and perform procedures specifically designed to identify any material matters which could indicate concern about the entity's ability to continue as a going concern.

SAS 130 (para 23) further notes that:

> The auditors may need to consider some or all of the following matters:
>
> - whether the period to which the directors have paid particular attention in assessing going concern is reasonable in the entity's circumstances . . .;
> - the systems [the entity has in place] for timely identification of warnings of future risks and uncertainties the entity might face;
> - budget and/or forecast information (cash flow information in particular) produced by the entity . . .;
> - whether the key assumptions underlying the budgets and/or forecasts appear appropriate in the circumstances;
> - the sensitivity of budgets and forecasts to variable factors both within the control of the directors and outside their control ;
> - any obligations, undertakings or guarantees arranged with other entities (in particular, lenders, suppliers and companies) for the giving or receiving of support;
> - the existence, adequacy and terms of borrowing facilities, and supplier credit; and
> - the directors' plans for resolving any matters giving rise to the concern (if any) about the appropriateness of the going concern basis. In particular, the auditors may need to consider whether the plans are realistic, whether there is a reasonable expectation that the plans are likely to resolve any problems foreseen and whether the directors are likely to put the plans into practice effectively.

In relation to the last matter, SAS 130 observes:

> [T]he auditors may need to consider whether the plans are realistic, whether there is a reasonable expectation that the plans are likely to resolve any problems foreseen and whether the directors are likely to put the plans into practice effectively. (para 23)

As regards determining the existence and terms of bank lending facilities, SAS 130 encourages meetings between the auditor and the entity's directors or, if appropriate, the auditor, directors and bankers, so that the auditor can form a view as to the likelihood of the continuation of loan facilities. In some circumstances, the auditor may seek written confirmation from bankers about their intentions. SAS 130, para 26, points out that auditors are more likely to seek confirmation of the existence and terms of bank facilities and the bank's intentions when:

- financial resources available to the audit client are limited;
- the auditee is dependent on borrowing facilities shortly due for renewal;
- correspondence between the bankers and the entity shows that the last renewal of facilities was agreed with difficulty;
- a significant deterioration in cash flow is expected;
- the value of assets granted as security is declining; or
- the auditee has breached the terms of borrowing covenants or there are indications of potential breaches.

During the course of the evidence-gathering phase of the audit [i.e. evaluation of the auditee's internal control system, compliance testing (where the auditor plans to rely on internal control procedures) and substantive testing] the auditor may encounter events or conditions that may cast doubt on the entity's ability to continue as a going concern. These might include some or all of the following:[11]

Financial factors:
- net liability or net current liability position;
- fixed term borrowings approaching maturity without realistic prospects of renewal or repayment;
- substantial operating losses or significant deterioration in the value of assets used to generate cash flows;
- inability to pay creditors on due dates;
- substantial sales of fixed assets not intended to be replaced.

Operational factors
- fundamental changes in the market or technology to which the entity is unable to adapt adequately;
- loss of key management;
- labour difficulties or shortages of important supplies.

Other factors
- pending legal or regulatory procedures against the entity which, if successful, may result in claims the entity cannot satisfy;

---

[11] More extensive lists of factors are provided in SAS 130, para 31, and ISA 570, para 8.

- changes in legislation or government policy that are expected to adversely affect the entity.

ISA 570 notes that when the auditor encounters events and conditions such as those outlined above, (s)he:

> inquires of management as to its plans for future action, including its plans to liquidate assets, borrow money or restructure debt, reduce or delay expenditures, or increase capital. . . . The auditor obtains sufficient appropriate audit evidence that management's plans are feasible and the outcome of these plans will improve the situation. (para 27)

Appropriate audit procedures in this situation generally include some or all of the following:

- analysing cash flow, profit and other relevant forecasts and discussing these forecasts with management;
- reviewing the terms of debentures and loan agreements to determine whether these have been breached;
- reviewing the minutes of directors' meetings and of other relevant committees (such as the audit committee) for any reference to financing difficulties;
- confirming the existence, legality and enforceability of arrangements to provide financial support to, or receive financial support from, related and third parties, and assessing the financial position of these parties;
- evaluating the entity's position with respect to unfilled customer orders.

(iii)   Completion and review phase

During the completion and review phase of the audit, auditors need to reconsider, and if necessary revise, their preliminary assessment of the entity's going concern status (made during the planning stage). They should determine and document the extent of their concern, if any, about the entity's ability to continue as a going concern and decide whether formal written representations from the client's directors are needed.

Whenever there are significant uncertainties regarding the auditee's ability to remain in existence, it is advisable for auditors to obtain a written statement from the directors confirming their (the directors') considered view that the entity is a going concern, together with supporting assumptions or qualifications, as necessary. However this is not the end of the story as far as auditors are concerned. They must also decide whether financial statement disclosure is required in respect of the uncertainty regarding the entity's continued existence. As expressed in ISA 570, paras 30 and 31):

> Based on the audit evidence obtained, the auditor should determine if, in the auditor's judgment, a material uncertainty exists related to events or conditions that alone or in aggregate, may cast significant doubt on the entity's ability to continue as a going concern.

A material uncertainty exists when the magnitude of its potential impact is such that, in the auditor's judgment, clear disclosure of the nature and implications of the uncertainty is necessary for the presentation of the financial statements not to be misleading.

(iv) Reporting phase

Where the auditor believes there is material uncertainty about the entity's ability to continue as a going concern, (s)he needs to determine whether the matters giving rise to the uncertainty are adequately disclosed in the financial statements. Where the auditor considers that the uncertainty is adequately disclosed, an unqualified audit opinion is appropriate. However, if the level of uncertainty is significant, the auditor is required to include in the section of the audit report which sets out the basis of the auditors' opinion, an explanatory paragraph (headed 'Fundamental Uncertainty'), drawing attention to the uncertainty.[12] Should the auditor consider that going concern uncertainties are not adequately disclosed in the financial statements, and that the deficiency is material to the truth and fairness of the financial statements, (s)he is required to express an 'except for' opinion. Such an opinion should also be expressed if the auditor considers the directors have not taken adequate steps to satisfy themselves that adoption of the going concern basis for their entity's financial statements is appropriate (SAS 130, paras 36, 42, 43 and 48).

In circumstances where auditors conclude that disclosures in the financial statements relating to going concern uncertainties are so inadequate as to cause the financial statements to be seriously misleading, they are required to express an adverse opinion. They are similarly required to express an adverse opinion if the financial statements have been prepared on a going concern basis and the auditors consider that adoption of this basis is inappropriate. However, it should be noted that the latter situation arises only in extreme circumstances, such as impending liquidation.

The various reporting options open to the auditor arising from a going concern uncertainty are depicted in Figure 12.5.

From the above discussion it is evident that auditors' responsibilities in relation to assessing auditees' ability to continue as going concerns are fairly demanding. However, by helping to ensure that uncertainties regarding the going concern assumption are detected, adequately disclosed in the financial statements and, where appropriate, referred to in the audit report, auditors help facilitate users of the financial statements to assess for themselves the impact of any major uncertainties and the consequent risk to the viability of the entity.

---

[12] Audit reports are discussed in Chapter 13.

Figure 12.5:   Auditors' reporting options arising from a going concern uncertainty

```
                    ┌──────────────────────────────┐
                    │  Material uncertainty about   │
                    │ status of entity as going     │
                    │      concern status           │
                    └──────────────────────────────┘
                                   │
                    Is uncertainty adequately disclosed?
                                   │
              ┌────────────────────┴────────────────────┐
              │                                          │
             Yes                                        No
              │                                          │
   ┌────────────────────┐                   ┌────────────────────┐
   │ Unqualified audit  │                   │ Other than         │
   │ report             │                   │ unqualified        │
   │                    │                   │ audit report       │
   └────────────────────┘                   └────────────────────┘
              │                                          │
   Is the level of uncertainty          Does inadequate disclosure
   significant (fundamental)?            render financial statements
              │                          seriously misleading?
              │                                          │
       ┌──────┴──────┐                          ┌────────┴────────┐
      Yes            No                         No               Yes
       │             │                          │                 │
┌───────────┐ ┌───────────┐          ┌───────────┐      ┌───────────┐
│Unqualified│ │Unqualified│          │Qualified  │      │Adverse    │
│opinion    │ │opinion    │          │'except    │      │opinion    │
│with       │ │without    │          │for'       │      │           │
│fundamental│ │uncertainty│          │opinion    │      │           │
│uncertainty│ │paragraph  │          │           │      │           │
│paragraph  │ │           │          │           │      │           │
└───────────┘ └───────────┘          └───────────┘      └───────────┘
```

12.5   MANAGEMENT REPRESENTATION LETTERS

When conducting an audit, the auditor may have cause to rely on information given to him or her by management[13] – especially when audit evidence from alternative sources is not available. Examples include management's responses to the auditor's enquiries about instances of fraud or other illegal acts known to management, and management's intentions with respect to holding or disposing of a long-term investment. As part of the completion and review stage of the audit, the auditor usually seeks to have significant representations made by

---

[13] Further to footnote 9, SAS 440: *Management representations*, notes:

  In the context of management representations, 'management' includes directors, officers and others who perform senior managerial functions. (para 5)

management recorded in writing. These are generally documented in what is known as a management representation letter.

These letters are technically written by the client's directors to the auditor but, in practice, they are normally prepared by the auditor and signed by the directors. Their purpose is essentially twofold:

- to obtain evidence that the client's directors acknowledge their responsibility for the entity's financial statements (and their truth and fairness);
- to place on record management's responses to enquiries made by the auditor during the course of the audit. This ensures there is no misunderstanding between management and the auditor as to what was said – and gives management the opportunity to correct any response which the auditor has misinterpreted. It also ensures that management assumes responsibility for its representations to the auditor.

Although management representation letters are normally obtained by the auditor as a matter of routine, opinion differs as to their value as audit evidence. This is clearly illustrated by the following quotations:

- The letter of representation is, at the very least, a useful piece of corroborative audit evidence. It can be of vital importance if the auditor is in any doubt as to whether he has been given all the information and explanations he requires. (Davey, 1980, p. 60)
- The audit utility of representation letters as primary evidence would appear to be limited. At best they may be corroborative, and then only to the extent that they support propositions on which the auditor should have formed his own judgment based on stronger forms of evidence. . . . While there may be circumstances unique to a particular audit that suggest the appropriateness of a representation letter, on balance there appears to be little audit justification for the representation letter to be formalised as a generally accepted auditing practice. (Pound and Besley, 1982, p. 13)

Notwithstanding Pound and Besley's stance, Auditing Standards make it clear that auditors are expected to obtain written confirmation of management's oral representations. This applies, in particular, where management's representations concern matters which are material to the financial statements and alternative audit evidence cannot reasonably be expected to exist. SAS 440: *Management Representations,* for example, states:[14]

---

[14] ISA 580: *Management representations,* paras 4 and 8, convey similar ideas to SAS 440, paras 11 and 16, but expresses them as follows:

> The auditor should obtain written representations from management on matters material to the financial statements when other sufficient appropriate audit evidence cannot reasonably be expected to exist. . . . In certain instances a representation by management may be the only audit evidence which can reasonably be expected to be available. For example, the auditor would not necessarily expect that other audit evidence would be available to corroborate management's intention to hold a specific investment for long-term appreciation.

Auditors should obtain written confirmation of representations from management on matters material to the financial statements when those representations are critical to obtaining sufficient appropriate audit evidence. (para 11)

In certain circumstances, such as where knowledge of the facts is confined to management (for example, when the facts are a matter of management's intentions), or when the matter is principally one of judgment or opinion (for example, on the trading position of a particular customer), management representations may be the only audit evidence available. (para 16)

However, despite the acknowledged need for auditors to obtain written representations from management, SAS 440 makes it clear that auditors cannot just accept those representations without question or further audit work. More specifically, it specifies:

When representations to the auditors relate to matters which are material to the financial statements, they:
(a) seek corroborative audit evidence;
(b) evaluate whether the representations made by management appear reasonable and are consistent with other audit evidence obtained, including other representations; and
(c) consider whether the individuals making the representations can be expected to be well-informed on the particular matters. (para 14)

Representations by management cannot be a substitute for other audit evidence that auditors expect to be available.[15] If auditors are unable to obtain sufficient appropriate audit evidence regarding a matter which has, or may have, a material effect on the financial statements, and such audit evidence is expected to be available, this constitutes a limitation on the scope of the audit, even if a representation from management has been received on the matter. (para 15)

SAS 440 further adds:

If a representation appears to be contradicted by other audit evidence, the auditors should investigate the circumstances to resolve the matter and consider whether it casts doubt on the reliability of other representations [by management]. (para 18)[16]

Indeed, if a representation from management contradicts other audit evidence, this would cause the auditor to re-assess management's integrity. As noted in Chapter 3 in relation to the concept of audit risk, management's integrity is a critical factor in the auditor's assessment of inherent risk.

Regarding the form and content of management representation letters, SAS 440 notes that:

[15] This corresponds to one of the principles enunciated by Moffit J in the *Pacific Acceptance* case discussed in Chapter 5, namely: An auditor has a paramount duty to check material matters for him or herself. However, reliance may be placed on enquiries from others where it is reasonable to do so. Nevertheless, reliance on others is to be regarded as an aid to, and not a substitute for, the auditor's own procedures (see Chapter 5, section 5.3).

[16] ISA 580, paras 6, 7 and 9, contain similar wording to SAS 440, paras 14, 15 and 18.

- [w]hen requesting a management representation letter, auditors request that it be addressed to them, that it contain specified information, and that it be appropriately dated and approved by those with specific knowledge of the relevant matters (para 20);
- [auditors should normally] request that the management representation letter be discussed and agreed by the board of directors, . . . and signed on their behalf by the chairman and secretary, before [the board approves] the financial statements. [This ensures] that the board as a whole is aware of the representations on which the auditors intend to rely [when] expressing their opinion on those financial statements (para 21);
- [the] management representation letter is normally dated on the date the financial statements are approved. If there is any significant delay between the date of the management representation letter and the date of the auditors' report, the auditors may consider it necessary to obtain further written representations regarding the intervening period (paras 22 and 23).[17]

An example of a management representation letter, appropriate for use in the audits of companies (derived from the appendix to SAS 440), is provided in Figure 12.6.

Before leaving the topic of management representation letters, it is pertinent to note that, should management refuse to confirm its representations in writing, this will normally constitute a limitation on the scope of the audit examination and, as such, may give rise to a qualified audit report.[18] Further, in such circumstances, it may not be appropriate for the auditors to place reliance on other representations made by management during the course of the audit (SAS 440, paras 24, 25, and ISA 580, para 15).

12.6 FINAL REVIEW, CONCLUSION AND CONFERENCE

12.6.1 Final review of audit working papers and conclusion

During the audit, as audit work is performed (and documented), it is reviewed by a member of the audit team who is senior to the assistant who undertook the work. This review is designed to ensure, *inter alia*, that appropriate audit procedures have been performed, conclusions reached are consistent with the results obtained, and specific audit objectives have been met. Any difficult issues or questions arising from the audit procedures performed are discussed, addressed and resolved (with appropriate notes recorded in the audit working papers).

---

[17] Similar provisions are found in ISA 580, paras 12–14.

[18] Scope limitations resulting in qualified audit reports are discussed in Chapter 13.

Figure 12.6: Example of a management representation letter

[Company letterhead]

[To the auditors]   [Date]

We confirm to the best of our knowledge and belief, and having made appropriate enquiries of other directors and officials of the company, the following representations given to you in connection with your audit of the financial statements for the period ended 31 December 20 . . .

1) We acknowledge as directors our responsibilities under the Companies Act 1985 for preparing financial statements which give a true and fair view and for making accurate representations to you. All the accounting records have been made available to you for the purpose of your audit and all the transactions undertaken by the company have been properly reflected and recorded in the accounting records. All other records and related information, including minutes of all management and shareholders' meetings, have been made available to you.

2) The legal claim by ABC Limited has been settled out of court by a payment of £258,000. No further amounts are expected to be paid, and no similar claims have been received or are expected to be received.

3) To the best of our knowledge and belief, having made enquiries of each member of the Board and key management personnel, the financial statements provide all the information required to be disclosed regarding related party transactions and control of the company that are required under FRS 8 and other applicable requirements. In particular we confirm that:

    • the disclosures include all related party transactions, of which we are aware, that have been made on a no charge basis;
    • where required by FRS 8, the materiality of related party transactions has been judged not only in terms of their significance to the company but also in relation to the other related party.

4) The company has not had, or entered into, at any time during the period any arrangement, transaction or agreement to provide credit facilities (including loans, quasi-loans or credit transactions) for directors or to guarantee or provide security for such matters.

5) Attached to this letter is a summary of the unadjusted differences that you have informed the company and the audit committee were identified during your audit of the financial statements. The company has made an adjustment to increase the provision for warranty costs. However, the company has decided not to make any of the other adjustments that you have identified on the basis that the extrapolations inherent in some of your audit findings are rather tenuous and in any event their cumulative effect is not material to the view presented by the financial statements taken as a whole.

6) There have been no events since the balance sheet date which necessitate revision of the figures included in the financial statements or inclusion of a note thereto.

As minuted by the board of directors at its meeting on .... (date).

....
Chairman   Secretary

Adapted from SAS 440, *Management representations* (APB, 1995), Appendix

At the conclusion of the audit, an overall review of the financial statements and the audit evidence gathered, and conclusions reached thereon, is conducted. In the words of SAS 470: *Overall review of financial statements*:

> Auditors should carry out such a review of the financial statements as is sufficient, in conjunction with the conclusions drawn from the other audit evidence obtained, to give them a reasonable basis for their opinion on the financial statements. (para 2)

In order to achieve this audit objective, the audit engagement partner reviews the audit work conducted – as documented in the audit working papers. The engagement partner's review is designed to establish that:

- sufficient appropriate audit evidence has been collected in each audit segment, and for the audit as a whole, on which to base an audit opinion;
- all audit work has been properly performed, documented and reviewed;
- conclusions reached in relation to specific audit objectives are consistent with the results obtained from the audit procedures performed;
- all questions and difficulties arising during the course of the audit have been resolved;
- the information presented in the financial statements complies with statutory requirements, and the accounting policies adopted are in accordance with accounting standards, are properly disclosed, are consistently applied, and are appropriate to the entity;
- the financial statements as a whole, and the assertions contained therein, are consistent with the auditor's knowledge of the entity's business and the results of audit procedures performed, and also that the manner of disclosure is fair.

A checklist may be used to ensure that all aspects of the financial statements are properly covered. When considering whether the accounting polices adopted by management are appropriate to the entity's circumstances, the auditor will have regard to:

- any policies commonly adopted in the particular industry to which the entity belongs;
- policies for which there is substantial authoritative support;
- whether any departures from applicable accounting standards are necessary in order for the financial statements to give a true and fair view;
- whether the financial statements reflect the substance of the underlying transactions and not merely their form (SAS 470, para 5).

On the basis of the review of the audit working papers, together with knowledge gained as the audit has progressed, the audit engagement partner forms an opinion as to whether the financial statements give a true and fair view of the reporting entity's state of affairs and financial performance. In order to ensure that this opinion is consistent with the audit evidence collected (as documented in the working papers), that sufficient appropriate audit evidence has been gathered, and that the working papers provide evidence that the audit has been carried out in accordance with auditing standards, a second audit partner (who has not been involved in the audit) may review the audit working papers. Indeed, SAS 240: *Quality control for audit work* (APB, 2000), states:

> [Audit f]irms should ensure that an independent review is undertaken for all audit engagements where the audited entity is a listed company. In addition, firms should establish policies setting out the circumstances in which an independent review should be performed for other audit engagements, whether on the grounds of the public interest or audit risk. (para 58)

12.6.2 Review of unaudited information

Even if everything is found to be in order, before the auditor can prepare the appropriate audit report, a further audit procedure needs to be performed. The auditor is required by SAS 160: *Other information in documents containing audited financial statements*, to review unaudited information in the entity's annual report (or other documents containing the audited financial statements), to determine that it is not materially inconsistent with the financial statements. This accords with the fundamental principle of external auditing included in *The Auditor's Code* (APB, 1996) – *Association*:

> Auditors allow their reports to be included in documents containing other information only if they consider that the additional information is not in conflict with the matters covered by their report and they have no cause to believe it to be misleading.

SAS 160 notes that two types of problems may be encountered: there may be an inconsistency between the financial statements and the other (unaudited) information, or the other information may contain misstatements. It explains:

> An inconsistency exists when the other information contradicts, or appears to contradict, information contained in the financial statements. An inconsistency may raise doubt about the audit conclusions drawn from audit evidence previously obtained and, possibly, about the basis for the auditors' opinion on the financial statements. (para 10)[19]
>
> A misstatement within the other information exists when the other information is stated incorrectly or presented in a misleading manner. It would potentially include an inconsistency between information obtained by the auditors during the audit (such as information obtained as part of the planning process or analytical

---

[19] ISA 720, para 3, defines an inconsistency in a similar manner to SAS 160, para 10, but refers to a 'material inconsistency' rather than to an inconsistency. In respect of a misstatement in other information it states:

> [A] 'material misstatement of fact' in other information exists when such information, not related to matters appearing in the audited financial statements, is incorrectly stated or presented. (para 15)

procedures, or as management representations) and information which is included in the other information. (para 11)

If the auditor discovers a material inconsistency, (s)he is required by SAS 160 to determine whether it is the financial statements or the other (unaudited) information which requires amendment, and to 'seek to resolve the matter through discussions with the directors' (para 9). If the financial statements are in error and the client refuses to make the necessary adjustments, the auditor is required to consider the implications for the audit report (SAS 160, para 12). Such an error will almost certainly result in a qualified or adverse opinion. If, however, it is the other information which is in error (or the other information contains a misstatement that is independent of the financial statements) and the client refuses to correct it, then the appropriate action depends on the particular circumstances.

- If the auditee is a company listed on the London Stock Exchange and the misstatement the directors refuse to correct relates to a disclosure the company is required to make in respect of its compliance (or otherwise) with the provisions of *The Combined Code,* and it is a matter Listing Rule 12.43A requires auditors to review, the auditor should refer to the misstatement in the opinion section of the audit report (APB, 1999, para 21).[20]
- If the auditee is a limited company and the directors' report is inconsistent with the financial statements, the auditor has a statutory responsibility to refer to the inconsistency in the audit report (SAS 160, para 13). Additionally, as SAS 160 (para 17) points out, auditors of limited companies have a right under the Companies Act 1985 (s.390) to be heard at any general meeting of the company's members on matters that concern them as auditors. Thus they have an opportunity to highlight any material inconsistency between the financial statements and other information in the company's annual report, or a misstatement in the other (unaudited) information.
- If the error is present in unaudited information other than the directors' report and the client's directors refuse to correct it, then the auditors may request the directors to consult with a qualified third party, such as the entity's lawyers. If the directors continue to refuse to effect the amendment the auditors consider necessary:

    the auditors consider including in the audit report an explanatory paragraph describing the apparent misstatement or material inconsistency. . . . When determining whether to add an explanatory paragraph to the audit report, or other appropriate action, auditors may need to take legal advice, including advice on whether they would be protected by qualified privilege from a

---

[20] Auditors' duties in respect of the Listing Rules of the United Kingdom Listing Authority (a division of the Financial Services Authority) are discussed in Chapter 5, section 5.5. Components of the audit report are discussed in Chapter 13.

defamation claim if they were to refer to the matters in their report or subsequently. (SAS 160, paras 15 and 16)[21]

- A further option open to the auditors when the directors refuse to correct a material inconsistency or misstatement is to resign from the engagement (SAS 160, para 18). As noted in Chapter 5, if auditors of a company resign, they are required (by the Companies Act 1985, s.394) to make a written statement of any circumstances they consider should be brought to the attention of the company's shareholders or creditors (or a statement that there are no such circumstances). A copy of this statement is sent to the Registrar of Companies. If the refusal by the auditee's directors to correct a material inconsistency or misstatement is sufficiently serious to prompt the auditor's resignation, it seems likely that it is sufficiently serious to qualify as a circumstance that should be drawn to the attention of the company's shareholders.

12.6.3 Final conference

Once all audit matters have been resolved and the audit engagement partner (in consultation with senior audit team members) has reached a conclusion with respect to the financial statements and prepared the audit report, a final conference is held between the client's directors (or, if it has one, its audit committee), the audit engagement partner and (usually) the audit manager. The conduct and findings of the audit are discussed, the financial statements are signed by one or more director[22] (if this has not already been done at a previous directors' meeting) and, finally, the audit report is signed and dated by the audit engagement partner (who signs for and on behalf of the audit firm). It is important that the auditor does not sign the audit report prior to the directors signing the financial statements. By signing the financial statements, the directors signal their responsibility for, and acceptance of, the statements as presented. The auditor's report expresses an opinion on the financial statements prepared, presented, and approved by the directors.

The date of the audit report is of the utmost importance because it signifies the end of the period considered by the auditor when expressing an opinion on the financial statements. It marks the end of the 'subsequent period' in which events may have occurred that impact on the truth and fairness of the financial statements as at the balance sheet date.

---

[21] ISA 720, paras 11, 12, 13 and 17, respectively, convey the key ideas expressed in SAS 160, paras 9, 12 and 15, respectively. However, unlike SAS 160, which deals with inconsistencies and misstatements in other information in the same paragraphs, ISA 720 devotes separate sections (blocks of paragraphs) to (i) 'material inconsistencies' and (ii) misstatements of fact in other information.

[22] The statutory requirement for one or more directors to sign the auditee's balance sheet is referred to in Chapter 5, section 5.2.6.

12.7   SUMMARY

In this chapter we have discussed the steps which constitute the completion and review phase of the audit. More specifically, we have examined the importance of, and procedures used for, the review for contingent liabilities and commitments, and the review for events (adjusting and non-adjusting) occurring subsequent to the balance sheet date. We have also discussed the auditor's duty with respect to the going concern assumption and the meaning and significance of management representation letters. Additionally, we have reviewed the steps involved in the final review of evidence gathered during the audit and the forming of an opinion with respect to the truth and fairness of the financial statements and their compliance with relevant legislation. In the concluding sections of the chapter, we have drawn attention to the need for the auditor to review unaudited information in the client's annual report (or other documents containing the audited financial statements), and explained the importance of the auditor signing the audit report after the directors have signed the financial statements. The significance of the audit report date has also been noted.

SELF-REVIEW QUESTIONS

12.1   Define: (i) contingent liabilities
              (ii) commitments
12.2   List five procedures auditors commonly use during their review for contingent liabilities and commitments.
12.3   (i) Briefly distinguish between adjusting and non-adjusting subsequent events.
        (ii) Give one specific example to illustrate each of these types of subsequent events.
12.4   (i) State the period which is subject to the auditor's review for subsequent events.
        (ii) List three procedures auditors commonly use during their review for subsequent events.
12.5   Explain briefly what is meant by the 'going concern' assumption.
12.6   Explain briefly the auditor's duty when (s)he has unresolved doubts about the ability of the auditee to continue as a going concern.
12.7   Explain briefly what is meant by a 'management representation letter' and outline its two primary purposes.
12.8   List five items which are commonly referred to in a management representation letter.
12.9   List four objectives of the final review of audit working papers.
12.10 Explain briefly the significance of dating the audit report.

REFERENCES

Auditing Practices Board (APB) (1994) *Reports by Auditors under Company Legislation in the United Kingdom,* Practice Note 8. London: APB.

Auditing Practices Board (APB) (1999) *The Combined Code: Requirements under the Listing Rules of the London Stock Exchange*, Bulletin 1999/5. London: APB.

Auditing Practices Board (APB) (2000) Statement of Auditing Standards 240: *Quality control for audit work*. Bulletin 1999/5. London: APB.

Committee on Corporate Governance (1998) *The Combined Code*. London: The London Stock Exchange Ltd.

Davey, J. (1980) Are letters of representation a waste of time? *Accountancy* **91**(1038), 59–60.

Dingell, J. (1985). Accountants must clean up their act. *Management Accounting* **66**(1), 21–23, 53–56.

Porter, B.A. (1993) An empirical study of the audit expectation–performance gap. *Accounting and Business Research* **24**(93), 49–68.

Pound, G. & Besley, R. (1982) Are representation letters needed? *Chartered Accountant in Australia* **52**(8), 11–13.

ADDITIONAL READING

Asare, S.K. (1992) The auditor's going-concern decision: interaction of task variables and sequential processing of evidence, *The Accounting Review* **67**(2), 379–393.

Behn, B.K., Kaplan, S.E. & Krumwiede, K.R. (2001) Further evidence on the auditor's going concern report: the influence of management plans. *Auditing: A Journal of Practice & Theory* **20**(1), 13–28.

Carey, P.J. & Clarke, B. (2001) An investigation of Australian auditors' use of the management representation letter. *British Accounting Review* **33**(1), 1–21.

Cuthbert, S. (1982) How easy to hoodwink the auditor! *Accountancy* **93**(1063), 136.

Fleak, S.K. & Wilson, E.R. (1994) The incremental information content of the going-concern opinion. *Journal of Accounting, Auditing & Finance* **9**(1), 149–166.

Grant Thornton (1990) *Audit Manual*. Chapter 21, Completion procedures. London: Longman.

LaSalle, R.E. & Anandarajan, A. (1997) Bank loan officers' reactions to audit reports issued to entities with litigation and going concern uncertainties. *Accounting Horizons* **11**(2), 33–40.

LaSalle, R.E., Anandarajan, A. & Miller, A.F. (1996) Going concern uncertainties: disclaimer of opinion versus unqualified opinion with modified wording. *Auditing: A Journal of Practice & Theory* **15**(2), 29–48.

Nogler, G.E. (1995) The resolution of auditor going concern opinions. *Auditing: A Journal of Practice & Theory* **14**(2), 54–73.

Rau, S.E. & Moser, D.V. (1999) Does performing other audit tasks affect going concern judgements? *The Accounting Review* **74**(4), 493–508.

Ricchuite, D.N. (1992) Working-paper order effects and auditors' going concern decisions. *Accounting Review* **67**(1), 46–58.

13 Auditors' Reports to Users of Financial Statements and to Management

---

LEARNING OBJECTIVES

After studying the material in this chapter you should be able to:
- state the auditor's statutory reporting obligation in respect of companies;
- explain what is required in order for financial statements to provide a true and fair view;
- explain what is meant by 'proper accounting records';
- describe the format of the standard audit report used for companies;
- explain the various types of audit opinion expressed in the United Kingdom and Republic of Ireland and the circumstances in which each is appropriate;
- explain how inherent uncertainties are reflected in standard audit reports;
- describe significant differences between the current standard 'expanded' audit report and the former 'short form' report;
- discuss the advantages and disadvantages of the 'expanded' audit report and 'short form' report;
- discuss the advantages and disadvantages of (i) a standard form of audit report and (ii) a 'free-form' report;
- explain the requirement for, and purpose and content of, auditors' communication of audit matters to those charged with the governance of companies.

The following publications and fundamental principles of external auditing are particularly relevant to this chapter:

Publications:
- Statement of Auditing Standards (SAS) 600: *Auditors' reports on financial statements* (APB, 1993)
- Statement of Auditing Standards (SAS) 610 (Revised): *Communication of audit matters to those charged with governance* (APB, 2001)
- *Revisions to the Wording of Auditors' Reports on Financial Statements and the Interim Review Report*, Bulletin 2001/2 (APB, 2001)
- *The United Kingdom Directors' Remuneration Report Regulations*, Bulletin 2002/2 (APB, 2002)
- International Standards on Auditing (ISA) 260: *Communication of audit matters to those charged with governance* (IFAC, 2000)
- International Standards on Auditing (ISA) 700: *The auditor's report on financial statements* (IFAC, 1994)

Fundamental principles of external auditing included in *The Auditor's Code* (APB, 1996)
- Clear communication
- Providing value

13.1 INTRODUCTION

The audit process culminates (in the case of companies) in the auditor's statutory report to shareholders. This report is the end product of the audit examination and communicates to shareholders, and other users of the company's financial statements, the auditor's conclusions about, among other things, the truth and fairness with which the statements portray the entity's financial position and performance and their compliance (or otherwise) with the Companies Act. The auditor is also required to communicate with those charged with the company's governance. This usually covers various aspects of the audit and the entity's financial affairs but also highlights any material weaknesses in the entity's internal control system discovered during the audit, and recommends ways in which these might be overcome. This communication is frequently referred to as a 'management letter' but it is broader in scope than the (former) traditional management letter (which focused almost exclusively on internal control weaknesses and how they might be rectified). However, like the traditional management letter, the auditor's communication with those charged with the entity's governance is a private communication and its contents are generally not revealed to shareholders or other third parties.

In this chapter we discuss the statutory reporting obligations of auditors of companies. We explore the issue of what is required for financial statements to be adjudged 'true and fair' and what is meant by 'proper accounting records'. We also examine the format of standard audit reports and consider the various types of audit opinion the auditor may express and the circumstances in which each is appropriate. We observe that the audit report is frequently the auditor's only opportunity to communicate with users of the audited financial statements and we discuss the differences between, and the advantages and disadvantages of, the 'expanded' audit report currently in use and its predecessor 'short form' report. We also consider the advantages and disadvantages of using a standard, rather than a 'free-flow' form of audit report. Before concluding the chapter we address the topic of auditors' communications to those charged with the governance of auditees, focusing in particular on their purpose and content.

13.2 AUDITORS' REPORTING OBLIGATIONS UNDER THE COMPANIES ACT 1985[1]

The Companies Act 1985 places a major duty on auditors. First, it specifies that the directors of every company must prepare financial statements comprising a balance sheet and profit or loss account. These financial statements are required

---

[1] As amended by the Companies Act 1989.

to give a true and fair view of the company's state of affairs and its profit or loss for the accounting period and to comply with the provisions of the Act as to form, content and notes.

The preparation of financial statements which meet the statutory requirements is a duty which belongs exclusively to the entity's directors. However, except in the case of exempt companies,[2] the Act places on auditors the responsibility of examining the financial statements and forming and expressing an opinion as to whether they give the required true and fair view and have been properly prepared in accordance with the Companies Act 1985. Additionally, auditors are required to form an opinion as to whether:

- proper accounting records have been kept by the company;
- proper returns have been received from branches not visited by the auditors;
- the financial statements are in agreement with the underlying accounting records;
- they have received all the information and explanations they required for the purposes of their audit;
- the information given in the directors' report is consistent with the financial statements.

In cases where auditors are of the opinion that any of these requirements have not been met, they are required to report that fact in their audit report. Additionally, auditors are required to ensure that the disclosure requirements relating to directors' emoluments and other benefits specified in the Companies Act 1985, Schedule 6, have been made and, insofar as they have not, to provide the required particulars in their audit report.

Two of the matters about which the auditors must form an opinion require some explanation, namely:

(i) proper accounting records;
(ii) a true and fair view.

(i) Proper accounting records

The Companies Act 1985 (s.221) requires all companies to maintain 'proper accounting records'. The Act explains that such records must be sufficient to show and explain the company's transactions and, among other things:

- enable the company's financial position to be disclosed, with reasonable accuracy, at any time;
- enable a balance sheet and profit and loss account which complies with the Companies Act to be prepared;

---

[2] See Chapter 5 (section 5.2.2) for an explanation of 'exempt' companies.

- record the day-to-day details of all receipts and payments of cash;
- provide details of the company's assets and liabilities;
- provide details of stock held by the company;
- provide details of trading goods bought and sold. The records must be in sufficient detail to enable the goods, the buyers and the sellers to be identified.

It can be seen from these requirements that the Act is both specific and strict as regards the criteria to be met in order for a company's accounting records to be considered 'proper accounting records'. It does not, however, lay down any detailed requirements for particular procedures or controls to be implemented.

It is important to appreciate that auditors must form an opinion in every audit as to whether or not proper accounting records have been kept by the auditee. However, this opinion is only stated in the audit report if the auditor considers that proper accounting records have *not* been kept.

(ii)   A true and fair view

Although the directors of companies are required to prepare financial statements which give a true and fair view of their company's financial position and performance, neither legislation nor the courts have explained what is meant by a 'true and fair view'. This has led to conflicting interpretations. As Johnston *et al.* (1982) observed:

> It is clear that the interpretation applied by most accountants is that the words 'true and fair' have a technical meaning. It is also clear that many lawyers (as well as investors) are of the opinion that these words have a popular meaning which should be followed by those responsible for their application. (p. 259)

The following quotations serve to illustrate the two opposing viewpoints. First the lawyers:

> . . . it is probably not an exaggeration to assert that company accounts remain almost unintelligible to the general public, including shareholders and intending investors, and that practices continue which are difficult to reconcile with the statutory obligations that balance sheets give a true and fair view of the company's affairs and that the auditors certify that the accounts give a true and fair view of the company's affairs . . . Essentially, the question is: are the accounts where there has been an undervaluation of assets[3] 'true'? . . . 'True and fair' are unambiguous words. Practice needs to conform to the legal obligation. (Northey, 1965, pp. 41–42)

Although this view may have intuitive appeal, it does not give guidance as to how it may be operationalised. It does not recognise for example, that a range of possible 'true values' exist – historical cost, net realisable value, current replacement cost, going concern value and net present value. Which should be used to give a 'true and fair' view of asset values?

---

[3] As a result of adherence to historical cost principles.

Recognising such difficulties, accountants assert that criteria are needed to provide benchmarks against which the 'true and fair' requirement can be judged. This has resulted in accountants giving the phrase a technical interpretation. The Inflation Accounting (Sandilands) Committee (1975) explained this as follows:

> Accounts drawn up in accordance with generally accepted accounting principles, consistently applied, are in practice regarded as showing a 'true and fair view'. . . . The Acts . . . give only limited guidance to the accountancy profession in interpreting the phrase 'true and fair' and it has been traditionally left to the profession to develop accounting practices which are regarded as leading to a 'true and fair view' being shown. (paras 50 and 52)

From the above quotation, it appears that the Sandilands Committee was of the opinion that financial statements prepared in accordance with accounting standards will provide a true and fair view. This stance was supported by Counsel, whose opinion on the matter was sought by the Accounting Standards Board. Counsel stated:

> Accounts which meet the true and fair requirement will in general follow rather than depart from standards and [any] departure is sufficiently abnormal to require to be justified. . . . [it is likely] that the Courts will hold that in general compliance with accounting standards is necessary to meet the true and fair requirement. (Arden, 1993, para 7)

However, Counsel went on to observe:

> . . . true and fair is a dynamic concept. Thus what is required to show a true and fair view is subject to continuous rebirth. (Arden, 1993, para 14)

It is interesting to note that some commentators have expressed the view that the legislature deliberately delegated to the accountancy profession the task of defining what qualifies as 'true and fair' financial statements at any point of time. For example, Ryan (1974) (Commissioner for Corporate Affairs in New South Wales) observed that, if a court were called upon to determine whether a particular set of financial statements presented a true and fair view, the fact that they had or had not been drawn up in accordance with the principles embodied in professional pronouncements would be very persuasive. He continued:

> I have come to the conclusion . . . that in selecting the phrase 'true and fair view' as the standard by which the profit or loss of a company and the state of its affairs are to be judged, the Legislature in effect conferred a legislative function on the accountancy profession. It is a legislative function of an ambulatory nature: what is 'true and fair' at any particular point of time will correspond with what professional accountants as a body conceive to be proper accounting principles. The evolution, development and general acceptance of those principles will cause the concept of what is 'true and fair' to shift accordingly. (p. 14)

Although accountants have applied a technical interpretation to the phrase 'true and fair', they nevertheless acknowledge that financial statements drawn up in strict conformity with accounting standards may not, in all circumstances, provide the required true and fair view. This point was emphasised by Flint (1980) when he observed:

> ... prescription by legislation and professional standards and guidance statements ... [is] necessary in the interests of good order and effective communication. .... But giving a 'true and fair view' must always be a standard of a higher order. Whatever may be the extent of prescription, an overriding requirement to give a 'true and fair view' is, at the lowest level of its utility, a safety valve protecting users from bias, inadequacy or deficiency in the rules; a fail-safe device for the unavoidable shortcomings of prescription. More positively, its real utility is in establishing an enduring conceptual standard for disclosure in accounting and reporting to ensure that there is always relevant disclosure – where necessary beyond the prescription – based on an independent professional judgment. (p. 9)

Similarly, as noted in Chapter 5 (section 5.2.2), the Companies Act 1985 acknowledges that compliance with the legislation and accounting standards may not always result in the provision of a true and fair view. The Act provides that where compliance with the Act results in financial statements that are 'not sufficient to give a true and fair view', additional information is to be provided [CA 1985, s. 226(4)]. The Act also provides that where compliance with the legislative provisions would result in financial statements not giving a true and fair view, the provisions should be departed from to the extent necessary to give a true and fair view. In this situation, the departure, the reasons therefor, and its effect, are to be disclosed in a note to the financial statements [CA 1985, S. 226(5)]. Presumably, such a departure could only be justified on the grounds of providing a true and fair view.

Given the recognition that compliance with generally accepted accounting practice does not always result in a true and fair view, it is suggested that the most appropriate interpretation of the phrase lies somewhere between the literal and the technical viewpoints. This interpretation may be explained by drawing a parallel with a good landscape painting. Such a painting portrays the landscape so 'truly and fairly' that anyone seeing the picture will gain an impression of the scene depicted, similar to the one they would have gained had they been present when the picture was painted. In similar vein, in order to meet the 'true and fair' requirement, financial statements must portray the financial affairs of the reporting entity in such a way that anyone reading the statements can gain an impression of the entity's financial position and performance similar to the one they would have obtained had they personally monitored the recording of the entity's transactions.

Many of the items presented in financial statements are subject to judgment.[4] As a consequence, in order to provide a good reproduction of the entity's finan-

---

[4] For example, what allowance should be made for debts which might prove to be 'bad'? For how many accounting periods are long-term assets likely to generate income?

cial picture (and to avoid the impressionist artist's creativity) some conventions or rules are needed to guide and direct the exercise of that judgment. Such 'rules' are embodied in accounting standards (or SSAPs and FRSs) and other generally accepted accounting principles. For financial statements to meet the required standard, they must be presented in such a way as to create the 'correct' impression of the entity's financial affairs (Porter, 1990). In most circumstances this will be achieved through judgmental application of accounting standards to the particular circumstances of the auditee.

Similar ideas were expressed by Tweedie (1983) when he provided a test for evaluating whether or not a set of financial statements presents a true and fair view:

> While the detailed requirements necessary to show a true and fair view will continually evolve as social attitudes and technical skills change, the basic question to be posed by both director and auditor will remain. 'If', they should ask, 'if I were on "the outside" and did not have the detailed knowledge of the company's trading performance and ultimate financial position that I have as I look at these accounts, would I be able to obtain a clear and unambiguous picture of that reality from these accounts?' If the picture is poorly painted, or worse, fails to represent reality, then the directors have failed to meet the paramount principle of financial reporting – to show a true and fair view. (p. 449)

Although the concept of 'a true and fair view' has not been defined by statute or by a court of law and has been subject to different interpretations, the Auditing Practices Board (APB) has provided guidance to auditors on the criteria financial statements should meet in order to be adjudged true and fair. In SAS 600: *Auditors' reports on financial statements*, the Board explains that:

> Save in exceptional circumstances, compliance with accounting standards[5] is necessary to give a true and fair view. (para 39)

> Financial statements are normally required to contain particulars of any material departure from an accounting standard which applies to the reporting entity, together with the financial effects of the departure unless this would be impracticable or misleading in the context of giving a true and fair view. (para 40)

> There is no specific legal requirement that companies should comply with accounting standards. However, legislation in the UK gives specific recognition to accounting standards and requires large companies to state in their financial statements whether those statements have been prepared in accordance with such standards and to give particulars of any material departure and the reasons for it – paragraph 36A of Schedule 4 to the Companies Act 1985. (para 42)

Following on from the last point, the APB concludes:

> It is likely that a Court would infer from this requirement, taken together with other changes introduced into UK company law by the Companies Act 1989, that . . . in general, compliance with accounting standards is necessary to meet the

---

[5] 'Accounting standards' means Financial Reporting Standards (FRSs) and Statements of Standard Accounting Practice (SSAPs) issued by the Accounting Standards Board (ASB).

requirement of company law that the directors prepare annual accounts which give a true and fair view of a company's (or group's) state of affairs and profit or loss. (para 43)

As noted earlier, if (in exceptional circumstances) compliance with accounting standards would result in financial statements which do not provide a true and fair view, the directors of the reporting entity should depart from the relevant standard(s) and/or provide additional information and explanations so that a true and fair view is given. In forming an opinion as to whether or not a set of financial statements presents a true and fair view, the auditor must give due consideration to the information presented in the financial statements as a whole – including any 'additional information and explanations' which are provided.

Regarding the evaluation of financial statements by auditors, it should be remembered that the Companies Act 1989 requires all auditors of the financial statements of companies to be members of a recognised auditing body.[6] Further, every member of a recognised auditing body who conducts an audit must conduct that audit in accordance with auditing standards issued by the APB. As a consequence of these requirements, all auditors of company financial statements judge whether or not a particular set of financial statements gives the required true and fair view based on the same criteria. This provides for some uniformity of opinion as between different auditors working in similar circumstances. Additionally, the auditors' reporting standard (SAS 600) ensures that auditors use a similar format to report their opinion.

13.3   FORMAT OF AUDIT REPORTS

The format of standard audit reports is prescribed by SAS 600. The unqualified audit report given by KPMG on the financial statements of Diageo plc, presented in Figure 13.1, is an example of an audit report prepared in accordance with this auditing standard.

SAS 600 (para 14) specifies that audit reports should include:

(a) title identifying the person or persons to whom the report is addressed;
(b) an introductory paragraph identifying the financial statements audited;
(c) separate sections, appropriately headed, dealing with:
  (i)   the respective responsibilities of the directors (or their equivalent) and auditors,
  (ii) the basis of the auditors' opinion,
  (iii) the auditors' opinion on the financial statements;

---

[6] See Chapter 5, section 5.2.3.

Figure 13.1:   An example of a standard unqualified audit report

**Report of the auditors
to the members of Diageo plc**

We have audited the financial statements on pages 18 to 41.

Respective responsibilities of the directors and auditors The directors are responsible for preparing the Annual Report and Accounts. As described above, this includes responsibility for preparing the financial statements in accordance with applicable United Kingdom law and accounting standards. Our responsibilities, as independent auditors, are established in the United Kingdom by statute, the Auditing Practices Board, the Listing Rules of the Financial Services Authority,[7] and by our profession's ethical guidance.

We report to you our opinion as to whether the financial statements give a true and fair view and are properly prepared in accordance with the Companies Act. We also report to you if, in our opinion, the directors' report is not consistent with the financial statements, if the company has not kept proper accounting records, if we have not received all the information and explanations we require for our audit, or if information specified by law or the Listing Rules regarding directors' remuneration and transactions with the group is not disclosed.

We review whether the statement on page 11 reflects the company's compliance with the seven provisions of the Combined Code specified for our review by the Financial Services Authority,[8] and we report if it does not. We are not required to consider whether the board's statements on internal control cover all risks and controls, or form an opinion on the effectiveness of the group's corporate governance procedures or its risk and control procedures.

We read the other information contained in the Annual Report, including the corporate governance statement, and consider whether it is consistent with the audited financial statements. We consider the implications for our report if we become aware of any apparent misstatements or material inconsistencies with the financial statements.

Basis of audit opinion We conducted our audit in accordance with Auditing Standards issued by the Auditing Practices Board. An audit includes examination, on a test basis, of evidence relevant to the amounts and disclosures in the financial statements. It also includes an assessment of the significant estimates and judgements made by the directors in the preparation of the financial statements, and of whether the accounting policies are appropriate to the group's circumstances, consistently applied and adequately disclosed.

We planned and performed our audit so as to obtain all the information and explanations which we considered necessary in order to provide us with sufficient evidence to give reasonable assurance that the financial statements are free from material misstatement, whether caused by fraud or other irregularity or error. In forming our opinion we also evaluated the overall adequacy of the presentation of information in the financial statements.

Opinion In our opinion the financial statements give a true and fair view of the state of affairs of the company and the group as at 30 June 2001 and of the profit of the group for the year then ended and have been properly prepared in accordance with the Companies Act 1985.

KPMG Audit Plc
Chartered Accountants
Registered Auditor
London, 5 September 2001

---

[7] The United Kingdom Listing Authority (which is responsible for the Listing Rules) was transferred from the Stock Exchange to the Financial Services Authority in May 2000.

[8] The seven provisions of the Combined Code specified for the auditors' review are listed in Chapter 5, section 5.5.

(d) a manuscript or printed signature of the auditors;

(e) the date of the auditors' report.[9]

Regarding the respective responsibilities of the directors and auditors, SAS 600 (para 20) states that auditors' reports should include:

(i) a statement that the financial statements are the responsibility of the reporting entity's directors;

(ii) a reference to a description of those responsibilities when set out elsewhere in the financial statements or accompanying information; and

(iii) a statement that the auditors' responsibility is to express an opinion on the financial statements.

In relation to the basis of the auditors' opinion, the Standard (para 24) required auditors to include in their report:

(a) a statement as to their compliance or otherwise with Auditing Standards, together with the reasons for any departure therefrom;

(b) a statement that the audit process includes

   (i) examining, on a test basis, evidence relevant to the amounts and disclosures in the financial statements,

   (ii) assessing the significant estimates and judgments made by the reporting entity's directors in preparing the financial statements,

   (iii) considering whether the accounting policies are appropriate to the reporting entity's circumstances, consistently applied and adequately disclosed;

(c) a statement that they planned and performed the audit so as to obtain reasonable assurance that the financial statements are free from material misstatement, whether caused by fraud or other irregularity or error, and that they have evaluated the overall presentation of the financial statements.[10]

As regards dating the audit report, it was noted in Chapter 12 that the audit report date is extremely important as it signifies the date to which the auditor has considered events, the occurrence of which might impact on the truth and fairness of the financial statements. SAS 600 further explains:

---

[9] ISA 700: *The Auditor's report on financial statements* (para 5) contains similar requirements to SAS 600, para 14, but distinguishes between (i) a title to the report (which, it notes, should usually include the term 'Independent Auditor') and (ii) the addressee. It also refers to:

   (a) an opening or introductory paragraph (i) identifying the financial statements audited and (ii) stating the respective responsibilities of the entity's management and auditor;

   (b) a scope paragraph describing the nature of the audit and including:

      (i) a reference to the ISAs or relevant national standards;

      (ii) a description of the work the auditor performed;

   (c) opinion paragraph containing an expression of opinion on the financial statements;

   (d) date of the report;

   (e) auditor's address and signature.

It also comments on the desirability of the standard form of audit report 'because it helps to promote the readers' understanding and to identify unusual circumstances when they occur.'

[10] ISA 700, paras 12–14, contain similar provisions to SAS 600, para 24. However, it adds (in para 15):

The report should include a statement by the auditor [in the scope paragraph] that the audit provides a reasonable basis for the [audit] opinion.' This provision is additional to the 'statement that the audit was planned and performed to obtain reasonable assurance about whether the financial statements are free of material misstatement. (para 13).

Auditors should not express an opinion on financial statements until those statements and all other financial information contained in a report of which the audited financial statements form a part have been approved by the directors, and the auditors have considered all necessary available evidence. (para 76)

The date of the auditors' report is, therefore, the date on which, following

   a) receipt of the financial statements and accompanying documents in the form approved by the directors for release;
   b) review of all documents which they are required to consider in addition to the financial statements (for example the directors' report, chairman's statement or other review of an entity's affairs which will accompany the financial statements); and
   c) completion of all procedures necessary to form an opinion on the financial statements (and any other opinions required by law or regulation) including a review of post balance sheet events

the auditors sign (in manuscript) their report expressing an opinion on the financial statements for distribution with those statements. (para 80)

If the date on which the auditors sign their report is later than that on which the directors approved the financial statements, the auditors take such steps as are appropriate

   a) to obtain assurance that the directors would have approved the financial statements on that later date. . . ; and
   b) to ensure that their procedures for reviewing subsequent events cover the period up to that date. (para 83)[11]

The APB has developed illustrative examples of audit reports incorporating the various requirements noted above, and these are presented in SAS 600, Appendix 2, as supplemented by APB Bulletin 2001/2: *Revisions to the Wording of Auditors' Reports on Financial Statements and the Interim Review Report*[12] and APB Bulletin 2002/2: *The United Kingdom Directors' Remuneration Report Regulations.*[13] The APB clearly expects the examples to be followed closely, for the Standard states:

---

[11] ISA 700, para 24, conveys similar ideas to SAS 600, para 76, but is less precise in its requirements. It states: 'Since the auditor's responsibility is to report on the financial statements as prepared and presented by management, the auditor should not date the report earlier than the date on which the financial statements are signed or approved by management.' ISA 700 does not contain equivalent paragraphs to SAS 600, paras 80 and 83.

[12] The APB explains that the purpose of Bulletin 2001/2 is to update example auditors' reports; in particular:

   (a) to incorporate reference to the Listing Rules of the Financial Services Authority (FSA) instead of to the Listing Rules of the London Stock Exchange. This reflects the transfer of the United Kingdom Listing Authority from the Stock Exchange to the FSA in May 2000;
   (b) to insert reference in the title of the auditor's report to 'Independent Auditor'. (This is in line with ISA 700: see footnote 8);
   (c) to expand the description of auditors' responsibilities, especially in respect of information in the Annual Report other than the financial statements.

[13] The APB explains the purpose of Bulletin 2002/2 is to update example auditors' reports to incorporate reference to the Directors' Remuneration Report, which will be effective for financial years ending on or after 31 December 2002, brought into force by the United Kingdom Government. Quoted companies are required 'to prepare a Directors' Remuneration Report, for each financial year, that contains specified information, some of which is required to be audited' (para 1). The 'APB recommends that the opinion paragraph of the auditors' report for quoted companies [includes a statement to the effect that] . . . the financial statements and the part of the Directors' Remuneration Report to be audited have been properly

The use of common language in auditors' reports assists the reader's understanding. Accordingly, Appendix 2 [to the Standard] includes examples of auditors' reports on financial statements to illustrate wording which meets the Auditing Standards contained in this SAS. (para 16)

However, the Standard also notes that '[a]uditors draft each section of their report on financial statements to reflect the requirements which apply to the particular audit engagement' (para 16), therefore some differences may be expected.

Referring to Figure 13.1, it should be noted that, in accordance with SAS 600, the report identifies the persons to whom it is addressed (the members of Diageo plc) and the financial statements on which the audit report is given (identified by reference to the pages on which the statements are presented: this is specifically permitted by Bulletin 2001/2).[14] The report also contains separate, suitably headed, sections dealing with the respective responsibilities of the directors' and auditors, the basis of the auditors' opinion and the auditors' opinion on the financial statements. The report also includes the auditors' signature (in printed form) and the report is dated (5 September 2001). The captions and the wording used follow the example of an unqualified audit report provided in APB Bulletin 2001/2, Appendix 1. (This example supersedes Example 1 in SAS 600, Appendix 2.)

13.4   TYPES OF AUDIT REPORT

13.4.1   Overview of types of audit report

There are basically two types of audit report:

- an unqualified report (that is, a 'clean' report);
- a qualified report.

However, there are three types of qualified report, namely, those containing:

- an 'except for' opinion;
- an adverse opinion;
- a disclaimer of opinion.

As shown below, each type of report is appropriate for particular circumstances.

---

[13] *continued*

prepared in accordance with the Companies Act 1985' (para 10). However, '[a]s the auditors are not required to audit all of the information contained in the Directors' Remuneration Report they will need, in their report, to describe accurately which elements of the Directors' Remuneration Report they have audited' (para 12). In addition, the auditors need to consider whether the information provided in the unaudited part of the Directors' Remuneration Report is consistent with the audited financial statements. The audit report also needs to explain that it is the directors' responsibilities for preparing the Directors' Remuneration Report.

Appendix 1 of the Bulletin show an illustration of an auditors' report with changes that need to be made highlighted (para 11). Such changes are incorporated in Figures 13.3 and 13.5.

[14] Notwithstanding the recommendation of Bulletin 2001/2, in common with many other audit reports issued during 2001 and 2002, the title of the auditors' report on Diageo's financial statements does not describe the auditors as 'Independent'.

Irrespective of the type of audit report issued, the auditor should provide a clear expression of opinion on the financial statements and on any further matters required by statute or the particular engagement. The opinion should be based on review and assessment of the conclusions drawn from evidence obtained during the audit (SAS 600, paras 2 and 30). As noted in a fundamental principle of external auditing included in *The Auditor's Code* (APB, 1996) – *Clear Communication*, the audit report should also contain sufficient information for a reader to gain a proper understanding of the auditor's opinion. In the words of the principle:

> Auditors' reports contain clear expressions of opinion and set out information necessary for a proper understanding of that opinion.

13.4.2 Unqualified audit reports

SAS 600 explains:

> An unqualified opinion on financial statements is expressed when in the auditors' judgment they give a true and fair view ... and have been prepared in accordance with relevant accounting or other requirements. This judgment entails concluding whether *inter alia*
> - the financial statements have been prepared using appropriate accounting policies, which have been consistently applied;
> - the financial statements have been prepared in accordance with relevant legislation, regulations or applicable accounting standards (and that any departures are justified and adequately explained in the financial statements); and
> - there is adequate disclosure of all information relevant to the proper understanding of the financial statements. (para 32)[15]

The report on the 2001 financial statements of Diageo plc is an example of an unqualified audit report (see Figure 13.1).

13.4.3 Qualified audit reports

According to SAS 600 (para 33), a qualified opinion is expressed when:

(a) there is a limitation on the scope of the auditor's examination [i.e. the auditor is unable to examine all of the evidence (s)he considers necessary to form an unqualified opinion]; or

(b) the auditor disagrees with the treatment or disclosure of a matter in the financial statements.

---

[15] The equivalent provision in ISA 700, para 27, is worded in rather more general terms, as follows:

An unqualified opinion should be expressed when the auditor concludes that the financial statements give a true and fair view . . . in accordance with the identified financial reporting framework. An unqualified opinion also indicates implicitly that any changes in accounting principles or in the method of their application, and the effects thereof, have been properly determined and disclosed in the financial statements.

Although SAS 600 recognises these factors as causes of qualified audit opinions, it also indicates that such opinions should be expressed only if, in the auditor's judgment, the effect of the matter giving rise to concern 'is or may be material to the financial statements' and, as a result, the 'statements may not or do not give a true and fair view of the matters on which the auditors are required to report or do not comply with relevant accounting or other requirements' (para 33).

In cases where the auditor considers the effect of the matter in question is material to the financial statements, the type of qualified opinion expressed depends on the circumstances.

- If the auditor considers the effect of a limitation on the scope of the audit, or the effect of a disagreement, is not so significant as to prevent the expression of an opinion, or to cause the financial statements to be seriously misleading, as the case may be, the auditor will express an *except for* opinion. (That is, the auditor states that, in his or her opinion, the financial statements give a true and fair view of the reporting entity's state of affairs and profit or loss except for the matter(s) specified in the audit report) (paras 35 and 37).
- If the auditor considers the effect of a limitation on the scope of the audit is so material or pervasive that (s)he is unable to obtain sufficient evidence to support an audit opinion, a *disclaimer* of opinion is expressed. (That is, the auditor states that (s)he is unable to form an opinion on the financial statements) (para 36).
- If the auditor considers the effect of a disagreement is so material or pervasive that he concludes that the financial report is seriously misleading, an *adverse* opinion is expressed (that is, the auditor states that, in his or her opinion, the financial report does not give a true and fair view) (para 34).[16]

13.5   CIRCUMSTANCES GIVING RISE TO AUDIT QUALIFICATIONS

13.5.1   Limitation of audit scope

Scope limitations arise when circumstances exist which prevent the auditor from obtaining all of the evidence considered necessary for the purpose of the audit. Examples of scope limitations include the following:

---

[16] ISA 700, paras 36–39, explains a qualified ('except for') opinion, disclaimer of opinion, and adverse opinion, in similar terms to SAS 600, paras 33–37, but deals with each type of opinion in turn (rather than, as in SAS 600, in terms of disagreement and limitation on scope). It adds (para 40):

> Whenever the auditor expresses an opinion that is other than unqualified, a clear description of all the substantive reasons should be included in the report and, unless impracticable, a quantification of the possible effect(s) on the financial statements. Ordinarily, this information would be set out in a separate paragraph preceding the opinion or disclaimer of opinion and may include a reference to a more extensive discussion, if any, in a note to the financial statements.

- the inability to carry out certain audit procedures as a result of:
  - circumstances related to the timing of audit work (for example, where the auditor is newly appointed and, as a consequence, was unable to attend the previous year's stocktake);
  - circumstances beyond the control of the client and the auditor (for example, where accounting records are destroyed in a fire or flood);
  - limitations imposed by the client (for example, where the client does not permit the auditor to send confirmation requests to certain debtors and the relevant balances cannot be verified by alternative procedures);
- significant weaknesses in the internal control system which cannot be compensated for by alternative auditing procedures.

When there has been a limitation on the scope of the auditor's work, the auditor must decide whether the limitation is sufficient to prevent him or her from forming an opinion on the entity's financial statements. In reaching this decision the auditor should assess:

a) the quantity and type of evidence which may reasonably be expected to be available to support the particular figure or disclosure in the financial statements; and

b) the possible effect on the financial statements of the matter for which insufficient evidence is available. When the possible effect is, in the opinion of the auditors, material to the financial statements, there will be insufficient evidence to support an unqualified opinion. (SAS 600, para 69)[17]

The next step is to decide whether the possible effect of the limitation on the scope of the auditor's work is so material or pervasive that a disclaimer of opinion is appropriate. If the limitation on scope is material in its effect, but not so significant as to warrant a disclaimer, an 'except for' opinion should be expressed. In this event, SAS 600 requires the opinion to be worded so as to indicate 'that it is qualified as to the possible adjustments to the financial statements that might have been determined to be necessary had the limitation not existed' [para 68(c)].

Whenever an 'except for' or disclaimer of opinion is issued as a result of a scope limitation, the auditor's report should include, in the opinion section of the report, a description of the factors leading to the limitation [SAS 600, para 68(a)]. This enables the reader of the financial statements to understand the reasons for the limitation and to distinguish between those limitations which are beyond the control of the auditor and the auditee (such as a fire which destroys accounting records) and those which are imposed on the auditor by the client (for example, preventing certain debtors from being approached for confirmations of their account balances) (SAS 600, para 71).

---

[17] ISA 700, paras 41 and 42, explains the circumstances giving rise to a limitation on scope qualification in similar terms to SAS 600, para 71, but does not contain an equivalent paragraph to SAS 600, para 69.

Figure 13.2:   An 'except for' opinion arising from a scope limitation

---

Report of the Auditors

To the Shareholders of SSL International plc
We have audited the financial statements on pages 38 to 59 which have been prepared under the historical cost convention and the accounting policies set out on pages 42 to 43. We have also examined the amounts disclosed relating to the emoluments, share options, long-term incentive scheme interests and pension benefits of the Directors which form part of the remuneration report on pages 32 to 35.[18]

Respective Responsibilities of Directors and Auditors
The Directors are responsible for preparing the Annual Report including, as described on page 36, preparing the accounts in accordance with applicable United Kingdom law and accounting standards. Our responsibilities, as independent auditors, are established in the United Kingdom by statute, the Auditing Practices Board, the Listing Rules of the Financial Services Authority, and by our profession's ethical guidance.

We report to you our opinion as to whether the accounts give a true and fair view and are properly prepared in accordance with the Companies Act. We also report to you if, in our opinion, the Directors' report is not consistent with the accounts, if the Company has not kept proper accounting records, if we have not received all the information and explanations we require for our audit, or if information specified by law or the Listing Rules regarding Directors' remuneration and transactions with the Company and the Group is not disclosed.

We review whether the corporate governance statement on page 29 reflects the Company's compliance with the seven provisions of the Combined Code specified for our review by the Financial Services Authority, and we report if it does not. We are not required to consider whether the Board's statements on internal control cover all risks and controls, or form an opinion on the effectiveness of the Company's corporate governance procedures or its risk and control procedures.

We read the other information contained in the Annual Report, including the corporate governance statement, and consider whether it is consistent with the audited accounts. We consider the implications for our report if we become aware of any apparent misstatements or material inconsistencies with the accounts.

Basis of Audit Opinion
We conducted our audit in accordance with Auditing Standards issued by the Auditing Practices Board except that the scope of our work was limited as explained below. An audit includes examination, on a test basis, of evidence relevant to the amounts and disclosures in the accounts. It also includes an assessment of the significant estimates and judgements made by the Directors in the preparation of the accounts and of whether the accounting policies are appropriate to the circumstances of the Company and of the Group, consistently applied and adequately disclosed.

We planned and performed our audit so as to obtain all the information and explanations which we considered necessary in order to provide us with sufficient evidence to give reasonable assurance that the accounts are free from material misstatement, whether caused by fraud or other irregularity or error. In forming our opinion we also evaluated the overall adequacy of the presentation of information in the accounts.

---

[18] Although auditors are required to ensure compliance with the disclosure requirements relating to directors' emoluments and other benefits specified in the Companies Act 1985, Schedule 6, they are not required to specify in their audit report that they have examined various items in the remuneration report, until financial years ending on or after 31 December 2002 (see note 13).

However, as described in notes 2(c) and 33 to the financial statements, during the year the Directors initiated a review of the Group's sales practices, including the appropriateness and timing of the recognition of sales over the last three financial periods, the accounting for sales returns and the appropriateness of the accounting treatment of certain amounts recorded as rebates, discounts and other payments to certain customers. As a result of this review, the Directors have concluded that there were irregularities in the treatment previously accorded to certain sales, returns, credits to customers and stock write-offs in the financial periods 1999 to 2001 ('the irregularities') and in correcting these irregularities have restated the financial statements for prior periods. The irregularities which have been identified as a result of this review as attributable to prior periods have been written off by restating reserves brought forward at 1 March 1999 and the profit and loss account for the period ended 31 March 2000. In making this restatement, the Directors have necessarily had to make a number of judgements in estimating the effect of the irregularities on the previous periods' financial statements and on the reserves brought forward at 1 March 1999.

The Directors' investigation of these alleged irregularities is ongoing.

Limitations of scope
In the context of the above ongoing investigation, we have been unable to obtain sufficient evidence to form an opinion as to the appropriateness or completeness of the prior period adjustments, or on the attribution of the transactions and write-offs identified between the current and prior periods.

In certain cases the documentary evidence to determine both the recognition and the timing of certain sales, sales returns, credits to customers and stock write-offs, is either incomplete or unavailable. Many of the key management responsible for the transactions in question are no longer with the Group. On the basis of legal advice, the Directors have requested us not to communicate with certain of the Directors and staff who were employed by the Group during the financial years 1999 to 2001. Further, in view of the commercial sensitivity of the customer relationships concerned, we were also asked not to seek confirmation from customers in relation to the specific customer orders concerned or more generally in respect of the trading arrangements in prior periods.

Qualified opinion arising from limitation in audit scope
Except for any adjustment that might have been found to be necessary had we been able to obtain sufficient evidence concerning the appropriateness and completeness of the prior period adjustments, in our opinion the financial statements give a true and fair view of the state of affairs of the Company's and Group's affairs as at 31 March 2001 and of the profit or loss and cash flows of the Company and Group for the year then ended and have been properly prepared in accordance with the Companies Act 1985.

In respect of the limitation of the scope of our work relating to the appropriateness and completeness of the prior period items, we have not obtained all of the information and explanations that we considered necessary for the purposes of our audit and have been unable to determine whether proper accounting records have been maintained.

In our opinion, the subject matter of the above qualification is not material for determining by reference to the financial statements whether the distribution of £15.9 million proposed by the Company is permitted under section 270 of the Companies Act 1985.

Arthur Andersen
Chartered Accountants and Registered Auditors

Bank House
9 Charlotte Street
Manchester
M1 4EU   5 June 2001

Figure 13.3:   A disclaimer of opinion resulting from the loss of accounting records

INDEPENDENT AUDITORS' REPORT TO THE SHAREHOLDERS OF DET PLC

We have audited the financial statements of DET plc for the year ended 31 March 2002 which comprise the Profit and Loss Account, Balance Sheet, the Cash Flow Statement, the Statement of Total Recognised Gains and Losses and the related notes. These financial statements have been prepared under the historical cost convention as modified by the revaluation of certain fixed assets and the accounting policies set out therein. We have also audited the information in the Directors' Remuneration Report that is described as having been audited.

Respective responsibilities of directors and auditors

The directors' responsibilities for preparing the Annual Report, the Directors' Remuneration Report and the financial statements in accordance with applicable law and the United Kingdom Accounting Standards are set out in the Statement of Directors' Responsibilities.

Our responsibility is to audit the financial statements and the part of the Directors' Remuneration Report to be audited in accordance with relevant legal and regulatory requirements and United Kingdom Auditing Standards.

We report to you our opinion as to whether the financial statements give a true and fair view and whether the financial statements and the part of the Directors' Remuneration Report to be audited have been properly prepared in accordance with the Companies Act 1985. We also report to you if, in our opinion, the directors' report is not consistent with the financial statements, if the company has not kept proper accounting records, if we have not received all the information and explanations we require for our audit, or if information specified by law regarding directors' remuneration and transactions with the company and other members of the group is not disclosed.

We review whether the Corporate Governance Statement reflects the company's compliance with the seven provisions of the Combined Code specified for our review by the Listing Rules of the Financial Services Authority, and we report if it does not. We are not required to consider whether the board's statements on internal control cover all risks and controls, or form an opinion on the effectiveness of the group's corporate governance procedures or its risk and control procedures.

We read other information contained in the Annual Report and consider whether it is consistent with the audited financial statements. This other information comprises only the Directors' Report, the unaudited part of the Directors' Remuneration Report, the Chairman's Statement, the Operating and Financial Review and the Corporate Governance Statement. Our responsibilities do not extend to any other information.

Basis of opinion

We conducted our audit in accordance with Auditing Standards issued by the Auditing Practices Board, except that the scope of our work was limited as explained below.

An audit includes examination, on a test basis, of evidence relevant to the amounts and disclosures in the financial statements and the part of the Directors' Remuneration Report to be audited. It also includes an assessment of the significant estimates and judgments made by the directors in the preparation of the financial statements, and of whether the accounting policies are appropriate to the company's circumstances, consistently applied and adequately disclosed.

We planned our audit so as to obtain all the information and explanations which we considered necessary in order to provide us with sufficient evidence to give reasonable assurance that the financial statements and the part of the Directors' Remuneration Report to be audited are free from material misstatement, whether caused by fraud or other irregularity or error. However, the evidence available to us was limited because, as stated in note 20 on page 41 of the financial statements, a fire at the company's head office destroyed many of the accounting records. The financial statements consequentially include a number of material amounts based on estimates.

In forming our opinion we also evaluated the overall adequacy of the presentation of information in the financial statements and the part of the Directors' Remuneration Report to be audited.

Opinion: disclaimer on view given by financial statements

Because of the possible effect of the limitation in evidence available to us, we are unable to form an opinion as to whether the financial statements give a true and fair view of the state of the company's affairs as at 31 March 2002, or of its profit for the year then ended. In all other respects, in our opinion, the financial statements and the part of the Directors' Remuneration Report to be audited have been properly prepared in accordance with the Companies Act 1985.

In respect alone of the limitation on our work resulting from the destruction of many of the company's accounting records:

- we have not obtained all the information and explanations that we considered necessary for the purpose of our audit; and
- we were unable to determine whether proper accounting records have been maintained.

....
Registered auditors
25 May 2002   Newcastle

Source: Adapted from SAS 600, Appendix 2, Example 9, as amended by APB Bulletins 2001/2 and 2002/2.

Examples of qualified audit reports arising from scope limitations are presented in Figures 13.2 and 13.3.

- Figure 13.2 illustrates an 'except for' opinion expressed on SSL International plc's 2001 financial statements. This has resulted from insufficient evidence being available to the auditors (Arthur Andersen) to enable them to form an opinion as to the appropriateness or completeness of prior period adjustments, or on the attribution of the transactions and write-offs identified between the current and prior periods. The auditors explain that, in certain cases, the documentary evidence to determine the recognition and timing of certain sales, sales returns, credits to customers and stock write-offs is either incomplete or unavailable.
- Figure 13.3 illustrates a disclaimer of opinion expressed on a company's financial statements which has resulted from the loss of a company's accounting records. Disclaimers of opinion are rare forms of audit report and, as a result, 'actual' examples are difficult to locate. As a consequence, Figure 13.3 presents a fictitious example (adapted from SAS 600, Appendix 2, as amended by APB Bulletin 2001/2).

13.5.2   Disagreement

When the auditor disagrees with the accounting treatment of a particular item in the financial statements or disagrees with the way in which an item is disclosed, and the auditor considers that the effect of the matter with which (s)he disagrees is material to the financial statements, a qualified audit opinion is expressed. The type of qualification depends on the severity of the effect of the matter giving rise to the disagreement.

- If the effect of the matter in question is, in the auditor's opinion, so material or pervasive as to render the financial statements seriously misleading, an adverse opinion is expressed.
- If the effect of the matter is material to the financial statements, but not so material as to warrant an adverse report, an 'except for' opinion is expressed.

Whenever an 'except for' or adverse opinion is expressed as a result of a disagreement, the auditor is required by SAS 600, para 74(a), to include in the opinion section of the audit report:

- a description of all substantive factors giving rise to the disagreement;
- the implications of these factors for the financial statements; and
- whenever practicable, a quantification of the effect on the financial statements of the matter with which the auditor disagrees.

The auditor may also draw attention to relevant notes in the financial statements but, as SAS 600 emphasises:

such reference is not a substitute for sufficient description of the circumstances in the auditors' report so that a reader can appreciate the principal points at issue and their implications for an understanding of the financial statements. (para 75)[19]

Examples of qualified audit reports arising from disagreement are presented in Figures 13.4 and 13.5.

- Figure 13.4 illustrates an 'except for' opinion expressed on Plantation & General Investments plc's 2000 financial statements which has resulted from the auditor's (Hacker Young) disagreement with the accounting treatment of the group's overseas plantations. These have not been professionally valued as required by FRS 15.
- Figure 13.5 illustrates an adverse opinion expressed on the financial statements of a company which has arisen from the auditors' disagreement over the need to provide for an expected loss. Adverse opinions are rare forms of audit report and, as a result, 'actual' examples are difficult to locate. As a consequence, Figure 13.5 presents a fictitious example (adapted from SAS 600, Appendix 2, as amended by APB Bulletins 2001/2 and 2002/2).

13.6 TREATMENT OF INHERENT UNCERTAINTIES

Inherent uncertainties are defined in SAS 600, para 12, to mean '[a]n uncertainty whose resolution is dependent upon uncertain future events outside the control of the reporting entity's directors at the date the financial statements are approved'. Such an uncertainty is defined as a 'fundamental uncertainty' when:

... the magnitude of its potential impact is so great that, without clear disclosure of the nature and implications of the uncertainty, the view given by the financial statements would be seriously misleading.

The magnitude of an inherent uncertainty's potential impact is judged by reference to the risk that the estimate included in financial statements may be subject to change [in terms of] the range of possible outcomes, and the consequences of those outcomes on the view shown in the financial statements. (para 13)

Inherent uncertainties may affect, at least to some degree, quite a wide range of items in the financial statements. They arise as a result of particular circumstances and, at the time the entity's directors approve the financial statements, it is not possible to remove the uncertainty. Examples include:

---

[19] ISA 700 does not contain paragraphs equivalent to SAS 600, paras 74 and 75. In respect of disagreement giving rise to a qualified audit report it merely states (para 45):

The auditor may disagree with management about matters such as the acceptability of accounting policies selected, the method of their application, or the adequacy of disclosures in the financial statements. If such disagreements are material to the financial statements, the auditor should express a qualified or adverse opinion.

Figure 13.4: **An 'except for' opinion resulting from the auditors' disagreement with the accounting treatment of overseas plantations**

Auditor's Report to the shareholders of Plantation & General Investments Plc

We have audited the financial statements on pages 11 to 35 which have been prepared under the historical cost convention as modified by the revaluation of certain fixed assets and the accounting policies set out on pages 15 and 16.

Respective responsibilities of directors and auditors
As described on page 6, the directors are responsible for preparing the Annual Report, including the financial statements. Our responsibilities, as independent auditors, are established by statute, the Auditing Practices Board, the Listing Rules of the London Stock Exchange, and by our profession's ethical guidance.

We report to you our opinion as to whether the financial statements give a true and fair view and are properly prepared in accordance with the Companies Act. We also report to you if, in our opinion, the directors' report is not consistent with the financial statements, if the company has not kept proper accounting records, if we have not received all the information and explanations we require for our audit, or if information specified by law or the Listing Rules regarding directors' remuneration and transactions with the group is not disclosed.

We review whether the corporate governance statement on page 9 reflects the company's compliance with the seven provisions of the Combined Code specified for our review by the Stock Exchange, and we report if it does not. We are not required to consider whether the board's statements on internal control cover all risks and controls, or form an opinion as to the effectiveness of the group's corporate governance procedures or its risk and control procedures.

We read the other information contained in the Annual Report, including the corporate governance statement, and consider whether it is consistent with the audited financial statements. We consider the implications for our report if we become aware of any apparent misstatements or material inconsistencies with the financial statements.

Basis of opinion
We conducted our audit in accordance with Auditing Standards issued by the Auditing Practices Board. An audit includes examination, on a test basis, of evidence relevant to the amounts and disclosures in the financial statements. It also includes an assessment of the significant estimates and judgements made by the directors in the preparation of the financial statements, and of whether the accounting policies are appropriate to the company's circumstances, consistently applied and adequately disclosed.

We planned and performed our audit so as to obtain all the information and explanations which we considered necessary in order to provide us with sufficient evidence to give reasonable assurance as to whether the financial statements are free from material misstatement, whether caused by fraud or other irregularity or error.

The evidence available to us was limited in that plantations, factories and ancillary properties located overseas have been included in the balance sheet at valuations determined by the directors and not by qualified external valuers. As explained in note 1, the directors believe that reliable full valuations, as defined in Financial Reporting Standard 15, Tangible Fixed Assets (FRS 15) cannot be obtained.

Accordingly, there were no satisfactory audit procedures we could adopt to confirm that these properties were valued at their depreciated replacement cost at the balance sheet date. However we are not aware of any reasons to doubt the directors' analysis or the valuations of the directors.

In forming our opinion we also evaluated the overall adequacy of the presentation of information in the financial statements.

Qualified opinion arising from the lack of professional valuations
Included in the fixed assets shown on the balance sheet is an amount of £21,479,000 representing the group's overseas plantations, factories and ancillary property. These assets are carried at their current value at the balance sheet date but the valuations have been prepared by the directors. Full valuations, involving professionally qualified external valuers, are required to be obtained at least once every five years, with interim valuations at least once every three years, by FRS 15, but for the reasons set out in note 1, these have not been obtained.

Except for any adjustments that might have been found to be necessary had there been a full valuation of the group's overseas assets within the last five years, in our opinion the financial statements give a true and fair view of the state of the group's and the company's affairs as at 31 December 2000 and of the group's profit for the year then ended and have been properly prepared in accordance with the Companies Act 1985.

In respect alone of the limitation on our work relating to asset valuations we have not obtained all the information and explanations that we considered necessary for the purpose of our audit.

Hacker Young
Registered Auditor
Chartered Accountants   23 April 2001

Figure 13.5:   Adverse opinion resulting from auditors' disagreement over need to provide for an expected loss

---

INDEPENDENT AUDITORS' REPORT TO THE SHAREHOLDERS OF DSE PLC

We have audited the financial statements of DSE plc for the year ended 31 December 2002 which comprise the Profit and Loss Account, Balance Sheet, the Cash Flow Statement, the Statement of Total Recognised Gains and Losses and the related notes. These financial statements have been prepared under the historical cost convention as modified by the revaluation of certain fixed assets and the accounting policies set out therein. We have also audited the information in the Directors' Remuneration Report that is described as having been audited.

Respective responsibilities of directors and auditors
The directors' responsibilities for preparing the Annual Report, the Directors' Remuneration Report and the financial statements in accordance with applicable law and the United Kingdom Accounting Standards are set out in the Statement of Directors' Responsibilities.

Our responsibility is to audit the financial statements and the part of the Directors' Remuneration Report to be audited in accordance with relevant legal and regulatory requirements and United Kingdom Auditing Standards.

We report to you our opinion as to whether the financial statements give a true and fair view and whether the financial statements and the part of the Directors' Remuneration Report to be audited have been properly prepared in accordance with the Companies Act 1985. We also report to you if, in our opinion, the directors' report is not consistent with the financial statements, if the company has not kept proper accounting records, if we have not received all the information and explanations we require for our audit, or if information specified by law regarding directors' remuneration and transactions with the company and other members of the group is not disclosed.

We review whether the Corporate Governance Statement reflects the company's compliance with the seven provisions of the Combined Code specified for our review by the Listing Rules of the Financial Services Authority, and we report if it does not. We are not required to consider whether the board's statements on internal control cover all risks and controls, or form an opinion on the effectiveness of the group's corporate governance procedures or its risk and control procedures.

We read other information contained in the Annual Report and consider whether it is consistent with the audited financial statements. This other information comprises only the Directors' Report, the unaudited part of the Directors' Remuneration Report, the Chairman's Statement, the Operating and Financial Review and the Corporate Governance Statement. Our responsibilities do not extend to any other information.

Basis of opinion
We conducted our audit in accordance with Auditing Standards issued by the Auditing Practices Board. An audit includes examination, on a test basis, of evidence relevant to the amounts and disclosures in the financial statements and the part of the Directors' Remuneration Report to be audited. It also includes an assessment of the significant estimates and judgments made by the directors in the preparation of the financial statements, and of whether the accounting policies are appropriate to the company's circumstances, consistently applied and adequately disclosed.

We planned and performed our audit so as to obtain all the information and explanations which we considered necessary in order to provide us with sufficient evidence to give reasonable assurance as to whether the financial statements and the part of the Directors' Remuneration Report to be audited are free from material misstatement, whether caused by fraud or other irregularity or error. In forming our opinion we also evaluated the overall adequacy of the presentation of information in the financial statements and the part of the Directors' Remuneration Report to be audited.

Adverse opinion
As more fully explained in note 18, no provision has been made for losses expected to arise on certain long-term contracts currently in progress, as the directors consider that such losses should be off-set against amounts recoverable on other long-term contracts. In our opinion, provision should be made for foreseeable losses on individual contracts as required by Statement of Standard Accounting Practice 9. If losses had been so recognised the effect would have been to reduce the profit before and after tax for the year and the contract work in progress at 31 December 2002 by £2,874,000.

In view of the effect of the failure to provide for the losses referred to above, in our opinion the financial statements do not give a true and fair view of the state of the company's affairs as at 31 December 2002 and of its profit for the year then ended. In all other respects, in our opinion the financial statements and the part of the Directors' Remuneration Report to be audited have been properly prepared in accordance with the Companies Act 1985.

....
Registered auditors
28 March 2003   Bristol

Source: Adapted from SAS 600, Appendix 2, Example 10, as amended by APB Bulletins 2001/2 and 2002/2.

- uncertainty as to the outcome of litigation, or a dispute with the Inland Revenue;
- doubts about the ability of the entity to continue as a going concern.

Although inherent uncertainties cannot be resolved at the time the financial statements are approved, the financial statements can reflect the directors' assumptions regarding their financial outcome and, where material, describe the circumstances giving rise to the uncertainties and their potential financial effect (SAS 600, para 55).

When forming an opinion on a set of financial statements, auditors are required to consider, in the light of evidence available at the date on which they express that opinion, the adequacy of the accounting treatment, estimates, and disclosures of inherent uncertainties in the financial statements. More specifically, SAS 600, paras 56 and 58, require auditors to consider:

- the appropriateness of the accounting policies dealing with the uncertain matters;
- the reasonableness of the estimates included in the financial statements in respect of the inherent uncertainties; and
- the adequacy of disclosures relating to the inherent uncertainties.

When an auditor concludes that an inherent uncertainty has been properly accounted for and adequately disclosed in the financial statements, providing (s)he has no other concerns regarding the financial statements, an unqualified audit opinion is appropriate. However, in some circumstances, the auditor may conclude that, although an inherent uncertainty has been properly accounted for and adequately disclosed, the degree of uncertainty about its outcome and potential impact on the view given by the financial statements is so significant (or fundamental) that attention should be drawn to it in the audit report. In such cases, SAS 600 [para 54(b)] requires auditors to include an explanatory paragraph referring to the fundamental uncertainty in the 'basis of opinion' section of the audit report. The Standard also notes:

> When adding an explanatory paragraph, auditors should use words which clearly indicate that their opinion on the financial statements is not qualified in respect of its contents. [para 54(c)]

An example of an unqualified audit report which includes an explanatory paragraph referring to a fundamental uncertainty (identified as 'Going Concern') is presented in Figure 13.6. This report has been issued on the 2001 financial statements of Wiggins Group plc.

If, after considering the adequacy of the accounting treatment and disclosure of an inherent uncertainty in the financial statements, the auditor concludes that an inappropriate accounting policy has been adopted and/or the estimate of the outcome of the uncertainty is materially misstated and/or the disclosures relating

Figure 13.6: An unqualified opinion with an explanatory paragraph referring to a fundamental uncertainty (about the entity's ability to continue as a going concern)

Independent auditors' report to the shareholders of Wiggins Group plc

We have audited the accounts of Wiggins Group plc for the year ended 31 March 2001, which comprise the profit and loss account, the statement of total recognised gains and losses, consolidated balance sheet, company balance sheet, consolidated cash flow statement and notes to the accounts. These accounts have been prepared under the historical cost convention and the accounting policies set out therein.

Respective responsibilities of directors and auditors
The directors' responsibilities for preparing the Annual Report and accounts in accordance with applicable law and United Kingdom Accounting Standards are set out in the Statement of Directors' Responsibilities.

Our responsibility is to audit the accounts in accordance with relevant legal and regulatory requirements, United Kingdom Auditing Standards issued by the Auditing Practices Board and the Listing Rules of the Financial Services Authority.

We report to you our opinion as to whether the accounts give a true and fair view and are properly prepared in accordance with the Companies Act 1985. We also report to you if, in our opinion, the Directors' Report is not consistent with the accounts, if the Company has not kept proper accounting records, if we have not received all the information and explanations we require for our audit, or if information specified by law or the Listing Rules regarding directors' remuneration and transactions with the Group and the Company is not disclosed.

We review whether the Corporate Governance Statement reflects the Company's compliance with the seven provisions of the Combined Code specified for our review by the Listing Rules, and we report if it does not. We are not required to consider whether the board's statements on internal control cover all the risks and controls, or form an opinion on the effectiveness of the Group's and Company's corporate governance procedures or its risk and control procedures.

We read the other information contained in the Annual Report and consider whether it is consistent with the audited accounts. This other information comprises only the Directors' Report, the Chairman's Statement, the Review of Operations and the Corporate Governance Statement. We consider the implications for our report if we become aware of any apparent misstatements or material inconsistencies with the accounts. Our responsibilities do not extend to any other information.

Basis of audit opinion
We conducted our audit in accordance with United Kingdom Auditing Standards issued by the Auditing Practices Board. An audit includes examination, on a test basis, of evidence relevant to the amounts and disclosures in the accounts. It also includes an assessment of the significant estimates and judgements made by the directors in the preparation of the accounts, and of whether the accounting policies are appropriate to the Group's and the Company's circumstances, consistently applied and adequately disclosed.

We planned and performed our audit so as to obtain all the information and explanations which we considered necessary in order to provide us with sufficient evidence to give reasonable assurance that the accounts are free from material misstatement, whether caused by fraud or other irregularity or error. In forming our opinion we also evaluated the overall adequacy of the presentation of information in the accounts.

Going Concern
In forming our opinion, we have considered the adequacy of the disclosures made in the accounting policies of the accounts concerning the uncertainty as to the continuation of the Group's borrowing facilities. In view of the significance of this uncertainty we consider that it should be drawn to your attention but our opinion is not qualified in this respect.

Opinion
In our opinion the accounts give a true and fair view of the state of the Group's and the Company's affairs as at 31 March 2001 and of the Group's loss and cashflows for the year then ended and have been properly prepared in accordance with the Companies Act 1985.

HLB Kidsons
Registered Auditors
Chartered Accountants
Ocean House, Waterloo Lane
Chelmsford, Essex CM1 1BD   14 August 2001

to the uncertainty are inadequate, the auditor is required to issue an 'except for' or adverse opinion, as appropriate, for disagreement (SAS 600, para 60).[20]

13.7   THE AUDIT REPORT – THE AUDITOR'S CHANCE TO COMMUNICATE

When considering the standard form of audit report, it should be remembered that this report is the auditor's primary opportunity to communicate with users of the financial statements. If the auditor's opinion is to provide credibility to the financial statements [statements prepared by the entity's management, which essentially report on their own (that is, management's) performance], it is essential that financial statement users read and understand the audit report. Yet, as is shown below, evidence from many parts of the English-speaking world suggests that, particularly until the 'expanded' (or 'long form')[21] audit report was adopted a decade or so ago, this was not the case. Indeed, it was principally as a result of concern about the apparent ineffectiveness of the audit report as a means of communication that the former 'short form' standard audit report was replaced by an 'expanded' form of audit report.

An example of the short form audit report used in the UK prior to the adoption (in 1993) of the expanded report, is presented in Figure 13.7. It can be seen from this Figure that the report was characterised by its brevity. It merely stated that the accounts had been audited in accordance with auditing standards, they gave a true and fair view of the company's state of affairs and profit (or loss) and cash flows for the year, and that they complied with the Companies Act 1985.

From about the early 1970s, the apparent deficiencies of the short form audit report attracted considerable attention, particularly in the USA, Canada, UK and Australia. Studies by Lee and Tweedie (1975) in the UK and Wilton and Tabb (1978) in New Zealand, for example, found that little more than 50% of financial statement users read audit reports. Further, in the USA, the Commission on Auditors' Responsibilities (CAR, 1978; the Cohen Commission) found that the standard short form audit report (then in use) served to confuse rather than inform financial statement users. The Commission noted, for example, that 'users are unaware of the limitations of the audit function and

---

[20] In Chapter 12, the auditor's reporting options with respect to a material uncertainty relating to the entity's status as a going concern are depicted in Figure 12.5. Similar options arise in relation to any material uncertainty.

[21] The equivalent of what is known in the UK as the 'expanded' audit report is referred to as the 'long form' report in countries such as the USA, Australia and New Zealand.

Figure 13.7:   Example of the standard unqualified (short form) audit report used until 1993

Report of the auditors

To the members of The Peninsular and Oriental Steam Navigation Company

We have audited the accounts on pages 27 to 49 in accordance with Auditing Standards.

In our opinion the accounts give a true and fair view of the state of affairs of the Company and the Group at 31 December 1991 and of the profit and cash flows of the Group for the year then ended and have been properly prepared in accordance with the Companies Act 1985.

London   KPMG Peat Marwick
24 March 1992   Chartered Accountants
                                                                                    Registered Auditor

---

are confused about the distinction between the responsibilities of management and that of the auditor' (p. 71). Surveys conducted by researchers such as Lee (1970) in the UK, Beck (1973) in Australia, the Macdonald Commission (CICA, 1988) in Canada, and Porter (1993) in New Zealand, provide support for the Cohen Commission's conclusions. These surveys found that a significant number of auditee representatives (directors, senior executives, chief accountants and internal auditors of companies), as well as financial statement users, believed that auditors are responsible for preparing auditees' financial statements, that auditors verify *every* transaction of the entity, and that a 'clean' audit report signifies the auditor guarantees that the financial statements are accurate and/or that the reporting entity is financially secure.

Woolf (1979), looking at the issue from a different perspective, drew attention to the irony of the long and complex audit process culminating in such a brief report. He highlighted his point by citing a study conducted in the USA by Seidler:

> Seidler of New York University observed that the 1975 annual report of Arthur Andersen and Co. [one of the world's 'Big 5' audit firms] revealed that 6.6% of the firm's total revenue was received from five clients . . . whose annual fees averaged about $5.1 million each. . . . The audit fee element in each approximated $3.4 million[22] and further analysis showed that this fee represented approximately 95 man years, or 128,000 hours of work – a truly prodigious expenditure of skilled auditing labour. On the assumption that the five clients were among the firm's largest, Seidler identified . . . [them] and then proceeded to count the number of words in the audit reports to their shareholders. He found that such lavish audit scrutiny – the equivalent of work of 95 professionals labouring for an entire year – had resulted, on average, in an expression of findings occupying no more than 175

---

[22] This $3.4 million average audit fee was in 1975 – nearly 30 years ago!!

words! . . . A situation, one has to concede, which has no parallel in any other sphere of investigative reporting. (pp. 223–224)

Concerned about the apparent shortcomings of the short form audit report, and stimulated by the Cohen Commission's (CAR, 1978) observation that 'the auditor's standard audit report is almost the only formal means used both to educate and inform users of financial statements concerning the audit function', the professional accountancy bodies in most parts of the English-speaking world developed and adopted an expanded form of audit report. More specifically, since 1988, new auditing standards prescribing the use of an expanded audit report have been issued by the American Institute of Certified Public Accountants (AICPA), the Canadian Institute of Chartered Accountants (CICA), the Auditing Practices Board (APB) (UK), the Australian Accounting Research Foundation (AARF), the New Zealand Society of Accountants (NZSA),[23] and the International Federation of Accountants (IFAC). In each case, unlike its predecessor short form report, the new expanded report included, *inter alia*:

- a statement explaining the respective responsibilities of the directors and auditor for the entity's financial statements;
- a brief description of the audit process;
- a statement that an audit is planned and performed so as to obtain sufficient evidence to give reasonable assurance that the financial statements are free (or not free, as the case may be) of material misstatement, whether caused by fraud, other irregularity or error.

An example of the expanded form of audit report adopted in the UK in 1993 is presented in Figure 13.8. This shows the unqualified audit report issued by Ernst & Young on the 1995 financial statements of British Airways plc.

The primary motive for the professional accountancy bodies adopting the expanded audit report was to educate financial statement users about the respective responsibilities of the directors and auditors for the financial statements, the audit process, and the level of assurance provided by the auditor's opinion. Studies by Kelly and Mohrweis (1989), Hatherly *et al.* (1991) and Zachry (1991), among others, suggest that use of the expanded report has achieved some success in meeting its objectives. However, this has been at the cost of changing the audit report into a longer and more complex document. Further, questions have been raised, for example by Alfano (1979), about the ease with which a financial statement user can determine whether or not the auditor has reservations about the financial statements, and the value of explaining *in the audit report* the responsibilities of the directors and auditors

---

[23] The NZSA is now known as the Institute of Chartered Accountants of New Zealand (ICANZ).

for the financial statements. To Alfano, this merely enables financial statement users to allocate blame if something is wrong. Additionally, commentators such as Elliott and Jacobson (1987) have questioned the ability of a few sentences in the audit report to convey adequately the essence of the audit process. Further, Epstein (1976) found that financial statement users 'are not interested in the details of an audit' but 'are looking for a seal of approval' (as reported, CAR, 1978, p. 164). As Alfano (1979) has expressed it: 'the reader wants to know whether the statements are right or wrong' (p. 39) – a fact they could glean by merely glancing at the former short form report. Certainly it seems pertinent to ask whether financial statement users require details of the auditor's and the

Figure 13.8: Example of the standard unqualified (expanded form) audit report adopted in the UK in 1993

Report of the auditors to the members of British Airways Plc

We have audited the accounts on Pages 16 to 47, which have been prepared under the historical cost convention as modified by the revaluation of certain fixed assets and on the basis of the accounting policies set out on Pages 20 to 22.

Respective responsibilities of Directors and auditors
As described above, the Company's Directors are responsible for the preparation of the accounts. It is our responsibility to form an independent opinion, based on our audit, on those accounts and to report our opinion to you.

Basis of opinion
We conducted our audit in accordance with Auditing Standards issued by the Auditing Practices Board. An audit includes examination, on a test basis, of evidence relevant to the amounts and disclosures in the accounts. It also includes an assessment of the significant estimates and judgements made by the Directors in the preparation of the accounts and of whether the accounting policies are appropriate to the Group's circumstances, consistently applied and adequately disclosed.

We planned and performed our audit so as to obtain all the information and explanations which we considered necessary in order to provide us with sufficient evidence to give reasonable assurance that the accounts are free from material misstatement, whether caused by fraud or other irregularity or error. In forming our opinion we also evaluated the overall adequacy of the presentation of information in the accounts.

Opinion
In our opinion the accounts give a true and fair view of the state of affairs of the Company and of the Group as at 31 March 1995 and of the profit of the Group for the year then ended and have been properly prepared in accordance with the Companies Act 1985.

Ernst & Young
Chartered Accountants
Registered Auditor
London   11 May 1995

directors' responsibilities for the financial statements, and a standard description of the audit process, in *every* audit report. Financial statement users need to be informed of these matters at least once, but ways more appropriate than including it in every audit report could perhaps have been found. According to critics of the expanded audit report (such as those named above), including the information in the audit report detracts from fulfilment of the report's primary function; that is, conveying the auditor's opinion on the accompanying financial statements.

Notwithstanding the criticism levelled against the expanded audit report, since 1993 its wording has been amended to provide even more information. Comparison of the unqualified audit report issued by Ernst & Young on British Airways' 1995 financial statements (which followed the example wording provided in SAS 600 in 1993; see Figure 13.8) with that issued by KPMG on Diageo's 2001 financial statements (reflecting the amended wording provided in the APB's Bulletin 2001/2; see Figure 13.1) shows that the current form of audit report is much longer than its 1993 counterpart. It provides, in particular, far more detail about the responsibilities of auditors. More specifically, it now includes information explaining:

(i)   the matters on which auditors are required to report if the entity has not complied with certain statutory and/or regulatory requirements (for example, if the entity has not disclosed required information relating to directors' remuneration and transactions with the group);
(ii) auditors' responsibility with respect to the seven provisions of *The Combined Code* they are required to review. It also highlights certain corporate governance matters that fall outside auditors' responsibilities (for example, forming an opinion on the effectiveness of the group's corporate governance, risk and control procedures);
(iii) that auditors read other information in the Annual Report to identify any apparent misstatements or material inconsistencies with the financial statements. [Although not referred to in KPMG's report on Diageo's 2001 financial statements, the example reports provided in Bulletin 2001/2 indicate that the audit report should identify the 'other information' the auditor is required to read, namely, the Directors' Report, Chairman's Statement, the Operating and Financial Review and Corporate Governance Statement, and to state that their responsibilities do not extend beyond these documents: see Figures 13.3, 13.5, and 13.6 which reflect the APB's guidance.]

The auditor's report is also to include, for accounts ending on or after 31 December 2002, reference to the auditor's responsibilities regarding the Directors' Remuneration Report referred to in the APB's Bulletin 2002/2: see Figures 13.3 and 13.5 and Note B.

The APB's Bulletin 2001/2 also recommends inclusion of the term 'Independent Auditor' in the title to the auditor's report;

> to better distinguish the auditors' report from reports that might be issued by others, such as by officers of the entity, the board of directors, or internal auditors who may not have to abide by the ethical guidance that applies to independent auditors. (para 6)[24]

['Independent Auditor' is included in the title of the audit reports presented in Figures 13.3, 13.5 and 13.6.]

A further change introduced by Bulletin 2001/2 is identification, in the introductory paragraph of the audit report, of the individual statements comprising the audited financial statements (i.e. the Profit and Loss Account, Balance Sheet, Cash Flow Statement, Statement of Total Recognised Gains and Losses, and related notes).[25] However, it notes that, while such identification is necessary for audit reports which are attached to entities' financial statements published on a website (or other electronic media), when the financial statements are published within an entity's Annual Report, the relevant statements; (and related notes) may be identified by means of page references. (The latter course has been followed by KPMG on Diageo's 2001 financial statements: see Figure 13.1.)

From Figures 13.1 to 13.6 it may be seen that the current expanded audit report is long and complex. Nevertheless, it provides the reader with useful information about the auditor's responsibilities and the basis for the auditor's opinion. This should increase the understanding of users of the financial statements about the audit and the reliance they may (justifiably) place on the auditor's opinion. Further, section headings reduce the report's complexity by providing guidance to readers about the content of the various sections.

Despite its apparent advantages, critics of the expanded report suggest that although it is informative there is a danger that, because of its standard format and length, as readers become familiar with it, it will not be read and important information will be missed. In other words, it will become a 'symbol' in the same way as the short form audit report came to be treated as a symbol.

One possibility that has been suggested to overcome this difficulty is that, instead of every audit report containing a standard description of the auditor's responsibilities and the audit process, each report could contain a description of any particular features or difficulties encountered during the audit in question and how they were resolved. Such a move away from standardised wording is

---

[24] In this requirement the APB has followed ISA 700, para 6.
[25] The Bulletin 2002/2 also requires reference to the Directors' Remuneration Report.

more likely to encourage each audit report to be read, and the particular context of each audit opinion to be better understood. However, the absence of standardised wording may cause confusion for financial statement users as to the auditor's precise meaning. Further, if each audit report were to be individually compiled, this would be time-consuming and costly for the auditors and may result in the inadvertent failure to meet all statutory and/or regulatory requirements.

13.8 THE COMMUNICATION OF AUDIT MATTERS TO THOSE CHARGED WITH GOVERNANCE (AND MANAGEMENT LETTERS)

In addition to issuing audit reports on the financial statements, it is standard practice for auditors to provide a report to the auditee's directors on various aspects of the audit. SAS 610 (Revised): *Communication of audit matters to those charged with governance,* provides guidance for auditors on these communications (which we refer to as 'governance communications'). It states:

> Auditors should communicate relevant matters relating to the audit of financial statements to those charged with governance of the entity.[26] Such communications should be on a sufficiently prompt basis to enable those charged with governance to take appropriate action. (para 2)

It goes on to explain that the purpose of these communications is to enable auditors to:

- ensure there is a mutual understanding of the scope of the audit and the respective responsibilities of the auditors and the directors;
- share information to assist both the auditors and the directors fulfil their respective responsibilities; and
- provide to the directors constructive observations arising from the audit process. (para 3)

Communicating audit matters to those charged with governance accords with the fundamental principle of external auditing included in *The Auditor's Code* (APB, 1996) – Providing Value. This states:

> Auditors add to the reliability and quality of financial reporting; they provide to directors and officers constructive observations arising from the audit process; and thereby contribute to the effective operation of business, capital markets and the public sector.

---

[26] In the case of companies, the directors are 'charged with the governance of the entity'. However, the board of directors may delegate their responsibilities in respect of the audit to a sub-committee of the board, i.e. the audit committee.

ISA 260: *Communication of audit matters with those charged with governance*, para 2, is almost identical to the first sentence of SAS 610, para 2. The need to communicate matters on a timely basis is referred to in ISA 260, para 13.

Although auditors should provide a governance communication as an outcome of all audits of companies' financial statements, the form, content and frequency of the communication varies widely – reflecting variations in the size, complexity, organisation and nature of auditees, as well as in auditors' views about the importance of matters relevant to the audit. The larger and more complex the organisation, the more formal the governance communication is likely to be.

The communication may be made orally and/or in writing. SAS 610 (para 15) observes that the auditor's decision as to the appropriate form of communication is affected by a number of factors including:

- the size, operating structure, legal structure and communication process of the entity being audited;
- the nature, sensitivity and significance of the matters being communicated;
- statutory and regulatory requirements; and
- the arrangements made with respect to periodic meetings or reporting of significant matters.

When audit matters are communicated orally (for example, by means of a presentation to the directors by the audit engagement partner and the audit manager), the matters so communicated, and the directors' response thereto, are generally confirmed in writing to the directors and also documented in the audit working papers.

Prior to communicating audit matters to the directors, auditors ordinarily discuss the matters to be communicated with the auditee's senior executives (termed 'management' in SAS 610). This enables facts and issues to be clarified and gives the executives an opportunity to provide further information and explanations. SAS 610 also notes (paras 19 and 20):

> If management agrees to communicate certain matters to those charged with governance, the auditors may not need to repeat the communication provided that they are satisfied that such communication is made and conveys, in an appropriate manner, relevant facts and conclusions.
> Auditors incorporate in their communication of matters to those charged with governance comments made by management, where those comments will aid the understanding of those charged with governance, and any actions management have indicated that they will take.

Such actions may relate, for example, to the rectification of weaknesses in internal control procedures identified by the auditor and reported to the executives.

Regarding the content of governance communications, SAS 610 identifies three groups of matters to be communicated, namely:

(i) relationships that may have some bearing on the audit firm's independence and the objectivity of the audit engagement partner and audit staff;

(ii)   audit planning information; and

(iii) findings from the audit.[27]

(i)   Independence relationships

In this regard, SAS 610 (para 24) specifies that, for auditees that are listed companies, auditors should, at least annually:

(a)   disclose in writing to the audit committee, and discuss as appropriate:
   - all relationships between the audit firm and its related entities and the client entity and its related entities that may reasonably be thought to bear on the firm's independence and the objectivity of the audit engagement partner and the audit staff; and
   - the related safeguards that are in place; and

(b)   where this is the case, confirm in writing to the audit committee that, in their professional judgment, the firm is independent within the meaning of regulatory and professional requirements and the objectivity of the audit engagement partner and audit staff is not impaired.

This requirement underlines the importance the auditing profession places on auditors being, and being seen to be, independent of their audit clients. It also accords with SAS 240: *Quality control for audit work,* which requires audit engagement partners to consider whether adequate arrangements are in place to safeguard their objectivity and the firm's independence (para 45). It similarly accords with the provisions of *The Combined Code* (Committee on Corporate Governance, 1998) which require the audit committees of listed companies to keep under review the independence and objectivity of the company's auditors

---

[27] In respect of the content of governance communications, ISA 260 is far more limited that SAS 610. Independence is not referred to and the remaining sections (modification of the audit report, audit planning and audit findings) are combined in a single paragraph as follows:

The auditor should consider audit matters of governance interest that arise from the audit of the financial statements and communicate then with those charged with governance. Ordinarily such matters include:

- The general approach and overall scope of the audit, including any expected limitations thereon, or any additional requirements;
- The selection of, or changes in, significant accounting policies and practices that have, or could have, a material effect on the entity's financial statements;
- The potential effect on the financial statements of any significant risks and exposures such as pending litigation, that are required to be disclosed in the financial statements;
- Audit adjustments, whether or not recorded by the entity that have, or could have, a significant effect on the entity's financial statements;
- Material uncertainties related to events and conditions that may cast significant doubt on the entity's ability to continue as a going concern;
- Disagreements with management about matters that, individually, or in aggregate, could be significant to the entity's financial statements or the auditor's report . . .;
- Expected modifications to the auditor's report;
- Other matters warranting attention by those charged with governance, such as material weaknesses in internal control, questions regarding management integrity, and fraud involving management;
- Any other matters agreed upon in the terms of the audit engagement. (para 11)

(Provision D.3.2). SAS 610 explains that, in order to assist audit committees fulfil this responsibility:

> [A]uditors make the audit committee aware of relationships that could reasonably be perceived as threatening their objectivity and the firm's independence (e.g. the total amount of fees the firm earns from the provision of other services to the entity) and of the safeguards that are in place. (para 28)

(ii) Audit planning information

Auditors are required to communicate to the directors (or audit committee):

> an outline of the nature and scope, including, where relevant, any limitations thereon, of the work they propose to undertake and the form of the reports they expect to make... Matters that might be communicated in outline include:
> - the concept of materiality and its application to the audit approach;
> - the way the auditors propose to address the risk of material misstatements, with particular reference to areas of higher risk;
> - the auditors' approach to the assessment of, and reliance on, internal controls;
> - the extent, if any, to which reliance will be placed on the work of internal audit and on the way in which the external and internal auditors can best work together on a constructive and complementary basis. ....(paras 29 and 30)[28]

However, SAS 610 does not envisage the communication to be solely one way – from the auditor to the entity's directors. It also highlights matters (in para 32) that auditors may find beneficial to discuss with the directors (or audit committee). For example:

- the views of the directors about the nature and extent of significant internal and external operational, financial, compliance and other risks facing the entity, their probability of occurrence and how they are managed;
- the control environment within the entity and whether the directors have a process for monitoring the effectiveness of the entity's internal control system. If a review of the effectiveness of the system has taken place, the results of that review;
- actions the directors propose to take in relation to developments in, for example, legislation, accounting standards, corporate governance reporting, listing rules, and other developments relevant to the entity's financial statements and annual report;
- actions taken by the directors and senior managers in response to previous communications from the auditors. If significant matters raised previously have not been dealt with effectively, the auditors should enquire as to why appropriate action has not been taken. They should also consider raising the

---

[28] We noted in Chapter 7, section 7.3, that information of this nature is generally included in the audit engagement letter. SAS 610 notes that 'matters that are included in the audit engagement letter need not be repeated [in the governance communication]' (para 31). Internal audit is discussed in Chapter 16.

matter(s) again, in the current communication, or they may give the impression that the matters are no longer of significance.

(iii) Findings from the audit

Auditors are required to communicate to the directors a number of matters arising from their audit. These include:

- expected modifications of the audit report;
- unadjusted misstatements in the financial statements and/or other information in the annual report;
- qualitative aspects of the entity's accounting practices and financial reporting;
- material weaknesses in the accounting and internal control systems identified during the audit.

Expected modifications of the audit report: According to SAS 610 (para 34), expected modification of the audit report should be discussed with the directors so as to:

- make them aware of the proposed modification, and the reasons therefor, before the report is finalised;
- make sure there are no disputed facts in respect of the matter(s) giving rise to the proposed modification;
- give the directors the opportunity to provide additional information and explanations in respect of the matter(s) giving rise to the proposed modification.

Unadjusted misstatements: Where the auditee's senior managers do not adjust misstatements identified by the auditor, such misstatements should be communicated to the directors with a request that the required adjustments be made. If the directors refuse to effect the adjustments, the auditor should discuss with them their reasons for, and appropriateness of, their refusal and also consider the implication of the effect of the unadjusted misstatements for the audit report. SAS 610 also notes:

> Auditors should seek to obtain a written representation from those charged with governance that explains their reasons for not adjusting misstatements brought to their attention by the auditors. ... [Such] a representation is obtained to reduce the possibility of misunderstandings concerning their reasons for not making the adjustments. A summary of the unadjusted misstatements [should be] included in, or attached to, the representation letter. (paras 36 and 37)[29]

Qualitative aspects of accounting practices and financial reporting: SAS 610 explains:

> In the course of their audit of the financial statements, auditors consider the qualitative aspects of the financial reporting process, including items that have a

---

[29] Management representation letters are discussed in Chapter 12, section 12.5.

significant impact on the relevance, reliability, comparability and materiality of the information provided by the financial statements. Auditors discuss in an open and frank manner with those charged with governance the auditors' views on the quality and acceptability of the entity's accounting practices and financial reporting. (para 41)

Matters likely to be discussed include:

- in cases where accounting standards provide some choice of accounting policy, the appropriateness of policies selected to the particular circumstances of the auditee.[30] Where the auditor considers that an inappropriate policy has been adopted, (s)he should request the directors to make appropriate changes. If the directors refuse to do so, the auditor needs to consider whether the effect of adopting the inappropriate policy is material to the truth and fairness of the financial statements and, if so, the implications for the audit report;
- the timing of transactions and the reporting period in which they are recorded;
- the appropriateness of accounting estimates (for example, the allowance for bad debts);
- the potential effect on the financial statements of any material uncertainties, including significant risks and exposures (such as pending litigation) and those that may cast doubt on the ability of the entity to continue as a going concern;
- the extent to which the financial statements are affected by unusual transactions including exceptional items such as non-recurring profits and losses recognised during the period;
- disagreements about matters that, individually or in aggregate, could be significant to the entity's financial statements or the audit report;
- apparent misstatements in information other than the financial statements included in the entity's annual report and material inconsistencies between the other information and the audited financial statements.

Material weaknesses in the accounting and internal control systems identified during the audit: SAS 610 defines a material weakness in the accounting and internal control system as:

> [A] deficiency in design or operation which could adversely affect the entity's ability to record, process, summarise and report financial and other relevant data so as to result in a material misstatement in the financial statements. (para 38)

Prior to publication of SAS 610: *Communication of audit matters to those charged with governance* (in 2001) and its predecessor SAS 610: *Reports to*

---

[30] Although some accounting standards provide a choice of accounting policies, FRS 18: *Accounting Policies*, states:

> Where it is necessary to choose between accounting policies . . . an entity should select [the policy] judged by the entity to be most appropriate to its particular circumstances for the purpose of giving a true and fair view. (para 17)

directors and managers (published in 1995), auditors routinely reported to the auditee's directors and/or senior managers, in what was called a Management Letter, material weaknesses in the accounting and internal control systems discovered during the audit. In addition to noting the existence and effect of the weaknesses, recommendations were made as to ways in which they might be rectified.

Management letters were usually provided at the conclusion of both the interim and the final audit. The interim letter, which reported accounting and internal control system weaknesses discovered during the interim audit, was sent to the audit committee or senior executives (such as the Managing Director and/or the Finance Director) as soon as possible after the interim audit so that weaknesses could be rectified on a timely basis. The final management letter was frequently broader in nature and usually included comments on the conduct and findings of the audit as a whole. However, the main focus was generally on matters relating to the entity's accounting and internal control systems and/or its financial affairs, where the auditor considered improvements could be made.

The governance communication now required by SAS 610 has, in essence, developed from the former final management letter but, as indicated above, it is much broader in scope than its predecessor. However, reporting material weaknesses in the client's accounting and internal control systems discovered during an audit remains a significant component of the communication. Further, in most audits, the auditor continues to send an interim management letter covering weaknesses discovered during the interim audit and, in many cases, the auditor supplements the governance communication with more detailed information about material weakness in the accounting and internal control systems, their effect and how they might be rectified. This supplementary information may be sent to the directors (or audit committee) and/or to the senior managers with day-to-day responsibility for the accounting and internal control systems and financial reporting process.

SAS 610 seems to acknowledge that auditors may send interim management letters and/or supplement their governance communications with details of accounting and internal control system weaknesses discovered during the audit as it states:

> Auditors normally do not need to communicate information concerning a material weakness of which those charged with governance are aware and in respect of which, in the view of the auditors, appropriate corrective action has been taken, unless the weakness is symptomatic of broader weaknesses in the overall control environment and there is a risk that other material weaknesses may occur. Material weaknesses of which the auditors are aware are communicated where they have been corrected by management without the knowledge of those charged with governance. (para 38)

Management letters are private communications between the auditor and the directors of the client entity. They constitute a valuable service to the client which, among other things, assists those responsible to improve the entity's accounting and internal control systems and financial reporting process. With improvements in these regards, the auditor's confidence about the completeness, accuracy and validity of the accounting data may well increase, and thus the audit work required to form an opinion about the financial statements (and hence audit fees) may, in subsequent years, be reduced.

13.9 SUMMARY

In this chapter we have discussed the reports that auditors provide for users of audited financial statements and for those charged with the governance of reporting entities. We have examined the standard form of audit report used for companies in the UK and Republic of Ireland and discussed the various types of audit opinion which may be expressed and the circumstances in which each is appropriate. We have also considered differences between the expanded form of audit report and its short form predecessor. We have noted that the expanded report was introduced to reduce misconceptions about the auditor's (*vis-à-vis* the directors') responsibility for the financial statements, the level of assurance provided by the audit report and the audit process. But we have also seen that the result has been a longer and more complex document which some commentators maintain is less effective than the former short form report in communicating the auditor's key message about the accompanying financial statements. However, notwithstanding the reservations of some commentators about the expanded audit report, we have observed that in recent years the APB has required additional information about auditors' responsibilities to be included.

In the final sections of the chapter we have given some attention to auditors' communications to those charged with the governance of auditees. We have noted that the auditor's report to users of the financial statements is a statutory requirement whose content is largely defined by the Companies Act 1985. It is required to be filed at Companies House and thus it is a public document. Governance communications are, however, private communications between the auditor and the auditee's directors. They are designed to ensure that the directors have no misconceptions about their responsibility for the financial statements or about the scope and nature of the audit process and that they are informed about key findings of the audit. The form and content of the communications vary widely according to the client and the particular circumstances encountered during the audit. However, in virtually all cases, one of the most important components of the governance communication is the section detailing the existence and effect of material weaknesses in the accounting and internal control systems discovered during the audit and how these might be rectified. In reporting these and similar matters, auditors provide a valuable service to those charged with the governance of auditees, assisting them improve their entity's accounting and internal control systems and other aspects of its financial affairs.

SELF-REVIEW QUESTIONS

13.1   List the elements which the Companies Act 1985 requires auditors to refer to in their audit reports.

13.2   The auditor of a company is required to form and express an opinion on the truth and fairness of the company's financial statements. Explain briefly:
(i)   the meaning frequently afforded the phrase 'true and fair' by lawyers;
(ii)   why this interpretation is not useful for preparers and auditors of financial statements;
(iii)   what is generally accepted by the accounting profession as being required for financial statements to provide the required true and fair view.

13.3   Describe briefly the format of the standard audit report currently in use in the United Kingdom and Republic of Ireland.

13.4   State the criteria which SAS 600 requires to be met before an auditor may issue an unqualified audit report.

13.5   List three types of qualified audit report and briefly explain the circumstances in which each is appropriate.

13.6   Explain briefly the difference between a scope limitation and an inherent uncertainty.

13.7   Distinguish between a material inherent uncertainty and a fundamental inherent uncertainty and explain how each is reflected in the auditor's report.

13.8   Explain briefly the ways in which the expanded audit report differs from its short form predecessor.

13.9   Discuss briefly advantages and disadvantages of:
(i)   a standard form of audit report compared to a free-flow form of report;
(ii)   a short form audit report compared to an expanded form of audit report.

13.10   Explain briefly the purpose, content and value of auditors' communications of audit matters to those charged with auditees' governance.

REFERENCES

Alfano, J.B. (1979) Making auditor's reports pure and simple. *CPA Journal* **46**(6), 37–41.

Arden QC, M. (1993) *The True and Fair Requirement* (Counsel's opinion). London: Accounting Standards Board. Also reprinted in Institute of Chartered Accountants in England and Wales (1994) *Members' Handbook, volume 2.* Appendix to the Foreword (pp. 13–20).

Beck, C.W. (1973) The role of the auditor in modern society: An empirical appraisal. *Accounting and Business Research* **3**(10), 117–122.

Canadian Institute of Chartered Accountants (CICA) (1988) *Report of the Commission to Study the Public's Expectations of Audits* (Macdonald Commission). Toronto: CICA.

Commission on Auditors' Responsibilities (CAR) (1978) *Report, Conclusions and Recommendations* (The Cohen Commission). New York: AICPA.

Committee on Corporate Governance (1998) *The Combined Code.* London: The London Stock Exchange Ltd.

Elliott, R.K. & Jacobson, P.D. (1987) The auditor's standard report: the last word or in need of change? *Journal of Accountancy* **164**(2), 72–78.

Epstein, M.J. (1976) The Corporate Shareholders' View of the Auditor's Rreport. In Commission on Auditors' Responsibilities. *Report, Conclusions and Recommendations.* New York: AICPA, p. 164.

Flint, D. (1980) *The Significance of the Standard of True and Fair View.* Invitation Research Lecture. New Zealand: New Zealand Society of Accountants.

Hatherly, D., Innes, J. & Brown, T. (1991) The expanded audit report: An empirical investigation. *Accounting and Business Research* **21**(84), 311–319.

Inflation Accounting Committee (1975) *Report of the Inflation Accounting Committee* (Sandilands Committee). London: HMSO, CMND 6225.

Johnston, T.R., Edgar, G.C. & Hays, P.L. (1982) *The Law and Practice of Company Accounting in New Zealand* (6th ed.). Wellington: Butterworths.

Kelly, A.S. & Mohrweis, L.C. (1989) Bankers' and investors' perceptions of the auditor's role in financial statement reporting: The impact of SAS No. 58. *Auditing: A Journal of Practice & Theory,* Fall.

Lee, T.A. (1970) The nature of auditing and its objectives. *Accountancy* **81**(920), 292–296.

Lee, T.A. & Tweedie, D.P. (1975) Accounting information: An investigation of private shareholder usage. *Accounting and Business Research* **5**(20), 280–291.

Northey, J. (1965) *Recommendations for Company Law Reform.* Business Law Symposium.

Porter, B.A. (1990) True and fair view: An elusive concept. *Accountants' Journal* **69**(110), Editorial.

Porter, B.A. (1993) An empirical study of the audit expectation–performance gap. *Accounting and Business Research* **24**(93), 49–68.

Ryan, S.J.O. (1974) A true and fair view revisited. *Australian Accountant* **44**(1), 8–10, 13–16 (Commissioner for Corporate Affairs in New South Wales).

Tweedie, D. (1983) True and fair rules. *The Accountant's Magazine* **87**(925), 424–428, 449.

Wilton, R.L. & Tabb, J.B. (1978, May) An investigation into private shareholder usage of financial statements in New Zealand. *Accounting Education* **18**, 83–101.

Woolf, E. (1979) *Auditing Today.* London: Prentice-Hall.

Zachry, B.R. (1991) Who understands audit reports? *The Woman CPA* **53**(2), 9–11.

ADDITIONAL READING

Bagshaw, K. (1994) Whatever happended to the audit report? *Accountancy* **113**(1206), 82–83.

Carcello, J.V. & Neal, T.L. (2000) Audit committee composition and auditor reporting. *The Accounting Review* **75**(4), 453–467.

Chitty, D. (2001) New words for old. *Accountancy* **123**(1295), 120–122.

Estes, R. (1982). *The Auditors' Report and Investor Behavior.* Lexington, MA: Heath.

Hatherly, D. (1992) Company auditing: a vision of the future? *Accountancy* **110**(1187), 75.

Holt, G. & Moizer, P. (1990) The meaning of audit reports. *Accounting and Business Research* **20**(78), 111–122.

Hopkins, L. (1996) A clear expression of opinion. *Accountancy* **117**(1232), 145.

Innes, J., Brown, T. & Hatherly, D. (1997) The expanded audit report – a research study within the development of SAS 600. *Accounting, Auditing & Accountability Journal* **10**(5), 702–717.

Jeter, D.C. & Shaw, P.E. (1995) Solicitation and auditor reporting decisions. *The Accounting Review* **70**(2), 293–315.

Krishnan, J., Krishnan, J. & Stephens, R.G. (1996) The simultaneous relation between auditor switching and audit opinion: an empirical analysis. *Accounting and Business Research* **26**(3), 224–236.

Lennox, C. (2000) Do companies successfully engage in opinion shopping? Evidence from the UK. *Journal of Accounting & Economics* **29**, 321–337.

Low, C.K. & Koh, H.C. (1997) Concepts associated with the 'true and fair view': evidence from Singapore. *Accounting and Business Research* **27**(3), 195–202.

Ludder, M.L., Khurana, I.K., Swayers, R.B., Cordery, C., Johnson, C., Lowe, J. & Wunderle, R. (1992) The information content of audit qualifications. *Auditing: A Journal of Practice & Theory* **11**(1), 69–82.

Manson, S. & Zaman, M. (2001) Auditor communication in an evolving environment: going beyond SAS 600 auditors' reports on financial statements. *British Accounting Review* **33**, 113–136.

Parker, R.H. & Nobes, C.W. (1991) 'True and fair': UK auditors' view. *Accounting and Business Research* **21**(84), 349–361.

Seidler, L.J. (1976) Symbolism and communication in the auditor's report. In Stettler, H.F. (ed.) *Auditing Symposium III.* University of Kansas: ToucheRoss/University of Kansas Symposium on Auditing Problems.

Stacy, G. (1997) True and fair view: a UK auditor's perspective. *The European Accounting Review* **6**(4), 705–709.

14 Legal Liability of Auditors

LEARNING OBJECTIVES

After studying the material in this chapter you should be able to:

- distinguish between auditors' statutory and common law duties;
- discuss auditors' contractual liability to their clients;
- discuss auditors' liability to third parties for negligence;
- explain how auditors' duty of care to third parties was extended by a series of cases starting in 1931 with *Ultramares* v *Touche* through to the 1980s with the cases of *Jeb Fasteners* and *Twomax Ltd*;
- explain the significance of the House of Lords' decision in the *Caparo* case (1990);
- describe how the law relating to auditors' liability to third parties has been extended since the *Caparo* judgment;
- discuss the effect of out-of-court settlements.

14.1   INTRODUCTION

When an auditor[1] accepts an audit engagement, this gives rise to the assumption that the auditor undertakes to perform the audit in accordance with certain statutory and common law obligations. If these obligations are not met, the auditor is liable to parties who suffer loss as a result. These parties include the client entity with whom the auditor has a contractual relationship, and may also include third parties who do not have a contractual relationship with the auditor but who, nevertheless, rely on the proper performance of the auditor's duties (more particularly, on the opinion expressed in the auditor's report).

In this chapter we address the issue of auditors' legal liability. More specifically, we examine auditors' contractual liability to audit clients and trace the development of their liability to third parties. We then consider in some detail the House of Lords' decision in the *Caparo* case (1990). This currently remains the most influential case in the United Kingdom with respect to auditors' liability and is notable for reversing the trend towards extending auditors' liability to third parties and returning the law to where it stood some 30 years ago. We also discuss some cases decided subsequent to *Caparo* and note how the law is gradually widening once again (albeit to a fairly limited extent) auditors' liability to third parties. Before closing the chapter we explore the effect of out-of-court settlements on the development of the law relating to auditors' liability and indemnity insurance.

14.2   OVERVIEW OF AUDITORS' LEGAL LIABILITY

14.2.1   Auditors' exposure to legal liability

As noted above, when an auditor accepts an audit engagement it is understood that (s)he agrees to perform the audit in accordance with certain statutory and common law obligations. If either of these sets of obligations are not met, the auditor is exposed to liability. Auditors' exposure to liability is depicted in Figure 14.1.

---

[1] As noted in Chapter 5, section 5.2.3, under the Companies Act 1989, s.25(2), an audit firm may be appointed as 'the auditor'. Thus, 'the auditor' should be taken to mean either an individual or an audit firm. The principles of legal liability apply equally in either case. If the audit firm is constituted as an ordinary partnership (as opposed to a Limited Liability Partnership), which is usually the case, the partners are jointly and severally liable. This means they are liable jointly with the other partners of the firm for any damages awarded by a court against any one of the firm's partners; they are also liable individually to meet damages awarded against any of the firm's partners, should the other partners of the firm not be able to pay. Limited Liability Partnerships (LLPs) are discussed in Chapter 15.

Figure 14.1: Auditors' exposure to legal liability

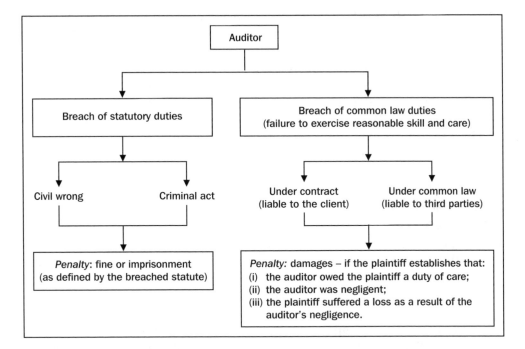

14.2.2 Breach of statutory duties

Some of the auditor's duties are specified by statute, for example in the Companies Act 1985 and the Theft Act 1968. If the auditor fails to perform these duties, the breach may constitute either:

- a civil wrong, whereby the client entity or some individual suffers loss as a result of the auditor failing to meet his or her statutory obligations; or
- a criminal act. This arises, for example, when an auditor deliberately signs a report knowing it to be false.

In either case, the maximum penalty the auditor will face (which will be in the form of a fine or imprisonment) is specified in the statute the auditor has breached. For example, under the Companies Act 1989 (s.28), if the auditor of a company becomes ineligible during his term of office to hold the position of auditor, (s)he is required to vacate the position and inform the company in writing. Failure to give such written notice renders the auditor liable:

(a) on conviction on indictment, to a fine, and
(b) on summary conviction, to a fine not exceeding the statutory maximum (currently, £5,000) (Companies Act 1989, s.28).

14.2.3 Breach of common law duties

In addition to statutory obligations which arise when an auditor agrees to perform an audit, a common law duty also arises, namely, a duty to perform the audit with reasonable skill and care appropriate to the circumstances. If the auditor fails to exercise reasonable skill and care, (s)he will be liable to make good any resultant loss suffered by those to whom a duty of care is owed. Such a duty of care may result from a contractual relationship or may arise under common law to parties outside a contractual arrangement. The circumstances in which the courts have held that auditors owe a duty of care to third parties are discussed in section 14.4.1 below.

The penalty for proven negligence (that is, failure to take due care) is the award of damages. However, before damages will be awarded against an auditor, the plaintiff must prove three facts, namely:

- that the auditor owed him or her a duty of care;
- that the auditor was negligent (that is, the auditor did not exercise a reasonable standard of skill and care in the particular circumstances); and
- the plaintiff suffered a loss as a result of the auditor's negligence.

Although these three requirements have been clearly established in law, two of them create difficulties for auditors as they are not static. These are as follows:

(i) What qualifies as negligence (what amounts to a reasonable standard of skill and care in the particular circumstances)?[2]

As noted in Chapter 5 (section 5.3), Moffit J made it clear in the Australian case of *Pacific Acceptance Corporation Limited v Forsyth and Others* (1970) 92 WN (NSW) 29, that compliance with generally accepted auditing standards may not be enough to protect the auditor from being judged negligent. Moffit J observed that professional standards and practice must change over time to reflect changes in the economic and business environment. Although the courts are guided by professional standards and current best auditing practice, they will not be bound by them and, if the courts see fit, they will go beyond them. It is for the courts, not the auditing profession, to determine, in the light of

---

[2] The concept of due care is discussed in Chapter 3, section 3.6.1. There we note that two significant characteristics of the concept are as follows:

    1. The standard of 'reasonable skill, care and caution' has become more exacting over the past 100 or so years, as society, and more particularly the commercial and corporate worlds, have become more complex and dynamic.

    2. Although Auditing Standards and other professional promulgations provide guidance to the court on what may reasonably be expected of auditors, it is up to the court, not the profession, to determine whether an auditor has taken due care in any particular audit.

society's norms of the time, what is reasonable skill and care in the particular circumstances of the case.

This leaves auditors in a difficult and unenviable position. Not only do they lack a clear standard to which they are expected to work (the standard of skill and care required of them varies over time and as between different sets of circumstances) but, additionally, when the courts evaluate whether or not they have exercised the required standard of skill and care, it is with the wisdom of hindsight.

(ii)   The parties to whom auditors owe a duty of care

As indicated in Figure 14.1, a duty of care may arise under either:

(a) *contract*, that is, as part of the contractual arrangement between the auditor and the client. This duty is generally clear-cut and does not give rise to uncertainty; or

(b) *common law*. This duty of care to third parties (that is, parties outside a contractual relationship) is imposed on auditors when the courts consider it reasonable and equitable to do so. As shown in section 14.4.1 below, between the early 1960s and the end of the 1980s, the parties to whom auditors were held to owe a duty of care were progressively extended. Then, as a result of the *Caparo* case, they were reduced significantly once more. The various changes leave auditors unsure as to whom they are liable should they fail to exercise a reasonable standard of skill and care in the particular circumstances of the audit.

14.3 AUDITORS' CONTRACTUAL LIABILITY TO THEIR CLIENTS

14.3.1 Auditors' contractual duties

When an auditor accepts an audit engagement, (s)he contracts with the client to perform certain duties. Some of these are specified in legislation (such as the Companies Act 1985); others have been determined over the years by the courts as a result of various cases being brought against auditors. (Some of these cases are discussed in Chapter 5, section 5.3.) If the auditor does not perform his or her duties with a reasonable standard of skill and care and, as a consequence, the client[3] suffers a loss, then the auditor is liable to make good the loss suffered.

---

[3] It should be noted that 'the client' is the client entity, not the entity's shareholders or any other interested party.

An example of an auditor being held liable for breach of contractual duties is provided by the Australian case of *AWA Limited v Daniels, trading as Deloitte Haskins & Sells & Ors* (1992) 10 ACLC 933. In this case, AWA's manager of foreign exchange operations, while appearing to trade profitably in foreign exchange dealings, in fact caused AWA to incur a loss of A$50 million. The manager concealed the losses by various means, including unauthorised borrowing from a number of banks, allegedly on behalf of AWA. AWA sued the auditors for damages in breach of contract, claiming that the loss suffered was caused by Deloittes' failure to draw attention to serious deficiencies in the company's internal controls and accounting records, and for failing to qualify their audit reports.

Rogers CJ found that Deloittes failed to perform their contractual duties in three ways. These are as follows:

(i)   It was clear that the books and records relevant to AWA's foreign exchange transactions were 'inaccurate and inadequate' and 'the auditors should have formed the opinion that proper accounting records had not been kept' (Rogers, C J at 959). They failed to fulfil this duty.

(ii) The auditors had doubts about the extent of the foreign exchange manager's authority to enter into foreign exchange transactions on behalf of AWA. In such circumstances the auditors had a duty to make enquiries from an appropriate level of management. This, Deloittes failed to do.

(iii) Notwithstanding that the auditors had discussed the inadequate system of recording foreign exchange transactions with the general manager of AWA, they did nothing to ensure that the matter was dealt with urgently and effectively, nor did they ensure that it was referred to AWA's board of directors. Rogers C J held that simply identifying shortcomings and bringing them to the attention of management below board level is insufficient discharge of an auditor's duty in cases where the auditor is aware that management fails to respond adequately. Management's failure to take action to rectify the position imposes on the auditor an obligation to inform the board. Further, this duty to report to the board is not discharged by relying on the possibility that the chief executive officer will have already done so.

In the AWA case it was decided that the auditors had been negligent in the performance of their duties and that their negligence had contributed to the loss suffered by AWA. However, AWA's senior management was also found to have contributed to the company's loss by virtue of deficiencies in its system of internal controls and record-keeping.

Deloittes appealed the trial judge's ruling but the Court of Appeal upheld Rogers CJ's findings.[4] Nevertheless, the Appeal Court gave greater weight

---

[4] *Daniels (formerly practising as Deloitte Haskins & Sells) v AWA Ltd*; 14 May 1995, (NSW) CA.

than did the trial judge to the part played by AWA's management in the loss suffered by the company. Taking due cognisance of the contributory negligence of AWA's management, the Court of Appeal reduced the damages awarded against Deloittes from A$17 million to A$6 million. In the Court of Appeal's view, the crux of Deloittes negligence lay in their failure to give appropriate advice to the board of directors regarding (i) the absence of controls over the foreign exchange operations and (ii) the failure of senior management to respond to their (the auditors') warnings regarding the absence of controls (Shanahan, 1995, p. 214).

With respect to auditors' contractual liability to their clients, the AWA case is particularly interesting as it illustrates both:

- a breach of auditors' statutory duties (that is, their failure to qualify their audit report for the company's failure to maintain proper accounting records, as required by section 331E(2) of the Australian Corporations Law[5]); and
- a breach of their common law duties [that is, their failure to make the necessary enquiries of AWA's senior management about matters of which they were uncertain (for example, the extent of the foreign exchange manager's authority), and their failure to report to the appropriate level of the entity's management (namely, the board of directors) serious deficiencies they had discovered in the entity's internal controls and record-keeping].

The case is also interesting in that it illustrates the exercise by the court of the principle of contributory negligence.

The recent English case of *Sasea Finance Ltd* v *KPMG* [2000] 1 All ER 676; [2000] 1 BCLC 236; [2001] 1 All ER (D) 127 (May), similarly involved a breach of auditors' contractual obligations to their client. In this case, Sasea Finance Limited (SFL), an English registered company which was part of the Swiss-based Sasea group of companies, sued its auditor, KPMG, for the negligent conduct of its audit for the year ending 31 December 1989. The audit was completed and the audit report signed in November 1990.

In 1992, the Sasea group collapsed and SFL went into liquidation. The affairs of the group were subject to criminal investigations and these revealed that the companies in the group had been vehicles for a massive fraud. SFL claimed that had KPMG acted with reasonable skill and care, it would have taken such action that would have allowed SFL to avoid suffering four losses between September 1990 and early 1991 (of £2.4 million, £113,000, £458,000

---

[5] This section contains the same provisions as section 237(2) of the UK Companies Act 1985.

and £8 million, respectively) which resulted from fraud and theft. KPMG contended that none of the losses was caused by any breach of contract or negligence on its part.

The High Court held that SFL's claims in respect of two of the losses (those of £2.4 million and £8 million, respectively) had insufficient bases to proceed to a trial, but it refused to strike out the other two claims. SFL appealed the Court's decision and KPMG cross-appealed. KPMG contended, among other things, that any negligence on its part was not the cause of the alleged losses.

The Court of Appeal overturned the High Court's decision and SFL's claim against KMPG for all four losses was reinstated. During the Court of Appeal hearing, Kennedy LJ explained some aspects of auditors' duties. He stated:

> Where a firm of accountants accepts instructions to audit the accounts of a company for a fiscal year, its primary obligation is, within a reasonable time, to exercise an appropriate level of skill and care in reporting to the company's members on the accounts of the company stating, in their opinion, whether the accounts of the company give a true and fair view of the company's financial affairs.

He then went on to clarify auditors' duty to report significant facts to their clients, and to do so in a timely fashion. He said:

> If, for example, the auditors discover that a senior employee of the company has been defrauding the company on a grand scale and is in the position to go on doing so, then it would normally be the duty of the auditors to report what had been discovered to the management of the company at once, not simply when rendering the auditor's report weeks or months later.

He concluded that the present case was concerned with losses brought about by fraud or irregularities the risk of which KPMG ought to have apprehended and reported. KPMG had a duty to warn the company's directors as soon as the fraud or irregularities had been detected.

It should be noted that, in order for contractual liability to be invoked, the aggrieved party must be a party to the contract. In the case of auditors appointed to perform a statutory audit under the Companies Act 1985, the contract is between the auditor and the company *per se*, *not* the company's shareholders as individuals. As the *AWA* and *Sasea* cases illustrate, if an auditor fails to perform his or her statutory duties, or fails to take due care in performing the audit, the client entity (in these cases, AWA Ltd and Sasea Finance Ltd) may sue for breach of contract. Should a shareholder wish to take action against the auditor(s), (s)he can do so only by exercising his or her rights as a third party under the common law (see section 14.4.1 below). However – worse news yet for shareholders – as a result of the House of Lords' decision in the *Caparo* case (1990), even this avenue of relief for them as individuals is of doubtful availability (see section 14.4.2 below).

14.3.2 The importance of engagement letters

Statement of Auditing Standards (SAS) 140: *Engagement letters* recommends that, when an auditor is engaged to perform an audit, an engagement letter be prepared to clarify the terms of the contract.[6] The engagement letter does not (indeed, cannot) excuse the auditor from performing his or her statutory or common law duties, or from performing those duties with a reasonable standard of skill and care appropriate to the circumstances of the audit. However, the letter can reduce to a minimum any misunderstanding between the client and the auditor with respect to the duties to be performed and the terms of the engagement.

Although engagement letters are important to clarify the terms of an audit engagement, as the United States (US) case of *1136 Tenants' Corporation* v *Max Rothenberg & Co* (1971) 319 NYS2d 1007 demonstrates, they are even more important when the engagement does not include an audit. In the *1136 Tenants' Corporation* case, a firm of certified public accountants was engaged to write up the books of a co-operative block of flats. It was successfully sued for negligence for not uncovering an embezzlement by the managing agent.

Damages were awarded against the accountants despite the fact that each set of accounts they submitted to the corporation was accompanied by a letter which began:

> Pursuant to our engagement, we have reviewed and summarised the statements of your managing agent, and other data submitted to us by the managing agent.

The letter concluded:

> The following statements were prepared from the books and records of the Corporation. No independent verifications were undertaken thereon . . .

Additionally, the financial statements themselves were marked:

> 'Subject to comments in letter of transmittal . . .'.

The accountants argued that the statement in the transmittal letter that 'no independent verifications were undertaken' was sufficient warning to all users of the financial statements that they were unaudited. The court nevertheless found them to be guilty of negligence (Woolf, 1979, p. 263). Had the accountants clarified the scope of their engagement and, more particularly,

---

[6] Engagement letters are discussed in Chapter 7, section 7.3.

specified that no audit would be undertaken, in an engagement letter, they may well have avoided the costly position in which they found themselves.

14.4 LIABILITY TO THIRD PARTIES UNDER COMMON LAW

14.4.1 *Development of auditors' duty of care to third parties – until the* Caparo *decision*

As noted above, if auditors breach their statutory duties, or fail to perform their duties with reasonable skill and care, they may be held liable to make good any consequential loss suffered by their client. This liability arises as a result of the contractual relationship between the auditor and the client.

Over the past 40 or so years, courts in the UK (and elsewhere) have held that auditors also owe a duty of care to certain third parties who suffer loss as a consequence of auditors failing to perform their duties with due care. Through a series of cases, beginning in 1931 in the USA, when it was held that auditors' liability should be restricted to contractual relationships and not extended to third parties, the parties to whom auditors have been held to owe a duty of care were widened progressively. This trend was reversed with the *Caparo* decision in 1990. The relevant cases are summarised in Figure 14.2.

In 1931, in the US case of *Ultramares Corporation* v *Touche* (1931) 255 NY 170, it was held that auditors' liability can arise only under a contractual relationship. Cardozo J decided that it would be too much to impose on accountants a liability to third parties for financial loss, as this may expose them to liability out of all proportion to the gravity of their actions. As Cardozo J expressed it (at 179):

> [it] may expose accountants to liability in an indeterminate amount for an indeterminate time to an indeterminate class.

In 1932, the English case of *Donoghue* v *Stevenson* (1932) AC 562 started the process of recognising a liability to parties outside a contractual relationship. This case involved a young man who purchased a bottle of ginger beer, complete with decomposed snail, and gave it to his girlfriend to drink. Not surprisingly, the girlfriend became ill. The court held that a duty of care is owed to third parties in circumstances where it can be reasonably foreseen that failure to take care may result in physical injury. Thus, this case established that liability may arise outside a contractual relationship in circumstances involving possible physical injury.

Figure 14.2: Summary of significant cases relating to auditors' liability to third parties – up to and including *Caparo* v *Dickman* (1990)

Case	Key finding(s) of the case
1. *Ultramares Corporation* v *Touche* (1931) 255 NY 170 [US case]	Accountants' liability should not be extended to third parties. It can only arise under a contractual relationship.
2. *Donoghue* v *Stevenson* (1932) AC 562 [UK case]	A duty of care is owed to third parties in circumstances where it can reasonably be foreseen that failure to take care may result in physical injury.
3. *Candler* v *Crane Christmas & Co.* [1951] 2 KB 164 [UK case]	No duty of care is owed to third parties in the case of financial loss. Lord Denning's dissenting judgment indicated things to come. He considered that accountants owe a duty of care to any third party to whom they know the accounts are to be shown in order to induce him or her to invest money or to take some other action on them. He did not think that the duty could be extended to include strangers, i.e. persons of whom the auditor knows nothing at the time of the audit.
4. *Hedley Byrne & Co Ltd* v *Heller and Partners* [1963] 2 All ER 575; [1964] AC 465 [UK case]	A duty of care is owed to third parties for financial loss where it can be shown that a 'special relationship' exists; i.e. where the provider of information knows, or ought to know, that a particular person is going to rely on the information for some specific purpose. The duty of care does not extend to strangers.
5. *Diamond Manufacturing Company* v *Hamilton* [1969] NZLR 609 [NZ case]	A 'special relationship' was said to exist because one of the auditors had been involved in negotiations with the investor; a duty of care therefore existed.
6. *MLC* v *Evatt* [1971] AC 793 [Australian case]	A 'special relationship' can arise only where the person giving the advice holds him or herself out to be an expert. (The *Hedley Byrne* principle was effectively narrowed.)
7. *Haig* v *Bamford* [1976] 3WW R331 (SC Can) [Canadian case]	No duty of care is owed to strangers. Auditors do not owe a duty of care to those whom, at the time of the audit, they are not aware will rely on the audited financial statements for a particular purpose.
8. *Anns* v *Merton London Borough Council* [1977] 2 All ER; 492 [1978] AC 728 [UK case]	The requirement for a 'special relationship' was replaced by a 'relationship of proximity or neighbourhood', and the test of 'knowledge' that someone would rely on the advice given and may suffer loss as a result of a failure to take care, was replaced by one of 'reasonable foreseeability'. This case extended quite considerably the third parties to whom a duty of care is owed in cases involving non-physical injury.
9. *Scott Group Ltd* v *McFarlane* [1978] 1 NZLR 553 [NZ case]	A duty of care is owed by auditors who could or reasonably should foresee that a particular person or group of persons will rely on the audited financial statements for a particular type of investment decision. The *Hedley Byrne* principle of knowledge of reliance on the audited financial statements was replaced by a test of reasonable foreseeability. Attention was drawn to the fact that audited financial statements of companies become a matter of public record through filing with the Companies Office.
10. *Jeb Fasteners Ltd* v *Marks, Bloom & Co* [1981] 3 All ER 289 [UK case]	Auditors owe a duty of care to any person or class of persons whom they do not know, but reasonably should foresee might rely on the audited financial statements when making investment decisions about the company. The case extended the *Scott Group* case from circumstances in which a takeover is reasonably foreseeable, to circumstances in which any form of financial support seems likely to be needed and reliance on audited financial statements could or should be expected.
11. *Twomax Ltd* v *Dickson McFarlane and Robinson* [1982] SC 113 [1983] SLT 98 [UK – Scottish case]	The duty of care owed by auditors to third parties established in the *Scott Group* case was extended to virtually anyone who can prove they relied on negligently audited financial statements when making an investment decision and suffered loss as a consequence.
12. *Caparo Industries plc* v *Dickman and Others* [1990] 1 All ER 568; [1990] 2 AC605; [1990] 2 WLR 358, HL [UK case]	In the absence of special circumstances, auditors owe a duty of care only to (i) the audit-client company and (ii) the company's shareholders as a body. A duty of care is owed to third parties only when the three tests of foreseeability of damage, proximity of relationship, and fairness of imposing a duty are satisfied.

Nearly 20 years later, in the case of *Candler* v *Crane Christmas & Co.* [1951] 2 KB 164, the court confirmed that no duty of care is owed to third parties in the case of financial loss. In this case, the defendant firm of chartered accountants negligently prepared a set of financial statements for their clients, knowing that they would be shown to the third party plaintiff for the purpose of making an investment decision. The investment failed and the plaintiff sued the accountants.

The majority of the court, re-iterating the fears expressed by Cardozo J in the *Ultramares* case, held that a duty of care is not owed to third parties in the case of financial loss. However, the dissenting judgment of Lord Denning signalled the way the law would develop in the future. He said:

> [Accountants] owe a duty, of course, to their employer and client and also, I think, to any third party to whom they themselves show the accounts or to whom they know their employer is going to show the accounts so as to induce him to invest money or to take some other action on them. But I do not think the duty can be extended still further so as to include strangers of whom they have heard nothing . . .

Twelve years later, in *Hedley Byrne & Co Ltd* v *Heller and Partners* [1963] 2 All ER 575; [1964] AC 465, the court accepted as correct the reasoning of Lord Denning in the *Crane Christmas* case. The *Hedley Byrne* case involved a telephone enquiry by a bank to a merchant bank (Heller & Partners Ltd) regarding the creditworthiness of a company for which Heller was banker. The bank communicated Heller's reply, that the company was 'considered good for its normal business engagements' and in particular for a proposed advertising contract, to one of its customers (Hedley Byrne & Co Ltd). The court held that a duty of care is owed to third parties where it can be shown that a 'special relationship' exists. Such a relationship will exist when the person giving the information knows, or ought to know, that another particular person is going to rely on the information for a specific purpose. However, the court emphasised that a duty of care does not extend to strangers; that is, persons of whom the person giving the information knows nothing at the time.

Hedley Byrne is a landmark decision in that it recognised third party liability in a case involving financial loss. Until then, liability to third parties had been limited to situations involving physical injury.

The next two cases in the series helped to clarify the meaning of a 'special relationship'. In the New Zealand case of *Diamond Manufacturing Company* v *Hamilton* [1969] NZLR 609, a member of an audit firm showed the financial statements the firm had audited to another party, knowing that the statements would be used in an investment decision. The court held that the auditors were liable to the third party as a special relationship existed and, therefore, a duty of care was owed. The special relationship arose because one of the auditors was involved in the negotiations with the investor. However, the court confirmed that a duty of care did not extend to strangers.

In 1971, in the Australian case of *Mutual Life & Citizens' Assurance Co Ltd* v *Evatt* [1971] AC 793, the circumstances in which a special relationship could arise were narrowed somewhat. This case involved an insurance agent who was negligent in giving financial advice. It was held that, in order for a special relationship to exist, the person giving the financial advice must not only know that someone is going to rely on the advice proffered but, further, he (or she) must be giving the advice in a professional capacity. The special relationship can only arise in circumstances where the person giving the advice holds him or herself out to be an expert.

Five years later (and 12 years after the *Hedley Byrne* principle was established) a Canadian court, in *Haig* v *Bamford* [1976] 3WW R331 (SC Can), confirmed that in cases involving financial loss, no duty of care is owed to a stranger: liability to third parties cannot arise in the absence of knowledge that a particular person will rely on the financial advice given (or the audited financial statements) for a specific purpose. This principle was to be tested in the UK just one year later.

The case of *Anns* v *Merton London Borough Council* [1977] 2 All ER 492; [1978] AC 728, involved the failure of a local authority to inspect a faulty building. The court held that the authority owed a duty of care to the occupiers of the building. Although not involving auditors or accountants, this case is of singular importance to the extension of auditors' liability to third parties. It introduced a 'relationship of proximity or neighbourhood' in place of a 'special relationship', and replaced the test of 'knowledge' that someone would rely on the advice given and may suffer damage or loss as a result of failure to take care, with one of 'reasonable foreseeability'. The court provided a two-step approach as a guideline for determining whether or not a duty of care exists in particular circumstances. In the words of Lord Wilberforce:

> In order to establish whether a duty of care arises in a particular situation, two questions must be asked:
> 1. As between the alleged wrongdoer and the injured party there must be a relationship of proximity or neighbourhood, such that in the reasonable contemplation of the former, carelessness on his part may be likely to cause damage to the latter, in which case a *prima facie* duty of care arises.
> 2. If the question is answered affirmatively, it is necessary to consider whether there are any considerations which ought to negative, or to reduce or limit the scope of the duty or class of person to whom it is owed.

The principles enunciated in this case extended quite considerably the third parties to whom a duty of care is owed in circumstances involving non-physical injury. However, it is pertinent to note that it also brought the law in such cases into line with that obtaining in situations involving physical injury: the reasonable foreseeability test was established in circumstances involving physical injury in *Donoghue* v *Stevenson* in 1932 (*supra*).

The courts did not have long to wait before the *Anns* case principles were applied in a case involving auditors. In the New Zealand case of *Scott Group Ltd* v *McFarlane* [1978] 1 NZLR 553, auditors failed to detect a basic double counting error which resulted in assets being significantly overvalued. At the time of the audit, the defendant auditor had no knowledge that the plaintiff had any intention of making a takeover offer. However, the court held that the company's rich assets and low profits situation made it a prime target for takeover or merger and, therefore, the auditor should have foreseen that some person or group of persons was likely to rely on the audited financial statements to make such an offer.

Thus, this case extended the *Hedley Byrne* test of *knowledge* to one of *reasonable foreseeability* in situations involving audited financial statements. It established that a duty of care is owed by auditors who can, or should, reasonably foresee that a particular person or group of persons will rely on the audited financial statements when deciding whether to make a takeover offer. Applying the two-part *Anns* test for a duty of care to be recognised, Woodhouse J identified four factors which give rise to a *prima facie* duty of care in the case of auditors. These are as follows:

1. Auditors are professionals in the business of providing expert advice for reward. If they did not intend their audited accounts to be relied upon, their work would be pointless.
2. Confidence in the ability of a company to handle its commercial arrangements would disappear if the audit report authenticating the company's accounts could not be relied upon.
3. In ordinary circumstances there is no opportunity for a person to make any intermediate examination of the company's accounts, nor is it practicable for many persons to do so.
4. Auditors are aware that the audited accounts will be filed with the Companies Office and therefore they become a matter of public record; they are available to the public, and anyone interested in the company has direct access to them.

Considering whether there are any factors which might negate or limit the scope of auditors' duty of care or the persons to whom it is owed, Woodhouse J found the only argument in favour of negating liability was that raised by Cardozo J in *Ultramares* v *Touche* (*supra*) over 45 years earlier; namely, the fear that auditors may be exposed to liability of indeterminate amount for an indeterminate time to an indeterminate class. However, his Honour considered that this need not be a matter of concern because of the difficulty of bringing a successful action for negligence. To succeed in such an action, the plaintiff must prove:

- it is reasonable to expect the auditors to have anticipated that the plaintiff would act on the audited financial information;
- the plaintiff actually relied on the audited financial information; and
- the auditors' failure to take care when auditing the financial information was the cause of the plaintiff's loss.

Woodhouse J concluded:

> [The auditors] must be taken to have accepted . . . a duty to those persons whom they can reasonably foresee will need to use and rely on [the audited financial statements] when dealing with the Company in significant matters affecting the Company's assets and business.

The *Scott Group* decision was applied and extended in the UK case of *Jeb Fasteners Ltd* v *Marks Bloom & Co* [1981] 3 All ER 289. In this case, the defendants conducted an audit for a company which they were aware was undergoing a liquidity crisis and needed to raise finance. The company's financial statements contained assets that were seriously overvalued, a fact the auditors failed to detect. The plaintiffs had reservations about the assets figure but nevertheless proceeded with the takeover. The court reaffirmed that the auditor owes a duty of care to any person or class of persons whom they do not know, but should be able to reasonably foresee might rely on the audited financial statements when making an investment decision relating to the company. Woolf J, citing the *Scott Group* decision with approval, stated:

> When he audited the accounts, Mr Marks would not know precisely who would provide the financial support, or what form the financial support would take, and he certainly had no reason to know that it would be by way of takeover by the plaintiffs. However, this was certainly one foreseeable method, and it does not seem to me that it would be right to exclude the duty of care merely because it was not possible to say with precision what machinery would be used to achieve the necessary financial support. Clearly, any form of loan would have been foreseeable, including the raising of money by debenture and, while some methods of raising money were more obvious than others, and a takeover was not the most obvious method, it was certainly one method which was within the contemplation of Mr Marks.

Woolf J concluded that the auditors should have foreseen that a person might rely on the audited financial statements for the purpose of making an investment decision and that the person could, therefore, suffer loss if the accounts were inaccurate.

Analysing Mr Justice Woolf's judgment (above) it appears that, although the case involved a takeover, he extended the *Scott Group* decision from circumstances in which a takeover is reasonably foreseeable, to circumstances in which any form of financial support seems likely to be needed, and reliance on audited financial statements can (or should) be expected.

In the Scottish case of *Twomax Ltd* v *Dickson, McFarlane & Robinson* [1982] SC 113; [1983] SLT 98, the facts are similar to those of the *Jeb Fasteners* case, and Lord Stewart had little hesitation in applying Woolf J's judgment. He held that although the auditors did not know the plaintiffs would rely on the audited financial statements to make an investment decision, they were aware that the auditee company (Kintyre Knitwear Ltd) needed capital. Given these circumstances, the auditors should have reasonably foreseen that some person (or group of persons) would rely on the audited financial statements and would suffer loss if they were inaccurate. This case is significant because it confirmed the *Scott Group's* and *Jeb Fasteners'* extension of auditors' duty of care to third parties whom they do not know but should reasonably foresee might rely on the audited financial statements when making an investment decision relating to the reporting entity. But, further, unlike the plaintiffs in the *Scott Group* and *Jeb Fasteners* cases, the plaintiffs in the *Twomax* case were able to prove to the satisfaction of the court that they not only relied on the financial statements when making their investment decision, they also suffered loss as a result of relying on those statements which had been audited negligently. As a consequence, damages were awarded against the defendant auditors.

Reviewing the cases outlined above, it is evident that between 1931 and 1983 the auditor's duty of care to third parties evolved from nothing to a very wide duty. Prior to 1963, influenced by the *Ultramares* case, auditors' liability was restricted to that arising under a contractual relationship. By the mid-1980s, auditors' duty of care extended to virtually anyone whom the auditors could, or should, reasonably foresee might rely on the audited financial statements when making an investment decision in respect of the reporting entity. When it is remembered that the audited financial statements of companies are filed with the Registrar of Companies and are readily available for public scrutiny, auditors' duty of care and their exposure to potential liability had become very wide indeed.

In this regard it is interesting to note the remarks of Savage (1981), made after the *Jeb Fasteners* but before the *Twomax* decision:

> [I]t is not beyond the bounds of possibility that a British Court might hold that an auditor owes a duty of care to anyone who consults audited accounts at the Companies Registry and sustains a loss as a result of a negligent audit. To that extent the Jeb decision only brings the law into line with the public's expectations. If the auditor carries out his work with reasonable care and competence . . . he has

nothing to fear.[7] If he fails to do so then, rightly, justice and equity demand that the law give remedy to those who have suffered as a direct result of his negligence. (p. 341)

Nevertheless, as is shown below, Savage's views were not shared by the House of Lords in the case of *Caparo Industries plc v Dickman & Others* [1990] 1 All ER 568; [1990] 2 AC 605; [1990] 2 WLR 358, HL. The Law Lords apparently felt the law had gone too far.

14.4.2 The Caparo decision

The facts of this case are briefly as follows. In June 1984 Caparo Industries plc (Caparo) purchased shares in Fidelity plc, a company listed on the London Stock Exchange. Prior to the purchase (in May 1984), Fidelity's directors announced that the company's profits for the year were £1.3 million – well short of the forecast profit of £2.2 million. Nevertheless, relying on the audited financial statements, Caparo purchased more shares in Fidelity and, later in the year, made a successful takeover bid for the company.

Subsequent to the takeover, Caparo brought an action against the auditors (Touche Ross) alleging that, notwithstanding the unqualified audit report, Fidelity's accounts were inaccurate; the reported pre-tax profit of £1.3 million should, in fact, have been a reported loss of £0.46 million. In bringing its action, Caparo claimed that Touche Ross, as auditors of Fidelity, owed a duty of care to investors and potential investors and, in particular, to Caparo, in respect of the audit of Fidelity's accounts. More particularly, Caparo asserted that:

- Touche Ross knew or ought to have known:
    (a)   that in March 1984 a press release had been issued stating that profits for the financial year would fall significantly short of £2.2 million;
    (b)   that Fidelity's price fell from 143 pence per share on 1 March 1984 to 75 pence per share on 2 April 1984; and
    (c)   that Fidelity required financial assistance.
- Touche Ross therefore ought to have foreseen that Fidelity was vulnerable to a takeover bid and that persons such as Caparo might well rely on the accounts for the purpose of deciding whether to take over Fidelity and might well suffer loss if the accounts were inaccurate.

---

[7] This has been demonstrated in the case of *Lloyd Cheyham & Co Ltd v Littlejohn & Co* [1987] BCLC 303. This case established that:

1. Auditors are not required to do any more than a person can or should do for himself. A person is not entitled to place unwarranted reliance on the financial statements.

2. Auditors who have performed good quality audits and who have good defensible working papers which show that their conclusions were justified on the basis of the evidence gathered, are able to defend themselves.

The Law Lords were unanimous in their decision that, in general, auditors do not owe a duty of care to individual shareholders or to potential investors. Rather, a duty of care is owed to the company's shareholders as a body. In reaching this decision, the Lords held that *Scott Group Ltd* v *McFarlane & Others* (*supra*), and the subsequent English and Scottish decisions which had relied on *Scott Group*, namely, *Jeb Fasteners Ltd* v *Marks Bloom & Co* (*supra*) and *Twomax Ltd* v *Dickson, McFarlane & Robinson* (*supra*), had been decided wrongly.

Analysis of the House of Lords' decision in the *Caparo* case reveals that the Lords were concerned to ensure that the scope of liability arising in professional negligence cases is not extended beyond reasonable limits. They referred with considerable respect to Cardozo J's statement in the *Ultramares* case (*supra*), namely, that auditors' liability should not be extended to the point where it may exist 'in an indeterminate amount for an indeterminate time to an indeterminate class'. Their concern is reflected in Lord Oliver's statement:

> To apply as a test of liability only the foreseeability of possible damage without some further control would be to create a liability wholly indefinite in area, duration and amount and would open up a limitless vista of uninsurable risk for the professional man.

Lord Bridge indicated what 'further control' might be imposed before the court would find that auditors (and other professional advisers) owe a duty of care to those who rely upon their statements. He stated:

> [T]here should exist between the party owing the duty and the party to whom it is owed a relationship characterised by the law as one of proximity or neighbourhood and the situation should be one in which the court considers it fair, just and reasonable that the law should impose a duty of a given scope upon the one party for the benefit of the other.

Following from these (and other similar) lines of reasoning, the Lords considered that, in order to establish that a duty of care exists, a three-part test needs to be satisfied, namely:

(i) *foreseeability of damage:* When a person (A) makes a statement for another (B) (either an individual or a member of an identifiable class) to rely upon, A should be able to reasonably foresee that B might suffer loss if the statement is incorrect;

(ii) *proximity of relationship:* With respect to the statement made, there must be a relationship of proximity between A and B. Such a relationship will exist if, when making the statement, A knew:
- that the statement would be communicated to B;
- that the statement would be communicated in relation to a particular transaction or a transaction of a particular kind; and
- that B would be very likely to rely on the statement when making a decision with respect to the transaction in question.

In determining whether there is a relationship of proximity between the parties, the court will determine whether the particular damage suffered by B is the kind of damage A was under a duty to prevent and whether there are circumstances from which the court can pragmatically conclude that a duty of care existed;

(iii) fairness: The court must consider it fair, just and reasonable to impose a duty of care on A for the benefit of B.

While recognising that audited financial statements might be used for a variety of purposes, including the making of investment decisions, the Lords were of the view that their primary purpose is to protect the interests of the company *per se*, and to enable shareholders and debenture holders to evaluate the quality of the stewardship exercised by the company's directors and 'to exercise such powers as are vested in them by virtue of their respective propriety interests' (per Lord Oliver). Their purpose is not to protect the interests of the general public or investors in particular who choose to use the financial statements for a particular purpose.

The banks saw the auditor's function within the context of this purpose of financial statements. Lord Oliver, for example, stated:

It is the auditor's function to ensure, so far as possible, that the financial information as to the company's affairs prepared by the directors accurately reflects the company's position in order, first, to protect the company itself from the consequences of undetected errors . . . and, secondly, to provide shareholders with reliable intelligence for the purpose of enabling them to scrutinise the conduct of the company's affairs and to exercise their collective powers to reward or control or remove those to whom that conduct has been confided.

Following from this view of the auditor's function, the Law Lords concluded that, in the absence of special circumstances, auditors owe a duty of care only to (i) the company *per se* and (ii) the company's shareholders as a body. More particularly, in general, auditors do not owe a duty of care to individual share-holders or potential investors, irrespective of any reliance they may place on the audited financial statements for their investment decision(s). In order for a duty of care to arise, other than to the company or the shareholders as a body, the three-part test of foreseeability of damage, proximity of relationship, and fairness of imposing a duty of care must be satisfied.

This returned the law roughly to where it stood nearly 30 years earlier at the time of *Hedley Byrne* v *Heller and Partners* (*supra*). However, many com-mentators consider the reversal of the law to be unfortunate. Baxt (1990), for example, notes that, as a result of the *Caparo* decision, both professional investors (such as Caparo) and ordinary individual investors are denied a possible avenue for relief when they suffer loss as a result of negligence on the part of auditors. He states:

> Clearly, we do not wish to see the prophecy come true of Chief Justice Cardozo, nor do we wish to identify any particular group of professionals as being more subject to liabilities than others. But some protection is needed for the investor in circumstances such as [Caparo], assuming (and this is important and tends to be overlooked in cases of this kind) that liability can be established. (Baxt, 1990b, p. 18)

Picking up on the last point made by Baxt in the above quotation, he (Baxt, 1990a), Gwilliam (1988), and others (including Woodhouse J in the *Scott Group* case), have emphasised the difficulty of an investor bringing a successful action against auditors. As noted in section 14.2 above, in order to do so, the investor must satisfy the court that:

- the auditor in question owed him a duty of care;
- the auditor was negligent in the performance of his duties;
- the investor suffered a loss as a result of relying on the negligently audited financial statements.

It seems that in the *Caparo* case, the House of Lords, in seeking to ensure that auditors are not exposed to unbounded liability, focused on the first requirement (above). They appear to have given little attention to the third factor. Yet, as cases such as *Scott Group* and *Jeb Fasteners* have demonstrated, this is the most difficult factor to prove. Most investors would find it difficult to prove to the satisfaction of the court that audited financial statements provided the sole or main basis for an investment decision. As Baxt (1990) observes:

> There must be a number of factors that will influence a shareholder to buy more shares in a company for investment purposes – a comparative analysis of other companies' performances, the market reaction to the information about those companies, the individual shareholder's financial position, his/her interests and needs, and a myriad of other individual factors. Each case will see different shareholders having to prove different things in order to show that the particular investment decision taken was based on the auditor's report, and that any loss is linked to the report, assuming further, that the report was negligent. (p. 9)

In the case of a large investor such as Caparo, it must surely be extremely difficult to prove reliance on negligently prepared audited financial statements. A large investor would almost certainly be expected to seek additional information from the company and elsewhere (that is, to undertake due diligence) before committing significant resources to the investment, such as occurs when a takeover offer is made.

14.4.3 Development of auditors' duty to third parties since the Caparo decision

As may be seen from Figure 14.3, since *Caparo* a number of cases relevant to auditors' duty of care to third parties have been decided in the UK. Some of these, such as *Al-Saudi Banque and Ors* v *Clark Pixley* [1990] Ch 313, have clarified aspects of the *Caparo* three-part test for a duty of care to be established; others, especially those in more recent years, such as *Barings plc* v *Coopers & Lybrand*; *Barings Futures (Singapore) Pte Ltd* v *Mattar* [2002] EWHC 461 Ch; [2002] All ER (D) 309 (Mar), have served to widen once more, albeit to a limited extent, the parties to whom auditors may be held to owe a duty of care. The cases have also shown that the law in this area remains 'transitional' and 'developing' [Court of Appeal, *Siddell* v *Sydney Cooper & Partners* (1999) PNLR 511].

The *Al Saudi Banque* case (*supra*) helped to clarify what is required for a 'special relationship' to exist, such as to give rise to auditors owing a duty of care to third parties. The case involved a company whose business consisted of providing finance to overseas customers in exchange for bills of exchange. The company then used the bills of exchange (which constituted virtually all of the company's assets) to negotiate advances from the ten plaintiff banks. In 1983 the company was compulsorily wound up and the bills of exchange were found to be worthless. The banks sued the auditors for negligence, alleging that they ought reasonably to have foreseen that the banks would rely on the auditors' reports when deciding whether to continue, renew or increase loans to the company, that they did so rely on the reports and were misled thereby. At the time of the relevant audit reports (1981 and 1982), seven of the plaintiff banks were existing creditors of the company but three were not.

Millet J held that the auditors did not owe the banks a duty of care:
- In respect of the three banks which were not existing creditors at the dates of the audit reports, the judge noted that the auditors had not reported directly to the banks and had not intended or known that the reports would be communicated to them. Even though it was foreseeable that a bank might ask a company for copies of its audited financial statements when making loan decisions with respect to the company, the element of proximity necessary to find a duty of care was lacking.
- Regarding the other seven banks, Millet J observed that, although their identities and amounts of exposure were known to the auditors when they signed their audit reports, their position was not comparable to that of the company's shareholders to whom the auditors owed a statutory duty to report. As the auditors had not sent copies of their reports directly to the banks, or sent copies to the company with the intention or knowledge that they would be supplied to the banks, the auditors owed no duty of care to the plaintiffs.

This case suggested that, in order for auditors to owe a duty of care to a third party (or, more particularly, the audit client's bankers) they must either give a

Figure 14.3: **Summary of significant UK cases relating to auditors' liability to third parties post the Caparo ruling**

Case	Key finding(s) of the case
1. *Al-Saudi Banque & Others* v *Clark Pixley* [1990] Ch 313	The court applied *Caparo* and held that in order for auditors to owe a duty of care to a third party they must have given the third party a copy of their audit report, or know that their audit report will be supplied to the third party.
2. *James McNaughton Papers Group Ltd* v *Hicks Anderson* [1991] 1 All ER 134; [1990] BCC 891; (1991) 9 ACLC 3,091	The court applied *Caparo* and held that when deciding whether a 'special relationship' exists, such as to give rise to a duty of care to a third party, the following need to be considered: the purpose for which a statement is made, the purpose for which it is communicated to the third party, the relationship between the maker of the statement and the third party, the size of the class to which the third party belongs, the knowledge of the maker of the statement, and the extent to which the third party relies on the statement advice.
3. *Morgan Crucible Co plc* v *Hill Samuel Bank Ltd* [1991] Ch 295; [1991] 1 All ER 148; [1991] 2 WLR 655; [1991] BCLC 178; [1991] BCC 82; [1990] NLJR 1605	Applying *Caparo* the court held that if during a contested takeover bid financial advisers of the target company make express representations after an identified bidder has emerged, intending the bidder to rely on those representations, a relationship of proximity exists such that the financial advisers owe the bidder a duty of care not to be negligent in making representations which might mislead him.
4. *Berg Sons & Co Ltd* v *Mervyn Hampton Adams* [1993] BCLC 1045	The court applied, but effectively narrowed, the *Caparo* decision. It held: 1. For a company to succeed in an action against its auditors it must show the company or its shareholders were misled. 2. To establish that auditors owe a duty of care to a third party it must be shown that: (a) a specific relationship exists between the audit function and the transaction in relation to which reliance was placed on the audit report, and (b) the case is brought within the period in which it is reasonably foreseeable that reliance may be placed on the audited financial statements.
5. *Galoo Ltd* v *Bright Grahame Murray* [1995] 1 All ER 16; [1994] 1 WLR 1360; [1994] 2 BCLC 492; [1994] BCC 319	Applying *Caparo* the court held that: 1. A plaintiff can claim for damages for breach of contract by an auditor only when the breach is the effective or dominant cause of his loss – not when the breach merely provides the opportunity to sustain a loss. 2. If an auditor is aware that a particular investor will rely on the audited financial statements for a particular share purchase or lending decision, and intends the bidder or lender to rely on them, a duty of care to the bidder or lender will arise.
6. *Henderson* v *Merrett Syndicates* [1995] 2 AC 145; [1994] 3 All ER 506; [1994] 3 WLR 761; [1994] NLJR 1204; [1994] 4 LRC 355	The House of Lords introduced 'assumption of responsibility' as an alternative to the three-part *Caparo* test in determining whether a professional adviser owed a duty of care to a third party. It also established that a professional adviser could owe a duty of care: • simultaneously to a party under a contractual relationship and to a third party; • to the same person under a contractual relationship and under the common law.
7. *White* v *Jones* [1995] 2 AC 207; [1995] 1 All ER 691; [1991] 2 WLR 187; [1995] 3 FCR 51; [1995] NLJR 251, 139 Sol Jo LB 83	The House of Lords applied the 'assumption of responsibility' criterion to establish that a professional adviser owed a duty of care to a third party in circumstances where not to do so would result in an injustice. It also extended the situations in which a 'special relationship' may be said to exist – to include those between a professional adviser and those intended to benefit from the task accepted by the professional adviser.
8. *ADT Ltd* v *BDO Binder Hamlyn* [1996] BCC 808	Binder Hamlyn was held to have assumed responsibility to a third party (ADT), and thus owed it a duty of care, because Binder Hamlyn's partner made (negligently prepared) oral representations to ADT, knowing the purpose for which the information was required and knowing that ADT would rely on it without independent enquiry.
9. *Peach Publishing Ltd* v *Slater & Co* [1997] BBC 751	The court held that Slater & Co (auditors and advisers to ASA) did not assume responsibility to Peach Publishing Ltd when it confirmed that management accounts it had prepared 'were right'. The information was given by Slater to its client (ASA) to enable it to decide whether or not to give Peach the requested warranty as to the accounts' accuracy.

Figure 14.3: *Continued*

Case	Key finding(s) of the case
10. *Coulthard & Ors* v *Neville Russell* (1998) PNLR 276; (1998) 1 BCLC 143; (1998) BCC 359	As a matter of principle accountants can owe a duty of care to a client company's directors. However, whether a duty is owed in a particular case depends on the facts of the case and, in particular, on whether the accountants can be shown to have assumed responsibility to the directors.
11. *Siddell* v *Sydney Cooper & Partners* (1999) PNLR 511	The Court of Appeal emphasised that: 1. in the area of the liability of professional advisers, the law is in a state of transition or development; 2. there is a distinction between breaches of duty by professional advisers that cause another's loss and those that merely provide the opportunity to sustain a loss. The type of loss sustained is a question to be decided on the facts; 3. whether or not professional advisers owe a company's individual shareholders and directors a duty of care depends on the facts of the particular case.
12. *Bank of Credit & Commerce International (Overseas) Ltd, BCCI Holdings (Luxembourg) SA, and BCCI SA* v *Price Waterhouse, and Ernst & Whinney* [1998] BCC 617, [1998] 15 LS Gaz R 32, 142 Sol Jo LB 86; [1998] 5 PNLR 564	A duty of care may be owed by the auditors of one company to another company where the business of the two companies is conducted as a single business. The courts noticed that leading decided cases considering the liability of professional advisers to third parties for financial loss had adopted two approaches: 1. the 'threefold test' – for a duty of care to be owed by an adviser to an advisee: (a) it must be foreseeable that if negligent advice is given, the recipient is likely to suffer damage; (b) there is a sufficient proximate relationship between the parties; and (c) it is just and reasonable to impose the liability; 2. the 'voluntary assumption of responsibility test'. Factors to be taken into account when deciding whether these tests have been met, include: (i) the precise relationship between the adviser and advisee; (ii) the precise circumstances in which the advice came into existence and in which it was communicated to the advisee; (iii) the degree of reliance the adviser intended or should reasonably have anticipated would be placed on the accuracy of his advice by the advisee and the reliance in fact placed on it; (iv) the presence or absence of other advisers on whom the advisee would or could rely; (v) the opportunity, if any, given to the adviser to issue a disclaimer.
13. *Electra Private Equity Partners* v *KPMG Peat Marwick & Ors* [2001] 1 BCLC 589, [1999] All ER (D) 415	The Court of Appeal's decision indicates that: 1. when deciding whether auditors owe a duty of care to a third party, the court will consider factors such as the auditor's knowledge or foreseeability that the third party will rely on the audited financial statements for a particular decision; any direct communications between the auditor and the third party; whether the auditor believed the third party would receive independent advice and, if so, whether the auditor appreciated the adviser would rely on the audited financial statements in giving the advice; 2. the law in relation to the liability of professional advisers is in a state of transition; 3. the fact that a third party receives independent advice will not necessarily negate an auditor's duty of care to the third party.
14. *Barings plc* v *Coopers & Lybrand & Ors, Barings Futures (Singapore) Pte Ltd* v *Mattar & Ors* [2002] EWHC 461 (Ch); [2002] All ER (D) 309 (Mar)	In circumstances where the auditor of a subsidiary forwards information to the parent company for use in the preparation of the consolidated financial statements, a duty of care may be owed by the auditor of the subsidiary to the parent company.

copy of their audit report to the third party or intend or know that their report will be supplied to that party. The case of *James McNaughton Papers Group Ltd* v *Hicks Anderson & Co* [1991] 1 All ER 134; [1990] BCC 891; (1991) ACLC 3091, indicated other factors the court will consider when deciding whether or not auditors owe a duty of care to a third party. In this case, James McNaughton Ltd was involved in the takeover of another company (MK). Draft accounts for use in the negotiations were prepared by Hicks Anderson and, at a meeting of the negotiators, a representative of that firm stated that MK was breaking even. After the takeover was completed, discrepancies were found in the draft accounts and MK was found to be insolvent. McNaughtons sued the accountants for negligent preparation of the accounts and stated that, in proceeding with the takeover, they had relied on the accounts and the statement made at the negotiating meeting by the accountants' representative.

The court of first instance found that the accountants owed McNaughton Ltd a duty of care but this decision was reversed on appeal. The Court of Appeal, applying the *Caparo* judgment, held that when a statement or advice is acted upon by a person (C), other than the person intended by the giver of the statement or advice (A) to act on it, the factors to be considered in determining whether A owes C a duty of care include:

- the purpose for which the statement is made;
- the purpose for which the statement is communicated;
- the relationship between A, C and any relevant third party;
- the size of any class to which C belongs;
- the state of knowledge of A;
- the reliance by C on A's statement or advice.

Considering these factors, the court found that the accountants owed no duty of care to McNaughton Ltd in respect of the draft accounts because:

- the accounts were produced for MK, not McNaughtons;
- the accounts were merely draft accounts and the accountants could not have reasonably foreseen that McNaughtons would treat them as final accounts;
- the accountants did not take part in the negotiations;
- McNaughtons were aware that MK was in a poor financial state and, thus, could have been expected to consult their own accountants;
- the statement made at the negotiating meeting was very general and did not affect the figures in the accounts. The accountants could not reasonably have foreseen that McNaughtons would rely on the statement without further inquiry or advice.

The *McNaughton* case added to the *Al Saudi* decision in that it provided guidance as to the matters (other than knowledge or intention of reliance on the audit report) the court would consider when deciding whether or not auditors owe a duty of care to a third party. These include the purpose for which an audit report is prepared, the purpose for which it is communicated to a third party, and the extent to which the third party relies (or sensibly should rely) on the auditor's statement or advice.

The case of *Morgan Crucible Co plc* v *Hill Samuel Bank Ltd* [1991] Ch 295; [1991] 1 All ER 148; [1991] 2 WLR 655; [1991] BCLC 178; [1991] BCC 82; [1990] NLJR 1605, provided an example of a situation in which auditors (and other professional advisers) were held to owe a duty of care to a third party. On 6 December 1985, Morgan Crucible (MC) announced a takeover bid for another company (FCE). On 19 December 1985, FCE's chairman sent to FCE's shareholders the first of a number of circulars recommending that the takeover offer be refused. Each circular, which was also issued as a press release by Hill Samuel Bank Ltd (HSB, the merchant bank advising FCE), referred to the company's audited financial statements for the years to 31 January 1984 and 1985 and its unaudited interim statements for the six months to 31 July 1985. A circular dated 24 January 1985 forecast a 38% increase in pre-tax profits for the year to 31 January 1985. It also contained (i) a letter from FCE's auditors stating that the profit forecast had been properly compiled in accordance with FCE's stated accounting policies, and (ii) a letter from HSB expressing the opinion that the forecast had been made after due and careful enquiry.

On 29 January 1985, MC increased its offer and this was accepted. MC subsequently found that FCE was worthless. MC sued the bank, the auditors and the directors of FCE alleging that it was foreseeable that it would rely on the representations contained in the pre-bid financial statements and the profit forecast. MC claimed that FCE's accounting policies were flawed, its pre-bid financial statements were prepared negligently, and that its profit had been grossly overstated. It asserted that, had it known the true facts, it would not have made the takeover bid, let alone increased it.

The court of first instance, relying on *Caparo*, held that neither the financial advisers (in this case, HSB and the auditors) nor the directors of a target company in a contested takeover bid owe a duty of care to a known takeover bidder regarding the accuracy of profit forecasts, financial statements, and defence documents prepared for the purpose of contesting the bid. Such documents are prepared for the purpose of advising shareholders whether or not to accept the bid, not for the guidance of the bidder. Hence, there is insufficient proximity between the financial advisers and directors of the target company and the bidder to give rise to a duty of care.

The Court of Appeal reversed this decision. It held that if, during the course of a contested takeover bid, the financial advisers and directors of the target company make express representations after an identified bidder has emerged, intending that the bidder will rely on those representations, they owe the bidder a duty of care not to be negligent in making representations which might mislead him. In the instant case, the defendants intended the plaintiffs to rely on the pre-bid financial statements and profit forecast for the purpose of deciding whether to make an increased bid and the plaintiff did so rely. There was, therefore, a relationship of proximity between each of the defendants and the plaintiff such as to give rise to a duty of care.

The case of *Berg Sons & Co Ltd* v *Mervyn Hampton Adams* [1993] BCLC 1045, focused primarily on auditors' duty of care to the auditee (that is, auditors' contractual duties) but it also explored, and to some extent further narrowed, auditors' duty of care to third parties. This case involved a small company in which all of the shares were held by the sole executive director, his wife and his son. In 1985 the company was put into liquidation and the company's liquidator, together with a discount house which had provided Berg Sons & Co with finance, sued the auditors for negligence. It was alleged that, as a consequence of the auditor's unqualified audit report on the company's 1982 financial statements, (i) the company was able to continue in business and borrow money which it had no prospect of repaying, and (ii) the discount house discounted bills receivable which should have been shown in the financial statements as irrecoverable.

Hobhouse J found that the auditors were not negligent even though they had received unsatisfactory assurances from both the acceptor of certain bills and Mr Berg, and this should have prompted an audit report qualified on grounds of uncertainty. His Honour, following the reasoning of the Law Lords in *Caparo*, stated:

> [T]he purpose of the statutory audit is to provide a mechanism to enable those having a proprietary interest in the company . . . to have access to accurate financial information about the company. Provided that those persons have that information, the statutory purpose is exhausted . . . In the present case the . . . plaintiffs have based their case not upon any lack of information on the part of the company's executive director but rather upon the opportunity that the possession of the auditor's certificate is said to have given for the company to continue to carry on business and borrow money from third parties. Such matters do not fall within the scope of the duty of the statutory auditor.

With respect to the auditors owing the company a duty of care, the court held that, in order for a company to bring a successful action against its auditors, it must show 'that the company or its members were in some way misled or left in ignorance of some material fact' (per Hobhouse J). A 'one-man' company such as Berg Sons & Co could never prove that it had been misled because its controlling director and shareholder would always know better than anyone else the true position of the company and its business.

The court also held that the auditors owed no duty of care to the discount house. Hobhouse J reaffirmed, but went beyond, the *Caparo* decision. He stated that, before a duty of care to third parties will arise, two criteria must be satisfied:

1. There must be a specific relationship between the function the defendant has been requested to perform and the transaction in relation to which the plaintiff relied upon the proper performance of that function (in this case, between the statutory audit and the discounting of bills receivable).
2. The case must be brought within a limited period of the alleged negligence. There is only a limited period of time within which it would be reasonably foreseeable that a bank or discount house would rely upon a given set of audited financial statements.

Commenting on this decision of Hobhouse J in the *Berg* case, Davies (1992) pointed out:

> The effect of these additional limitations is to place such stringent restrictions on the circumstances in which the creditors of a company can sue its auditors that it is now difficult to imagine any circumstances when such a claim could succeed arising out of the statutory audit function. (p. 4)

He also noted that, as a result of the *Berg Sons & Co* judgment, it is most unlikely that a successful case can be brought in the UK against auditors by their small company audit clients or by such clients' creditors.

The case of *Galoo Ltd* v *Bright Grahame Murray* [1995] 1 All ER 16; [1994] 1 WLR 1360; [1994] 2 BCLC 492; [1994] BCC 319, served to confirm the difficulty a company's creditors will experience in trying to establish that the company's auditors owed them a duty of care. It also helped to clarify what the UK courts will accept (in the wake of the *Caparo* decision) as a 'special relationship' which may give rise to auditors owing a duty of care to a third party.

The facts of this case are briefly as follows. Hillsdown Holdings (HD) purchased 51% of the shares in GM; GM, in turn, held 100% of the shares in Galoo Ltd (GL). The acquisition agreement stated that the purchase price of the shares was to be 5.2 times the net profit of GM, as reflected in the audited financial statements of GM and GL for the year ending December 1986. The financial statements were audited by Bright Grahame Murray and delivered by them to HD for the specific purpose of establishing the share price. Between 1987 and 1992, HD advanced £30 million in loans to GM and GL and, in 1991, purchased a further 44% of shares in GM on terms set out in a supplemental share purchase agreement.

In 1992, HD, GM and GL sued the auditors, claiming that the audited financial statements of GM and GL for the years 1985 to 1989, and the draft audited financial statements for 1990, contained substantial inaccuracies. In auditing the financial statements without discovering or reporting such inaccuracies, the auditors had been negligent and in breach of their duties owed to the plaintiffs. If the auditors had performed their duties with reasonable skill and care, the insolvency of GM and GL would have been revealed and they would have ceased trading immediately. They would not have accepted, or continued to accept, advances from HD, and HD would not have purchased shares in GM or made loans to GM and GL.

The Court of Appeal was asked to rule on whether there was a sustainable cause of action against the auditors. It found there was – but only in respect of HD's initial 51% investment. The court held:

1. A plaintiff's claim that it had suffered loss by entering into a loan agreement did not give rise to any damages since the mere acceptance of a loan could not be described as a loss giving rise to damages. The mere acceptance by GM and GL of loans from HD in reliance on the auditors' statements did not give rise to any cause of action against the auditors.
2. A plaintiff is entitled to claim damages for breach of contract by the defendants where the breach is the effective or dominant cause of his loss – rather than merely providing him with the opportunity to sustain loss. Based on the facts in the instant case, the auditors' breach of duty clearly provided GM and GL with the opportunity to incur, and to continue to incur, trading losses, but it could not be said to have caused those losses.
3. The fact that it is foreseeable that a potential investor in a company might rely on a company's audited financial statements is not of itself sufficient to impose on the auditor a duty of care to the investor. However, if the auditor has been made aware that a particular identified bidder for shares or lender will rely on the audited financial statements, and the auditor intends that that party should so rely, the auditor owes a duty of care to the identified party and may be liable in the event of any breach of this duty. In respect of the 1987 acquisition of shares in GM by HD, it is clear that the auditors knew the audited financial statements for the year to December 1986 would be relied upon by HD for calculating the purchase price of the shares and they were required to submit the audited financial statements to HD for that specific purpose. Thus, the auditors owed a duty of care to HD in that regard. However, with respect to HD's loans to GM and GL and additional shares purchased in GM, it was not alleged that the auditors either knew or intended that HD would rely on the audited financial statements of GM and GL when deciding whether to make the loans or when calculating the purchase price of the shares in GM under the supplemental share price agreement. Hence, no duty of care was owed by the auditors to HD in respect of the loans or the additional shares purchased.

From the post-*Caparo* cases reviewed above, it is evident that subsequent to *Caparo* it was (and, indeed remains) extremely difficult for third parties to establish that auditors owe them a duty of care. To do so, they must show that the auditors knew, or intended, that they would place reliance on the audited financial statements for a specific transaction, that there is a nexus between the audit and the transaction, and that they brought their case against the auditors within a limited period of the auditors' alleged negligence. However, as the cases outlined below bear witness, in recent years the courts have modified the *Caparo* decision to some extent and have recognised a duty of care to third parties in situations where strict application of the three-part *Caparo* test (foreseeability of damage, proximity of relationship, and fairness of imposing a duty) would have precluded such a duty being owed. The most significant modification of the *Caparo* ruling is the court's recognition of a duty of care arising when auditors (or other professional advisers) 'assume responsibility' to a third party. This principle was enunciated by the House of Lords in *Henderson v Merrett Syndicates* [1995] 2 AC 145; [1994] 3 All ER 506; [1994] 3 WLR 761; [1994] NLJR 1204; [1994] 4 LRC 355.

In the *Henderson* case the plaintiffs were Lloyd's names[8] who were members of syndicates that were managed by the defendants. The plaintiffs fell into two groups:

(i) 'direct names' – names who belonged to syndicates that were managed by the members' agents. Thus, the agents were both the members' and managing agents;[9]

(ii) 'indirect names' – names who were placed by their members' agents with syndicates that were managed by other agents. The members' agents entered into sub-agency agreements with the managing agents of those syndicates.

The relationship between the names, members' agents and managing agents was regulated by agency and sub-agency agreements. These gave the managing agent 'absolute discretion' in respect of underwriting business conducted on behalf of the names but also contained an implied term that the agents would exercise due care and skill in the exercise of their functions as managing agents.

Following very poor performance in the Lloyd's insurance market, the plaintiffs sued the defendants, alleging that they had been negligent in the conduct

---

[8] Names are persons who underwrite (or accept the risks – and hence the financial consequences – attaching to) insurance contracts within the Lloyd's insurance market. As the potential liability attaching to an insurance contract can run into many millions of pounds, the names are organised in syndicates which operate as single entities to underwrite one or more insurance contract and also, in appropriate circumstances, to re-insure the syndicate against the risks attaching to insurance contracts they have accepted.

[9] Names are members of Lloyd's and each member has an agent (which, almost invariably, is a firm of professional insurance underwriters) who looks after their interests within the Lloyd's insurance market. Additionally, each syndicate has a managing agent (also a firm of professional insurance underwriters) who conducts the business of the syndicate.

and management of the plaintiffs' syndicates. The key issues for the court to decide included the following:

(i) whether the members' (and managing) agents owed a common law duty of care to the direct names, notwithstanding that a contractual relationship existed between them;

(ii) whether the managing agents appointed as sub-agents by the members' agents owed a duty of care to the indirect names (who were third parties in respect of the sub-agency agreements);

(iii) whether the members' agents were responsible to the indirect names for any failure on the part of the managing agents to whom they had delegated underwriting duties under the sub-agency agreements.

The court of first instance found in the plaintiffs' favour on all three issues. The defendants appealed to the Court of Appeal. When that court dismissed their appeal, they appealed to the House of Lords. The Law Lords also dismissed their appeal, explaining their reasons as follows.

1. Where a person assumes responsibility to perform professional services for another who relies on those services, the relationship between the parties is sufficient, in itself, to give rise to a duty by the person providing the services to exercise reasonable skill and care in so doing. Accordingly, the managing agents at Lloyd's owed a duty of care to the names who were members of the syndicates they managed. By holding themselves out as possessing special expertise to advise the names on the suitability of risks to be underwritten, on when, and the extent to which, re-insurance should be taken out, and on claims that should be settled, the agents clearly assumed responsibility towards the names in their syndicates. Moreover, names, as the managing agents well knew, placed implicit reliance on that expertise in that they gave authority to the managing agents to bind them (the names) to contracts of insurance and re-insurance, and to the settlement of claims.

2. An assumption of responsibility by a person rendering professional services, coupled with reliance on those services by the person for whom they are rendered, can give rise to a common law duty of care irrespective of any contractual relationship between the parties. In the case of the direct names, their contract with their members' agents did not operate to exclude the common law duty of care because an implied term of the agency agreements was that the agents would exercise due care and skill in the exercise of their functions as managing agents; that duty of care is no different from the duty of care owed by the managing agents to the names under the common law. Likewise, the indirect names were not prevented by the chain of contracts contained in the agency and sub-agency agreements from suing the managing agents under the common law. In particular, the fact that the managing agents had, with the consent of the indirect names, assumed responsibility in

respect of their managing activities to the members' agents under sub-agency agreements (thus, under contract), did not prevent the managing agents from also assuming responsibility in respect of the same activities to the indirect names as third parties to those agreements.

Thus, in *Henderson* v *Merrett Syndicates,* the House of Lords recognised the criterion of 'assumption of responsibility' as an alternative to the three-part *Caparo* test to apply when determining whether or not a professional adviser (or professional services provider) owed a duty of care to a third party who relied on his or her advice (or services). The Law Lords also established that a professional adviser (or services provider) may simultaneously owe a duty of care to a party with whom the adviser has a contractual relationship and to a third party. Additionally, the fact that a person is in a contractual relationship with a professional adviser does not preclude that person from also being owed a common law duty of care by the adviser.

The House of Lords applied the criterion of 'assumption of responsibility' to determine whether or not a professional adviser owed a duty of care to a third party in *White* v *Jones* [1995] 2AC 207; [1995] 1 All ER 691; [1991] 2 WLR 187; [1995] 3 FCR 51; [1995] NLJR 251, 139 Sol Jo LB 83. This case concerned a testator who, on 17 July 1986, instructed solicitors to prepare a will including gifts of £9,000 for each of his two daughters. Nothing was done to effect the testator's instructions until the managing clerk of the solicitors' firm arranged to visit him on 17 September 1986. However, the testator died on 14 September and the daughters sued the solicitors for negligence.

The court of first instance held that the solicitors owed no duty of care to the plaintiff daughters. The daughters appealed and the Court of Appeal over-turned the decision. The solicitors then appealed to the House of Lords contending that, as the plaintiffs' claim was for a purely financial loss, it could only lie in contract and there was no contract between the solicitor and the disappointed beneficiaries.

The House of Lords held that, where a solicitor accepts instructions to prepare a will and, as a result of his negligence an intended beneficiary is reasonably foreseeably deprived of a legacy, the solicitor is liable for the loss suffered. The Law Lords explained their reasons as follows:

1. The assumption of responsibility by a solicitor towards his client should be extended in law to an intended beneficiary who is reasonably foreseeably deprived of his intended legacy as a result of the solicitor's negligence in circumstances where there is no contractual or fiduciary relationship and neither the testator nor his estate has any remedy against the solicitor.

Unless the intended beneficiary can claim there is no remedy against the solicitor's negligence and an injustice will occur.
2. Adopting the incremental approach by analogy with established cases giving rise to a duty of care, the principle of assumption of responsibility should be extended to a solicitor who accepts instructions so that he is held to be in a special relationship with those intended to benefit under those instructions, so that he owes a duty to the intended beneficiary to act with due expedition and care in relation to the task he has accepted.

Thus, in *White* v *Jones* (*supra*) the House of Lords applied the 'assumption of responsibility' criterion to establish that a professional adviser (a solicitor) owed a duty of care to a third party (a beneficiary under a will) in circumstances where not to do so would give rise to an injustice. The Law Lords also extended the situations in which a 'special relationship' may be said to exist – to include those between a solicitor (or other professional adviser) and the parties intended to benefit from the task accepted by the solicitor (or, more generally, the parties intended to benefit from a task accepted by a professional adviser).

The case of *ADT Ltd* v *BDO Binder Hamlyn* [1996] BCC 808, also shows that, when justice demands it, the courts will go beyond the *Caparo* ruling and impose a duty of care on a professional adviser (in this case auditors) to a third party. Binder Hamlyn issued an unqualified audit report on the 1989 financial statements of Britannia Securities Group (BSG) – a company ADT Ltd was contemplating purchasing. In January 1990, a partner of Binder Hamlyn attended a meeting with a director of ADT and confirmed that BSG's 1989 audited financial statements showed a true and fair view of BSG's state of affairs. On the strength of this representation ADT purchased BSG for £105 million. It was subsequently found that BSG's true value was £40 million.

The question to be decided by the court was whether, as a result of the oral assurance given by Binder Hamlyn's partner to the ADT director in respect of BSG's audited financial statements, Binder Hamlyn had assumed responsibility to ADT and thus owed it a duty of care. May J held that Binder Hamlyn had assumed responsibility to ADT at the meeting in January 1990 when its partner gave (negligently prepared) information or advice directly to ADT, knowing the purpose for which it was required and knowing ADT would place reliance on it without further enquiry. The judge also noted that the defendants were negligent when conducting the 1989 audit; their standard of professional competence did not achieve that of ordinarily skilled auditors. The judge awarded damages against Binder Hamlyn of £65 million for the difference in the amount paid for BSG (£105 million) and its true value (£40 million).

Application of the *ADT* decision was limited somewhat by the Court of Appeal's ruling in *Peach Publishing Ltd* v *Slater & Co* [1997] BBC 751. Peach Publishing

Ltd was incorporated by Mrs Land for the purpose of acquiring Anthony Sheil Associates Ltd (ASA). During the negotiations, ASA was advised by its auditors, Slater & Co, and Mrs Land received independent advice from Ernst & Young.

During the course of negotiations, ASA was asked to produce up-to-date management accounts. Based on information provided by ASA, Slater produced a balance sheet and a profit and loss account for the 10 months to October 1990 (when the acquisition was planned) and handed the statements to Mrs Land. At a subsequent meeting, Mrs Land asked ASA to warrant the accuracy of the accounts provided. This ASA would not do. Considerable pressure was then put on Mr Slater to confirm that the accounts 'were right' in order for a warranty to be given. Mr Slater told the meeting that the balance sheet and profit and loss account 'were right', subject to the qualification that they had not been audited. ASA then gave Mrs Land the requested warranty. It was subsequently found that the accounts were misleading. Peach sued Slater & Co claiming that Mr Slater's representation had induced Peach to buy all the shares of ASA.

The court of first instance held that Slater & Co owed Peach a duty of care in respect of the assurance given. However, this decision was reversed by the Court of Appeal. The key issue for the court to decide was whether Mr Slater had assumed responsibility to Peach for the accuracy of the financial statements. The Appeal court held that, on the facts of the case, he had not. The judge explained that when Mrs Land asked Mr Slater for the assurance, her real interest was getting a warranty from ASA. Thus, Mr Slater did not assume responsibility to Peach but merely gave his client, ASA, information on which it could decide whether or not to give the warranty. The judge also noted that a prudent purchaser would not have relied on the management accounts without asking their own advisers to check the figures.

Like the *ADT* case considered above, those of *Coulthard & Ors v Neville Russell* (1998) PNLR 276; (1998) 1 BCLC 143; (1998) BCC 359, and *Siddell v Sydney Cooper & Partners* (1999) PNLR 511, extended the *Caparo* decision by recognising that an accountant's duty of care is not limited to the company *per se* and the company's shareholders as a body, but may also be owed to the company's directors and shareholders as individuals. However, in each case, the court emphasised that whether or not a duty of care is owed by a professional adviser to a third party depends upon the particular circumstances of the case.

The *Coulthard* case involved Neville Russell's failure to advise its client company's directors that loan payments to a shell company to pay for shares the company was purchasing in the parent company might infringe section 151 of the Companies Act 1985. The High Court judge refused to uphold Neville

Russell's assertion that the plaintiff's action against it had insufficient legal grounds to proceed. Neville Russell appealed the decision but the Court of Appeal confirmed the lower court's ruling. The Court of Appeal held that, as a matter of principle, accountants can owe a duty of care to a client company's directors but whether or not a duty is owed in a particular case depends upon the facts of the case and, in particular, on whether it can be shown that the accountants had assumed responsibility to the directors.

In *Siddell* v *Sydney Cooper & Partners* (*supra*), the defendants (SCP) were the auditors and management accountants of a small family-run company with four shareholders and directors (Mr and Mrs Siddell and Mr and Mrs Fellows). Following the departure of the company's finance director (Mrs Jefferies – the only 'outside' director) in 1992, irregularities were found in the accounting records. Soon afterwards the company, which had been thought to be profitable, went into receivership with a deficit of more than £1 million. The plaintiffs sued SCP for breach of their duty of care to them as shareholders and directors. The court of first instance held that the plaintiffs' claim had insufficient legal grounds to proceed. Following *Caparo*, the judge held that auditors do not normally owe a duty of care to a company's shareholders.

The plaintiffs appealed the decision and the Court of Appeal overturned the lower court's ruling. Mummery LJ and Clarke LJ explained their reasons as follows:

1. Where, as in the case of the liability of professional advisers, the law is in a state of transition or development, an order to disallow an action to proceed should not be made unless the court can be properly persuaded that the claim is bound to fail. This is not the position in this case.
2. The judge (in the court of first instance), relying on *Caparo* v *Dickman* (1990) and *Galoo Ltd* v *Bright Grahame Murray* (1994), disallowed the appellants' action to proceed on the basis that SCP owed them, as third parties, no duty of care. The judge also submitted that, as in *Caparo*, liability did not arise unless it could be shown that the advisers intended or knew that the third parties were personally relying on the services being provided to the company and there was actual reliance. While accepting for present purposes these requirements for liability to arise (although noting that the law is in a state of transition or development), the facts in this case are very different from those in *Caparo*. SCP were not simply acting as auditors but were providing broader services to the company, including the preparation of quarterly and annual accounts and the giving of advice. Following *Henderson* v *Merrett Syndicates Ltd* (1995) 2 AC 145, it cannot be maintained that the existence of a contract between the parties necessarily precludes a co-extensive duty of care at common law (that is, to third parties).

3. The judge in the first court also disallowed the appellants' action to proceed on the basis that the alleged breaches of duty did not cause the appellants' loss but merely provided an opportunity to sustain loss. Only the former kind of loss is recoverable. It is for the court to decide, by applying common sense, which type of loss has been suffered. However, it is important to note that the question of whether a particular loss has been caused by a breach of duty is a question of fact and, as such, an action should not be prevented from proceeding on this ground unless it is bound to fail. That is not the position in this case.

In the course of its judgment, the Court of Appeal noted:

> The principles upon which *Caparo* was based cannot be restricted to large companies [but] whether a duty of care [to third parties] exists depends upon all the circumstances of the particular case. Those circumstances will include the size of the company and the number and type of shareholders (or indeed directors) to whom the duty is said to be owed (as quoted in Scott, 1999).

By recognising that auditors (or accountants) may owe a duty of care to their client company's shareholders and/or directors as individuals, *Coulthard* v *Neville Russell* and *Siddell* v *Sydney Cooper & Partners* clearly extended the *Caparo* decision. However, the story does not end here. In the case of *Bank of Credit & Commerce International (Overseas) Ltd, BCCI Holdings (Luxembourg) SA*, and *BCCI SA* (Plaintiffs) v *Price Waterhouse and Ors*, and *Ernst & Whinney and Ors* (Defendants) [1998] BCC 617; [1998] 15 LS Gaz R 32, 142 Sol Jo LB 86; [1998] 5 PNLR 564, the Court of Appeal held that the auditor of one company may owe a duty of care to another [third-party] company. In this case the court also took the opportunity to summarise the approaches to the liability of professional advisers for financial loss which had been adopted in leading cases where the issue had been considered.

The facts of the case are briefly as follows. On 5 July 1991, after evidence had emerged of a large scale global fraud extending back several years, an international swoop co-ordinated by the Bank of England closed down the Bank of Credit & Commerce International (BCCI) group of companies.

Until 1987, when BCCI was persuaded to engage Price Waterhouse (PW) as its sole auditors, it was able to obscure its world-wide fraudulent operations by engaging different auditors for its different banking subsidiaries. While Ernst & Whinney (E&W) acted as the auditors of BCCI Holdings (Luxembourg) SA and BCCI SA (located in Luxembourg), PW acted as auditors of BCCI (Overseas) (located in the Cayman Islands).

The liquidators of all three banks brought proceedings against PW [as auditors of all the banks for the years 1987, 1988 and 1989 and of BCCI (Overseas) prior to 1987] and E&W [as auditors of BCCI (Holdings) and BCCI SA prior to 1987] for negligently performed audits; audits that failed to detect massive frauds being perpetrated on BCCI's creditors and shareholders. In addition to suing PW for breach of its contractual duties, BCCI (Overseas) alleged that E&W also owed it a duty of care on the grounds that the business and operations of Overseas and BCCI SA (BCCI's two principal banking subsidiaries) were managed as if they were the business and operations of a single bank (Lascelles and Donkin, 1991).

In the trial court, Laddie J held that BCCI (Overseas)'s claim against E&W could not proceed. He said that, in order to proceed, Overseas had to show that E&W had provided it with information, knowing or intending that Overseas would rely on it for a particular purpose, and that Overseas had in fact relied on the information for that purpose. (Expressed in terms of the *Caparo* ruling, it had to meet the requirements for a relationship of proximity to be established.) Laddie J ruled that Overseas had not succeeded in pleading a case that contained the required elements.

Upon appeal the Court of Appeal overturned the decision. During its judgment, the court noted:

> The liability of accountants and of other professional advisers for economic loss caused by reason of their alleged negligence to persons other than their clients has been the subject of a substantial number of leading cases. In *Smith* v *Eric S Bush* (1990) I AC 83 'the threefold test' as to whether a duty of care is owed by an adviser to those who act on his advice was stated to be: (a) it must be foreseeable that if the advice is negligent the recipient is likely to suffer the kind of damage that has occurred; (b) there is a sufficient proximate relationship between the parties and (c) it is just and reasonable to impose the liability (Lord Griffiths at (1990) 1 AC 864H). To this test has been added 'the voluntary assumption of responsibility test' referred to in *Henderson* v *Merrett Syndicate Ltd* (1995) 2 AC 145 by Lord Goff and extended from the principle underlying the decision in *Hedley Bryne* v *Heller and Partners Ltd* (1964) AC 465.

The court pointed out that the 'threefold test' and the 'assumption of responsibility test' indicated the criteria that had to be satisfied in order for liability to be attached to the appellants. It also noted that the authorities had provided guidance on factors to be taken into account in deciding whether these criteria had been met. These include:

(a) the precise relationship between the adviser and advisee;
(b) the precise circumstances in which the advice came into existence and in which the advice was communicated to the advisee, and whether the communication was made by the adviser or by a third party;
(c) the degree of reliance the adviser intended or should reasonably have anticipated would be placed on its accuracy by the advisee and the reliance in fact placed on it;

(d) the presence or absence of other advisers on whom the advisee would or could rely;

(e) the opportunity, if any, given to the adviser to issue a disclaimer.

The court also observed that decided cases concerning the liability of professional advisers to third parties had established that any development in the law in this area ought only to made incrementally. It further noted:

> It needs to be borne in mind that . . . a barrier exists between an adviser and any person who is not his immediate client [i.e. a third party] which has to be overcome before the adviser can be said to owe a duty to that person, a barrier which will be all the stronger if that person is in receipt of independent advice. However, the reality in the present case is that any barrier between Ernst & Whinney and BCCI (Overseas) was a mere shadow. Overseas' and BCCI SA's banking activities were conducted as those of a single bank, such was the intermingling of their operations and the constant exchange of information between them. Ernst & Whinney were, in effect, the supervising auditors of both banks, as well as the auditors of BCCI Holdings (Luxembourg) SA.

The court held that, if the threefold test or the assumption of responsibility test were applied to the facts of the case, it would be quite wrong to dismiss the claims of Overseas against E&W on the grounds that they had no legal foundation.[10] However, the court noted that the facts of the case were very unusual and, therefore, the case ought not to be regarded as setting a precedent. Nevertheless, the court's decision is very significant in terms of auditors' liability to third parties as it shows that, in certain circumstances (such as where the business of two companies is conducted as if it were a single business), the court will recognise that the auditors of one company may owe a duty of care to another (third party) company.

Since the Court of Appeal's summary of the law relating to the liability of accountants and other professional advisers to third parties for financial loss suffered as a result of the professional adviser's negligence, two other cases of note have reached the courts, namely, *Electra Private Equity Partners* v *KPMG Peat Marwick & Ors* [2001] 1 BCLC 589; [1999] All ER (D) 415, and *Barings plc* v *Coopers & Lybrand & Ors, Barings Futures (Singapore) Pte Ltd* v *Mattar & Ors* [2002] EWHC 461 (Ch); [2002] All ER (D) 309 (Mar).

The *Electra* case concerned venture capital fund managers who, in May 1992, invested IR£10 million in unquoted convertible loan stock and thereby acquired effective control of C plc, an Irish leasing company. Eighteen months

---

[10] BCCI's liquidators originally filed claims against PW and E&W for $11 billion (approximately £6.5 billion). However, in September 1998, PW and E&W agreed an out-of-court settlement with the liquidators for an amount reputed to be in the region of $95–100 million (Nisse, 1999; *The Financial Times*, 1998).

later the plaintiffs lost all of their investment when C plc went into receivership. The plaintiffs sought to recover their losses from two firms of accountants:

(i) KPMG – whom the plaintiffs had instructed to investigate and report on the suitability of the investment, and
(ii) SKC (an Irish partnership which was part of the KPMG international firm) – who, as auditors of C plc had provided, or concurred in C plc producing, to the plaintiffs prior to the investment, C's audited financial statements (complete with 'clean' audit report) for the year ending 29 February 1992.

Carnwath J disallowed Electra's claim against SKC from proceeding on the basis that, in order for a duty to arise to a third party, the claimant would need to show that the auditors had consciously assumed responsibility to the third party. The plaintiffs appealed the ruling and the Court of Appeal found in their favour. Reasons advanced by the court for its decision included the following:

1. The court's determination in a case such as the present might depend, in particular, on:
   (a) knowledge or foreseeability by the auditor that the potential investor would rely on the accuracy of the audited financial statements in deciding whether to invest – as distinct from insisting on audited reports and an unqualified auditor's report as a condition of investment;
   (b) the fact and nature of any direct communications between the auditor and the potential investor;
   (c) whether the auditor reasonably believed that the potential investor would obtain independent advice on the suitability of the investment; and
   (d) if he did so believe, whether he appreciated that the independent adviser would rely on his (the auditor's) figures for the purpose of advising the potential investor.
   The court held that Carnwath J had wrongly focused on a 'conscious assumption of responsibility' as the test of the existence of a duty of care, and this could have resulted in too high a threshold for the plaintiffs. Electra's claim against SKC gave rise to a triable issue, namely, whether SKC knew or foresaw the purpose for which the plaintiffs required the audited financial statements, and whether they assumed responsibility for their accuracy by providing them to the plaintiffs in the alleged circumstances (i.e. for the purpose of making an investment decision).
2. The court should proceed with great caution in exercising its power to disallow cases from proceeding on the basis of the facts presented when:
   (a) all the facts are not known by the court;
   (b) the facts, and the legal principles turning on them, are complex; and
   (c) when the law, as in the instant case, is in a state of development.

Actions by a third party against auditors and other professional advisers for negligence are notable examples of facts-sensitive cases where the law is still in a state of transition.

3. Carnwath J wrongly held that the involvement of KPMG as independent advisers was fatal to the plaintiffs' claimed duty of care by SKC. It was not necessary to the success of the claim that KPMG be acting as agents for Electra in their dealings with SKC. Further, there had been considerable direct contact between Electra and SKC. At the very least, it was arguable that such a tripartite relationship, particularly having regard to the close professional association between KPMG and SKC, created a 'special relationship' between the plaintiffs and SKC.

The *Barings* case (*supra*) or, more correctly, the portion of the case of relevance to the theme of this section of the chapter, namely, auditors' liability to third parties, essentially turned on the question of whether Coopers & Lybrand Singapore (C&LS) owed a duty of care to Barings plc. During 1992 and 1993, Deloitte & Touche (D&T) were the auditors of Barings Futures (Singapore) Pte Ltd (BFS) – a subsidiary of Barings Securities Ltd (BSL) which was, in turn, an indirect subsidiary of Barings plc, a non-trading group holding company based in London. In 1994, D&T were replaced by C&LS as auditors of BFS. Coopers & Lybrand (C&L) were the auditors of both BSL and Barings plc throughout the relevant period. As auditors of BFS, D&T and C&LS were required to provide Barings plc's directors with consolidated schedules (and a copy of BFS's audit report) which the directors used in preparing the group's consolidated financial statements.

The Barings Group collapsed in February 1995 as a result of the unauthorised and heavily loss-making trading of Nick Leeson, general manager of BFS. In 1996, the liquidators of the Barings Group sued C&L, C&LS and the Singapore partners of D&T for £1 billion,[11] claiming that their negligent auditing of the group accounts (by C&L) and of BFS's accounts (by D&T and C&LS) was responsible for the collapse of the Barings Group in 1995. C&L, C&LS and D&T maintained that the collapse of the group was due to management failings and fraud, not to the work of the auditors (Perry, 2001a). Irrespective of the outcome of that fundamental and overarching argument, at a more detailed level, C&LS and D&T challenged the claims brought against them by Barings plc and BFS, respectively.[12]

---

[11] As reported, for example, Perry (2001b).

[12] The portion of the case which addressed the question of whether D&T had sufficient grounds to negate claims brought against it by BFS did not concern auditors' liability to third parties. However, as the key issue in dispute is the reliance auditors may place on letters of representation, a topic we discussed in Chapter 12 (section 12.5), we have reported this portion of the case in an Appendix to this chapter.

C&LS sought to have Barings plc's claim against it dismissed as having no legal foundation. The firm submitted that it owed a duty of care to BFS (its audit client) but not to Barings plc: any claim for damage suffered as a consequence of its negligence could only be claimed by the subsidiary that had suffered damage (i.e. BFS) and not by its shareholder (Barings plc). The information C&LS was required to supply to Barings plc was simply so that Barings plc's directors could comply with their legal obligation to prepare consolidated financial statements. The High Court found in favour of C&LS but Barings plc appealed its ruling.

Unlike the High Court, the Court of Appeal did not accept C&LS's arguments. Leggatt L J pointed out that at no time during the audit of BFS's consolidation schedules, prepared for the purpose of the group's consolidated financial statements, did the auditors detect or report the unauthorised trading of Leeson or the losses that had resulted. On the contrary, those schedules showed BFS to be profitable. He cited with approval the decision in *George Fischer (Great Britain) Ltd* v *Multi Construction Ltd* [1995] 1 BCLC 260, where it was held that there was no legal principle preventing a holding company from recovering damages for loss in the value of its subsidiaries resulting directly from a breach of duty owed to it, as distinct from a duty owed to the subsidiaries themselves.

Leggatt LJ also noted that C&LS could not have supposed that the only responsibility it assumed to Barings plc was to submit BFS's schedules in a form suitable for incorporation into the consolidated financial statements and that it did not matter whether they showed a true and fair view of BFS's financial affairs. His Honour observed that an auditor's task is to conduct the audit so as to make it probable that material misstatements in financial documents will be detected. That did not occur and C&LS had a case to answer. The Court of Appeal concluded that C&LS must have appreciated that their audit report and consolidated schedules would be used for the purpose of producing the consolidated financial statements. That was enough to establish that C&LS owed a duty of care to Barings plc in addition to that owed to BFS.[13]

According to Leggat L J, a critical point in this case is that Barings plc pleaded a direct relationship between it and C&LS arising from the circumstances in which work was done for, and information was supplied by, C&LS to Barings

---

[13] Rather than pursue their case through the courts, in October 2001, C&L and C&LS (now part of PwC) reached an out-of-court settlement with the liquidators of the Barings Group for an undisclosed sum (Perry, 2001b). [A prior settlement, expected to be finalised in September 2001 but which failed at the last minute, was rumoured to be for between £70 million and £100 million (Perry, 2001a).] By the time the settlement was finalised (in October 2001), legal costs involved in the cases brought by the Barings Group against C&L, C&LS, and D&T had exceeded £100 million (Perry, 2002).

plc and its auditors in England (C&L) relating to the preparation of the group's accounts. This seems to limit future application of the decision to cases in which the facts are fairly similar. Nevertheless, as a result of the court's ruling in this case, it seems likely that where the auditor of a subsidiary forwards information to the parent company for use in the preparation of the group's consolidated financial statements, a duty of care will be owed, more or less routinely, by the auditor of the subsidiary to the parent company.

From our review of cases decided in the post-*Caparo* era, it is evident that since the House of Lords' momentous decision in the *Caparo* case in 1990, which essentially returned the law relating to auditors' liability to third parties to where it had stood at the time of *Hedley Bryne* v *Heller and Partners* (*supra*) nearly 30 years previously, the courts have gradually adopted a slightly more liberal approach to the question of the parties to whom auditors may be held to owe a duty of care.

The *Caparo* decision appeared to be a definitive statement of auditors' duty of care for economic loss owed to third parties (Berwin Leighton, 1999) and, seemingly, served to create a fairly certain and protected environment for auditors in terms of their exposure to liability. In order for auditors to owe a duty of care to a third party the three-part test of (i) forseeablity of damage, (ii) proximity of relationship between the auditor and the third party, and (iii) fairness of imposing a duty on the auditor, had to be satisfied. However, despite the apparent certainty of the position established by the Law Lords, as we have noted, in recent years the courts have emphasised that the law in this area is far from certain; indeed, as judges have noted, 'it is in a state of transition and development' (for example, in the *Siddell* and *Electra* cases cited above). Nevertheless, whilst acknowledging this characteristic of uncertainty and transition, some key factors of the law relating to the liability of auditors to third parties as it currently stands can be distilled from the cases we have reviewed. These are as follows:

1. In addition to the 'three-part *Caparo* test', the courts may apply the 'voluntary assumption of responsibility test' to determine whether or not an auditor owed a duty of care to a third-party plaintiff in a particular case.
2. Although the law relating to the liability of auditors to third parties for economic loss is transitional and developmental, it will be developed only incrementally (i.e. in small steps). Apparently, the courts are not anxious to return (at least, not rapidly) to the situation which existed in the early 1980s following the *Jeb Fasteners* and *Twomax* decisions (see section 14.4.1 above) which left auditors exposed to potentially extremely onerous liability.
3. In cases in which a third party has received independent advice, this will serve to strengthen the barrier between the auditor and the third party which will need to be overcome before the auditor will be held to owe a duty of care

to the third party. However, the fact that a third party has received independent advice will not necessarily negate the auditor's duty of care to that party.

4. When a third party claims to have suffered financial loss as a consequence of the auditor's negligence, the court will evaluate the facts of the case to determine whether the auditor's negligence actually caused the loss or whether it merely provided an opportunity for the plaintiff to sustain a loss. Only the former type of loss will give rise to damages.

5. In order to succeed in a case alleging financial loss caused by an auditor's negligence, a third party must commence proceedings within the period in which it is reasonably foreseeable that reliance may be placed on the audited financial statements.

6. Whether or not an auditor will be held to owe a duty of care to one or more third parties in a particular case depends upon the facts of that case. The courts have demonstrated that, notwithstanding the *Caparo* decision, auditors may, in principle, be held to owe a duty of care to, *inter alia*, individual shareholders and directors of auditee companies, to a 'sister' subsidiary company and/or the parent company of the auditee and to the auditors of the parent company. However, in each of the cases, such as those noted above, where the auditor has been held to owe a duty of care to a third party, the court has emphasised that its decision is case specific; that is, it applies only in the circumstances of the particular case being considered by the court (see, for example, the *ADT, Coulthard, Siddell, BCCI* and *Barings* cases cited above).

Although we can identify these and other elements of the law relating to auditors' liability to third parties as it currently stands, a more general common theme may be discerned from the cases we have reviewed. This theme was given explicit recognition by the New Zealand Court of Appeal in *South Pacific Manufacturing Co Ltd v New Zealand Security Consultants & Investigations Ltd* [1992] 2 NZLR 282.[14] The court held that proper standards of care should be imposed on people who undertake tasks which require skill and judgment and on whom others are dependent. However, this must be balanced by the need to preserve a proper balance between the differing interests of people (such as the plaintiffs and defendants) going about their business or daily lives. The court concluded that, irrespective of whether judges follow the *Anns* rule (cited in section 14.4.1 above) or adopt a more conservative approach (such as that enunciated in *Caparo*) they essentially seek to decide whether it is just and

---

[14] The case involved insurance assessors who reported suspected arson in two separate incidents of suspicious fires preceding insurance claims. The insured sued the assessors for preparing their reports negligently. The Court of Appeal was asked to decide whether a duty of care was owed by insurance assessors to an insured.

reasonable that a duty of care should be imposed on one party for the benefit of another in the particular circumstances of the case before them.

14.5   THE EFFECT OF OUT-OF-COURT SETTLEMENTS

Woolf (1983) has observed that the development of the law relating to auditors' liability and, more particularly, auditors' common-law liability to third parties, has been hampered by the predisposition of the auditing profession to settle out of court. However, the issue is complex and is worthy of further examination.

As noted in section 14.2.3, one of the major difficulties faced by auditors with respect to their liability for breach of their common law duties is that neither the parties to whom they owe a duty of care, nor the requirements which constitute a reasonable standard of skill and care, is static. This leaves auditors uncertain as to their legal obligations and may incline them towards going on the defensive, 'playing safe', and agreeing an out-of-court settlement with those who bring an action against them. Added to this are the enormous costs involved in lengthy court hearings – costs that are not limited to hefty legal fees[15] but also include the lost earnings of partners who spend days, if not weeks or months, in court, and the costs associated with damaged reputations resulting from allegations (whether justified or not) of negligent auditing. Given the legal uncertainties and high costs involved, it is not surprising that auditors are disposed to settle out of court – even in circumstances where they believe they may be able to defend successfully a case brought against them. This action is encouraged by their indemnity insurers who frequently pressure them to settle out of court as they consider this to be the least-cost option.

Nevertheless, auditors' propensity to settle out of court has some serious adverse consequences for the profession. For example, it prevents the underlying legal issues with respect to auditors' liability from being resolved and thus stifles clarification and development of the law in this area. It also causes indemnity insurance premiums to rise to unnecessarily high levels. As Woolf (1983) has explained:

> Treating insurance as an escape leads to an increase (not a decrease) in the risks against which further insurance cover is then needed – and so on, until the premiums exceed, by a very substantial margin, the damages which would be awarded against us if the issues in question were tested in the courts. (p. 65)

---

[15] As noted in footnote 13, by the time PwC reached an out-of-court settlement with the liquidators of the Barings Group, legal fees alone had exceeded £100 million.

A further damaging outcome is that, when news of an out-of-court settlement reaches the media headlines (which inevitably it does), it seems to signify to interested parties, and to the public at large, that the auditors concerned accept they are in the wrong and that they are unable to defend successfully the claims brought against them. It is arguable that, in general, this is more damaging to the reputation of the auditors involved, and to the auditing profession as a whole, than having the facts of the case exposed in court – and the possibility that the case will be decided in the auditors' favour.

Whatever the advantages and disadvantages of auditors settling out of court, decided cases have demonstrated that the courts will not impose an unfair burden on auditors. *Caparo,* and subsequent cases (including those discussed in section 14.4.3), show that the courts have been concerned to limit the parties to whom auditors owe a duty of care, so as not to leave them exposed to liability which is indeterminate in amount for an indeterminate time to an indeterminate class. Similarly, examples such as the *Littlejohn* case (see footnote 7) may be cited to show that the courts have also been concerned to keep the standard of skill and care required of auditors within reasonable bounds. Additionally, as Gwilliam (1988) has shown:

> While the courts reserve for themselves the ultimate right to determine what reasonable skill and care entails, they have always been very reluctant to impose on professions standards higher than those regarded as appropriate by the profession itself. (p. 22)

14.6 SUMMARY

In this chapter we have addressed the issue of auditors' legal liability. We have distinguished between a breach of auditors' statutory duties and a breach of their common law duties, and between auditors' contractual and third-party liability. We have also traced the development of auditors' duty of care to third parties and noted the effect of the decision in the *Caparo* case. We have further noted that, since *Caparo*, the law relating to auditors' liability to third parties has continued to evolve but the courts have been concerned to ensure that auditors are not exposed to an unreasonable liability burden.

In the final section of the chapter we have considered the effect of out-of-court settlements on the development of the law relating to auditors' liability, on auditors' indemnity insurance, and on auditors' (and the profession's) reputation. In the next chapter we discuss measures that both audit firms, and the auditing profession as a whole, have taken (and are taking) to try to reduce auditors' exposure to liability through the performance of consistently high quality audits and other means.

SELF-REVIEW QUESTIONS

14.1 Distinguish briefly between a breach of auditors' statutory duties and a breach of their common law duties.

14.2 Distinguish briefly between auditors' contractual liability and their liability to third parties.

14.3 List the three facts a plaintiff must prove before a court will award damages against auditors for negligence.

14.4 Explain the position adopted in the case of *Ultramares* v *Touche* (1931) with respect to auditors' liability to third parties. What reason did the judge give for his decision in this case?

14.5 Explain briefly the significance of the decision in *Hedley Byrne & Co Ltd* v *Heller and Partners* (1963) to the development of auditors' liability to third parties.

14.6 Explain the position adopted in the cases of *Jeb Fasteners* (1981) and *Twomax Ltd* (1983) with respect to auditors' liability to third parties.

14.7 Explain briefly the principles enunciated in the *Caparo* decision (1990) with respect to the parties to whom auditors are liable.

14.8 Identify the parties to whom auditors may be held to owe a duty of care as a result of the *Coulthard*, *Siddell*, *BCCI and Barings* cases.

14.9 List six factors of the law relating to the liability of auditors to third parties that have emerged from cases settled subsequent to the *Caparo* decision, and identify the common theme that can be discerned from the courts' decisions.

14.10 Explain briefly the impact of out-of-court settlements on:
    (i) the development of the law as it relates to auditors' liability;
    (ii) auditors' professional indemnity insurance; and
    (iii) the reputation of the auditors concerned and, more generally, on the auditing profession.

REFERENCES

Baxt, R. (1990) Shutting the gate on shareholders in actions for negligence – the Caparo decision in the House of Lords. *Companies and Securities Forum*, pp. 2–12. CCH Australia Ltd.

Berwin Leighton (1999) *Electra* v *KPMG: auditors' duty to third parties re-examined.* Berwin Leighton. *www.icclaw.com/devs/uk/ma/ukma_076.htm.*

Davies, J. (1992) *Auditors' Liabilities: Who can sue now?* Unpublished paper written for Reynolds Porter Chamberlain, UK.

Gwilliam, D. (1988) Making mountains out of molehills. *Accountancy* **101**(1135), 22–23.

Lascelles, D. & Donkin, R. (1991) The bank that liked to say yes. *The Financial Times*, 8 July 1999, p. 10.

Nisse, J. (1999) Pots of money appear on the horizon for BCCI's creditors. *The Times*, 29 September 1999.

Perry, M. (2001a) Coopers' Barings settlement collapses. *Accountancy Age*, 31 July 2001.

Perry, M. (2001b) Analysis – Battle of Barings rages on. *Accountancy Age*, 11 October 2001.

Perry, M. (2002) Barings' case against Deloitte set for May. *Accountancy Age*, 21 March 2002.

Savage, N. (1981) The auditor's legal responsibility to strangers? *The Accountant's Magazine* **85**(904), 338–341.

Scott, A. (1999) Another year in court: 1998's key liability cases. *Accountancy* **123**(1266), 106.

Shanahan, J. (1995) The AWA case: an auditor's view. Reported in *Butterworths Corporation Law Bulletin* (Australian Corporation Law), No. 10, 19 May 1995, 213–214.

Sued, P.W. (1998) *The Financial Times*, 19 November 1998, p. 14.

Woolf, E. (1979) *Auditing Today*. London: Prentice-Hall.

Woolf, E. (1983) Auditing and staying out of court. *Accountancy* **94**(1074), 65–66.

ADDITIONAL READING

Baker, C.R. & Quick, R. (1996) A comparison of auditors' legal liability in the USA and selected European countries. *European Business Review* **96**(3), 36–44.

Chitty, D. (1999) No end of a lesson. *Accountancy* **123**(1269), 108–9.

Erickson, M., Mayhew, B.W. & Felix, Jr, W.L. (2000) Why do audits fail? Evidence from Lincoln Savings and Loan. *Journal of Accounting Research* **38**(1), 165–194.

Gwilliam, D. (1997) Changes in the legal environment. In M. Sherer and S. Turley (eds) *Current Issues in Auditing*, 3rd ed., Chapter 6. London: Paul Chapman Publishing.

Howard, J. (2000) Is Caparo still good law? *Accountancy* **125**(1280), 149.

Kadous, K. (2000) The effects of audit quality and consequence severity on juror evaluations of auditor responsibility for plaintiff losses. *The Accounting Review* **75**(3), 327–341.

Kubrin, D. (1997) Auditor of subsidiary may owe duty of care to parent. *Accountancy* **119**(1243), 106.

McLean, D. (1995). Auditors' liability: all they want is a level playing field. *Accountancy* **115**(1221), 83.

O'Leary, C. (1998) Auditors' liability to third parties – the door remains open. *Managerial Auditing Journal* **13**(9), 521–524.

O'Sullivan, N. (1993) Auditors' liability: its role in the corporate governance debate. *Accounting and Business Research* **23**(91A), 412–420.

Passmore, C. (1997) The professional's bane. *Accountancy* **119**(1246), 80.

Power, M. (1998) Auditor liability in context. *Accounting, Organizations and Society* **23**(1), 77–79.

Scott, A. (1998) A year in court: What were 1997's key liability cases? *Accountancy* **121**(1254), 106.

Shu, S.Z. (2000) Auditor resignations: Clientele effects and legal liability *Journal of Accounting and Economics* **29**, 173–205.

Swinson, C. (1986) The Littlejohn case. *The Accountants' Magazine* **90**(956), 49–50.

Woolf, E. & Hindson, M. (2000) See you in court, *Accountancy* **125**(1279), 96–97.

Woolf, E. & Hindson, M. (2000) Wrong again. *Accountancy* **125**(1280), 150–151
Woolf, E. & Hindson, M. (2000) Routes to court. *Accountancy* **126**(1285), 94–95.

APPENDIX

Barings plc v Coopers & Lybrand & Ors, and Barings Futures (Singapore) Pte Ltd v Mattar & Ors [2002] EWHC 461 (Ch); [2002] ALL ER (D) 309 (Mar)

The facts of this case are as set out in Chapter 14, section 14.4.3. The part of the case reported here concerns the action brought by Barings Futures (Singapore) (BFS) against Deloitte & Touche (D&T) for negligent auditing in 1992 and 1993.

D&T sought to have BFS's action dismissed on the grounds that Jones, qualified accountant and finance director of BFS at the relevant time, signed letters of representation addressed to D&T prior to the 1992 and 1993 audit reports being signed. D&T claimed that, when signing the audit reports, it had relied on statements in the letters, namely: that there had been no irregularities involving employees that could have a material effect on the financial statements; the financial statements were free of material errors and omissions; transactions with related parties and losses on sale and purchase commitments had been properly recorded; BFS had recorded or disclosed all of its liabilities; and there had been no post-balance sheet events requiring adjustment to the financial statements.

D&T explained to the court that it routinely requires audit clients to provide a representation letter, signed by a suitably knowledgeable director or senior employee, before it will sign an unqualified audit report on the statutory accounts (and on which, in this case, its audit report on the consolidated schedules was dependent).

It was undisputed that Jones had signed the letters but, unknown to D&T, his contact with BFS during the 1992 and 1993 accounting periods was so small that he had no relevant knowledge which would render him properly able to sign the letters. D&T claimed that had Jones not signed the letters it would not have issued an unqualified audit report and, had it refused to issue an unqualified report on the accounts, the subsequent damage to BFS would have been averted. Therefore, Jones' reckless signature was a cause of D&T's exposure to the claims of negligence made against it. Jones signed the letters as a director of BFS, in the course of acting as such a director. It followed that BFS was vicariously liable for the consequences. It also followed that D&T had a claim against BFS for the consequences of Jones' fraud. That claim mirrored the claim against D&T and so gave them an absolute defence of circuity.

The court held that Jones' action in signing the letters was not recklessly fraudulent. D&T had not proved to the court's satisfaction that when he signed the representation letters he did so:

(i) knowing that the statements in the letters were untrue, without honest belief in their truth, or with indifference as to whether or not they were true; or

(ii) knowing that he had no reasonable grounds for making the statements, without an honest belief that he had such grounds, or with indifference as to whether he had or not.

Hence D&T's claim was dismissed. Evans-Lombe J ruled that, although the letters signed by Jones were inaccurate, BFS's negligence claim against D&T for £200 million could proceed. Perry (2002) reports that unless D&T agrees a settlement with the Barings group liquidators, it is expected that this case (which has been long delayed by C&L's attempts to reach an out-of-court settlement) will last well into 2003. She also observes:

> The trial and its outcome will be closely scrutinised by the profession to see how much auditors can rely on information from company management.

Expressed slightly differently, this case should establish the validity of regarding management representation letters as appropriate audit evidence.

REFERENCE

Perry, M. (2002) Barings hearings to focus on former FD. *Accountancy Age*, 25 January 2002.

15 Avoiding and Limiting Auditors' Liability

LEARNING OBJECTIVES

After studying the material in this chapter you should be able to:
- describe and evaluate measures audit firms are required to implement in order to ensure that high quality audits are performed;
- explain the objectives, process and outcomes of monitoring auditors' performance in the United Kingdom;
- discuss the advantages and disadvantages of limited liability companies, limited liability partnerships, statutory caps and proportionate liability as means of limiting auditors' liability.

The following publications are particularly relevant to this chapter:
- Statement of Auditing Standards (SAS) 240: *Quality control for audit work* (APB, 2000)
- International Standard on Auditing (ISA) 220: *Quality control for audit work* (IFAC, 1994)
- *Audit Regulations and Guidance* (Institute of Chartered Accountants in England and Wales, Institute of Chartered Accountants of Scotland, Institute of Chartered Accountants in Ireland, December 1995).

15.1 INTRODUCTION

In Chapter 14 we reviewed a number of cases involving auditors being sued by their clients and/or by third parties for (allegedly) performing their duties negligently (that is, without due skill and care). Although the 1990 *Caparo* decision reduced very significantly the numer of parties to whom auditors owe a duty of care and, thus, those who can succeed in an action against them, auditors continue to face staggering claims for damages. For example, as we noted in Chapter 14, Price Waterhouse (PW) and Ernst & Young (E&Y) faced a claim for $11 billion (about £6.5 billion) as a consequence of their (allegedly) negligent auditing of the failed Bank of Credit and Commerce International (BCCI) Group's accounts,[1] and Coopers & Lybrand (C&L), Coopers & Lybrand Singapore (C&LS) and Deloitte and Touche (D&T) faced a claim for £1 billion for their (allegedly) negligent auditing of the Barings Group's accounts.[2]

In some cases, damages awarded by the courts against auditors have been enormous. For instance, in December 1995, damages of £65 million were awarded against the former BDO Binder Hamlyn partnership for its negligent auditing of Britannia Security Group's 1989 financial statements.[3] Similarly, in June 2001, $7 million (about £4.5 million) was awarded against Arthur Andersen (AA) in the USA, in enforcement actions brought by the Securities and Exchange Commission (SEC)[4] and, in May 2002, the Phoenix court (USA) approved a settlement by AA with the Baptist Foundation of Arizona (BFA) for $217 million (about £143 million) for its negligent auditing of BFA's accounts (in particular, its failure to discover a massive fraud) (accountingweb.com, 2002).

Damages claims and settlements of a magnitude such as those cited above have prompted auditing firms to call for, and adopt, ways to limit their liability. Of particular concern to the firms is the fact that damages settlements bear no relationship to the size of the audit fee or the extent of the auditors' negligence. However, notwithstanding the successful actions that have been brought

---

[1] We also noted that, in September 1998, PW and E&Y agreed a settlement with the liquidators of the BCCI Group for an amount reputed to be in the region of $95 – 100 million (see Chapter 14, footnote 10).

[2] We also noted that, in October 2001, C&L and C&LS (now part of PricewaterhouseCoopers) agreed a settlement with the liquidators of the Barings Group for an undisclosed sum. A previous settlement, which collapsed in September 2001, was rumoured to be for between £70 and £100 million (see Chapter 14, footnote 13). D&T still face a claim of £200 million for their (allegedly) negligent auditing of the accounts of Barings Futures Singapore Ltd (BFS) in 1992 and 1993 (see Chapter 14, Appendix).

[3] See Chapter 14, section 4.4.3.

[4] The SEC successfully claimed 'that Andersen's audit reports on . . . the annual financial statements of Waste Management, Inc. for the years 1992 through 1996 . . . were materially false and misleading and that Andersen [had] engaged in improper professional conduct' (SEC Press Release, 2001).

against auditors, as we observed in Chapter 14 (section 14.5), the courts have, in general, shown themselves reluctant to impose on auditors a standard of skill and care higher than that generally regarded as appropriate by the auditing profession. It seems to follow that the most effective way for auditors to address the problem of their liability for negligence is to avoid it by performing high quality audits.

In this chapter we explore ways in which auditors may avoid or limit their exposure to liability. More specifically, we discuss measures implemented by audit firms, and by the profession as a whole, which are designed to ensure that auditors perform consistently high quality audits. We also examine moves by audit firms to form limited liability companies (LLCs) or limited liability partnerships (LLPs) and the advantages and disadvantages of each. Additionally, we discuss proposals to limit auditors' liability by means of imposing a statutory cap or enshrining the principle of proportionate liability in legislation.

15.2 MAINTAINING HIGH QUALITY AUDITS

15.2.1 The need for quality control

It is essential that auditors perform high quality audits not only so they can avoid exposure to legal liability but, arguably more importantly, so they fulfil adequately their function in society. In order to ensure that high quality audits are performed, quality controls are needed.

In Chapter 3 (section 3.6.2) we discussed the concept of quality control, and we noted that Flint (1988) explained the importance of quality control as follows:

> Auditors have both a legal duty and a professional obligation to work to the highest standards which can reasonably be expected to discharge the responsibility that is placed on them. . . . In a profession whose authority is dependent among other things on public confidence . . . a demonstrable concern, individually and collectively on the part of the members of the profession, to control and maintain the highest quality in its work, is a matter of basic principle. The basis of continuing public confidence and trust in professional competence is a belief that the standards of the members of the profession will be maintained and can be relied on. (pp. 159, 161)

The key issue is minimising the prospect of audit failure; that is, failing to detect material misstatements that are present in the financial statements under audit, or failing to report those that are detected but not corrected by the auditee's directors. Flint explains, 'this is what society in general, and those who rely on audit in particular, expect'. He adds, 'this is what the professional accountancy bodies as the regulatory authority[5] have an obligation to pursue in the public interest' (Flint, 1980, p. 64).

Whether it be prompted by concern for the public interest, concern for the interests of users of financial statements, concern about potential damage to the profession's reputation if poor quality audits are performed, or concern about possible exposure to legal liability (or a mixture of these factors), both individual firms and the auditing profession as a whole have established procedures designed to ensure that all audits are performed to the highest standards.

15.2.2   Quality control within audit firms

Guidance is provided for audit firms in the UK in Statement of Auditing Standards (SAS) 240: *Quality control for audit work* on measures they should take to ensure that high quality audits are performed. The standard, noting that 'quality control is of paramount importance to the independent audit function' (para 1), explains:

> In order to carry out an audit in a manner that meets the reasonable expectations of users of audited financial statements, it is essential that audit work is carried out with due regard for audit quality. The firm never compromises the demands of audit quality in order to achieve financial success. In developing quality control policy and processes, and in order to preserve audit quality, management structures within firms are designed to prevent commercial considerations taking precedence over the quality of audit work. (para 9)

It is interesting to note in the above quotation that SAS 240 implicitly addresses the criticism frequently levelled against auditors – that they compromise their independence (their objective, unbiased attitude of mind) in order to acquire or retain a (potentially) lucrative or otherwise desirable audit client – especially one offering high fee income from non-audit services.[6] SAS 240, para 9, leaves auditors in no doubt as to where their professional duty lies: irrespective of how financially attractive a particular client or course of action may appear to be, the quality of audit work must always come first.

Regarding measures that audit firms should implement in order to secure high quality audits, SAS 240 (para 6) identifies four parties with particular responsibilities, namely:

---

[5] As explained in Chapter 5 (section 5.2.3), only auditors registered with one of the five Recognised Supervisory Bodies [RSBs – the Institutes of Chartered Accountants in England and Wales (ICAEW), of Scotland (ICAS) and in Ireland (ICAI), the Chartered Association of Certified Accountants (ACCA) and the Association of Authorised Public Accountants (AAPA)] are eligible for appointment as company auditors in the UK. Hence, strictly speaking, in respect of auditing, the RSBs rather than the professional bodies constitute the 'regulatory authority' in the UK.

[6] Threats to auditors' independence are discussed in Chapter 4, section 4.2.

- *the audit firm* itself – which is responsible for providing 'an environment to support audit engagement partners and the necessary processes to facilitate their role';
- *the audit engagement partner* – who 'has an especially important role in promoting a quality culture within the audit team';
- *all members of an audit team* – who are 'responsible for the performance of their work in accordance with professional standards';
- *a senior audit partner within the firm* – who has 'overall responsibility for [the firm's] quality control policy and processes'.[7]

To assist the clarity of our discussion of firms' quality controls, we separate them into two groups as follows:

(a) firms' environmental quality controls; and

(b) quality control responsibilities of audit engagement partners.

(a) Firms' environmental quality controls

As indicated above, SAS 240 requires audit firms to maintain an environment that is conducive to high quality audit work. The standard also identifies characteristic elements of such an environment. These include the following:

(i)   quality control policy and processes;

(ii)   a senior audit partner with overall responsibility for the firm's quality control;

(iii) procedures for evaluating new and continuing audit engagements;

(iv)   sufficient audit engagement partners and staff with the requisite competencies;

(v)   appropriate assignment of audit engagement partners and audit staff to audit engagements;

(vi)   procedures to facilitate and encourage consultation;

(vii) independent review of audit engagements;

(viii) post-event monitoring of the quality of audit engagements.

As may be seen from Figure 15.1, each of these elements of an audit firm's quality control environment (which are discussed below) makes a unique, but complementary, contribution towards ensuring high quality audit work.

(i) Quality control policy and procedures

According to SAS 240 (para 8) quality control policy and processes need to be established and communicated to audit engagement partners, audit staff, and

---

[7] Unlike SAS 240, ISA 220: *Quality control for audit work* does not identify parties within the audit firm with particular responsibilities for securing high quality audits. Instead it states: 'Quality control policy and procedures should be implemented at both the level of the audit firm and on individual audits' (para 2).

Figure 15.1: Key elements of an audit firm's quality control environment

Element	Contribution to securing high quality audit work
Quality control policy and processes	Help to ensure an appropriate audit report is issued and regulatory requirements (including Auditing Standards and Ethical Guidelines) are adhered to.
Senior audit quality control partner	Responsible for developing, documenting, and communicating to relevant people, the firm's quality control policies and processes.
Procedures for evaluating new and continuing audit engagements	Provides reasonable assurance that only appropriate audit engagements are accepted.
Sufficient audit engagement partners and staff with the requisite competencies	Crucial for adequate staffing of all audits and, hence, for the performance of high quality audit work.
Appropriate assignment of audit engagement partners and audit staff to audit engagements	Engagement partners are responsible for the quality of audit work on engagements to which they are assigned. They need to be supported by staff competent to perform work assigned to them.
Procedures to facilitate and encourage consultation	Help to prevent technical errors and errors of judgment occurring during an audit.
Independent review of individual audit engagements	Independent assessment of the quality of audit engagements, including key decisions and significant judgments made.
Post-event monitoring of audit engagements (conducting audit compliance reviews) by an audit compliance partner	Systematic review of a sample of completed audit engagements and implementation of appropriate courses of action where failures are identified.

others who need to be aware of them. Such policy and processes are those that are:

> designed to provide reasonable assurance as to the appropriateness of the auditors' report, and of adherence to Auditing Standards, ethical and other regulatory requirements. [para 7(k)]

The Standard explains that the key benefit of developing quality control policy and processes lies in the fact that they provide a framework for ensuring that all relevant regulatory requirements, including those of Auditing Standards and Professional Ethical Guidelines, are met. SAS 240 notes that appropriate documentation of the policy and processes is necessary for their effective communication to audit engagement partners and audit staff, and that such communication 'is an essential prerequisite to their implementation' (para 13). Communication may be through the firm's internal training sessions, staff manuals and/or electronic or paper circulars. The means of communication is immaterial; what is important is that quality control policy and processes are established and effectively communicated to all those involved in audit work so that they can be properly implemented.[8]

(ii)   *Audit partner with overall responsibility for the firm's quality control*
SAS 240 (para 8) requires a senior audit partner to be appointed to take responsibility for the firm's quality control policy and processes. The authority and responsibility of this senior audit quality control partner includes developing, documenting, and communicating to relevant people, the firm's quality control policy and processes. Where firms have more than one office, each office may appoint an individual to be responsible for control matters within that office but one senior audit partner, with the necessary experience, seniority and authority, is to be assigned overall responsibility for quality control within the firm. SAS 240 also observes that this partner should have sufficient 'influence to help ensure that the quality of audits conducted by the firm is never compromised by commercial considerations' (para 11).

(iii)   *Procedures for evaluating new and continuing audit engagements*
Procedures are required for evaluating the propriety of accepting a new or continuing audit engagement (SAS 240, para 15). When making the evaluation firms should consider, among other things:

(a) their competence to undertake the work (paying due regard to factors such as the firm's knowledge and experience of the (potential) audit client's business sector, any potential conflict with another client in the same sector, and the availability of audit staff with the required levels of competence and experience to conduct the audit);

(b) whether the engagement poses threats to the firm's independence and, if so, whether adequate safeguards can be established (this factor is discussed below in relation to the responsibilities of the audit engagement partner);

(c) the integrity of the (potential) client's owners, directors and senior managers;

---

[8] ISA 220 contains similar but less detailed provisions to those in SAS 240. It states:

The audit firm should implement quality control policies and procedures designed to ensure that all audits are conducted in accordance with ISAs or relevant national standards or practices. . . . The firm's general quality control policies and procedures should be communicated to its personnel in a manner that provides reasonable assurance that the policies and procedures are understood and implemented. (paras 4 and 7)

(d) compliance with the profession's ethical requirements relating to a change of auditor.[9]

Pre-engagement investigations and procedures for accepting new and continuing audit engagements are discussed in detail in Chapter 7, section 7.2.3.

(iv) Sufficient audit engagement partners and staff with the requisite competencies

Clearly, it is fundamental to the performance of high quality audits to have sufficient audit engagement partners and audit staff, with the necessary competencies, to undertake the firm's audit work. To achieve this, audit firms need to have recruitment procedures that help to identify individuals with integrity and the ability to develop the competencies needed to perform the firm's work, and appropriate plans for staff members' appraisal and career development (SAS 240, paras 24 and 25).[10]

The importance of staffing audits with personnel who possess high ethical standards (especially integrity and objectivity), who are intelligent, and who have the ability and willingness to learn, is discussed in Chapter 6, section 6.5. We discuss the concept of competence, and how competencies may be acquired, in Chapter 3, section 3.3.2.

(v) Appropriate assignment of audit engagement partners and staff to audit engagements

Responsibility for the conduct and quality of an individual audit is that of the audit engagement partner who is assigned to the particular engagement. However, it is not just a case of assigning engagement partners to audits. SAS 240 (para 30) explains that audit firms require policies and procedures to ensure that:

(a) audit engagement partners have the competencies necessary to perform their role;
(b) audit engagement partners' responsibilities are clearly defined and communicated to them;

---

[9] Regarding quality controls relating to the acceptance and retention of audit clients, ISA 220 provides less detailed guidance than SAS 240 but it contains a provision that is similar in substance. This states:

> An evaluation of prospective clients and a review, on an ongoing basis, of existing clients is to be conducted. In making a decision to accept or retain a client, the firm's independence and ability to serve the client properly and the integrity of the client's management are to be considered. [para 6(f)].

However, it also provides illustrative examples of appropriate procedures for implementing this provision in Appendix F.

[10] ISA 220 contains similar, but narrower and less detailed requirements than SAS 240. It requires 'The firm to be staffed by personnel who have attained and maintain the technical standards and professional competence required to enable them to fulfil their responsibilities with due care' [para 6(b)]. However, it also provides illustrative examples of appropriate procedures for implementing this provision in Appendix B.

(c) the identity and role of the audit engagement partner is known to the directors and senior management of the audited entity;

(d) audit engagement partners have appropriate support (e.g. another partner), where necessary, at meetings with the directors and senior management of the audited entity that will involve matters that are, or may be, material to the auditors' report; and

(e) audit engagement partners have sufficient time to discharge their responsibilities.

Given that audit engagement partners are responsible for the conduct of audit work on individual audits, they clearly have a pivotal role in securing high quality audits. The requirements cited above are designed to enable these partners to discharge their role satisfactorily. (We discuss the responsibilities of audit engagement partners in more detail below.) However, it is not only engagement partners that need to be appropriately assigned to individual audits; as has been implied above, it is equally important to assign audit staff, with the competencies required to perform the audit work expected of them, to individual audit engagements.[11]

(vi) Procedures to facilitate and encourage consultation

Procedures are required to ensure that proper consultation takes place whenever difficult or contentious matters are encountered. In this regard, SAS 240 explains:

> Consultation brings to bear the collective experience and technical expertise of the firm and reduces the possibility that significant technical errors or errors of judgement may occur. Firms . . . encourage partners and staff to consult . . . individuals of appropriate seniority and experience within the firm . . . whenever they are considering a difficult or contentious matter. (paras 35 and 37)[12]

Whenever the results of consultation are relevant to audit conclusions they should be fully and properly documented.

(vii) Independent review of audit engagements

In order to ensure that audits of a high quality are performed, audit engagements should be independently reviewed prior to the audit report being issued.

---

[11] ISA 220 does not differentiate between audit engagement partners and audit staff being assigned to audit engagements, nor does it identify procedures to assist engagement partners fulfil their role. It merely specifies: 'Audit work is to be assigned to personnel who have the degree of technical training and proficiency required in the circumstances' [para 6(c)]. However, it also provides illustrative examples of appropriate procedures for implementing this provision in Appendix C.

[12] As for the quality control elements we have already considered, ISA 220 makes brief reference to consultation – yet captures the essence of the provisions contained in SAS 240. It simply states: 'Whenever necessary, consultation within or outside the firm is to occur with those who have appropriate expertise' [para 6(e)]. A key difference between ISA 220 and SAS 240 in respect of consultation is that SAS 240 refers only to consulting *within* the firm. ISA 220 envisages consulting experts from *inside or outside* the audit firm. Further, illustrative examples of appropriate procedures for implementing its provision on consultation are provided in ISA 220, Appendix E.

SAS 240, para 58, requires firms to conduct independent reviews for all listed company audit engagements and to establish procedures prescribing the circumstances when other engagements should be subject to such reviews.[13] An example of such a circumstance is when audit risk is high (that is, when the risk of expressing an inappropriate audit opinion is high) and the audit firm needs to attain a particularly high level of assurance that the opinion expressed in the audit report is appropriate.

An independent review largely rests on reviewing the audit working papers (which must, therefore, be properly prepared, complete, and adequate for the purpose), supplemented by making enquiries of relevant members of the audit team. To be effective, it needs to be conducted by a reviewer who acts as an objective but knowledgeable outside observer. As we noted in Chapter 6 (section 6.6.4), the review should be performed by one or more partners who have not been involved in the audit but who are sufficiently knowledgeable and experienced to fulfil the reviewer role.

SAS 240 emphasises that:

> The independent review does not involve a detailed review of all audit working papers, nor does it affect the responsibilities of the audit engagement partner. Its purpose is to provide an independent assessment of the quality of the audit including the key decisions and significant judgements made. (para 62)

In order to achieve this objective, SAS 240 (para 61) explains that the independent reviewer should consider the following matters:

(a) the objectivity of the audit engagement partner and key audit staff and the independence of the firm . . .;

(b) the rigour of the planning process including the analysis of the key components of audit risk identified by the audit team and the adequacy of the planned responses to those risks;

(c) the results of audit work and the appropriateness of the key judgements made, particularly in high risk areas;

(d) the significance of any potential changes to the financial statements that the firm is aware of but which the management of the audited entity has declined to make;

(e) whether all matters which may reasonably be judged by the auditors to be important and relevant to the directors, identified during the course of the audit, have been considered for reporting to the board of directors and/or the audit committee . . .; and

(f) the appropriateness of the draft auditors' report.[14]

---

[13] ISA 220 does not include a requirement for independent review. Indeed, it seems lukewarm to the notion. It observes: 'The process of reviewing an audit may include, particularly in the case of large complex audits, requesting personnel not otherwise involved in the audit to perform certain additional procedures before issuing the auditor's report' (para 17).

[14] SAS 240, paras 61 and 62, are also cited in Chapter 6, section 6.4.4. However, we have repeated them here as they are of particular relevance to securing high quality audits.

(viii)   Post-event monitoring of the quality of audit engagements

As indicated in Figure 15.1, an audit firm's quality control environment should include procedures for post-event monitoring of the quality of audit engagements. This is usually referred to as an audit compliance review. SAS 240, para 69, explains that the objective of such a review is:

> to provide an independent assessment of:
> (a)   the appropriateness of the auditors' report, and the conduct of the audit in accordance with Auditing Standards, ethical and other regulatory requirements;
> (b)   whether the firm's own quality control policy and processes have been applied in practice and appropriate consultation has taken place in relation to difficult or contentious issues.[15]

Given its nature, the monitoring process should clearly be the responsibility of a senior audit partner (or other senior person to whom the necessary authority and responsibility are delegated) within the firm – preferably one who is independent of those directly engaged in audit work. According to SAS 240, para 70, this partner (who we refer to as the audit compliance partner) should develop procedures to ensure that a sample of completed audit engagements is reviewed systematically (i.e. an audit compliance review is conducted regularly – usually annually) and, where failures in audit work are identified, appropriate courses of action are implemented. Such action may include:

(a)   communicating the findings to relevant people (for example, all those engaged in audit work) within the firm so that future failings may be avoided;

(b)   additional training and professional development for the errant audit staff member(s);

(c)   changes to the firm's policies and procedures;

(d)   disciplinary action against those who repeatedly fail to comply with the firm's standards.

(b)   Quality control responsibilities of audit engagement partners

Although the eight elements of a firm's quality control environment presented above provide a structure for ensuring that high quality audits are conducted by the firm, responsibility for the quality of an individual audit is that of the audit engagement partner. The responsibility of this partner is limited in scope in that it is restricted to the particular audit engagement but, in respect of that engagement, it is all-embracing. The engagement partner has responsibility for the quality of all the audit work performed on the engagement, for applying the firm's quality control policy and processes to the engagement, and for finalising

---

[15] ISA 220's provision with respect to monitoring the quality of audit work is limited to noting: 'The continued adequacy and operational effectiveness of quality control policies and procedures is to be monitored' [para 6 (g)]. However, ISA 220, Appendix G, also provides guidance on procedures for implementing this provision.

and signing the audit report on behalf of the firm (SAS 240, paras 39 and 40).[16] While acknowledging this overall responsibility for the audit engagement, SAS 240 specifies three sets of duties for which the engagement partner is particularly responsible, namely:

(i) assuring the firm's, the partner's and the audit team's independence;
(ii) directing, supervising and reviewing audit work performed during the engagement;
(iii) reading the audit report, the financial statements, and information issued with the financial statements.

We discuss each of these below.

(i)   Independence of the firm, engagement partner and audit team
When discussing the firm's environmental quality controls relating to the acceptance of new or continuing audit engagements, above we noted that one of the factors firms must consider when evaluating the propriety of accepting an audit engagement is whether the firm's independence might be at risk if the engagement were to be accepted and, if so, whether adequate safeguards could be established. To assist with this evaluation, SAS 240 (para 47) requires audit firms to prepare a summary of:

(a) any factors that may reasonably be thought to bring into question the independence of the firm or the objectivity of the audit engagement partner or staff to be employed on the engagement; and
(b) related safeguards that are in place.

It also notes:

> The summary includes a record of all non-audit work, other than that which is insignificant individually and in aggregate, that the firm has agreed to perform for the audited entity. (para 47)

The last requirement addresses the thorny issue of the provision of non-audit services by auditors and its impact on auditor independence. (We examine this issue in detail in Chapter 4.)

Notwithstanding these general (firm-based) provisions, SAS 240 specifically requires audit engagement partners to:

> consider whether adequate arrangements are in place to safeguard their objectivity and the firm's independence, and [to] document their conclusions. (para 45)[17]

---

[16] As for the provisions in ISA 220 relating to the firm's quality control environment, those relating to the responsibility of audit engagement partners are similar in substance to those in SAS 240 but are far less detailed and specific. The equivalent provision to SAS 240, paras 39 and 40 states: 'The auditor [i.e. engagement partner] should implement those quality control procedures which are, in the context of the policies and procedures of the firm, appropriate to the individual audit' (ISA 220, para 8).

[17] The equivalent provision in ISA 220 merely states: 'Personnel in the firm are to adhere to the principles of independence, integrity, objectivity, confidentiality and professional behaviour' [para 6(a)]. However, illustrative examples of procedures for implementing this provision are provided in Appendix A.

As part of this consideration, engagement partners are required to 'conclude on the summary [prepared as noted above] as to whether adequate safeguards have been established' (para 47). To assist engagement partners fulfil these responsibilities, SAS 240 provides that audit firms should:

> have in place appropriate procedures to ensure that the audit engagement partner is made aware of any other relationship which exists between the firm . . . and the client entity . . . that may reasonably be thought to bear on the firm's independence and the objectivity of the audit engagement partner and the audit staff. (para 48)

Thus, SAS 240 places squarely on the shoulders of the audit engagement partner responsibility for assessing whether or not the audit engagement can be performed in an independent, objective manner – and whether it would be so perceived by an outside observer. If this independence cannot be assured, either the engagement should not be accepted (if the firm's independence is in doubt) or the proposed audit engagement partner and/or senior audit staff members whose objectivity may be questioned should not be used on the engagement.

(ii) Direction, supervision and review of audit work

As the audit engagement partner is responsible for all of the audit work performed during the audit engagement, it is evident that (s)he is responsible for ensuring the work is directed, supervised and reviewed 'in a manner that provides reasonable assurance that the work has been performed competently' (SAS 240, para 49).[18]

The direction, supervision and review of audit work by audit team members is discussed in detail in Chapter 6, section 6.5: *Staffing an audit* and we will not repeat it here. However, in addition to ensuring the work of audit staff is appropriately directed, supervised and reviewed, audit engagement partners are responsible for conducting an overall review of the audit working papers.[19] SAS 240 (para 55) explains the extent, purpose, focus and timing of the review in the following words:

> The review is sufficient for [the audit engagement partner] to be satisfied that the working papers contain sufficient appropriate evidence to support the conclusions reached and for the auditors' report to be issued. Although the review may not cover all working papers, it covers:
> (a) all critical areas of judgement, especially any relating to difficult or contentious matters identified during the audit;
> (b) audit evidence relating to high risk areas;
> (c) any other areas which the audit engagement partner considers important.
> Audit engagement partners document the extent of their review and its timing so as to demonstrate that it was completed before the auditors' report was signed.

---

[18] ISA 220 [para 6(d)] similarly provides: 'There is to be sufficient direction, supervision and review at all levels to provide reasonable assurance that the work performed meets appropriate standards of quality.' It also provides illustrative examples for implementing the provision in Appendix D.

[19] This section should be read in conjunction with Chapter 12, section 12.6.1: Final review of audit working papers and conclusion.

As noted above [under firms' environmental quality controls (vii)], for all listed company audit engagements and for other engagements where the audit firm considers it appropriate, once the audit engagement partner is satisfied with the performance, documentation and review of the audit engagement, it is subject to an independent review.

(iii) Reading the audit report, the financial statements, and information issued with the financial statements

The audit engagement partner is not only responsible for ensuring that a high quality audit is conducted, (s)he is also responsible for finalising and signing the audit report on behalf of the firm. SAS 240 explains that this involves reading 'the auditors' report, the financial statements and the information issued with the financial statements' (para 56).

This might seem like a simple, quickly executed final step. However, as we observed in Chapter 12, section 12.6, before signing the audit report, the audit engagement partner is required by SAS 470: *Overall review of financial statements*, and by SAS 160: *Other information in documents containing audited financial statements*, respectively:

- to conduct an overall review of the financial statements which is sufficient, together with conclusions drawn from evidence gathered during the audit, to provide a reasonable basis for his or her opinion on the financial statements (SAS 470, para 2); and
- to review the unaudited information in the auditee's annual report (or other documents containing the audited financial statements) to determine that it is not materially inconsistent with the financial statements or misleading. If the information is inconsistent with the audited financial statements and/or misleading, the audit engagement partner is required to 'seek to resolve the matter through discussion with the [auditee's] directors' (SAS 160, para 9).

Once the engagement partner is satisfied with the conduct of the audit and has

(a) performed an overall review of the audit working papers and the financial statements;
(b) read the unaudited information in documents containing the financial statements and resolved any difficulties; and
(c) decided on the appropriate wording for the audit report,

(s)he should (re)read the draft audit report to ensure that its wording is appropriate and complies with SAS 600: *Auditors' reports on financial statements*. If the audit engagement is subject to independent review, this should be performed once the audit engagement partner is entirely satisfied with the conduct and outcomes of the audit – but before the audit report is signed. Although the engagement partner has responsibility for signing and dating the audit report on behalf of the firm, as explained in Chapter 12 (section 12.6.3), this step is not completed until the auditee's directors have signed the financial statements.

In order for audit firms to be assured that audits conducted by the firm are of a high quality, they need to ensure that all of the quality controls outlined above are implemented and adhered to throughout the firm. As noted above, each audit firm is required to appoint a quality control partner and an audit compliance partner. In multi-office firms, these senior audit partners need to satisfy themselves (usually by visiting each office of their firm) that each office of the firm is adhering to the firm's quality control policy and processes (in the case of the quality control partner) and performing high quality audits (in the case of the audit compliance partner).

Where audit firms have a number of offices internationally, intra-firm quality control reviews may be conducted. These involve teams of about five senior audit partners, drawn from different countries, who visit various offices of the firm around the world to review the adequacy of, and level of compliance with, the firm's quality control procedures. Such reviews are internal matters of the firms concerned and are designed to ensure that the risk of members of the firm performing poor quality audits and, thus, of exposing the firm's partners to liability, is kept to a minimum. At the same time, ensuring that all offices of the firm (internationally) maintain adequate quality control procedures helps to enhance the reputation of the firm for the professional quality of its audit work.

15.2.3 Quality control within the profession

In addition to individual audit firms developing, implementing and monitoring quality controls, the professional bodies in the UK have introduced measures designed to ensure that high quality audits are performed by all registered auditors throughout the UK. Similar measures have been introduced in many other parts of the world – for example, in the USA, Canada, Australia and New Zealand (NZ). Although the professional bodies in the various countries have given different titles to what we might call 'quality control monitoring mechanisms' (for instance, the term 'monitoring' is used in the UK, 'peer review' in the USA, and 'practice review' in NZ), all of the schemes are designed to serve three key purposes, namely:

- to ensure auditors meet their obligation to society to provide professional work of the highest quality. Monitoring provides a means of ensuring that all members of the profession adhere to the profession's technical and professional standards;
- to sustain public confidence in the profession by demonstrating a concern for maintaining high standards of professional work;

- to demonstrate to the public, and more particularly to the government, that the professional bodies are discharging satisfactorily their self-regulatory (or, in the case of Recognised Supervisory Bodies, delegated statutory) responsibilities. This is reflected, for example, in Cook and Robinson's (1979) observation that the 'AICPA [American Institute of Certified Public Accountants] leadership hoped that a strong self-regulatory program [that is, peer review] . . . would satisfy the profession's critics in Congress who were calling for direct government regulation' (p. 12).[20]

We explain in Chapter 5 (section 5.2.3) that in the UK only registered auditors are eligible for appointment as company auditors. Such auditors may be either individuals, or firms with a majority of individuals, who have qualified with a Recognised Qualifying Body and registered with a Recognised Supervisory Body (RSB). In order to become an RSB, a professional body must have, *inter alia:*

(i)   rules relating to auditors being fit and proper persons;
(ii) technical standards applying to audit work;
(iii) procedures for:
    (a) maintaining auditors' competence,
    (b) investigating complaints,
    (c) meeting claims arising out of audit work,
    (d) monitoring compliance with, and enforcing, the RSB's rules.

Thus, monitoring auditors' compliance with auditing standards and other rules is a condition of a professional body gaining RSB status.

The monitoring function of the five RSBs[21] is discharged by two units: the Joint Monitoring Unit (JMU), which monitors auditors registered with the three Institutes, and the ACCA monitoring unit, which monitors those registered with the two Associations. The remit of the monitoring units is to ascertain

---

[20] In the UK, in 2001, the professional accountancy bodies, in conjunction with the Department of Trade and Industry, established The Accountancy Foundation. The Foundation, which was heralded in the Labour Party's 1997 Business Manifesto, is designed:

> to ensure there [is] a framework of independent regulation for the accountancy profession. . . . The aims of the new system of regulation are to ensure that the accountancy profession operates in the public interest and to secure public confidence in the impartiality and effectiveness of the accountancy bodies' systems of regulation and discipline. (Accountancy Foundation Review Board, 2002, p. 3)

Although The Accountancy Foundation Review Board (a component of The Accountancy Foundation) has general oversight of the regulation of the accountancy profession, the professional bodies remain responsible, among other things, for the registration and monitoring of auditors. Nevertheless, the Review Board of the Foundation is responsible for scrutinising the activities of the professional bodies in these (and other) regards.

[21] Institutes of Chartered Accountants in England and Wales (ICAEW), of Scotland (ICAS) and in Ireland (ICAI), the Chartered Association of Certified Accountants (ACCA) and the Association of Authorised Public Accountants (AAPA).

whether registered auditors are complying with the audit regulations. Thus, their monitoring activities embrace registered auditors' compliance with all aspects of the regulations including, for example, those relating to technical auditing standards, ethical guidelines, independence, professional competence and professional indemnity insurance.

The focus of monitoring is the audit firm rather than individual auditors. At 31 December 2000, there were nearly 12,000 registered audit firms in the UK but the number and profile of firms registered with the three Institutes and the two Associations differed markedly. Nearly 8,630 firms were registered with the Institutes: about 63% were sole practitioners, some 36% had between 2 and 20 principals, and less than 1% (49 firms) had more than 20 principals. Of the Institutes' registered audit firms, 102 (slightly more than 1%) had listed company clients, with the largest 16 firms, with more than 50 principals, auditing approximately 75% (and the largest 51 firms, with more than 10 principals, auditing nearly 98%) of such companies (ICAEW *et al.*, 2000, p. 6). By comparison, nearly 3,250 firms were registered with the Associations; approximately 85% were sole practitioners and the remaining 15% had between 2 and 20 principals. Only two of the Associations' audit firms had listed company clients.

It is possibly as a result of differences in the number, size and nature of audit firms registered with the Institutes and Associations, respectively, that the JMU and ACCA monitoring unit approach the task of monitoring rather differently. We discuss the approach adopted by each below.

Monitoring by the JMU[22]
The JMU's monitoring process, which is depicted in Figure 15.1, has two key elements:
(a) Desk top monitoring; and
(b) JMU visits.

Desk top monitoring: Every audit firm registered with the three Institutes is required to send to the JMU a completed annual return. This is tested for any inconsistencies or omitted information followed by a detailed risk assessment. This involves subjecting the annual return to more than 150 risk and public interest checks – for example, checking whether the firm conducts an audit compliance review, updates its accounting disclosure checklist and audit programme, has an audit manual or similar document, and whether the firm has 'public interest' auditees such as listed companies, charities and pension

---

[22] Information on JMU monitoring has been derived from the JMU's annual reports for the years 1997 to 2001 and the joint annual reports of the ICAEW, ICAS and ICAI to the Department of Trade and Industry (DTI) on Audit Regulation for the years 1992 to 2000.

schemes. Where significant risk characteristics are identified, the system generates a risk report.

The firm's annual return, risk report and file (records from previous years) is reviewed by the desk top monitoring team. Largely based on its review of these documents, the team selects the firms to be visited by JMU inspectors.

JMU visits: Audit firms are selected for visits in one of five ways:

- As a result of desk top monitoring: About 80% of firms are selected by this means. (In the year to 31 December 2000, 705 of the 881 firms selected for visits were in this category.)
- Random selection: About 10% of firms visited are selected at random, without reference to potential risks identified by desk top monitoring. The main focus of these visits is verifying the integrity of the firms' annual returns and the completion (and quality) of their audit compliance reviews (see section 5.2.2 above).
- For follow-up visits: About 1% of visits are follow-ups to a previous visit where improvements were promised. Follow-up visits are designed to test implementation of the promised improvements.
- At the request of the Audit Registration Committee of the RSB with which the firm is registered: These visits (about 3% of the total) are usually prompted by complaints lodged against the firm in question. In recent years, approximately 24% of complaints received by the Institutes' Audit Registration Committees have concerned 'inadequate audit work', and a further 10% have questioned auditors' independence or being 'fit and proper persons'.[23]
- Firms have listed company audit clients: In 1997, the three Institutes and the Department of Trade and Industry (DTI) agreed that the largest firms with listed company clients (the 'Big Five' and 'Group A' firms; 20 firms in total) should receive full JMU visits every three years, with interim visits in the two intervening years (JMU, 2001, p. 7). The other audit firms with listed company clients (numbering 82 in 2000) are mostly visited every four (or, at a maximum of every five) years. In the year to 31 December 2000, of the 881 audit firms selected for JMU visits, 34 firms with listed company clients were selected for full JMU visits and 12 for interim visits.

As may be seen from Figure 15.2, a JMU visit begins with an opening meeting. At this meeting, the JMU inspectors discuss with the audit compliance

---

[23] While the proportion of complaints relating to inadequate audit work has remained relatively unchanged over the years from 1998 to 2000 (when the proportions were 23% and 24%, respectively), those concerning auditors' independence and being fit and proper persons has declined markedly. In 1998 and 2000, 5% and 3% of complaints, respectively, related to auditors' independence; in the same years 18% and 6%, respectively, concerned auditors' being fit and proper persons. In 1999 and 2000 about half of the complaints received by the Audit Registration Committees related to non-reporting of matters under the Pensions Act 1998. The ICAEW explains that these complaints originate in difficulties the firms and others experienced in interpreting the requirements of legislation relating to pension funds (ICAEW *et al.*, 1998, 1999, 2000, Appendix 5).

partner,[24] and other audit partners who wish, or are requested (by the JMU or the firm) to be present, the firm's quality control policy and processes – and adherence thereto. As noted in section 15.2.2 above, a key element of an audit

Figure 15.2: JMU's monitoring process

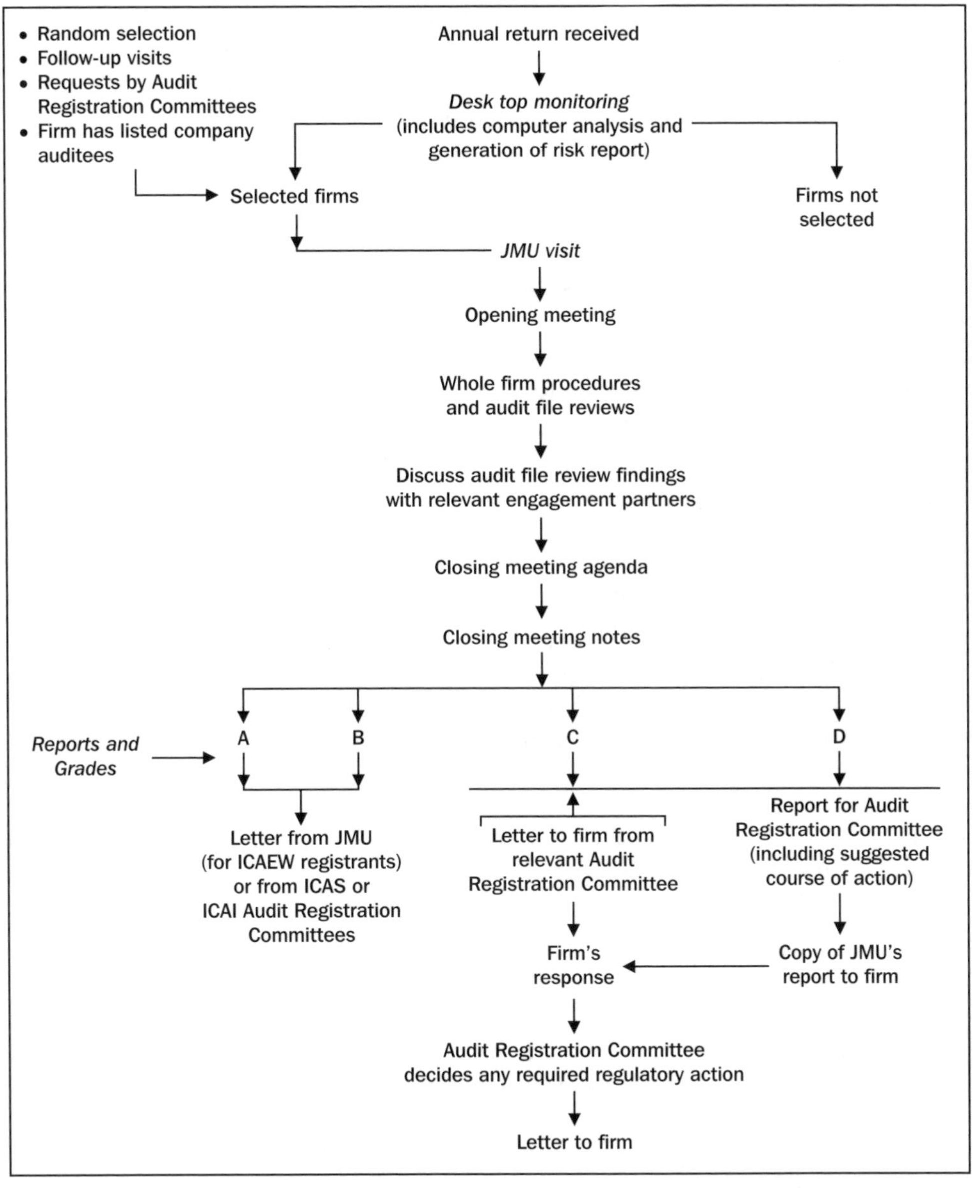

Source: Adapted from JMU 2001, p. 6

[24] The senior audit partner responsible for the firm's audit compliance review.

firm's environmental quality controls is its audit compliance review – the firm's internal review conducted to ensure, among other things, that the firm and its audit engagement partners and audit staff are complying with audit regulations and auditing standards. It is not surprising, therefore, that a significant portion of a JMU visit focuses on the firm's audit compliance reviews; more specifically, on how they were conducted, their results, and the remedial actions implemented. During the meeting the JMU inspectors also discuss with the audit compliance partner the firm's 'whole firm procedures' (procedures covering, for example, quality control, independence, consultation, competence, appointment to, and retention of, audit clients, and compliance with statutory requirements) and individual audit engagement files they wish to review.

The JMU inspectors then conduct a detailed review of the firm's whole firm procedures and selected audit engagement files. At the time the audit files are reviewed, the inspectors discuss the findings with the relevant engagement partners and any minor issues are clarified and resolved. The major points arising from the reviews are summarised in a closing meeting agenda. These points are usually expressed as actual or potential instances of non-compliance with the audit regulations and/or auditing standards resulting in risks to the firm's audit work. They are discussed in the overall context of the audit regulations.

At the conclusion of the visit, the JMU inspectors meet with the audit compliance partner and other partners who wish, or are requested, to be present at a closing meeting. The partners give the firm's initial response to the issues identified by the JMU and the JMU's suggestions for improvement. The firm sends typed notes of the closing meeting (known as closing meeting notes) to the JMU noting, in particular, its response to matters raised during the visit and how it plans to address them.

Upon receipt of the firm's closing meeting notes, the JMU finalises its visit report. As indicated in Figure 15.2, the results of visits are graded A to D. These signify the following outcomes:
- *Grade A* – there are no regulatory issues to deal with.
- *Grade B* – any regulatory issues have been dealt with adequately in the firm's closing meeting notes and no further action is required.
  [Firms with Grade A or Grade B visits receive a letter from the JMU (in the case of ICAEW registered auditors) or from the Audit Registration Committee of ICAS or ICAI, as applicable, continuing their audit registration.]
- *Grade C* – the findings of the JMU were not satisfactory. The firm needs to confirm in due course to the relevant RSB that promised improvements have been effected but no other restrictions or conditions on audit registration are imposed.

- *Grade D* – the findings of the JMU were not satisfactory and the deficiencies were more serious than warrants a Grade C. In these cases, the JMU submits a detailed report, together with the closing meeting notes, to the relevant Audit Registration Committee; a copy is also sent to the firm concerned.[25] The Audit Registration Committee reviews the JMU's report and the firm's comments thereon, and decides upon appropriate regulatory action. It may accept the firm's proposals for corrective action and/or ask for, or impose, additional requirements. If the Audit Registration Committee considers that a firm's non-compliance with the audit regulations, although serious, does not warrant withdrawal of registration, it may require a follow-up visit by the JMU to confirm that required remedial action has been taken. It may also impose restrictions or conditions on the firm's registration; for example, it may prohibit the firm from accepting any new audit clients. (Restrictions or conditions were imposed on 78 firms (9% of firms visited) registered with the three Institutes in the year to 31 December 2000.) As a final measure, the Audit Registration Committee may withdraw a firm's registration. This action was applied to ten Institute registered firms in the year to 31 December 2000 and a further 11 voluntarily surrendered their registration following the JMU visit (ICAEW *et al.*, 2000).

The results of JMU visits (and, in the case of C and D Grades, reviews by the relevant Audit Registration Committee) for the years 1992 to 2000 are presented in Figure 15.3 below.

As might be expected, the time taken for JMU visits varies with the size of audit firms. Most visits to single office practitioners take one day on site. Interim visits to the 20 largest firms with listed company clients last up to 30 days; full visits to these firms may take 100 days. In respect of the largest firms, the JMU notes (2001, p. 7) that it seeks, over the three year visit cycle that applies to these firms to visit most, if not all, of the offices of the firm. It also explains, in respect of large multi-office firms:

> A full visit breaks down into a Head Office and local office visits. A visit to a large firm local office is not dissimilar from a visit to a single office firm. The visiting inspector will have a local opening meeting with the local partner responsible for audit matters, consider whole firm matters, carry out a number of detailed file reviews (both reperformance of the firm's ACR [audit compliance review] and other JMU risk based [audit file] selections, discuss the detailed individual [audit file] findings with the [relevant engagement partner] and consolidate the significant findings for a local closing meeting. The results of all the local closing meetings will then be consolidated for the national closing meeting with the national audit compliance principal. (JMU, 2001, p. 7)

---

[25] The JMU also sends a detailed report to the relevant Audit Registration Committee for all audit firms with listed company clients visited by the JMU, irrespective of the grade awarded. This reflects the high level of public interest associated with listed company audits.

(ii) Monitoring by the ACCA monitoring unit[26]

The ACCA monitoring unit follows a similar process to the JMU but places greater emphasis on visits to registered auditors rather than on analysis of annual returns. This difference can be explained by reference to the number of registered auditors monitored by each unit. The ACCA unit, which monitors about 3,250 registered auditors, is able to visit each at least once every five years; this would be difficult for the JMU which has about 8,630 registered auditors to monitor. Hence, as we have seen, the JMU adopts a risk-based approach and selects firms to visit largely based on their size, the number and nature of their audit clients, and the results of desk top monitoring. All registered audit firms with listed company clients are visited at least once every five years (the 20 largest firms, with the majority of such clients, being visited annually) but for firms not selected for a visit, the JMU largely relies on the desk top monitoring of their annual returns. Nevertheless, in the year to 31 December 2000, the JMU visited 881 registered audit firms compared with 468 firms visited by the ACCA monitoring unit.

The ACCA has a policy of renewing practising certificates (which are required by all registered auditors) annually. To renew their certificates, registered auditors must confirm their compliance with the relevant Association's Authorisation Committee's[27] rules with respect to them being fit and proper persons, holding adequate professional indemnity insurance, having arrangements for practice continuity, and undertaking continuing professional development (CPD). All practice certificate applications are scrutinised and, providing they are satisfactory, they are approved by the relevant Authorisation Committee. Information provided on the applications is subject to verification during monitoring visits to the audit firm concerned.

Like the JMU, the ACCA monitoring unit selects audit firms for visits in a number of ways. These are as follows:

(a) For routine visits: These firms, which account for about 70–75% of firms visited, are selected according to their risk profiles and monitoring cycle. (In the year to 31 December 2000, 328 of the 468 firms visited were in this category.) As noted above, all registered audit firms are visited at least once every five years but firms with a high risk profile may be visited more frequently. These firms are identified by factors such as the outcome of a previous monitoring visit, the number and type of audit clients, the nature and organisation of the firm, and the length of time since the last visit. The ACCA (2000) explains:

---

[26] Information on ACCA monitoring has been derived from the ACCA's report to the DTI on Audit Regulation for the years 1992–2000.

[27] Chartered Association of Certified Accountants (ACCA) and Association of Authorised Public Accountants (AAPA) (see footnote 21).

> Firms which have public interest clients or are carrying out a significant amount of audit work or those where the firm's structure indicates that control problems may exist will be visited sooner than those which do not. (p. 22)

(b) For follow-up visits: About 16–18% of visits are follow-ups to previous unsatisfactory visits. (In the year to 31 December 2000, these visits accounted for 85 of the 468 visits made.)

(c) As follow-ups to complaints received: These visits are prompted by complaints received by the Associations that indicate a failure in the firm's procedures. Complaints generally give rise to about 5% of visits but, in the year to 31 December 2000, only six visits (1% of the total) were complaint-responsive.

(d) At the request of an Authorisation Committee: These visits are requested as a result of unsatisfactory first or second visits. They generally account for about 2% of total visits but, in the year to 31 December 2000, they amounted to 10% of visits made (49 of 468).

An ACCA monitoring unit visit follows essentially the same process as the JMU – with an initial meeting, reviews of 'whole firm procedures' and individual audit engagement files, and a final meeting. At the initial meeting, the ACCA compliance officer generally meets with all, rather than just a few, of the firm's partners. This again reflects differences in the registered audit firms the two units monitor: while 12% (1,066) of the firms monitored by the JMU have four or more partners, this applies to only 1% (35) of the firms monitored by the ACCA unit. During the meeting, factual information about the firm, its partners, staff and clients is confirmed, and checks are made on the firm's continuing eligibility for registration as an auditor and its compliance with audit regulations. Additionally, the ACCA compliance officer ascertains the firm's quality control policy and processes (including its procedures for ensuring compliance with auditing standards) and its approach to audit work.

Following the initial meeting, the ACCA compliance officer selects a sample of audit engagement files for review – ensuring that the audit work of every audit partner and every office of the firm (where there is more than one) is reviewed. Additionally, the firm's records are reviewed to confirm eligibility for audit registration, compliance with continuing obligations (such as the qualifications of audit partners and staff, and procedures to ensure that all partners and staff involved in audit work are fit and proper), and compliance with Rules of Professional Conduct (including the independence requirements).

At the conclusion of the monitoring visit, the ACCA compliance officer, like the JMU inspectors, meets with the firm's partners to discuss the visit's findings and agree, where applicable, the remedial action to be taken. In any case where deficiencies in audit work or non-compliance with audit regulations have been found, the firm may be required to provide written details of proposed correct-ive action and/or to confirm in writing action taken to correct the identified weaknesses.

After the visit, the compliance officer drafts a report covering the matters dis-cussed at the meeting. The draft report, together with the completed pro-gramme, file inspection checklists and any supplementary working papers, is reviewed by another member of the monitoring staff and then sent to the relevant registered audit firm. As for the JMU, ACCA visits result in a grading from A to D. As may be seen from the descriptions below, in all material respects the grades coincide with those of the JMU. The main difference is the subdivision, by the ACCA unit, of grade C.

- *Grades A and B* – satisfactory: These firms comply in all material respects with the audit regulations and, where any deficiencies were found in audit work, these were minor in nature and considered unlikely to have under-mined the audit opinion issued.
- *Grade C* – less than satisfactory: The ACCA (2000, p. 23) explains that these firms:

  have controls which are either weak or not consistently effective and they have produced at least one audit opinion which was not properly supported by docu-mentary evidence. Such firms fall into two categories:

  (C+) firms which appear to have a fairly clear idea of the required standards and have procedures in place but those procedures are not adequate to deliver a consistent level of compliance with auditing standards.

  (C–) firms which are less willing or able to produce work of an adequate quality. Typically, the individuals concerned lack the experience and training neces-sary to distinguish adequately between an audit and accounts preparation, or else exhibit a degree of scepticism about the audit of the smaller com-pany, the need to comply with standards or the need for regulation.

  All grade C firms are subject to a re-visit. In the case of a C+ firm, a re-visit is accorded a low priority; for C– firms an early re-visit is provided for.

- *Grade D* – unsatisfactory, referred to Authorisation Committee: Firms may receive this grade as a consequence of doubts about the firm's eligibility for registration as an auditor or about its compliance with the audit regulations. The regulations include a requirement to comply with auditing standards, hence, serious breaches of auditing standards result in a Grade D. However, ACCA (2000) explains that 'many referrals to the Committee arise from issues such as control of a firm or shortfalls in [continuing education] and do not reflect problems concerning the conduct of audit work' (p. 23).

If a follow-up visit consequent upon a C– grading reveals no improvement, then the audit firm is automatically graded D and referred to the Authorisation Committee. If such a visit shows some improvement (the firm has improved from C– to C+), the firm is given a further opportunity to effect improvements and a second follow-up visit is made. If this second visit does not result in a satisfactory grade (A or B), the firm is referred to the Authorisation Committee.

Like JMU visits, the time taken for ACCA monitoring unit visits varies according to the number of the firm's offices, audit partners and audit clients, and the degree to which the firm has adopted standard compliance procedures. Most visits to sole practitioners (which, as noted earlier, account for some 85% of ACCA registered auditors) can be completed, on site, by one compliance officer within a day. (This is the same time as that taken by the JMU.) However, 'where the firm is large or complex, it requires correspondingly more time and staff' (ACCA, 2000, p. 64).

15.2.4 *Effectiveness of monitoring auditors' performance*

As may be seen from Figure 15.3, the outcome of monitoring visits indicates that, in general, auditors' performance has improved since 1992 (when

Figure 15.3: Results of visits by the JMU and ACCA monitoring unit 1992 to 2000

	1992	1993	1994	1995	1996	1997	1998	1999	2000
JMU visits	%	%	%	%	%	%	%	%	%
A & B Satisfactory	40	31	38	63	60	63	65	56	57
C Appropriate plans for improvement	–	58	48	22	24	26	28	33	32
D Restriction on audit registration	–	5	7	9	10	7	4	8	9
D Audit registration									
• withdrawn	–	4	4	3	3	2	1	1	1
• surrendered	–	2	3	3	3	2	2	2	1
Concerns about audit work or non-compliance with regulations	–	60	–	–	–	–	–	–	–
ACCA unit visits									
A & B Satisfactory	45	44	49	54	54	56	53	52	46
C Not satisfactory:									
C+ Revisit a low priority	27	27	21	16	17	12	12	13	15
C– Early revisit required	20	19	12	14	17	14	16	19	22
D Referred to Authorisation Committee	8	10	18	16	12	18	19	16	17

Source: ICAEW *et al.*, *Reports to the DTI, 1992 to 2000*; ACCA, *Reports to the DTI, 1992 to 2000*

monitoring was introduced). Perhaps not surprisingly, greatest improvement was noted in the early years (between 1992 and 1995) as audit firms became more acquainted with the standard of work required and more accustomed to having their performance monitored. However, the improvement does not seem to have been sustained; the proportion of both JMU visits and ACCA unit visits resulting in a satisfactory outcome (Grades A and B) has declined since 1998. This may partly be a result of the JMU and ACCA monitoring unit demanding rather higher standards – now that the audit regulations are well known and the monitoring system is well established. However, the JMU cautions:

> It is important to appreciate that, generally, different firms are visited each year. Thus it is not appropriate to talk in terms of changes in standards when comparing successive years. [Monitoring visit results show that] the large majority of firms are conducting audit work in accordance with the [audit] regulations and auditing standards or have appropriate plans to make improvements . . . Matters raised on a visit are mainly of a procedural nature and would not be critical to the audit opinion. Raising these issues with the firm contributes to the educational element of the visit. (ICAEW *et al.*, 2000, pp. 8–9)

Whatever the detailed outcomes of monitoring visits, the results of surveys conducted during the early years of monitoring in both the UK and USA indicate that, in general, monitoring of audit work has resulted in an overall improvement in its quality or, probably more precisely, its documentation. This improvement has been achieved primarily through improved quality control systems and documentation procedures (see, for example, Evers and Pearson, 1990; Wallace and Wallace, 1990; Fearnley and Page, 1992, 1993; Moizer, 1994). The surveys also reveal that the deficiencies most frequently identified by monitoring visits in both countries are those of inadequate audit planning and, more particularly, documentation.

The ACCA (2000, pp. 65–69) reports that the problems its monitoring unit encounters most frequently result from firms' quality controls not ensuring compliance with auditing standards. More specifically, it highlights the following deficiencies as those occurring most frequently:

- poor or inadequate documentation of audit work;
- failure to plan, or failure to record the plan, or, in some cases, just completing a standard planning checklist without giving sufficient additional details of matters arising in the particular audit or without considering their effect on the audit approach;
- inappropriate use of proprietary audit programmes and the failure to tailor standard programmes to the needs of the particular audit; also initialling or ticking audit tests listed in the audit programme indicating their completion but without giving details of the work performed;

- inadequate documentation of the review of audit work and, more particularly, the failure to clarify how significant issues raised during the review were dealt with;
- lack of appreciation of the importance of documenting and evaluating the client's accounting systems and of gaining sufficient knowledge of the client's business to be able to identify events, transactions and practices that may have a significant impact on the financial statements or the audit thereof;
- over-reliance on management representations especially in relation to the physical existence and condition of tangible fixed assets, the existence and ownership of stock, and the collectability of debtors' balances;
- inadequate or non-existent financial statement disclosure checklists which are needed in order to ensure clients' financial statements comply with statutory and professional requirements;
- inadequate consideration of clients' going concern status (i.e. failure to comply with the requirements of SAS 130: *Going concern*);
- inadequate reporting (in the audit report) of uncertainties – especially in respect of the appropriateness of adopting the going concern basis for the financial statements.

In relation to deficiencies in audits reports, the ACCA (2000, p. 69) notes that a few firms still try to issue a qualified opinion using 'subject to'. This form of qualification, formerly used to signify disagreement with an aspect of the financial statements, disappeared from use (or should have!) in September 1993 when the APB's SAS 600: *Auditors' reports on financial statements* became effective.

Considering the overall effectiveness of the monitoring of registered auditors, it is clear (from the professional bodies' annual reports to the DTI) that both the JMU and the ACCA monitoring unit have uncovered numerous instances of non-compliance with professional standards – and generated innumerable suggestions for improvements in auditing practices. It also seems likely that the 'threat' of monitoring visits has motivated practitioners to effect improvements in their auditing procedures and quality control systems. Additionally, the professional bodies (or, more correctly, the RSBs), when reporting on the effectiveness of their monitoring schemes, have drawn attention to the large number of audit firms which received a less than satisfactory grade as the outcome of their initial monitoring visit (and, hence were subject to a re-visit) but which had 'cleaned up their act' before the follow-up visit. The RSBs have also noted that auditors who persist with their defective performance are disciplined and, if necessary, excluded from the profession. In this regard it is pertinent to note that monitoring seems to have resulted in the removal of a number of 'bad eggs' from the profession's nest and restricted the auditing activities of others. In the nine years since the inception of monitoring in 1992 to 2000, 164 auditors registered with the ICAEW, ICAS or ICAI had their audit registration withdrawn, another 169 surrendered their registration following a JMU visit, and a further 559 either had their registration suspended (pending, for example, further training) or had restrictions imposed on them until required training and/or improvements in performance had been effected (and verified through a follow-up visit). Examples of restrictions include prohibition on accepting new audit clients and precluding certain partners from appointment as audit engagement partners or, even, from engaging in audit work (ICAEW *et al.*, 1992 to 2000).

Given the improvements in auditors' compliance with auditing standards which monitoring appears to have brought, it may be asked why instances of auditor negligence still occur. In answer, commentators such as Wood and Sommer (1985) note that it is not known how many audit failures have been avoided as a result of auditors being required to conform to prescribed standards in the performance of their audit work. They also point out that the monitoring process focuses on firms' quality controls and that no quality control system can prevent *all* undesirable events from occurring. The JMU (in ICAEW *et al.*, 2000) similarly notes that, although the large majority of firms are conducting their work in accordance with audit regulations and auditing standards, 'it is unlikely that there could ever be 100% achievement at this level given the nature of any monitoring process' (p. 9). Woodley (1991) echoed this theme when he stated, on the eve of monitoring being introduced in the UK:

> It would be foolish to believe that there will be no audit failures in the future. No amount of monitoring can eliminate the possibility of errors of judgement or failures to follow laid down procedures. But . . . the extra emphasis on quality control procedures, the possibility of a [monitoring] visit, and the dire consequences of failing to comply with the regulations [should] result in fewer audit failures in the future. (p. 61)

It is pertinent to emphasise that monitoring is largely concerned with assessing audit firms' quality control policy and processes and compliance therewith, rather than with the substance of audit judgments. Thus, although audit firms may effect improvements in their control procedures, faulty audit judgments may persist. However, as Wood and Sommer (1985), among others, have observed, although monitoring cannot prevent all audit errors from occurring, society has other checks in place to ensure that those responsible for causing harm to others as a result of sub-standard professional work do not go unpunished. For example, when questions of audit failure arise, authorities such as the DTI in the UK and the Securities and Exchange Commission (SEC) in the USA investigate and, if justified, appropriate sanctions are imposed on the culprits. Further, as evidenced by cases such as those discussed in Chapter 14, in some instances, those harmed as a result of auditors' sub-standard work may seek redress through the courts.

15.3   PROPOSALS FOR LIMITING AUDITORS' LIABILITY

When investors and others suffer loss as a consequence of a company collapsing unexpectedly, they seek to recover their loss from any hopeful avenue. Although a company's failure is frequently the result of mismanagement by (or, sometimes, dishonesty of) its directors and/or senior executives, when the company fails, the fortunes of its directors often go with it. As a consequence, suing the directors is usually perceived as an option which is unlikely to bear fruit. However, auditors are known to carry indemnity insurance and, if any fault can be found with the way in which they performed their duties, they are often regarded as a potential source from which losses may be recouped. It is generally accepted that this 'deep pocket' syndrome has been a prime motivator in the increasing number of suits brought against auditors over the last couple of decades in English-speaking countries, particularly in the USA, UK and Australia.

In some cases, as is noted in the introduction to this chapter, auditors have faced enormous claims for damages amounting to many millions of pounds. Further, the damages awarded against auditors frequently bear no relation to the size of the audit fee or the extent of the auditors' negligence. The extent of such potential liability has caused some commentators, such as Hardcastle (1988), to conclude that there is a very real risk that it will result in a shortage of suitable people prepared to enter the auditing profession. Hardcastle states, for example:

> There is no doubt that, if current trends in litigation continue without check, the flow of people prepared to enter the professions will slow up and professional standards will fall, as the most able people come to regard a professional career as too risky. (p. 15)

Similar concerns were expressed by Pasricha when commenting on Ernst & Young (E&Y) becoming a limited liability partnership (LLP: such partnerships are discussed below). He observed:

> Without our conversion to an LLP I could have seen a time in the future where it would have become difficult to attract the high calibre of person needed to become a partner in a professional services firm. (Pasricha, 2002)

The potential liability burden auditors face has given rise to calls by auditing firms and others for auditors' liability to be limited in some way. The four main proposals which have been adopted or suggested are:

(i)   permitting auditors to form limited liability companies (LLCs);
(ii) permitting auditors to form limited liability partnerships (LLPs);
(iii) placing a statutory cap on auditors' liability;
(iv) enshrining proportionate (or contributory) liability in statute law.

We discuss each of these options below.

(i) Limited liability companies (LLCs)

Prior to the Companies Act 1989, a body corporate was precluded from being appointed as auditor. Audit firms had to exist as sole practitioners or partnerships. As noted in Chapter 14, under partnership law (which does not cover LLPs), all partners within a firm have joint and several liability. If a court awards damages against a partner in a non-LLP audit firm (or the firm reaches an out-of-court settlement with the plaintiffs) for an amount that exceeds the firm's indemnity insurance cover, the personal assets of the errant partner are used to make good the deficit. If there is still a shortfall, the assets of the other partners in the firm are called upon to rectify the deficiency. Thus, a particular partner may lose his or her personal assets as a consequence of negligence on the part of another partner in the firm – a partner whom (s)he may not even know if the firm is large and has many offices.

The Companies Act 1989 changed the law to permit audit firms to form limited liability companies (LLCs). In cases where firms take advantage of this option, to the extent that any damages awarded against the company (or out-of-court settlement agreed to by the company) exceed the company's insurance cover, the assets of the company are called upon to meet the damages claim. Additionally, the personal assets of the individual 'partner' (or, more correctly, shareholder/director) responsible for the negligence giving rise to the damages (or settlement), may be pursued through the corporate front and used to meet any deficiency. However, the personal assets of 'partners' not associated with the defective audit cannot be called upon.

Thus, incorporation benefits audit 'partners' (shareholder/directors) who are not themselves guilty of negligence in that their personal assets are safe from seizure to meet damages awarded to (or settlement agreed with) a successful plaintiff. However, it does not alter the fact that, if the damages awarded against the audit company exceed the company's indemnity insurance cover, the damages (or settlement) might still result in the company losing all of its assets (forcing the auditors out of business) and the successful plaintiffs not recovering all of their losses.[28]

Another argument raised against auditors forming LLCs is that auditors are members of a profession and, as such, they are accorded certain rights and

---

[28] It should be recalled that, in order to be successful, plaintiffs must prove to the satisfaction of the court that, *inter alia,* they have suffered loss as a result of the auditor's negligence (i.e. they made an economic decision based on financial statements which the auditor audited without exercising due skill and care). The damages awarded by the court make good that loss suffered.

privileges in society. As a consequence, they should not be permitted to hide behind a corporate front while retaining their professional status. One of the recognised hallmarks of a member of a profession is a preparedness to stand by the quality of his or her work and reputation as an individual. Although this argument has merit, as indicated above, incorporation does not result in the identity of the professional responsible for the audit being lost. The individual can still be traced through the corporate front in the event of failing to perform an audit without due skill and care.

Notwithstanding the apparent benefits of changing from a partnership to an LLC in terms of reduced exposure to potential liability, audit firms have demonstrated some reluctance to take advantage of this option. Only about 200 audit firms have taken the incorporation route – including just one of the 'Big Five' firms, namely, the audit section of KPMG which became KPMG Audit plc in 1996. The reasons for audit firms' reluctance to incorporate appear to be associated with company (as compared with individual) tax and, more particularly, National Insurance, rules[29] and the requirement to produce an annual report – complete with audited financial statements which show a true and fair view of the audit company's financial position and its profit or loss for the year. It is also possible that some firms have reservations about whether an incorporated entity provides the appropriate environment within which professional services should be performed. Another possible reason may lie in the emergence of an attractive alternative – LLPs – which are, in the words of Davies (2001, p. 24):

> a modern hybrid combining the internal flexibility of the partnership with the legal protection provided by the limited company.

(ii)   Limited liability partnerships (LLPs)

LLPs were first accorded serious consideration as a possible means of reducing auditors' exposure to liability in 1996 – the year the auditing section of KPMG incorporated as KPMG Audit plc. E&Y and Price Waterhouse (PW), perceiving that the disadvantages of LLCs outweighed their benefits, emerged as stalwart proponents of LLPs. As it seemed that the UK Government could not be persuaded to embrace the LLP notion, the two firms lobbied the Jersey Parliament. Their efforts were rewarded and, in May 1998, the Jersey Parliament enacted LLP law, rendering it possible to establish LLPs in Jersey from September 1998.

However, the UK Government became concerned at the prospect of many UK professional firms (particularly accounting and legal firms) moving their Head

---

[29] These rules result in the 'partners' being subject to significantly higher taxes (and, more particularly National Insurance contributions) than those to which they are subject under a partnership.

Offices' to Jersey and setting up as LLPs there. In 1999, an LLP Bill was drafted and the DTI 'pledged that Limited Liability Partnerships would be up and running by 2000' (Kemeny, 1999). Howells, Minister of Consumer and Corporate Affairs, observed that the LLP Bill was 'very important' and explained:

> One of the functions [of LLPs] will be to help partnerships attract new partners who have been fearful of taking up leadership roles because of unlimited liability . . . [However], in return for LLP status, firms will be expected to offer greater disclosure in the form of filed audited annual accounts. If you have limited liability you have disclosure so that someone who deals with the firm can make an informed decision. (as quoted, Kemeny, 1999)

The Limited Liability Partnerships Act was enacted by the UK Parliament in 2000. Under the Act, businesses could register as LLPs from 6 April 2001; on that date, E&Y became the first organisation in the UK to be issued with an LLP certificate (Hinks, 2001b). Welcoming moves by E&Y to become the first 'Big Five' firm to assume LLP status, Howells (Minister of Consumer and Corporate Affairs) stated:

> I know this new Act [Limited Liability Partnerships Act 2000] will be welcomed by many firms. . . . The new LLP structure is likely to benefit a wide range of businesses, including start-ups. It gives members the freedom to arrange their internal relationships as they wish while retaining the benefit of limited liability . . . I am confident that the Act and [associated] Regulations strike the right balance between the interests of those who want to become Limited Liability Partnerships and those who will do business with them. (as quoted, Hinks, 2001a)

Compared with ordinary partnerships and LLCs, it seems that LLPs provide accounting (and other) firms with four main advantages. These are as follows:

(a) *Limited liability*: This is probably the most important advantage as far as the large accountancy firms are concerned. As noted earlier, under partnership law, all partners are jointly and severally liable for losses caused by the negligence (or other wrongful acts or omissions) of any partner acting in the ordinary course of the partnership's business. Under the Limited Liability Partnerships Act 2000, partners (who are referred to as members) are able to limit their liability to the capital they invest in their firms (Loxton, 2001b). The importance of this advantage is reflected in two comments by Land, E&Y's Chairman:

> • The introduction of LLPs is an important step forward in beginning to provide a fair and reasonable measure of protection for businesses such as ours in an increasingly litigious society. (as quoted, Smith, 2001)
> • I think it is easy for people to forget that in our profession . . .there was real concern that, in an increasingly litigious environment, the law was unfair to us. The doctrine of joint and several liability is a pretty harsh doctrine. (as quoted, Hinks, 2001b)

(b) *The firm has a separate legal personality*: Under partnership law, a partnership does not have a legal personality: it exists as a network of relationships between individual partners. Each partner is an agent, not of the firm, but of the other partners. Under LLP law, the firm is established as a corporate body with a separate legal personality similar to that of an LLC. Each partner is an agent of the LLP in the same way as a director is an agent of his or her company (Davies, 2001, p. 24).

(c)   *Taxation*: As we observed above, incorporation as an LLC is tax disadvantageous to the shareholder/directors of the company (partners of the 'converted' partnership). However, under LLP law, members continue to be taxed as partners (that is, as individuals). Thus, while gaining the advantages of being a separate legal entity (as a corporate body), LLPs have the advantage over LLCs in that, for tax and National Insurance purposes, they are treated as businesses conducted by partners (Loxton, 2001a).

(d)   *Internal flexibility*: LLPs are able to organise their management structure and internal affairs in any way they wish. As in ordinary partnerships, all members ('partners') are able to participate in the management of the LLP. There is no need to elect a Board of Directors or to comply with any of the other organisational requirements attaching to companies.

While there are distinct advantages to be gained by accounting firms converting to LLPs, there are also some disadvantages. These include the following:

(a)   *Preparation of audited financial statements*: One of the 'costs' to accounting firms of becoming LLPs is that the provisions of the Companies Act 1985 regarding the preparation, audit and filing of annual financial statements apply to LLPs. Like LLCs, all LLPs are required to prepare annually, and to file with the Registrar of Companies, audited financial statements that give a true and fair view of the LLP's financial position and its profit or loss for the year. Additionally, where an LLP's profit exceeds £200,000 in any year, it must report the profit attributable to the member with the largest entitlement to profit under the firm's internal agreement.

However, just as the Companies Act's provisions relating to the preparation, audit and filing of financial statements apply to LLPs, so too do the exemptions. Thus, an LLP meeting the Companies Act's criteria to be classed as 'small' is entitled to take advantage of the same limited reporting requirements as a small company. Further, any LLP with a turnover of less that £1 million and a balance sheet total of less than £1.4 million need not have its financial statements audited.

The reporting requirements applying to LLPs are viewed by some (for example, Davies, 2001) as onerous and as likely to be an obstacle to firms becoming

LLPs. However, it is pertinent to observe that most accounting firms' clients are companies and these entities (which are probably less familiar with the financial reporting and auditing requirements than the accounting firms) do not seem to find the reporting obligations too burdensome.

(b) *Consent of third parties may be required to transfer partnership loans and leases.* Where an existing partnership has, for example, a bank loan and/or overdraft, the partnership will need the bank's consent before the loan and/or overdraft can be transferred to an LLP. Further, because the liability of members of an LLP is limited, the bank's security is reduced when a partnership (with joint and several liability) converts to an LLP. Thus, the bank may require personal guarantees for the loan and/or overdraft from the LLP's members before granting its consent to the transfer. Similarly, if a partnership wishes to transfer a lease to an LLP, the landlord's consent will be required. As for the bank, because the landlord's security will be reduced by the transfer of the lease to an LLP, the LLP's members may be required to give personal guarantees in respect of the lease (Tutty, 2001).

(c) *Creditor safeguards are included in the Limited Liability Partnerships Act 2000.* The provisions of the Insolvency Act 1986 relating to a business trading when insolvent apply to LLPs. This means that if an LLP goes into liquidation as a result of insolvency, its members may be personally liable for the debts of the LLP if they knew, or ought to have known, that their firm was heading for insolvency and did not take appropriate action (Davies, 2001). However, the bad news for LLPs does not end here. As Davies (2001, p. 25) explains:

> [The Limited Liability Partnerships Act 2000 includes] a brand new provision for a liquidator to 'claw back' any withdrawal of funds made by a member of an LLP in the two-year period leading up to the firm's liquidation if, at the time of the withdrawal or as a result of it, he knew, or should have concluded that the firm could no longer pay its debts.

In addition to these disadvantages for audit firms converting to LLPs is the (potential) disadvantage to innocent parties who suffer loss as a result of negligence (or other wrongdoing) by a member ('partner') of an LLP. If the loss suffered by a plaintiff exceeds the capital contribution of the member concerned (and, possibly, also his or her personal assets), then, to the extent of the shortfall, the consequences of the members' wrongdoing are borne by the plaintiff. When it is remembered that the evidence suggests that plaintiffs do not succeed easily in actions brought against auditors (see Chapter 14, section 14.5), preventing those who are successful from recovering, in full, the amount lost as a result of auditors' negligence may be viewed as inequitable.

We noted above that, on 6 April 2001, E&Y became the first firm in the UK to take advantage of the opportunity to become an LLP. On 3 May 2002,

KPMG followed its example and became the second Big Five firm to adopt LLP status. As we have seen, the audit section of KPMG was incorporated as KPMG Audit plc in 1996; the LLP covers all of KPMG's operations in the UK and embraces KPMG Audit plc as an element of the LLP. Another Big Five firm – PricewaterhouseCoopers (PwC) – has signalled its intention to convert to an LLP. PW (now part of PwC) was a strong advocate of LLPs when they first attracted serious consideration in 1996. Indeed, as noted above, PW, together with E&Y, was instrumental in Jersey's Parliament enacting LLP law. PwC planned to adopt LLP status in mid-2002 but, as a result of the firm floating off its consultancy arm in July 2002, the move was deferred. It seems likely that the firm will join the LLP fold during 2003. Deloitte & Touche is also reported to be seriously considering converting its partnership to an LLP (Perry, 2002).

Notwithstanding the interest the Big Five firms have shown in becoming LLPs, it seems that other accounting firms are less anxious to follow their example. In May 2002, Lee reported that since April 2001, 'well over 1,000 LLPs have been registered at Companies House but take up among accountancy firms has been slow'. However, he explains:

> I believe the apparent disinterest [in forming LLPs] is merely the consequence of two key factors that are delaying the inevitable. [Firstly] most accountancy firms will only incorporate as an LLP at the start of an accounting period (typically 1 April or 1 May) and after the partners have made time to consider all relevant factors including the recommended creation and adoption of an appropriate members' agreement. . . . [Secondly] until a definitive SORP [Statement of Recommended Practice] is issued later this year, accountancy firms will not know for certain all of the implications of reflecting their results as an LLP. Last year's draft SORP, if adopted without any change, would have resulted in many firms reflecting increased taxable profits and future annuity obligations in the LLP accounts. (Lee, 2002)

Just as Lee seems to think that accounting firms' conversion to LLPs is "inevitable" (see above), Land (Chairman of E&Y) believes that 'LLP status will become commonplace for professional services firms in the next few years' (as quoted, Smith, 2001). However, others appear to hold a contrary view. For example, Crofton-Martin [Senior tax partner of Pannell Kerr Forster (PKF), a middle tier firm] observed that, although conversion to an LLP may be an attractive and effective option for large firms:

> the cost and management time involved . . . may be disproportionately high for small partnerships. . . . . Changing to LLP status is time-consuming and expensive due to financial accounting and administrative requirements. (as reported, Zea, 2001)

Crofton-Martin's views seem to be supported in the marketplace as a survey conducted by an accountancy support company, SWOT, in October 2001 found that '90% of high street [accountancy] partnerships are not planning to become LLPs' (as reported, Zea, 2001). Whether LLPs will become commonplace among accounting firms or whether they will remain the province of the large firms remains an open question.

(iii) Statutory cap on auditors' liability

As an alternative to audit firms incorporating as LLCs or LLPs in order to limit their liability, it has been suggested that legislation should be enacted to 'cap' the liability to which they may be exposed. A widely supported proposal (especially by audit firms!) is that a cap or limit on auditors' liability should be fixed as a factor of the audit fee (for example, ten times the fee). Such arrangements are already in place, for example, in Germany.

This suggestion possesses the advantages of simplicity, linking the size of the sanction associated with a negligently performed audit to the size of the reward resulting from the audit, and preventing (or reducing) the likelihood of auditors being forced out of business by a single negligently performed audit. However, as with LLCs and LLPs, limiting auditors' liability by means of a statutory cap has some disadvantages. These include the following:

(a) The possibility that auditors would be encouraged to reduce the size of their audit fee to a minimum so as to limit their exposure to liability. This may result in a reduction in audit work and, hence, in audit quality, if cost-cutting measures were put in place in an attempt to adjust audit work to the (reduced) audit fee. Along similar lines, it is also possible that auditors would be motivated towards doing less audit work (even less than that justified by a reduced audit fee) – thus increasing their risk of exposure to liability – because the adverse consequences associated with substandard audit work are capped at a known level (i.e. a factor of the audit fee).

(b) It would result in auditors being treated differently from other professional groups and may well result in the government imposing some compensating restrictions on the profession. For example, the government may assume responsibility for regulating or controlling the profession.

(c) As for LLCs and LLPs, a statutory cap on auditors' liability could result in an innocent client or third party, who suffered loss as a consequence of auditors failing to perform their duties with reasonable skill and care, being prevented from recovering the full amount of the loss suffered.

Pratt (1990, p. 78) points out that rather than an innocent party, who relies in good faith on an auditor's skill and professional judgment, bearing the cost of the auditor's negligence (as a consequence of auditors' liability being limited), it is preferable for the audit firm to shoulder the burden. Indeed, to Pratt, a particularly strong argument against any form of limitation of auditors' liability is that an audit firm can spread the risk of potential damages for negligence through professional indemnity insurance. Referring to claims, such as those made by Hardcastle (1988) and Pasricha (2002) (see above), that auditors' liability may be reaching the point where it is prejudicial to the survival of the auditing profession, Pratt observes:

> [T]he accountancy profession will only continue to offer services if it can achieve a satisfactory return. Given that the market for statutory audit services is not a free one (public companies are required by law to have an audit and the qualifications of auditors are likewise prescribed), these oligopolistic characteristics would suggest, according to fundamental economic theory, that higher [indemnity insurance] costs will simply be passed on to audit clients in the form of increased fees. (p. 79)

A federal judge, in the American case of *Rusch Factors* v *Levin* [1968] 284 F Supp. 85, cited by Pratt in support of his argument, asks:

> Why should an innocent reliant party be forced to carry the weighty burden of an accountant's professional malpractice? Isn't the risk of loss more easily distributed and fairly spread by imposing it on the accounting profession, which can pass the cost on to the entire consuming public? (as reported, Pratt, 1990, p. 79)

Against these views, audit firms would point to the decline in the capacity of the insurance market and their inability (particularly for the large firms) to secure – at any cost – the level of professional indemnity insurance they desire and need.

(iv) Enshrining contributory negligence (or proportionate liability) in statute law

An alternative suggestion for limiting auditors' liability, other than through incorporation as LLCs or LLPs or imposing a statutory cap, is that of enacting legislation to give statutory recognition to the principle of contributory negligence (or, equivalently, proportionate liability). Under this principle, damages are awarded against those responsible for a plaintiff's loss in proportion to their responsibility for (or contribution to) that loss. For example, if a court held that a plaintiff's loss was caused equally by negligence on the part of the company's auditors and its directors, then the auditors and the directors would each be responsible for meeting half of the damages awarded.

At present in the UK, the law relating to negligence falls within the ambit of common (that is, court) law rather than statute law. The principle of contributory negligence (proportionate liability) already exists within the common law but, to date, judges in the UK appear not to have applied the principle in cases involving auditors. Hence, it has been proposed that legislation be enacted requiring the courts, in any case involving auditors (or other professional groups to which it applies), to ascertain the extent of the auditor's negligence *vis-à-vis* that of any other party, for example, the auditee's directors, and apportioning blame, and hence damages, accordingly. Such legislation already exists in the USA and, as the AWA case discussed in Chapter 14 (section 14.3.1) shows, it is also in place in Australia. It is being pursued as a favoured option by the auditing profession in the UK (Palmer, 2001, para 9.553.1) but so far the proposal has not found favour with the Government.[30]

Proportionate liability offers significant advantages for auditors and plaintiffs alike. For example, auditors are, in most cases, called upon to meet only part, rather than the full amount, of damages awarded to a successful plaintiff. As a result, there is less likelihood of audit firms being forced out of business as a result of meeting damages settlements. Similarly, because damages awarded to a successful plaintiff are derived from more than one source (i.e. errant auditors and company directors), there is greater likelihood than under the alternative means of limiting auditors' liability of him or her recouping the full amount of the loss suffered. Although these benefits are clearly important, probably the single most important advantage of the principle of contributory negligence is the equity it introduces; it attempts to apportion damages against errant parties according to their proportion of (or contribution towards) the cause of the loss suffered by the plaintiff. It remains to be seen if, and when, the UK Government may be persuaded of the merits of this means of reducing auditors' exposure to liability.

15.4 SUMMARY

In this chapter we have considered how auditors' exposure to legal liability may be avoided or limited. More particularly, we have discussed measures individual audit firms may implement in order to ensure that audits conducted by the firm are of a consistently high standard. We have also examined the monitoring activities of the auditing profession (or, more correctly, the RSBs) in the UK which are designed to monitor the performance of registered auditors in order to ensure they are complying with the profession's auditing and other relevant standards.

Additionally, we have discussed four means by which auditors' exposure to liability may be limited, namely, the incorporation of audit firms as LLCs, or as LLPs, the introduction of a statutory cap on liability, and the enactment of legislation to give statutory recognition to the principle of contributory negligence (or proportionate liability). We have observed that, although the law has been changed to enable audit firms to form LLCs or LLPs, so far relatively few

---

[30] It is pertinent to note that (as was pointed out to one of the authors by a senior audit partner in one of the Big Five firms) out-of-court settlements are, in effect, applications of the principle of proportionate liability. In reaching the agreed settlement, the auditors implicitly acknowledge their portion of the 'blame' for losses suffered by a client or third party and agree the settlement on this basis.

firms have taken advantage of this opportunity although four of the the Big Five firms have formed, or have signalled their intention of forming, LLPs. We have further noted that, as a means of limiting auditors' liability, proportionate liability has much to recommend it. It is an option favoured by the UK auditing profession but, to date, it is not a proposal that has found favour with the UK Government.

SELF-REVIEW QUESTIONS

15.1. List eight environmental quality control elements audit firms should implement to help ensure that high quality audits are performed by the firm.

15.2 List three specific quality control responsibilities of audit engagement partners.

15.3. Explain briefly the rationale underlying the auditing profession's introduction of mechanisms designed to monitor auditors' performance.

15.4. Describe briefly the key features of the Joint Monitoring Unit's monitoring process.

15.5 List two ways in which monitoring by the Joint Monitoring Unit and the ACCA monitoring unit differ and give reasons to explain these differences.

15.6. Evaluate briefly the effectiveness of monitoring auditors' performance in the UK.

15.7. Given that quality control policy and processes have been established in audit firms and that auditors' performance is monitored by the Recognised Supervisory Bodies, audit failures should be a thing of the past. Explain briefly:
   (a) why audit failures still occur, and
   (b) the checks which society has in place to ensure that those responsible for causing harm to others as a result of sub-standard work do not go unpunished.

15.8. List two advantages and two disadvantages for each of the following forms of organisation for audit firms:
   (a) limited liability companies (LLCs)
   (b) limited liability partnerships (LLPs)

15.9. List two advantages and two disadvantages of the introduction of a statutory cap on auditors' liability.

15.10 Discuss briefly the merits of the principle of contributory negligence (or proportionate liability) as a means of limiting auditors' liability.

REFERENCES

Accountancy Foundation Review Board (2002) *Protecting the Public Interest: Introducing the Work Programme of the Review Board*. London: The Accountancy Foundation Ltd.

Accountingweb.com (2002) Andersen reaches settlement in Baptist Foundation lawsuit. *www.accountingweb.com* (7 May 2002).

Chartered Association of Certified Accountants (ACCA) (1992) (1993) (1994) (1995) (1996) (1997) (1998) (1999) (2000) *Annual Reports on Audit Regulation to the Secretary of State for Trade and Industry*. London: ACCA.

Cook, J.M. & Robinson, H.G. (1979) Peer review – the accounting profession's program. *CPA Journal* **49**(3), 11–15.

Davies, J. (2001) Insight: LLPs – safety in numbers. *Accountancy Age*, 28 March 2001, pp. 24–25.

Evers, C.J. & Pearson, D.B. (1990) Lessons learned from peer review. *Singapore Accountant* (June), 19–23.

Fearnley, S. & Page, M. (1992) Counting the cost of audit regulation. *Accountancy* **109**(1181), 21–22.

Fearnley, S. & Page, M. (1993) Audit regulation – one year on. *Accountancy* **111**(1193), 59–60.

Flint, D. (1980) Quality control policies and procedures – the prospect for peer review. *Accountant's Magazine,* **84**(884), 63–66.

Flint, D. (1988) *Philosophy and Principles of Auditing*. London: Macmillan.

Hardcastle, A. (1988) Going to the Government, cap in hand. *Accountancy* **101**(1133), 15–16.

Hinks, G. (2001a) Howells welcomes E&Y into LLP fold. *www.accountancyage.com/News/1120208* (6 April 2001).

Hinks, G. (2001b) Ernst & Young is first LLP. *Accountancy Age*, 12 April 2001, p. 3.

Institute of Chartered Accountants in England and Wales (ICAEW), Institute of Chartered Accountants of Scotland (ICAS), Institute of Chartered Accountants in Ireland (ICAI) (1992) (1993) (1994) (1995) (1996) (1997) (1998) (1999) (2000). *Audit Regulation: Annual Reports to the DTI*. London: ICAEW, ICAS, ICAI.

Joint Monitoring Unit (JMU) (1997) (1998) (1999) (2000) (2001) *The JMU Annual Reports*. London: JMU.

Kemeny, L. (1999) LLPs set for fasttrack through Parliament. *Accountancy Age*, 2 December 1999, p. 6.

Lee, M. (2002) The debate: LLPs – Just delaying the inevitable. *Accountancy Age*, 2 May 2002, p. 12.

Loxton, L. (2001a) Full steam ahead for LLPs. *www.accountancyage.com/news/1118722*. (7 March 2001).

Loxton, L. (2001b). Limited liability partnerships 'normal' in five years. *Accountancy Age*, 29 March 2001, p. 1.

Moizer, P. (1994) *Review of Recognised Supervisory Bodies: A Report to the Department of Trade & Industry on the Audit Monitoring Process*. Unpublished.

Palmer, Sir F.B. (2001) *Palmer's Company Law, Volume 2*. 25th edition (Principal editor G. Morse,). London: Sweet & Maxwell.

Pasricha, N. (2002). The debate: LLPs – Changing nature of our business. *Accountancy Age*, 2 May 2002, p. 12.

Perry, M. (2002) Deloittes considers move to LLP status. *Accountancy Age*, 28 February 2002, p. 2.

Pratt, M.J. (1990) *External Auditing: Theory and Practice in New Zealand*. New Zealand: Longman Paul.

Securities Exchange Commission (SEC) (2001) *Arthur Andersen LLP Agrees to Settlement Resulting in First Antifraud Injunction in more than 20 Years*. New York: SEC, Press Release, 19 June.

Smith, P. (2001) E&Y reaches LLP landmark. *www.accountancyage.com/News/ 1122573*, (28 June 2001).

Tutty, R. (2001) Headstart: LLPs – Is an LLP the right choice for you? *Accountancy Age*, 29 March 2001, p. 26.

Wallace, W.A. & Wallace, J.J. (1990) Learning from peer review. *CPA Journal* **60**(5), 48–53.

Wood, A.M. & Sommer, Jr, A.A. (1985) Statements in quotes. *Journal of Accountancy* **156**(5), 122–131.

Woodley, K. (1991) Introducing audit regulation. *Accountancy* **107**(1159), 60–61.

Zea, A. (2001) LLPs too costly for small businesses. *Accountancy Age*, 4 October 2001, p. 3.

ADDITIONAL READING

Acher, G. (1996) Jointly, severally and unfairly liable. *Accountancy* **117**(1232), 80.

Brown, P. (1995) Partial incorporation: will it work? *Accountancy* **115**(1227), 81.

Carcello, J.V., Hermanson, R.H. & McGrath, N.T. (1992) Audit quality attributes: the perceptions of audit partners, preparers, and financial statement users. *Auditing: A Journal of Practice & Theory* **11**(1), 1–15.

Colbert, G. & Murray, D. (1998) The association between auditor quality and auditor size: an analysis of small CPA firms, *Journal of Accounting, Auditing and Finance* **13**(2), 135–150.

Douglas, P. (1994) Liability capping is the wrong solution. *Accountancy* **113**(1209), 70.

Favere-Marchesi, M. (2000) Audit quality in ASEAN. *The International Journal of Accounting* **35**(1), 121–149.

Fogarty, T.J. (1986) The imagery and reality of peer review in the US: Insights from institutional theory. *Accounting, Organizations and Society* **21**(2/3), 243–268.

Garvey, H. & Dickson, A. (1996) What the JMU found; and found again. *Accountancy* **117**(1234), 126–127.

Institute of Chartered Accountants in England and Wales (ICAEW) (1996) *Finding a Fair Solution. A Discussion Paper on Professional Liability*. London: ICAEW.

Institute of Chartered Accountants in England and Wales (ICAEW) (2000) *Towards Better Auditing*. London: ICAEW, Audit and Assurance Faculty.

King, R.R. & Schwartz, R. (2000) An experimental investigation of auditors' liability: implications for social welfare and exploration of deviations from theoretical predictions, *The Accounting Review* **75**(4), 429–451.

O'Sullivan, N. (2000) The impact of board composition and ownership on audit quality: Evidence from large UK companies. *British Accounting Review* **32**(4), 397–414.

Singleton-Green, B. (1996) 'Convincing arguments' against liability reform. *Accountancy* **117**(1233), 81.

Swinson, C. (1994) Professional standards – is monitoring a big mistake? *Accountancy* **114**(1214), 77.

Warming-Rasmussen, B. & Jensen, L. (1998) Quality dimensions in external audit services – An external user perspective. *The European Accounting Review* **7**(1), 65–82.

16 Internal Audits

LEARNING OBJECTIVES

After studying the material in this chapter you should be able to:

- identify the key differences between internal audits and external audits;
- explain the relationship between risk and control and the role of internal audit within this relationship;
- discuss the benefits of internal audits for organisations;
- list the key objectives of an internal audit;
- outline the internal audit process;
- describe the various types of internal audit;
- explain the relationship between risk management and internal audit;
- describe the key features of a Control Risk Self Assessment (CRSA) system;
- explain the interface between internal audits and external audits.

16.1 INTRODUCTION

In Chapter 1 we distinguish between external audits and internal audits. We note, in particular, that external audits are performed for shareholders and other parties external to the entity and that they are conducted in accordance with statutory and regulatory requirements by independent, external auditors. Internal audits, on the other hand, are performed for the entity's management (primarily its senior executives and directors) and are conducted in accordance with management's requirements by personnel internal to the entity, if the entity has an internal audit function, or external to it, if the internal audit function is outsourced.

As a consequence of external audits being governed by the law and regulations, apart from minor differences resulting from variations in the size and complexity of auditee entities[1] and additional industry-specific requirements applying in some cases, the external audits of all companies are similar in their objective, process and outcomes. They relate to the truth and fairness of the financial statements of the entity being audited and cover the entire organisation. By contrast, internal audits are governed by the requirements of the entity's senior management and, as a result, vary widely in their scope (that is, the extent of the functions or activities of the organisation covered by a particular audit) and in their objective(s). They may, for example, have as their objective providing assurance to the company's directors and senior executives that appropriate controls are in place and operating effectively to mitigate identified risks to which the organisation is exposed; alternatively, they may be conducted to investigate a concern of the Chief Executive Officer about a function or activity within the company not performing to the expected standard of effectiveness or efficiency,[2] or about adherence to the company's strategic plan, objectives, policies or procedures.

Although a variety of internal audits may be conducted, in recent years, as societal and regulatory concern about corporate governance and risk management has grown, the attention of company directors and senior executives has focused increasingly on the risks to which their companies are exposed and the controls in place to mitigate those risks. Greater demands have been placed on risk managers to ensure that all of the organisation's risks are identified, and on

---

[1] It is pertinent to note that in the context of external audits the term 'auditee' applies to the unit subject to audit which is the entity as a whole; in the context of internal audits the term similarly applies to the unit subject to audit but, in this case, it may be the entity as a whole or, more commonly, a function or activity within it.

[2] Audits investigating the effectiveness, efficiency and economy of a company, or a part thereof, are usually referred to as value for money (VFM) audits. As economy is, in essence, a subset of efficiency, for reasons of succinctness and clarity, in this chapter we refer to effectiveness and efficiency, rather than effectiveness, efficiency and economy.

internal auditors to ensure that appropriate and effective controls are in place to counter those risks. At the same time, the benefits of devolving primary responsibility for the risks and controls of individual functions and activities within the company to the managers of those functions or activities have come to be recognised. These managers are better placed than more remote risk managers and internal auditors to identify the risks to which their function or activity is exposed and to establish appropriate controls to mitigate those risks. As a consequence, Control Risk Self Assessment (CRSA) has been adopted by many (especially larger) companies. Under CRSA, functional or activity managers have primary responsibility for identifying the risks, and for checking the adequacy and continued operation of controls in their unit of the organisation and the company's risk managers and internal auditors have a general oversight role.

External audits have been the focus of the first 15 chapters of this book. In this chapter we turn our attention to internal audits. We first explore the relationship between risk and control and explain the role of internal audit within this relationship. We then discuss the key objectives of internal audits, explain the desirability of conducting internal audits with specialist internal auditors, outline the internal audit process, and review the various types of internal audit that may be performed. We devote a significant portion of the chapter to examining the relationship between internal audit and risk management – and we do this in the context of CRSA. In the concluding section, we address the question of how internal auditing interfaces with external auditing.

16.2   RISK, CONTROL AND THE ROLE OF INTERNAL AUDIT

16.2.1   Relationship between risk and control

In Chapter 2 (section 2.2) we observe that, as economic and technological developments occurred during the past couple of centuries, so the size and nature of the dominant form of business enterprise evolved – from individual traders and family owned and operated businesses, through small local, and later large national, companies with small groups of professional managers and hundreds if not thousands of employees, to huge multinationals, similarly managed by professional managers but with, in many cases, hundreds of thousands of employees located in many parts of the world.

In order to function effectively (that is, achieve a stated purpose such as earning a given level of profit or selling a given volume of products or services in particular markets), companies require a broad strategic plan, specific objectives, and means of ensuring that their employees strive towards achieving the stated plan and objectives (that is, controlling their activities). Developing the strategic plan, defining the objectives, and establishing the means of controlling employees' activities, is the task of a company's board of directors. However, as companies develop and expand, they outgrow the ability of any one person or small group of people (such as the board of directors) to closely manage every aspect of their operations. Management responsibilities need to be delegated to subordinates – and, the bigger and more complex the company (or group of companies), the greater the delegation involved. Thus, responsibility for ensuring that activities are performed which will enable the company's strategic plan and objectives to be achieved is delegated to managers subordinate to the board of directors. However, this gives rise to the possibility that the subordinate managers will not fulfil their delegated responsibilities as intended and, as a result, achievement of the organisation's strategic plan and/or objectives may be threatened or put at risk. In the corporate setting, when we speak of 'risk' we mean the possibility that events may occur which will prevent (or threaten) achievement of the company's strategic plan and objectives.

Companies, like people, operate in an environment where risks of all kinds exist. For people, simply travelling to work or to a holiday destination are activities that are prone to risk; events may occur that prevent arrival at work or at the holiday destination, or prevent arrival in the manner or at the time planned. For companies, simply using a building to house employees and equipment is a risk – the building might burn down or get flooded; similarly, dealing in cash is a risk since cash might be stolen. However, companies' risks are not limited to the possibility of cash or other tangible assets being lost, stolen or damaged; they include, for example, the loss of information or technical knowledge. For instance, if a direct marketing company fails to establish proper back-up facilities and a fire destroys its entire customer database, the company loses an asset of far greater value than the computer hardware on which the database was stored. Further, companies may lose key employees – together with their knowledge of the organisation's internal activities and/or external customer and supplier networks, or the company's strategic plan may come under threat. If the chosen strategy of the board of directors is undermined – perhaps through a lack of understanding by the managers to whom the board has entrusted responsibility for its implementation, or through a lack of an appropriate response to changing market conditions, then the company's very existence could be at risk.

For a company to survive and be successful it is essential that it identifies, assesses and manages its risks. We use the term 'manages' rather than 'eliminates' for the following reasons:

- Some risks *cannot* be eliminated because they are outside the control of the company. For example, a change in the regulatory or tax environment which renders the company's products less attractive for customers, more expensive to produce or sell, or less profitable, cannot be eliminated. However, such risk can be managed by having appropriate contingency plans in place.
- Other risks *could* be eliminated but to do so is not cost-effective: the costs involved in eliminating the risk of an identified adverse event occurring would outweigh the potential damage to the company if the event occurred. Alternatively, measures established to prevent a damaging event from occurring may also preclude potentially beneficial events from taking place. This is particularly the case when measures designed to mitigate identified risks result in suppressing entrepreneurial flair – thus preventing the possibility of gaining potentially rich rewards.

Identifying and assessing risks

Before risks can be managed they need to be identified and assessed. Companies can identify the risks to which they are exposed in various ways but perhaps the most common is to analyse each functional area of the company (for example, marketing, sales, production, distribution, administration, human resources, etc.) to identify events that could occur which, if they did so, would have an adverse impact on the function concerned.

Once identified, the events can be assessed to determine: (i) their probability of occurrence if appropriate controls were not in place, and (ii) their likely adverse impact if they should occur. From this 'dual assessment', a single 'risk score' may be derived for each potentially harmful event that threatens the company, and the risks prioritised accordingly. Greatest effort in managing the company's risks can then be accorded to those that pose the greatest threat.

To illustrate the areas of a business organisation that may be vulnerable to risk, in Figure 16.1 we list the risk categories used by a major UK company to classify the threats it has identified to the achievement of its objectives.

Managing risks

Managing risks involves establishing and maintaining controls to prevent identified potentially damaging events from occurring or mitigating their harmful effects. However, risk and control may be viewed as the two extremes of a risk-control continuum. A company could operate without establishing any controls; its costs would be kept to a minimum but potential threats would exist (some more likely to occur and/or potentially more damaging than others), any one of which could result in serious loss or damage to the company's assets or operations, or even in the demise of the company itself. If a company's

Figure 16.1: Risk categories used by a major UK company to classify identified threats to the achievement of its objective

- Strategy (risks that could impact achievement of the strategic plan)
- Cash
- Physical assets
- Information (risks relating to the loss of valuable customer, financial, sales and/or strategic data)
- Knowledge (risks relating to the loss of intellectual capital)
- Goodwill/reputation/brand

management adopted this risk-exposed stance it would be gambling the company's possible survival against enhanced profits. At the opposite extreme, a company could spend time and effort identifying all possible threats to which it might be exposed and then designing a complex and expensive web of controls to prevent them from occurring or to lessen their impact if they did occur. If a company followed this maximum control course of action it would be sacrificing profit, perhaps even incurring losses, in favour of eliminating all risk. Neither of these approaches is a wise option; business enterprises thrive and prosper by taking risks – but in a controlled manner. Thus, the art of managing risks has two essential strands:

(i) understanding the potential risks facing the company, their likely impact if they should occur, and the probability of their occurrence if no controls were present; and

(ii) designing the optimum control environment to counter identified risks by balancing the costs of preventing the risks from occurring, or lessening their impact, against the benefits of so doing. In such an environment, greatest attention is given to mitigating the risks with the highest risk scores.

As we noted earlier, as companies grow in size and complexity, so it becomes necessary for management responsibilities to be delegated. However, ultimate responsibility for the company's management – selecting its strategy, designing its strategic plan, defining its objectives, establishing required controls, and so on – remains that of the board of directors. Therefore, the board needs to be confident that subordinate managers to whom responsibilities have been delegated are fulfilling those responsibilities – and doing so in the desired manner. The board needs to be assured, for example, that subordinate managers understand its chosen strategy and are adhering to its strategic plan. Suppose, for instance, that a company's strategy includes the goal of gaining a foothold in Europe for its main product line and that its strategic plan includes the objective of securing 10% of the European market for the product. Suppose further that implementation of this objective is delegated to the Director of Sales and Marketing and that (s)he is responsible for developing and implementing the tactics to achieve it. In this situation, the board of directors will require regular updates on how well the tactics are being deployed and the likelihood of the strategic goal being achieved. The Sales and Marketing Department will be responsible for taking remedial action to counter any minor threats to achievement of the objective but the board will need to be notified immediately of any major threats, such as a trade embargo or penal taxes being introduced in targeted European markets, so that it can decide, for example, whether a change in strategic direction is called for.

Where managers below board level delegate responsibilities to their subordinates, they need similar assurances to those required by the board of directors about fulfilment of those responsibilities. In order to ensure the required assurances can be provided, networks of checks and balances (collectively known as 'the control environment') are established throughout the company. Managers at all levels are responsible for ensuring that an effective control environment is operating at all times within their sphere of responsibility; that appropriate controls are in place to prevent 'threats' to achievement of the company's objectives from occurring or, failing this, ensuring they are detected in a timely manner and, if possible, mitigated. For example, a system of passwords might be established throughout a company to ensure that only authorised employees with valid passwords can log into the computer system. This is a powerful preventive control, designed to protect the company's information from theft, sabotage or corruption. Similarly, reconciling a company's bank statement with its General Ledger cash account helps to verify that all of the company's cash transactions are legitimate and are correctly recorded in the company's books. This is a detective control which would uncover, for example, theft of funds from the company's bank account. It is less powerful than the preventive (password) control mentioned above because it is performed after the event (i.e. the control will detect the theft of funds but only after they have been stolen when it may be too late to remedy the situation).

16.2.2   Role of internal audit

A company's controls are generally embedded in its systems and implemented by employees. However, no system is perfect and as individuals are human they are prone to make mistakes. As a result, it is necessary to have a review process in place to monitor the effectiveness of the control environment – a process that constitutes part of the role of the internal audit function.

An effective control environment means more than having mechanisms in place to prevent, or failing that, to detect and if possible mitigate threats to

quate feedback mechanisms are in place to ensure that managers are notified by their subordinates of the emergence of potential threats and steps taken to counter them. Verifying that such mechanisms are in place is another important element of the role of internal auditors. In general, people do not like reporting bad news. Sometimes this is manifested as reluctance by subordinates to report matters to their managers which might be perceived as reporting a failure on their part. This situation is exacerbated if a portion of the managers' remuneration is based on their overall performance – including that relating to implementing and maintaining effective internal controls. Additionally, potential threats may not be reported to superiors because of the misguided belief that, provided a threat has been identified and remedial action has been implemented and is on track, senior managers need not be 'bothered' with the issue. However, this overlooks the fact that until the remedial action is successfully concluded the threat still exists and, depending on its severity, the relevant level of the company's management needs to be made aware of it. Once informed, the senior managers may simply endorse the remedial action already underway but, with their wider perspective of the company and its business, they may require a different course of action to be taken.

Thus, internal auditors have a critical role within the risk-control relationship. As we noted above, in a business context, risk refers to the possibility that events may occur which threaten achievement of the company's objectives. Controls are measures that are put in place to prevent, or failing this to detect, the occurrence of such events. The role of the internal audit function is, principally, to review the company's control environment to ensure that:

(i) controls are in place and functioning effectively to prevent or detect the occurrence of potentially damaging events; and
(ii) adequate feedback mechanisms are in place and functioning effectively so that relevant levels of management are informed promptly of potential threats to achievement of the company's objectives, and of the remedial action that has been taken.

16.3 INTERNAL AUDIT OBJECTIVES AND SPECIALISTS

16.3.1 Objectives of internal audit

Although the internal audit function is internal to a company, it is not part of the control environment; instead it is a mechanism for conducting an independent review of that environment on behalf of the directors and senior executives. Its principal objective is to effect change. Unlike external auditors, internal auditors do not simply report their audit conclusions (generally expressed in terms of control weaknesses they have encountered); they also formulate, together with the manager of the function or activity that has been audited, appropriate actions to remedy the identified weaknesses. They then follow up on the agreed actions to ensure they have been implemented and the control weaknesses eradicated.

In order to convey the unique position of an internal audit function within a company, in Figure 16.2 we reproduce the Internal Audit Charter of a major UK public listed company. Key features of this charter include the following:

(i) internal audit is an activity that is independent of, but reviews, all of the company's other functions;

(ii) it is an activity that is conducted for the company's executive (its most senior managers) and the Audit & Compliance Committee.[3] In accordance with this, the Head of Internal Audit reports directly to the Chief Executive Officer (CEO) and also reports to the chairman of the Audit & Compliance Committee;

(iii) the remit of internal audit is to evaluate internal control throughout the company in order to ensure that the company's controls are adequate to prevent, or detect and remedy, events that may threaten the company's operations, financial security and/or reputation;

(iv) the work of the internal audit function is facilitated by the right to unimpeded access to all of the company's functions, property, records and personnel, with the exception of any pension scheme established by the company. In relation to pension schemes, an internal audit service is to be provided if such is requested by the scheme's trustees;

(v) as an outcome of their work, internal auditors are expected to make recommendations for control improvements and also for remedial action if potentially threatening events are detected. However, any recommendation is to be agreed with the line manager concerned; in the event that agreement cannot be reached between the internal audit function and the relevant line manager, a resolution process is provided;

(vi) the CEO is kept informed of the state of risk control throughout the company through regular meetings with the Head of Internal Audit. Prior to these meetings, the internal audit function is expected to review the risk profile[4] (signed off by the relevant manager) of each functional area

---

[3] It is interesting to note that this illustrative company has an 'Audit & Compliance Committee'. In many companies its equivalent would be referred to as the 'Audit Committee'. These committees are discussed in Chapter 4, section 4.4.

[4] A risk profile captures data concerning: (i) potential adverse events that may affect the function, (ii) the likely impact of the events should they occur, (iii) the probability of the events occurring if no controls were present, and (iv) the effectiveness of the controls in place to prevent the events from occurring or, failing this, to mitigate their impact.

Figure 16.2:   Internal Audit Charter of a major UK public listed company

CHARTER

Internal Audit is an independent appraisal activity within [X] plc for the review of all operations as a service to the Executive and the Audit & Compliance Committee.

The function provides an evaluation of internal control throughout the company with the intention of ensuring that management operates adequate controls to mitigate significant operational, financial and reputational risks to the business.

The Head of Internal Audit reports directly to the Chief Executive Officer with an additional reporting responsibility to the chairman of the Audit & Compliance Committee.

In carrying out their duties, Internal Auditors will have full and unrestricted access to all company functions, records, property and personnel necessary for the performance of their work. This authority does not extend to any pension scheme set up by the company; however, Internal Audit will, at the request of the trustees of the scheme, provide them with an Internal Audit service.

Internal Audit will adhere at all times to the professional standards of the Institute of Internal Auditors (UK) to which the department is affiliated.

Internal Audit's routine activities will give rise to recommendations for remedial action and control improvement. Recommendations will need buy-in from the line managers affected by a recommendation. In the normal course of events, no issues will be reported to the Chief Executive Officer until such support has been obtained. In the event that an audit recommendation cannot be agreed to by the line manager concerned, then the matter will be elevated to the Head of Internal Audit and the relevant functional Executive. Should agreement still not be possible, then both parties will discuss the matter with the Chief Executive Officer whose decision on the matter will be final. Should the Head of Internal Audit still feel there is a significant control risk that is not being addressed, then the matter will be reported to the Audit & Compliance Committee at the next available meeting. There may, however, be circumstances where this reporting process is inappropriate; for example, the identification by Internal Audit of activities which could result in the company losing its licence, or having its licence suspended. In such cases, the Head of Internal Audit is expected to report these matters to the Chief Executive Officer as soon as possible.

The Head of Internal Audit will hold regular meetings with the Chief Executive Officer to discuss the state of risk control within the business. Internal Audit will be expected to comment on the standard of control in each functional area and for the company as a whole. These commentaries will be based upon the Risk Profiles prepared for each area and signed off by the functional managers. Prior to the meeting, the Head of Internal Audit will meet with each Director or Officer to discuss his report in order to ensure there are 'no surprises' at the meeting. In the event that agreement as to the standard of control cannot be reached, then this fact is to be reported to the Chief Executive Officer at the meeting. If necessary, the Director or Officer has the right of attendance at the meeting.

There will arise from time to time issues which cut across functional lines which may require Internal Audit input; for example, organisational or cultural changes, the introduction of new technology or new product development. The Chief Executive will ensure that the Head of Internal Audit has sufficient access to the various committees to allow for the necessary technical audit input. It is the responsibility of the Head of Internal Audit to ensure that he is aware of all major projects scheduled to be undertaken and to ensure that sufficient Internal Audit input occurs at the correct time on all relevant projects.

Chief Executive

of the company and to discuss the relevant risk profiles with the senior executive responsible for each function. At the meetings with the CEO, the Head of Internal Audit is expected to comment (based on the risk profiles) on the standard of risk control within each functional area and for the company as a whole. Through this process, the risk-control awareness of all relevant players within the company is kept high and neither the company, nor any part within it, should be exposed to 'nasty surprises';

(vii) provision is made for the Head of Internal Audit to provide input to any cross-functional developments in the company, such as changes in organisational structure, and to any new developments such as new products, markets or technology. However, it is the responsibility of the Head of Internal Audit to be aware of all major projects that are planned and for ensuring that appropriate internal audit input is provided at the relevant time;

(viii) the standard of work performed by the internal auditors is to accord with the professional standards of the Institute of Internal Auditors (IIA) (UK). As for the professional standards applying to external auditors, the professional standards of the IIA include both technical auditing standards and ethical guidelines.

16.3.2 Internal auditors vs external auditors to fulfil the internal audit function

Reviewing the features of the internal audit function outlined above, it may well be thought that external auditors could readily fulfil the internal audit role. As we saw in earlier chapters, during the course of their work, external auditors need to gain a thorough understanding of their clients' risk exposures and internal control systems. This is especially true for audit firms that have adopted the business risk approach to auditing (see Chapter 2, section 2.2.6). These firms, in particular, are concerned to ensure that they understand fully the operations and assets of their audit clients – including assets such as information, knowledge, goodwill, reputation and brands, all of which impact the financial results – as well as the current and fixed assets that normally appear in financial statements. In this regard there is much common ground between the work of external and internal auditors as all aspects of a company's operations and all of its assets are prone to risk and it is the task of the internal auditors to ensure that the company's control environment is effective in providing adequate protection. Given this common ground, it could be argued that if external auditors were to fulfil the internal audit role, duplication would be avoided and external auditors would gain a deeper understanding of their clients' risk-control environments.

However, such reasoning loses sight of the fact that, while external audits are conducted as a service for shareholders and other parties external to the audit client, internal audits are performed as a service for the organisation's directors and senior executives. If external auditors were to fulfil the internal audit role, then serious questions would arise about their independence and their ability to express an unbiased opinion on the truth and fairness of the entity's financial statements.

Further, the perspective of external and internal auditors in relation to a company's risk exposures and control environment tends to differ. Generally, external auditors are primarily interested in risks that could threaten the company's continued viability, and in the effectiveness of the control environment in preventing, or detecting and correcting, errors and irregularities in the financial data. Internal auditors, on the other hand, have rather more of an all-embracing approach. They are interested in all of the risks that could threaten achievement of the entity's objectives (particularly those with the highest risk scores that pose the greatest threat) and in ensuring that the control environment is effective in protecting all of the company's operations and assets. Additionally, internal auditors are concerned with the company's effectiveness and efficiency in achieving its objectives. These matters are not usually within the remit of external auditors; if they should encounter areas of the organisation that are not operated efficiently or effectively, they are not generally responsible for reporting these findings to the company's directors or senior executives, although they may do so as a matter of good practice. The contrary applies to internal auditors; their role normally includes responsibility for identifying and reporting ineffectiveness and inefficiency in the company's operations – and for recommending, and following up on, remedial action. In order to fulfil their wide-ranging role, unlike external auditors who are largely drawn from the ranks of qualified accountants, internal auditors frequently come from a wide range of backgrounds. These include professionally qualified internal auditors (those with IIA qualifications), qualified accountants, information technology experts, and specialists such as engineers and actuaries.

A further restricting factor as regards external auditors fulfilling the role of internal auditors is the limited time external auditors spend in their audit clients. External auditors are usually only present at certain times of the year (generally for the interim and final audits). However, as we observed earlier in this chapter, it is of the utmost importance to those responsible for managing companies that they are informed of threats to achievement of the company's objectives as soon as they arise so that action can be taken to prevent the potentially damaging events from occurring or to minimise their impact.

16.4   INTERNAL AUDIT PROCESS

The internal audit process can usefully be divided into four sub-processes, namely:

(i)   planning
(ii) executing
(iii) reporting
(iv) following up.

(i)   Internal audit planning

As we noted above, internal auditors are responsible for reviewing all functional areas of a company and to facilitate this they are given the right to unimpeded access to all of the company's assets, records and personnel. This all-embracing responsibility of the internal audit function is often referred to as its portfolio.

If internal auditors were to try to review all elements of their portfolio every year, a higher complement of staff would be required than the company actually needs – or is likely to be willing to pay for. Consequently, the internal audit portfolio is prioritised so that greatest attention is given to those functional areas that are perceived to present the greatest risk – either because they deal with large volumes of valuable (and easily removable) items such as cash or negotiable instruments, or because previous internal or external audit work has identified significant problems. However, care is also taken to ensure that all areas of the company are audited within a reasonable timeframe. Thus, it might be decided that all of the company's functional areas must be audited at least once every three years but those that engage in activities that could potentially threaten achievement of the company's strategic plan should be audited at least once a year.

In order to identify the areas that warrant more frequent and/or more rigorous audit attention, risk matrices are produced for all functional areas in the internal audit portfolio (an example of a typical risk matrix is presented in section 16.6.2 below). Data in the risk matrices are grouped into various risk categories, and these are incorporated into what is known as the *annual internal audit planning model*. This model combines the risk data with other factors such as the complexity of the functional area, the time since the last audit, and other relevant matters, and generates a list of audits to be conducted during the ensuing year.

The internal audit function can then determine its staffing requirements – the number of staff and the skills and experience – necessary to complete the various audits. Where the planning model signals a likely shortfall, this can usually be covered by employing short-term supplementary staff from external sources for specific, usually specialised, audits. This approach, known as 'co-sourcing', is more efficient than employing sufficient staff to cover peak audit times and having to find alternative work for surplus staff at other times.

(ii)   Executing an internal audit

Typically, an internal audit commences with a memorandum being sent to the senior manager responsible for the area to be audited. It sets out the activities to be audited and those, if any, that fall outside the scope of the audit, how the progress of the audit is to be monitored, and the process to be adopted for reporting audit issues. These matters are then discussed at the start of the audit at a meeting with the senior managers of the area concerned.

The audit work progresses in accordance with a predetermined plan (or audit programme) which sets out the audit tests to be performed. The audit tests conducted (and their documentation) broadly resemble those of an external audit which we discuss in Chapters 6 to 12. The internal audit process includes, for example:

(a) a 'walk through' test whereby the internal auditor traces one or more transactions or other specific data items through the information systems of the area being audited to ascertain whether the systems, in fact, operate as described to the internal auditor by personnel in the area concerned; for example, tracing data relating to the recruitment of a new employee through the relevant information systems of the human resources department to establish whether the systems operate as described;

(b) the completion of Internal Control Questionnaires (ICQs). These comprise a series of questions which are asked of relevant staff members in the area being audited in order to determine whether or not certain internal controls are present and are being complied with. The only practical way to 'test' the operation of some controls is to ask questions of the relevant person; for example, if large sums of cash are regularly taken to the bank on foot, a security control may require the time of banking and the route taken to be varied. The most efficient way to test this control is to ask the person concerned when they bank the cash and the route they take. Such questions are included in the ICQ;

(c) compliance testing, that is gathering evidence to determine whether or not internal control procedures are being complied with. These tests are primarily conducted by the following means:

- observation – watching while a particular activity of a controlling nature is performed; for example, observing whether the receptionist always checks security passes before admitting people into the offices;

- interviewing – conducting interviews with employees who perform control activities to establish whether they understand the controls they are operating and why they are operating them; for example, interviewing employees who perform bank reconciliations;
- examination of documentation – reviewing a small sample of documentary evidence to establish whether the control is operating as intended; for example, reviewing a selection of cheque requisitions (documents prepared by someone in the area being audited to support a cheque to be paid to, say, a supplier) to ascertain that two valid signatures appear;

(d) substantive testing – tests of transactions and balances, and procedures such as analytical review, which seek to obtain audit evidence regarding the completeness, accuracy and validity of information in the accounting records, financial statements and management information systems generally, including, for example, sales and production data expressed in both financial and non-financial terms. Substantive tests are particularly important to verify the completeness, accuracy and validity of information in the records of the area being audited in respect of activities where internal controls are considered to be weak – either because they are adjudged by the internal auditors to be inadequate or not operating satisfactorily, or because required controls are absent. Substantive testing is also used to determine whether a perceived risk, resulting from inadequate or unsatisfactory controls has, in fact, manifested itself; for example, if a weak control environment gives rise to the possibility that 'ghost' employees could appear on the payroll, verifying the existence of the employees listed on each payroll for a specified period (say, a month or a quarter).

Where internal auditors need to examine a large volume of data in order to form an opinion about the adequacy of the overall control environment or to determine whether a perceived potential risk has materialised, they generally use Computer Assisted Audit Techniques (CAATs). These are sophisticated computer programs that are capable of searching through huge databases to identify and highlight individual pieces of data that conform to certain criteria specified by the auditor.[5]

(iii)   Reporting
At the conclusion of the audit, the internal auditors have an exit meeting with the senior manager(s) of the area being audited. At this meeting, any control deficiencies the auditors have identified are discussed and corrective action is

---

[5] The use of CAATs in external audits is discussed in Chapter 11, section 11.9.

agreed. These matters are then incorporated into a formal audit report, along with the managers' response to the matters raised by the auditors, and a target date for completion of the remedial action is agreed.

(iv) Following up

One of the most important elements of an internal auditor's role is ensuring that agreed action to remedy control deficiencies actually takes place. In most cases such action cannot be effected immediately after the audit. It may, for instance, require changes to be made to the relevant function's systems, or more staff may need to be recruited. As a result, the internal auditors need to monitor progress and, as the agreed date for completion approaches, work with the manager(s) of the area concerned to ensure the agreed action is effected.

This important part of an internal auditor's work does not have a direct parallel in an external audit. In general, the responsibilities of external auditors are complete when the audit report on the financial statements and the management letter are issued.[6] Unlike internal auditors, it is not incumbent upon external auditors to follow up on the matters detailed in the management letter to ensure they are remedied. However, in most cases this is done as a matter of good practice at the beginning of the following year's audit.

16.5   TYPES OF INTERNAL AUDIT

Internal auditors' key responsibility is providing assurance to the company's directors and senior executives about all aspects of the company's control environment. However, the internal audit requirements of the directors and senior executives can vary widely and, as a result, the type of internal audit work performed, and the way in which it is carried out, can differ markedly. The internal audit function performs, for example, financial audits, operational audits, value for money (VFM) audits, and special projects. We discuss each of these in turn.

(i) Financial audits

When discussing financial audits we need to distinguish between financial statement audits conducted by external auditors and financial audits performed by internal auditors. As explained in earlier chapters, a financial statement audit is an examination, by qualified accounting professionals external to the entity, of the entity's financial statements and supporting

---

[6] Audit reports and management letters are discussed in Chapter 13.

evidence. Its purpose is to provide assurance to the shareholders and other interested parties outside the entity that the financial statements present a true and fair view of the company's (or group's) financial position and performance. In contrast to this, the purpose of financial audits conducted by internal auditors is to ensure that the financial systems within the company (or group) are appropriately designed, implemented and maintained so as to be effective in preventing, or detecting and correcting, errors and/or irregularities in the financial data and records that underlie the summary figures which appear in the financial statements.

Reviews of the company's financial systems may form part of the internal auditors' routine, rotational examination of all aspects of the company, or they may be specifically commissioned by the directors or senior executives. This might occur, for example, if there is some concern over a particular aspect of the organisation's financial activity. The internal auditors may, for instance, be requested to examine all bank account reconciliations performed during – say – the previous six months, to ensure they were completed promptly and accurately and that all identified differences were cleared.

Financial audits conducted by internal auditors, especially in cases similar to the bank reconciliations example, are clearly of interest to the external auditors. The outcome of the bank reconciliation investigation, for example, would provide the external auditors with valuable evidence as to the completeness and accuracy of the bank account in the company's accounts.

(ii) Operational audits

The primary purpose of an operational audit is to examine the control environment of a particular function of an organisation (for example, information technology, production, sales, or human resources), or an aspect of its operations, such as a specific process (for example, cash receipts or customer data processing), or a particular product. It should be noted that the manager responsible for the function or activity concerned is also responsible for establishing its control environment.

Internal auditors are responsible for assessing the adequacy of the overall control environment of the function or activity being audited (that is, the auditee).[7] To achieve this, they first identify all of the potential risks likely to affect the auditee and then evaluate the adequacy of the controls in place to mitigate each risk. From this they can assess the adequacy of the control environment as a whole.

---

[7] See footnote 1.

In order to illustrate some of the risks that might be examined in an operational audit, we reproduce in Figure 16.3 a brief extract from a risk report for a bank. It should be noted that the risk report not only describes the bank's risk exposures but also records, for each potential risk (or, more correctly, potential adverse event), the asset under threat (cash in this case) if the identified adverse event should occur, the likely impact if the event occurred, and the probability of the event occurring.

As indicated in Figure 16.3, internal auditors evaluate the control environment relating to each risk on two bases, namely, the 'target environment' and the 'actual environment'.

- *The target environment* refers to the effectiveness of the control environment in mitigating the identified risk if the appropriate controls were in place and operating as intended. This does not necessarily mean that the potential risk is fully mitigated. As we noted earlier, the cost of mitigating risks must be balanced against the benefits to be gained from so doing. The target environment represents the level of control determined by the manager responsible for the auditee to be the optimum; almost invariably it lies somewhere between a totally risk free, but enormously expensive, control environment and one which is inexpensive to maintain but is prone to losses through the occurrence of (unchecked) adverse events.
- *The actual environment* refers to the effectiveness of the control environment in mitigating the identified risk in practice (i.e. as the controls in place actually operate). It is possible, or even likely, that the controls established by the manager responsible for the auditee do not always operate as intended – and some may not be operating at all. In this situation, the level of risk the manager was prepared to accept when establishing the controls required to attain the target environment will be exceeded, possibly to a level that is unacceptable. For example, in order to safeguard funds in a company's bank account, a control may be established in the finance department whereby the bank statement and company's cash account is to be reconciled at the end of each week. In establishing this control, the Finance Director accepts that it is not perfect; theft of cash could occur at the start of the week and not be detected until some days later, by which time the perpetrator and cash may have disappeared. Nevertheless, the control reflects the target control environment desired by the Finance Director; in order to avoid the additional cost of having the bank account reconciled daily, (s)he is prepared to accept the small risk of error or fraud going undetected for up to five days and the possibility that the situation will not be able to be rectified. However, if as a result of, say, staff shortages, the bank statement and cash account entries were only reconciled at the end of each month, the risk of loss is far greater than originally envisaged by the Finance Director because theft of cash could remain undetected for up to 30 days, giving far less chance of rectifying the situation.

Figure 16.3:   Brief extract from a bank's risk report

Risk no.

10. *Purchasing fraud*
     Purchasing fraud whereby dummy or
     associated companies are used to obtain
     monies or services

Asset – Cash
Impact size – Medium
Probability – High

	Control Environment Score[1]	
Target[2]		83
Actual[3]	A[4]	83

20. *Ghost employees on payroll*
     Ghost employees entered on payroll

Asset – Cash
Impact size – Medium
Probability – High

	Control Environment Score	
Target		83
Actual	B	167

30. *Leavers accidentally left on payroll*
     Leavers are accidentally left on the payroll
     system but continue to retain the pay

Asset – Cash
Impact size – Medium
Probability – Medium

	Control Environment Score	
Target		55
Actual	A	55

40. *Leavers deliberately left on payroll*
     Leavers are deliberately left on the payroll
     to enable the person to continue to be paid
     or the payroll employee to obtain the
     payment

Asset – Cash
Impact size – Medium
Probability – Medium

	Control Environment Score	
Target		55
Actual	C	167

The following factors are explained in greater detail in the text (especially in section 16.6.2):

[1] The control environment score is derived from the scores of four factors: (i) the importance of the asset affected should the adverse event occur, (ii) the size of the impact on that asset if the event occurred, (iii) the probability of the event occurring if no controls were present, (iv) the effectiveness of the controls in mitigating the risk of the event occurring and/or its impact.

[2] The target (control) environment reflects the effectiveness of the control environment in mitigating the identified risk if the appropriate controls were in place and operating as intended.

[3] The actual (control) environment reflects the effectiveness of the control environment in mitigating the identified risk in practice (i.e. as the controls in place are actually operating).

[4] The letters (on a scale from A to D) indicate the effectiveness of the controls in place to mitigate the identified risk(s): A signifies highly effective controls; D indicates ineffective (or absent) controls.

As an outcome of the audit of a particular function or activity of the company, internal auditors report to the relevant manager on how the controls relating to the function or activity are functioning. If, as in the bank reconciliation example cited above (when staff shortages occur), the controls are defective in some way, this fact is reported to the manager and the resultant additional risk exposures are highlighted. Additionally, the auditors recommend action(s) the manager should take to remedy the situation. It should be noted that all the time the actual control environment deviates from the target environment, the function or activity of the company concerned has a greater risk exposure than that desired by the relevant manager and (s)he needs to be on heightened alert for the emergence of additional risks.

(iii)   Value for money (VFM) audits

VFM audits are similar to operational audits in that they can cover any area of an organisation's activity and they can be part of routine, rotational internal audit work or specifically commissioned by management. The objective of VFM audits is to ascertain the efficiency and/or effectiveness[8] of a particular area or aspect of the company's activities. For example, the Finance Director may commission an examination of the company's use of consultants. The purpose of the examination could be:

(a) to determine whether the use of consultants was justified or whether the work could have been done by the company's own staff; and

(b) whether the cost involved is one-off or continuous and, thus, whether cost savings could be achieved by employing someone permanently.

An audit of this nature would investigate matters such as:

- who has authority to commission the use of consultants;
- whether competitive quotes are obtained;
- whether the organisation secures maximum skills transfer during a consultancy in order to obviate the need for repeat consultancies in respect of the same area or issue;
- whether the consultants are properly managed so as to ensure non-productive time is kept to a minimum;
- whether there are clear deliverables so as to ensure consultancy projects are completed to the organisation's satisfaction.

One such review was commissioned recently by the Finance Director of a major international bank when he observed that the overall cost of consultancy had increased significantly during the previous two years. The internal auditors discovered that two years previously, as a means of addressing rising costs, an

---

[8] See footnote 2.

embargo had been imposed on recruitment of new staff and significant staff reductions had been required in all areas. The bank's functional managers were monitored on how well they achieved savings through a reduction in staff numbers and salary costs but their expenditure on consultants was not monitored. No productivity gains were achieved by the cost-cutting initiative; the cost was merely redistributed from staffing to consultancy.

(iv) Special projects

Internal auditors are often asked to undertake *ad hoc* work ranging from reviews of major organisation-wide projects to specific fraud investigations. The latter can involve fraud against the company by external sources, such as computer hackers, money launderers or crooked suppliers, or similar acts by one or more employees – for example, theft of cash; illegal use or theft of organisational assets such as vehicles, equipment or stock; and theft of trade secrets. In the case of more serious fraud, the police or other external agencies are usually informed and the internal auditors work in conjunction with these parties.

16.6   INTERNAL AUDIT AND THE LINK TO RISK MANAGEMENT

16.6.1   Relationship between internal auditors and risk managers

Internal audit and risk management are two separate professional disciplines that have co-existed in a number of large organisations for many years. Traditionally, the role of the internal auditor was to ensure that established control environments continued to operate as intended, any deficiencies were identified promptly and appropriate remedial action was taken. This was complemented by the role of the risk manager which was to ensure that the company identified its major (or 'key') risks and had controls or contingency plans in place to mitigate them.

As companies became larger and more complex, their boards of directors required increased assurance about the adequacy of their control environments. This resulted in internal auditors and risk managers reporting more frequently and in greater detail on identification of the company's risks and the effectiveness of its controls. At the same time, significant control failures were held responsible for some spectacular business collapses – for example, Barings Bank, the Maxwell Empire, and the Bank of Credit & Commerce International (BCCI). Internal controls came to be identified as a key element of companies' governance mechanisms and, following publication of corporate governance reports such as those of the Committee on the Financial Aspects of Corporate Governance (Cadbury Committee, 1992), the Study Group on Directors' Remuneration (Greenbury Committee, 1995), the Committee on Corporate Governance (Hampel Committee, 1998a) and the Combined Code (Committee on Corporate Governance, 1998b), the directors of major companies became acutely aware of the need for them to remain fully informed about the standard of corporate governance within their organisation. This resulted in increased demands being placed on internal auditors and risk managers, who became jointly responsible for monitoring and reporting on the companies' corporate governance mechanisms and their adequacy for identifying and rectifying potential problems.

Notwithstanding boards of directors' increased expectations of internal auditors and risk managers, in general, they were opposed to increasing staff levels to the extent necessary to provide annual operational audits for every function and activity of the business. A solution adopted by many companies was Control Risk Self Assessment (CRSA) – a system originally developed by the internal audit function in Gulf Canada. Under CRSA, each function within a company (or other organisation) is responsible for identifying its own key risks and for ensuring that appropriate controls are embedded in its procedures to mitigate those risks. Periodically (perhaps half-yearly), the manager responsible for the function completes a return for the board of directors reporting whether the function's controls have been operating as intended throughout the period and, if not, the remedial action taken. The relevant manager also expresses an opinion about the effectiveness of the overall control environment of the function. The returns from all of the functions provide the company's directors with the information needed to compile a corporate governance statement for inclusion in the company's annual report. As we noted in Chapters 5 and 13, all companies listed on the London Stock Exchange are required to publish a corporate governance statement in their annual reports or to explain why they have not done so.

16.6.2 Establishing a CRSA system

We need to emphasise that, under CRSA, the managers responsible for each function or activity of a company are responsible for identifying the risks to which the function or activity is exposed and for ensuring that effective controls are in place to mitigate them. It is the task of risk managers to ensure that all of the risks have been identified, and that their probability of occurrence and potential adverse impact on the relevant function or activity have been quantified. It is the role of the internal auditors to verify that appropriate controls are in place to mitigate the identified risks and, if not, to recommend remedial action – and also to follow up to ensure the corrective action has been taken.

The respective roles of the functional or activity managers, internal auditors and risk managers may, perhaps, be best clarified by explaining the steps taken to establish a CRSA system. We do this by reference to a factual example, and much of what follows is derived from the procedures manual of a major UK listed company.

Our illustrative company's procedures manual first sets out the fundamental assumption on which the company's CRSA system is predicated. It states:

> An organisation's aim should not be to eliminate all risks from its operations but to sensibly manage them via an appropriate control environment.

It then explains:

> Any system designed to meaningfully evaluate and consistently report on the standard of an organisation's control environment must be capable of dealing with the 'Eight Facts of Business Life'. These detail the complex interactions, the one-to-many relationships, which exist between risks and controls:
> 1. You cannot evaluate controls unless you understand the risks.
> 2. Risks affect different assets and some assets could be more important to an organisation than others.
> 3. The quantity/size/value/volume of the asset at risk varies depending upon the type of exposure.
> 4. If there were no controls in place it does not follow that all risks would occur – i.e. there are degrees of probability.
> 5. Preventative controls are more effective than detective controls.
> 6. All controls have a degree of effectiveness depending upon the risks they are addressing.
> 7. It is quite usual for more than one control to be required to fully mitigate a single risk.
> 8. The thoroughness with which a control is applied will impact on the effectiveness of the control.

The starting point of establishing a CRSA system is categorising the company's assets. This is necessary because, as explained in Fact of Business Life 2: 'Risks affect different assets and some assets could be more important to an organisation than others'. To reflect the differential importance of assets to a company, 'score weights' are attached to each category of assets. These 'score weights' reflect the relative adverse impact on the company should the asset concerned be lost or destroyed.

The asset categories (and their score weights) used by our illustrative UK listed company are shown in Figure 16.4. (In practice, these entries are incorporated in the company's CRSA computer program and we present them as they would appear on the computer screen.)

The next step in establishing a CRSA system is identifying the entities that constitute the components of the system. The entities are defined functions or activities within the company which are the responsibility of an identifiable

Figure 16.4: An example of asset categories used in a CRSA system

Asset type	Description	Score weight[1]
C	Cash	200
G	Goodwill	400
I	Information	300
K	Knowledge	200
L	Legal	50
P	Physical assets	100

[1] The score weights represent the relative adverse impact on the company if the asset concerned was lost or destroyed.

senior manager. Each entity is analysed to determine the risks to which it is exposed and a 'risk profile' is prepared. However, before this process can commence, what are known as 'impact value fields' need to be defined. As each risk in an entity is identified it is assigned an impact value, reflecting its potential adverse impact on the entity, of 'High', 'Medium' or 'Low'. In order to ensure that all entities within the company assign these impact values on the same basis, their parameters need to be defined. For example, a risk that could give rise to a loss of between £1 and £5 million might be assigned a 'low' impact value, losses of between £5 and £10 million might be categorised as 'medium', and losses of £10 to £1,000 million as 'high'.[9] These figures are inserted into the CRSA system's impact value fields as minimum and maximum values. In Figure 16.5 we reproduce some of the entries that appear in our illustrative company's CRSA system.

Once the entity and impact values have been defined, data can be captured about each potential risk (or potential adverse event) to which the entity is exposed and the asset category or categories which may suffer loss or damage should the identified adverse event occur. Sufficient detail is captured to identify the asset(s) at risk should the event occur, the potential value impact of the event, and the probability of the event occurring if no controls were present. This process addresses three more of the 'Eight Facts of Business Life', namely:

- Fact 1: 'You cannot evaluate controls unless you understand the risks.' This means that before appropriate controls can be put in place, it is necessary to understand the risks to which the entity may be subject; controls should be established to mitigate specifically identified risks.

---

[9] It might be thought that the 'high' impact value might be defined as 'losses in excess of £10 million'. However, an upper limit must be specified as no computer field can be left unfilled. Hence, a figure well in excess of that thought likely to apply is usually used.

Figure 16.5:   An example of impact value fields in a CRSA system

Short description	Corporate risks – Generic	
Responsibility	Main board	
Impact values		
	Minimum	Maximum
Low impact	1,000,000	4,999,999
Medium impact	5,000,000	9,999,999
High impact	10,000,000	1,000,000,000

- Fact 3: 'The quantity/size/value/volume of the asset at risk varies depending upon the type of exposure.'
- Fact 4: 'If there were no controls in place it does not follow that all risks would occur – i.e. there are degrees of probability.'

Most of the data relating to the risks to which a company's entities are exposed (and, subsequently, the data relating to the controls in place to mitigate these risks) are normally captured in a workshop environment. This enables senior managers, assisted by risk managers and internal auditors, to benefit from input from a broad cross-section of interests in the company. Further, the impact of adverse events occurring is frequently not confined to just one of the company's entities. In an interactive workshop setting, the entity managers may be better able to identify the risks to which their particular entity might be exposed, the potential impact of such risks, and their probability of occurrence.

In Figure 16.6 we reproduce some of the entries relating to a risk that has been identified and recorded in our illustrative company's CRSA system. With reference to Figure 16.6, the following points should be noted:

- The *short description field* records a brief description of the risk. To be useful, the description needs to be meaningful in its own right.
- The *long description field* provides a fuller description of the risk [or, more correctly the potential adverse event(s)] identified in the short description.
- The *asset type field* identifies the asset category under threat should the adverse event(s) occur.
- The *impact* and *probability fields* record the likely impact on the entity should the adverse event(s) occur and the probability of the event(s)

Figure 16.6:   An example of entries relating to an identified risk in a CRSA system

		Related controls	
Risk no.	10		
Short description	Strategic risks		
		No.	Short description
Long description	A strategy may not exist, it may not suit the marketplace or the marketplace may change while the strategy does not. Even in situations where a well thought-out strategy exists it can be jeopardised if it is poorly communicated or poorly implemented. Equally, if the management information system available to management is poor, or the data is suspect, the strategy itself may be flawed or the company may lack feedback on its strategic performance. Alternatively, such feedback may be incorrect leading to erroneous remedial action.	10	5-yr business plan
		20	Budgetary control
Asset type	G		
	Goodwill		
Impact	○ Low ○ Medium ⊙ High		
Probability	⊙ Low ○ Medium ○ High		

occurring should no controls be present. In each case, quantification is based on three broad measures – high, medium and low.

Once all the potential risks to which an entity may be exposed have been captured (as outlined above), the controls embedded within the entity's procedures are identified and recorded in a similar manner. Initially, the risk exposures are ignored and controls existing in the entity are recorded as they are thought of. It is important to compile a comprehensive list of controls – whether or not they mitigate the identified risks. Any redundant controls (controls not mitigating an identified risk) can be discarded at a later stage, and the list (as compiled) can be used to check whether a particular risk has been inadvertently omitted from the list of risks (i.e. a control which appears to be redundant may, in fact, be negating a risk not originally identified and therefore not recorded on the list of risks).

When the controls are identified they are classified into one of five categories: preventative, corrective, detective, deterrent and entity. The last category signifies that the control is effected from outside the function or activity being profiled. For example, if the finance department checks all invoices before the purchases (i.e. creditors) ledger department pays them, then the finance department constitutes an 'entity control' in the purchases ledger department's risk profile. When classifying their entities' controls (and identifying how improvements may be made), the senior managers of the entities concerned need to be cognisant of Fact of Business Life 5: 'Preventative controls are more effective than detective controls'.

Once the controls have been identified and classified, the results of compliance testing (including an evaluation of the effectiveness of the controls in mitigating the identified risks) are introduced into the analysis. It would be convenient if such testing resulted in a simple yes/no answer to the question of whether a control operates in the intended manner. Unfortunately this is not the case and Fact of Business Life 8 comes into play: 'The thoroughness with which a control is applied will impact on the effectiveness of the control'. Compliance testing generally results in an evaluation signifying that the control operates effectively 'Always', 'Mostly', 'Sometimes' or 'Never'.

In Figure 16.7 we reproduce some of the entries relating to a control that has been identified and recorded in our illustrative company's CRSA system. The following points should be noted:

- The *short description field* records a brief description of the control.
- The *long description field* provides a fuller description of the control identified in the short description.
- The *control type field* records the category to which the control belongs – preventative, corrective, detective, deterrent or entity.
- The *compliance test field* records the results of compliance tests to which the control has been subjected. Five options are offered indicating the control is complied with: 'always', 'mostly', 'sometimes', 'never' or the control has not been tested. The last applies to the control recorded in Figure 16.7.

It would be extremely helpful if the list of risks to which the entity being profiled is exposed could be neatly matched against the controls the entity has in place, and any shortfall in the controls identified. However, business life is not so straightforward. This brings us to Facts of Business Life 6 and 7:

**Figure 16.7:   An example of entries relating to an identified control
in a CRSA system**

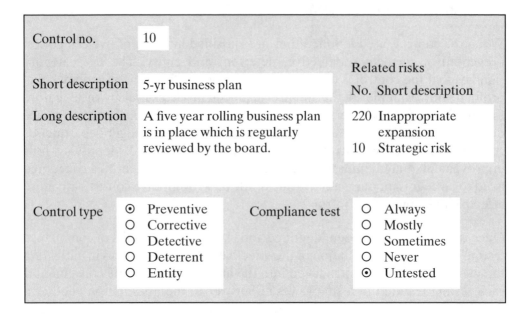

- Fact 6: 'All controls have a degree of effectiveness depending upon the risks they are addressing.' In most cases an identified risk could be mitigated by a number of different controls and a choice must be made as to which to select. This is largely a cost-benefit decision where the cost of implementing, maintaining and monitoring the control is balanced against the potential impact on the entity's assets should the adverse event occur and the probability of its occurrence. Evaluated on this basis, the most effective control to mitigate an identified risk may not be selected; instead a cheaper alternative may be adopted.
- Fact 7: 'It is quite usual for more than one control to be required to fully mitigate a single risk.' In other words, there is a 'one-to-many' relationship between risks and controls. There is also a many-to-one relationship where one control mitigates more than one risk. With this additional factor incorporated into an already complex analysis, the evaluation of the risk and control data is best handled by a matrix approach.

In Figure 16.8 we reproduce part of a risk-control matrix for our illustrative company. It shows the risk number (as recorded in the list of risks: see Figure 16.6 where we present the relevant information for risk number 10) along the top horizontal axis,[10] and the control's number, short description, type, and the

---

[10] Further details of individual risks (i.e. the short description of the risk, the type of asset at risk, the risk's likely impact and probability of occurrence) are shown in a separate computer screen window.

Figure 16.8: An example of a control-risk matrix in a CRSA system

Corporate risks – Generic

No	Control description	Type	Test	10	20	30	40	50	60	70	80	90	100	110	120	130	140	150	160	170	180	190	200	210	220	230	240	250
10	5-yr business plan	P	U	3																								
20	Budgetary control	T	U	3										3											3	3		
30	Internal audit	E	U			3																						
40	Formal physical security	P	U														4											
50	Dual signatures	P	U																									
60	Purchasing policy	P	U																									
70	Passwords	P	U														3											
80	Formal contracts with key suppliers	C	U									3	3															
90	Legal department	E	U			4																			4			
100	Board of management	P	U			4																						
110	Tax authority audits	T	U			3																						
120	External auditors	P	U				3																					
130	Shareholder department	E	U					4																				
140	Bonus scheme	D	U						3																			
150	Staff appraisals	D	U						3																	3		
160	Training for staff	T	U						3																	3		
170	Training for directors	D	U							3																		
180	Government regulation re takeover	P	U								5																	
190	Performance targets for suppliers	C	U										4															
200	Cashflow forecasts	P	U											4														
210	BSCS used for debtor control	P	U											4														
220	Data backup	P	U												2													
230	IT – Operations department	E	U													4												
240	Link with a media company	C	U																			4						
250	Media department	E	U																			4						
260	Finance function	P	U																				4	4			4	
270	Fraud matrix	P	U		5																							
280	IT – Business support department	E	U																									
290	IT – Infrastructure department	E	U																									
300	IT – Interface department	E	U																									
	Target environment			A	A	A	A	A	A	A	A	A	A	A	A	A	A	A	A	A	A	A	A	A	A	A	A	A
	Actual environment			C	A	A	D	B	B	D	A	D	A	A	D	B	A	D	D	D	A	B	B	D	A	C	A	D
	Target score (1259)			33	67	100	50	100	33	33	33	100	67	33	33	100	75	22	89	45	100	11	45	11	45	45	6	50
	Actual score (2803)			100	67	100	200	200	67	133	33	400	67	33	133	200	75	89	178	100	22	89	44	133	6	133	6	200

result of any compliance testing (as recorded in the list of controls: see Figure 16.7 where we present the relevant information for control number 10) down the left hand vertical axis. The impact of each control on each risk is plotted using a scale of 1 to 5, where 1 signifies a weak impact and 5 a powerful impact. At this point the controls are scored as if they operate as intended; the result of compliance testing is introduced later. Key controls, defined as controls which are particularly effective in mitigating the identified risks (with scores of 4 or 5), are highlighted in Figure 16.8 in bold italics.

The results of compliance tests are now introduced into the analysis – and are incorporated in the scores shown for the 'actual control environment' (explained below). The frequency of testing a control depends on its importance in mitigating identified risks, as reflected in the matrix scores of 1 to 5. Controls with a high score are tested more frequently that those with a low score as the potential adverse effect, should the control fail to operate as intended, is greater.

Below the control descriptions in Figure 16.8, two types of control environments are shown – the target environment and actual environment. As we explained in section 16.5 above:

- *The target environment* reflects the effectiveness of the control environment in mitigating the identified risks if the appropriate controls are in place and operating as intended. (Remember, this does not always mean the risk(s) are eliminated as this is not cost-effective; when all the controls operate as intended, some risk may remain.)
- *The actual environment* refers to the effectiveness of the control environment in mitigating the identified risks as the controls in place actually operate – as established through compliance testing. This will differ from the target environment if one or more of the controls fails to operate or does not operate as intended.

Below the body of the matrix there are two rows of letters. These denote the quality of the controls in place with respect to each identified risk for: (i) the target environment and (ii) the actual environment. The letters range from A to D, where A signifies highly effective controls (i.e. the controls mitigate the risk to the desired extent) and D indicates ineffective (or absent) controls. Below the letters are two rows of scores for each risk – one relating to the target environment, the other to the actual environment. These scores are derived by multiplying the scores attributed to the identified risk for each of the following factors:

- the importance of the asset that would be damaged or lost if the identified adverse event occurred (as reflected in Figure 16.4);

- the high, medium or low adverse impact on the asset(s) should the event occur;
- the high, medium or low probability of the event occurring if no controls were present;
- the effectiveness of the controls in place to mitigate the risk of the event occurring (derived from scores from 1 to 5 as explained above and the results of compliance tests).

For example, the best-case scenario, with the lowest score, would reflect a situation where a relatively unimportant asset would suffer a small negative impact if the risky event occurred; there is a low probability of the event occurring and, in any event, adequate controls are in place to mitigate the risk and compliance tests indicate that they always operate as intended. In contrast to this, the worst-case scenario, with the highest score, would result if the company's most important asset would suffer a large negative impact if the risky event occurred, there is high probability that the event would occur if no controls were present, and compliance tests suggest that the controls in place are ineffective.

The scores for each of the identified risks (shown at the foot of the matrix) may be added together to produce an overall score for the entity – again reflecting the target and the actual environments. These summary scores are presented at the bottom left of the matrix. The greater the difference between the target and actual environment scores, the greater the unplanned risk exposure of the entity concerned.

CRSA is an extremely useful tool for identifying, assessing and controlling the risks to which companies (and other organisations) are exposed. It ensures that managers who are responsible for the organisation's functions or activities are fully aware of (and responsible for) the risks to which their functions or activities are exposed – and the controls in place to mitigate those risks. Formal CRSA analysis also enables risk managers to review the identified risks of the organisation's entities to ensure that all relevant risks have been identified, and that their likely impact and probability of occurrence have been appropriately quantified. From the risk profiles of the individual entities, risk managers can build up a risk profile for the organisation as a whole and identify those areas that are most exposed to risk.

Similarly, CRSA analysis provides a sound basis for internal auditors to verify that the controls each function or activity has in place have been properly identified, are effective in mitigating the identified risks, and have been appro-priately evaluated. Further, from the risk-control profiles of the individual entities, internal auditors can draw conclusions about the overall control environment of the organisation. We noted in section 16.3 above that the Head of Internal Audit typically discusses with the organisation's Chief Executive (and, possibly, also the chairman of a committee such as an Audit Committee) the state of risk control throughout the organisation. Such discussions are most effective if they are based on an analysis of the risk profiles of the organisation's sub-units (or entities). Risk-control matrices, derived from CRSA, provide the ideal basis for such discussions.

16.6.3 Audit of the risk management function and the effect of a compliance function

From our review of CRSA it is evident that the internal audit and risk management functions address different aspects of the same issue. Today, internal auditors and risk managers work closely together and in some companies the heads of both functions report to the same senior executive or director (for example, the Director of Group Audit and Risk). Nevertheless, the risk management function, like all other functions within a company, is an element of the internal audit portfolio and, as such, is audited in the same way as all other functions. The internal auditors need to ensure that the risk management function has adequate controls over its activities because, if such controls are not in place, the company will be exposed to the risk of loss in the same way as if, for example, the finance department did not perform regular bank reconciliations.

One major risk that the risk management function of any large company must be prepared for is the unknown – some unforeseen event that might emerge 'out of the woodwork' unnoticed to threaten the company in some way. An example might be a change of government followed by a nationalisation programme for the industry in which the company operates (such as transport), or a terrorist attack that destroys the company's head office and all its records and/or kills its key executives. Such risks are termed 'emerging risks'. In a company whose risk management function is well managed, 'emerging risks' feature as an element of its risk profile – and a strategy is in place to help it identify such risks as soon as they arise, thus enabling the company to take prompt defensive action when necessary (i.e. the risk management function has 'controls' in place). It is part of the role of the internal audit function to conduct regular audits of the risk management function and, if it finds that 'emerging risks' are not included in its risk profile, to report this fact to the Head of Risk Management and ensure that remedial action is taken. This would include ensuring that emerging risks were explicitly recognised as one of the function's risks and that appropriate controls were established to mitigate it. Without such action, the company as a whole is exposed to the 'emerging risks' threat.

In recent years, the dramatic increase in statutory and regulatory requirements with which companies must comply has prompted many large companies to establish a specific compliance function. In this context, the word 'compliance' means 'operating in accordance with all of the legal and regulatory requirements that apply to the organisation concerned'. The role of the compliance function is to conduct regular, structured checks to ensure that all aspects of the company that are subject to legal and/or regulatory requirements are complying with those requirements. Testing is conducted in much the same way as financial statement audit compliance testing[11] but the sample sizes are significantly larger. Testing undertaken by the compliance function usually replaces work that would otherwise be performed by internal auditors and, therefore, the latter do not need to perform detailed compliance tests in these areas; instead they focus on reviewing the work performed in the relevant areas by the compliance function.

16.7 INTERFACE BETWEEN INTERNAL AND EXTERNAL AUDITORS

As may be discerned from the previous sections of this chapter, the work of internal and external auditors is closely aligned. If this alignment is well managed, companies can achieve significant savings in their external audit fees. However, to gain cost savings without compromising either the internal or the external audit function requires careful management.

At one end of the spectrum is the situation where internal auditors do not get involved with the company's financial systems or financial data at all; they focus almost exclusively on the effectiveness and operation of controls established to mitigate identified risks. In this case, the external auditors need to perform relatively extensive compliance and substantive testing before they can form an opinion about the truth and fairness of the figures and other disclosures in the company's financial statements. This is obviously expensive. In contrast to this, the company may have a highly professional, well staffed, internal audit function which routinely performs periodic, detailed examinations of the internal controls that are designed to protect (or assure) the integrity of the financial statement data. In this case, once the external auditors are satisfied regarding the professionalism (in particular, the independence, integrity and competence) of the internal audit staff,[12] they can place reliance on the work

---

[11] Financial statement audit compliance testing is discussed in Chapter 9, section 9.9.4.

[12] External auditors usually satisfy themselves about the quality of the internal audit staff by reviewing the working papers from a sample of internal audits.

performed by the internal auditors, thus saving external audit time – and, hence, saving the company external audit fees.[13]

This raises the question of why companies do not give their internal auditors responsibility for all external audit support work and request the external auditors to rely upon it. Two reasons may be advanced to explain why this does not happen:

1. If internal auditors were to undertake all of the support work for the external auditors, they would need either to reduce significantly the other work they perform for the company or to recruit extra staff – the costs of which would, almost certainly, outweigh the savings gained in external audit costs.
2. External auditors have a legal obligation to express their opinion on the truth and fairness of the company's financial statements and it is likely that certain aspects of the financial statements are so central to forming their opinion that they will want to check the evidence supporting these aspects for themselves, irrespective of any work the internal auditors may have done. Thus, in these regards, even if the internal auditors performed the work, savings in external audit time and fees would not be realised.

The maximum benefit can be derived from the internal–external audit interface if both sets of auditors agree where on the continuum (from no internal audit assistance to internal auditors performing all of the support work) their respective responsibilities meet. In this regard, the company's audit committee can play a key role. If both the internal auditors and the external auditors submit their annual audit plan to the audit committee, that committee is then in a position to ensure that the company derives maximum benefit from the skills and expertise available to the two separate disciplines.[14]

16.8 SUMMARY

In this chapter we have explored, in some depth, the relationship between risks that may threaten a company and the controls in place to mitigate those risks. We have seen how the role of internal auditors focuses on examining the controls to ensure they are appropriate to mitigate the identified risks and operating effectively. We have discussed the benefits to companies (and other organisations) of having an internal audit function, staffed by internal audit

[13] In respect of external auditors relying on the work of internal auditors, reference should be made to Chapter 6, section 6.5. The same requirements apply when external auditors rely on the work of internal auditors as when they rely on the work of experts.

[14] The responsibilities of audit committees, including their role in overseeing the internal and the external audit functions, is discussed in Chapter 4, section 4.4.

specialists, to perform internal audit work. We have also identified the objectives of an internal audit and outlined the internal audit process – explaining how an internal audit is planned, executed, reported and followed up. Additionally, we have examined different types of internal audits (financial, operational, value for money, and special projects), explored the relationship between risk and control within the context of a CRSA system and discussed the value of such a system to company managers, internal auditors and risk managers alike. We have also considered how internal auditors interface with external auditors and how a company may derive maximum benefit from this interface.

SELF-REVIEW QUESTIONS

16.1 Give two reasons to explain why a company usually seeks to manage rather than eliminate its risks.

16.2 State the key objectives of an internal audit.

16.3 Outline the steps involved in:
  (a) planning
  (b) executing
  (c) reporting
  (d) following up
  an internal audit.

16.4 Distinguish between a financial statement audit, performed by external auditors, and a financial audit, performed by internal auditors.

16.5 Outline the principal features of:
  (a) an operational audit, and
  (b) a value for money audit.

16.6 Explain the relationship between risk managers and internal auditors.

16.7 Briefly describe the key features of a Control Risk Self Assessment (CRSA) system.

16.8 State the advantages of a CRSA system for:
  (a) company managers
  (b) risk managers
  (c) internal auditors
  (d) companies as a whole.

16.9 Explain the role of a compliance function and how it impacts the work of internal auditors.

16.10 Briefly explain:
  (a) the advantage to external auditors and companies of external auditors relying (in part) on the work of internal auditors; and
  (b) why internal auditors do not perform all of the support work for an external audit.

REFERENCES

Committee on the Financial Aspects of Corporate Governance (1992) *Report of the Committee on the Financial Aspects of Corporate Governance* (Cadbury Committee). London: Gee and Co Ltd.

Committee on Corporate Governance (1998a) *Final Report of the Committee on Corporate Governance* (Hampel Committee). London: The London Stock Exchange Ltd.

Committee on Corporate Governance (1998b) *The Combined Code.* London: The London Stock Exchange Ltd.

Study Group on Directors' Remuneration (1995) *Report of the Study Group on Directors' Remuneration* (Greenbury Committee). London: Gee and Co Ltd.

ADDITIONAL READING

Campbell, A. (1994) Measuring auditors' reliance on internal auditors: A test of prior scales and a new proposal. *Behavioural Research in Accounting* **6**, 110–120.

Committee of Sponsoring Organisations of the Treadway Commission (COSO) (1992) *Integrated Control – Integrated Framework*, Executive Summary. New Jersey: COSO.

Edge, W.R. & Farley, A.A. (1991) External auditor evaluation of the internal audit function. *Accounting and Finance* **31**(1), 69–83.

Maletta, M.J. (1993) An examination of auditors' decisions to use internal auditors as assistants: the effect of inherent risk. *Contemporary Accounting Research* **9**(2), 508–525.

Mills, T.Y. (1996) The effect of cognitive style on external auditors' reliance: decisions on internal audit functions. *Behavioural Research in Accounting* **8**, 49–73.

Whittington, R. & Margheim, L. (1993) The effects of risk, materiality, and assertion subjectivity on external auditors' reliance on internal auditors. *Auditing: A Journal of Practice & Theory* **12**(1), 50–64.

17 Environmental Audits

LEARNING OBJECTIVES

After studying the material in this chapter you should be able to:

- define an (internal) environmental audit and an (external) environmental verification or assurance engagement;[1]
- describe the various forms of environmental reports and distinguish between 'environmental' and 'sustainability' reports;
- outline the requirements for organisations to register for ISO 14001 and Europe's Eco-management and audit scheme (EMAS) and highlight the key differences between the two sets of requirements;
- explain the objective, scope and process of (i) an environmental audit, and (ii) an environmental verification engagement;
- outline the contents of reports resulting from (i) an environmental audit, and (ii) an environmental verification engagement;
- discuss the professional requirements for performing environmental audits and verification engagements, and identify the professional groups which may be equipped to undertake such work;
- explain the major difficulties facing environmental auditors and verifiers;
- discuss the advantages and disadvantages to companies of voluntarily undergoing environmental audits and/or having their environmental or sustainability reports externally verified;
- discuss the relevance of environmental matters to external financial statement auditors.

The following publications are particularly relevant to this chapter:

- ISO 14001: *Environmental management systems – specification with guidance for use* (International Organization for Standardization, 1996)
- ISO 14010: *Guidelines for environmental auditing – general principles* (International Organization for Standardization, 1996)
- *Eco-management and audit scheme* (EMAS) (Regulation (EC) No 761/2001 of the European Parliament and of the Council, 2001)[2]
- *FEE discussion paper: providing assurance on sustainability reports* (Fédération des Experts Comptables Européens (FEE), 2002)

---

[1] For reasons we explain in this chapter, we use the term 'environmental audit' to mean an internal environmental audit and 'verification engagement' to mean (in essence) an external audit of environmental (or sustainability) reports. The term 'verification engagement' is used to denote the same meaning as 'assurance engagement'.

[2] In this chapter we cite this reference as EMAS, 2001.

17.1 INTRODUCTION

During the past 20 or so years, society's awareness of the need to take care of the environment and, more particularly, of the need for businesses to operate in an environmentally considerate manner, has grown at a phenomenal rate. Society's level of concern about the environment today is reflected in almost daily reports in the news media about environmental issues. These cover, for example, industrial plants' chimneys belching forth clouds of unsightly, odorous and potentially dangerous gaseous wastes, reputedly harmful radioactive emissions from radio and mobile telephone masts, and spillages of hazardous chemicals from tankers causing motorway closures and warnings to house-holders to keep windows and doors closed. Society's concern is also reflected in the growth of 'green parties' in political circles and in the emergence of formal standards such as ISO 14001: *Environmental management systems – specifications with guidance for use* and Europe's *Eco-management and audit scheme* (EMAS).

As a response to society's significant and growing concern for the environment, companies are increasingly reporting on their environmental performance. However, the form of this reporting varies widely – from brief reports in companies' annual reports to extensive stand-alone environmental reports, complete with photographs, graphs and other diagrammatic representations of relevant information. Added to this, in the absence of environmental reporting standards, the range and quality of the information provided differs significantly. Further, while some companies report only on environmental issues, others report their performance in respect of both environmental and social issues, and still others issue wide-ranging 'sustainability' reports – covering environmental, social and economic matters. The credibility of the information provided also differs markedly; some reports are not subject to any external verification (or audit) and where they are verified, in the absence of generally accepted environmental reporting and verification standards, the level of assurance given as to the reliability of the information varies widely.

In this chapter we explore what we may loosely refer to as 'environmental auditing'. We first clarify some of the highly confusing terminology associated with this topic and trace the development (albeit briefly) of environmental reporting and auditing. We then examine in some detail the requirements for organisations wishing to qualify for ISO 14001 or EMAS, and outline the objectives, scope and process of environmental audits and the reports issued as an outcome of these engagements. We also discuss the professional requirements for performing such audits, identify the groups which may be equipped to under-take such work, and explain the difficulties facing those who conduct environ-mental audits. Before concluding the chapter we explore the advantages and disadvantages attaching to environmental reporting and auditing and consider the relevance of environmental matters to external financial statement audits.

17.2 ENVIRONMENTAL AUDITING AND REPORTING – CLARIFYING THE JARGON

In the environmental auditing and reporting arena there is considerable confusion about the meaning of various terms. For example, some commentators use the term 'environmental reporting' to mean reporting about a company's performance in relation to certain environmental factors; others use the term to embrace the company's performance in respect of social (and also, in some cases, economic) as well as environmental matters. Lightbody (2000) reports similar confusion in respect of the term 'environmental audit'. She explains:

> At present [the term] is used both in practice and in the literature to refer to a wide range of environmental assessments and reviews. . . . For example, a recent publication jointly sponsored by IFAC [International Federation of Accountants] and AARF [Australian Accounting Research Foundation][3] referred to 'environmental audits' as including:
> - assessments of site contamination;
> - environmental impact assessments of planned investments;
> - environmental due diligence audits (pre-acquisition audits);
> - the audit of corporate environmental performance reports; and
> - the audit of the entity's compliance with environmental laws and regulations.
> (p. 152)

A review of these various types of audits reveals that most are internal audits – audits conducted for a company's directors or senior executives. However, the term also embraces 'the audit of corporate environmental performance reports' which is similar in nature to an external financial statement audit. In order to ensure that we and our readers apply the same meaning to terms we use in this chapter, we have drawn on EMAS (2001), ISO 14001 (1996), and the FEE discussion paper: *Providing assurance on sustainability reports* (FEE, 2002) to define them as set out in Figure 17.1.

For the purposes of this chapter we need to highlight two sets of distinctions within these definitions, namely, those between:

(a) an *environmental audit,* which is concerned with an organisation's environmental management system (EMS) and its outcome in terms of environmental performance, that is conducted for *internal management purposes,* and a *verification engagement* which is concerned with reporting and verifying of information about the organisation's environmental performance for *parties external to the organisation;*

---

[3] Lightbody cites the relevant reference as: International Federation of Accountants (1995). *The audit profession and the environment.* Caulfield, Australia: Australian Accounting Research Foundation, p. 6.

Figure 17.1: Definitions of terms associated with environmental auditing and reporting

Term	Definitions
Environment	Surroundings in which an organisation operates, including air, water, land, natural resources, flora, fauna, humans, and their interrelationships.
Environmental policy	An organisation's intentions and principles in relation to its overall environmental performance which provides a framework for action and for setting its environmental objectives and targets.
Environmental objective	An overall environmental goal, arising from the environmental policy, that an organisation sets itself to achieve, and which is quantifiable where practicable.
Environmental target	A detailed performance requirement, quantified where practicable, that is applicable to all or part(s) of an organisation. It arises from the environmental objectives and needs to be set and met in order to achieve those objectives.
Environmental performance	The results of an organisation's management of its environmental aspects; that is, the potential interaction of its activities, products or services with the environment.
Environmental aspect	An element of an organisation's activities, products or services that can interact with the environment.
Environmental impact	Any change to the environment, whether adverse or beneficial, wholly or partially resulting from an organisation's activities, products or services.
Environmental management system (EMS)	The part of the organisation's overall management system that includes the organisational structure, planning activities, responsibilities, practices, procedures, processes and resources that are concerned with developing, implementing, achieving, reviewing and maintaining its environmental policy.
Environmental audit	A systematic, documented, periodic and objective evaluation of an organisation's EMS and environmental performance, and communication of the results of the process to the organisation's directors or senior executives. It is conducted with the aim of: (i) establishing the conformity of the organisation's EMS with the criteria set by the directors or senior executives; (ii) assessing compliance with the organisation's environment policy and achievement of its environmental objectives and targets; (iii) facilitating improvement in the organisation's environmental performance.
Internal environmental auditor	An individual (or a team), internal or external to the organisation, who acts on behalf of the organisation's directors or senior executives. The individual or team possesses individually or collectively the competences required to conduct an environmental audit and is sufficiently independent of the activities audited to make an objective judgment.
Sustainability	The concept of meeting the needs of the present generation without compromising the ability of future generations to meet their own needs. It encompasses environmental, social and economic factors. A sustainability report contains disclosures about the sustainability performance of an organisation.
Environmental report	A report of an organisation dealing with the environmental dimension of sustainability.
Economic	The dimension of sustainability dealing with the economic impacts of an organisation, that is, the effects of the organisation's activities, products or services on the economy or economies in which it operates.
Social	The dimension of sustainability that relates to the human impacts of an organisation; These include the organisation's working conditions and community involvement.
Assurance or verification engagement	An engagement designed to provide assurance about, and thus to enhance the credibility of, information provided for external parties by an organisation's directors or senior executives.

(b) an organisation's *environmental* performance and reporting, and its *sustainability* performance and reporting; that is, its performance (and reporting thereof) in relation to environmental, social and economic factors.

These distinctions arise from, and reflect, the development of what we may loosely refer to as environmental auditing and reporting – the topic we now explore.

17.3 DEVELOPMENT OF ENVIRONMENTAL AUDITING AND REPORTING

17.3.1 Development of environmental audits

Environmental auditing is not new. Indeed, in 1991 the International Chamber of Commerce (ICC, 1991) noted that Arthur D Little, a firm of consultants in the USA specialising in environmental issues, has been conducting environmental audits around the world since the 1920s. Nevertheless, interest in environmental audits remained slight until the 1980s. Since then they have burgeoned and today they are commonplace in major companies (particularly those in the extractive, manufacturing and chemicals sectors) throughout the industrialised world. Their rapid growth during the past couple of decades seems to be linked to two related stimuli – environmental catastrophes and regulation.

Since the 1970s catastrophes have caused immense harm to humans, the environment and property. They include, for example:

- dioxins released into the air by a chemical plant in Sevsoin, Italy, in 1976 which harmed 250 people, including pregnant women (Natu, 1999, p. 133);
- a huge oil spill in the English Channel in 1978 when the supertanker *Amoco Cadiz* split into two. Much marine life was killed and the French coastline was badly polluted (Natu, 1999, p. 133);
- tons of toxic gas escaping from the Union Carbide plant in Bhopal, India, in 1984. An estimated 3,800 people died as a result of the emissions (*Encyclopaedia Britannica*, 2002);
- radioactive material released into the atmosphere from the nuclear power station at Chernobyl, Ukraine, in 1986. 'Beyond 32 immediate deaths, several thousand radiation-induced illnesses and cancer deaths were expected in the long term' (*Encyclopaedia Britannica*, 2002);
- a spillage of 10.9 million tons of crude oil from the supertanker *Exxon Valdez* when it ran aground on a reef in Prince William Sound, South Alaska, in 1989. The spillage had disastrous effects on marine life and coastal ecology in the sound (*Encyclopaedia Britannica*, 2002).

Disasters such as these have caused a global outcry and demands that corporate activities be regulated so that organisations responsible for environmental damage are made to suffer severe financial penalties and other sanctions.

Since the mid-1970s, perhaps prompted by reports of environmental disasters, industrialised nations have become more aware of the damage businesses (and individuals) can – and do – inflict on the environment and the need to implement preventive measures. Governments, first in the USA but rapidly followed by the UK, Continental Europe, Australia, New Zealand and else-where, have responded to society's concerns and pressures exerted by environ-mental activities and have introduced a wealth of laws and regulations designed to protect aspects of the environment. Such laws and regulations have had a major impact on businesses and how they conduct their activities. This is noted by Roussey (1992), for example, who explains:

> Entities operating in this country [the US] are now subject to a growing number of environmental laws and regulations. As a result, these entities may be responsible for significant clean-up costs and liabilities if they have not appropriately disposed of hazardous wastes. They may also be liable for personal injury claims from employees and customers if there are toxic problems in the workplace or associ-ated with their products. These concerns relate not only to the original owners, operators, or users of waste disposal sites, but they also relate to other third parties not originally associated with a contaminated site, or disposal at such a site. (pp. 47–48).

Of the plethora of laws and regulations which exist in the USA at both the Federal and State level, perhaps the most far-reaching and significant are The Congressional Comprehensive Environmental Response, Compensation and Liability Act 1980 (known as CERCLA or 'the Superfund' legislation) and The Superfund Amendment and Reauthorization Act 1986. In the European Union (EU) the key legislative provision was enacted as Article 130R of the Single European Act 1987. This states:

1. Action by the [European] Community relating to the environment shall have the following objectives:
   (i)   to preserve, protect and improve the quality of the environment,
   (ii) to contribute towards protecting human health;
   (iii) to ensure a prudent rational utilization of natural resources.
2. Action by the Community relating to the environment shall be based on the principles that preventive action should be taken, that environmental damage should as a priority be rectified at source, and that the polluter should pay. Environmental protection requirements shall be a component of the Com-munity's other policies. (as cited in Vinten, 1996).

Guided by this Article, member States have enacted their own body of laws and regulations. In the UK, probably the most significant and far-reaching environ-mental legislation is enshrined in the Environmental Protection Act 1990. Vinten (1996) explains that this Act:

represents the beginning of the practical manifestation of the principle that the polluter pays. It also introduces the notion of integrated pollution control. Previously each component of the environment – air, land and water – had its own separate laws and systems of control. Now Her Majesty's Inspectorate of Pollution will control the releases of air, water and land from most polluting industrial processes. . . . Companies have to . . . pay penalties for breaking the specified emission limits. There is a requirement for environmental impact assessments for new developments such as new shopping centres or factories. There is also a legal obligation to minimise waste production using the principle that goes by the acronym BATNEEC – 'best available technology not entailing excessive cost'. Best available technology under the act include technology, use of personnel, and the design, layout and maintenance of buildings. . . . Industries covered by the act have to apply for authorization to continue to operate, to make major changes to their plants, or to build new ones. Various bodies, such as the Health and Safety Executive, have to be consulted, and then there has to be public advertisement in a local newspaper. Attempting to avoid compliance is a high risk strategy, with serious consequences for the company and those within it. (pp. 15–16)

Since the mid-1980s, faced by the huge volume of highly complex environmental laws and regulations – and their exposure to liability should it wittingly or unwittingly breach one or more of them – company managements have increasingly adopted environmental (compliance) audits. These audits are designed to ensure that the company is complying with all relevant laws and regulations, and to generally assess matters such as the company's compliance with:

- occupational health and safety requirements;
- emissions limits and other requirements attaching to a licence to operate;
- regulations governing the generation, storage and disposal of hazardous wastes;
- potential liability for the past disposal (on- and off-site) of hazardous substances.

During the late 1980s and early 1990s, as liability for contamination of land and other breaches of environmental law were held to attach not only to the perpetrator but also to third parties such as the purchaser of polluted land, environmental (due diligence) audits also came to be conducted in order to determine whether liability may attach to a transaction such as the purchase of property. Such environmental (due diligence) audits are now commonplace, as the costs of cleaning up contaminated land can run into many millions of pounds and the net to capture those who may be held responsible seems to be spread ever wider. Roussey (1992) reports that in the USA:

> The courts have held four classes of parties responsible for clean-up of hazardous waste sites: (1) current owners and operators, (2) owners and operators at the time of the waste disposal, (3) hazardous waste generators, and (4) hazardous waste transporters. . . . A recent court decision has also found lenders potentially responsible for the hazardous waste problems of borrowers. (p. 47)

These single transaction environmental (due diligence) audits are also important to ensure that projects can proceed as planned. Hamilton (1997), for example, reports a case where a group of friends purchased land (without an environmental audit) with the intention of finding a developer to build a block of luxury condominiums. They held the property for two years before they found a developer who was interested. Before signing the agreement, the developer's financial backers insisted on an environmental audit. During the audit, broken thermometers were found at the site and the soil was found to be contaminated with mercury and other toxic materials. Perhaps needless to say, the developer walked away from the project and the owners faced enormous clean-up costs and the costs of trying to track down the previous owners to pin liability on them.

Although environmental audits were initially reactive and somewhat single focused in nature – designed to ensure compliance with relevant laws and regulations or to avoid liability or other adverse consequences attaching to a transaction – since the early 1990s they have become more proactive and wide-ranging in character. They are now regarded by many companies as a means of providing management with valuable information (especially where environmental management systems have been established) and of protecting and enhancing the company's reputation.[4]

The trend towards establishing environmental management systems (EMS) has been encouraged by the emergence of environmental certification schemes such as the British Standard (BS 7750), Europe's eco-management and audit scheme (EMAS), and the international standard ISO 14001. BS 7750, the world's first structured environmental scheme for companies, was introduced in 1992 as a voluntary environmental management and audit scheme to which companies could seek to gain certification. It was revised in 1994 but withdrawn in 1997 following the introduction of ISO 14001 in 1996. EMAS, which was launched in 1993, was originally intended to be a compulsory environmental management and audit scheme applicable to specific industrial sites. However, faced by industry opposition, it was introduced as a voluntary scheme applicable to all companies (or parts thereof). It is similar to, but (as we explain below) rather more rigorous than, BS 7750 and ISO 14001. ISO 14001 was developed primarily as a result of the 1992 Rio Earth Summit which resulted in a commitment to protection of the environment across the world. Like EMAS, companies or parts thereof (such as individual sites, divisions or subsidiaries), may apply for ISO 14001 certification.

EMAS and ISO 14001 are very similar in their approach and requirements. Both require registrants to be committed to (i) continuous improvement in

---

[4] The advantages for companies of conducting environmental audits are discussed in section 17.5.

environmental performance and (ii) compliance with applicable environmental laws and regulations. Both schemes are structured around the operation of an environmental management system (EMS). As indicated in Figure 17.2, the starting point for establishing a system is an initial review. This enables the company (or part thereof) to gain a thorough understanding of the potential environmental impacts of its activities, products and services and it also provides the 'baseline' from which the entity can strive to improve its environmental performance.

As shown in Figure 17.2, an EMS comprises a set of elements that together facilitate companies achieving environmental performance improvements. They include the following:

(i)   *An environmental policy:* this specifies the environmental principles promoted by the organisation and provides the framework for setting and reviewing environmental objectives and targets.

(ii)   *Objectives and targets:* these are the specific goals (often set for the ensuing year) towards which environmental performance is to strive and against which performance can be evaluated.

(iii) *Performance procedures or an environmental programme:* this sets out the means by which the objectives and targets are to be achieved.

(iv)   A *mechanism for monitoring and controlling environmental performance:* this comprises the environmental audit whereby the company's environmental performance is evaluated against the set objectives and targets, the operation and effectiveness of the EMS is assessed, and the company's compliance with relevant environmental laws and regulations is reviewed. The audit generates one or more reports which are communicated to the company's board of directors, environmental committee of the board and/or senior executives. They report the audit findings and generally include recommendations for improvement.

(v)   *Management review:* based on the audit report(s) and other relevant information, the board of directors (or other appropriate body) reviews the suitability and effectiveness of the EMS and achieved environmental performance. From this review, together with the auditors' recommendations, the board of directors is able to identify and implement any required changes to the environmental policy and other elements of the EMS.

For organisations registered with EMAS, in addition to establishing and maintaining an EMS as outlined above there is a requirement for the environmental audit to be conducted by an external 'verifier' and to publish, annually, an externally verified (or audited) environmental statement. (We discuss this statement in the next section.)

Figure 17.2: Elements of an environmental management system (EMS)

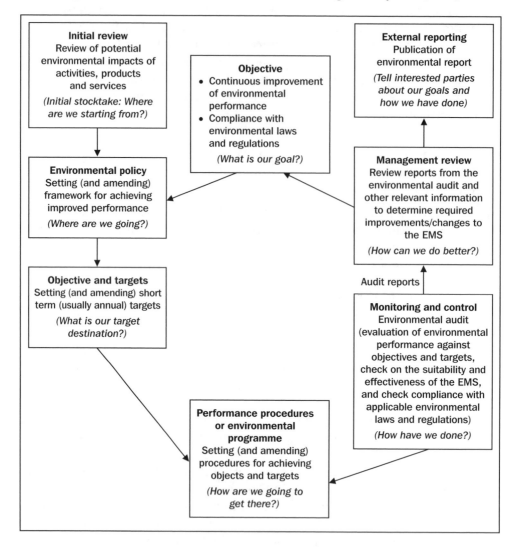

Reviewing the components of an EMS, it is evident that environmental audits are crucial to the effective functioning of the system and the achievement of improved environmental performance. They enable evaluation of the suitability and effectiveness of the EMS and appraisal of actual environmental performance against planned performance. From this, opportunities for improvement in the design and operation of the system and in the company's environmental performance can be identified.

Although we have outlined the requirements for organisations wishing to gain ISO 14001 or EMAS registration, relatively few companies seek to do so. (In

2002, 52 of the FTSE 350 companies had ISO 14001 certification and just six – J Sainsbury, Shell, BP, Scottish Power, British Gas and British Energy – had EMAS certification: these six companies also had ISO 14001 certification.) Nevertheless, it is evident from their environmental reports that virtually all major companies either have a full EMS or a well developed environmental programme. It is also evident that although the primary motivator for environmental audits, at least until the mid-1990s, was seeking to avoid liability – either through failure to comply with the 'vast tomes of environmental legislation' (*Economist*, 1990, p. 19) or through unwittingly 'inheriting' liability through a transaction such as an acquisition – today many (if not most) internal environmental audits are proactive in nature, designed to help organisations improve their environmental performance.

17.3.2 Development of environmental reporting

In June 2000, MacKay (2000) reported:

> The number of companies publishing some sort of environmental report has increased exponentially over the last 10 years. The bigger corporate polluters in the energy, extraction and construction sectors have been publishing health, safety and environmental data for a long time. (p. 1)

The extent of environmental reporting – and industry sector variations – is reflected in Gilmour and Caplan's (2001) observation:

> PricewaterhouseCoopers took a snapshot of what the top 100 global companies by market capitalisation (taken from last year's *Financial Times* 500 listings) are disclosing. Almost all of these publish some kind of commentary on social and environmental issues in their annual reports and accounts. Just under half also produced a separate report covering either environmental or corporate citizenship or both. . . . [A]ll of the automotive companies in the top 100 are producing separate environmental reports. In the energy and utilities sectors, 80% of the companies are providing separate information on their environmental and/or social impact; industrial products, 75%; pharmaceuticals, 64%; . . . At the other end of the spectrum are the service companies that do not convert or handle physical material, and deal mostly in business-to-business transactions. In the entertainment, media and broadcasting sector, only 20% of the companies [produce separate environmental and/or social information]. (p. 45)

Given the extent of environmental reporting, the question arises as to what has prompted companies to engage in this activity. MacKay (2000) throws some light on the issue. She explains:

> Companies produce environmental reports partly out of a growing concern for the environment, but mostly because they get into trouble if they don't. There is now significant pressure from the government and the environmental lobby for companies to report environmental and social data. . . . Large companies that don't report are 'named and shamed' by environmental pressure groups. (pp. 1–2)

However, it seems that companies are coming under rather wider stakeholder pressure to provide environmental information than that identified by MacKay. Indeed, at least four sources of pressure may be identified. These are as follows:

(i)   *Increased accountability.* As a consequence of increased media coverage and improved information technology, companies' activities are subject to greater scrutiny than ever before and, as a result, companies are being held to higher levels of accountability by their stakeholders. This is manifested, among other ways, as demands for increased disclosures – including those relating to companies' environmental performance.

(ii) *Increased expectations.* As Gilmour and Caplan (2001) explain:

> The global investor community has begun to develop a consensus view of the behaviour companies are expected to exhibit, and the kind of information they should report. . . . Analysts and investors are now asking about sustainability-related performance issues alongside financial measures. BP and Coca-Cola are two examples of large companies that faced questions on environmental and social issues at their recent annual general meetings. BP was asked about adapting to climate change, and Coca-Cola about the extent to which its bottles and cans could be recycled. (p. 44)

(iii) *Investment decisions.* A growing body of shareholders is interested in investing in 'environmentally friendly' and 'socially and ethically responsible' companies. In the USA, ethical investment funds are well established: in 1999 it was estimated that $2 trillion was invested in such funds (Gilmour and Caplan, 2001). In the UK, the FTSE has created an index of leading ethical companies known as FTSE4Good; in 2002, 176 of the FTSE 350 companies were also FTSE4Good companies. Given the increasing incidence of investors selecting 'environmentally friendly' (and similar) companies in which to invest their funds, it is clearly advantageous, at least for listed companies, to disclose relevant information to aid investors' decisions.

(iv) *Concern about companies' environmental liabilities.* Companies (especially in the USA, but increasingly in the UK) are facing enormous actual or potential liabilities as a result of breaching environmental laws or regulations or through 'inheriting' them through transactions such as acquisitions. Beets and Souther (1999) (citing Chadwick *et al.*, 1993) reported the extent of these liabilities in the USA in 1993 in the following words:

> The overall known environmental liability in the United States is currently estimated to be between 2 and 5 percent of the gross national product. Environmental cleanup costs under the Comprehensive Environmental Response, Compensation and Liability Act of 1980, or 'Superfund', are approximately $500 billion and will take 40 to 50 years to complete. (p. 130)

Against this background, it is understandable that current and potential shareholders are putting pressure on companies to report their environmental performance and policy.

Possibly as a response to the growing concern of investors, other stakeholders and society at large about companies' environmental performance and liabilities, regulatory and similar bodies are demanding or encouraging increased environmental disclosures by companies. In the USA in 1993, for example, the SEC prescribed increased, and more prominent, disclosure of existing and potential environment-related liabilities. In June 1994, SEC Commissioner Richard Roberts observed that increased public awareness of environmental issues had brought:

> Increased pressure to bear on the SEC to ensure that publicly-held companies are disclosing in a full, fair, and timely manner the present and potential environmental costs of an economically material nature. My view is that the company owes this to the investing public. (as cited in Beets and Souther, 1999, p. 130)

In the USA, companies have also come under increased pressure from the Environmental Protection Agency (EPA). Since 1998, companies in the oil, steel, metal, automobile and paper industries have been required by the EPA to disclose in an internet database:

> the number of plant inspections they underwent in the past two years, non-compliance ratings, dates and amounts of penalties imposed, the number of spills, pounds of materials spilled and any resulting injuries or deaths, a hazard rating for each factory based on the toxicity of the chemicals released, the ratio of pollution releases to production, the racial and income profiles of those living within three miles of each plant, and information from the Toxic Release Inventory. (Beets and Souther, 1999, pp. 130–131)

In Europe too, companies are facing increasing regulatory pressure to disclose environmental information. In Denmark and the Netherlands, for example, legislation has been passed that requires environmental reporting by major companies. Further, as we have already noted, companies registered with EMAS are required to publish annually, an externally validated (or audited) environmental statement. EMAS (2001), Annex III, explains:

> The aim of the environmental statement is to provide environmental information to the public and other interested parties regarding the environmental impact and performance and the continual improvement of environmental performance of the organisation. . . . The minimum requirements for this information shall be as follows:
> (a) a clear and unambiguous description of the organisation registering under EMAS and a summary of its activities, products and services . . . ;
> (b) the environmental policy and a brief description of the environmental management system of the organisation;
> (c) a description of all the significant direct and indirect environmental aspects which result in significant environmental impacts of the organisation and an explanation of the nature of the impacts as related to these aspects;[5]
> (d) a description of the environmental objectives and targets in relation to significant environmental aspects and impacts;

---

[5] Definitions of environmental aspects and impacts, as defined by EMAS (2001), are included in Figure 17.1.

(e) a summary of the data available on the performance of the organisation against its environmental objectives and targets with respect to its significant environmental impacts. The summary may include figures on pollutant emissions, waste generation, consumption of raw material, energy and water, noise . . . The data should allow for year-by-year comparison to assess the development of the environmental performance of the organisation . . . ;

(f) other factors regarding environmental performance including performance against legal provisions with respect to their significant environmental impacts.

In order to meet EMAS certification requirements, the information published in the company's environmental statement must be:

(a) accurate and non-deceptive;
(b) substantiated and verifiable;
(c) relevant and used in an appropriate context or setting;
(d) representative of the overall environmental performance of the organisation;
(e) unlikely to result in misinterpretation;
(f) significant in relation to the overall environmental impact. (EMAS, 2001, Annex III, para 3.5)

As noted earlier, J Sainsbury, Shell, BP, Scottish Power, British Gas and British Energy are all EMAS accredited and all publish environmental statements that comply with the above requirements.

In the UK, investors (particularly institutional investors) have been urged by influential bodies such as the Association of British Insurers to pay regard to companies' environmental, social and similar performance, in addition to financial indicators, when making their investment decisions. This, in turn, has put greater pressure on companies to disclose the relevant information. However, perhaps more significantly, Government Ministers (such as John Prescott, Deputy Prime Minister in 1997 and Michael Meacher, Minister for the Environment, in 1998) have expressed their belief in the importance of environmental reporting (Newsmedia, 1998) and, in October 2001, the Prime Minister (Tony Blair) called upon FTSE 350 companies to voluntarily publish annual environmental reports (separate from their annual reports) by the end of 2001. In the event, only 43 did so (Fettis, 2002). Perhaps Blair's 'request' was an indication that, if companies did not voluntarily disclose environmental information, they would be forced to do so through legislation and/or regulation. That this may, indeed, become a reality is signalled in the draft clauses of the Companies Bill published in July 2002 [Department of Trade and Industry (DTI), 2002]. Clauses 73, 75 and 81 indicate that all major companies will be required to publish in their annual reports a fully audited operating and financial review (OFR) and that company directors will be required to form an opinion as to whether certain specified matters should be included in the OFR. These matters include:

- the company's policies in relation to employment by the company;
- the company's policies on environmental issues relevant to the company's businesses;
- the company's policies on social and community issues relevant to the company's business;
- the company's performance, in the financial year to which the operating and financial review relates, in carrying out the policies mentioned.

The provisions outlined above are interesting in that they encompass both environmental and social policies and performance. Until the late 1980s, companies' voluntary disclosures related, almost exclusively, to environmental issues, and reports issued separately from the annual report were generally entitled 'Environmental Report'. (This coincides with the period when environmental audits were, in the main, limited to environmental compliance and environmental due diligence audits.) During the 1990s, companies came under increasing pressure to pay due regard to social issues and to disclose information relating to their social performance. Many companies began to publish both environmental and social information – either within their annual reports or as separate reports. While some significant companies (such as J. Sainsbury) continue to publish 'Environmental Reports', more than 2,000 organisations worldwide issue 'Social and Environmental Reports' (Perry, 2002). A review of relevant internet sites reveals that this applies to a number of FTSE 350 companies, including, for example, BP and British Gas.

A few companies, like Shell for instance, have gone a step further. They have recognised that both social and economic concerns are inextricably linked with environmental issues and have started to produce 'Sustainability Reports'. The Fédération des Experts Comptables Européens (FEE, 2001) explains:

> 'Sustainability' and 'sustainable development' are terms which came to prominence following the Brundtland Report[6] which argued that human development should meet the needs of the present without compromising the ability of future generations to meet their own needs. . . . In the context of corporate reporting, the term 'sustainability' is generally used to indicate that the subject of the report includes environmental, social and economic issues. Sustainability reports have evolved from a process – which started with the appearance of environmental reports. . . . Separate environmental and social reports are still being produced, but 'sustainability' reports aim to give a more comprehensive 'triple bottom line' approach to stakeholder accountability. It should be emphasised that it is still a minority of, typically, larger organisations, which is producing such reports – but the numbers are increasing all the time. (p. 1)

It needs to be borne in mind that, at least in the UK at the present time, environmental, social and sustainability reporting is voluntary. Nevertheless, a

---

[6] World Commission on Environment and Development (1987) *Our Common Future*. Oxford: Oxford University Press.

significant (and growing) number of companies have adopted the view that, in order to enhance the credibility of the information provided in their reports, it should be externally verified (or audited). In 2001, Gilmour and Caplan reported that 49 of the top 100 UK companies by market capitalisation which issued 'a separate report covering either environmental or citizen issues or both . . . included an external assurance statement from the external auditors or other specialists' (p. 45). As noted earlier, companies like Shell, British Gas and J Sainsbury which have EMAS certification are required to have their environmental reports externally verified.

17.4 INTERNAL AND EXTERNAL ENVIRONMENTAL AUDITS

Having looked at the evolution of environmental auditing [from compliance to environmental management system (EMS) and environmental performance audits] and environmental reporting (from environmental to sustainability reports) we now turn our attention to environmental auditing *per se* – its objectives, scope, process and outcomes. We first consider *internal* environmental audits (that is, those conducted as an aid to management) and then address *external* environmental audits (that is, those conducted to provide assurance to parties outside the organisation).

17.4.1 Internal environmental audits

The starting point for an internal environmental audit is a definition of its objectives and scope, and identification of those who are to perform the audit. Like the internal audits we discussed in Chapter 16, the objectives and scope of the audit are defined by management – generally the board of directors, a committee of the board (such as an audit or environmental issues committee), or senior executives. The audits are designed to suit management's needs.

The objective of the audit may be defined narrowly or broadly. It may be, for example:

- to ensure that the organisation is complying with applicable environmental laws and regulations (or even a subset of these – such as those relating to hazardous wastes);
- to evaluate the effectiveness of an existing waste control or treatment;
- to identify the environmental impacts of current processes, products and services (with a view to identifying alternatives which are more 'environmentally friendly');

- to identify potential cost savings from waste minimisation and recycling of waste products;
- to identify ways to reduce materials, water and/or energy usage.

Alternatively, the objective may be broader, such as applies in the case of audits performed in accordance with the EMAS or ISO 14001 schemes. The objective may be, for instance:

- to ensure that the EMS is appropriate to the company's activities, products and services (and their environmental impacts) and is operating effectively;
- to ensure that environmental performance complies with the company's established environmental policy and procedures and also with regulatory requirements.

It should be noted that, whether narrowly or broadly defined, the objective of an internal environmental audit almost invariably includes (implicitly or explicitly) the formulation of recommendations for improvement.

It may be that a particular audit is one in a series of audits, or an element of an audit cycle, whereby all of the company's activities are to be audited but over a period of time such as three years.[7]

The scope of the audit (that is, its extent and boundaries in terms of factors such as the physical location(s), subject matter and organisational activities to be audited) is dependent on the audit objective(s). The audit may, for instance, cover the entire organisation (a comprehensive audit), or focus on a department or process (an activity audit) or on one or more sites (a site audit). However, for every audit it is important that the scope, like the audit objective and expected audit outcomes, are clearly defined in writing and agreed with the director(s) or senior executive(s) requesting the audit. In particular, reference should be made to:

(i)   the subject matter and activities to be covered by the audit;
(ii) the environmental criteria to be established or used to evaluate performance;
(iii) the period to be covered by the audit.

---

[7] For organisations with EMAS certification, EMAS (2001) Annex II explains:

> Over a period of time all activities in a particular organisation shall be subject to an audit. The period of time taken to complete audits of all activities is known as the audit cycle. For small non-complex organisations, it may be possible to audit all activities at one time. For those organisations the audit cycle is the interval between these audits. ... The audit or audit cycle shall be completed ... at intervals no longer than 3 years. (paras 2.1, 2.9)

Companies registered with the ISO 14001 scheme are required to have 'periodic environmental management system audits' (ISO 14001, para 4.5.3) but no time-frame is specified. However, the audit programme is required to include details of audit frequency (ISO 14001, Annex A para A.5.4).

As for all other audits, in order to ensure objectivity and freedom from bias, it is important that all members of the audit team are independent of the subject matter and activities to be audited. It is also important that audit team members, individually or collectively, possess the necessary knowledge, skills and experience to achieve the audit objective(s). Because of the range of knowledge and skills that are required for environmental audits, most audit teams are interdisciplinary in nature. The audit team may comprise employees from the part of the organisation being audited, employees from other parts of the organisation, external consultants or auditors, or a combination thereof. Where internal staff are used, their independence from the subject(s) and activities to be audited is of particular importance. The audit objective(s) and scope determine the required size, knowledge, skills and experience of the audit team but, as Maltby (1995) points out:

> The environmental audit potentially requires a knowledge of the legal framework within which the company operates, and also of any forthcoming changes in the law, an understanding of the company's processes, raw materials, products, wastes and energy usage, the effects of each of these on the environment locally and globally, and the ability to suggest ways in which the company might change or improve what it does. Only the largest companies can afford to maintain all these skills permanently in-house. For this reason, it is likely that, whatever the form and purpose of environmental audits, most audit work will be carried out for companies by consultants. (p. 16)

The audit process is much the same as that for an external financial statement audit and it follows a similar set of logical steps, namely:

(i)   gaining an understanding of the organisation, the subject matter and activity(ies) to be audited;
(ii) planning the audit;
(iii) collecting audit evidence;
(iv) evaluating the evidence, forming conclusions and developing recommendations;
(v)   reporting the audit findings, conclusions and recommendations to the director(s) or senior executive(s) who requested the audit.

These steps are present in all environmental audits but their details vary according to the audit objective(s); for example, the details of a compliance audit will differ from those of a comprehensive or site audit. For purposes of illustration we describe below the steps that usually apply in an comprehensive audit.

(i)   Gaining an understanding of the company, its environmental impact and its EMS

In order to gain a thorough understanding of the organisation, its environmental impact and its EMS, the audit team leader usually reviews all relevant documentation. This includes, for example, the company's environmental policy, specifications of environmental objectives and targets, procedures manual, staff training records (insofar as they relate to training in environmental-related issues), regulatory requirements to which the company is subject, the findings and conclusions of previous environmental audits (whatever their objectives, whether broad or narrow), reports of management reviews of the environmental audit reports (including reports on the suitability and effectiveness of the EMS),[8] and records of accidents and emergencies and how they were dealt with.

The audit team should also visit the company to meet key personnel and to familiarise themselves with such matters as organisational structure, the attitude of the directors, senior executives and employees to environmental issues, the organisation's functional areas (such as marketing, public relations, legal, production and finance), its operating factors (such as process discharges – including air, water and noise; site tidiness; water, energy and materials usage; waste and recycling; and occupational health and safety).

(ii) Planning the audit

Based on their understanding of the organisation, its environmental impact and its EMS, the audit team can develop the audit plan. This should specify, among other things:

(a) the organisational, functional and operating units to be audited;

(b) those elements of the organisation's EMS that are of high priority (because their effective operation is of particular importance to the effective operation of the entire EMS, or because past audits have identified significant problems, or for some other reason);

(c) the procedures to be used for auditing the various elements of the EMS and the company's environmental performance, and responsibility for performing and reviewing these procedures (that is, devising the audit programme);

(d) the dates and locations where the audit procedures are to be performed;

(e) the time to be taken for the audit as a whole and major segments thereof;

(f) a schedule of meetings to be held with the director(s) or senior executive(s) who requested the audit;

(g) the content and format of the audit report, its expected date of issue and the parties to whom it is to be distributed.

As for an external financial statement audit, the audit plan and audit programme should be sufficiently flexible to allow changes to be made if they are deemed appropriate as information is gathered during the audit.

---

[8] As noted in section 17.3.1, management review of environmental audit reports and other relevant information is an integral element of the company's EMS.

(iii)   Collecting audit evidence

Sufficient appropriate audit evidence needs to be collected on which to base conclusions about the suitability of the EMS to the company, its activities, products and services and their environmental impact, and about the effectiveness of the system's operation and its ability to effect improved environmental performance and ensure compliance with relevant regulatory requirements.

As for financial statement audits, the evidence is gathered by a variety of procedures including:
(a) *observation* of activities and conditions to evaluate whether these comply with the company's established EMS criteria;
(b) *enquiry* of relevant personnel (asking people about the activities they perform and whether they can identify ways in which their – or their area's – environmental performance could be improved);
(c) *acquiring information from outside sources* – for example, ascertaining measures used by other similar companies or industry norms that afford appropriate benchmarks for evaluating the company's environmental objectives and targets, or about alternative processes that result in less waste, reduced consumption of water and/or energy, or are otherwise more 'environmentally friendly' than those currently used by the company;
(d) *examination of records and documents* – for example, records of emissions, water and energy usage, waste created and disposed of, health and safety, and staff training;
(e) *analytical review* – for example, analysing the proportion of inputs to outputs of a process, and evaluating the extent and rate of change in the environmental impact of a particular activity, product or service from one period to the next;
(f) *tests of details* – for example, testing samples of records of factors such as energy and water usage, emissions, waste created and disposed of, and so on, to evaluate whether recorded results correspond with actual results.

(iv)   Evaluating the evidence, forming conclusions and developing recommendations

After the audit evidence has been gathered, the audit team should review the results of the audit procedures performed to ascertain whether sufficient appropriate evidence has been gathered for each audit segment and the audit as a whole on which to form conclusions about, for example:
(a) the suitability of the EMS for the organisation and its activities, products and services and their environmental impact;
(b) whether the environmental objectives and targets set for the period being audited have been reached or exceeded;
(c) whether the organisation has complied with all applicable environmental regulatory requirements.

Any material instances of non-conformance with the EMS criteria and procedures should be evaluated to determine their nature (for example, whether they are isolated instances or systemic) and their effect. Additionally, opportunities for the organisation to improve its EMS or environmental performance should be determined and, where appropriate, formulated as recommendations.

(v)   Reporting the audit findings, conclusions and recommendations

Before the audit report is prepared, the audit team generally holds a 'closing meeting' with the directors and/or senior executives responsible for the organisation's EMS, environmental performance, and compliance with environmental regulatory requirements, and also those responsible for the functions and activities audited. The purpose of the meeting is to present the audit findings in a factual manner and to ensure that those present understand and acknowledge the findings. It also provides an opportunity for the company personnel to challenge or question the findings and for any misunderstandings or disagreements to be resolved.

Following the closing meeting the audit report is prepared. It is normally addressed to the company's directors or senior executives who requested the audit and includes the following information:

(a) the agreed objectives and scope of the audit;
(b) identification of the functions and activities audited;
(c) identification of company personnel responsible for the functions and activities audited;
(d) the criteria against which the audit was conducted;
(e) the period covered by the audit and the dates of the audit;
(f) the audit findings, together with reference to supporting evidence;
(g) conclusions about:
  • the level of compliance with the company's environmental policy,
  • the company's environmental performance and progress,
  • the suitability of the EMS for the company, its activities, products and services and their environmental impacts,
  • the company's environmental objectives and targets,
  • the effectiveness of the EMS's operation,
  • the effectiveness and reliability of the company's arrangements for monitoring its environmental impacts,
  • the company's compliance with applicable regulatory requirements;
(h) recommendations for corrective action, where appropriate, or for improvements to the company's EMS, its environmental performance and/or its compliance with applicable regulatory requirements.

The report is also dated and signed by the audit team leader.

17.4.2   External environmental verification (or 'audit')

In section 17.3.2 we noted that virtually all major companies report some environmental information – either in their annual reports or in separate environmental reports.[9] We also observed that a number of companies choose to have their environmental information verified (or audited). This verification is voluntary; it is not associated with legal or regulatory requirements[10] or with those of ISO 14001. ISO 14001 requires registrants to publish their environmental policy but it does not require any other disclosures or that externally reported environmental information be verified. Further, it does not require registrants to have their EMS externally verified. This contrasts with EMAS, which requires registrants to publish annually an externally verified environmental statement (see section 17.3.2 above) and also to have their EMS audit programme,[11] and all other 'elements required for registration verified in a period not exceeding 36 months' (EMAS, 2001, Annex 5).

It is pertinent to note that we use the word 'verify' rather than 'audit' in relation to external environmental reporting. FEE (2002) prefers the term 'assurance'. It explains:

> The term 'assurance' is preferable to terms such as 'verification' or 'review' . . . because it avoids confusion with terms such as 'audit' and 'verification' that have more specialised meanings (para. 19)

In its Glossary, FEE defines assurance as 'that which enhances the credibility of information'. It defines 'audit' and 'verification' in the following terms:

Audit: An assurance engagement in which the credibility of information is enhanced to a high level, for example a statutory audit of financial statements.

Verification: A test of detail in which a matter is confirmed by reference to very persuasive evidence, such as checking a disclosure to third party documentation.

EMAS (2001) does not define 'verification' but seems to impute a meaning akin to FEE's definition of assurance. We use the term in the same way; that is, interchangeably with assurance. In the context of providing credibility to externally reported environmental information, use of the term 'audit' is inappropriate as generally it is not possible to provide the implied high level of assurance. This stems from three main factors, namely:

---

[9] We also noted that environmental information may be published in environmental reports, environmental and social reports, or sustainability reports.

[10] If proposed changes to the Companies Act are enacted, all major UK companies will be required to comment in their operating and financial review (OFR) on their environmental policies and performance, and on community, social, ethical and reputational issues, whenever these are material to the company's activities and performance. Also, the OFR will be subject to audit (see section 17.3.2 above).

[11] We noted in section 17.3.1 that 'a mechanism for monitoring and controlling environmental performance' (that is, an environmental audit) is an element of an EMS.

(i) the lack of generally accepted criteria or standards for environmental reporting;

(ii) the absence of generally accepted quantitative performance indicators, and the subjective and qualitative nature of much of the reported information;[12]

(iii) the lack of generally accepted verification (or assurance) standards and the general absence of conclusive evidence.

These factors combine to generate a situation where, as Beets and Souther (1999) express it:

> [C]orporate environmental reports can disclose as much or as little information as corporations prefer in whatever format they prefer. . . . While some corporations genuinely want to be environmentally friendly and share information related to their efforts with the public, the absence of environmental reporting [and verification] standards enables other corporations to publish 'green glosses', i.e., attractive environmental reports that disseminate little useful information but are designed to enhance public relations. . . . Corporations may be especially tempted to publish few tangible details about their environmental efforts if their competitors' environmental programs and efforts are more substantive than their own. (pp. 136–137)

The absence of generally accepted environmental reporting criteria and standards means there are no generally accepted benchmarks against which a company's environmental performance and the quality of its environmental reports can be judged. It also results in the environmental reports of a single company lacking consistency over time, and those of different companies lacking comparability at any point in time, as regards performance measures used and reported, and in the scope, format and quality of the information disclosed. Additionally, without recognised reporting and verification standards, environmental information is open to challenge as being incomplete, biased and/or inaccurate.

Notwithstanding the current difficulties for preparers, verifiers and users of environmental reports resulting from the absence of generally accepted reporting standards, constructive steps are underway to resolve the difficulty. The Global Reporting Initiative (GRI), in particular, is developing a comprehensive environmental reporting framework. FEE (2001) explains the origins and objectives of the GRI as follows:

> The GRI was originally convened in 1997 by CERES (Coalition for Environmentally Responsible Economies) in partnership with UNEP (United Nations Environment Programme) and has been developed by a steering committee representing a mix of stakeholders. . . . The GRI seeks to make sustainability reporting[13] as routine and credible as financial reporting in terms of comparability, rigour, and verifiability. Specifically, the GRI's goals are to:

---

[12] Beets and Souther (1999) point out that even a term like water usage 'can be defined differently from company to company and industry to industry' (p. 36).

[13] Reporting on environmental, social and economic issues (see section 17.3.2).

- Elevate sustainability reporting practices worldwide to a level equivalent to financial reporting;
- Design, disseminate, and promote standardised reporting practices, core measurements, and customised, sector-specific measurements;
- Ensure a permanent and effective institutional host to support such reporting practices worldwide.

  . . . In June 2000 GRI published its *Sustainability Reporting Guidelines* which have already formed the basis for a number of Sustainability Reports. . . . The GRI Guidelines are continuously updated, at present an update is taking place with the help of various GRI working parties.[14] (p. 2)

Under the GRI's guidelines, companies' environmental (and, where applicable, social and economic) performance is reported through the disclosure of quantitative or qualitative performance indicators. To put these indicators in their proper context, companies are encouraged to disclose relevant objectives and environmental, social and economic programme information as well as commenting on unusual events and identified trends (FEE, 2002, para 169).

The GRI's guidelines were developed with the assistance of more than 30 large companies including British Airways, Ford and Shell (Gilmour and Caplan, 2001). That companies are using the guidelines as a basis for their environmental reports is reflected in statements by, for example, Shell and J Sainsbury. In its 2001 Report, *People, Planet and Profits*, Shell states:

> Shell is a Charter Group member of the GRI and a pilot test company of the GRI reporting guidelines. This report has been produced within the broad framework of the guidelines. We will continue to evolve the Shell Report and provide learning into the further development of the guidelines. (p. 48)

Similarly, J Sainsbury's 2001 Environmental Report notes:

> For the first time we have followed the environmental sections of the Global Reporting Initiative (GRI) sustainability reporting guidelines which sets standards for clear, coherent and responsible reporting. These are designed to help companies communicate information about their environmental, social and economic performance more effectively. In so doing we join a number of leading UK companies using this methodology. (p. 1)

In addition to some major UK companies adopting the GRI's guidelines as a basis for reporting their environmental (or sustainability) performance, a relatively small but increasing number of major UK companies are having such information externally verified (MacKay, 2000). For the six UK companies with EMAS certification (Shell, BP, Scottish Power, British Gas, British Energy and J Sainsbury), external verification of their environmental statement is compulsory; for all other companies it is voluntary. Presumably, these companies believe it is cost-effective to have the credibility of the information in their reports enhanced in this way. This belief is reflected, at least to some extent, in the fact that most companies which have their environmental (or sustainability)

---

[14] Gilmour and Caplan (2001) report that the updated guidelines are expected to be issued in 2002.

information verified engage in 'stakeholder dialogue' (FEE, 2002)[15] or 'stakeholder consultation' (Larsson and Ljungdahl, 2001). Larsson and Ljungdahl explain that this activity is one of a number of techniques that are:

> developed and deployed [by companies] to deal with the multidimensional nature of sustainability issues, and the relative immaturity of corporate information collection and reporting systems.

FEE (2002) explains rather more specifically that:

> A company may use stakeholder dialogue relating to a sustainability report to ascertain:
> - what matters stakeholders want in a sustainability report (and whether past reports have met their needs)
> - the levels at which matters become significant enough to be included [that is, materiality levels]
> - what imprecision in measurement or degree of approximation is acceptable [that is, the tolerable error][16]
> - what assurance [external verification], if any, stakeholders value. (para 160)

Unlike an external financial statement audit where the objectives and scope are defined by statute, and the level of assurance with respect to, *inter alia*, the truth and fairness of the financial statements must, by definition, be high, the objectives, scope and level of assurance to be provided by an environmental (or sustainability) verification engagement need to be specified by the company concerned. In many companies where such engagements take place, the directors reach a decision about these matters as an outcome of stakeholder dialogue. For EMAS registrants the objectives of, and level of assurance to be provided by, the external verification are defined in general terms by EMAS requirements. EMAS (2001), Article 3, requires all EMAS registrants to:

(a) have their environmental management system and audit programme verified at least once every 36 months; and

(b) publish annually validated updates of their environmental statements.

Although EMAS (2001) does not define the terms 'verify' and 'validated', it is clear that something akin to a financial statement audit that provides a reasonably high level of assurance is envisaged. It specifies in Annex V (para 5.4.1) for example that:

---

[15] FEE (2002) defines stakeholders and stakeholder dialogue as follows:

> Stakeholders: Individuals or organisations that have, or could have, a non-trivial interest in a sustainable development decision of a company. The interest could be influencing the decision or simply through being affected by the outcomes of a decision. For a company, stakeholders include: investors, government agencies, workers, suppliers, customers, and those potentially affected by environmental and other impacts. (para 155)
> Stakeholder dialogue: Interaction between a company and its stakeholders to ascertain stakeholder views and communicate information relevant to stakeholders. (Glossary)

[16] Materiality levels and tolerable error are discussed in the context of external financial statement audits in Chapter 8.

The function of the environmental verifier is to check . . .

(a) compliance with all of the requirements of this Regulation [that is, EMAS 2001]: initial environmental review if appropriate, environmental management system, environmental audit and its results and the environmental statement;

(b) the reliability, credibility and correctness of the data and information in the environmental statement[17] . . .

The environmental verifier shall, in particular, investigate in a sound professional manner, the technical validity of the initial environmental review, if appropriate, or audit or other procedures carried out by the organisation, without unnecessarily duplicating those procedures. Inter alia, the environmental verifer should use spot checks to determine whether the results of the internal audit are reliable.

As for the internal environmental audits we discussed in section 17.4.1, the external verification of environmental or sustainability disclosures proceeds in much the same way as an external financial statement audit. The verification engagement must be planned and conducted so as to obtain sufficient appropriate evidence to express a conclusion with the desired level of assurance about the reliability of the information. It proceeds in a series of logically ordered steps as follows:

(i) Determining the acceptability of the engagement

Among other matters, the potential verifier needs to consider whether:

- the verification team possesses the necessary multidisciplinary skills to undertake the engagement;
- there are adequate verification team resources at appropriate locations to conduct the verification work within a reasonable time frame;
- verification team members possess the necessary degree of independence from the client. (As for external auditors, unless verification team members are, and are perceived to be, independent of the client, the verification statement will not provide the intended credibility to the published information);
- the information to be verified is suitable for verification and suitable criteria exist to enable the intended level of assurance to be achieved.

(ii) Agreeing with the client the subject matter, scope and terms of the engagement

The scope of a particular verification engagement may be limited to less than the whole of the environmental or sustainability report. As FEE (2002) explains:

---

[17] The detailed requirements specified in EMAS 2001, Annex III, para 3.5 (reproduced in section 17.3.2 above) for information published in companies' environmental statements help to indicate the high level of assurance that EMAS seems to envisage for verification of externally reported environmental information. The requirements specify, for example, that published environmental information must be accurate and non-deceptive, substantiated and verifiable, and relevant and used in an appropriate context or setting.

This may be because the company does not want assurance on all of the report (perhaps because of cost or other assurance providers being involved),[18] or because there are limitations through lack of suitable criteria or evidence that preclude some matters being included. [Additionally], for a given set of subject matter, the objectives of the assurance engagement may be restricted. For example: assurance may be given on the implementation of a policy, but not its enforcement; or on the operation of a system but not on the accuracy of performance indicators that depend on data from it. [Further], for a given objective, a company may request in advance that the assurance provider does not employ the full range of possible evidence gathering procedures. For example, visits to sites may be restricted or stakeholder dialogue prevented. (paras 117–119)

When considering the external validation of environmental or sustainability disclosures, it needs to be borne in mind that, unlike external financial statement audits, companies are reporting, and having validated, the relevant information voluntarily and that there are no generally accepted reporting or verification standards. Nevertheless, where the scope of the engagement is limited to less than the full environmental or sustainability report, or the procedures to be performed are restricted in some way, the external verifier needs to assess whether sufficient appropriate evidence can be collected to support a conclusion and whether (s)he will be able to define sufficiently clearly for users of the environmental or sustainability report the parts that have been subject to external verification.

(iii)   Gaining a thorough understanding of the client company and its environment-related affairs

Before commencing the engagement, the verifier needs to gain a thorough understanding of the client company, the environmental regulatory requirements pertaining to it, the environmental impacts of its activities, products and services, its environmental policy, EMS, environmental objects and targets, environmental audit programme and the results thereof, and environmental performance. This understanding is necessary in order to provide a context for evaluating the quality of the information that is to be verified.

(iv)   Planning the engagement

This step in a verification engagement includes defining the parts of the environmental (or sustainability) report that are to be verified, identifying appropriate evaluation criteria, determining materiality levels, assessing the likelihood of the report containing material misstatements, and designing appropriate verification procedures.

---

[18] For example, Ernst & Young were assisted in their external verification of BP's 'Health, Safety and Environment Facts 1996' by Environmental Resources Limited 'in respect of data collection processes' (Ernst & Young's 1996 Report, reproduced in Beets and Souther, 1999, Appendix B).

(v) Performing compliance procedures

Where the steps of 'gaining an understanding of the client company' and 'planning the engagement' have indicated that the company's EMS and other management information systems are effective in preventing, or detecting and correcting, errors in the company's data or information, the verifier may plan to rely on the systems to generate reliable environmental information. However, as in an external financial statement audit, irrespective of how reliable the company's systems may appear to be, before the verifier can place reliance on them, (s)he must test the suitability of the systems' design to prevent, or detect and correct, material misstatements in the environmental (or sustainability) information, and the effectiveness of the operation of the systems' internal controls throughout the reporting period.

(vi) Performing substantive procedures

As in a financial statement audit, analytical review and tests of details are used to test the completeness, accuracy and validity of the information in the company's environmental (or sustainability) report that is subject to external verification.

(vii) Conducting completion and review procedures

This step in a verification engagement is very similar to that conducted in an external financial statement audit. It includes procedures such as:

- obtaining a management representation letter to support all significant representations made by management on which the external verifier is placing reliance;
- reviewing the entire environmental or sustainability report to check, in particular, that the overall presentation of the report is not misleading and that the report is 'balanced'; that is, it 'fairly' reflects both positive and negative aspects of the company's environmental or sustainability performance;
- reviewing other information issued by the company (including its financial statements) that may be inconsistent with its environmental (or sustainability) disclosures.

(viii) Issuing the verification report to management

As for environmental reporting and verification, there are no standards governing the external verification report on environmental information. However, for verifications conducted for EMAS registered companies, EMAS (2001) Annex V, requires the verifier's report to management to specify:

    (a) all issues relevant to the work carried out by the environmental verifier;
    (b) the starting point of the organisation towards implementation of an environmental management system;

(c) in general, cases of nonconformity with the provisions of this Regulation [i.e. EMAS 2001], and in particular:
–   technical defects in the environmental review, or audit method, or environmental management system, or any other relevant process,
–   points of disagreement with the draft environmental statement, together with details of the amendments or additions that should be made to the environmental statement;
(d) the comparison with the previous [environmental] statements and the performance assessment of the organisation.

In addition to a report to management which is often in the nature of a 'management letter'[19] (i.e. a report that contains detailed, and often confidential, feedback to management about the verification engagement and its findings), the external verifier usually issues a verification report for publication with the company's environmental (or sustainability) report. In most cases, the content and format of this report are not dissimilar from that of an external financial statement auditor's report. Reference to the two example reports presented in Figures 17.3 and 17.4, issued respectively by Ernst & Young LLP on BP's 2001 Environmental and Social Review and PricewaterhouseCoopers on J Sainsbury's 2001 Environment Report, reveals that each has:

(a) a title indicating the type of report issued;
(b) an addressee (BP plc and Sainsbury plc);
(c) an introductory paragraph identifying the subject matter and nature of the engagement and the responsibilities of the company's directors in respect of the report;
(d) the basis of the conclusions reached and expressed;
(e) the verifier's conclusions/opinion based on the work done;
(f) the name and address of the verifiers;
(g) the date of the report.

One factor we have not yet discussed in relation to the external validation of companies' environmental reports is the providers of this service. The two key requirements for external verifiers of environmental reports are independence and competence. Unless the verifiers possess these two characteristics, a report issued by them will do little to enhance the credibility of the environmental information published by the relevant companies. At present, external verification is performed almost exclusively by 'Sustainability (or similar) Units' of the Big Five accountancy firms or by large firms of environmental (or, increasingly, sustainability) consultants such as Ashridge, Lloyd's Register or Aspinwall. MacKay (2000) explains:

There is something of a turf war going on between these two camps. The Big Five trade on their audit experience, their sophisticated audit methodologies and their

---

[19] Management letters issued as an outcome of an external financial statement audit are discussed in Chapter 13, section 13.8.

Figure 17.3:   Ernst & Young LLP's 'attestation statement' on BP's 'Environmental and Social Review'

Attestation statement

To BP p.l.c
We have reviewed BP's Environmental and Social Review 2001 (the Review), as outlined below, in order to substantiate its contents.

The Review has been prepared by the company, which is responsible for selecting the information and collecting the data for presentation therein.

This attestation statement in itself should not be taken as a basis for interpreting BP's performance in relation to its non-financial policies.

Approach
There are currently no statutory requirements or generally accepted standards in the UK relating to the preparation, publication and attestation of corporate environment and social reports. We have therefore used a customized attestation process involving detailed challenge of the contents of the Review, selected document review, interviews with executives and managers, and site-based reviews to understand how the non-financial policies are being implemented and reported upon.

Basis of our review
Our terms of reference agreed with BP were to:
1. Discuss, with a selection of BP executives and senior managers, each of the four non-financial policies (Health, Safety and Environmental Performance, Ethical Conduct, Employees, and Relationships) to understand objectives and priorities for embedding the policies, the means to accomplishing those objectives and the degree to which those objectives were met.
2. Review selected documents which provide internal assurance to BP management that policy objectives and priorities are being met.
3. Review a selection of external media sources for reports relating to BP's adherence to its policies, as a check on the appropriateness of the information reported and statements made in the Review.
4. Test evidence supporting the Review's data, statements, and assertions at a sample of BP sites.
5. Review relevant documents, such as minutes of meetings of the board of directors and the board's Ethics & Environment Assurance Committee, to assess management awareness and review of policy commitments.
6. Review HSE data management systems and samples of data reported by sites to assess whether data has been collected, consolidated and reported accurately.
7. Challenge the Review to substantiate its content.

Conclusions
On the basis of our review, in accordance with the terms of reference for our work, we conclude that:
- Assertions and claims made in the Review are supported by the evidence obtained during the attestation process.
- The objectives for implementation of the non-financial policies described in the Review are consistent with those which the board and senior managers have set in the course of the year.
- The board has monitored the implementation of the non-financial policies over the period. As part of such monitoring, it is the responsibility of management to identify any material issues or concerns that may be arising, together with the actions they are taking to address them. In the course of our review, we have seen evidence of this process working in practice.
- The Review covers a selection of issues highlighted in the media over the reporting period. Decisions regarding the inclusion of such material and the degree to which the Review contents address key stakeholder concerns are based on BP's judgement.
- We have made observations to BP management as a result of the visits to sites (sites visited are listed in the Review Approach section of our statement, which can be found on *bp.com*). Among these observations are:
  - At the sites visited it was observed that in some cases data reporting procedures and data quality assurance processes are not adequately documented. However, we are not aware of any material modifications that should be made to the HSE data which would affect assessment of group-wide HSE performance.
  - The policies are understood and responsibilities for implementing them have been made clear across relevant functions. Communication of the non-financial policy expectations to contractors and suppliers tends to focus on the Health, Safety and Environment Policy expectations, but less often extends to the other non-financial policies.
  - We have observed leadership and commitment to the non-financial policies. We have seen continuing effort to develop training programmes, guidelines and procedures to achieve the aims of the non-financial policies.
  - There is variation in regional and business unit implementation of the non-financial policies. For example, we observed increased management effort on the Ethical Conduct Policy implementation in areas where the risks are perceived to be most significant. At some sites we observed that work had been undertaken to increase the proportion of local employees in the workforce, but not all sites visited had set formal targets relating to wider diversity issues.
  - We saw evidence that significant progress has been made in embedding the HSE policy expectations within the former Burmah Castrol site visited. Site management recognize the need to focus on embedding the other non-financial policies.
  - We saw evidence that the non-financial policy expectations are considered in the evaluation and design of projects in Indonesia and Vietnam.
  - There are few measures established for the Relationships and Ethical Conduct Policies, which makes it difficult for BP to demonstrate performance improvement.
  - Social impact assessments were conducted in several countries visited during the reporting period. The findings of the social impact assessments were being used to develop social investment strategies.

Ernst & Young LLP
London   20 March 2002

global brands. The consultants trade on their specialisation in environmental consultancy and their environmental expertise. The Big Five employ environmental specialists and the consultants employ auditors. They both poach each other's staff and KPMG'S environmental audit division was augmented some years ago by a mass defection of environmental audit experts from a client – The Body Shop. . . . The consultants can . . . be relied on to use words such as correct, accurate and complete in their reports; auditors generally balk at saying anything stronger than 'properly collated'. . . . Whatever the reasons, . . . more environmental reports in the UK are verified by firms of consultants than by firms of auditors. (p. 2)

FEE (2002) similarly notes the apparent shortfalls in the competence of accountancy firms and consultants to act as external verifiers. More particularly, it notes the need for accountancy firms to better communicate how they meet the need for specialist expertise and for consultants to 'convince users (of validated environmental and similar reports) that they are competent in assurance [verification] itself as well as being experts in the subject matter' (para 77).

It should be noted that in order to act as an external verifier for an EMAS registrant, individuals or organisations must be accredited environmental verifiers. Under EMAS (2001), Article 4, all European Union member countries are required to establish a system for the accreditation of environmental verifiers and for the supervision of their activities: Annex V provides details of the requirements for the accreditation and supervision of environmental verifiers. In order to qualify for accreditation, Annex V requires that an individual or organisation must possess:

   (a) knowledge and understanding of the Regulation [that is, EMAS 2001], [and] the general functioning of environmental management systems....;
   (b) knowledge and understanding of the legislative, regulatory and administrative requirements relevant to the activity subject to verification;
   (c) knowledge and understanding of environmental issues, including the environmental dimension of sustainable development;
   (d) knowledge and understanding of the technical aspects, relevant to environmental issues, of the activity subject to verification;
   (e) understanding of the general functioning of the activity subject to verification in order to assess the appropriateness of the management system;
   (f) knowledge and understanding of [internal] environmental auditing requirements and methodology;
   (g) knowledge of information audit (Environmental Statement).

Additionally, environmental verifiers are to be independent, impartial and objective. Among other requirements they (and where the verifier is an organisation, its staff) are to be:

free of any commercial, financial or other pressures which might influence their judgment or endanger trust in their independence of judgment and integrity in relation to their activities.

**Figure 17.4: PricewaterhouseCoopers' verification of J Sainsbury's
Environmental Report**

VERIFICATION

To J Sainsbury plc

The 2001 J Sainsbury plc Environment Report ('the Report') covers the J Sainsbury plc UK retail business (Sainsbury's Supermarkets Limited), Sainsbury's Bank and Shaw's (the US supermarket business). This statement relates to the verification of the Report, posted on the Internet as a pdf file, that was carried out by PricewaterhouseCoopers (PwC).

The Directors of J Sainsbury plc are responsible for the content of the Report, including the reliability of the information presented, and for making available to us information necessary to carry out our responsibilities. The maintenance and integrity of the J Sainsbury plc Environment Report web site is also the responsibility of the Directors and PricewaterhouseCoopers accept no responsibility for any changes that may have occurred to the verified content of the Report since being placed on the internet. The work described below has been carried out for J Sainsbury plc and PwC have no responsibility for any use or interpretation of the work by third parties.

Objectives

PwC was engaged to:

1. Review certain information in the Report to confirm to the Directors that nothing came to our attention to suggest the information reviewed is materially misstated and
2. Comment on the current status of environmental management and reporting at J Sainsbury plc based on the observations made during the review process.

It should be noted that there are no common standards for reporting or review of environmental performance information and that environmental data are subject to a number of inherent limitations compared to financial data, due to both their nature and the methods used in determining or estimating the data. There are also no current standards on the reporting of information on the Internet. Our work was planned and conducted to obtain moderate rather than high assurance on the reliability of selected information in the Report.

Basis of our opinion

Our opinion is based on the following work:

a) a review of the reliability of internal controls at Group level governing information collected for the Report
b) examination, on a sample basis, of information and supporting evidence for selected Key Performance Indicators (KPIs), text and targets for Sainsbury's Supermarkets Ltd and Shaw's and review of progress made against selected targets for Sainsbury's Bank and
c) a review of the Report to check for consistency with the findings of our work.

Information which has been subject to review is indicated by the presence of a $\boxed{V}$ symbol. It should be noted that where this symbol appears next to a graph, the review is related to 2000/01 data only.

Our work did not include visits to supermarkets, stores or offices but was carried out at Group Head Office in the UK and through dialogue with appropriate J Sainsbury plc staff and review of supporting documentation.

Our opinion

On the basis of the work undertaken, nothing came to our attention to suggest that the information is materially misstated.

Comments

During the review process, we made a number of observations and recommendations on the reporting process and the wider development of environmental management at J Sainsbury plc, which we reported to management. Key comments were:

a) The inclusion of environmental data for Shaw's for the first time in this year's Environment Report has allowed J Sainsbury plc to provide a more complete Group report of environmental performance. The reporting of environmental data for all operating companies is necessary to achieve a comprehensive report on Group performance.
b) There is an ongoing challenge for J Sainsbury plc to improve the quality of data in the Report. Progress has been made by J Sainsbury's Supermarkets Ltd through the establishment of improved systems for the reporting and recording of environmental data, including the use of standard data reporting templates. There is a need, however, for further standardisation of measuring and reporting methods across the Group to provide appropriate data on a timely basis for all of the Group's business operations.
c) Progress has been made on the further development of processes for environmental management and reporting since last year's Report (1999/00). Further work is required to achieve clearer definition of roles and responsibilities for environmental management across the Group and to formalise a comprehensive Group-wide environmental management system.
d) In line with emerging practice amongst leading companies, the management should consider the benefits of closer integration of the Group environmental management programme with integration with wider corporate social responsibility activities.

PricewaterhouseCoopers
London: August 2001

They are also required

> to have documented methodologies and procedures, including quality control mechanisms and confidentiality provisions, for the verification requirements of this Regulation. (Annex V, para 5.2.1)

In respect of the supervision of environmental verifiers, EMAS (2001), Annex V, requires the national accreditation bodies with which the particular accredited environmental verifier is registered, to ensure, at regular intervals not exceeding 24 months, that:

> the environmental verifier continues to comply with the accreditation requirements and to monitor the quality of the verifications undertaken. Supervision may consist of office audit, witnessing in organisations, questionnaires, review of environmental statements validated by the environmental verifier and review of validation reports. (Annex V, para 5.3.1)

This system of 'supervision' is very similar to the 'monitoring' of registered auditors undertaken by the JMU and ACCA monitoring unit on behalf of the auditor 'accreditation bodies' (that is, the Recognised Supervisory Bodies) which we discussed in Chapter 15.

17.5 ADVANTAGES AND DISADVANTAGES OF ENVIRONMENTAL AUDITING AND REPORTING

Given that, at least in the UK at the present time, all internal environmental auditing and external environmental reporting and verification is undertaken voluntarily, the question arises as to why companies pursue these activities. Expressed slightly differently, what advantages may accrue to companies – and what disadvantages may result – as a result of them engaging in environmental auditing and reporting?

17.5.1 Advantages of environmental auditing and reporting

As may be seen from Figure 17.5, we have identified eight advantages accruing to companies from internal environmental audits and a further six from reporting environmental information and having the information verified. We discuss each of these advantages below.

(i) Avoidance (or minimisation) of environment related liabilities

Probably the most important advantage of internal environmental audits for companies is that they help to ensure that they (the companies) comply with the myriad of environmental laws and regulations to which they are subject and thereby avoid (or at least minimise) financial penalties or other sanctions.

As we noted in section 17.3.1, many companies initially instituted environmental audits as a response to the ever increasing volume and complexity of

Figure 17.5: **Advantages and disadvantages of internal environmental audits and external reporting and verification**

Internal environmental audits	External environmental reporting and verification
Advantages	
(i) Avoidance (or minimisation) of environment related liabilities	(ix) Enhanced corporate image or reputation
(ii) More efficient operating processes (i.e. cost savings)	(x) Enhanced credibility of published environmental and financial information
(iii) Reduced insurance premiums	(xi) Reduced risk of regulatory investigations relating to environmental matters
(iv) Improved managerial decisions resulting in enhanced financial and environmental performance	(xii) Reduced risk of litigation for misrepresentation by users of published environmental information
(v) Improved environmental management and enhanced environmental protection	(xiii) Improved investment decisions by investors and increased potential funding
(vi) Improved risk management	(xiv) Improvements in the environmental management system, internal controls and reporting systems
(vii) Satisfaction of customer requirements and enhanced customer relations	
(viii) Enhanced corporate image or reputation	
Disadvantages	
(i) Resources required to develop, implement and maintain an environmental auditing programme	(iv) Possible adverse consequences of reporting environmental information
(ii) Disruption caused in facilities being audited	(v) Absence of generally accepted environmental reporting and verification standards
(iii) Adverse consequences of audits uncovering breaches of environmental regulatory requirements	(vi) High costs of producing environmental reports and having them verified

environmental regulations (and the increasing severity of penalties), and the resultant ease of inadvertently breaching them. Internal audits – whether conducted as focused environmental compliance audits or broader (comprehensive) environmental audits – enable companies to be alert to any compliance problems and thus to take appropriate corrective action in a timely manner. In some cases this may be limited to adjusting procedures or adopting new technologies (such as installing new plant or equipment that reduces emissions of toxic gases to permitted levels); in others it may involve taking costly remedial action – for example, cleaning up contaminated sites where hazardous waste has been dumped. By identifying potential compliance problems as soon as they arise, companies can avoid fines and other penalties for breaching regulatory requirements and the costs imposed by the court for remediation. It also avoids the adverse publicity and damage to the company's reputation that inevitably follows an environmental prosecution (Quality Network, 1996).

(ii)   More efficient operating processes (cost savings)

One of the key objectives of internal environmental audits is ascertaining ways in which environmental management can be improved. This involves, among other things, reviewing current and alternative operating processes, and resource and energy sources (or types), in order to identify opportunities for cost savings. These may be achieved through, for example, reduced resource and energy usage, and minimalisation of waste with a consequential reduction in storage and disposal costs.

(iii)   Reduced insurance premiums

Quality Network (1996) points out that insurance companies are very aware of the risk that attaches to poor environmental performance by organisations they insure. Companies with a sound and effective EMS (in which, environmental audits are an integral part: see section 17.3.1) are able to demonstrate to their insurance companies that they pose less risk. As a result, they are generally able to secure reduced insurance premiums. Indeed, according to Quality Network (1996), some insurance companies require an internal environmental audit of the insured organisation as a condition to agreeing insurance cover.

(iv)   Improved managerial decisions

All management decisions are made on the basis of available information and, all other things being equal, the more comprehensive and the higher the quality of relevant information, the better the decisions reached. Internal environmental audits generate a wealth of data that enhance the information on which management formulates decisions about, for example, resource allocation, products and services to be produced, operating processes, plant and equipment to acquire, procedures to be adopted in respect of the storage and disposal of hazardous wastes, and action to be taken in the event of, for instance, an environmental or health or safety emergency or disaster. These and similar decisions have a direct impact on the company's financial and non-financial performance. Hence, as commentators such as Bowman (1999) have noted:

> Voluntary [internal] environmental audit is an integral part of good environmental management and good environmental management should be seen as good business'. (p. 395)

Given the avoidance of fines and costs of remediation through ensuring compliance with environmental laws and regulations, the cost-saving opportunities identified through environmental audits, and an improved basis for decision-making, it is not surprising that good environmental management results in enhanced financial, as well as environmental, performance.

Supporting the notion that good environmental management is good for business, Quality Network (1996) has observed that the financial performance of 'green portfolios' (that is, portfolios of companies that feature in indices such as FTSE4Good, signifying good environmental performance and ethical conduct), has 'been good in comparison to more traditional investments' (p. 2).

(v)   Improved environmental management and enhanced environmental protection

Where companies conduct environmental audits, it indicates a commitment by their directors and senior executives to environmental protection. It also signals a willingness by the directors and executives to give due consideration to the environmental audit findings and to implement the accompanying recommendations designed to improve the company's environmental management system and environmental performance.

Further, the audits themselves generally have the effect of raising awareness within the company of environmental matters and, more specifically, the audit remit usually includes assessment of the suitability and adequacy of training programmes for company personnel on environmental issues. Additionally, the audits facilitate comparison of environmental practices at various sites, divisions and, if applicable, subsidiaries of the company and, through their feedback and recommendations, help to ensure that best practices are adopted throughout the organisation. By these means, environmental audits help to improve companies' environmental management – and thereby enhance environmental protection.

(vi)   Improved risk management

A recent development in the realm of environmental auditing is the use of these audits to evaluate potential business risks. Audits with this objective attempt to identify environmental issues that pose the greatest risk to continuing business operations. Such risks may be reflected in factors such as significant capital expenditure requirements (for example, for the purchase of new plant or equipment to reduce emissions to permitted levels, the cost of cleaning up contaminated land, or removing asbestos from buildings), limitations on production (for instance, because products or processes and, in particular, resultant gaseous, liquids or solid wastes do not meet newly announced environmental or health and safety regulations), or other factors (Bowman, 1999).

(vii)   Satisfaction of customer requirements and enhanced customer relations

The news media frequently report the concerns of various groups in society about matters such as the harmful effects of 'factory farming', the use of pesticides and chemical fertilisers to aid agricultural and horticultural production, 'overfishing' the oceans, and the removal of slow-regeneration hardwoods from tropical rainforests for building materials and furniture manufacture.

Increasingly, companies whose directors and senior executives are themselves sensitive to environmental issues, or who are aware of their customers' preferences in this regard, seek suppliers and sub-contractors who can demonstrate that they are good environmental citizens. Thus, 'supplier' and 'sub-contracting' companies that conduct environmental audits are well placed to reassure their customers of their commitment to good environmental management and performance.

(viii) and (ix)   Enhancement of the company's image or reputation

A company's image and reputation may be enhanced through both conducting environmental audits and publishing independently verified information about its environmental performance. Where companies conduct environmental audits they are able to demonstrate their commitment to improved environmental performance. This in itself may enhance their image – or, alternatively, may help them counter (or mitigate) adverse publicity about their attitude to the environment.

However, companies are likely to be able to enhance their reputation more effectively if they report publicly on their environmental performance – particularly if their report is independently verified. Such reporting and verification may also translate into more tangible benefits in that, if the company is portrayed as being 'environmentally friendly', it may be favoured by environmentally concerned customers and investors. As Beets and Souther (1999) observe:

> positive public relations . . . may accrue from issuing a verified environmental report; that is, 'being green' may have a positive impact on revenues and stock prices. (p. 135)

(x)   Enhanced credibility of published environmental and financial information

If a company's environmental report is not verified by an independent, competent environmental verifier, some users of the report may consider the information to be biased, incomplete, or otherwise unreliable. Some may go as far as regarding the company's environmental disclosures as 'greenwash', that is, as an exercise in public relations rather than responsible environmental reporting. Independent verification of the environmental information may render it more credible – and thus more useful – to users.

However, independent verification of a company's environmental report may do more than enhance its credibility. For companies whose activities, products or services have a significant environmental impact (such as companies in the extractive, chemicals and manufacturing industries), publishing independently verified environmental information can enhance the credibility of the company's published financial statements. For example, if a company has material environmental remediation liabilities (possibly resulting from the storage and disposal of hazardous waste contaminating large areas of the company's land at various locations on- and off-site), both the company's directors and its external auditor will be concerned about the appropriateness and adequacy of disclosures in the financial statements in respect of the liabilities. The independent verification of information relating to the liabilities in the company's environmental report will help to assure the directors and auditor about the adequacy of the disclosures (Beets and Souther, 1999).

(xi)   Reduced risk of regulatory investigations relating to environmental matters

When a company publishes comprehensive environmental information – when, for example, it reports its environmental policy, environmental objectives and targets, achieved environmental performance measured against the targets, its environmental audit programme, the effectiveness of controls within its environmental management system, and the level of its compliance with environmental laws and regulations – the implication is that the company is environmentally aware and open and frank about its environmental issues. Where the information is independently verified, this impression is strengthened. It seems likely that such companies are less likely to attract regulatory investigations in respect of their environmental matters, and less likely to breach environmental regulatory requirements, than companies which do not issue informative environmental reports, whether within their annual report or separately.

(xii) Reduced risk of litigation for misrepresentation by users of published environmental information

A reduced risk of litigation resulting from misrepresentation derives from companies having their environmental disclosures independently verified. Where companies publish (unverified) environmental information they may believe it is complete, unbiased and a fair representation of the facts. However, without independent verification of the relevant information, companies run the risk of inadvertently disclosing inaccurate or misleading information – and, hence, of being exposed to the risk of being sued (or subjected to other adverse actions) by parties who act in reliance on the environmental information provided and thereby suffer loss.

(xiii)   Improved investment decisions by investors and increased potential
funding

Like management decisions, investors' decisions are based on available information and, all other things being equal, the more comprehensive and the higher the quality of the information, the better the decisions made. Thus, where companies publish environmental reports – particularly if these are externally verified – investors have additional information on which to base their investment decisions.

Further, the results of a number of studies of investor preferences indicate that many investors are concerned about companies' environmental performance and are more likely to invest in companies with a good environmental track record (see, for example, *The Accountant*, 1998; *Investors Chronicle*, 1998; Krumsiek, 1998). Hence, for companies with a good environmental record, publishing information about their environmental performance may result in a rise in their share price (as demand for their shares increases) and in their increased ability to attract new capital.

(xiv)   Improvement in the environmental management system, internal
controls and reporting systems

As a consequence of having their published environmental information independently verified, companies benefit from the expertise and experience of a competent knowledgeable professional, who is divorced from the day-to-day operation of the company's environmental management system and its procedures, controls and reporting mechanism. As part of their work, external verifiers are likely to review the various elements of the company's environmental management system, identify weaknesses or opportunities for improvement, and make recommendations.

Thus, as a by-product of having their external environmental reports externally verified, companies' environmental management systems, performance and reporting mechanisms may be improved. This, in turn, should enhance many of the advantages accruing to companies as a result of internal environmental audits and external environmental reporting which we have discussed.

17.5.2   Disadvantages of environmental auditing and reporting

Reference to Figure 17.5 reveals that we have identified three disadvantages attaching to internal environmental audits and a further three that are associated with external environmental reports and their verification. We discuss each of these disadvantages below.

(i) Resources required to develop, implement and maintain an environmental auditing programme

A significant disadvantage of internal environmental audits is their cost. To design, implement and maintain an environmental audit programme so that each function, process and site of the organisation is audited on a regular basis (at least once every three years for EMAS registrants) is a costly undertaking. As we noted in section 17.3.1 above, the audits may be conducted by personnel internal or external to the organisation. However, because of the range of skills required for environmental audits, it is beyond the resources of all but the largest companies to maintain an in-house audit team, and the majority of companies rely on environmental consultants to perform their audits. But, irrespective of whether the audits are conducted by an internal or external team of environmental auditors, internal environmental audits are both time-consuming and costly.

(ii) Disruption caused in the facilities being audited

Whatever function, process or site of a company is audited at a particular point in time, the activities of the facility are disrupted by the audit. The disruption is generally greatest during the on-site visit by the environmental audit team as personnel have their activities observed, are asked questions, or asked to locate and provide relevant documents and records – or their normal work routines are disrupted in some other way. However, the disruption is not limited to the period of the on-site visit but extends to the pre- and post-visit phases: work is disrupted during the preparation for the audit and when any resultant recommendations for improvement are implemented.

(iii) Adverse consequences of audits uncovering breaches of environmental regulatory requirements

One of the most serious consequences of an environmental audit for a company is the possibility that the audit will uncover past or present breaches of environmental laws or regulations. Companies fear that regulators or third parties may impose liability for the previously unknown violations. The legal or regulatory breaches may not even be those of the company itself. For example, soil or groundwater on the company's property may have been contaminated by a previous owner but the present company may be faced with enormous remediation costs and, possibly, also claims for damages by third parties who have been harmed in some way by the contamination.

In the USA, the costs of audit discovery came to prominence in 1992 when Coors Brewing Company, based in Colorado, undertook a voluntary investigation of its volatile organic compound (VOC) emissions. As Volokh (1997, p. 28) explains:

The investigation found that when beer is spilled during the making, packaging, and disposal process, large quantities of VOCs are released into the air. As the producer of about 20 million barrels of beer per year, Coors alone was releasing 650 to 750 tons of VOCs – about 17 times more than originally thought. [Coors voluntarily disclosed their finding to Colorado state officials]. . . . In July 1993, the Colorado Department of Health – allegedly under pressure from the federal EPA [Environmental Protection Agency] issued Coors a compliance order containing a $1.05 million civil penalty for violations of state pollution laws. The fine was also to include a to-be-determined-later 'economic benefit payment' to the state for money the company had saved by not complying with the laws. . . . Coors argued that it was being unfairly punished for voluntarily revealing problems that both regulators and major brewers had missed,[20] and warned that such fines would go a long way to discourage other companies from conducting self- [i.e. voluntary internal] audits. (Coors had already spent 18 months and $1.5 million conducting the study.) In February 1994, the fine was reduced. Coors agreed to pay a $100,000 fine and a $137,000 economic benefit payment.

The Coors' experience has prompted at least 24 states in the USA (including Colorado) to enact 'audit privilege' laws (Dailey and Bolduan, 1997). These states are keen to foster environmental protection and believe that companies are more likely to conduct voluntary environmental audits, and correct any discovered violations of environmental laws and regulations, if their audit findings will not be used as a basis for imposing sanctions upon them. In most states the audit privilege laws apply to 'voluntary, internal and comprehensive environmental audits designed to identify past non-compliance and improve future compliance with state and federal environmental requirements' (Kass and McCarroll, 1995, p. 13). They generally have two components, namely:

(a) a *privilege component* whereby neither information obtained as a result of the audit nor the audit documents are admissible as evidence against a company in administrative, civil or criminal proceedings. In order to take advantage of this 'evidential privilege', companies are required to inform the relevant state's environmental regulatory agency of any regulatory violation and to institute corrective action in a timely manner;

(b) an *immunity component* whereby companies that find, report and correct environmental regulatory breaches are given immunity from sanctions. The company may be required to take certain steps to control or rectify environmental damage but punitive sanctions are outlawed. Immunity is not generally available where regulatory violations are intentional or reckless, or where violations have caused on-site injury or substantial harm to people, property or the environment (Volokh, 1997).

In most states the audit privilege laws grant privilege and immunity. However four (Minnesota, Montana, Pennsylvania and South Dakota) only grant

---

[20] Official EPA figures had grossly underestimated brewing company emissions.

immunity,[21] and a further four (Arkansas, Illinois, Indiana and Oregon) only grant privilege (Lauren, 1997; Strader, 1997).

The federal Environmental Protection Agency (EPA) has consistently been opposed to states' evidential privilege for environmental audits – contending that such privilege 'invites secrecy' and weakens the states' power of environmental law enforcement (Morley, 1997; Dailey and Bolduan, 1997). The EPA has also made it clear that protection afforded by state audit privilege laws does not extend to violations of federal environmental laws (Sobnosky, 1999). This means that companies which report violations of federal environmental laws, discovered as a result of an environmental audit, remain liable to prosecution under the federal laws. This is a major concern for companies as many federal environmental laws embody a requirement for companies discovering violations of federal environmental regulations to report them to the EPA (or a state environmental agency acting for the EPA) – and provide severe penalties (including fines and imprisonment) for failure to do so (Dailey and Bolduan, 1997). Thus, companies are exposed to prosecution if they report violations of federal environmental laws – or if they violate the law by failing to report the violations.

Notwithstanding its opposition to state audit privilege laws, recognising the benefits of environmental audits in terms of enhanced environmental protection, in December 1995, the EPA issued its *Final Policy Statement of Incentives for Self-Policing: Discovery, Disclosure, Correction and Prevention of Violation*, 60 Fed. Reg. 66, 706. This policy provides that, if companies meet all of the specified conditions, gravity-based (i.e. non-economic benefit) penalties will not be imposed and the EPA will not refer cases for criminal prosecution.[22] Morley (1997, p. 6) explains that:

> The conditions [to be met] are the heart of the policy, and include the following:
> 1. The violation was discovered through a systematic procedure implemented by the company, such as an environmental audit or due diligence program.
> 2. The violation was identified voluntarily and not through a required monitoring program or pursuant to an [environmental protection] agency inspection or third party complaint; once identified, the violation was promptly disclosed.
> 3. The violation was expeditiously corrected.
> 4. The company agreed to take steps to prevent further violations.
> 5. Same or closely related violations must not have occurred within a certain period in the past.
> 6. The company must co-operate and provide necessary information to determine whether the policy is applicable.

---

[21] Another 11 states grant immunity against civil but not criminal prosecution (Lauren, 1997).

[22] The EPA has maintained its policy of not mitigating economic benefit civil penalties, noting that it has 'full discretion to recover any economic benefit gained as a result of non-compliance' (as cited in Morley, 1997, p. 6).

Although companies which meet the EPA's conditions gain some immunity from penalties they would otherwise incur as a consequence of breaching federal environmental laws, their violations are made public. The same applies in states whose 'audit privilege' laws grant immunity but not evidential privilege to companies that report violations of the state's environmental laws discovered as a result of an internal environmental audit. These companies remain exposed to liability resulting from actions brought by non-governmental third parties (for example, organisations or individuals who suffer harm as a consequence of the company's breach of environmental regulations). Similarly, environmental activists are able to use information about companies' violations to generate negative publicity about the companies concerned.

In order to avoid the adverse consequences of having their reports of environmental regulation violations made public, some companies employ environmental lawyers to conduct their internal environmental audits and claim lawyer–client privilege (or confidentiality) to protect the audit findings from being placed in the public domain. Other companies, who use specialist environmental consultants, similarly try to prevent disclosure of their audit results through privilege by requiring the consultants to report the audit findings to the company's lawyers who then report them to the company (McKinney and Steadman, 1998).

Companies are faced with something of a dilemma. If they demonstrate their commitment to good environmental management and conduct environmental audits, they risk prosecution in respect of any breaches of environmental laws and regulations the audit may uncover. If they do not conduct environmental audits they risk prosecution in respect of violations they might have discovered and corrected that come to light in other ways – for example, through an inspection by an environmental regulatory agency, or another organisation or individual suffering consequential harm.

Environmentally-oriented companies stress that the goal of environmental laws and regulations is to protect and enhance the environment rather than to collect fines, therefore the regulators should provide protection for companies that voluntarily conduct environmental audits and uncover, report and remedy violations of environmental regulations. They also argue that it is better to allocate companies' financial resources to remediation of damage caused by past or present breaches of environmental regulations rather than to defending prosecutions and paying hefty fines. Additionally, they observe that it is cost-effective for the regulators to focus their scarce resources on pursuing organisations that are habitually poor environmental performers rather than prosecuting those that demonstrate their commitment to good environmental management by conducting environmental audits and other similar means.

(iv)   Possible adverse consequences of reporting environmental information

A disadvantage accruing to companies that publish information about their environmental performance is that their reports need to be – and need to be accepted by users as – complete and unbiased (that is, reporting both 'good' and 'bad' environmental performance). However, if a company's report discloses detrimental environmental effects caused by its activities, products or services that were not previously known, this may generate negative publicity and/or prompt an adverse reaction by environmental regulators. It may, for example, trigger regulatory investigations and, possibly, litigation.

(v)   Absence of generally accepted environmental reporting and verification standards.

In the absence of generally accepted standards that prescribe the information to be included in published environmental reports and how quantitative items are to be identified, measured and reported, the content, format and quality (in terms of completeness, accuracy and validity) of environmental reports varies widely. Similarly, without generally accepted verification standards, the rigour of the verification investigation to which the reports are subject varies markedly and, as Beets and Souther (1999) have highlighted, questions arise as to the value of the verification process. They report:

> In 1996, the Global Environmental Management Initiative (GEMI) . . . published the results of a study of environmental reports and their perceived value. This study involved a series of interviews of environmentalists, investors, media, regulators and corporations. These parties consistently indicated that third party attestation of environmental reports is currently of little value because of the lack of guidelines and standards related to the reports and their verification. (p. 134)

A further disadvantage for companies resulting from the absence of environmental reporting standards is the potential for users of their reports to misinterpret statements made or data provided. Such misunderstanding may result in adverse consequences for the company; it may, for example, result in unjustified negative publicity or even in a court action alleging misrepresentation. Along similar lines, in the absence of verification standards there is a danger that users of verified environmental reports may not properly understand the nature and level of the assurance provided. If informed users are familiar with externally audited financial statements, they may mistakenly conclude that a similar high level of assurance is provided by the verification of environmental reports (FEE, 2002).

(vi)   High costs of producing environmental reports and having them verified

As for internal environmental audits, a significant disadvantage for companies that publish verified environmental reports is the cost involved. Many companies that publish a separate environmental (or sustainability) report produce a document that is as 'thick' as their annual report and one which contains significantly more photographs, graphs and diagrams. Such reports are extremely expensive to compile (in terms of gathering relevant information and data, deciding what to include and what to leave out, and how to present the material to be included). They are also expensive to produce in hard and/or electronic form and to publish.[23] Companies that have their environmental reports independently verified also incur the costly professional fees of the verifiers.

Notwithstanding the financial resources that are consumed by publishing verified environmental reports, companies engage in this activity only if they believe those resources are used to good effect. By implication, these companies consider that the financial costs involved, together with the other disadvantages attaching to environmental reporting and verification, are outweighed by the advantages to be gained: in other words, they believe the exercise makes good business sense.

17.6 THE RELEVANCE OF ENVIRONMENTAL ISSUES TO EXTERNAL FINANCIAL STATEMENT AUDITS

Although this chapter is concerned with internal environmental audits and external environmental reports and their verification, the primary focus of this book is external financial statement audits. It is, therefore, appropriate to consider the relevance of environmental issues to external financial statement audits. That environmental matters are relevant to such audits has been noted by commentators such as Owen and Collison. Owen (1992) for example observes:

> [T]he fact that environmental issues, and particularly company shortcomings in response to these issues, have ever-increasing financial consequences for business means that the financial auditor must pay due regard to them now in the conduct of current statutory audits. (as cited in Collison, 1996, p. 326)

Collison (1996) further explains:

> A company's environmental policy and obligations and its reaction to environmental developments, such as the changing attitudes of consumers are clearly a concern to the financial auditor to the extent that they are material to the financial statements. (p. 328)

Reviewing the content of statutory financial statements, it could justifiably be asserted that environmental issues impact, at least to some extent, all aspects of the financial statements and their audit. However, the areas where they are probably of greatest significance for external auditors include the following:

---

[23] A number of companies, such as J Sainsbury in 2001, have sought to reduce the cost – as well as reducing the use of resources such as paper and ink – by publishing their reports only on the internet.

(i) Gaining an understanding of the client and assessing its risks

Given society's increasing awareness of environmental issues, the increasing
volume and complexity of environmental laws and regulations, and the increasing importance of incorporating environmental considerations into business
decisions, it is clearly important that auditors gain a thorough understanding of
their clients' environmental policy, the environmental impacts of their activities, processes, products and services, and their environmental regulatory
obligations. In this context it is pertinent to note that among the matters listed
in the Appendix to Statement of Auditing Standards (SAS) 210: *Knowledge of
the business* that auditors should consider are:

- Environmental requirements and problems (in a section headed: *The
  industry – conditions affecting the client's business*); and
- Legislation and regulations that significantly affect the entity (in a section
  headed: *The entity's business – products, markets, suppliers, expenses,
  operations).*[24]

However, not only must auditors gain an understanding of the environmental
matters that affect their clients (and *vice versa*), they must also consider
environment-related issues when assessing their clients' financial, operational,
business and other risks, and the impact of these risks on the financial statements.

*(ii) Ascertaining audit clients' compliance with environmental laws and
       regulations*

SAS 120: *Consideration of law and regulations* explains:

> For audit purposes laws and regulations relevant to the audit can be regarded as
> falling into two main categories:
> (a) those which relate directly to the preparation of . . . the financial statements of
>   the entity, and
> (b) those which provide a legal framework within which the entity conducts its
>   business and which are central to the entity's ability to conduct its business
>   and where non-compliance may reasonably be expected to result in the entity
>   ceasing operations, or call into question its continuance as a going concern.
>   (para 21)

Clearly, environmental laws and regulations fall within the latter category. SAS
120, para 29, illuminates the meaning of non-compliance with laws and regulations possibly 'calling into question the entity's continuance as a going concern'
by providing as an example:

> Where the non-compliance accounts for a substantial portion of profits, or
> through the level of fines or damages which could result.

---

[24] These two matters are also listed in the Appendix to International Standard on Auditing (ISA) 310:
Knowledge of the business.

Throughout this chapter we have noted that virtually all companies are, to a greater or lesser extent, subject to environmental laws and regulations. However, for organisations in industrial sectors such as chemicals, manufacturing and the extractive industries, environmental laws and regulations may well be central to their ability to conduct their business. For audit clients for whom environmental laws and regulations are particularly significant, SAS 120 requires auditors to:

> Perform procedures to help identify possible or actual instances of non-compliance with those laws and regulations which provide a legal framework within which the entity conducts its business and which are central to the entity's ability to conduct its business[25] and hence to its financial statements, by:
> (a) obtaining a general understanding of the legal and regulatory framework applicable to the entity and the industry, and of the procedures followed to ensure compliance with that framework
> (b) inspecting correspondence with relevant licensing or regulatory authorities
> (c) enquiring of the directors as to whether they are on notice of any such possible instances of non-compliance with law or regulations, and
> (d) obtaining written confirmation from the directors that they have disclosed to the auditor all those events of which they are aware which involve possible non-compliance, together with the actual or contingent consequences which may arise therefrom. (para 28)

Thus, for audit clients where environmental laws and regulations are central to their ability to conduct their business, ascertaining their compliance (or, more pertinently, instances of non-compliance) with these laws and regulations is an important element of an external financial statement audit.

(iii) Evaluating the adequacy of disclosures relating to contingent liabilities and the adequacy of provisions

If a company breaches environmental laws and regulations it is exposed to liabilities in the form of, for example, fines, damages and remediation costs (that is, costs to remedy any harm to the environment, property or people that results from the breach). In some cases the liabilities may be minor in relation to the financial affairs of the company but in others they may be of sufficient size to be material to the company's financial statements.

SAS 120 explains external auditors' responsibilities in these circumstances. It states:

> When the auditors become aware of information which indicates that non-compliance with law or regulations may exist, they should obtain an understanding of the nature of the act and the circumstances in which it has occurred

---

[25] For example, in a waste disposal company, the terms of licences under which the company is allowed to dispose of hazardous waste are central to its ability to conduct its business. If the company should breach the terms of the licences, it is likely that it will be unable to continue in business.

and sufficient other information to evaluate the possible effect on the financial statements. (para 37)

When evaluating the possible effect on the financial statements, the auditors consider

- the potential financial consequences, such as fines, penalties, damages, threat of expropriation of assets, enforced discontinuance of operations and litigation;
- whether the potential financial consequences require disclosure, and if so, the adequacy of any disclosure, and
- whether the potential financial consequences are so serious as to call into question the view given by the financial statements [that is, whether the going concern assumption is valid]. (para 38)

Where the potential financial consequences of one or more violations of environmental regulatory requirements is material to an audit client's financial statements, the auditor needs to evaluate the adequacy of disclosures relating to the associated contingent liabilities, both in terms of the likely amount involved and the explanation of the relevant circumstances.[26]

Additionally, for audit clients whose activities, processes, products or services have (or are likely to have) a significant impact on the environment, external auditors need to evaluate the adequacy of their clients' insurance cover for the possible consequences of breaching environmental regulatory requirements (including the associated legal costs) and for potential environment-related emergencies and disasters. Similarly, they need to evaluate the adequacy of their provisions in respect of these matters.

(iv) Reviewing the valuation of fixed assets and stock

Among other matters to which external auditors need to pay special regard for clients for whom environmental matters are particularly significant is the value of fixed assets – in particular, land and buildings – and of stock, as shown in the pre-audited financial statements. The value of land may be altered dramatically by factors such as the discovery of hazardous waste, or contaminated soil or underground water, at any of the client's locations (anywhere in the world) irrespective of whether the hazardous waste was dumped, or the soil or water was contaminated, by the client or a previous occupier of the site(s) concerned.

Similarly, the value of buildings and plant may be altered by, for instance, the discovery that they breach health and safety or environmental regulations – for

---

[26] It should be remembered that when an audit client has been prosecuted for non-compliance with environmental laws or regulations and the resultant fine, damages, remediation costs, etc. have been settled by the regulatory authority or the court but are not yet paid, an actual liability exists and should be recorded as such in the financial statements. Contingent liabilities relate, among other things, to breaches of environmental laws or regulations which have been discovered but the resultant financial consequences are, as yet, uncertain as to their amount.

example, that the present arrangement for storage of waste poses a fire or health hazard, or radio-active or gaseous emissions exceed permitted levels. In some cases, violation of regulations may be caused by changes in the regulations themselves: for example, permitted levels of emissions may be reduced as a result of a regulatory change. Whatever their cause, where buildings or plant (or, indeed, any other productive asset) breaks current or soon-to-be-implemented regulations, considerable capital expenditure may be required to bring existing assets into line with the required standards. Apart from affecting the value of the assets as stated in the balance sheet, planned capital expenditure may give rise to commitments to be disclosed in the financial statements: the external auditor will need to review the adequacy of any such disclosures.

Along similar lines, for clients with processes or products that have a significant influence on the environment, external auditors need to be alert to the fact that the value of stock may be diminished, or items of stock may be rendered obsolete through 'environmental concerns, storage and disposal costs of environmentally-maligned materials and recycling commitments' (Collison, 1996, p. 32). The value of stock stated in the balance sheet may need to be adjusted accordingly.

Before leaving the topic of the relevance of environmental issues to external financial statement audits, we should make reference to the draft clauses of the proposed Companies Bill (DTI, 2002). As we noted in section 17.3.2, these clauses embody the proposal that the directors of all major companies will be required to include within their annual reports an operating and financial review (OFR) and that, for companies where environmental issues are significant, the directors will be required to report in their OFR on the company's impact on the environment. The draft clauses also propose that the OFR (and therefore the directors' report on the company's impact on the environment) will be subject, along with the company's financial statements, to external audit.

17.7 SUMMARY

In this chapter we have highlighted the importance of environmental issues for all companies, especially those in industrial sectors such as manufacturing, the extractive industries and chemicals which have (or are likely to have) a significant environmental impact. We have noted, in particular, that companies are subject to a huge volume of highly complex environmental laws and regulations – and also that they may gain significant advantages by incorporating environmental considerations into their business decisions.

We have traced the development of internal environmental audits from 'single issue' audits (such as compliance and due diligence audits) to 'comprehensive' audits (those covering organisations' environmental management systems and their environmental performance); similarly, we have traced the development of external environmental reporting, from 'single topic' environment reports to broadly based sustainability reports, covering social and economic, as well as environmental, matters. We have also noted that, in order to enhance the credibility of their published environmental (or sustainability) reports, a number of companies voluntarily submit their reports to independent verification (or assurance).

Additionally, we have reviewed the objectives, scope and process of, and the reports associated with, internal environmental audits and external verification (or assurance) engagements, and discussed the advantages and disadvantages that may accrue to companies through engaging in these activities. We observed that, notwithstanding the significant disadvantages that may result from companies conducting internal environmental audits and publishing environmental reports (and having these reports independently verified), companies seem to find that pursuing these activities makes good business sense. In the final section of the chapter we have considered some of the ways in which environmental matters may impact the statutory audit of companies' financial statements.

SELF-REVIEW QUESTIONS

17.1 Define the following terms:
(i)   an environmental management system;
(ii) an internal environmental audit;
(iii) an external verification (or assurance) engagement.

17.2 Explain briefly how the scope of internal environmental audits has developed over the past 20 or so years.

17.3 Outline the various forms in which a company may report its environmental performance and distinguish between an 'environmental report' and a 'sustainability report'.

17.4 Discuss briefly the objective and requirements of the ISO 14001 scheme and Europe's eco-management and audit scheme (EMAS), and list the key differences in the requirements of the two schemes.

17.5 Explain briefly the difficulties for internal environmental auditors and external environmental verifiers that result from the absence of environmental reporting and verification standards.

17.6 List the professional requirements for internal environmental auditors and external environmental verifiers and identify the groups which may be equipped to undertake this work.

17.7 Outline the usual contents of:
   (i) an internal environmental audit report to management;
   (ii) a verification (or assurance) report attached to a company's published environmental report.
17.8 List and briefly explain the advantages that may accrue to companies as a consequence of conducting internal environmental audits and publishing independently verified environmental (or sustainability) reports.
17.9 List and briefly explain the disadvantages that companies may experience as a consequence of conducting internal environmental audits and publishing independently verified environmental (or sustainability) reports.
17.10 List four ways in which environmental factors may impact upon the statutory audit of companies' financial statements.

REFERENCES

Accountant, The (1998) Going green, *The Accountant*, 14 April.
Beets, S.D. & Souther, C.C. (1999) Corporate environmental reports: The need for standards and an environmental assurance service. *Accounting Horizons* **13**(2), 129–145.
Bowman, M. (1999) New legislative 'protection' of voluntary environmental audits: Incentive or indictment. *Australian Business Law Review* **27**(5), 391–406.
British Standard 7750 (1992) *Environmental Management Systems*. London: British Standards Institute.
Collison, D.J. (1996) The response of statutory financial auditors in the UK to environmental issues: A descriptive and exploratory case study. *British Accounting Review* **28**, 325–349.
Dailey, D.K. & Bolduan, L.M. (1997) Voluntary environmental audits: Will Congress act? *Corporate Legal Times* **7**(73), 59.
Department of Trade and Industry (DTI) (2002) *Modernising Company Law – Draft Clauses*. London: HMSO.
Economist (1990) Managing greenly. *Economist*, 9 August, **316**(7671), 18–20.
Encyclopedia Britannica Ready Reference Encyclopedia 2002 Edition (on CD Rom)
Fédération des Experts Comptables Européens (FEE) (2001) *FEE Update on Sustainability Issues*, November. Brussels: FEE.
Fettis, L. (2002) FD's back environmental reports. *Accountancy Age* 20 June, p. 3.
Gilmour, G. & Caplan, A. (2001) Who cares? *Accountancy* **128**(1297), 44–45.
Hamilton, E. (1997) The top ten pitfalls of environmental audits and how to avoid them. *Journal of Environmental Law & Practice* **4**(5), 29–35.
International Chamber of Commerce (ICC) (1991) *An ICC Guide to Effective Environmental Auditing*. Paris: ICC Publishing.
Investors Chronicle (1998) Survey – ethical investment: Pensions with principles. *Investors Chronicle*, 17 July, 44.
Kass, S.L. & McCarroll, J.M. (1995) Environmental audits: How they can help – and hurt – the Corporation. *Directorship* **21**(9), 12–14.
Krumsiek, B.J. (1998) The emergence of a new era in mutual find investing: Socially responsible investing comes of age. *Journal of Investing*, Winter, 84–99.

Larsson, L. & Ljungdahl, F. (2001) Seeking sustainability. *Accountancy* **128**(1295), 155.

Lauren, J. (1997) The dangers in coming clean. *CFO* **13**(9), 83–6.

Lightbody, M. (2000) Environmental auditing: The audit theory gap. *Accounting Forum* **24**(2), 151–169.

MacKay, E. (2000) Environmental reporting – creating the right environment. *www.accountancyage.com/News/1103312* (14 June 2000), 1–3.

Maltby, J. (1995) Environmental audit: Theory and practices. *Managerial Auditing Journal* **10**(8), 15–26.

McKinney, M.M. & Steadman, M.E. (1998) EPA challenges privilege issue in environmental self-audits. *CPA Journal* **68**(8), 9.

Morley, S.J. (1997) Environmental self-audit review: New EPA policy and self-audit privilege developments. *Journal of Environmental Law & Practice* **4**(4), 5–8.

Natu, A.V. (1999) Environmental audit – A tool for waste minimisation for small and medium scale dyestuff industries. *Chemical Business* **13**(9), 133–137.

Newsmedia (1998) On corporate environmental standards – Follow a green giant's example. *www.accountancyage.com/News/53463* (8 May).

Owen, D. (1992) *Green Reporting: Accountancy and the challenge of the nineties.* London: Chapman and Hall

Perry, M. (2002) Adding credibility to value. *Accountancy Age*, 16 May, p. 8.

Quality Network (1996) Benefits of eco-management systems. *www.quality.co.uk/eco/benefits* (12 February).

Roussey, R.S. (1992) Auditing environmental liabilities. *Auditing: A Journal of Practice & Theory* **11**(1), 47–57.

Sobnosky, K.J. (1999) The value-added benefits of environmental auditing. *Environmental Quality Management* **9**(2), 25–32.

Strader, J. (1997) Tell before we ask. *Executive Report* **15**(7), 1.

Vinten, G. (1996) The objectives of the environmental audit. *Environmental Management and Health* **7**(3), 12–21.

Volokh, A. (1997) Carrots over sticks. *Washington Monthly* **29**(6), 28–31.

World Commission on Environment and Development (1987) *Our Common Future.* Oxford: Oxford University Press.

ADDITIONAL READING

The Canadian Institute of Chartered Accountants (1992) *Environmental Auditing and the Role of the Accounting Profession.* Toronto: CICA.

Confederation of British Industry (CBI) (1990) *Narrowing the Gap: Environmental Auditing.* London: CBI.

Corporate Board (1994) Environmental audits have risks as well as benefits. *Corporate Board* **15**(86), 27.

DeFeo, V.J. & Falk, H. (1998) Audited social responsibility disclosures. *Critical Perspectives on Accounting* **9**, 193–199.

Elkington, J. (1989) *The Environmental Audit.* London: World Wide Fund for Nature.

Elliott, D. & Patton, D. (1998) Environmental audit response: The case of the engineering sector. *Green Management International* **22**(Summer), 83–95.

Graham-Bryce, I. (1988) The approach to environmental auditing in the Royal Dutch/Shell Group of companies. In UNEP, *Industry and Environment: Environmental Auditing.* Paris: UNEP, pp. 8–10.

Gray, R. & Collinson, D. (1991) The environmental audit: Greengage or whitewash. *Managerial Journal of Auditing* **6**(5), 17–25.

Hillary, R. (1988) *The Eco-management and audit scheme: A Practical Guide.* Letchworth: Technical Communications (Publishing) Ltd.

Lewis, L. (2000) Environmental audits in local government: A useful means to progress in sustainable development. *Accounting Forum* **24**(3), 296–319.

Owen, D.L., Swift, A., Humphrey, C. & Bowerman, M. (2000) The new social audits: Accountability, managerial capture or the agenda of social champions? *The European Accounting Review* **9**(1), 81–98.

Power, M. (1997) Expertise and the construction of relevance: Accountants and environmental audit. *Accounting, Organisations and Society* **22**(2), 123–146.

Price Waterhouse (1995) PW survey: more companies give priority to environmental issues. *CPA Journal* **65**(4), 9.

Sutton, S.G. & Arnold, V. (1998) Towards a framework for a corporate single audit: Meeting financial statement users' needs. *Critical Perspectives on Accounting* **9**, 177–191.

Appendix: Summary of Steps in a Statutory Financial Statement Audit

The steps in the audit process are depicted in Figure A.1.

Step 1 – Appointment (see Chapter 5)

The external auditor of a company is formally appointed (or re-appointed) by the shareholders at their annual general meeting (AGM). However, in practice, the company's directors usually arrange the appointment and this is ratified by the shareholders at the AGM.

Step 2 – Engagement letter (see Chapter 7)

At the commencement of the audit, an engagement letter is prepared by the auditor and sent to the client. This is to ensure there are no misunderstandings between the auditor and the client, and it sets out things such as:

- the scope (extent) of the audit, including any work the auditor is to do in addition to that required for the statutory audit;
- confirmation of any verbal agreements, including the basis on which fees are to be charged;
- confirmation of any work to be performed by the client [for example, the preparation of schedules such as stock on hand (prior to stocktaking) and an aged analysis of debtors];
- a statement emphasising that, under the Companies Act 1985, the financial statements are the responsibility of the auditee's management[1] and that the statements are required to give a true and fair view of the company's financial position and performance and comply with relevant legislation;
- an indication of how the auditor will approach his or her work and guidance as to the approximate timing of the work to be done;
- a statement noting that the objective of the audit is to form an opinion on the truth and fairness of the financial information, not to detect fraud. However, it is also pointed out that audit procedures are designed to give reasonable assurance that any material frauds will be detected.

---

[1] Readers are reminded that the term 'management' is used to mean the company's executive and non-executive directors and non-director senior executives. (See the Preface to this text.)

Figure A1: Summary of the audit process

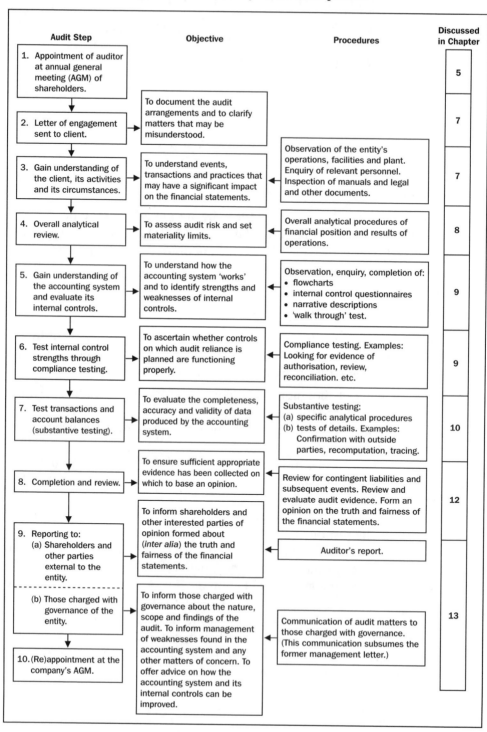

The auditor prepares two copies of the engagement letter. They are both sent to the client for signing; one is retained by the client, the other is returned to the auditor for inclusion in the audit file.

It should be noted that the engagement letter does not absolve the auditor from any statutory, common law or professional duties in relation to the audit. Its principal purpose is to clarify the role and scope of the audit and to confirm that the client entity's management is aware of the nature of the audit engagement. It also outlines some administrative matters.

Step 3 – Understanding the client (see Chapter 7)

It is essential that the auditor gains a thorough understanding of the client entity, its business, its operations, its industry and its key personnel. This understanding:
- makes the auditor aware of any particular events, transactions or accounting practices which may have a significant impact on the financial statements;
- enables the auditor to assess whether there are circumstances which increase the likelihood of errors being present in the (pre-audited) financial statements;
- provides a background against which evidence gathered during the course of the audit can be evaluated to see if it 'makes sense' and 'looks right'.

This understanding of the client is acquired primarily through the following procedures:
- visiting the client company, touring its premises and meeting key personnel (for example, the managing director, the finance director, and the marketing, production and human resources department managers);
- discussing with key personnel, in relation to the past year, the trading and financial position of the company, problems and successes experienced, and any significant changes in activities, accounting or personnel policies and procedures;
- reviewing the company's legal documents (including, for example, its Memorandum and Articles of Association, and any debenture trust deeds), policy and procedures manuals, and any significant commercial agreements (e.g. franchise and leasing agreements).

Step 4 – Overall analytical review (see Chapter 8)

In this step of the audit process, meaningful relationships in the entity's accounting data are examined. Primarily by means of trend and ratio analysis, the auditor gains a better understanding of the entity's financial position and the results of its operations and its cash flows, as presented in the financial statements. The results of this analysis are evaluated against the auditor's expectations, based on his or her understanding of the client's circumstances. Key indicators such as net profit to sales, return on shareholders' funds, debt to equity ratio, and working capital ratio, are compared with the averages for these indicators in the client's industry (or business sector). Based on the auditor's knowledge of the client, its 'usual' position in its industry and any known exceptional circumstances, the auditor can assess whether the financial statement data 'look right', or whether it appears that there are errors in the data.

Based on this overall analytical review the auditor can assess:

- audit risk: the likelihood that material error is present in the (pre-audited) financial statements;
- materiality limits: the amount of error the auditor is prepared to accept in individual financial statement account balances, and in the financial statements as a whole, before concluding that they are materially misstated. (A material misstatement is one which is likely to affect a decision or action of a reasonable user of the financial statements.)

Step 5 – Understanding the accounting system and evaluating its internal controls (see Chapter 9)

Before the auditor can assess the truth and fairness with which the financial statements portray the company's financial position and performance, (s)he must understand the accounting system and the controls which are 'built into' the system to prevent, or detect and correct, errors and irregularities in the accounting data (i.e. the internal accounting controls). The auditor must understand how the transactions data is captured, how it is processed through the accounting system, and how it is 'converted' into financial information in the form of financial statements. (S)he also needs to know which personnel are responsible for performing what tasks.

The auditor gains this understanding of the accounting system primarily through:

- observation: observing various aspects of the client's accounting system;
- enquiry: asking questions of client personnel;
- completing a (or using a client-prepared) flowchart of the system;
- completing an Internal Control Questionnaire (ICQ). This usually consists of a list of questions which require 'yes', 'no' or 'not applicable' answers. The auditor completes this on the basis of observation and enquiry.

The flowchart and/or ICQ, together with any narrative descriptions of parts of the accounting system, are important audit documents and are kept in the audit file.

In order to test his or her understanding of the accounting system, the auditor conducts a 'walk through' test. For this test, one or two transactions are followed through the accounting system, from their recording on a source document (e.g. sales invoice) at the time the transaction takes place, through the journals, ledger, trial balances, etc., to their presentation in the financial statements (that is, as an element of account balances presented in the financial statements; e.g. as an element of 'Sales' and 'Debtors').

In addition to gaining knowledge of how the accounting system 'works', the auditor makes a preliminary evaluation of the system's internal controls. More specifically, the auditor identifies internal control 'strengths' and 'weaknesses'.

- *Strengths* are controls within the accounting system which, if operating properly, will prevent, or detect and correct, errors and irregularities.
- *Weaknesses* are aspects of the system which are susceptible to error or irregularities, but which lack a control to prevent or detect such occurrences.

Based on the results of the overall analytical review and preliminary evaluation of the internal controls, the auditor can make decisions concerning the nature, timing and extent of audit procedures.

- *The nature of audit procedures* refers, for example, to whether the auditor will rely primarily on:
  - compliance tests: audit procedures designed to test whether the internal controls on which the auditor plans to rely to protect the integrity of the accounting data are functioning as intended (i.e. are being complied with); or
  - substantive tests: audit procedures designed to test the validity, completeness and accuracy of transactions and/or account balances.

  Both types of test are used in virtually every audit, but the emphasis on one or the other largely depends on the auditor's preliminary evaluation of the internal controls. Where internal controls are considered to be effective, greater reliance is placed on compliance testing than on substantive testing. Where internal controls are regarded as weak, the emphasis is on substantive tests. Because the auditor is required to express an opinion on the truth and fairness of the information presented in the financial statements, some substantive testing of that information *must* be undertaken in *every* audit.

  The 'nature of audit procedures' also refers to the procedures the auditor chooses from the alternatives available to accomplish a particular audit objective: for example, whether the auditor uses analytical procedures or tests of transactions to evaluate the accuracy, validity and completeness of the interest paid account balance.

- *The timing of audit tests* refers to whether (and the extent to which) the auditor conducts audit tests during an interim audit (that is, some months before the end of the financial year) rather than during the final audit (that is, around and shortly after the balance sheet date). Some testing must always be done during a final audit but, where internal controls are strong, some tests may be conducted earlier in the year. This enables the auditor to spread audit work more evenly throughout the financial year and to complete the final audit in a shorter period.
- *The extent of audit procedures* refers to the amount of evidence the auditor needs to gather before (s)he can be confident that the financial statements do or do not contain material error and/or inadequate disclosures. In general, the more effective the internal controls in preventing, or detecting and correcting, errors, the more likely it is that the financial statements will be free from error and, therefore, the less the evidence the auditor needs to gather in order to form an opinion that this is, in fact, the case.

Step 6 – Testing internal control strengths through compliance testing (see Chapter 9)

Before the auditor can rely on 'strengths' in the accounting system (i.e. effective internal controls) to prevent or detect errors in the accounting data, tests must be conducted to make sure that:

- these controls are, in fact, working effectively; and
- they have been so working throughout the financial year.

To illustrate a compliance test: one objective of internal controls is to ensure that all transactions are properly authorised. A control might be that, before any credit sale is made to a customer, it must be authorised by the credit manager. The credit manager is required to initial the sales invoice to indicate that the sale has been authorised. An audit procedure to test whether this control has been complied with is to examine copies of sales invoices for the credit manager's initials.

Step 7 – Testing the validity, completeness and accuracy of transactions and account balances (substantive testing) (see Chapter 10)

Because the auditor is required to express an opinion as to whether or not the company's financial statements give a true and fair view of its financial position and performance and comply with relevant legislation, (s)he must always conduct some substantive tests. There are two main types of substantive tests:

(i) analytical procedures;
(ii) tests of details.

(i)   Analytical procedures: In these tests the relationships in accounting data are examined to determine the 'reasonableness' of individual account balances. For example, in order to verify the interest paid account balance, the auditor may ascertain the entity's average debt and average interest rate for the year. By applying the interest rate to the debt, an indication of the interest that should have been paid (or payable) during the year can be determined. By comparing the interest paid account balance with the calculated amount, the auditor can decide whether or not the recorded amount is 'reasonable'. If it is, in many cases, no further testing of this account will be performed. However, if it is not, then the disparity between the recorded and calculated amounts will need to be investigated.

(ii)   Tests of details: In these tests, the validity, completeness and accuracy (as to amount, account classification and reporting period) of transactions and account balances are examined. For example, the auditor, may:

- compute such items as depreciation and allowance for bad debts, and reperform bank reconciliations, etc. This checks for arithmetical errors;
- trace transactions forwards from source documents to financial statements. This checks for completeness: to make sure all relevant transactions have been included in the financial statement account balances and that none has been 'lost' on its way through the system;
- trace transactions backwards from financial statements to source documents. This checks for validity: to make sure that account balances shown in the financial statements reflect the totals of genuine transactions;
- request confirmations from outside parties. For example, a sample of customers may be asked to confirm that they owed the client company the amount stated in the company's debtors' ledger account, and banks are asked to confirm the client's bank balances as at the balance sheet date;
- observe such items as stock. This usually includes attendance at the company's stocktake when stock is counted. However, it also includes observing the type and quality of stock on hand in order to assess whether, and how much of it, is obsolete or substandard;
- inspection of documents such as marketable securities (for example, share certificates) and loan, lease or hire purchase contracts.

Step 8 – Completion and review (see Chapter 12)

This step, which completes the evidence gathering and evaluation phase of the audit, comprises four separate sub-steps:

(i)   review for contingent liabilities and commitments;
(ii) review for subsequent events;
(iii) re-assessment of the validity of the going concern assumption;
(iv) final review of evidence gathered during the audit and formation of opinion.

(i)   Review for contingent liabilities and commitments: Before concluding the audit, the auditor must ascertain whether the entity has any contingent liabilities or commitments which should be disclosed in the financial statements.

- A *contingent liability* is a possible obligation which is expected to arise from a past event but which, at the balance sheet date, is uncertain as to existence or amount. An example is litigation for infringement of, say, environmental or product safety regulations. The outcome of the litigation will not be known until the case is heard in court.
- A *commitment* is a contractual undertaking; for example, an undertaking to purchase a certain amount of raw materials at a fixed price at a particular time in the future, or an agreement to lease or buy fixed assets at an agreed price on a specified future date.

The auditor faces two major problems when reviewing for contingent liabilities and commitments:

(a) management may not wish to disclose these items in the financial statements;
(b) it is more difficult to discover unrecorded transactions and events than it is to evaluate recorded information.

However, financial statements are required to show a true and fair view of the reporting entity's state of affairs and this necessitates disclosure of any material contingent liabilities and commitments. Therefore, the auditor must attempt to ascertain whether they exist. This is accomplished primarily through:

- making enquiries of management;
- reviewing the minutes of directors' (or equivalent) meetings;
- reviewing correspondence files;
- reviewing audit working papers prepared during the course of the audit for information that may indicate a potential contingent liability;
- obtaining confirmation from the client's solicitor(s) regarding known, pending or expected liabilities or commitments.

(iii)   Review for subsequent events: The auditor is required to review transactions and events which occur during the period between the balance sheet date and the date of the audit report to see if anything has happened which might affect the truth and fairness of the financial statements as at the balance sheet date. Two types of subsequent events may have occurred:

(a) *Adjusting events:* These are events which clarify conditions existing at the balance sheet date and/or which permit more accurate valuation of account balances as at that date. For example, the commencement of bankruptcy proceedings against a major customer during the subsequent events period may indicate that his or her financial position was not sound at the balance sheet date. In this case, some adjustment to the allowance for bad debts account might be called for.

(b) *Non-adjusting events:* These are events which indicate conditions that have arisen subsequent to the balance sheet date. As these conditions do not affect the financial position or performance of the entity as at the balance sheet date, they should not be incorporated in the financial statements. However, where a non-adjusting post balance sheet event is material, it should be disclosed by way of a note to the financial statements, so that users of the financial statements can gain a proper understanding of the entity's financial position and performance. An example of this type of event is a major expansion (or retraction) of the organisation, such as a purchase (or sale) of a subsidiary subsequent to the balance sheet date.

If the post balance sheet event is such that it brings into question the validity of the going concern concept (for example, as a consequence of a fire or flood occurring after the balance sheet date which results in a significant loss not covered by insurance), then it should be considered in the re-assessment of the going concern assumption.

(iii) Re-assessment of the validity of the going concern assumption: In normal circumstances, financial statements are prepared on the basis of an assumption that the reporting entity will continue as a going concern for the foreseeable future. As part of their audits, auditors are required to consider whether adoption of this assumption is justified. Under SAS 130 they are required (among other things) to:

- plan and perform procedures specifically designed to identify material matters which might indicate that adoption of the going concern assumption might not be valid;
- determine and document the extent of their concern (if any) about the company's ability to continue as a going concern.

If auditors believe that the company's ability to continue as a going concern is in question, they are required to consider whether the relevant information is adequately disclosed in the financial statements. Where auditors believe the relevant matters relating to the company's (uncertain) future are adequately disclosed (assuming the auditors are satisfied in all other respects), they are required to express an unqualified opinion. However, they are also required to include an explanatory paragraph referring to the uncertainty in respect of the company's status as a going concern in the 'basis of opinion' section of the audit report. If auditors consider the relevant information is not adequately disclosed, they are required to express an 'except for' or 'adverse' audit opinion, as appropriate (see Step 9 below).

(iv)   Review of evidence gathered during the audit and formation of an opinion: At the conclusion of the audit, the auditor must carefully review the audit working papers. (S)he must consider:

- the objectives, nature, timing and extent of audit procedures performed, the results obtained, and the conclusions reached;
- problems encountered during the audit and how these have been resolved;
- whether sufficient, appropriate audit evidence has been gathered in each audit segment and for the audit as a whole, on which to form an opinion.

As part of the 'completion and review' stage of the audit, the auditor usually obtains a letter of representation from the client's management. This is ostensibly written by the client's management but, in practice, it is usually written by the auditor and signed by management. The purpose of the letter is essentially:

- to obtain evidence that the client's directors acknowledge their responsibility for the company's financial statements (and their truth and fairness);
- to place on record management's responses to enquiries made by the auditor during the audit. This ensures there is no misunderstanding between management and the auditor as to what was said – and gives management the opportunity to correct any response which the auditor has misinterpreted. It also ensures that management assumes responsibility for its representations to the auditor.

Once the auditor is satisfied that sufficient appropriate audit evidence has been gathered, (s)he must form an opinion (based on the evidence collected and documented in the working papers) as to whether or not:

- the financial statements present a true and fair view of the company's financial position and performance;
- proper accounting records have been kept by the company;
- proper returns have been received from branches not visited by the auditors;
- the financial statements are in agreement with the underlying accounting records;
- the auditor has received all the information and explanations (s)he required for the purposes of the audit;
- the information given in the directors' report is consistent with the financial statements.

Step 9 – Reporting (see Chapter 13)

The concluding step in the audit process is the preparation of reports addressed to:

(i) the company's shareholders. (This report may also be read by other stakeholders external to the entity);
(ii) those charged with the company's governance.

(i)   Report to shareholders

Auditors are required by the Companies Act 1985 to report to shareholders their opinion as to the truth and fairness of the company's financial statements and their compliance (or otherwise) with the Companies Act 1985. The report may be unqualified or qualified.

- An *unqualified audit report* indicates that, in the auditor's judgment, the financial statements give a true and fair view of the company's financial position and performance and comply with the Companies Act 1985.
- A qualified audit report indicates that:
  - there has been a limitation on the scope of the auditor's examination; or
  - the auditor disagrees with the treatment or disclosure of a matter in the financial statements,

  and, in the auditor's opinion, the effect of the scope limitation or the matter with which (s)he disagrees is material to the financial statements. The qualified audit report may be of three types: 'except for', adverse or disclaimer.
  A *qualified audit report* will also be issued if the auditor considers:
  - the company has not kept proper accounting records;
  - all of the required information and explanations have not been received;
  - the financial statements are not in agreement with the underlying accounting records;
  - proper returns have not been received from branches not visited by the auditor;
  - the information given in the directors' report is not consistent with the financial statements.

(iv)   Report to management: In addition to the auditor's report to shareholders, auditors are required to communicate audit matters to those charged with the company's governance (that is, the company's directors). In particular, they are required to communicate matters relating to:

(a) relationships that may bear on the auditor's independence and the objectivity of those engaged on the audit;
(b) audit planning information; and
(c) findings from the audit.

The purpose of these communications is to:

- help ensure there is a mutual understanding between the auditor and the company's directors about the scope of the audit and the respective responsibilities of the auditor and directors;
- share relevant information that will assist the auditor and the directors fulfil their respective responsibilities; and
- provide the directors with constructive observations (and recommendations for improvement) arising from the audit process.

The content of the auditor's communication to those charged with governance varies widely in practice – depending on the auditor, the client and the circumstances. The communication has subsumed, and is broader in content than, the former 'management letter' but an important component of the letter (like the management letter) is commenting on any internal control weaknesses which have come to light during the audit, explaining the effect of these weaknesses, and recommending steps which could be taken to rectify them.

Index

Note: Page references in *italics* refer to Figures